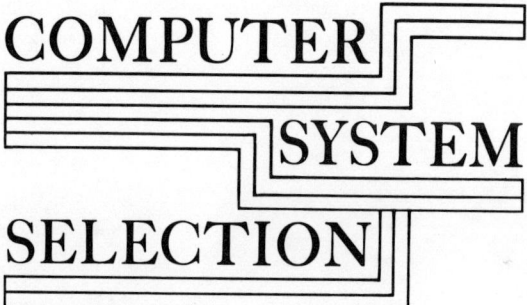

COMPUTER SYSTEM SELECTION

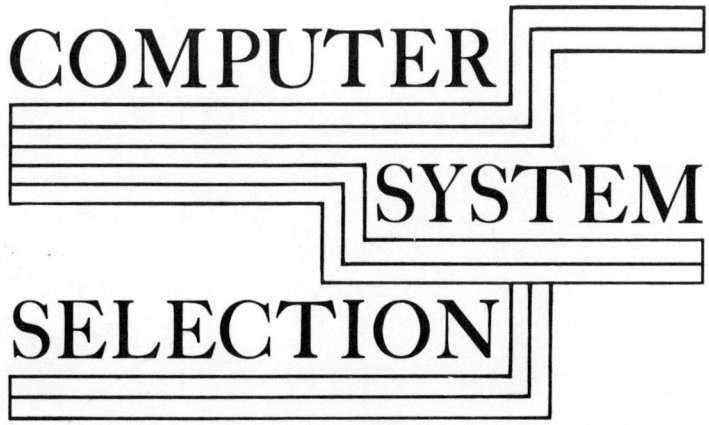

COMPUTER SYSTEM SELECTION

An Integrated Approach

Jon D. Clark
Arnold Reisman

PRAEGER

PRAEGER SPECIAL STUDIES • PRAEGER SCIENTIFIC

Library of Congress Cataloging in Publication Data

Clark, Jon.
    Computer system selection.

    Includes bibliographies and index.
    1. Electronic digital computers--Purchasing.
I. Reisman, Arnold, 1927 (Aug. 2)-   II. Title.
QA76.5.C533   001.64   80-21496
ISBN 0-03-057888-4

Published in 1981 by Praeger Publishers
CBS Educational and Professional Publishing
A Division of CBS, Inc.
521 Fifth Avenue, New York, New York 10017 U.S.A.

123456789 145 987654321

Printed in the United States of America

PREFACE

Applied methods for computer system selection vary as widely as do requirements, motivations, and administrative environments. The academic literature is replete with specialized methods to handle considerations of taxation, depreciation, and even subjective evaluation of software performance and quality. What is missing, however, is a unified methodology that will allow a decision maker to trade-off various measures of computer systems whether they be tangible, intangible, financial, or non-financial. This book presents such a methodology. Although it consists of components drawn from data processing and accounting, among others, integration is provided by concepts taken from decision theory and engineering economics.

The target audience to be served by this book is composed of senior or first-year graduate students in business information systems, computer science, and industrial engineering. In addition, it is designed to serve the reference needs of the practitioner and the scholar within each of these fields.

CONTENTS

LIST OF TABLES

LIST OF FIGURES

1

INTRODUCTION

THE ECONOMIC SIGNIFICANCE OF
THE SELECTION DECISION

Electronic data processing (EDP) was the most burgeoning industry of the past decade, and it is likely to continue growing at an extreme rate through the 1980s. Pushed along by the increasing demands for data, storage, retrieval, analysis, reporting, and so on, and by needs in scientific and engineering communications for analytical power, the industry's projected revenues are expected to grow at an average annual rate of 16 percent to 18 percent.[1] This degree of growth, moreover, is not confined to the United States, as can be seen in Table 1.1. IBM derived approximately 46 percent of its revenues in 1977 from abroad. The corresponding figures for other manufacturers are: Univac 49 percent; Honeywell 50 percent; Burroughs 37 percent; Control Data 43 percent; NCR 46 percent; and Digital Equipment 43 percent. (For more current general market data, see [1, 10-13].)

Certain segments of this vast industry are just beginning to develop beyond the level of infancy. The minicomputer market, although not as large as that of the midi and maxi range, is experiencing explosive development. The personal computer market is even more explosive with a projected change from $63 million in shipments for 1977 to over $300 million in 1980.

The extremely high growth rate of this portion of the market reflects, in part, three major points:

TABLE 1.1
Computer Mainframe Base by Manufacturer
(in millions of dollars for 1977)

Company	United States			International			Total	
	Through 12/77	Percent of Total	Percent of Firm	Through 12/77	Percent of Total	Percent of Firm	Through 12/77	Percent of Total
IBM	29,682	70.6	54.4	24,906	71.7	45.6	54,588	71.1
UNIVAC	2,961	7.0	51.5	2,794	8.1	48.5	5,755	7.5
Honeywell	2,898	6.9	50.4	2,851	8.2	49.6	5,749	7.5
Burroughs	2,811	6.7	63.3	1,629	4.7	36.7	4,440	5.8
Control Data	1,483	3.5	56.7	1,134	3.3	43.3	2,617	3.4
NCR	961	2.3	54.4	805	2.3	45.6	1,766	2.3
Digital Equipment	329	0.8	57.4	244	0.7	42.6	573	0.7
Other	926	2.2	72.3	355	1.0	27.7	1,281	1.7
Total	42,051	100.0	54.8	34,718	100.0	45.2	76,769	100.0

Source: Some of these statistics were reported in Standard & Poors Industry Surveys, Office Equipment and Services: Basic Analysis, July 27, 1978, Section 2, p. 14.

- With typical investments, including all hardware and software, ranging from $1,000 to $100,000, many small, would-be users may now be able to afford such equipment for a wide variety of uses.
- Whether or not the user is small, the number of potentially cost-justifiable applications has grown considerably.
- As students of data processing from both secondary and college levels begin infiltrating the work force, increased demand will certainly follow.

Considering the range in size of potential computer uses, as well as the variety of both economic and noneconomic factors relevant to the selection of hardware systems, a unified methodology is needed to systematically bring all of the factors into proper perspective. The consequences of a failure to do so could be costly and, at most, disastrous.

Frequently, computer systems are intended to serve as support for some type of management information system (MIS). Table 1.2 displays some facts regarding MIS development failures as found in a recent study [9]. The data should highlight the potential dangers of an incomplete cost-benefit analysis.

The California State Department of Human Resources[2] reported that over 1,000 programs had to be converted at a cost of $3 million, representing 80 man-years of effort. With financial commitments at such high levels, one cannot afford to make unwise decisions.

In yet another vein, Ruth M. Davis, director of the National Bureau of Standards, Institute for Computer Sciences and Technology, said, "It is 'technological suicide' to introduce computer or telecommunications equipment into one part of the organization without considering the effects of that change on other parts of the process."[3] That is to say, the introduction of EDP or any change to an existing system affects the organization as a whole and, therefore, the way it performs. One must be conscious of this fact and attempt to estimate its total impact in any cost-benefit analysis.

CURRENT STATE-OF-THE-ART

Considering the vast sums of money at stake, it is surprising that standard methodologies of cost-benefit analysis have not been developed and used in the field of EDP. Certainly, there have been attempts, and they can be roughly classified as academic and practical or common.

The academic approach can be typified by a conceptual all-inclusiveness: measure everything of value and rank the respective alternatives relative to either cost, weighted costs, cost/effectiveness ratio, or in terms of cost/value [2, 4, 6, 7]. To be sure, there are a variety of other techniques. In general, each attempts to convert every factor into monetary terms regardless of whether it is naturally expressible in these terms. The most serious failing of these methods is that a general methodology is not developed that will permit a prospective decision maker to select the relevant portions of the overall methodology. It is

TABLE 1.2
Prototypal MIS Development Failures

Industry	Application	Original Development Cost Estimate in $(mm)	Original Payback Period Estimate in Years	Development Cost at Abandonment in $(mm)	Development Cost Estimate at Abandonment in $(mm)	Payback Period Estimate at Abandonment in $(mm)
Electric utility	Customer information	2.5	4	7.0	15.0	15
Consumer goods	Order processing	0.9	3	2.5	5.5	net cost increase
Banking	Integrated loan	1.5	–	1.3	2.5	net cost increase
Petroleum	Well information	1.0	–	0.9	–	net cost increase
Insurance	Customer accounting	1.3	4	1.9	4.0	12

Source: Howard L. Morgan and John V. Soden, "Understanding MIS Failures," *Data Base* 5, Nos. 2, 3, and 4 (Winter 1973): 157-67.

4

felt that the manager should have the option of using a methodology that includes consideration of such factors as federal, state, and local taxes, the investment tax credit, not to mention a host of nonfinancial attributes.

The other end of the spectrum is represented by practitioners who, because of the lack of suitable methods, are forced to use quick and dirty procedures typified by the "general impression," or perhaps a cost-only weighted scoring method. Corporate or institutional politics play a heavy role in the decision-making process and are too often underestimated by those affected. It is a generally accepted practice that if a project is the least bit uncertain, it would be better to fail with a large vendor such as IBM than with one of the smaller companies. The ready excuse, "if IBM couldn't do it," is often sufficient to save the manager involved, at least temporarily. While the academicians have a relatively complete conceptual model, the models employed by practitioners are easy to use, if somewhat inaccurate.

There is a middle ground, however, that is espoused by many of the articles contained in some of the popular trade journals [3, 5, 8]. The articles dealing with cost-benefit analysis are more precise mathematically than those commonly used by practitioners. They are often easy to use, albeit narrow in scope.

GOALS OF THE BOOK

In a broad sense, the goal of this book is to fill the methodological void that exists between the academician's and practitioner's approach. Most of the ground that will be covered is not new. However, the work of other authors will be put together into a pragmatic yet sound unified methodology. To be sure, some new ground will be broken, but this too will be integrated into the overall procedure.

More specifically, the goals are as follows:

- To integrate current theory, practice, and provide extensions.
- To develop a taxonomical and yet pragmatic approach to computer selection specifically to assist the decision maker in selecting from a generalized methodology a method relevant to his or her needs.
- To provide a number of realistic examples of the various techniques presented so as to aid in the understanding of concepts discussed.

In order to accomplish these goals, this book is partitioned into seven chapters. Chapter 2 will lay the groundwork for the problem of computer system selection using a taxonomic approach. Chapters 3 and 4 develop the theory required to handle various discounted cash flow models and a variety of tax considerations. Chapter 5 presents a general decision model capable of handling both financial and nonfinancial factors as well as uncertainty. Finally a unified methodology of financial and nonfinancial factors is addressed in Chapter 6, followed by an example case study in Chapter 7.

NOTES

1. See Standard & Poors Industry Surveys [11,12] for more detailed information.
2. Marvin Smalheiser, "Mammoth D.P. Conversion Involves 1100 Programs," *Computerworld,* October 10, 1973, p. 6.
3. Ruth M. Davis, "Introduction of D.P. into Firm 'Not End in Itself,' " *Computerworld,* March 13, 1974, p. 39.

REFERENCES

[1] Barna, Becky. "The Datamation 50." *Datamation,* May 1979.

[2] Borovitz, Israel and Ein-Dor, Philip. "Cost Utilization: A Measure of System Performance." *Communications of the ACM* 20, no. 3 (March 1977): 185-91.

[3] Brandon, Dick H. "Computer Acquisition Method Analysis." *Datamation,* September 1972, pp. 76-9.

[4] Ein-Dor, Philip. "A Dynamic Approach to Selecting Computers." *Datamation,* June 1977, pp. 103, 104, 108.

[5] Heckman, Randall J. "The Best Time to Purchase Your Computer." *Datamation,* December 1972, pp. 59-60, 62.

[6] Joslin, Edward O. *Computer Selection.* Reading, Mass.: Addison-Wesley, 1968.

[7] King, John L. and Schrems, Edward L. "Cost-Benefit Analysis in Information Systems Development and Operation." *Computing Surveys,* 10, no. 1 (March 1978): 19-34.

[8] Martin, Donald D. "Taxation in the Lease-Purchase Decision." *Datamation,* February 1974, p. 59.

[9] Morgan, Howard L. and Soden, John V. "Understanding MIS Failures." *Data Base* 5, nos. 2, 3, and 4, (1973): 157-67.

[10] Solomon, Laurence. "The Top Foreign Contenders." *Datamation,* May 1979, pp. 79-81.

[11] Standard & Poors Industry Surveys, Office Equipment Systems and Services: Basic Analysis, July 27, 1978, Section 2.

[12] Standard & Poors Industry Surveys, Office Equipment Systems and Services: Current Analysis, September 13, 1979, Section 3.

[13] Withington, Frederic G. "The Changing Profile." *Datamation,* May 1979, pp. 10-12.

2
PROBLEM DEFINITION
AND FORMULATION

FACTORS TO BE CONSIDERED

The computer system selection decision involves many factors, some of which can be described in dollars and cents, some of which can be measured or counted, and yet others which may be difficult to quantify. The methods presented in this book require that all factors be quantified. Means for quantifying the many factors are, of course, discussed. In order to assist in the process of delineating the various factors to be considered in choosing between alternatives, a full taxonomy or a classification of computer selection attributes will be presented.[1]

In this chapter, only a top slice of the taxonomy will be presented. Each major area or subarea will be explored in Appendix A and should be referred to during an application of this methodology to ensure completeness.

An additional and important point to be made is that the general methodology is modular in nature and, therefore, tailorable to specific user needs. The taxonomy will help define broad-based modules that may or may not be included in the final decision aid or rule.

The outline in Table 2.1 delineates the major areas to be considered in the computer selection process. It includes costs, hardware, expansion potential, vendor support, and software (CHEVS). Each of the major modules described by the CHEVS taxonomy has a characteristic scale of measurement. Financial costs are handled exclusively by the C module of the CHEVS taxonomy through various capital budgeting techniques presented in Chapters 3 and 4. The

TABLE 2.1
The CHEVS Taxonomy

C   Costs
      Initial and one-time
      Continuing

H   Hardware characteristics
      Speed and capacity
         Central processor
         Peripheral equipment
         Auxiliary equipment
      Compatibility
      Switchability
      Reliability
      Special features and other characteristics

E   Expansion potential

V   Vendor support
      Programming assistance
      Training
      Maintenance
      Backup
      Documentation
      Personnel loaned

S   Software
      Systems
      Utilities
      Application

Source: Compiled by the authors.

remaining modules, due to their typically nonfinancial nature, will be dealt with analytically through concepts drawn from economic theory and/or utility theory; these will be addressed in Chapter 5. At a later point (Chapter 6), a methodology will be developed to combine both financial and nonfinancial components into a single decision rule, figure of merit, index, scoring model, or criterion function.

Examples of factors involved in each of the major modules of the CHEVS taxonomy and a few suggested scales of measurement are contained in the succeeding paragraphs. It should be noted that each of these areas has a sub-taxonomy delineating specific factors for the general case. These can also be referred to in Appendix A.

C   Costs or net profits are exclusively tangible dollar cash flows, for example, projections of payments to be made to the hardware manufacturer, the software supplier, and all those involved in the installation and continued use of the hardware/software system and the surrounding facilities wherever applicable. This also includes projections of all revenues attributable to the use of the system. Examples of the scales of measurement are dollars, pounds sterling, or any other currency or item of value, such as gold.

H   Hardware characteristics include a tremendous variety of factors, such as primary memory capacity, basic instruction cycle time, or possibly the required power supply. The generally accepted scale of measurement for each are, respectively, K words (1,000s of words), nsec (billionths of a second), 110 or 220 volts, and so on.

E   Expansion potential typically consists of factors representing either the amount of slack time in the current system expressed on a time scale, or an indication of maximum expansion in terms of numbers of certain physical units such as printers, or add-on memory expressed in K words or characters, and so on.

V   Vendor support involves such factors as programming assistance, training, and personnel loaned — probably best measured on a man/day scale. While maintenance and backup typically might be measured in terms of either miles to the source, travel time between, or simply some measure of availability.

S   Software rating might occur in several dimensions, including execution time in seconds or minutes, or size in K words of primary memory required. Alternately, software may be rated subjectively on an arbitrary scale. If, for example, a specific software package provides 80 percent of the desired capabilities, then a rating of 80 percent would be given, for example, a 0-100 scale could be used.

Arbitrary scales may be used in all major areas of the CHEVS taxonomy. The most difficult operational characteristic of using arbitrary scales is gaining a fair appraisal of the performance of a hardware candidate or alternative on the factor in question. A very useful tool for this type of rating, or for decisions requiring subjective inputs is the Delphi Method. A description of the Delphi Method[2] is included in Chapter 4.

A SENSE OF PERSPECTIVE

After the development of the CHEVS model and a brief explanation of the various factors and scales of measurement of each, it might be beneficial to take a second look at precisely where it fits in the general scheme of methodologies used by academicians and practitioners.

In Chapter 1, three general approaches were discussed: the academic, typified by Edward O. Joslin[3]; the practical, characterized by a "general impression"; and finally a middle ground, espoused in trade journals such as *Datamation*. The approach being advocated here attempts to borrow the strong points of each and, more importantly, fill the voids that have been left. Figure 2.1 pinpoints some of these areas.

A VIEW THROUGH CHEVS

In order to demonstrate the various techniques in a coherent fashion, a single example will be used throughout this book. It involves the selection among five alternatives for mainframe, peripherals, software, and support. The quantities cited are taken from an actual equipment analysis completed recently. The identities of the various participants will be omitted. Note that in the example one of the alternatives to be considered is that of retaining the current system.

A report intended for top management is presented in Table 2.2. It is necessarily brief; nevertheless, it contains at least one factor in each of the major areas of the CHEVS model. Table 2.3 classifies the same information within the context of the CHEVS model. In Chapters 5 and 6, techniques will be demonstrated that apply financial and nonfinancial considerations, respectively; and many of the examples will originate from data contained in this volume.

FIGURE 2.1
The Advocate/Characteristic Matrix

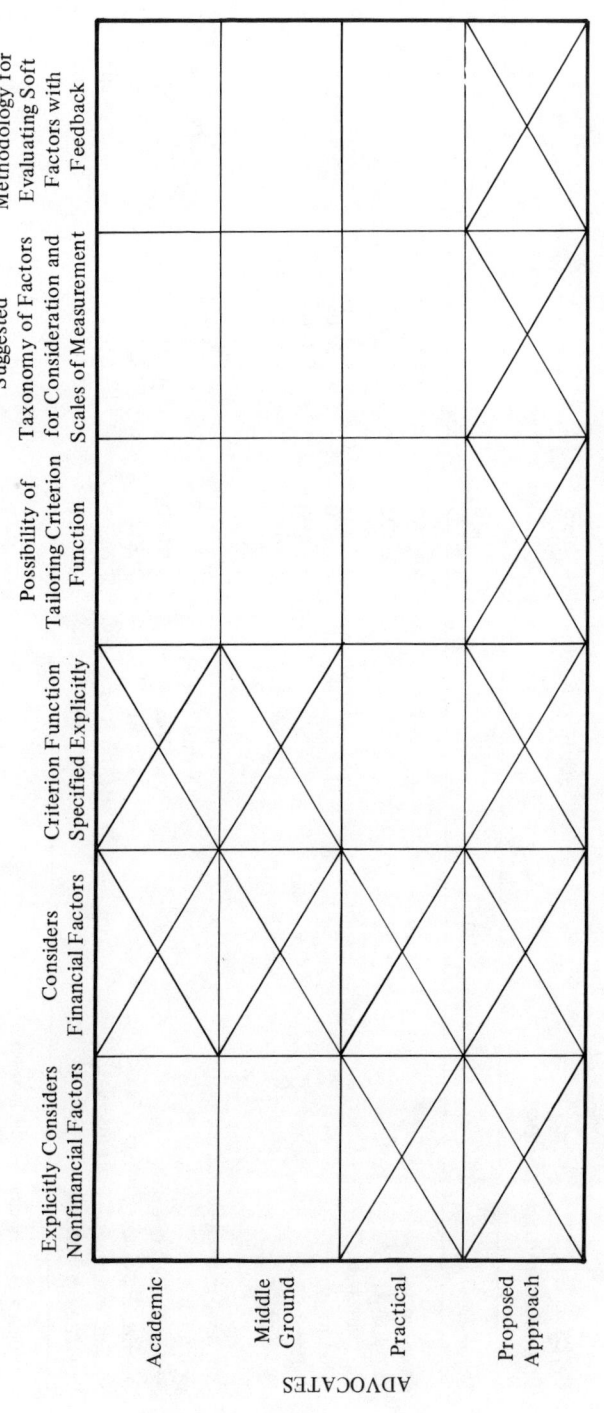

Source: Compiled by the authors.

11

TABLE 2.2
Top-Management Report

Major Item	Now	A	B	C	D
Basic rental	41,967	42,284	39,767	47,608	58,694
Extra shift	1,200		2,500	3,106	3,900
Maintenance	1,950				
Education	200		300	300	1,200
Software			1,400	1,400	2,000
Totals	45,317	42,284	43,967	52,414	65,794
Conversion requirements	No	Yes	No	No	Yes
Conversion cost	0	Minimal	0	0	30,000 to 60,000
Expansion increments	11,000	2,000	11,000	11,000	8,000
Operating system rating	Bad	Good	Bad	Bad	Good
System engineering support	None	100% Req.	None	None	None
Benchmark results	6-8 hrs.	45 min.	—	55 min.	40 min.

Source: Compiled by the authors.

12

TABLE 2.3
A View through the CHEVS Taxonomy

Financial factors (C)
    One-time costs: conversion costs
    Continuing costs: basic rental
                       extra shift
                       maintenance
                       education

Nonfinancial factors
    Hardware (H): benchmark results
    Expansion potential (E): increments
    Vendor support (V): systems engineering support
    Software (S): operating system rating

Source: Compiled by the authors.

NOTES

1. See [1]-[4] for more information on computer performance evaluation methods and, in particular, [4] for a series of useful taxonomies.

2. In particular, see O. Helmer, *Social Technology* (New York: Basic Books, 1966); O. Helmer and N. Rescher, "On the Epistemology of the Inexact Sciences," *Management Science* 6 (1959): 47; and N. Dalkey and O. Helmer, "An Experimental Application of the Delphi Method to the Use of Experts," *Management Science* 9 (1963): 458.

3. Edward O. Joslin, *Computer Selection* (Reading, Mass.: Addison-Wesley, 1968).

REFERENCES

[1] Drummond, Mansford E. Jr. *Evaluation and Measurement Techniques for Digital Computer Systems.* Englewood Cliffs, N.J.: Prentice-Hall, 1978.

[2] Ferrari, Domenico. *Computer Systems Performance Evaluation.* Englewood Cliffs, N.J.: Prentice-Hall, 1978.

[3] Hellerman, Herbert and Conroy, Thomas F. *Computer System Performance.* New York: McGraw-Hill, 1975.

[4] Svobodova, Liba. *Computer Performance Measurement and Evaluation Methods: Analysis and Application.* New York: American Elsevier, 1976.

3

FINANCIAL CONSIDERATIONS

TIME VALUE OF MONEY CONCEPTS

A Basic Model: ERBS

We shall next develop a model that will be applicable to any investment decision [10]. This model will reduce to their present worth all disbursements and receipts involved in the possession and operation of computer hardware and software. Mathematical relationships for the less complicated cases may be obtained by merely dropping or simplifying certain terms in the model expression. The section that follows will define all of the cases that may arise in data processing investment policy decisions. Subsequent sections will treat some of these cases individually.

Let E   symbolize the operating expenses or disbursements for each individual piece of hardware/software;

    R   will symbolize the revenues or receipts that are due to the possession and/or operation of a piece of hardware/software;

    B   symbolizes the purchase price of the hardware/software; and

    S   represents the salvage value.

Thus, the case involving E, R, B, and S (ERBS) is the most complex situation considered by this model. It involves each alternative in terms of its individual purchase price and salvage value, operating income, and expense relationships. Many of management's decisions, however, are based on the comparison of cases less complicated than ERBS, but from it they all may be derived. For example, should owners, managers, and/or consultants be faced with a decision among several alternative items of hardware/software that will be leased rather than purchased, a comparison of the ER subcase will be required. Furthermore, should the hardware/software in question not have any assignable income or revenue function, only E need be considered. This classification scheme includes all possible cases to be formulated. Figure 3.1 presents graphically all major subgroupings.

FIGURE 3.1
Structure of Special Cases of the General Model ERBS

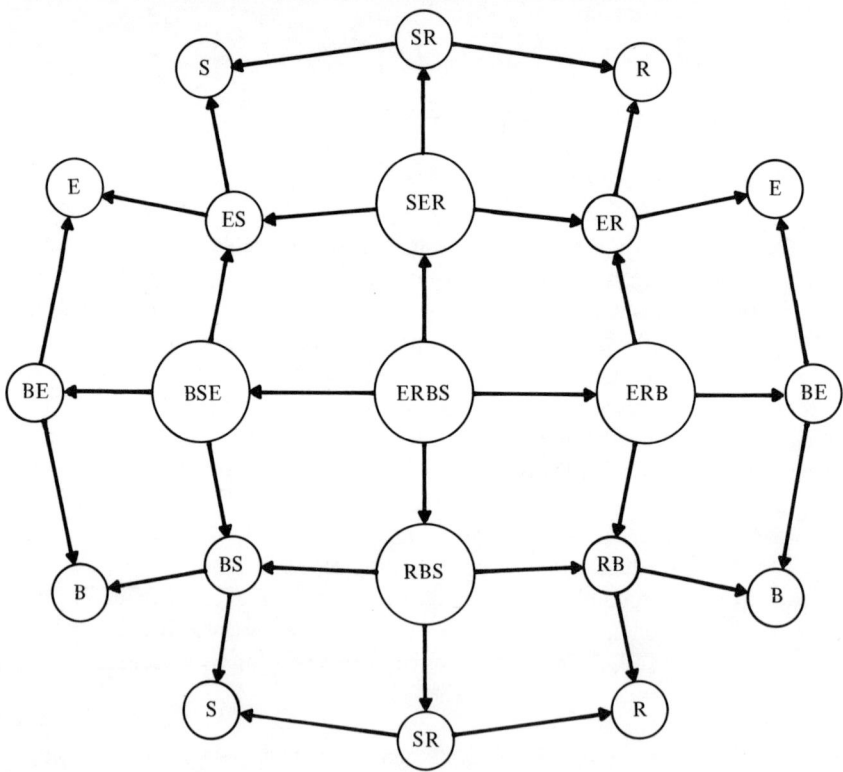

E = Operating disbursements   B = Capital investments
R = Operating receipts   S = Salvage value

Source: Compiled by the authors.

Essential Concepts

Time Value of Money

A given amount of money, properly invested, may earn interest and thus grow in magnitude. Alternatively, there is a cost associated with borrowed money. Opportunities are foregone when such money is allowed to sit idle. Thus, such costs are time-dependent. Cash flows must be identified in terms of timing as well as amount.

If the interest charge for any one period of time is based on the original principal amount only, and not on the accumulated, due to interest amount up to that point in time, then the interest is said to be "simple interest," which is given by the formula:

$$I = Pi*N$$

where P = principal: amount borrowed or invested; i* = the simple interest rate; N = the number of periods before repayment or withdrawal; and I = total interest for N periods.

If the interest charge for any period is based on the original principal plus any accumulated interest charges up to that period, then it is "compound interest," which is given by the formula:

$$I = P(1 + i)^N - P$$

where i = the compound interest rate; P = the original principal; N = the number of periods before repayment or withdrawal; and I = total compound interest for N periods.

We observe that in the above two cases we had interest that accrued at the end of each time period. The rate (i or i*)[1] was considered for one time period. We could also consider the discount factor that is distributed continuously over time. This is called the continuous interest rate, r, as opposed to the discrete rate i. The continuous rate r and discrete rate i are related by the formula:

$$i = e^r - 1 \text{ or } r = \ln(1 + i)$$

Thus a 20 percent continuous interest rate is equal to a 22.14 percent discrete interest rate. Table 3.1 shows how the principal grows with respect to time, for the same interest rate of 8, 10, or 12 percent per annum, when the interest is discrete and continuous.

A comparison of the relation between discrete and continuous processes is afforded by an examination of Figure 3.2. When time t is measured in units of time equal to the interest period of the discrete model, the two cases will

TABLE 3.1
Compounded Amount for $1,000 Investment

Time in Periods, t = N	Values of r = i .08 Discrete	.08 Continuous	.10 Discrete	.10 Continuous	.12 Discrete	.12 Continuous
1	$1,080	$1,083	$1,100	$1,105	$1,120	$1,128
2	$1,166	$1,174	$1,210	$1,221	$1,254	$1,271
3	$1,260	$1,271	$1,331	$1,350	$1,405	$1,433
4	$1,360	$1,377	$1,464	$1,492	$1,574	$1,616
5	$1,469	$1,492	$1,611	$1,649	$1,762	$1,822
6	$1,587	$1,616	$1,772	$1,822	$1,974	$2,054
7	$1,714	$1,751	$1,949	$2,014	$2,211	$2,316

Source: Compiled by the authors.

yield the same compounded amount at t = 0, 1, 2, . . . , if r is chosen equal to ln(1 + i). If r is chosen equal to i, the continuous method will give a compound amount larger than that obtained with the discrete process.

Thus at the end of 4.5 years, we see that the amount in the account is F_S if the interest is based on simple interest calculations, and F_D if it is based on compound discrete interest calculations. Obviously $F_D > F_S$ because of the compounding. Again, if the interest is continuously compounded, we observe that the amount at the end of 4.5 periods is F_C. We see that $F_C > F_D$ during the compounding period. This is not surprising since in the case of continuous compounding, the interest on interest is being calculated every time instant; whereas in the discrete case it accrues only at the end of the year. Therefore, if the proper r is used, then $F_C = F_D$ at the end of every period.

It should be noted that if r is incorrectly assumed to be numerically equal to i, then F_C^1 is the amount at the end of the 4.5 periods. Clearly, under these circumstances $F_C^1 > F_C$.

these circumstances $F_C^1 > F_C$

Example 3.1. A person invests $100.00 at 5 percent simple interest per annum; 5 percent compound interest per annum; and 5 percent continuous compounding. How much does he or she receive in interest at the end of eight years in each of these cases?

1. Simple interest for eight years =
   PiN = 100 (0.05)(8)
   = 40

FIGURE 3.2
Compound Amount versus Time-Discrete and
Continuous Compounding

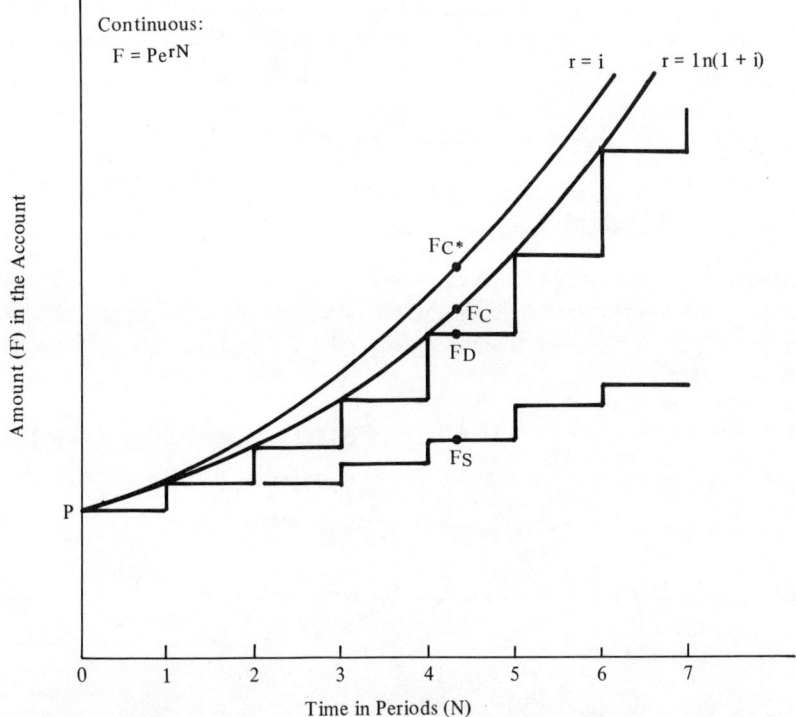

Continuous:

$F = Pe^{rN}$

$r = i$ $r = 1n(1 + i)$

Amount (F) in the Account

F_C*

F_C

F_D

F_S

P

0   1   2   3   4   5   6   7

Time in Periods (N)

Discreet:

$F = P(1 + i)N, N \leqslant j < 1,$

$N = 0, 1, 2. . .$

Source: Compiled by the authors.

2. Compound interest for eight years when discrete rate is used

$= P(1 + i)^N - P$

$= 100(1 + 0.05)^8 - 100$

$= 1.4775(100) - 100$

$= 47.75$

3. Continuous compound for eight years when continuous rate is used

$= Pe^{rn} - P$

$= 100e^{0.05(8)} - 100$

$= 100 (1.4918) - 100$

$= 49.18$

As expected, $49.18 > 47.75 > 40.$

Present Worth

Similar to the notion that a sum of money on hand at this moment has potentially higher value some time in the future, the expenditure that takes place in the future has a lower present value or "present worth." The present worth of a sum of money F to be given N periods hence is calculated by these formulas:

$$P_S = F/iN = F\,(iN)^{-1}$$

$$P_D = F/(1 + i)^N = F\,(1 + i)^{-N} \quad \text{if the interest is compounded discretely}$$

$$P_C = F/e^{rN} = Fe^{-rN} \quad \text{if the interest is compounded continuously}$$

Example 3.2. What is the present worth of $1,000, which is due ten years hence, if the interest is simple; if the interest is compounded annually; and if the interest is continuously compounded. Take the interest rate as 5 percent in all the cases.

1. Present worth $P_S = F\,(1 + iN)^{-1} = 1000\,[1 + 0.05(10)]^{-1} = 666.67$

2. Present worth $P_D = F\,(1 + i)^{-N} = 1000\,(1 + 0.05)^{-10} = 613.91$

3. Present worth $P_C = F\,(e^{-rN}) = 1000\,[e^{-.05 \times 10}] = 606.53$

Again, as could have been guessed, $P_S > P_D > P_C$.

The General Model

The economic component of the computer selection decision rule must consider the expenses (E), the revenues (R), the purchases (B), and the salvage value (S) aspects of the ERBS model and employ the time value of money concepts. The interest on money borrowed, on money owed, or on opportunities foregone may be treated either on a continuous or discrete basis; any algebraic statements must reflect the above. The continuous basis of treating interest or cost of capital is conceptually much more sound. This is because investments need not await the beginning nor the end of any arbitrary calendar period.

Therefore the economic model[2] in terms of continuous discount rate and continuous cash flows can be stated as follows:

$$P = B - S + E - R = B - \int_{0}^{T} [R(t) - E(t)]\,e^{-rt}dt - Se^{-rT}$$

The definite integral from 0 to T is necessary due to the expense E(t) or revenue R(t) streams typically being a function of time t, where T is the projected economic life of the hardware/software component.

The corresponding algebraic statement when the cash flows are assumed to be discrete and discounting[3] continuous is:

$$P = B - \sum_{p=0}^{k} (R_p - E_p) e^{-r \sum_{q=0}^{p} T_q} - Se^{-rT}$$

where

$$\sum_{q=0}^{p=k} T_q = T$$

Moreover, when the cash flows and discounting are both discrete[4], the equation becomes

$$P = B - \sum_{p=0}^{k} (R_p - E_p)[1 + i]^{-\sum_{q=0}^{p} T_q} - Se[1 + i]^{-T}$$

and again

$$\sum_{q=0}^{p=k} T_q = T \; .$$

The above equations can be used to calculate P the present worth of the cash flow streams associated with the various alternative configurations. It represents the economic yardstick for comparison purposes. In all of the above equations time must be expressed in the same units as the respective rate of discount; for example, if i is the annual rate then T_q must be expressed in years.

METHODS OF MANAGERIAL AND ENGINEERING ECONOMICS

Decisions involving a choice between competing computer hardware/software alternatives are made at various levels of corporate or institutional management. Thus as part of his responsibilities, a system designer must choose between alternate components for the system or subsystem being designed. This choice is rarely based on technical considerations alone. The designer more often than not has a choice of several standard items that will perform the basic function required. The choice, therefore, is to a large extent an economic one. Alternately, a data processing (DP) manager must choose between alternative ways of securing various services required. Where such services require the use of hardware/ software systems, the choice might be between keeping an outdated version or replacing it with newer and/or more efficient components. There might be several manufacturers offering such systems and each manufacturer may offer several types, each having its own advantages as well as purchase price and operating cost characteristics. In addition, there might be the alternative of replacing the existing components with leased items.

We shall next turn our attention to the various methods developed over the years by management to handle computer system selection problems. We shall first state the underlying concepts involved in each methodology and then deduce the required mathematical models from the general model for cases of varying complexities. Each model so deduced will of course be classified on the basis of our ERBS scheme. Next, we shall turn our attention to a discussion of the advantages and disadvantages of the various methodologies and to some of the pitfalls inherent in them.

The Present Worth Method

This is a method that traditionally has been used to either evaluate the present worth of a future outlay or the present worth of an anticipated cash flow stream. Of equal, if not greater, importance, however, is the application of this methodology in choosing between alternate investment opportunities. The investments discussed here are not necessarily of the one-time variety. Specifically, these investments may involve both immediate outlays as well as commitments to future expenditures. Moreover, the investments might bring forth revenues at various times in the future (as with DP facilities management). Expenditure as well as revenue cash flows might either be discrete or distributed over time. The time pattern of either the required or anticipated disbursements or the expected revenues in one system may be very different from that of the competing systems. Thus, one configuration may have high initial costs and low time distributed or operating costs. In a competing alternative the reverse may be true, low initial costs but high time distributed commitments while revenues are either of the same pattern in both or also characteristic of the investment proposal. Yet another competitor or alternative might have no initial costs at all, as in the case of leased equipment, while still another may have no operating expenses though very high initial costs, as is the case with equipment carrying a service guarantee.

Thus we may see that when presented with as varied a list of alternatives as above, we must somehow be able to reduce all of these cash flow patterns to some "common denominator"; for otherwise we are presented with a choice based on conflicting measures. The present worth of these various cash flow streams is one such common denominator; as we shall see later, there are others.

In order to calculate the present worth of any investment program, in addition to projecting the cash flows for the life cycle of the investment, it is necessary to make the correct choices for the value of the discounting (continuous) rate r, or alternately, the (discrete) rate i. What these rates ought to be in any given analysis has been the subject of much debate in the literature of the last decade or so. The problem has yet to be resolved to everyone's satisfaction. It is because of this very problem that various scholars and practitioners have advocated other methodologies for decisions involving a choice between alternative investment opportunities. Specifically, the rate of return method, which is described in the next section, has been advanced as a way around this problem. We shall see later that the rate of return method also is not completely free of difficulties in application; and so the present worth approach has yet to be discarded. As a matter of fact, this approach has many advantages and is widely used. Returning to the question of the discounting or capitalization rate, we will take the position that somehow it can be evaluated. Reference [10] will present several of the best approaches to the problem thus far advanced in the literature.

The following example demonstrates the use of present worth as a means of comparing computer system alternatives.

Example 3.3. In this example we will consider the choice between five alternative approaches to the problem of satisfying a five-year $(N = 5)$ computer service requirement. Several simplifying assumptions will be made: there is no salvage value at the end of the fifth year $(S = 0)$; all alternatives have the same life, $T_A = T_B = T_C = T_D$; the interest rate is a discrete 10 percent (that is, $i = 10$ percent, $r = 9.531$ percent). The relevant cash flows for each alternative are as follows:

	Alternatives				
	Current Service	A	B	C	D
Monthly expense	45,317	42,284	43,967	52,414	65,794

The present value of these cash flows can be obtained as follows[5]:

$$P = B - \sum_{p=0}^{k} (R_p - E_p)e^{-r\sum_{q=0}^{p} T_q} - Se^{-rT}$$

Since no mention is made of a purchase price, B can be assumed to be zero $(B = 0)$. Similarly, $R_p = 0$. Moreover, in the absence of any statement to the contrary, all discounting periods can be assumed to be equal to each other and to those of the cash flows indicated. Hence, all $T_q = 1$ month. Thus, in five years there are 60 such periods, and the discounting term [see Appendix B for values of e^x, e^{-x}, $(1+i)^j$, and $\sum_{j=0}^{N} e^{-rj}$]

$$e^{-r \sum_{q=0}^{p} T_q}$$

can be replaced by e^{-rx60}. However, since the discounting time period is now one month, the discount rate must reflect this; hence, $r = 9.531/12 \cong 0.8$ percent and the present worth P is simply

$$P = 0 - \sum_{p=0}^{k} (0 - E_p)e^{-.09531/12 \sum_{q=0}^{p} T_q} - 0$$

At this stage we must make a choice as to whether the cash flows occur at the beginning or the end of each period. If the former is true, the term $\sum_{p=0}^{k}$ will read $\sum_{p=0}^{59}$, for otherwise we would count 61 payments. If, however, the payments are assumed to occur at the end of each period, then the above term should read $\sum_{p=1}^{60}$.

Assuming beginning of the period payments

$$P = \sum_{p=0}^{k} E_p e^{-(.09531/12 \sum_{q=0}^{p} T_q)}$$

$$= E_p \sum_{p=0}^{k=59} e^{-(.008 \sum_{q=0}^{p} T_q)}$$

The bracketed term can be found in Appendix Table B.3, for example, the "SUM OF E^{-RX}" column for R = .08 and x = 59 reads 4.7842913E + 01. The E + 01 means that the decimal point must be shifted one place to the right. Moreover, we can round off the above so that the term reads 47.84. The E_p's are simply the monthly figures for each of the alternatives. Hence, the present worth values can be obtained.

		Alternatives			
	Current Service	A	B	C	D
Monthly Expense	45,317	42,284	43,967	52,414	65,794
Σe^{-rj}		47.84	47.84	47.84	47.84	47.84
	2,167,965	2,022,867	2,103,381	2,507,486	3,147,585

Inasmuch as the present worth (of expenses) of alternative A is the lowest, then it is the least cost approach and, therefore, should be selected providing that this is the only criterion.

The above are the only cash flows and the present worths to be considered. However, the above example did not include purchase price, revenue, and/or salvage value considerations. Let us now enlarge the problem to include these one at a time.

Let us assume that the following investments must be made at T_0 to prepare the computer sites before the installation. This will give us a problem of the EB subcase of ERBS.

		Alternatives			
	Current Service	A	B	C	D
Present worth of monthly expenses	2,167,965	2,022,867	2,103,831	2,507,486	3,147,585
Capital investment	0	100,000	15,000	40,000	60,000
Present worth of EB	2,167,965	2,122,867	2,118,831	2,547,486	3,207,585

The least cost alternative now has become B.

Each alternative might also have a salvage value in five years and thus become the EBS subcase of ERBS. Note that the salvage value must be discounted to T_0 (assume $r = .095$).

		Alternatives			
	Current Service	A	B	C	D
Present worth of monthly expenses and capital investment	2,167,965	2,122,867	2,118,381	2,547,486	3,207,585

Salvage value	-25,000	-30,000	-30,000	-65,000	-105,000
$e^{-.095(5)}$	.622	.622	.622	.622	.622
Present worth of salvage value	-15,550	-18,660	-18,660	-40,430	-65,310
Present worth of EBS	2,152,415	2,104,207	2,099,721	2,507,056	3,142,275

In this case the least cost alternative is again B.

Finally, let us assume that the following revenue streams are attributed to each alternative so that we can see an example of the general ERBS case.

	Alternatives				
	Current Service	A	B	C	D
Present worth of EBS	2,152,415	2,104,207	2,099,721	2,507,056	3,142,275
Monthly revenues	-42,000	-45,000	-43,000	-55,000	-60,000
$\Sigma e^{-.008(60)}$	47.84	47.84	47.84	47.84	47.84
Present worth of revenues	-2,009,280	-2,152,800	-2,057,120	-2,631,200	-2,870,400
Present worth of ERBS	143,135	(48,593)	42,601	(124,144)	271,875

The highest return alternative is now C. The last several illustrations should convince one to consider all relevant cash flows since any exclusion of one may cause a different decision to be made.

The Rate of Return Method

This method is also used to evaluate alternative computer system investment opportunities[6] and the general model equation, or special cases of it, may be applied in various circumstances. The question here is: For a given cash flow, what is the rate r which renders the "present worth" equal to zero? The "present worth," however, takes on a somewhat different meaning depending on whether the problem at hand is one of evaluating a possible future investment or one of establishing a historical fact; that is, the return realized on past investments and the attendant cash flow streams. In the former case, the "present worth" is the current value of the investment, assuming that the investment program is to be initiated immediately. In the latter case, we are referring to the present worth at the time the investment was initiated. Thus we see that in either case the present worth commonly referred to in the use of this methodology is the worth at the time the investment program was, is, or will be begun.

In applying this methodology to evaluate alternative investment possibilities, we first must decide upon the minimum acceptable rate of return, inasmuch as all projects yielding less than this cut-off rate are unacceptable for investment consideration. All the other investment alternatives, that is, those yielding a rate of return above the given threshold (if they are not mutually exclusive as in the previous examples) are then ranked in order of preference based on the anticipated return rate thus calculated. However, the decision as to what value to use for the cut-off or threshold rate of return is not an easy one. Clearly, it is a function of the risk class or category to which the particular investment belongs. Similar to the problem of the choice of a discounting rate in present worth type analysis, recent literature is quite concerned with the establishment of a correct and proper cut-off rate.

Let us next demonstrate the uses of this methodology, first as a means of evaluating historical or actual rates or return, and second as a means of choosing between alternative investments. We will now consider the application of this method to evaluate the actual return realized on a given investment.

Example 3.4. Two years ago $200,000 was invested in a computer system; one year ago a $100,000 portion was sold. The estimated value of the system today due to some rather significant developments in specialized software is $132,000. Several approaches can be taken in applying the general model to this problem. The $100,000 sale at the end of the first year may be considered a revenue and, hence, the revenue function would be retained in the resulting equation. Alternatively, this could be considered a two-step "salvage value" problem. In either case, the general model reduces to

$$P = 200{,}000 - 100{,}000e^{-rT_1} - 132{,}000e^{-r(T_1 + T_2)}$$

where $T_1 = T_2 = 1$ year. We force P to zero and calculate r. The calculation, as is often the case in these problems, involves the use of trial and error. Thus, using the tables of Appendix B, let us try $r = 0.09$, giving

$$200{,}000 = 100{,}000e^{-0.9 \times 1} + 132{,}000e^{-.09 \times 2}$$
$$= 91{,}393 + 132{,}000 \times 0.8353$$
$$= 201{,}653 \text{ (not quite)}$$

Since the resulting figure is too high (exceeds 200,000), further discounting is necessary; hence a larger r is selected for trial.

Let us next try r = 0.095

$$200{,}000 = 100{,}000 \times 0.909 + 132{,}000 \times 0.8267$$
$$= 200{,}024 \text{ (close enough)}$$

therefore r = 0.095 or 9.5 percent.

From this simple example several important points emerge. First, the general model is applicable in calculating the expected rate of return on future investments as well as the realized rate of return on past investments. It should be apparent especially from the second example that the labor involved in extracting the rate of return r becomes great especially in the more complicated cases of ERBS.

In the past, two ways have been developed to reduce the tedium. Tables such as those in Appendix B showing present values of lump sums and of income streams arising from annuities and bonds have been produced. With the tables available, one can often cast one's problem in a form where the tables are useful. The other method of circumventing the problem has been through the use of formulas that provide approximate answers in the hope that they are "good enough."

Now there is another way to avoid the tedium. An algorithm has been developed [2] for computer-based solution of what is, perhaps, the most complex of all common compound interest problems: the determination of a realized rate of return on an investment portfolio where funds have been added to and withdrawn from the portfolio after the initial investment. Because this is a rather general algorithm, it can also be applied to a great number of simple cases such as finding the promised yield of a bond.

In applying this method to choose between alternative investments we merely compute the expected rate of return for each and rank the various possible investments in decreasing order according to the magnitude of this criterion. As shown in the following example, alternative C is by far the best with a return of 11 percent followed by alternatives A and B with returns of 9.5 percent and 8.1 percent.

	Alternatives		
	A	B	C
Initial investment	200,000	225,000	168,000
Portion sold after 1 year	100,000	115,000	80,000
Estimated current value	132,000	140,000	120,000
Rate of return	0.095	0.081	0.110

In summary, then, this method may use any of the ERBS subgroups of the general model.

The Equivalent Annual Cost Method

The literature provides yet another method for choosing between alternative computer system investments. Very simply put, this method requires that the entire cash flow stream associated with an investment be reduced to an equivalent series of uniform annual payments over the expected system life cycle. Thus, if the expected life of an investment is N years, and the present worth of all projected cash flows associated with this venture is calculated as above to be P, then the equivalent annual cost can be seen to correspond to an annuity of some value A. The annuity A is the equivalent series of uniform annual costs payable at the beginning of each year and running a period of N years, at the interest rate r. For this particular situation the general model can be shown to reduce to

$$P = A \sum_{j=0}^{N-1} e^{-rj}$$

or

$$A = P / \sum_{j=0}^{N-1} e^{-rj}$$

Alternatively, if the payments are to be made at the end of each year, the above expression must be modified to read

$$P = A \sum_{j=1}^{N} e^{-rj}$$

or

$$A = P / \sum_{j=1}^{N} e^{-rj}$$

which for convenience in using the tables in Appendix B can also be expressed as

$$P = A \left[\left(\sum_{j=0}^{N} e^{-rj} \right) - 1 \right]$$

or

$$A = P / \left[\left(\sum_{j=1}^{N} e^{-rj} \right) - 1 \right]$$

Where $1/ \left[(\sum_{j=1}^{N} e^{-rj}) - 1 \right]$ is called the capital recovery factor.

Having formulated by deduction the present worth equation for the problem, we calculate the value of P for the expected cash flow stream. In order to arrive at the equivalent annual cost, we multiply the calculated value of P by the "capital recovery factor" with the same values for r and N as used in calculating P in order to calculate A.

As a method of comparison of alternative investment proposals this procedure is straightforward, assuming that all proposals being considered have equal expected lives. (Chapter 6 discusses the issue of differential lives.) One merely ranks the alternatives according to the uniform annual cost associated with each.

There is some question, however, regarding the applicability of this as well as other methods for the comparison of alternative investments, the economic lives of which are of differing magnitudes. For instance, a possible investment X has an economic or useful life of say N years, and a competing investment Y has a life of M years while N ≠ M. If, in addition, both investments are to serve the same function as would be the case in alternate plant or equipment proposals, then how is the advantage of the longer life of investment X incorporated into the equivalent annual cost? Grant [4] takes the position that from fundamental economic considerations involved in the calculations, the shorter-lived investment used a correspondingly shorter "capital recovery factor." Thus, at least the interest on money invested and also the recovery of such money has been properly apportioned. This he amplifies by pointing out that the consideration of longer life investment implies that a service of at least this duration is required by the investor. This means that the service will still be required after the shorter-lived investment Y is retired; and "presumably, although not necessarily, the annual costs of continuing the service will be of the same general order of magnitude."[7] If it is assumed that as good an estimate as any is that each replacement will have the same first cost, salvage value, and annual disbursements as the item being replaced, the annual cost will be repeated during the second and subsequent life cycles.

A somewhat more sophisticated view of the matter recognizes that the present decision between a long-lived and short-lived alternative is simply a decision as to what to do now. In aiming to have the decision now turn out to be the best decision in the long run, it is appropriate to consider what may happen after the expiration of the life of the shorter-lived alternative.

A prospect that N years hence a replacement structure with a much lower annual cost is likely to be available should be given weight in the present choice as a factor favorable to "Investment Y." Similarly, the prospect that "M" years hence the replacement structure will have higher annual costs is a factor favorable to the present selection of "Investment X." In general, prospects for technological improvements, changes in service requirements, and price reductions are favorable to the selection of short-lived alternatives; prospects for price increases and for extra costs incident to replacements are favorable to the selection of longer-lived alternatives. The extent to which such prospects may be evaluated numerically in the cost comparison and the extent to which they must be considered only as irreducible data naturally will depend on circumstances.

Example 3.5. As an illustration of the equivalent annual cost method of comparing alternative proposals, we shall use the cash flow streams (note the already calculated present worths of each) shown in Table 3.2.

TABLE 3.2
Equivalent Annual Cost Method Summary Table

Year	Cash Flow Streams			
	Alternative 1		Alternative 2	
0	B_0	13,000	B_0	25,000
1	B_1	2,000	B_1	1,000
2	B_2	2,200	B_2	1,000
3	B_3	5,000	B_3	2,000
4	B_4	2,600	B_4	3,000
5	B_5	3,000	B_5	5,000
5	$S(5)$	(1,000)		
5	B_1	13,000		
6	B_1	2,000	B_6	2,000
7	B_2	2,200	B_7	3,000
8	B_3	5,000	B_8	4,000
9	B_4	2,600	B_9	5,000
10	B_5	3,000	B_{10}	5,000
10	$S(10)$	(1,000)	$S(10)$	(3,000)
Calculated present worth		$40,289		$42,070

Source: Compiled by the authors.

Under the equivalent annual cost methodology, we merely perform one more calculation. We convert the total present worths of each competing proposal to a uniform series of payments lasting ten years at the same rate of capitalization used to find the present worth, namely, 7.7 percent for this example. We can now modify the equation to reflect the fact that we know P but are looking for A. Consequently,

$$A = P / \left[\sum_{j=0}^{10} e^{-rj} - 1. \right]$$

Now, using Appendix B, we find that the denominator is equal to $7.709 - 1 = 6.709$. Therefore, the equivalent annual cost for Alternative 1 is $A = 40,289/6.709 = 6,020$, and for Alternative 2, $A = 42,070/6.709 = 6,270$. Thus we see Alternative 1 to be more attractive still than Alternative 2. Specifically, Alternative 1 offers an equivalent annual saving of $250 over a period of ten years.

We should note at this stage that many practicing managers and accountants would arrive at the equivalent annual cost of the above example by merely adding all of the projected undiscounted cash flows for each alternative and dividing the sum by the projected time horizon. Thus, in this case, Alternative 1 would yield a net cash flow of $53,600, while Alternative 2 has a net cash flow of $53,000. Since the planning time horizon is ten years under this system of calculations, Alternative 2 has a lower average annual payment and is therefore preferable.

According to yet another incorrect practice, managers find the present worth of the projected cash flows, as was done in the example; but then they simply spread this value over the time horizon merely by dividing it by the number of years under consideration. Under this practice Alternative 1 would show an average annual cost of

$40,289/10 = \$4,029$

and Alternative 2 would indicate a cost of

$42,070/10 = \$4,207$

Thus the choice made by the previous decision rule has been reversed; and in this case it is in concert with the correct choice as calculated by spreading the present worth over the life of the project using the capital recovery factor. However, if one were interested in arriving at the rental payments to be associated with the lease of the above equipment, it is clear that one must use the correct application of the time value of money both in reducing the actual payments to their present worth and in spreading this present worth in equal installments over the planning time horizon.

The Payback Method

The payback period is defined as the length of time required for the sum of net cash returns to equal the initial capital outlay. This method has been widely used as a rule-of-thumb measure of the desirability of an investment opportunity. Under the above definition, the payback period for an inconstant stream of expected revenues is determined by adding the proceeds of successive years until the total is equal to the initial outlay. However, in practice the payback period is often computed by dividing the original amount invested by the average cash inflow. Thus, different answers may be obtained depending on which of the above methods are used. In common practice, this method does not recognize the time value of money; that is, there is no discounting involved. This method is simple to apply and simple to explain, hence its popularity. However, because of its simplicity, it does embody some major deficiencies: it ignores the benefits received after the payback period; and it ignores the pattern of returns within the period; that is, it does not consider the time value of money.

Example 3.6. Let us assume that we have the following expense and revenue streams for a proposed system to be installed.

$$E_1 = 2,000 \qquad R_1 = 5,000$$
$$E_2 = 2,200 \qquad R_2 = 8,200$$
$$E_3 = 5,000 \qquad R_3 = 10,500$$
$$E_4 = 2,600 \qquad R_4 = 8,600$$
$$E_5 = 3,000 \qquad R_5 = 5,000$$

In addition the system will cost $13,000 at T_0 and will have a salvage value at T_5 of 1,000. The net revenues are:

$$R_0 = -13,000$$
$$R_{1_{net}} = 3,000$$
$$R_{2_{net}} = 6,000$$
$$R_{3_{net}} = 5,500$$
$$R_{4_{net}} = 6,000$$
$$R_{5_{net}} = 2,000$$
$$\text{Salvage value} = 1,000$$

We find that at the end of the third year the system has more than paid for itself. That is, the net revenues, at the end of the third year, total $15,000, which is, of course, $1,500 more than the initial outlay. Therefore, the payback period in this case is less than three years.

It should be apparent from the definition of the payback period and from the example that this method is applicable only when there is a revenue to be derived from the investment. Thus, in a straightforward manner, at least this method cannot be applied to the comparison of alternatives where the economics dictate consideration of cost minimization.

Moreover, this method can be applied to any of the cases considered by ERBS, excepting, of course, those cases that do not involve revenue (R) or salvage value (S). That is, some form of income stream must be present and this stream must, within a finite time horizon, be greater than the cost or outgo stream in order for the payback period method to be applicable. In using any of the special cases of the general model with this method, it is, of course, understood that r, the rate of discount, is taken as being equal to 0 (zero).

The Average Rate of Return Method

The average rate of return method consists of adding all the earnings after depreciation and dividing them by the project's economic life. When this figure for average earnings over the period is obtained, it is divided by the average investment over the period. The calculation of the average return method will be demonstrated with the following example.

Example 3.7. Let us consider two alternatives. Alternative 1 has an initial cost of $1,000 and a four-year life. Using a straight-line depreciation method, its annual depreciation is, therefore, $250. Its earnings are listed in Table 3.3.

TABLE 3.3
Calculation of Average Return on Investment

Year	Earnings	Depreciation	Earnings after Depreciation*
		Alternative 1	
1	$500	$250	$250
2	400	250	150
3	300	250	50
4	100	250	(150)
			$300

300/4 / 1,000/2 = 75/500 = 15 percent

Year	Earnings	Depreciation	Earnings after Depreciation*
		Alternative 2	
1	$100	$167	$ (67)
2	200	167	33
3	300	167	133
4	400	167	233
5	500	167	333
6	600	167	433
			$1,098

1,098/6 / 1,000/2 = 183/500 = 37 percent

*Figures in parentheses indicate losses.
Source: Compiled by the authors.

Alternative 2 has an initial cost similar to that of the other alternative, namely $1,000, but its economic life is six years, hence the $167 annual depreciation.

Since straight-line depreciation was assumed in this case, the average investment in the project is the amount at the beginning of the period, plus the amount at the end of the period, divided by 2. The amount at the end of the period is zero in both cases; thus, the average investment is one half of the original investment. We thus see that the net (after depreciation) earnings are $300 and $1,098, respectively, for Alternatives 1 and 2, and the average annual earnings are $75 and $183, respectively. Inasmuch as $500 is the average undepreciated investment in both cases, Alternative 1 yields an average return on investment of 15 percent, while Alternative 2 yields 37 percent.

The average return method of ranking investment proposals is seen to be superior to the payback method in that it does take into account earnings over the entire economic life of a project. It still, however, carries one of the fundamental weaknesses of payback period; namely, it disregards the time value of money.

According to Weston [11], the average rate of return method involves a further weakness. It typically provides for the deduction of depreciation expenses in calculating the average rate of return. The payback method did not involve this error. Why deduction of depreciation involves error needs to be set forth explicitly, because there tends to be considerable confusion on this point. It is perfectly proper for accounting statements such as the income statement and the balance sheet to take depreciation into account as a part of one of the fundamental tenets of accounting procedure for accrual accounting. These financial statements, however, are historical in their orientation. They seek to take costs historically incurred and allocate them to the appropriate subsequent accounting periods.

Investment decisions are by their nature forward-looking. Costs that have been incurred are sunk costs. They are sunk in the sense that, once having been made, they cannot be recovered except through future cash flows. Hence, for investment decisions that are forward-looking in their orientation, only cash flows that occur subsequent to the sinking of funds into investments are relevant for decision-making purposes. The use of the average rate of return method in ranking investment proposals is, therefore, grossly in error.

The Pitfalls

In the chapter we have presented several methods that have been widely used in the literature and by practitioners for the evaluation of various economic alternatives. Some of these methods take into account the time value of money, others do not. Each of these methods has certain advantages and many of them have their unique disadvantages and pitfalls. Thus, we will use this opportunity to further discuss these pitfalls.

The payback period in all of its 250 variations does not take into account the time value of money. It ignores the pattern of returns within the payback period. Moreover, the payback period ignores the benefits received subsequent to the payback of the money invested. Yet it is a rather simple decision rule to use and to understand. This decision rule is very widely used in industry. Sloane [7] attempted to place the payback period in its perspective, vis-a-vis the rate of return method. He develops a relatively general decision rule: "When using the rate of return method of ranking investment opportunities, a slow payback is desirable in those investments promising an above average rate of return; a fast payback is desirable in those investments promising a rate of return below the average."[8]

The average rate of return he refers to is the rate of return for the industry of which the firm making the decision is part. He offers this statement as a general principle but cautions that it must be modified in light of the individual firm's circumstances. In addition, it must be recognized that this principle was based on a specific definition of the payback period; the definition requiring that the expected proceeds are added for each successive year until the total of such revenues are equal to the initial outlay. Dividing the initial outlay by the average expected income, on the other hand, or using any other means of calculating the payback will violate the above definition and therefore may violate this principle.

Turning now to an earlier part of the chapter, specifically to the various approaches that do in fact take into account the time value of money, we find the present worth method to be a very powerful tool. Its use is widely gaining in acceptance by financial managers, managerial economists, and most recently by accountants; as well as by many writers in the computer literature. However, the power of the present worth method is somewhat negated by the fact that it requires, for its application, the choice of a rate at which cash flows are to be discounted. This choice often involves consideration of the cost of capital that has inherent problems relating to its determination. In order to circumvent these problems the rate of return method has been widely advocated in recent years. However, this method does contain several pitfalls in its application. Some of these pitfalls are rather subtle. For one thing, it is indeed possible under certain conditions to obtain several solutions for the rate of return. This is because one is solving a polynomial for the exponent. Assuming that the initial investment, say C_0, is negative, that is, the proposal would require an initial investment, Pitchford and Hagger [6] have found sufficient conditions for the rate of return to be unique. One is that each of the other net incremental returns, C_j, where $j = 1, 2, \ldots$, from the project be positive. If, however, one or more of these net incremental returns is negative, the project may have no internal rate of return or more than one internal rate of return. Soper [9] shows that the sufficient conditions for the rate of return to be unique are that the final return, C_N, in the life of the project be positive, assuming that the initial investment C_0 was negative and that

$$-C_0 > \sum_{j=1}^{N} C_j/(1 + i)^j$$

for $j = 1, 2, 3, \ldots, N - 1$.

It is not difficult to find examples in the world of industry or commerce for which the terminal value C_N is not positive and hence for which the rate of return is not unique. Even if the terminal value of an investment is positive, Soper's second condition for a unique value of the internal rate of return may not be satisfied. Hirshleifer [5] presents several numerical values of patterns of net incremental returns that do not lead to a unique value of the internal rate of return. For some such values there is more than one value of the internal rate of return, while for others there is no real value of same. Bernhard [1] goes through an extensive analysis of the fundamental meaning of the internal rate of return method as opposed to the present worth method, indicating the reasons for the nonunique values of the internal rate of return as well as for the opposite rankings of projects, and goes on to define an average rate of return first suggested by Solomon [8], which is defined as follows:

$$-C_0(1 + i)^n = C_1 (1 + i_2) (1 + i_3) \ldots (1 + i_N)$$
$$+ C_2 (1 + i_3) (1 + i_4) \ldots (1 + i_N) + \ldots C_N$$

or

$$i = (C_1 (1 + i_2)(1 + i_3) \ldots (1 + i_n) + C_2 (1 + i_3) \ldots (1 + i_N)$$
$$+ \ldots C_N / -C_0)^{1/N} - 1$$

Fleischer [3] discusses several other problems with the rate of return method. One of these he calls the ranking error and the other the preliminary selection error. As the simplest illustration of the ranking error, he offers

the case where only two alternatives are being considered, and these alternatives are usually exclusive in the sense that acceptance of one automatically excludes the other. Mutual exclusiveness may occur either because each of the alternatives is technically capable of fulfilling the same required function, or because insufficient capital is available for the financing of both alternatives. Regardless of the cost, selection of the proposal having the highest rate of return may result in an economically inferior decision.[9]

Another example illustrating the ranking is

the case where more than two alternatives are being considered but, due to limited funds, not all of the projects may be accepted in the final capital budget. In this event the notion of "financial mutual exclusiveness at the margin" is introduced to indicate that the last alternative accepted automatically precludes all others.[10]

He suggests that the proper approach to this problem is "based upon the definition of alternative capital budget package, each of which is mutually exclusive."[11] Once these packages have been completely determined, the optimum package may be selected by any one of the several methods commonly used in the economic analysis. These methods take into account the amount and timing of cash flows and the time value of money. If the rate of return method is used, it is essential that the optimum package be chosen by an iterative technique in which successive increments of investment are examined to determine if they yield incremental rates of return in excess of the required minimum. As an example of the preliminary selection error, he offers a problem "which arises when selection of alternatives takes place prior to determination of the final capital budget."[12] This case generally occurs in one of two situations. First, some sort of screening may take place at organizational levels subordinate to (or other than) the senior executive level at which the final budget is structured. Second, a proposal may be selected from among two or more alternatives, each of which is mutually exclusive for technical reasons, prior to consideration as a contender for limited capital funds. "If investment funds are limited, it may be better to accept the inferior of two or more technically mutually exclusive alternatives in order to 'free' capital for investment in one or more other projects."[13]

SUMMARY

This chapter developed the notions of time value of money and present worth. The application of these, in whole or in part, are used in a number of classic methods of managerial and engineering economics: present worth, rate of return, equivalent annual cost, payback, and average rate of return. The following chapter considers yet another dimension of financial analysis: tax considerations.

NOTES

1. Assuming r is chosen so that $e^r - 1 = i$, or $r = \ln(1 + i)$.
2. This corresponds to equation 3.4-1.5 in [10].
3. Ibid.
4. This corresponds to equation 3.4-2.1 in [10].
5. The sign convention in this equation is cost minimization problem solving, for example, facilities cost terms are plus (+) and income terms are negative (−). This is purely arbitrary.
6. For actual investments made at some prior time, this methodology is used in evaluating the realized or actual rate of return.
7. See Grant[4].
8. See Sloane [7].
9. See Fleischer [3].

10. Ibid.
11. Ibid.
12. Ibid.
13. Ibid.

REFERENCES

[1] Berhnard, R. H. "Discount Methods for Expenditure Evaluation – A Clarification of Their Assumptions." *Journal of Industrial Engineering* 29, no. 1, (January-February 1962): 19-27.

[2] Fisher, L. "An Algorithm for Finding Exact Rates of Return." *Journal of Business* 39 (January 1966): 111-18.

[3] Fleischer, G. A. "Two Major Issues Associated with the Rate of Return Method for Capital Allocation: The 'Ranking Error' and 'Preliminary Selection.' " *Journal of Industrial Engineering* 17, no. 4 (April 1966): 202-08.

[4] Grant, E. L. *Principles of Engineering Economy,* 3d ed. New York: Ronald Press, 1960.

[5] Hirshleifer, J. "On the Theory of Optimal Investment Decisions." *Journal of Political Economy* 66, no. 5 (August 1958).

[6] Pitchford, J. D. and Hagger, A. J. "A Note on the Marginal Efficiency of Capital." *Economic Journal* 68, no. 271 (September 1958): 597-610.

[7] Sloane, W. R. "Payback in Perspective." *Business Perspective* 1 (Summer 1965): 17-19.

[8] Solomon, E. "The Arithmetic of Capital Budgeting Decisions." *Journal of Business* 29, no. 2 (April 1956).

[9] Soper, C. S. "The Marginal Efficiency of Capital: A Further Note." *Economic Journal* 66, no. 273 (March 1959): 174-77.

[10] Reisman, Arnold. *Managerial and Engineering Economics.* Boston: Allyn and Bacon, 1971.

[11] Weston, J. F. and Brigham, E. F. *Essentials of Managerial Finance,* 5th ed. Hinsdale, Ill.: Dryden Press, 1979.

4

TAXATION CONSIDERATIONS

There are a variety of ways of acquiring a given data processing system. Typically, one of the following means is chosen: rental from the manufacturer, leasing from a third party, or outright direct or installment purchase. A decision among these alternatives should consider the discounted cash flow and a desirable fit with other corporate cash flows as well as certain intangible factors. Leverage with the contractor is considerably increased if payments are still due; and it is potentially an excellent way of gaining attention if services provided are poor. Naturally the manufacturer should provide equal services regardless of the acquisition method; however, this is not always the case.

Obsolescence is frequently considered when choosing a method of acquisition. Obsolescence can be segregated into three basic types. Physical obsolescence simply relates to the operational condition of the system. Maintenance will surely increase, if not extend indefinitely, the physical life of almost any piece of equipment. Under normal circumstances this is not a major consideration.

Technical obsolescence, on the other hand, relates to how close the given piece of equipment is to the state-of-the-art. Rather fast and dramatic changes have characterized the data processing field since its inception. Although there is some evidence pointing to a general slowing of this trend, the future is quite uncertain.

Economic obsolescence is the most important criterion and simply relates to how well the system in question satisfies the needs of the user. Undoubtedly, it is this type of obsolescence that is of most concern to managers in a typical environment.

In this section we shall consider each of the acquisition alternatives and the effects on taxation. A matrix will be constructed that will assist in defining suitable modifications to the financial portion of the criterion function to be presented in a subsequent chapter.

TABLE 4.1
Acquisition Method/Economic Factor/Tax Provision Matrix

	Rent	Lease	Purchase
Economic Factors			
Lease/rental payments	x	x	
Excess use payments	x		
Maintenance		x	x
Initial purchase cost			x
Cost of capital			x
Insurance			x
Residual value			x
Tax provisions			
Federal income tax	x	x	x
Investment tax credit		x*	x
Depreciation		x*	x
State tax	x	x	x
Local property tax			x

*Allowed if asset is on the books of the user and not on those of a third party.

Source: Compiled by the authors.

From a tax standpoint the rental alternative permits one to expense all rental payments, but this precludes gaining any advantage through depreciation since the asset is not owned by the user. Typically, local property tax is not charged since it is usually allocated on the basis of owned assets. This alternative spreads over time the burden of the various cash flows required. The owner of the asset, however, may pass on a portion of the investment tax credit usually on the order of one-third.

The lease alternative also requires the expensing of costs as they are incurred, as does the rental alternative; but typically the user must pay for maintenance, which of course is a deductible expense. The lessee may receive, as is usually the case, the full investment tax credit from the owner. In addition, there are lease arrangements with an option to buy, which take on, from a tax point of view, some of the characteristics of both the standard lease and the purchase. In the case where there is a lease with an option to buy, the lessee is permitted to capitalize a portion of the lease cost as if it were an asset and in turn depreciate it by one of the accepted methods to be covered. The amount that is capitalized depends upon the terms of the lease as well as current Internal Revenue Service (IRS) rulings and, therefore, in a specific analysis one should consult with tax specialists to arrive at the proper expenses and capitalization as well as depreciation. The effect of this type of lease on state and local taxes must also be checked for each specific case to insure correctness.

If the purchase alternative is selected, there still will be a variety of deductible expenses such as maintenance or interest. However, the tax savings due to the depreciation of the asset and to the investment credit provisions of the Internal Revenue Code are normally significant. In this acquisition method, due to the fact that an asset of considerable value is owned, local property tax may now be assessed.

We will now begin to investigate each of the relevant provisions of federal income tax, state tax, and local property tax law.

FEDERAL TAX PROVISIONS

The federal tax rate on income for corporations is as follows: 17 percent for the first $25,000, 20 percent for the second $25,000, 30 percent for the third $25,000, 40 percent for the fourth $25,000 and 46 percent thereafter.[1] In any case, the resulting tax rate, exclusive of very low taxable income corporations ($< 100,000$), is 46 percent.[2] The significance of the tax rate can be seen when one realizes that expenses are directly deductible from income before the tax is allocated. Therefore, an additional dollar spent or written off as depreciation and deducted as an expense does not result in a dollar less of profit. Only a portion of that profit dollar affects the year end statements. In effect the government subsidizes the depreciation. This is often a significant portion of "expenses." At a rate of 46 percent for tax the net cost to the user is actually only 54 percent. Consider the following cases where there is an income of $100.00 and an expense, real or as depreciation, of $50.00 and $51.00, respectively.

	Case 1	Case 2	Net Change
Income	$100.00	$100.00	
Expense	50.00	51.00	+ 1.00
Gross profit	50.00	49.00	− 1.00
Tax rate	.46	.46	
Tax liability	23.00	22.54	− .46
Net profit	27.00	26.46	− .54

The result is clear: a dollar addition to "expenses" is offset $0.46 by the tax liability, thus resulting in a net reduction in profit of but $0.54.

The required modification of the present value equations previously developed is almost trivial since they need to be multiplied only by a factor representing $(1 - .46)$ or $.54$. Our familiar problem of selecting among five alternative systems will be used and the original present worth equation modified as follows:

$$P = \sum_{j=1}^{5} (R_j - E_j)e^{-rj} \qquad \text{(original equation)}$$

$$P = (1 - FTR) \sum_{j=1}^{5} (R_j - E_j)e^{-rj} \qquad \text{(including federal tax consideration)}$$

where the federal tax rate $(FTR) = .46$

Again, running through the same calculations we arrive at the net present worth of the expense stream projected for each of the five alternatives on an after-tax basis.

Sometimes there will be a revenue stream R, which must be considered before an acquisition method is chosen. It is easier by far to include both E and R along with the suitable tax provisions in an overall expression than it is to consider them separately. For the purposes of calculating federal income tax (not including allowances for depreciation and the investment tax credit), we simply subtract expenses from total revenues, and if the resultant is positive, multiply it by the FTR to obtain the tax liability. Since in most analyses involving both revenue and expense streams one is primarily interested in the resulting profit (may be either positive, if a gain, or negative, if a loss), the total value of expenses must be added to the federal income tax liability with that being subtracted from total revenues. In a discounted cash flow analysis we are interested in the present worth of the revenue and expense streams, which can be expressed as follows:[3]

$$P = \sum_{j=1}^{N} [R_j - (R_j - E_j)(FTR) - E_j]e^{-rj} = \sum_{j=1}^{N} [(R_j - E_j)(1 - FTR)]e^{-rj}$$

Now let us use the parameters specified in a previous example involving revenues of $100 for each of two cases as well as expenses of $50 and $51, respectively, at T_0. Note that in this case since all revenues and expenses were incurred at T_0, e^{-rj} is simply 1.00 and the $\sum_{j=1}^{N}$ can be eliminated from the equation. Thus we obtain the following:

$$P_0 \text{ (case 1)} = \frac{(100 - 50)(.54)}{27}$$

$$P_0 \text{ (case 2)} = \frac{(100 - 51)(.54)}{26.46}$$

An example that involves both revenues and expenses over time to be discounted to T_0 can be constructed similar to the familiar five alternative problem assuming the following revenue and expense streams:

Let $N = 5$ years

    $r = 9.531$ percent (as it was previously)

Projected Annual Revenue and Expense Streams

Alternatives

	Current Service	A	B	C	D
R_j	478,632	512,820	490,028	626,780	683,760
E_j	516,433	481,868	501,048	597,310	749,788

Substituting the required parameters into the equation we obtain:

$$P_0 = \sum_{j=1}^{5} [(478,632 - 516,433)(.54)] e^{-rj}$$

Since all the parameters remain constant over time we can simply take the sum of the e^{-rj}'s and multiply this by the factors remaining in the brackets.

$$P_{0_{\text{Current}}} = 3.794 (478,632 - 516,433)(.54)$$
$$3.794 (-19,657) = -77,445$$
$$P_{0_A} = 3.794 (512,820 - 481,868)(.54)$$
$$3.794 (16,095) = 63,413$$
$$P_{0_B} = 3.794 (490,028 - 501,048)(.54)$$
$$3.794 (-5,730) = -22,577$$
$$P_{0_C} = 3.794 (626,780 - 597,310)(.54)$$
$$3.794 (15,324) = 60,377$$
$$P_{0_D} = 3.794 (683,760 - 749,788)(.54)$$
$$3.794 (-34,335) = -135,576$$

It should be quite apparent in this example that Alternative A results in the largest present value for net profit and, therefore, is to be preferred in this analysis.

Let us assume that each of the above alternatives also have an initial capital investment at T_0 as well as a salvage value at T_5. This can be handled quite easily by considering them as expenses and revenues, respectively. Note, however, that these are not repetitive and must be discounted to T_0 to be included in the above cash flow analysis. The following equation will be used to calculate the after tax discounted cash flows of the Bs and Ss.

$$P_0 = (1 - FTR) \sum_{j=1}^{N} (S_j - B_j)e^{-rj}$$

Since we are, in this example, only concerned with the Bs at T_0 and the Ss at T_5 the expression reduces to

$$P_0 = (1 - FTR)[S_5(e^{-rx5}) - B_0 (e^{-rx0})]$$
$$(.54) (S_5 (.622) - B_0)$$

Using the following S and B streams we can obtain the net contribution of the initial investments and salvage values to the previously calculated R and E streams.

	Alternatives				
	Current Service	A	B	C	D
B_0	0	100,000	15,000	40,000	60,000
S_5	25,000	30,000	30,000	65,000	105,000
$e^{-.095x5}$	.622	.622	.622	.622	.622
Present worth of Ss	15,550	18,660	18,660	40,430	65,310
Present worth of $S_5 - B_0$	15,550	−81,340	3,660	430	5,310
$(1-FTR)$	.54	.54	.54	.54	.54
After tax present worth of Ss and Bs	8,397	−43,924	1,976	232	2,867
Previously calculated after tax present worth of Rs and Es	−77,445	63,413	−22,577	60,377	−135,576
Total present worth	−69,048	19,489	−20,601	60,609	−132,709

Note that with the added decision criteria of initial investment (Bs) and salvage value (Ss) the resulting best decision is Alternative C.

Depreciation Concepts

Depreciation is a provision of the Internal Revenue Code, which allows the owner of a property, in this case a computer system, to recoup the investment by deducting an amount from taxable income. This permits the investor to assign the cost of an asset purchased at some point, over the life of the asset. The depreciation expense allowed as a deduction from taxable income is unique in that it does not represent a true cash outflow over time since the entire investment was made at some initial point. However, since it reduces the cash outflow to the tax collector, for example, it is treated as an expense, it is a ready source of capital for the enterprise and should be exploited to its fullest. If the funds thus saved can be invested profitably in the interim, that is, before the asset needs replacement, a substantial increase in corporate profitability can result. It should be noted that the effect of depreciation is not to reduce the total amount of tax paid, but rather to defer the payment of the tax. One essentially obtains an interest-free loan and can make whatever investments that seem appropriate.

Several types of depreciation procedures are acceptable to the Treasury Department.[4] The three procedures in most common use are those allowed specifically by the Internal Revenue Code:[5] the straight-line method,[6] the declining-balance method[7] and the sum of the years' digits method.[8] These three methods differ not so much in the amount of total depreciation allowable over the life of the asset as in the fraction of the total depreciation that may be taken in the early years of the asset's useful life. In general it is desirable to take as much depreciation as possible as early as possible so that the funds thus generated can be invested for a longer period of time.[9] The purpose of this section is to provide quantitative guidelines for use by management in reviewing current depreciation policy and for suggesting ways of improving that policy.

Clearly the desirability of using an accelerated depreciation schedule depends upon the amount of profit that can be made by investing the funds thus generated. For this reason, a quantitative comparison of the various depreciation procedures requires that a measure of profitability for the invested funds be available. We have therefore decided to use a discounted cash flow analysis. As indicated in the earlier chapters, the discounted cash flow method is the uniquely correct method to use when the earnings of a firm over time are known with certainty. For most firms it is correct enough to make discounted cash flow a highly practical measure of profitability.

The Treasury Department recognizes both item accounting and class accounting procedures for depreciation. In the former, depreciation is computed separately for each depreciable capital asset. The individual results are then added to find the total depreciation deductible by that corporation for the year. In class accounting, each capital asset owned by the firm is put into one of several asset classes. Depreciation is then computed separately for each class of assets on the basis of the average life of the assets within the class. Whether item or class accounting is used, depreciation procedures are similar and the results of the present section apply. For ease of presentation, however, we shall speak as though only item accounting were being carried out.

The analysis presented herein is applicable to property held for the production of income, not for capital gains. Due to the somewhat different legal restrictions involved, setting quantitative guidelines for the latter type of property would require a slightly different form of analysis. Furthermore, we shall restrict our attention to the usual corporate situation in which the incremental tax rate is constant over time and depreciation is fully covered by pretax earnings.

The definitions given below are necessary for the subsequent discussion and are consistent with the current version of the Internal Revenue Code.

Depreciable Property: Any property, personal[10] or real, tangible or intangible, which is used in the conduct of a trade or business or is held to produce income, which was acquired in a bona fide transaction and has a limited and estimatable life exceeding one year (property having a useful life of one year or less is expensed, not depreciated).

Basis of Property: For purposes of computing depreciation, the basis of any item of depreciable property purchased by the taxpayer is the cost of the property plus the cost of any capital additions made to the property; that of property inherited is equal to the fair market value of the property at the time of the inheritance. Determination of the basis of an asset obtained in other ways can be quite intricate.[11]

Useful Lives: The useful life of the property, which is used for purposes of calculating depreciation, can be estimated by the taxpayer subject to review and possible disallowance by the IRS. Alternatively, one may obtain from the IRS an agreement in writing fixing the useful life of the property in question. Such an agreement is binding both upon the IRS and the taxpayer.

Salvage Value: The salvage value of an asset is the taxpayer's estimate of the market value of the asset at the end of its useful life. The Revenue Act of 1962 stipulates that in calculating depreciation for certain property the taxpayer may elect to reduce the salvage value by up to 10 percent of the basis of the property. In order to qualify for this election, the property must be depreciable personal property acquired after October 16, 1962, having a useful life of at least three years.[12] The election may be applied only in tax years beginning after January 1, 1962. Clearly, it is to the taxpayer's advantage to make this election whenever possible.

Salvage value enters explicitly into calculation of depreciation by the straight-line[13] and sum of the years' digits methods, but not in computing depreciation by means of the declining balance method. No matter which method is used for calculating depreciation, however, the total depreciation taken may not exceed the basis minus the salvage value.

Throughout our analysis, we shall employ the following symbols: N is the depreciable life of the asset in years, B is the original basis of the asset, S is the estimated salvage value of the asset after N years (possibly reduced as indicated above), T is the effective incremental income tax rate, i is the rate of return on investment, and P is the present value of the earnings on the cash flow accruing from the use of a certain method of depreciation.

Methods of Depreciation

Twenty Percent First-Year Depreciation

On qualifying property, 20 percent of the first $10,000 of the cash cost (or the first $20,000 of the cash cost if a joint return is filed) of newly purchased property may be deducted the first year.[14] In order to qualify, property must be tangible personal property with a useful life of at least six years and must be acquired by purchase after December 31, 1957.

If the property was purchased on trade-in, the cash cost does not include that portion of the basis of the new property that is due to the residual basis of the property traded in, but rather includes that portion paid for in cash or its equivalent. The basis of the new property is reduced by the amount of the first-year depreciation; the property is then depreciated by some suitable method using the new basis. The total amount of first-year depreciation is shown in Figure 4.1 as a function of the cash cost of the property. In Figure 4.2, the

FIGURE 4.1
First-Year Depreciation as a Function of the Cash Cost of Property during the Year

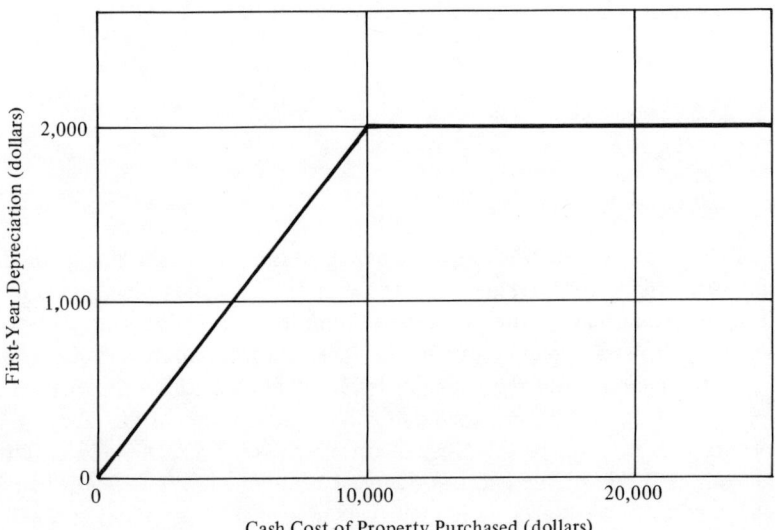

Source: Compiled by the authors.

effective rate of first-year depreciation is shown as a function of the cash cost of the property. The effective rate of first-year depreciation is constant at 20 percent out to a cash cost of $10,000, after which it decreases hyperbolically as shown in the figure.

FIGURE 4.2
The Effective Rate of First-Year Depreciation

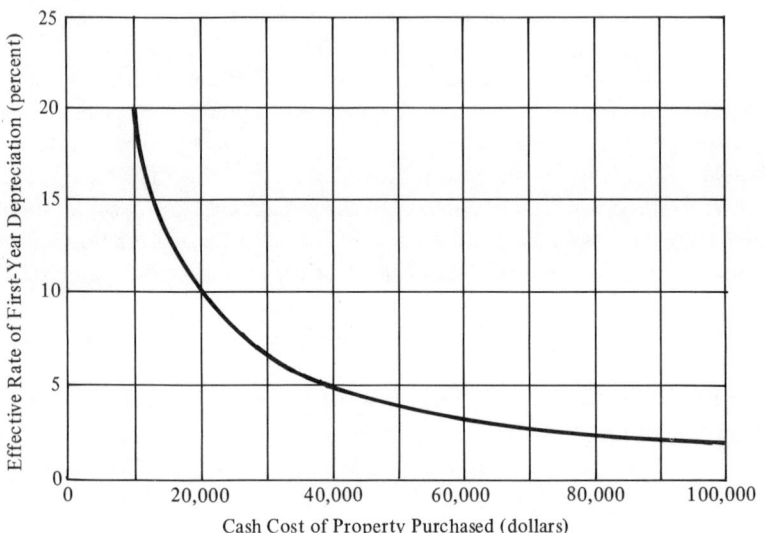

Cash Cost of Property Purchased (dollars)

Source: Compiled by the authors.

The Straight-Line Method.

Of all the procedures for computing depreciation, the straight-line method[15] is the most widely usable. It may be used on any depreciable property and is the only method that may be used on intangible property such as patents or copyrights. For the straight-line method, the rate of depreciation is constant and equal to the reciprocal of the depreciable life of the asset in years. The annual depreciation deduction is computed by dividing the basis minus the salvage value by N. Thus, if the basis or the original cost of an asset is $12,000 and the anticipated salvage value at the end of a ten-year economic life is $2,000, then the annual depreciation for each of the ten years in the life of the asset is (12,000 − 2,000)/10 = $1,000. Obviously, the deduction is constant over the life of the asset.

No other method of depreciation is of universal applicability. For example, in order to use any one of the other methods of depreciation, the asset must be tangible property with a useful life of at least three years. Of the other methods, the common attribute is that they produce more cash than the straight-line method early in the life of the asset. For this reason they are generally more profitable than the straight-line method, everything else being equal.

The Declining Balance Method.

The declining balance method[16] may be used on any tangible property having a useful life of at least three years. Depreciation for any one year is computed by multiplying the depreciation rate, which is constant throughout the life of the asset, by the current basis of the asset. The basis is then reduced by the amount of the depreciation taken during that year and the procedure is repeated for the next year. This cycle continues until either the useful life of the asset is expended or the total depreciation taken is equal to the original basis minus the salvage value. Thus the current basis of the asset declines with time. The depreciation rate is larger than that used for the straight-line method. The maximum rate that can be used with the declining balance method is twice that of the straight-line method or $2/N$. This rate applies if the property was acquired new or erected by the taxpayer after December 31, 1953; otherwise, the maximum rate is $1.5/N$. The latter rate is used if the property was acquired used or acquired before January 1, 1954.

We shall now calculate the amount of the declining balance left after the jth year and the amount of depreciation allowable using the declining balance method during the nth year. Let α/N be the rate of depreciation to be used with the declining balance method. The value of α is indicated above. If α is equal to 2, the method is called the double declining balance method or, less commonly, the 200 percent declining balance method. If α is equal to 1.5, the method is called the 150 percent declining balance method. Let A_j be the amount of the declining balance after the jth year and D_j be the depreciation taken during the jth year. Then

$$A_1 = B - B\,\alpha/N = B(1 - \alpha/N)$$
$$A_2 = A_1 - A_1\,\alpha/N = B(1 - \alpha/N)^2$$
$$A_j = A_{j-1} - A_{j-1}\alpha/N = B(1 - \alpha/N)^j$$

and

$$D_j = A_{j-1}\alpha/N = B\,\alpha/N(1 - \alpha/N)^{j-1}$$

Since A_N is not equal to zero, there is a salvage value of the asset implicit in the declining balance method. This salvage value is different for different values of α and N. Its variation with N for the two most common values of α is shown in Figure 4.3 and in Table 4.2. For a given basis and α, the salvage value increases monotonically as N increases, gradually approaching the limit,

$$\lim_{N \to \infty} A_N = \lim_{N \to \infty} B\,(1 - \alpha/N)^N = Be^{-\alpha}.$$

Example 4.1. Let the initial basis of an asset be \$10,000 and let us further assume that the asset has an economic life of five years. If we use $\alpha = 2$, then

FIGURE 4.3
Salvage Value Versus Life of Asset

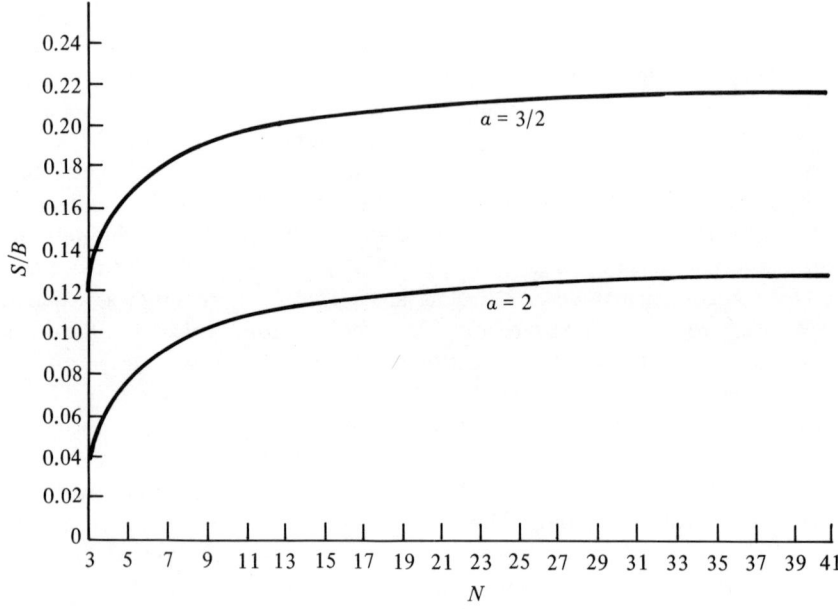

Note: In a strict sense, "salvage value" is only an estimated value, not the fallout of a depreciation formula. Nevertheless, when this residual value occurs, the IRS allows a switch over to another method such as straight line, which will fully depreciate the asset.

Source: Compiled by the authors.

the amounts of the declining balance after each of the five years are as follows:

$$A_1 = 10,000 \,(1 - 2/5) = 6,000$$
$$A_2 = 6,000 \,(1 - 2/5) = 3,600$$
$$A_3 = 3,600 \,(1 - 2/5) = 2,160$$
$$A_4 = 2,160 \,(1 - 2/5) = 1,296$$
$$A_5 = 1,296 \,(1 - 2/5) = 778$$

Therefore, $A_5 = \$778$ is the salvage value we could have calculated by using the values of Table 4.2. For a five-year life and $\propto = 2$, the table yields a value of .077760, which when multiplied by the original basis of $\$10,000$ yields $\$777.60$ as a "salvage value."

TABLE 4.2
Salvage Value Inherent in the Declining Balance Method as a
Fraction of the Basis

	α	
N	3/2	2
3	0.125000	0.037037
4	0.152588	0.062500
5	0.168070	0.077760
6	0.177979	0.087792
7	0.184864	0.094865
8	0.189927	0.100113
9	0.193807	0.104160
10	0.196874	0.107374
11	0.199361	0.109989
12	0.201417	0.112157
13	0.203146	0.113983
14	0.204620	0.115543
15	0.205891	0.116891
16	0.206999	0.118067
18	0.208836	0.120020
20	0.210298	0.121577
25	0.212910	0.124364
30	0.214639	0.126213
35	0.215867	0.127528
40	0.216785	0.128512
45	0.217497	0.129276
50	0.218065	0.129886
∞	0.223130	0.135335

Source: Compiled by the authors.

Thus the depreciation deduction schedule for our $10,000 asset would be

$$D_1 = 10,000 - 6,000 = 4,000$$
$$D_2 = 6,000 - 3,600 = 2,400$$
$$D_3 = 3,600 - 2,160 = 1,440$$
$$D_4 = 2,160 - 1,296 = 864$$
$$D_5 = 1,296 - 778 = \underline{518}$$

$$\sum_{j=1}^{5} D_i = 9,222,$$

and $\sum\limits_{j=1}^{5} D_j$ + Salvage Value = 9,222 + 778 = $10,000.

The Sum of the Years' Digits Method

The sum of the years' digits method[17] may be used on property qualifying for the double declining balance method as stipulated above. Using this method the current year's depreciation deduction is calculated by subtracting the salvage value from the original basis of the property and multiplying this quantity by a fraction that differs from year to year. The fraction has a denominator that is constant with time and that is equal to the sum of the digits representing the number of years of useful life of the asset. For example, for N = 5, the denominator equals 1 + 2 + 3 + 4 + 5 = 15. The numerator changes each year and is equal to the number of useful years of life left in the asset at the beginning of the current year. For example, if an asset originally had a useful life of five years, at the end of the second year it has three years of useful life remaining so that the fraction for the third year would be three-fifteenths or one-fifth. In general, for an asset with N years of useful life the denominator of the fraction is equal to N(N + 1)/2 and the numerator of the fraction is equal to N − j + 1, so that the entire fraction is equal to 2(N − j + 1)/N(N + 1). Thus,

$$D_j = (B - S)2(N - j + 1)/N(N + 1),$$

and the amount of depreciation deducted in any given year is proportional to the useful remaining life of the asset at the beginning of that year [2,3].

Example 4.2 Let us now consider the deduction schedule for the asset of example 4.1, that is, for a $10,000 item having a five-year life and no inherent salvage value. Therefore:

$$D_1 = 10,000 \times 2 \times (5 - 1 + 1)/5(5 + 1)$$
$$= 20,000/30 \times 5 = 3,333$$

$$D_2 = 20,000/30 \times 4 = 2,667$$

$$D_3 = 20,000/30 \times 3 = 2,000$$

$$D_4 = 20,000/30 \times 2 = 1,333$$

$$D_5 = 20,000/30 \times 1 = 667$$

and

$$\sum_{j=1}^{5} D_j = 10,000$$

These are the three methods of depreciation that are specifically allowed by law. In addition, the Internal Revenue Code of 1954 states that "any other consistent method productive of an annual allowance which, when added to all allowances for the period commencing with the taxpayer's use of the property and including the taxable year, does not, during the first two-thirds of the useful life of the property, exceed the total of such allowances which would have been used had such allowances been computed under the method described in paragraph two."[18] The method described in the paragraph referenced is the declining balance method. Thus the declining balance method produces as fast a write-off as is allowable during the early life of asset. In this sense, it is a limiting method of depreciation.

When constructing the criterion function for the financial factors in an investment decision, be sure to include the depreciation D in the expense stream so that both federal and state income taxes are allocated on the correct basis. Note, too, that the depreciation method has an effect on state property tax, as will be covered later.

The Investment Credit

The 7 percent investment credit[19] was instituted by the Revenue Act of 1962 in order to encourage investment in new plant and equipment; later it was changed to 10 percent.[20] That act provided that a certain fraction of the amount of money invested by an individual or a firm in new capital assets is deductible as an investment credit from the taxpayer's income tax liability. The basis of the asset was then reduced by the amount of the investment credit. The Revenue Act of 1964 leaves the amount of the investment credit unchanged but stipulates that, starting with tax years beginning in 1964, the basis of the capital asset is not reduced by the amount of the investment credit.

In order to qualify for the investment credit, property must be either tangible personal property or other tangible property — but not including buildings or their structural components — which is used as an integral part of manufacturing, production, or extraction, or to furnish transportation, communication, electricity, gas, water, or sewage disposal services, or constitutes a research or storage facility used in connection with the above. It includes only depreciable property with a usable life of at least four years constructed or acquired by the taxpayer after December 31, 1961.

The amount of the investment credit is not always simply 10 percent of the total amount invested by the taxpayer during the current tax year in new plant and equipment. The effective rate used for computing the investment credit varies with the estimated life of the asset as shown in Table 4.3. Moreover, the maximum amount of investment credit that is allowable in a single year depends upon the taxpayer's total tax liability during that year, in the manner illustrated in Figure 4.4. Thus in practice, the effective rates used for computing

TABLE 4.3
Effective Tax Rate versus Life

Life (years)	Fraction of Basis Subject to Credit	Effective Rate (percent)
3 or more but less than 5	1/3	3 1/3
5 or more but less than 7	2/3	6 2/3
7 or more	1	10

Note: The table assumes a 10 percent basic tax rate.

Source: Compiled by the authors.

the investment credit may not be those shown in Table 4.3 under some circumstances.

FIGURE 4.4
The Maximum Investment Credit Allowed

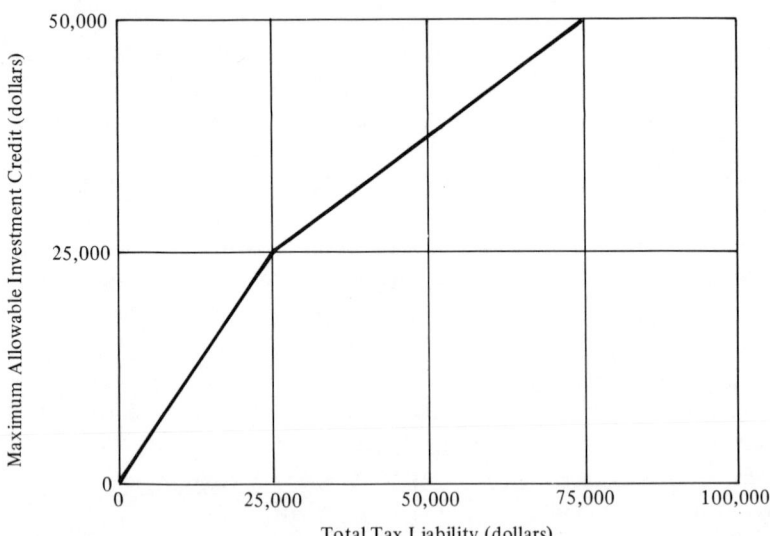

Note: The slope of the total tax liability line from $25,000 up will change (increase) each year through 1982. See regulation 1.46-9, paragraph 53IV.011 of [1], Vol. 1.

Source: Compiled by the authors.

Example 4.3. Suppose a manufacturing company purchased a new computer on January 1, 1979, for $65,000 cash. Clearly, its basis in the property is $65,000. The system has a useful life, N, of ten years. The manufacturer estimates that at the end of its useful life the system will have a salvage value of $10,000.

On its 1979 tax return, it reports an investment credit of $6,500 (10 percent of $65,000); this does not affect its basis in the property. Using the new basis, the company then proceeds to depreciate the property through its life by the straight-line method, the double declining balance method, or the sum of the years' digits method, giving rise to further deductions (see Table 4.4).

TABLE 4.4
Depreciation Deductions Based on Various Methods of Depreciation

Year	Straight-Line Method	Double Declining Balance Method	Sum of the Years' Digits Method
1979	$5,500	$13,000	$10,000
1980	5,500	10,400	9,000
1981	5,500	8,320	8,000
1982	5,500	6,656	7,000
1983	5,500	5,325	6,000
1984	5,500	4,260	5,000
1985	5,500	3,408	4,000
1986	5,500	2,726	3,000
1987	5,500	2,181	2,000
1988	5,500	1,745	1,000

Source: Compiled by the authors.

At the corporate tax rate (46 percent of all income of $100,000) the tax savings produced by reporting these depreciation deductions, not counting investment credit, are contained in Table 4.5.

TABLE 4.5
Tax Savings at the Corporate Tax Rate, by Method of Depreciation

Year	Straight-Line Method	Double Declining Balance Method	Sum of the Years' Digits Method
1979	$2,530	$ 5,980	$ 4,600
1980	2,530	4,784	4,140
1981	2,530	3,827	3,680
1982	2,530	3,062	3,220
1983	2,530	2,450	2,760
1984	2,530	1,960	2,300
1985	2,530	1,568	1,840
1986	2,530	1,254	1,380
1987	2,530	1,003	920
1988	2,530	803	460

Source: Compiled by the authors.

TABLE 4.6
Discounted Tax Savings, by Method of Depreciation

Year	Straight-Line Method			Double Declining Balance Method			Sum of the Years' Digits Method		
	Savings	e^{-rx}	Discounted Savings	Savings	e^{-rx}	Discounted Savings	Savings	e^{-rx}	Discounted Savings
1979	$2,530	.905	$2,290	$5,980	.905	$5,412	$4,600	.905	$4,163
1980	2,530	.819	2,072	4,784	.819	3,918	4,140	.819	3,391
1981	2,530	.741	1,875	3,827	.741	2,836	3,680	.741	2,727
1982	2,530	.670	1,695	3,062	.670	2,052	3,220	.670	2,157
1983	2,530	.607	1,536	2,450	.607	1,487	2,760	.607	1,675
1984	2,530	.549	1,389	1,960	.549	1,076	2,300	.549	1,263
1985	2,530	.497	1,257	1,568	.497	779	1,840	.497	914
1986	2,530	.449	1,136	1,254	.449	563	1,380	.449	620
1987	2,530	.407	1,030	1,003	.407	408	920	.407	374
1988	2,530	.368	931	803	.368	296	460	.368	169
			$15,211			$18,827			$17,453

Source: Compiled by the authors.

Discounting these tax savings at 10 percent per year yields a present value of $15,211 for the tax savings due to reporting depreciation using the straight-line method, $18,827 for the double declining balance method, and $17,453 for the sum of the years' digits method, as shown in Table 4.6. Even greater tax savings often can be obtained by using the declining balance method for the first several years of the asset's life, then switching to the straight-line method.[21]

If a taxpayer owns a depreciable asset for only a portion of the year, all of the 20 percent first-year depreciation and the 10 percent investment credit may be taken, but only a pro-rata share of the regular depreciation allowance may be deducted. Table 4.7 recapitulates the conditions under which the investment credit and the various methods of depreciation may be used in computing depreciation allowances for various kinds of assets. Figure 4.5 shows how cumulative depreciation calculated by the various methods varies throughout the life of a typical asset.

STATE TAX

Typical state income taxes are simply based on net profits as are federal income taxes. Thus a suitable expression of the state tax liability at the state tax rate (STR) would be:

$$ST_j = [(R_j - E_j)(STR)]$$

When applying discounted cash flow concepts to obtain the equation representing the present worth of the projected cash flows considering state taxes, we arrive at the identical equation developed when we considered federal income tax only:

$$P_0 = \sum_{j=1}^{N} [R_j - (R_j - E_j)(STR) - E_j] e^{-rj}$$

LOCAL PROPERTY TAX

Local property tax in most instances is allocated on the basis of the depreciated value of the asset. However, this assumes that the discount rate fairly represents the deterioration in the value of the asset. If one of the accelerated depreciation methods is used, the local tax authorities may disallow the use of book value in the tax calculation. The equations to be developed assume that the book value is allowed for this purpose.

TABLE 4.7
Property Types versus Credits and Depreciation

Qualifying Property	Allowable Credit and Methods of Depreciation*					
	20 percent First-Year Depreciation	Straight-Line	Double Declining Balance	150 percent Declining Balance	Sum of the Years' Digits	10 percent Investment Credit
Intangible Property		x				
Tangible Property						
Useful life 2 years		x				
Useful life 3 years						
Constructed or acquired new after December 31, 1953		x	x	x	x	
Constructed or acquired on or before December 31, 1953, or acquired used		x		x		
Useful life 4 or 5 years						
Constructed or acquired new after December 31, 1953						
Buildings used as an integral part of manufacturing, production, or extraction		x	x	x	x	
Other property		x	x	x	x	x

Constructed or acquired on or before December 31, 1953, or acquired used					
Buildings used as an integral part of manufacturing, production, or extraction		x			x
Other property		x		x	
Life of at least 6 years					
Constructed or acquired new after December 31, 1953					
Buildings used as an integral part of manufacturing, production, or extraction		x	x	x	
Other real property		x	x	x	x
Personal property		x	x	x	x
Constructed or acquired before December 31, 1953, or acquired used					
Buildings used as an integral part of manufacturing, production, or extraction	x	x			
Other real property		x		x	x
Personal property	x	x		x	x

*For conditions under which switching is allowed and for optimal switching strategies, see [4].

Source: Compiled by the authors.

FIGURE 4.5
The Cumulative Fraction of the Basis Depreciated

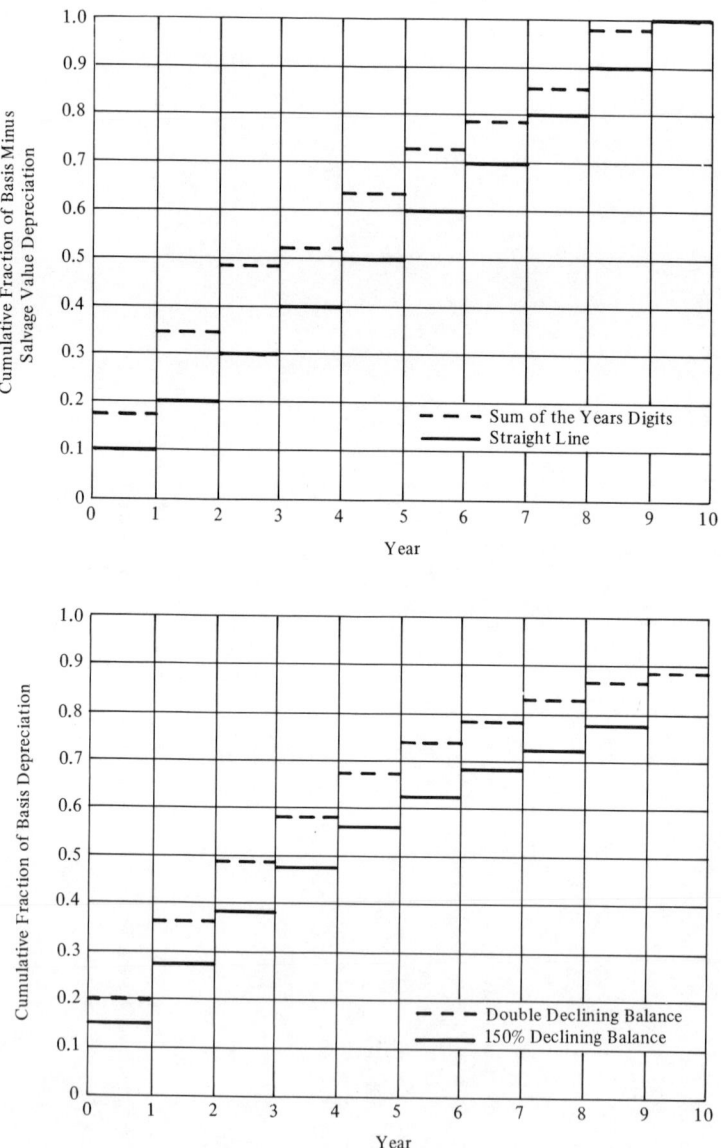

Note: These figures represent the cumulative fraction of the basis (or basis minus salvage value) that is depreciated by the various methods for each year during the life of an asset whose useful life is ten years.

Source: Compiled by the authors.

$$LT_j = (B - \sum_{j=1}^{N} D_j)\,(LPR)$$

where B is the original basis of the property and LPR is the local property tax rate.

Again applying discounted cash flow techniques we derive the following:

$$P_0 = (B - \sum_{j=1}^{N} D_j e^{-rj})LPR$$

SUMMARY

Before we embark upon the solution to a fairly realistic-size problem of computer selection as is done in Chapter 7, a general equation should be developed that will take into consideration the federal, state, and local property tax structures, depreciation, expense and revenue streams, the investment credit and, of course, the time value of money.

We will begin with the basic equation for the present worth of the revenue and expense streams including consideration for federal income tax only.

$$P_0 = \sum_{j=1}^{N} \left[(R_j - E_j)(1 - FTR) \right] e^{-rj}$$

But depreciation is deductible for federal tax purposes as are state and local taxes.

$$P_0 = \sum_{j=1}^{N} \left[(1 - FTR)(R_j - E_j - ST_j - LT_j - D_j) \right] e^{-rj}$$

Let us next add consideration for the investment credit (IC) as it reduces the tax liability in the year when it is taken.

$$P_0 = \sum_{j=1}^{N} \left[(1 - FTR)(R_j - E_j - ST_j - LT_j - D_j) + IC_j \right] e^{-rj}$$

Although one could expand each of the terms ST, LT, D, and IC into an overall equation of the present worth, this will not be done since substitution from the various sections of the chapter of the relevant terms and expressions will achieve this end quite properly. As a quick but effective method of checking the validity of the last equation, let us create an income statement with a variety of relevant parameters and determine whether the same results are produced.

Income Statement		
Revenues (R)		100.00
Expenses (E_j)	50.00	
State Tax (ST_j)	4.00	
Local Tax (LT_j)	1.00	
Depreciation (D_j)	6.00	
		61.00
Taxable Income		39.00
Tax Rate (Federal)		.46
Federal Tax Liability		17.94
Net Income After Taxes		21.06

In order to simplify the test, let us assume that all cash flows occurred at T_0 and therefore $e^{-rt} = 1.00$. Then substituting the above parameters into the equation, we obtain

$$P_0 = \sum_{j=0}^{0} \left[(1 - FTR)(R_j - E_j - ST_j - LT_j - D_j)IC_j \right] e^{-rj}$$

$$= [(1 - .46)(100 - 50 - 4 - 1 - 6)]$$
$$= [(.54)(100 - 61)]$$
$$= 21.06$$

Since the results are comparable, we should proceed to the next chapter where a comprehensive computer selection problem will be defined and analyzed using the methodologies developed.

NOTES

1. See regulation 1.11-1, paragraph 477.053 of [1], Vol. 1.
2. All calculations from this point forward assume a 46 percent federal tax rate. Since this is not appropriate for a relatively low-income firm, it must be adjusted accordingly.
3. Please note that the sign convention in the following calculations is opposite from that used previously as the focus now is profit maximization as opposed to cost minimization.
4. It should be recognized that certain depreciation procedures may be disallowed during conditions of national economic strains. Such is especially the case with some of the accelerated depreciation schemes.
5. See regulation 1.167 (b) - 0 (c), paragraph 1733 of [1], Vol. 2.
6. See regulation 1.167 (b) - 1, paragraph 1734 of [1], Vol. 2.
7. See regulation 1.167 (b) - 2, paragraph 1735 of [1], Vol. 2.

8. See regulation 1.167 (b) - 3, paragraph 1736 of [1], Vol. 2.

9. By doing so, one not only saves due to the timing difference in tax payment but also due to the differential tax rate if the taxable income can be kept below, say, $100,000.

10. Personal property is used here in the legal sense, as any property that is not realty.

11. See regulation 1.167 (g) - 1, paragraphs 1745-6, [1], Vol. 2.

12. See regulation 1.167 (f) - 1, paragraph 1744, [1], Vol. 1.

13. Each of these methods will be discussed subsequently in this chapter.

14. See code 179, paragraph 1966A, [1], Vol. 3.

15. See regulation 1.167 (b) - 1, paragraph 1734 of [1], Vol. 2.

16. See regulation 1.167 (b) - 2, paragraph 1735 of [1], Vol. 2.

17. See regulation 1.167 (b) - 3, paragraph 1736 of [1], Vol. 2.

18. S. Davidson and D. S. Drake, "Capital Budgeting and the 'Best' Tax Deprec-iation Method," *Journal of Business* 34 (October 1961): 442-52.

19. See regulation 1.38-1, paragraph 509D of [1], Vol. 1.

20. The application, if not the existence, of the investment tax credit has varied since its institution in 1962. It is advisable to check on its current status prior to use.

21. For calculations under which switching is allowed and for optimal switching strategies see [4].

REFERENCES

[1] Commerce Clearing House. *Standard Federal Tax Reporter,* Vol. 1-10, 1980.

[2] Myers, J. H. "Useful Formulae for DDB and SYD Depreciation." *Accounting Review* 33 (1958): 93-95.

[3] VanNess, P. H. "The Mathematics of Accelerated Depreciation." *N.A.A. Bulletin,* April 1961, pp. 5-14.

[4] Reisman, A. *Managerial and Engineering Economics.* Boston: Allyn and Bacon, 1971.

5

A GENERAL DECISION MODEL

In the previous chapters, we have developed some general models that provide us with information regarding the economic or financial aspects of the decision-making process. However, when we are actually faced with having to choose among various investment policies, allocate resources among competing projects, select the "best" system design, or make any other type of important decision, we find that the costs or financial aspects represent but one input to the problem. Usually we must weigh the relative importance of many factors, not only relative to each other, but also the degree to which they satisfy the needs, goals, objectives, and constraints or restrictions of the decision maker.

In addition, since the outcomes of most decisions will be affected by what will happen in the future, we of necessity must take future conditions into consideration in our present decisions. Since the future is not known to us with certainty, we can only consider it in probabilistic terms, that is, we can make educated guesses regarding the "chances" that certain conditions, scenarios, or states of nature will occur. The probabilities of occurrence of various possible future states must somehow be combined and related in the current decision procedure.

We generally like to measure objective facts on a linear scale. This is especially true when quantifying subjective information or judgments. Yet in either case the value we place on a little more or a little less of a certain attribute has in general a nonlinear relationship with the linear scale of this attribute.

The old saying, "once you have made your first million the second does not mean as much," is a good example of such considerations. The concept of utility as developed in modern economic theory allows us to recognize the essentially nonlinear and subjective relationships between values and the respective and linear attribute scales.

Lastly, many decisions require multiple decision makers or panels. The usual processes for arriving at consensus in committees or panels have been shown to be both inefficient and ineffective due to the many human frailties that are exacerbated by open debate. The Delphi Method will be introduced as a means of efficiently reaching an effective consensus by a panel of expert individuals.

In light of the above, we require a model general enough to incorporate any combination of the considerations in the previous paragraph. Specifically we need a unified methodology that will be applicable in decision-making situations where there may be several alternative solutions, several criteria, several future states of nature, economic utility considerations, and multiple decision makers. Such a model was designed in detail and with considerable rigor by Melvin W. Lifson in 1965 [4] and enlarged upon and heavily used by one of the authors of this book. In this chapter, we will borrow heavily from his methods. First we will lay the groundwork for the development of a general decision and utility model. In attempting to determine the proper input values, we will concentrate on three major kinds of activities. First, we will have to gather information regarding the past and organize it in such a way that it will be useful in making some statements regarding the future. Second, we will actually have to work out a procedure by which we can forecast the future. It will be necessary to provide a means for obtaining agreements regarding a number of highly speculative questions. Since we will have to rely upon the subjective judgment of experienced people regarding events that will occur in the future, we will be forced to make some probabilistic statements that summarize the collective opinions of the group. Finally, we will need some formal explicit relationships with which to combine the predicted information into a form that is usable in the decision-making process.

INFORMATION GATHERING AND ORGANIZATION

A considerable amount of controversy exists in industry today regarding the possibility of forecasting or predicting the future values of the inputs required for rational decision making. How can an engineer or manager of a firm foretell the future with certainty? The answer is that forecasts do not need to be certain. How is it possible, then, that forecasts can be of much help in planning and decision making? It is possible for long-range planning to be effective without dealing in certainties. The underlying assumption upon which our inputs are based is that our aim is not to gain a hard and fast outline of the future but an evaluation of probability upon which to make informed decisions.

It is typically necessary to narrow the scope of the process of gathering input data so that it will be compatible with elapsed time, manpower, and other resource constraints surrounding the entire decision-making process. The amount of resources to be expended in this process depends, by and large, upon the economic benefits to be derived from such an effort. Decisions regarding the allocation of resources for the solution of a given problem are usually based upon previous experience with similar problems. Note, however, that the amount predicted for any given variable for a given period of time will not normally correspond to the realized value, but will be distributed about this value.

In the presentation of information regarding alternative design configurations, policies, investment programs, or computer system selection, it is helpful to state the desirable alternatives on similar scales and in close proximity to each other so that effective comparisons of the data can be made. This can be done in the form of graphs, tables, or probability distributions.

PREDICTION OF THE FUTURE

An effective methodology for the determination of input values for future states[1] in the absence of "hard facts" is the Delphi Technique. The Delphi Technique replaces direct debate [1, 2, 3, 6] by a carefully designed program of sequential individual interrogation (best conducted by questionnaires) interspersed with information and opinion feedback derived by computed consensus from an earlier part of the program. The participants (experts) may be asked to state the reasons for previously expressed opinions; and a collection of such reasons may then be presented to each of the participants in the group together with an invitation to reconsider and possibly revise the earlier estimates. The inquiry into the reasons and the subsequent feedback of the reasons adduced by others may serve to stimulate the experts into taking due account of considerations that they might through inadvertence have neglected, and to give due weight to factors they were inclined to dismiss as unimportant on first thought.

An excellent description of the framework of the Delphi Method is given by E. S. Quade [5]. Consider the common situation of having to arrive at an answer to the question of how large a particular number — N — should be. For example, N might be the estimated cost or the value of a particular software attribute for any of the basic areas in the CHEVS model. One might proceed as follows:

Have each expert independently give an estimate of N. Arrange the responses in order of magnitude, and determine the quartiles, Q_1, M, Q_3, so that the four intervals formed on the N-line by these three points each contain one-quarter of the estimates. In this case, M is used instead of Q_2 to represent the median point. One-half of the responses lie below M and the other half are above (see Figure 5.1).

FIGURE 5.1
A Graphic Scheme for Presenting the Results of
One Round of the Delphi Method

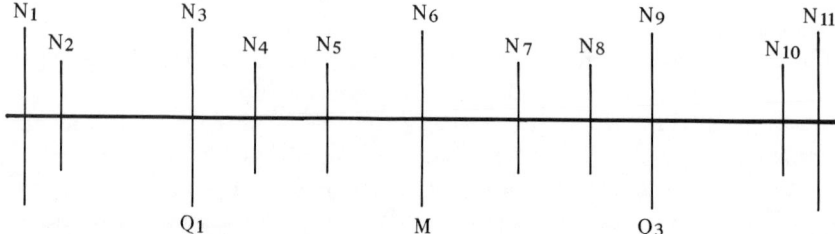

Source: Compiled by the authors.

Communicate the values of Q_1, M, Q_3 to each respondent; ask him or her to reconsider the previous estimate; and if this new estimate lies outside the interquartile range (Q_1, Q_3) to briefly justify why the answer should be lower (or higher) than what corresponds to the majority opinion expressed in the first round.

The results of this second round (which, as a rule, will be less dispersed than the first) are again fed back to the respondents in summary form, including the new quartiles' limits. In addition, the reasons for raising or lowering the values (elicited in Round 2 and suitably collated and edited) are also given to the respondents (always, of course, preserving anonymity of the proponents). Now the experts are asked to first consider these reasons, giving them the weight they deserve and then, using the new information, to revise their previous estimates. Moreover, if the revised estimates fall outside the second-round interquartile range, the respondent is asked to state briefly why arguments were found unconvincing that might have drawn the estimates toward the median. It should be noted here that the participants are now being exposed (all with ambiguities) to argument and counterargument before they are asked to vote on the next round.

Finally, in a fourth round, both the quartiles of the third distribution of responses and the counterarguments elicited in Round 3 are submitted to the respondents, who are encouraged to make one last revision of their estimates. The median of these Round 4 responses may then be taken as representing the group position as to what N should be (see Figure 5.2).

THE CONCEPT OF UTILITY

While criterion function generally offers a composite "measure of goodness" for all the germane criteria (see Chapter 6), they typically do not explicitly relate achievement on any given criterion with the objective of the organization or the project. It is not sufficient to know that the present worth of a decision

FIGURE 5.2
Convergence toward Consensus: A Graphic Representation

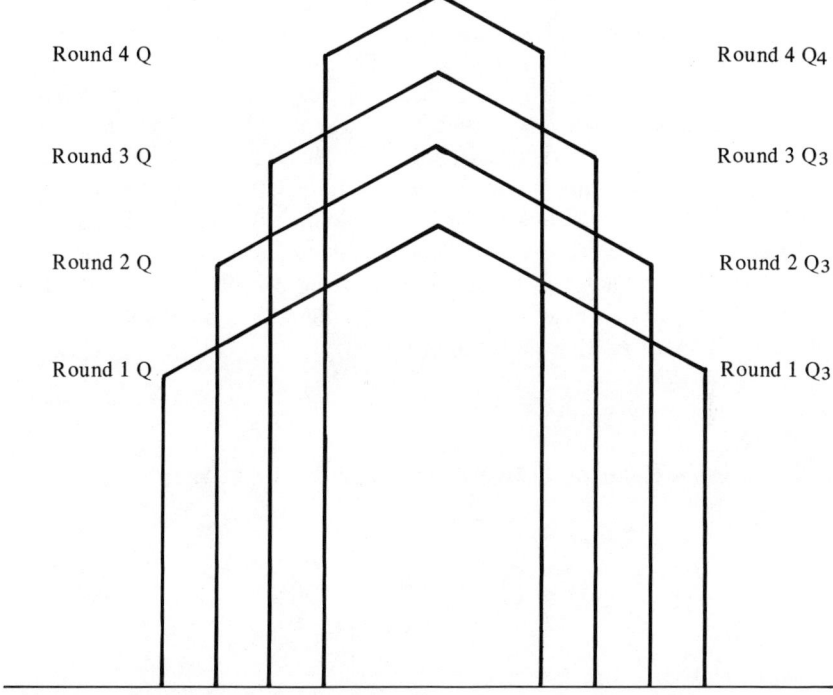

Round 4 Q   Round 4 Q$_4$

Round 3 Q   Round 3 Q$_3$

Round 2 Q   Round 2 Q$_3$

Round 1 Q   Round 1 Q$_3$

Scale
Source: Compiled by the authors.

alternative is more important to the project than reliability; rather, it is necessary to know how much a specific amount of present worth contributes to
the success of the enterprise and similarly how much a specific measure of
reliability contributes to the same objective.

The needed measure of relative contribution to the success of the enterprise has been referred to as system worth, figure of merit, cost effectiveness,
cost benefit, and utility. For our purposes here, we will use the term "utility"
to denote the measure of contribution to success of the enterprise, that is, of the
relative fulfillment of needs, goals, and objectives. We usually measure the units
of utility in utiles. A brief but comprehensive historical background for the
concept of utility as well as the fundamental assumptions and related theory is
available [4]. It is necessary to find explicit functional relationships between
utility and each of the criteria under consideration. For example, in considering
the present worth of the costs associated with a computer, we notice that
achieving a present worth of $30,000 has some value or utility to the achieve-
ment of the enterprise's goals, objectives, and needs; but a present worth of

$50,000 has perhaps a much lower utility. Furthermore, as indicated earlier, the relationship between utility and present worth, U = f(P), is usually nonlinear. This idea can be seen by means of a simple example.

Assume that utility can be given on a scale of values from 0 to 100. An analysis of historical data combined with experience suggests that the present worth of a given alternative investment lies between $30,000 and $50,000. Any present worth values that lie outside this range would effectively represent a different investment alternative situation. Furthermore, it is known that in terms of the organization's competitive position in the market, the present worth of the given investment alternative should not exceed $50,000. This $40,000 figure, which separates the desirable magnitudes of the criterion from the undesirable, is known as the "threshold" value. Sometimes such a threshold is called the "aspiration level." One possible functional relationship between utility and present worth is shown in Figure 5.3.

FIGURE 5.3
A Functional Relation between Utility and Present Worth

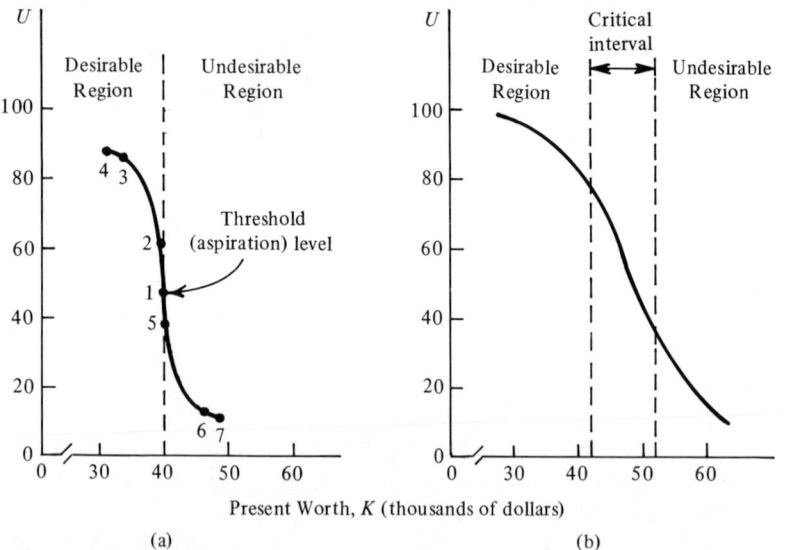

Present Worth, K (thousands of dollars)

(a)   (b)

Source: Compiled by the authors.

To determine the curve shown on the diagram, it is necessary to estimate a sufficient number of points so that a curve can be drawn. The first and most obvious point might be that which is defined by the threshold level of $40,000 and a utility value of 50 (a point half way up the utility scale). If the present worth can be made even a little bit smaller than the aspiration level, the value to the enterprise is considerably increased. Thus, if the present worth were $39,000, the utility might increase from 50 to 60. This would give us a second point on our curve. The rate of increase of utility decreases as the present worth decreases and levels off at some value in the vicinity of $30,000. Below the $30,000 value it might be expected that the utility would begin to drop because we would be operating out of the reasonable range of value for the given decision alternative. Since we expect the maximum utility value to occur at approximately $30,000, we can introduce points 3 and 4, both of which have utility values that are approximately equal. With points 1, 2, 3, and 4, we are able to draw a reasonable curve in the "desirable region."

On the other hand, if the present worth turns out to be greater than the threshold level, the utility drops considerably to a point that is denoted on the diagram as point 5. The utility drops rapidly with increasing present worth and levels off at a utility of approximately 10 utiles. The reason that the utility does not approach zero in value is because it is assumed that no matter how large the present worth there is some value in terms of achieving the enterprise objectives. As long as the decision makers make their assumptions explicit and consistent with respect to all decision alternatives, the maximum and minimum utility values are not crucial.[2]

In some situations the utility function is not discontinuous, but there is a critical interval in which there is a very rapid change in utility with respect to a given criterion. Such a situation is depicted in part (b) on Figure 5.3. A sufficient number of points can determine any utility function, be it continuous or discontinuous, by using the Delphi methodology in conjunction with an appropriate group of knowledgeable and experienced people.

Once a utility function has been obtained for each criterion, it is necessary to estimate a performance level or achievement level for each criterion in order to use the utility relationship. In some cases, a constant numerical value can be calculated for a criterion, but in other cases there may be a distribution of values. Such distributions, or probability densities as they are often called, may be obtained by experimental measurement, an appropriate set of analytical calculations, or by using the distribution of estimates provided by a group of experts. The relationship between the frequency of occurrence and a given criterion measure usually may be represented or approximated by a normal distribution curve. A considerable simplification of the calculations can be accomplished by taking the mean of the distribution curve and using this single mean value to determine the utility of that criterion.

These concepts can also be applied to nonfinancial factors and this will be illustrated by means of a relatively simple example. Suppose that you are considering alternatives A_1, A_2, A_3, A_4, A_5 involving the benchmark results of each.[3] Furthermore, you anticipate three possible conditions in the user environment, the states of nature N_1, N_2, and N_3 (N_1 = a 50/50 mix of compilations and production runs, N_2 = mostly compilations, N_3 = mostly production runs).

Analysis of each potential decision under each possible state of nature yields the following results (mean values):[4]

A_1 (continue with existing system)
    achieve benchmark results of 7 hours if N_1 occurs
    achieve benchmark results of 9 hours if N_2 occurs
    achieve benchmark results of 6 hours if N_3 occurs
A_2 (lease system A)
    achieve benchmark results of 45 minutes if N_1 occurs
    achieve benchmark results of 55 minutes if N_2 occurs
    achieve benchmark results of 40 minutes if N_3 occurs
A_3 (lease system B)
    achieve benchmark results of 60 minutes if N_1 occurs
    achieve benchmark results of 55 minutes if N_2 occurs
    achieve benchmark results of 50 minutes if N_3 occurs
A_4 (lease system C)
    achieve benchmark results of 55 minutes if N_1 occurs
    achieve benchmark results of 40 minutes if N_2 occurs
    achieve benchmark results of 60 minutes if N_3 occurs
A_5 (lease system D)
    achieve benchmark results of 40 minutes if N_1 occurs
    achieve benchmark results of 45 minutes if N_2 occurs
    achieve benchmark results of 35 minutes if N_3 occurs

You have sufficient confidence in your analysis (that is, the variance of your estimates is sufficiently small to justify your using the mean values of your estimate) to represent the probability densities of the outcome.

You estimate the probabilities of the three market conditions as follows:

Prob. $(N_1) = .3$
Prob. $(N_2) = .2$
Prob. $(N_3) = .5$

The foregoing information is summarized in Table 5.1. The entries in the matrix represent your expected benchmark results under each decision for each condition of the user environment. With this information we can now compute an expected benchmark result.

$EB_1 = .3(7) + .2(9) + .5(6) = 6.9$ hours
$EB_2 = .3(45) + .2(55) + .5(40) = 45.5$ minutes
$EB_3 = .3(60) + .2(55) + .5(50) = 54.0$ minutes
$EB_4 = .3(55) + .2(40) + .5(70) = 59.5$ minutes
$EB_5 = .3(70) + .2(45) + .5(30) = 45.0$ minutes

TABLE 5.1
Benchmark Results for Each User Condition

	N_1	N_2	N_3
	Prob. $(N_1) = .3$	Prob. $(N_2) = .2$	Prob. $(N_3) = .5$
A_1	7 hours	9 hours	6 hours
A_2	45 minutes	55 minutes	40 minutes
A_3	60 minutes	55 minutes	50 minutes
A_4	55 minutes	40 minutes	60 minutes
A_5	40 minutes	45 minutes	35 minutes

Source: Compiled by the authors.

Under the foregoing assumptions, the best alternative is A_2. It can be seen that the expected benchmark results (EBs) represent utility in terms of time. Since there has been no explicit statement of the relationship between the benchmark timings and their value to the organization, the foregoing expected benchmark results can best be considered as a criterion function rather than a utility.

Now suppose that benchmark results of 60 minutes or more are highly undesirable. On the other hand, results of 30 minutes or less, although good, are not worth as much on a marginal basis as those in the 40- to 55-minute range. The above considerations may be graphed as shown in Figure 5.4. Substituting the utility of benchmark time from Figure 5.3 for the benchmark times themselves in a second decision matrix, the results shown in Figure 5.4 are obtained.

The expected utility may now be computed from the values contained in Table 5.2 to identify the best alternative:

$$U_1 = .3(-2.00) + .2(-2.00) + .5(-2.00) = -2.0$$
$$U_2 = .3(.67) + .2(-.83) + .5(.83) = .45$$
$$U_3 = .3(-1.25) + .2(-.83) + .5(0.0) = -.54$$
$$U_4 = .3(-.83) + .2(.83) + .5(-1.08) = -.62$$
$$U_5 = .3(.83) + .2(.67) + .5(1.00) = .88$$

The best alternative now is A_5, not A_2, as chosen without the application of utility theory. This result emphasizes a significant characteristic of the application of the utility concept, namely, that attitudes toward risk[5] are automatically incorporated into the value of alternatives by introducing the utility idea.

FIGURE 5.4
Utility Function of Benchmark Timings

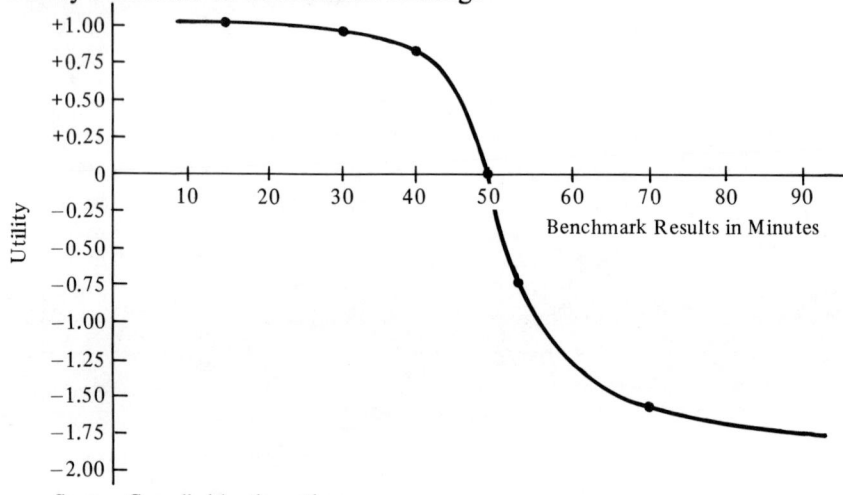

Source: Compiled by the authors.

TABLE 5.2
Utility Values of Benchmark Results for Each User Condition

	N_1	N_2	N_3
	Prob. (N_1) = .3	*Prob. (N_2) = .2*	*Prob. (N_3) = .5*
U_1	−2.00	−2.00	−2.00
U_2	.67	− .83	.83
U_3	−1.25	− .83	0.00
U_4	− .83	.83	−1.08
U_5	.83	.67	1.00

Source: Compiled by the authors.

CONSIDERATION OF MULTIPLE CRITERIA

When considering alternative investment decisions, one must systematically include other quantitative factors before a final decision is made. The decisions as to which criteria to use, in addition to present worth, are strongly dependent upon the long-range goals, short-range objectives, and the needs of the organization. These three items should be stated explicitly by the management before any of the evaluative criteria are determined. According to Melvin Lifson [4], a goal is considered to be a long-range qualitative, perhaps nebulous, type of achievement extending over a period of time; it is a direction in which to aim rather than a target at which to shoot. In the data processing environment, a goal might be described as follows: to continue operating as a growing but efficient department serving the computational and/or informational needs of the organization. An "objective" is an event that is believed to represent progress toward achievement of its goals; it is a specific step, milestone, or accomplishment in the direction of goal fulfillment. Some of the objectives of an MIS department run as an investment center might be: to make a 20 percent return on investment during each of the next five fiscal years; to begin selling services to the outside business community; and so on.

The accomplishment of a set of objectives implies that a corresponding set of needs must be satisfied. Thus, if the MIS department is to begin selling services outside the home organization, it must have a data processing system that meets certain specifications in addition to promoting its availability to the potential user community.

The process of specifying the goals, objectives, and needs of the organization may be aided by the Delphi Method, some extensions or variations of it, or any other methods that appear to be suitable. Once the goals, objectives, and needs are stated explicitly, it is relatively easier to list the major evaluative criteria that are to be used in the decision-making process. In attempting to achieve certain objectives, it becomes obvious that in addition to considerations of costs, such criteria as reliability, maintainability, aesthetics, ease of use, and so on, become perhaps of equal importance. It also becomes possible to judge the relative importance of each of the evaluative criteria.

The HEVS subcase of the CHEVS taxonomy will assist in the specification of objectives by suggesting a variety of criteria. The decision maker is certainly not limited to its offerings and, in fact, should be encouraged to go beyond them for criteria that are compatible with the organizational objectives. Appendix A details many of the factors that might be considered.

There are several ways of handling multiple criteria: one can treat each criterion as an independent entity until it is incorporated into a single valued function; one may separately consider all nonfinancial factors in a subcriterion function that later will be combined with the financial portion. Either way, the results are the same. In some situations, managers may feel more comfortable with a clear distinction between financial and nonfinancial factors throughout the analysis procedure. For demonstration purposes we will, however, treat each criterion as a separate entity until the point at which the criterion function is used. The reader should realize that this is a purely arbitrary decision and if the other approach is desired, one can simply apply the principles set out in Chapter 6 to achieve this end.

PROBLEMS OF MEASUREMENT

The area of nonfinancial factor analysis is characterized by a tremendous variety of scales of measurement for the factors involved. This implies that a correspondingly large number of utility curves, if the utility concept is to be used, will be necessary. The construction of utility curves is both time consuming initially and also likely to require maintenance over time as risk aversion changes. It therefore behooves the decision maker to limit the number of utility conversions to a manageable number that is dependent upon the amount of time allowed for the decision process, among others.

A potential remedy to this is to work directly in utiles. This should be attempted only by those who are comfortable with utility theory and certainly a great deal of caution is necessary. A major problem with working directly with utility is that it does not provide the control and inherent documentation of the sensitivity of a given factor to the overall corporate goals. It is probably best applied to criteria that are inherently soft, that is, that are evaluated by purely subjective judgment and may not even have suggested scales of measurement as might be in the case of estimating the aesthetic value of a specific piece of equipment.

Another issue that applies to factors both involved in the nonfinancial area and more specifically to those expressed in utiles is that of their overall effect on the final decision. In either case, the result of their inclusion in the final criteria function can be dramatic and, therefore, a great deal of care is necessary in their administration. It should suffice to say that one could easily bias the final decision through the subtle manipulation of any of the included factors. It is suggested that the Delphi Method can be applied here to a great advantage and thus may reduce the risk of the previously mentioned manipulations.

NOTES

1. It is also useful in the determination of present states.

2. The Delphi Technique can be used to develop utility curves for various enterprises [7, 8, 9].

3. This is the actual timing of a run or a series of runs of software that are considered to be representative of a normal job stream. For an in-depth treatment of this technique, as well as a variety of suitable alternatives, see M. E. Drummond, Jr., *Evaluation and Measurement Techniques for Digital Computer Systems* (Englewood Cliffs, N.J.: Prentice-Hall, 1973).

4. That is to say, if system A is selected and run with a 50/50 mix of compilations and production runs, the actual time to complete the test job stream (benchmark) is 55 minutes; if the environment is changed for the same system and is mostly one of production jobs (few compilations) the benchmark is 40 minutes.

5. An adequate definition of "risk" is simply a situation in which several states of nature can exist, all identifiable, and with attributable probabilities of occurring.

REFERENCES

[1] Dalkey, N. and Kelmer, O. "An Experimental Application of the Delphi Method to the Use of Experts." *Management Science* 9 (1973): 458.

[2] Helmer, O. *Social Technology.* New York: Basic Books, 1966.

[3] Helmer, O. and Rescher, N. "On the Epistemology of the Inexact Sciences." *Management Science* 6 (1959): 47.

[4] Lifson, M. W. "Applications of Criteria and Measures of Value in Engineering Design." Hughes Aircraft Company, TM-818, May 1965.

[5] Quade, E. S. *Cost Effectiveness: Some Trends in Analysis.* Santa Monica, Calif.: The Rand Corporation, March 1967, p. 3529.

[6] Reisman, A. *Managerial and Everyday Economics.* Boston: Allyn and Bacon, 1971.

[7] Reisman, A., Herling, J., Fancher, M. G., Kaminski, G., and Srinivasan, S. "Timeliness of Library Materials Delivery: A Set of Priorities." *Socio-Economic Planning Sciences* 6, no. 2 (1972): 145-52.

[8] Service, Allen. "A Social System Measurement Model." Technical Memorandum No. 329, Department of Operations Research, Case Western Reserve University, Cleveland, Ohio, January 1974.

[9] Mantell, S. J., Jr. et al. "A Social Service Measurement Model." *Operations Research* 23, no. 2 (March-April 1975): 218-40.

6

THE CRITERION FUNCTION:
AN INTEGRATION OF FINANCIAL
AND NONFINANCIAL FACTORS

A GENERAL METHODOLOGY

Computer selection decisions, as stated over and over in the previous chapters, must consider a number of tangible and intangible criteria. A full analysis of all relevant criteria should be undertaken in order to obtain an estimate of the total effectiveness of the various alternatives available. This effectiveness is made up of the sum of the effects of the individual factors and of interactions. The benefit of the interaction of two factors, beyond that of simple addition, is known as synergism. A well-known example of this effect is illustrated by the factors success and wealth; each additively desirable, and each increasing the effect of the other. In the case of a choice between two investment policies, for, say, computer central processing units, the factors of reliability and maintainability can be estimated or calculated independently of each other, but it is recognized that there is some implicit relationship between these two factors. We have not as yet advanced far enough in the state-of-the-art to include the interactions and relationships in an equation, but their presence should be known and acknowledged as we proceed with our analysis. Sometimes such interactions are lumped into a factor that is sometimes called the interaction parameter, "Finagle's constant," the correction factor, and so forth. In analytical problems, where there is an equation that relates the variables to each other, all of the independent variables are multiplied by such a correction factor. Alternately, in some cases it may be possible to add a term reflecting these interactions. However, in choosing between alternative investment programs or in making any types of decisions between alternatives, such a factor can usually be ignored because it is the same for all alternatives and we are only trying to obtain relative values.

The overall effectiveness of a given alternative may be measured by an expression called the "criterion function." In the current literature, it is sometimes called the "objective function," "measure of effectiveness," and so on. The criterion function (CF) is the sum of the individual effects K_x of each of the criteria x, each weighted or proportioned with respect to its relative importance by the weighting coefficient W_x. Thus the criterion function may be written as:

$$CF = \sum_{x=1}^{a} W_x K_x \tag{6.1}$$

where W_x = weighting coefficient, measuring respective importance; and K_x = criterion variable, as a system function or a parameter.

Quantitative solutions for the decision problem can be reached by substituting numbers for each of the criteria and estimating numbers for each of the weighting factors, so that a CF value can be computed for each alternative. Of course, the alternative having the best CF is the "winning" or best alternative. The CF equation given above is just one way of writing the relationship between the criteria; any other relationship that will explicitly satisfy the objectives set forth may be used. Since state-of-the-art knowledge regarding the relationships between criteria is rather limited at the present time, the simple linear function is assumed to be satisfactory for purposes of computer system selection.

Since the criterion function is a decision maker's tool, he or she can do anything to it that is logical. Weighting factors that may be chosen so that they vary between zero and one, their sum equals to one or is greater than one. Digits can be used for and just as well as the weighting factors, rather than decimals. This might be done in order that additional criteria and their weighting factors can be added later in the decision process if the need arises. The choices, together with their advantages, are listed below:

$0 < W_x < 1; \Sigma W_x = 1$ (proportions most easily recognized)
$0 < W_x < 1; \Sigma W_x > 1$ (convenient to modify)
W_x digits; $\Sigma W_x \gg 1$ (approximate relations are indicated)

The first relationship is the one that is usually used. It is easy to recognize the proportion and it is consistent with our thinking about percentages. Thus, if there were three criteria, the most important criterion might be given a weighting factor of 0.5; the criterion of next importance is a factor of 0.3; and the criterion of least importance might be given a factor of 0.2. It can be seen that the sum of these factors is 1.0. On the other hand, if an additional factor were to be considered after many calculations had been made, then it would certainly be possible to add an additional factor such as 0.2. It should be recognized that the addition of this new term would effectively reduce the original three terms by 20 percent.

There is still another method for assigning the relative weights, W_x, which will be used in the forthcoming illustrative examples. In this method, we rank order all of the criteria from the most important criterion all the way down to the least important criterion. Then, the most important criterion is assigned a value of 1.0. The question is then asked, "If the first criterion has a value of 1.0, what must the relative weight of the second criterion be?" This question is answered by seriously considering how important the second criterion is in achieving the objectives set forth by the organization or in the project in comparison with the importance of the first criterion. Thus, if a relative weight of 0.5 is assigned, it implies that the second criterion is half as important as the first in achieving the objectives. The sum of the relative weights by this method does not necessarily add up to a constant value. It is still possible to add additional criteria at some later date and not be forced to change any of the initial assigned relative weight values.

An inspection of the various terms of the criterion function equation indicates that the various terms in the equation usually have different units of measurement. Thus, one criterion may have units of cost; another criterion may have units of speed; and still another may have dimensionless units. Moreover, due to the scales used, some of the terms will be numerically so much smaller in magnitude than any of the others that they will have a negligible effect upon the criterion function, irrespective of the magnitude of W_x. For example, the present worth values may be in the range from \$500,000 to \$1,000,000, whereas reliability may be evaluated on a scale between 0 and 100, while maintainability might be evaluated on a scale between 0 and 1.

It is possible to convert each term in the criterion function equation to the same set of units as any other term. This may be accomplished in a number of ways. Each of the terms could be nondimensionalized, that is, divided by some reference value in the same unit as the given term. This method, however, does not produce criterion values that are of the same order of magnitude. A simple and perhaps more satisfactory approach consists of calculating a unit conversion factor for each term. The unit conversion factor, F_x, is equal to the average value of K for a specific criterion chosen for this purpose, divided by the average K_x for the criterion in question.[1] The formula for obtaining F_x in the case where it is desired to convert all of the terms of the equation to the units and the scale range of the first criterion is

$$F_x = \overline{K}_1 / \overline{K}_x \qquad (6.2)$$

where F_x is taken as the median value or rating that is assigned on criterion X to all the feasible alternatives.

We can now write a more complete equation for the criterion function, which will include the units conversion factor, F_x; thus

$$CF = \sum_{x=1}^{a} F_x W_x K_x = F_1 W_1 K_1 + F_2 W_2 K_2 \dots + F_a W_a K_a \tag{6.3}$$

An application of the criterion function theory presented thus far is given in the following example. We return to the computer system selection case presented in Chapter 2 and consider the use of multiple criteria, including financial and nonfinancial factors. It can be seen that, in addition to the present worth of the rental arrangements for each alternative, it is also desired to consider such factors as the operating system rating, system engineering support available, and the benchmark results. Just as in the case of present worth, the benchmark results can be determined by a variety of techniques available in the literature. It is beyond the nature of this study to discuss such calculations or methodologies.

In considering such a factor as the operating system rating, it is clear that at the present time such criteria can be evaluated by the Delphi Method or by some other procedure that takes qualitative factors into consideration and seeks a consensus from a panel of knowledgeable people. If the amounts of resource that are to be allocated as a result of the decision-making process are very great, then it is advisable that a number of experienced personnel be polled to arrive at reasonable estimates for these criteria.

It can be seen in Table 6.1 that each criterion has a range of values, which are enumerated in the second column. An average or median value for each criterion, $\overline{K}_x$, can be estimated by taking a value somewhere near the middle of the range of values. Thus, in the case of expansion increment, an average value of $6,500 is used because this is halfway between $2,000 and $11,000. It should be noted that the range of values that will be used can be obtained by looking at the data that have been collected. The unit conversion factor, F_x, can be obtained in a straightforward manner by substitution into equation 6.2. In this problem it was decided that all terms in the criterion function equation should be expressed in the same units as the present worth, namely dollars. Therefore, since the reference criterion is the first one, its average criterion value is used as the numerator in calculating all of the unit conversion factors.[2]

A summary of the additional information that is required in order to make a decision regarding the five alternative computer systems is given in Tables 6.2 to 6.5. It may be recalled from the previous illustrative problem that there were three states of nature regarding the type of jobs being submitted during the benchmark process. The first state had a probability of 0.3; the other two had probabilities of 0.2 and 0.5, respectively. It can be seen that if the benchmark

TABLE 6.1
Range of Values, Average Value, and Units Conversion Factor for the Computer Selection Problem

Major Criteria, K_x	Range of K_x	Average* Value of K_x $\overline{K}_x$	Units Conversion Factor, F_x $F_x = \overline{K}_1/\overline{K}_x$
K_1 = Present worth	\$2,006,498 3,167,118	\$2,586,808	1.0
K_2 = Conversion requirements	0-1	0.5	5,173,616
K_3 = Expansion increments	\$2,000-11,000	\$6,500	398
K_4 = Operating system rating	0-1	0.5	5,173,616
K_5 = System engineering support	0-1	0.5	5,173,616
K_6 = Benchmark results	35-540	283	8,982

*In order to avoid the possibility (remote) of problems associated with the use of F_x, the true (actual data) median should be sought.

Source: Compiled by the authors.

TABLE 6.2
Composite Criterion Function Calculations for N_1

Criteria K_x (1)	Relative Weight of K_x, W_{x-1} (2)	Alt. A_1 K_{x11} (3)	Alt. A_2 K_{x21} (4)	Alt. A_3 K_{x31} (5)	Alt. A_4 K_{x41} (6)	Alt. A_5 K_{x51} (7)
Present worth ($)	1.0	-2,150,427	-2,006,498	-2,086,365	-2,487,199	-3,167,188
Conversion requirements	.4	0	1	0	0	1
Expansion increments	.3	11,000	11,000	2,000	11,000	8,000
Operating system rating	.5	0	1	0	0	1
System engineering rating	.3	0	-1	0	0	0
Benchmark results	.4	-420	-45	-	-55	-45
Criterion function						
$CF_{yz} = \sum\limits_{x=1}^{6} F_x W_{x-z} K_{xyz}$		-2,346,087	1,174,786	-772,965	-1,317,414	2,300,616

for the yth alternative and the zth state of nature

Source: Compiled by the authors.

86

TABLE 6.3
Composite Criterion Function Calculations for N_2

Criteria K_x (1)	Relative Weight of K_x, W_{x-1} (2)	Alt. A_1 K_{x12} (3)	Alt. A_2 K_{x22} (4)	Alt. A_3 K_{x32} (5)	Alt. A_4 K_{x42} (6)	Alt. A_5 K_{x52} (7)
Present worth ($)	1.0	−2,150,427	−2,006,498	−2,086,365	−2,487,199	−3,167,118
Conversion requirements	.6	0	1	0	0	1
Expansion increments	.3	11,000	2,000	11,000	11,000	8,000
Operating system rating	.5	0	1	0	0	1
System engineering rating	.2	0	−1	0	0	0
Benchmark results	.4	−540	−55	—	40	−35
Criterion function						
$CV_{yz} = \sum\limits_{x=1}^{6} F_x W_{x-z} K_{xyz}$		−2,777,247	2,690,942	−772,965	−1,317,519	3,353,305

for the yth alternative and the zth state of nature

Source: Compiled by the authors.

TABLE 6.4
Composite Criterion Function Calculations for N_3

Criteria K_x (1)	Relative Weight of K_x, W_{x-3} (2)	Alt. A_1 K_{x13} (3)	Alt. A_2 K_{x23} (4)	Alt. A_3 K_{x33} (5)	Alt. A_4 K_{x43} (6)	Alt. A_5 K_{x53} (7)
Present worth ($)	1.0	−2,150,427	−2,006,498	−2,086,365	−2,487,199	−3,167,118
Conversion requirements	.2	0	1	0	0	1
Expansion increments	.3	11,000	2,000	11,000	11,000	8,000
Operating system rating	.5	0	1	0	0	1
System engineering rating	.5	0	−1	0	0	0
Benchmark results	.5	−360	−40	−	−60	−40
Criterion function						
$CF_{yz} = \sum_{x=1}^{6} F_x W_{x-z} K_{xyz}$		−2,130,507	−876,695	−772,965	−1,389,379	1,265,893

for the yth alternative and the zth state of nature

Source: Compiled by the authors.

88

TABLE 6.5
Composite Criterion Function for the yth Alternative

$$CF_y = \sum_{z=1}^{3} (N_z)CF_{yz}$$

$CF_1 = .3(-2,346,087) + .2(2,777,247) + .5(-2,130,507)$	$=$	$-2,324,529$
$CF_2 = .3(1,174,786) + .2(2,690,942) + .5(-876,695)$	$=$	$452,276$
$CF_3 = -772,965$		
$CF_4 = .3(-1,371,414) + .2(-1,317,519) + .5(-1,389,379)$	$=$	$-1,369,618$
$CF_5 = .3(2,300,616) + .2(3,353,305) + .5(1,265,893)$	$=$	$1,993,793$

Source: Compiled by the authors.

result alone is used as the selection criterion, A_5 is preferable, since it is the fastest system. As can be seen in Tables 6.2 to 6.5, we are expanding the previous example to include six criteria, of which the benchmark result is only one. In the second column of Table 6.2-6.4 we can see the relative weights that were assigned to the various criteria. The present worth criterion was assigned a relative weight, W_1, of 1.00. The relative weights of the other criteria were assigned by means of the Delphi Method, or simply by the use of subjective judgment on the part of the decision maker. It is important to note that the relative weights are not the same for all states of nature. A multitude of reasons can be given for choosing different values. For instance, the relative weights given to conversion requirements and system engineering support may be partially a function of the amount of compilations versus production runs to be made. In an environment catering mostly to compilations, excessive conversion requirements may degrade the total level of performance from a throughput standpoint; while system engineering support will be largely insignificant, since its importance lies in the area of design. Thus the weights of W_2 and W_5 might be 0.6 and 0.2, respectively. If, however, the state of nature three, N_3, existed, W_2 and W_5 would more likely be 0.2 and 0.5 in our hypothetical case.

Numerical values for each of the criteria, K_x, are either calculated or assigned, and these are given in columns 3, 4, 5, 6, and 7 in Tables 6.2-6.4. It should be noted that we are trying to find the investment alternative that will maximize each of the criteria other than present worth. These criteria represent benefits rather than costs. Since we have criteria that represent both costs and benefits, we recognize the difference between them by placing a minus sign in front of each of the present worth (cost) values. We will then choose the investment alternative that produces the highest criterion function.

In view of the fact that there are multiple states of nature, multiple decision alternatives, and multiple criteria, we are forced to introduce triple subscripts on some of the variables. Thus, K_{xyz} represents the xth criterion for the yth decision alternative and the zth state of nature. The nomenclature for the rest of the variables is reasonably self-explanatory.

Once all of the numerical values have been either calculated or assigned, it becomes a rather simple matter to substitute the numbers into equation 6.3. When we multiply the corresponding F, W, and K values together and sum the products, we obtain the alternative of remaining with the present system for the first state of nature, which has a criterion function value of −2,346,087. We can combine the states of nature into a single estimate of the criterion function for each alternative by carrying out the indicated procedure in Table 6.5. Thus we can obtain the combined criterion for the first alternative by multiplying the probability of the first state of nature by its corresponding criterion function and adding to it the probability of the second state of nature and its corresponding criterion function. In this way we obtain −2,324,529, as shown in Table 6.5. In a similar manner, for the second alternative, we obtain 452,276. It can now be concluded that even when we take additional criteria into account (other than the simple benchmark results), alternative A_5 is still superior. It might be expected that if other criteria were used, if the relative weighting factors were to be changed, or if different states of nature were considered, the criterion functions for each of the decision alternatives might turn out quite differently.

At this point, the reader may be prompted to inquire whether this exercise can really accomplish anything; whether he or she should run through all of these calculations and estimates in a real project. If the project is of any consequence to the enterprise, then the answer to both parts is "definitely" yes. In a real situation, the decision maker must manipulate all of the foregoing variables and states of nature, and he usually does this in his head. It is assumed that he is capable of carrying out all of the operations mentally, but it is an established psychological fact that the human mind cannot handle more than five or six variables at a time; and that number, albeit small, is usually handled very inefficiently. It is always better to estimate the values of small pieces of a problem than to try an overall estimate of a complex system as a whole. Errors tend to cancel out when component pieces are looked at. When estimates, no matter how crude, are made explicitly, it is possible to revise them in a systematic manner and to establish corroboration or disagreement with those values between individuals or groups of knowledgeable people. Since some sort of evaluation is going on continuously in any project, whether consciously or not, the explicit quantification of subjective judgments makes it possible to improve the decision-making process whenever new data and experience are obtained.

In this section we have shown that the criterion function is a measure of the relative value of a given decision alternative in relation to other alternatives based upon relative performance with respect to a limited number of criteria. It should be stressed that the foregoing analysis did not explicitly take into account the utility or value to the "organization" of performance on any of the criteria. In the case study to be presented in Chapter 7, the utility concept will be used in the final criterion function as it was in Chapter 4 relative to nonfinancial factors.

POTENTIAL PROBLEMS

There are a variety of potential problems that the practitioner should be aware of before applying these methods. The first two problems to be discussed are not conceptual weaknesses, but rather operational ones, which can be easily avoided.

It should be noted with regard to the previous example, involving the decision among five alternatives, that alternative A_3 had no value for its benchmark runs. Although, for exemplary purposes, we proceeded with the required calculations, this should not be permitted. Either the alternative should have been eliminated from consideration because no value was available, or a value should have been determined or, possibly, estimated. The reason for this is that a null value for any factor, unless it is intended to be zero, unfairly biases the criterion function. In this case, since the criterion function considered the benchmark results to be inversely related to its effects on the criterion function itself, a null value would have given alternative A_3 an artificially high score. On the other hand, had it been directly related, the result would have been an artificial lowering of the score.

Another point of interest concerning the overall methodology relates to the effects of using zero-one variables. In the previous example, three of the six criteria were of this class and had a marked effect on the final values of the criterion function. Whenever this type of variable is used and, in addition, has a relatively high weight, K_x, associated with it, it may cause rather significant swings in the value of the criterion function as a result of a change. This is dramatically demonstrated by considering that all of the alternatives had present worths (actually costs) ranging from \$2,006,498 to \$3,167,118, while the final criterion function values had the range of $-2,324,529$ to $1,993,793$. This does not suggest an "invalid property of the method," but rather that it can magnify the apparent relative difference between alternatives.

Another series of issues that must be dealt with are the following: differential lives of alternatives, probability of success, and inflation. Due to the significance of each on the decision process, a section will be devoted to the individual issues.

DIFFERENTIAL LIVES OF ALTERNATIVES

Relative to EDP two types of lives are relevant: economic and technological. The functional life is that period of time within which the system functionally pays for itself, while the technological life relates to the period of time that the system is at the state-of-the-art in relation to commercially available systems. While both may be important to the user and can certainly be evaluated by decision theory, only the functional life will be dealt with in this book.

John R. Canada and Harrison M. Wadsworth [1] discussed the significance of differential lives of competing alternatives.

> There is little question that project life is an important element in determining the prospective worth or relative desirability of an investment project. The dispersion or variability which can occur in project life is a prime candidate for consideration whenever the effect of risk is taken into account in an economic analysis of a prospective project. This is because of the typically high degree of sensitivity of project worth, or relative desirability, to changes in project life.[3]

> The inherent inaccuracies in project life estimates may often be so great as to make the refinement of considering the effect of life dispersion on expected values of these key factors unneeded or unrealistic.[4]

Although the literature far from abounds with treatments of this topic, the National Association of Accountants [2] has said:

> Differences in project lives, when two competing projects are being compared, present another type of problem. The precise comparison of two projects requires that the two lives be made equal and a terminal value be established for the longer lived project. This approach is uncommon in practice, according to our findings and other studies of this subject. The most common technique is to evaluate the potential profitability of each project separately using whatever life estimates apply in each case. Then the cash flows are examined to see what their impact is on the company's cash projections. The project whose cash flow best meshes with company cash flows may be chosen even though it shows a lower profit potential.[5]

Certainly, fitting the projected cash flows to the given company for a decision alternative is a must; however, it does not help in the selection of the best alternative providing a variety of alternatives can be potentially serviced through the resources at hand. Therefore, in order to isolate the major alternatives relative to this issue it would be advisable to consider the following relationship:

$$P = B - S + E - R$$

where: P = present value, B = purchase price, S = salvage value, E = expense function, and R = revenue function.

By attempting to manipulate each of the BSER components we will be able to enumerate the important alternatives available to differential lives as follows:

Owned asset: Adjust differential lives through the use of salvage value. This, however, is not applicable to leases or rental situations since title to the resource is not held by the user. This is undoubtedly the cleanest method for adjustment since it can be accomplished physically and is therefore not artificial.

Leased Asset: If it is possible to break the lease with a penalty, then this too can be done in the model by treating all lives as equal but using the lease-breaking penalty as an expense in whatever period it is incurred. Since most leases, if they contain such a clause, charge a large penalty, this will probably poison that alternative in the selection process. The lease or leases that have the shorter time frames can have extension cash flows estimated. Many leases provide for extensions and therefore this method is not artificial and is only subject to errors in estimation.

Marginal analysis can be used. That is, determine which alternative is most profitable for its individual life. This really assumes that all factors but life are equal. Note that this method is actually that which has been suggested by the National Association of Accountants [2]. It inherently assumes that future system replacements will be the same as those currently available, a dangerous assumption in such a dynamic industry.

Express each present value calculation for every alternative in closed form so that it is taken to perpetuity, thus equalizing the lives at infinity. The fact that the present worth reaches a saturation point especially quickly at relatively real current rates of discount, for example, cost of capital, and so on, can also be used with advantage Both of these, in this case, assume that future replacements will essentially be the same. This may have been considered undesirable in so dynamic an industry as data processing until the advent of double digit interest rates. Other things being equal, select the alternative that is most beneficial for long-range projections. That is, if computer prices are declining rapidly in relation to computing capabilities, take the shortest lease and renegotiate the contract more frequently. This, however, could be potentially disastrous and might well backfire if an unexpected conversion had to take place or the lease price were increased rather than decreased as expected.

The "Null": ignore any life difference. For very long-lived alternatives this will probably work quite well due to the present value calculations reaching their threshold values (obviously, high interest rates can have the same effect); however, for relatively short-lived alternatives the most desirable may be eliminated due to this technique.

Certainly most of the above alternatives have shortcomings, however, it is felt that the third is the best overall for leased assets involving computer hardware and software since it most closely follows the generally accepted practice. It is also felt that extension prices for leases can be gathered quite easily and, therefore, there is a reduced risk of an estimation of error.

PROBABILITY OF SUCCESS

It is quite likely that several computer system manufacturers will submit proposals that, if not virtually identical, will at least be quite similar. The question for the decision maker then becomes: Are the proposals actually equivalent? This issue is perhaps the most difficult to analyze objectively due to the fact that implicitly it suggests evaluating the various states of nature. For our purposes, however, we simply would like to express the best estimate of the system living up to its projected success. This can be done through the use of a probability expression that when applied against the evaluated factors provides us with an expected value. Certainly expected value concepts have received their share of attention and do not require repetition here.

One major potential pitfall must be mentioned: that is, implicitly imbedding the probability judgment in both the factors to be evaluated and explicitly in the expected value calculation, thus double weighting the effect.

Since the determination of this probability will have potentially significant effects on the decision outcome, all possible care should be exercised. Completely objective estimates are neither published nor held in the professional community and, therefore, the suggested method for its determination is through the Delphi Technique or through any other form of establishing a value judgment.

INFLATION

The whole issue of considering, at least explicitly, the effects of inflation on economic decisions involving computer hardware or software has been successfully avoided in the literature to this point. The reasons for this are easy to understand and probably include the following:

- Projecting inflation, like any other economic indicator, is an art and, therefore, not easily accomplished.
- Until recently, inflation in the United States has been a relatively small factor for decision analysis, but, more importantly, it has been relatively stable.

Traditionally, the cost of capital estimates made for use in economic decision making have included an estimate of inflation combined with the opportunity loss component, but neither explicitly. For years, countries such as Brazil and Japan have endured inflation rates ranging from 10 to upwards of 30 percent, and now the United States, too, seems to be heading in that direction.

The time is past when the rate of inflation can be combined with the rate of opportunity loss for decision making. Each deserves a separate estimation due to their assumed independence (this may be an interesting side issue to consider) and magnitude. A look at Table 6.6 will further suggest the effect of inflation on the cost of capital and discounting in general (Let i = opportunity loss, θ = inflation rate).

TABLE 6.6
Discount Factors for i = .08, θ = Variable

Year n	$\theta = .04$	$\theta = .08$	$\theta = .12$	$\theta = .16$	$\theta = .20$
1	.890	.858	.826	.798	.772
2	.792	.735	.684	.637	.595
3	.706	.630	.565	.508	.459
4	.628	.540	.467	.406	.354
5	.559	.463	.386	.324	.274

Source: Compiled by the authors.

It should be quite apparent that the inflation rate becomes a significant factor in a cash flow analysis very quickly as n increases where n is the number of years in the discounted cash flow stream.

In order to explicitly control, at least in our decision model, the respective rates of opportunity loss and inflation independently of one another, we simply substitute the following throughout our decision equations:

$$(1.0 + i) * (1.0 + \theta)$$

where i is the opportunity loss and Theta (θ) represents the inflation rate. Note that θ is multiplicative with respect to i, not additive.[6]

In terms of the buy/lease decision to be made in the example problem, high inflation will have the following effects:

- Make leasing more advantageous since one will pay the later years with "cheap" dollars.
- Make purchasing less advantageous due to the fact that most cash outflows occur at T_0 when cash is at a high value, and then allowing depreciation (a virtual cash inflow) to occur with "less valuable" dollars.

The significance of inflation, however, is also related to the degree of significance of the cash flows that are attributed to it in relation to the nonfinancial benefits to accrue over the life of the asset.

NOTES

1. Given a range of values of a particular K_x, say 30,000 to 50,000, the $\bar{K}$ is the arithmetic average of the extremes, namely $(30,000 + 50,000)/2 = 40,000$.

2. It should be noted that in certain cases a change of the range of K_x and the corresponding change of F_x may alter the decision outcome.

3. See page 15 of [1].

4. See page 22 of [1].

5. See pages 96-97 of [2].

6. For a more extensive treatment of inflation see [3] and [4].

REFERENCES

[1] Canada, John R. and Wadsworth, Harrison M. "The Effects of Project Life Dispersion on Key Interest Factors for Economic Analysis of Capital Investment." *Engineering Economist* 11, no. 4 (Summer 1966).

[2] National Association of Accountants. *Financial Analysis to Guide Capital Expenditure Decisions,* Research Report 43. New York, 1967.

[3] Reisman, A. *Managerial and Engineering Economics.* Boston: Allyn and Bacon, 1971.

[4] Reisman, A. and Rao, A. K. "Discounted Cash Flow Analysis: Stochastic Extensions." American Institute of Industrial Engineers, 1973.

7

A CASE STUDY

THE ALTERNATIVES

The hypothetical problem on which the various decision techniques will be applied and about which the major issues will be discussed is as follows. C & W Enterprises is just beginning to outgrow its second-generation hardware system and has already accepted vendor proposals for advanced third-generation hardware and software in the medium-size range. Virtually all of its current software is written in assembler, and since this is not supported by any current system, all software must be converted (a microprogrammable computer, however, could emulate the older hardware with a degraded level of performance). A certain set of "must" features were specified. All of the proposals under consideration meet the "must" features requirements as well as some, if not all, of the desired features. The system is to satisfy the corporate requirements, which change over time, for five to seven years. Tables 7.2-7.4 present the relevant cash flows for each proposal.

The analysis of attributes (Table 7.4) contains 39 items. The first such feature, the present value of the cash flows, is not shown as it is to be calculated later. The set of 39 features may not be representative of an actual situation; however, the number and degree of aggregation within each is intended to reduce the clerical labors and yet demonstrate the approach.

TABLE 7.1
Common One-Time Costs for All Alternatives

Site preparation	
Wiring modifications	400
Space for equipment	
Facilities	
Walls	1,800
Painting	800
False flooring	2,500
Security provisions	
Fire protection	3,500
Secured area for critical software storage	1,200
Equipment installation	
Wiring (general hookup of peripherals, etc.)	400
General moving labor	200
Total	10,800

Source: Compiled by the authors.

THE ARITHMETIC SOLUTION

The objective of the computer system selection procedure set out here is to calculate and choose the investment alternative that has the maximum value for the criterion function. Many of the techniques developed thus far will be used for purposes of illustration. In order to complete the analysis begun in the preceding section, some additional tables will be necessary and are included in this section — see Tables 7.5-7.8. These tables were used exclusively to derive the present value of each alternative subject to federal and state income tax regulations. The nonfinancial factors are derived from Table 7.4 and are extended and normalized through techniques that will be provided in Tables 7.9 and 7.10-7.14. (The Appendix contains all of the relevant formulas and parameters used for the various calculations and conversions.)

This method of analysis essentially converts all criteria into a common unit of choice, which results in criterion function values of 7,415K, 10,726K, 10,458K, 8,335K, and 11,180K utiles, respectively, for Alternatives 1 through 5.

TABLE 7.2
Alternative-Dependent Cost Factors, 1, 2, and 3

	1		*2*	*3*
Cost	*Purchase Cost*	*Maintenance for Purchase*	*Closed-end Lease*	*Third Party Lease*
One-time cost				
Equipment transfer including insurance	800		800	800
Vendor support: program and data conversion	10,000		15,000	10,000
Consideration if shipped late or installed late			5,000	
Total	10,800		20,800	10,800
Continuing costs and capital equipment costs				
System equipment				
Central processing unit and associated equipment				
Mainframe	909,500	1,045	15,182	18,978
Real-time clock	3,000	15	50	63
Floating point option	4,000	5	68	85
Console	8,000	50	136	170
Total	924,500	1,115	15,436	19,296

TABLE 7.2 (continued)

	1		2	3
	Purchase Cost	Maintenance for Purchase	Closed-end Lease	Third Party Lease
Peripheral equipment				
Printer	34,000	200	720	900
Controller	45,000	125	480	600
Train cartridge	2,000		80	100
Card reader/punch	15,000	51	208	260
Disk (6 drives)	312,000	1,020	6,240	7,800
Controller	13,000	30	262	327
Tape (6 drives)	134,400	4,800	2,760	3,450
Controller	26,000	100	560	700
Total	581,400	6,326	11,310	14,137
Personnel (systems programmer)		1,800	1,800	1,800
Supplies				
Magnetic tape	1,500		31	31
Disk packs	7,200		120	150
Paper		500	500	500
Forms		300	300	300
Cards		180	180	180
Total	8,700	980	1,131	1,161

Unbundled software				
Systems				
Operating system				
COBOL	3,400	20	56	70
FORTRAN	6,200	50	104	130
Utilities				
Data management	8,600	45	144	180
Sort/Merge	4,800	30	80	100
Application				
Accounts payable	11,980	60	200	250
Accounts receivable	13,200	75	220	275
Total	48,180	280	804	1,005
Total continuing costs and capital equipment	1,562,780	10,501	30,481	37,399
Total at T_0	1,573,580		20,800	10,800
Total for each period (month)	10,501		30,481	37,399

Note: Since the third-party alternative involves a different vendor than the current one, a penalty is charged if the new equipment is late and the existing must be retained.

Monthly penalty	5,000
Expected delay	1 month
Expected delay cost	5,000

This, of course, does not consider opportunity losses that would be quite difficult to calculate.

Source: Compiled by the authors.

TABLE 7.3
Alternative-Dependent Cost Factors, 4 and 5

	4		5
	Purchase Cost	*Maintenance for Purchase*	*Closed-end Lease*
One-time cost			
Equipment transfer including insurance	700		700
Vendor support: Program and data conversion	35,000		35,000
Consideration if shipped or installed late	3,750		3,750
Total	39,450		39,450
Continuing costs and capital equipment costs			
System equipment			
Central processing unit and associated equipment			
Mainframe	704,500	950	15,499
Real-time clock	3,500	20	77
Floating point option	3,800	20	84
Console	7,000	55	154
Total	718,800	1,045	15,814
Peripheral equipment			
Printer	58,000	350	1,276
Controller	42,000	130	924
Train cartridge	2,200	40	48
Card reader/punch	12,500	55	275
Disk (6 drives)	290,000	1,000	6,380
Controller	12,000	30	264
Tape (6 drives)	124,000	4,500	2,728
Controller	25,000	80	550
Total	565,700	6,185	12,445
Personnel (systems programmer)		1,500	1,500
Supplies			
Magnetic tape	1,400		29
Disk packs	7,000		148
Paper		600	600
Forms		300	300
Cards		180	180
Total	8,400	1,080	1,257

(continued)

TABLE 7.3 (continued)

	4		5
	Purchase Cost	Maintenance for Purchase	Closed-end Lease
Unbundled software			
Systems			
Operating system	20,000	250	800
COBOL	3,800	30	120
FORTRAN	6,000	50	200
Utilities			
Data management	9,000	55	280
Sort/merge	4,800	35	150
Application			
Accounts payable	12,000	80	300
Accounts receivable	14,000	100	350
Total	69,600	600	2,200
Total continuing costs and capital equipment	1,362,500	10,410	33,216
Total at T_0	1,402,950		39,450
Total for each period (month)	10,410		33,216

Note: Since the above alternatives involve systems from a different manufacturer than the existing one, a late installation will result in the need for keeping the old equipment at a significant monthly penalty cost.

Monthly penalty	5,000
Expected delay	.75 month
Expected delay cost	3,750

This, of course, does not consider opportunity losses, which would be quite difficult to calculate.

Source: Compiled by the authors.

TABLE 7.4
Alternative-Dependent Noncost Factors (Benefits)

	Alternative 1	Alternative 2	Alternative 3	Alternative 4	Alternative 5	K_n
Speed and capacity of hardware						
Central processing unit						
Memory						
Speed nanosecond	540	540	540	500	500	2
Capacity kilobytes	512	512	512	512	512	3
Instructions						
Speed microsecond	2,100	2,100	2,100	400	400	4
Capability number of	152	152	152	99	99	5
Peripheral equipment						
Card reader/punch						
Speed cards/minute (read)	800	800	800	800	800	6
Speed cards/minute (punch)	250	250	250	300	300	7
Printer						
Speed lines/minute	1,100	1,100	1,100	1,720	1,720	8
Capacity characters/line	132	132	132	132	132	9
Magnetic tape						
Speed kilo-characters/second	200	200	200	96	96	10
Capacity bytes/inch	1,600	1,600	1,600	800	800	11
Disk						
Access time millisecond	60	60	60	20	20	12
Speed kilo-characters/second	312	312	312	300	300	13
Capacity million bytes	29	29	29	20	20	14

Controllers						
Printer capacity	4	4	4	6	6	15
Tape capacity	6	6	6	8	8	16
Disk capacity	6	6	6	6	6	17
Compatibility						
Hardware (arbitrary scale, AS)	100	100	100	90	90	18
Software AS	90	90	90	80	80	19
Switchability						
Hardware AS	95	95	95	85	85	20
Software AS	90	90	90	80	80	21
Reliability						
Hardware AS	95	95	95	98	98	22
Software AS	85	85	85	90	90	23
Expansion potential						
Hardware slack time hours/day	8	8	8	12	12	24
Software AS	30	30	30	70	70	25
Vendor support						
Program assistance Percent	90	90	40	90	90	26
Training AS	85	85	60	80	80	27
Maintenance AS	60	60	50	70	70	28
Backup AS	90	90	85	65	65	29
Documentation	90	90	90	95	95	30

(continued)

105

TABLE 7.4 (continued)

	Alternative 1	Alternative 2	Alternative 3	Alternative 4	Alternative 5	K_n
Existing software						
Systems						
Operating system AS	85	85	85	95	95	31
COBOL AS	80	80	80	95	95	32
FORTRAN AS	90	90	90	80	80	33
Access methods AS	6	6	5	5	5	34
Utilities						
Sort/merge AS	80	80	80	85	85	35
Data management AS	75	75	75	90	90	36
Application						
Accounts payable AS	80	80	80	90	90	37
Accounts receivable AS	85	85	85	90	90	38
Inventory AS	90	90	90	90	90	39

Source: Compiled by the authors.

Alternative	Description	Present Value Financial Cost	Total Value Criterion Function
1	Purchase IBM XXXX	1,244,869	7,415K
2	Lease IBM XXXX	417,070	10,726K
3	Third Party Lease XXXX	340,874	10,458K
4	Purchase Burroughs YYYY	1,134,432	8,335K
5	Lease Burroughs YYYY	432,193	11,180K

In Order of Present Value Financial	In Order of Total Value of Criterion Function
Alt. 5	Alt. 5
3	2
1	3
4	4
2	1

Although the calculations of these are relatively straightforward, several points should be made.

The total value of the criterion function indicates the rank order of the alternatives and is an approximation to the relative benefit of each alternative. It assumes each factor to be independent of all others and the scales used for evaluating the alternatives in the respective factors to be linear.

Only K_1 (present worth) is naturally expressed on a dollar scale and, therefore, a dollar cost. However, K_{12} (access speed) is inversely related to benefit (as is cost); a high value is worth less to a user than a low one. Therefore, these were evaluated as if they were negative benefits.

It would be a relatively minor extension to obtain the expected value of each criterion function using, say, a Delphi panel to determine the confidence band for each factor. This will not be attempted here because little will be gained for demonstration purposes by doing so.

It should be apparent that Alternative 5 (lease the Burroughs YYYY) is the best overall system even though in purely financial terms it would have followed Alternative 3 (lease IBM XXXX from a third party).

TABLE 7.5
Factors for Tax Consideration

Yearly Depreciation and Life of Asset	Alternative 1	Alternative 2	Alternative 3	Alternative 4	Alternative 5
Projected life of asset	5	5	5	5	5
Capitalized value at T_0 (hardware and software)	1,562,780			1,362,500	
Estimated salvage value	250,000			200,000	
Value to be depreciated	1,312,780			1,162,500	
Capitalized value at T_0 of program and data conversion	10,000	10,000	15,000	35,000	35,000
...of common items (see Table 7.1)	10,800	10,800	10,800	10,800	10,800
Total capitalized value	1,333,580	20,800	25,800	1,208,300	45,800
Straight-line depreciation per year	266,716	4,160	5,160	241,860	9,160
Expenses					
Expensed items					
Equipment transfer	800	800	800	700	700
Late consideration		5,000		3,750	3,750
One-time expenses at T_0	800	5,800	800	4,450	4,450
Repeatable monthly expenses	10,501	30,481	37,399	10,410	33,216

Book Value of Assets

At:					
T_0	1,572,780	10,000	15,000	1,398,500	35,000
T_1	1,308,224	8,000	12,000	1,158,800	28,000
T_2	1,043,668	6,000	9,000	919,100	21,000
T_3	779,112	4,000	6,000	679,400	14,000
T_4	514,556	2,000	3,000	439,700	7,000
T_5	250,000	0	0	200,000	0

Investment Credit

Capitalized value of computer hardware	1,505,900	1,285,500
Less salvage value	250,000	200,000
Total depreciable value	1,255,900	1,085,500
Effective investment credit rate	.0233	.0233
Investment credit	29,262	25,292

Source: Compiled by the authors.

TABLE 7.6
Time-Phased Cash Flows

Time	Alternative 1	Alternative 2	Alternative 3	Alternative 4	Alternative 5
T_0 One-time costs computer hardware and software	10,800	20,800	10,800	39,450	39,450
	924,500			718,800	
	581,400			565,700	
	8,700			8,400	
	48,180			69,600	
	1,573,580	20,800	10,800	1,401,950	39,450
T_{1-12} Monthly costs					
Hardware	6,426	14,137	11,310	6,185	12,445
Personnel	1,800	1,800	1,800	1,500	1,500
Supplies	980	1,161	1,131	1,080	1,257
Software	280	1,005	804	600	2,200
	9,486	18,103	15,045	9,365	17,402
T_{12} Interest on undepreciated portion of assets	157,278	1,000	1,500	139,850	3,500
T_{13-24} Monthly cost same as T_{1-12}					
T_{25-36} ,, ,, ,,					
T_{37-48} ,, ,, ,,					
T_{49-60} ,, ,, ,,					
T_{24} Interest	130,822	600	1,200	115,880	2,800
T_{36} Interest	104,369	600	900	91,910	2,100
T_{48} Interest	77,911	400	600	67,940	1,400
T_{60} Interest	51,456	200	300	43,970	700
T_{60} Salvage value	250,000			200,000	

Source: Compiled by the authors.

TABLE 7.7
Present Value Calculations

Assume: i = 10 percent, r = .09531, $r_{mo.}$ = .008

		One-Time Costs		
Alternative 1	Alternative 2	Alternative 3	Alternative 4	Alternative 5
1,573,580	20,800	10,800	1,401,950	39,450

Expenses by Year

Alternative 1

9,486*11.396 = 108,102
108,102* .908 = 98,157
108,102* .825 = 89,184
108,102* .750 = 81,077
108,102* .681 = 73,617
450,137

Alternative 2

18,103*11.396 = 206,302
206,302* .908 = 187,322
206,302* .825 = 170,199
206,302* .750 = 154,727
206,302* .681 = 140,492
859,042

Alternative 3

15,045*11.396 = 171,453
171,453* .908 = 155,679
171,453* .825 = 141,449
171,453* .750 = 128,590
171,453* .681 = 116,759
713,930

Alternative 4

9,365*11.396 = 106,724
106,724* .908 = 96,905
106,724* .825 = 88,047
106,724* .750 = 80,043
106,724* .681 = 72,679
444,398

(continued)

TABLE 7.7 (continued)

Alternative 5

$17,402*11.396 = 198,313$
$198,313* \quad .908 = 180,068$
$198,313* \quad .825 = 163,608$
$198,313* \quad .750 = 148,735$
$198,313* \quad .681 = \underline{135,051}$
$\qquad\qquad\qquad 825,775$

Interest Expense

Alternative 1

$157,278* \quad .908 = 142,808$
$130,822* \quad .825 = 107,928$
$104,369* \quad .750 = 78,277$
$77,911* \quad .681 = 53,057$
$51,456* \quad .619 = \underline{31,851}$
$\qquad\qquad\qquad 413,921$

Alternative 3

$1,500* \quad .908 = 1,362$
$1,200* \quad .825 = 990$
$900* \quad .750 = 675$
$600* \quad .681 = 409$
$300* \quad .619 = \underline{186}$
$\qquad\qquad\qquad 3,622$

Alternative 2

$1,000* \quad .908 = 908$
$800* \quad .825 = 660$
$600* \quad .750 = 450$
$400* \quad .681 = 272$
$200* \quad .619 = \underline{124}$
$\qquad\qquad\qquad 2,414$

Alternative 4

$139,850* \quad .908 = 126,984$
$115,880* \quad .825 = 95,601$
$91,910* \quad .750 = 68,933$
$67,940* \quad .681 = 46,267$
$43,970* \quad .619 = \underline{27,217}$
$\qquad\qquad\qquad 365,002$

112

Alternative 5

3,500* .908 = 3,178
2,800* .825 = 2,310
2,100* .750 = 1,575
1,400* .681 =   953
  700* .619 =   433
             8,449

Depreciation by Year

Alternative 1

266,716* .908 = 242,178
266,716* .825 = 220,041
266,716* .750 = 200,037
266,716* .681 = 181,634
266,716* .619 = 165,097
              1,008,987

Alternative 4

241,860* .908 = 219,609
241,860* .825 = 199,535
241,860* .750 = 181,395
241,860* .681 = 164,707
241,860* .619 = 149,711
               914,957

Salvage Value in Year 5

Alternative 1

250,000* .619 = 154,750

Alternative 4

200,000* .619 = 123,800

Source: Compiled by the authors.

TABLE 7.8
Summary of Present Values for Each Alternative: Financial Cost Components Only

Assume: federal tax rate = 46 percent, state tax rate = 4 percent (S), total effective rate = (.46 + S)

	Alternative 1	Alternative 2	Alternative 3	Alternative 4	Alternative 5
Costs					
Expenses	450,137	859,042	713,930	444,398	825,775
Interest	413,921	2,414	3,622	365,002	8,449
	864,058	861,456	717,552	809,400	834,224
Federal tax rate	.46	.46	.46	.46	.46
After tax present value	397,467	396,270	330,074	372,324	383,743
Initial costs	1,573,580	20,800	10,800	1,401,950	39,450
Total present value of costs	1,971,047	417,070	340,874	1,774,274	423,193
Less present value salvage value	154,750			123,800	
	1,816,297			1,650,474	
Less benefit of depreciation * .54 (for tax)	544,858[1]			494,077[2]	
Less investment credit	26,570[3]			22,965[4]	
Total tax benefit	571,428			517,042	
Total present value cost	1,244,869	417,070	340,874	1,133,432	423,193

[1]Total depreciation at present value equals 1,008,997 times the federal and state tax of 54 percent equals 544,858.
[2]Same as note 1 except 914,957 and 494,077, respectively.
[3]Investment credit of 29,262 discounted to T_0 equals 26,570.
[4]Investment credit of 25,292 discounted to T_0 equals 22,965.

Source: Compiled by the authors.

114

TABLE 7.9
Conversion of Criteria

| Criteria number | Range | | | Factor |
	Low	High	Average	
K_1	340,874	1,244,869	792,872	1
2	500	540	520	1,575
3	512	512	512	1,599
4	400	2,100	1,250	655
5	99	152	125.5	6,525
6	800	800	800	1,024
7	250	300	275	2,978
8	1,100	1,720	1,410	581
9	132	132	132	6,204
10	96,000	200,000	148,000	5.5
11	800	1,600	1,200	683
12	20	60	40	20,471
13	300,000	312,000	306,000	2.7
14	20	29	24.5	33,423
15	4	6	5	163,773
16	6	8	7	116,981
17	6	6	6	136,478
18	90	100	95	8,620
19	80	90	85	9,634
20	85	95	90	9,099
21	80	90	85	9,634
22	95	98	96.5	8,486
23	85	90	87.5	9,359
24	8	12	10	81,887
25	30	70	50	16,378
26	40	90	65	12,598
27	60	85	72.5	11,295
28	50	70	80	10,236
29	65	90	75.5	10,846
30	90	95	92.5	8,852
31	85	95	90	9,099
32	80	95	87.5	9,359
33	80	90	85	9,634
34	5	6	5.5	148,885
35	80	85	82.5	9,926
36	75	90	82.5	9,926
37	80	90	85	9,634
38	85	90	87.5	9,359
39	90	90	90	9,099

Source: Compiled by the authors.

115

TABLE 7.10
Analysis of Alternative 1

Criteria	Relative Weight	Factor	Value	Weight Value (1,000s)
K_1	−4.0	1	1,244,869	−4,979
2	.15	1,575	540	127
3	.15	1,599	512	122
4	.2	655	2,100	275
5	.2	6,525	152	198
6	.3	1,024	800	245
7	.2	2,978	250	148
8	.4	581	1,100	255
9	.2	6,204	132	163
10	.3	5.5	200,000	330
11	.2	683	1,600	218
12	−.5	20,471	60	−614
13	.3	2.7	312,000	251
14	.4	33,423	29	591
15	.1	163,773	4	66
16	.1	116,981	6	70
17	.1	136,478	6	81
18	.6	8,620	100	517
19	.6	9,634	90	520
20	.3	9,099	95	259
21	.3	9,634	90	260
22	.8	8,486	95	644
23	.8	9,359	85	536
24	.6	81,887	8	393
25	.7	16,378	30	343
26	.6	12,598	90	580
27	.4	11,295	85	384
28	.5	10,236	60	307
29	.5	10,846	90	488
30	.5	8,852	90	398
31	.6	9,099	85	464
32	.6	9,359	80	449
33	.4	9,634	90	346
34	.7	148,885	6	625
35	.5	9,926	80	397
36	.6	9,926	75	446
37	.6	9,634	80	462
38	.6	9,359	85	477
39	.7	9,099	90	573
Totals	19.3			7,415K

Source: Compiled by the authors.

TABLE 7.11
Analysis of Alternative 2

Criteria	Relative Weight	Factor	Value	Weight Value (1,000's)
K_1	−4.0	1	417,070	−1,668
2	.15	1,575	540	127
3	.15	1,599	512	122
4	.2	655	2,100	275
5	.2	6,525	152	198
6	.3	1,024	800	245
7	.2	2,978	250	148
8	.4	581	1,100	255
9	.2	6,204	132	163
10	.3	5.5	200,000	330
11	.2	683	1,600	218
12	−.5	20,471	60	−614
13	.3	2.7	312,000	251
14	.4	33,423	29	591
15	.1	163,773	4	66
16	.1	116,981	6	70
17	.1	136,478	6	81
18	.6	8,620	100	517
19	.6	9,634	90	520
20	.3	9,099	95	259
21	.3	9,634	90	260
22	.8	8,486	95	644
23	.8	9,359	85	536
24	.6	81,887	8	393
25	.7	16,378	30	343
26	.6	12,598	90	580
27	.4	11,295	85	384
28	.5	10,236	60	307
29	.5	10,846	90	488
30	.5	8,852	90	398
31	.6	9,099	85	464
32	.6	9,359	80	449
33	.4	9,634	90	346
34	.7	148,885	6	625
35	.5	9,926	80	397
36	.6	9,926	75	446
37	.6	9,634	80	462
38	.6	9,359	85	477
39	.7	9,099	90	573
Totals	19.3			10,726K

Source: Compiled by the authors.

TABLE 7.12
Analysis of Alternative 3

Criteria	Relative Weight	Factor	Value	Weight Value (1,000's)
K_1	−4.0	1	340,874	−1,363
2	.15	1,575	540	127
3	.15	1,599	512	122
4	.2	655	2,100	275
5	.2	6,525	152	198
6	.3	1,024	800	245
7	.2	2,978	250	148
8	.4	581	1,100	255
9	.2	6,204	132	163
10	.3	5.5	200,000	330
11	.2	683	1,600	218
12	−.5	20,471	60	−614
13	.3	2.7	312,000	251
14	.4	33,423	29	591
15	.1	163,773	4	66
16	.1	116,981	6	70
17	.1	136,478	6	81
18	.6	8,620	100	517
19	.6	9,634	90	520
20	.3	9,099	95	259
21	.3	9,634	90	260
22	.8	8,486	95	644
23	.8	9,359	85	536
24	.6	81,887	8	393
25	.7	16,378	30	343
26	.6	12,598	40	304
27	.4	11,295	60	271
28	.5	10,236	50	255
29	.5	10,846	85	460
30	.5	8,852	90	398
31	.6	9,099	85	464
32	.6	9,359	80	449
33	.4	9,634	90	346
34	.7	148,885	5	521
35	.5	9,926	80	397
36	.6	9,926	75	446
37	.6	9,634	80	462
38	.6	9,359	85	477
39	.7	9,099	90	573
Totals	19.3			10,458K

Source: Compiled by the authors.

TABLE 7.13
Analysis of Alternative 4

Criteria	Relative Weight	Factor	Value	Weight Value (1,000's)
K_1	−4.0	1	1,134,432	−4,538
2	.15	1,575	500	118
3	.15	1,599	512	122
4	.2	655	400	52
5	.2	6,525	99	129
6	.3	1,024	800	245
7	.2	2,978	300	178
8	.4	581	1,720	399
9	.2	6,204	132	163
10	.3	5.5	96,000	158
11	.2	683	800	109
12	−.5	20,471	20	−204
13	.3	2.7	300,000	241
14	.4	33,423	20	267
15	.1	163,773	6	98
16	.1	116,981	8	93
17	.1	136,478	6	81
18	.6	8,620	90	465
19	.6	9,634	80	462
20	.3	9,099	85	232
21	.3	9,634	80	231
22	.8	8,486	98	665
23	.8	9,359	90	673
24	.6	81,887	12	589
25	.7	16,378	70	802
26	.6	12,598	90	580
27	.4	11,295	80	361
28	.5	10,236	70	358
29	.5	10,846	65	352
30	.5	8,852	95	420
31	.6	9,099	95	518
32	.6	9,359	95	533
33	.4	9,634	80	308
34	.7	148,885	5	521
35	.5	9,926	85	421
36	.6	9,926	90	535
37	.6	9,634	90	520
38	.6	9,359	90	505
39	.7	9,099	90	573
Totals	19.3			8,335K

Source: Compiled by the authors.

119

TABLE 7.14
Analysis of Alternative 5

Criteria	Relative Weight	Factor	Value	Weight Value (1,000's)
K_1	−4.0	1	423,193	−1,693
2	.15	1,575	500	118
3	.15	1,599	512	122
4	.2	655	400	52
5	.2	6,525	99	129
6	.3	1,024	800	245
7	.2	2,978	300	178
8	.4	581	1,720	399
9	.2	6,204	132	163
10	.3	5.5	96,000	158
11	.2	683	800	109
12	−.5	20,471	20	−204
13	.3	2.7	300,000	241
14	.4	33,423	20	267
15	.1	163,773	6	98
16	.1	116,981	8	93
17	.1	136,478	6	81
18	.6	8,620	90	465
19	.6	9,634	80	462
20	.3	9,099	85	232
21	.3	9,634	80	231
22	.8	8,486	98	665
23	.8	9,359	90	673
24	.6	81,887	12	589
25	.7	16,378	70	802
26	.6	12,598	90	580
27	.4	11,295	80	361
28	.5	10,236	70	358
29	.5	10,846	65	352
30	.5	8,852	95	420
31	.6	9,099	95	518
32	.6	9,359	95	533
33	.4	9,634	80	308
34	.7	148,885	5	521
35	.5	9,926	85	421
36	.6	9,926	90	535
37	.6	9,634	90	520
38	.6	9,359	90	505
39	.7	9,099	90	573
Totals	19.3			11,180K

Source: Compiled by the authors.

APPENDIX A

THE CHEVS TAXONOMY:
ITEMS TO BE CONSIDERED
FOR COMPUTER SELECTION

COSTS

I. One-time costs
    A. Site preparation
        1. electrical
            a) air conditioning
                (i)   cooling
                (ii)   heating
                (iii) humidity
                (iv)   dust or particulate control
            b) power supply
                (i)   wiring
                (ii)   auxiliary generator
                (iii) voltage regulator
        2. space for equipment
            a) facilities
                (i)   walls
                (ii)   ceiling
                (iii) painting
                (iv)   draperies
                (v)   carpeting (nonstatic)
            b) false flooring (including bracing)
        3. security provisions
            a) badge readers
            b) closed circuit TV (central monitoring)
            c) limited entry points
            d) fire protection (fire/smoke detectors)
            e) noncombustible furnishings
            f) flood protection
            g) secured area for critical software storage
    B. Equipment installation
        1. carpentry
        2. wiring
        3. plumbing
        4. general moving labor
        5. initial diagnostic checkout

C. Equipment transportation including insurance
D. Vendor support
  1. personnel
     a) analysts
     b) programmers
     c) operators
     d) instructors
  2. training (including transportation and living costs, if training is not on site)
  3. existing programs
  4. backup facilities
  5. machine time for checkout
  6. documentation
  7. program and data conversion
  8. special consideration if used as a test site
  9. consideration if shipped or installed late

II. Continuing costs
  A. Procurement of computer system equipment
    1. central processor and associated equipment
       a) double precision arithmetic
       b) real-time clock
       c) special instruction set
       d) floating point instructions
       e) firmware
       f) hardware multiply and divide
       g) hardware square root
       h) real-time interrupt
       i) memory
       j) digital/analog conversion
       k) hardware monitor
       l) console
    2. peripheral computer equipment
       a) remote terminals
       b) card reader/punch
       c) printer
       d) magnetic tape
       e) disk
       f) drum
       g) data cell
       h) paper tape reader/punch
       i) controllers
       j) magnetic ink character reader
       k) optical scanner
       l) communications controller

      m) cathode ray tube (CRT)

      n) teletypes

      o) communications lines

      p) microfiche equipment

      q) special devices

   3. auxiliary equipment

      a) key punches

      b) verifyers

      c) key tape

      d) key disk/drum

      e) communications equipment

      f) data set

      g) modem

      h) concentrators

      i) message switching equipment

      j) card sorters

      k) collators

      l) interpreters

      m) bursters

      n) off-line printers

      o) shredder

B. Operation and maintenance of all equipment

C. Personnel

   1. manager

   2. analysts

   3. programmers (application and system)

   4. operators

   5. key operators

D. Program development

   1. application

   2. system

E. Supplies

   1. magnetic tape

   2. disk packs

   3. paper tape

   4. printer paper 1, 2, 3, 4, . . . n part)

   5. forms

   6. punch cards

F. Indirect costs

   1. space used

   2. heat

   3. electricity

   4. miscellaneous services and maintenance

G. Unbundled software
  1. operating system
     a) real-time
     b) time sharing
     c) teleprocessing
     d) disk
     e) multiprogramming
     f) multiprocessing
     g) multitasking
  2. utilities
     a) data management
     b) sort/merge
  3. data base management systems
  4. application software
     a) accounts receivable
     b) accounts payable
     c) inventory control
     d) bill of material
     e) sales forecasting
     f) miscellaneous

HARDWARE CHARACTERISTICS

I. Speed and capacity
(This section is intended to serve as a key of scales of measurement for speed [S] and capacity [C] factors.)
  1. accuracy, resolution, number of places
  2. arbitrary scale (AS)
  3. average latency
  4. average seek + latency
  5. baud = bits/second
  6. bits/operand
  7. bpi = bytes/inch (7 & 9 track tape only)
  8. characters/record
  9. characters recognized
  10. characters/line
  11. characters/second
  12. cpm = cards/minute
  13. digits/second
  14. inches
  15. inches/second
  16. KB = kilobytes
  17. pounds/minute

18. lines
19. lpm = lines/minute
20. MB = million bytes
21. msec = millisecond
22. number of lines
23. number of devices handled
24. number of instructions
25. number of interrupt types
26. number of places monitored
27. nsec = nanosecond
28. ppm = part/minute
29. seconds/exposure
30. size
31. usec = microsecond
32. percent overhead

A. CPU
1. double precision arithmetic (S: usec, C: bits/operand)
2. real-time clock (S: percent overhead)
3. instruction set (S: nsec, C: number of instructions)
4. floating point option (S: usec, C: bits/operand)
5. firmware (S: nsec, C: number of instructions, KB)
6. multiply/divide (S: usec, C: bits/operand)
7. hardware square root (S; usec, C: bits/operand)
8. real-time interrupt (S: usec, C: number of interrupt types)
9. memory (S: nsec, C: MB)
10. digital/analogue conv. (S: digits/second, C: number of places, accuracy, resolution)
11. hardware monitor (S: percent overhead, C: number of places monitored)
12. console (S: characters/second, C: characters/line)

B. Peripheral computer equipment
1. remote terminals (S: characters/second, C: characters/line)
2. card reader/punch (S: cpm, C: characters)
3. printer (S: lpm, C: characters/line)
4. magnetic tape (S: characters/second, C: bpi)
5. disk (S: characters/second, average seek + latency, C: MB)
6. drum (S: characters/second, average latency, C: MB)
7. data cell (S: characters/second, average seek + latency, C: KB)
8. paper tape reader/punch (S: characters/second)
9. controllers (C: number of devices handled)
10. magnetic ink character readers (S: characters/second, C: characters recognized)
11. optical scanner (S: characters/second, C: characters recognized)
12. plotter (S: inches/second, C: inches)

13. communications controller (C: number of devices handled)
14. CRT (S: characters/second, C: characters/line, lines)
15. teletypes (S: characters/second)
16. dedicated communications lines (S: baud)
17. microfiche (S: seconds/exposure, C: size)
18. special devices (as required)

C. Auxiliary equipment
   1. key punches (C: characters/recognized)
   2. verifyers (C: characters/recognized)
   3. key tape (C: characters/recognized)
   4. key disk (C: characters/recognized)
   5. communications equipment (S: baud)
   6. data set (S: baud, C: number of characters recognized)
   7. modem (S: baud, C: number of characters recognized)
   8. concentrators (S: baud, C: number of lines)
   9. message switching equipment (S: baud, C: number of lines)
   10. card sorters (S: cpm)
   11. collators (S: cpm)
   12. interpreters (S: cpm)
   13. bursters (S: ppm)
   14. off-line printers (S: lpm, C: characters/line)
   15. shredders (S: pounds/minute)

II. Compatibility

Compatibility refers to the degree to which the proposed system interfaces with previous and remaining system components. For example, the character set generated by a model 026 key punch may be satisfactory for existing hardware, but the replacement may expect the character set of a model 029. In reality, this relative incompatibility is handled by a hardware converter, usually at an extra cost. Typically, however, compatibilities are much more significant to the system designer: can the 96-column card files used on the IBM System 3 be used with a UNIVAC 1110? For purposes of comparison between alternatives, one would include whatever costs would be incurred in order to arrive at a completely compatible system including the sale of incompatible hardware and the acquisition of new.

III. Switchability

Switchability is that quality that indicates the inherent flexibility of the proposed system to change. If the system designer were partially in error, could the proposed system be modified or adjusted to accommodate that change? Unfortunately, no hard and fast numbers are assignable to this factor and, therefore, a best estimate based on an arbitrary scale will normally be used. One would expect an IBM system to rate quite high due to its being a virtual standard for the industry, while another vendor might be rated lower for the converse reason.

IV. Reliability

Reliability is frequently taken for granted in hardware systems; in some cases this may be justified due to the built-in error checking; however, occasionally even the best manufacturer will design and offer for sale a piece of equipment that develops a reputation for poor reliability. Perhaps the safest strategy is to avoid all such cases if possible. Since the frequency of error or breakdown rates are not published, it is very difficult to quantify this factor except on an arbitrary scale. The industry standard, when the information is available, is the mean time before failure (MTBF). The degree to which critical components have been built with redundancy may serve as a basis for establishing a value for the reliability factor.

Telecommunications hardware frequently have published or guaranteed error rate limits, and if applicable, these should be used. The typical scale used is the number of successful bit transmissions between errors (that is, 1 in 10^9 bits).

V. Special features and other characteristics

Special features serve to narrow the field of alternatives considerably, provided they are mandatory. Due to their relative degree of nonstandardization, it is difficult to establish beforehand the infinite variety of potential quantifiable characteristics. However, speed, capacity, compatibility, switchability, and reliability should all be considered in addition to cost. Special features, on the negative side, must be approached with caution since they often tend to lock one into a specific implementation, thus reducing switchability. Special features may include memory lockout, parallel processing, virtual memory, and data collection devices for inventory control. Certainly there are a variety of other characteristics that are relevant, such as size and weight of the equipment. However, in most cases the alternatives being considered, usually all of which come from the same or similar technology, will not vary significantly. Others, such as the line voltage required to run a computer, may permit one alternative to be simply plugged in, while the other may require special wiring. In this case the normalization of this factor can be simply handled by allocating a cost to those alternatives for the proposed hardware modifications to support the special voltage. In other cases an arbitrary scale may be used as in special features.

EXPANSION POTENTIAL

Expansion potential for a growing organization is, of course, quite important. In this effort, upward compatibility to larger, more sophisticated pieces of hardware is desirable to avoid conversion costs in the future. Upward compatibility can also be gained within a given series of computer hardware by implementing the current applications on a limited but nevertheless expandable version of the vendor's equipment. At even a lower level, expansion can be gained through the addition of more shifts or weekend operations. Examples of measures of the expansion potential of a system, in addition to an arbitrary scale, would include:

slack time: the amount of available free time on each piece of system equipment

maximum expansion: the number of units of various types of resources that can be added to the system (channels, controllers, disk drives, and so on)

VENDOR SUPPORT

A. Program assistance
    1. development (percent or hours)
    2. writing (percent or hours)
    3. conversion (percent or hours)
    4. test (percent or hours)
B. Training
    1. analysts (AS for net relevant hours of training)
    2. programmers (same as above)
    3. operators (same as above)
C. Maintenance (AS for convenience of maintenance and completeness)
D. Backup availability (AS or miles away)
E. Documentation
    1. ease of use (AS)
    2. completeness (AS)
    3. kept up to date (AS)
F. Personnel lent
    1. analysts (hours)
    2. programmers (hours)
    3. operators (hours)

SOFTWARE

Traditionally, computer system selection methods have focused on hardware, perhaps due to the tremendous technological breakthroughs that have been made. The user, however, is results-oriented and, although interested in satisfactory hardware performance, is more interested in the software capabilities provided. This last section of criteria will be devoted to the analysis of software.

The major criteria to be evaluated for each piece of software include:

cost ($)
size (KB storage space used)
speed of execution (time)

special features offered (AS)
ease of use (AS)
special devices required (AS or $)
how well documented and maintained (AS)
level of use (how many other installations use the same package)

The following categories of software should all be considered in the user analysis. Obviously, if the user plans to simply convert existing application software, then those segments will be omitted except in the determination of conversion costs.

I. Systems software
   A. Operating system
      1. executive and control functions
         a) job management
            (i) job control
               (1) scheduling
               (2) resource allocation
               (3) program loading
               (4) event monitoring
               (5) program termination processing
            (ii) input/output control
               (1) input/output scheduling
               (2) data transfer
               (3) device manipulation
               (4) remote terminal support
            (iii) system communication
               (1) system start up
               (2) job control communication
               (3) input/output stream control
               (4) resource status modification
               (5) system status interrogation
            (iv) recovery processing
               (1) checkpointing
               (2) restarting
            (v) diagnostic error processing
               (1) hardware error control
               (2) program error control
               (3) interface error control
            (vi) processing support
               (1) time service
               (2) testing and debugging service
               (3) logging and accounting
               (4) program accessible system description maintenance
      2. system management functions
         a) operating system management

               (i)   system generation
               (ii)   system maintenance
       b)   program maintenance
       c)   library and directory maintenance
               (i)   load module generation
       d)   compiler interfaces
               (i)   executive routine support
               (ii)   library support
               (iii)   system utility program support
       e)   management support utilities
               (i)   peripheral device support
               (ii)   system simulation routines
               (iii)   system measurement routines
               (iv)   stand-alone utilities

    3.   data manipulation functions
       a)   data management
               (i)   file management facilities
               (ii)   input/output support facilities
               (iii)   data management system facilities
       b)   data handling utilities
       c)   sorting and merging

  B. Assemblers
  C. Compilers (FORTRAN, COBOL, PL1, RPG, and so on)
  D. Simulators
  E. Emulators
  F. Software performance monitor
  G. Access methods

II. Utilities
  A. Sort/merge
  B. Data compaction
  C. Data management
  D. Data base management system
  E. Data encription/decription routine

III. Application software
  A. Accounts receivable
  B. Accounts payable
  C. Inventory control
  D. Bill of material
  E. Sales forecasting
  F. Financial reporting
  G. Open order and order processing
  H. General ledger
  I. Investment analysis
  J. Payroll
  K. Statistical analysis

TABLE B.1

Values of e^x and e^{-x}

x	e^x	e^{-x}	x	e^x	e^{-x}	x	e^x	e^{-x}
0.00	1.0000E+00	1.0000E+00	.50	1.6487E+00	6.0653E-01	1.00	2.7182E+00	3.6787E-01
.01	1.0100E+00	9.9004E-01	.51	1.6652E+00	6.0049E-01	1.01	2.7456E+00	3.6421E-01
.02	1.0202E+00	9.8019E-01	.52	1.6820E+00	5.9452E-01	1.02	2.7731E+00	3.6059E-01
.03	1.0304E+00	9.7044E-01	.53	1.6989E+00	5.8860E-01	1.03	2.8010E+00	3.5700E-01
.04	1.0408E+00	9.6078E-01	.54	1.7160E+00	5.8274E-01	1.04	2.8292E+00	3.5345E-01
.05	1.0512E+00	9.5122E-01	.55	1.7332E+00	5.7694E-01	1.05	2.8576E+00	3.4993E-01
.06	1.0618E+00	9.4176E-01	.56	1.7506E+00	5.7120E-01	1.06	2.8863E+00	3.4645E-01
.07	1.0725E+00	9.3239E-01	.57	1.7682E+00	5.6552E-01	1.07	2.9153E+00	3.4300E-01
.08	1.0832E+00	9.2311E-01	.58	1.7860E+00	5.5989E-01	1.08	2.9446E+00	3.3959E-01
.09	1.0941E+00	9.1393E-01	.59	1.8039E+00	5.5432E-01	1.09	2.9742E+00	3.3621E-01
.10	1.1051E+00	9.0483E-01	.60	1.8221E+00	5.4881E-01	1.10	3.0041E+00	3.3287E-01
.11	1.1162E+00	8.9583E-01	.61	1.8404E+00	5.4335E-01	1.11	3.0343E+00	3.2955E-01
.12	1.1274E+00	8.8692E-01	.62	1.8589E+00	5.3794E-01	1.12	3.0648E+00	3.2627E-01
.13	1.1388E+00	8.7809E-01	.63	1.8776E+00	5.3259E-01	1.13	3.0956E+00	3.2303E-01
.14	1.1502E+00	8.6935E-01	.64	1.8964E+00	5.2729E-01	1.14	3.1267E+00	3.1981E-01
.15	1.1618E+00	8.6070E-01	.65	1.9155E+00	5.2204E-01	1.15	3.1581E+00	3.1663E-01
.16	1.1735E+00	8.5214E-01	.66	1.9347E+00	5.1685E-01	1.16	3.1899E+00	3.1348E-01
.17	1.1853E+00	8.4366E-01	.67	1.9542E+00	5.1170E-01	1.17	3.2219E+00	3.1036E-01
.18	1.1972E+00	8.3527E-01	.68	1.9738E+00	5.0661E-01	1.18	3.2543E+00	3.0727E-01
.19	1.2092E+00	8.2695E-01	.69	1.9937E+00	5.0157E-01	1.19	3.2870E+00	3.0422E-01
.20	1.2214E+00	8.1873E-01	.70	2.0137E+00	4.9658E-01	1.20	3.3201E+00	3.0119E-01
.21	1.2336E+00	8.1058E-01	.71	2.0339E+00	4.9164E-01	1.21	3.3534E+00	2.9819E-01
.22	1.2460E+00	8.0251E-01	.72	2.0544E+00	4.8675E-01	1.22	3.3871E+00	2.9523E-01
.23	1.2586E+00	7.9453E-01	.73	2.0750E+00	4.8190E-01	1.23	3.4212E+00	2.9229E-01
.24	1.2712E+00	7.8662E-01	.74	2.0959E+00	4.7711E-01	1.24	3.4556E+00	2.8938E-01
.25	1.2840E+00	7.7880E-01	.75	2.1170E+00	4.7236E-01	1.25	3.4903E+00	2.8650E-01
.26	1.2969E+00	7.7105E-01	.76	2.1382E+00	4.6766E-01	1.26	3.5254E+00	2.8365E-01
.27	1.3099E+00	7.6337E-01	.77	2.1597E+00	4.6301E-01	1.27	3.5608E+00	2.8083E-01
.28	1.3231E+00	7.5578E-01	.78	2.1814E+00	4.5840E-01	1.28	3.5966E+00	2.7803E-01
.29	1.3364E+00	7.4826E-01	.79	2.2033E+00	4.5384E-01	1.29	3.6327E+00	2.7527E-01
.30	1.3498E+00	7.4081E-01	.80	2.2255E+00	4.4932E-01	1.30	3.6692E+00	2.7253E-01
.31	1.3634E+00	7.3344E-01	.81	2.2479E+00	4.4485E-01	1.31	3.7061E+00	2.6982E-01
.32	1.3771E+00	7.2614E-01	.82	2.2704E+00	4.4043E-01	1.32	3.7434E+00	2.6713E-01
.33	1.3909E+00	7.1892E-01	.83	2.2933E+00	4.3605E-01	1.33	3.7810E+00	2.6447E-01
.34	1.4049E+00	7.1177E-01	.84	2.3164E+00	4.3171E-01	1.34	3.8190E+00	2.6184E-01
.35	1.4190E+00	7.0468E-01	.85	2.3396E+00	4.2741E-01	1.35	3.8574E+00	2.5924E-01
.36	1.4333E+00	6.9767E-01	.86	2.3631E+00	4.2316E-01	1.36	3.8961E+00	2.5666E-01
.37	1.4477E+00	6.9073E-01	.87	2.3869E+00	4.1895E-01	1.37	3.9353E+00	2.5410E-01
.38	1.4622E+00	6.8386E-01	.88	2.4108E+00	4.1478E-01	1.38	3.9749E+00	2.5157E-01
.39	1.4769E+00	6.7705E-01	.89	2.4351E+00	4.1065E-01	1.39	4.0148E+00	2.4907E-01
.40	1.4918E+00	6.7032E-01	.90	2.4596E+00	4.0656E-01	1.40	4.0551E+00	2.4659E-01
.41	1.5068E+00	6.6365E-01	.91	2.4843E+00	4.0252E-01	1.41	4.0959E+00	2.4414E-01
.42	1.5219E+00	6.5704E-01	.92	2.5092E+00	3.9851E-01	1.42	4.1371E+00	2.4171E-01
.43	1.5372E+00	6.5050E-01	.93	2.5345E+00	3.9455E-01	1.43	4.1786E+00	2.3930E-01
.44	1.5527E+00	6.4403E-01	.94	2.5599E+00	3.9062E-01	1.44	4.2206E+00	2.3692E-01
.45	1.5683E+00	6.3762E-01	.95	2.5857E+00	3.8674E-01	1.45	4.2631E+00	2.3457E-01
.46	1.5840E+00	6.3128E-01	.96	2.6116E+00	3.8289E-01	1.46	4.3059E+00	2.3223E-01
.47	1.5999E+00	6.2500E-01	.97	2.6379E+00	3.7908E-01	1.47	4.3492E+00	2.2992E-01
.48	1.6160E+00	6.1878E-01	.98	2.6644E+00	3.7531E-01	1.48	4.3929E+00	2.2763E-01
.49	1.6323E+00	6.1262E-01	.99	2.6912E+00	3.7157E-01	1.49	4.4370E+00	2.2537E-01

x	E	E̅		x	E	E̅		x	E	E̅
1.50	4.4816E+00	2.2313E-01	*	2.00	7.3890E+00	1.3533E-01	*	2.50	1.2182E+01	8.2084E-02
1.51	4.5267E+00	2.2090E-01	*	2.01	7.4633E+00	1.3398E-01	*	2.51	1.2304E+01	8.1268E-02
1.52	4.5722E+00	2.1871E-01	*	2.02	7.5383E+00	1.3265E-01	*	2.52	1.2428E+01	8.0459E-02
1.53	4.6181E+00	2.1653E-01	*	2.03	7.6140E+00	1.3133E-01	*	2.53	1.2553E+01	7.9659E-02
1.54	4.6645E+00	2.1438E-01	*	2.04	7.6906E+00	1.3002E-01	*	2.54	1.2679E+01	7.8866E-02
1.55	4.7114E+00	2.1224E-01	*	2.05	7.7679E+00	1.2873E-01	*	2.55	1.2807E+01	7.8081E-02
1.56	4.7588E+00	2.1013E-01	*	2.06	7.8459E+00	1.2745E-01	*	2.56	1.2935E+01	7.7304E-02
1.57	4.8066E+00	2.0804E-01	*	2.07	7.9248E+00	1.2618E-01	*	2.57	1.3065E+01	7.6535E-02
1.58	4.8549E+00	2.0597E-01	*	2.08	8.0044E+00	1.2493E-01	*	2.58	1.3197E+01	7.5774E-02
1.59	4.9037E+00	2.0392E-01	*	2.09	8.0849E+00	1.2368E-01	*	2.59	1.3329E+01	7.5020E-02
1.60	4.9530E+00	2.0189E-01	*	2.10	8.1661E+00	1.2245E-01	*	2.60	1.3463E+01	7.4273E-02
1.61	5.0028E+00	1.9988E-01	*	2.11	8.2482E+00	1.2123E-01	*	2.61	1.3599E+01	7.3534E-02
1.62	5.0530E+00	1.9789E-01	*	2.12	8.3311E+00	1.2003E-01	*	2.62	1.3735E+01	7.2802E-02
1.63	5.1038E+00	1.9592E-01	*	2.13	8.4148E+00	1.1883E-01	*	2.63	1.3873E+01	7.2078E-02
1.64	5.1551E+00	1.9398E-01	*	2.14	8.4994E+00	1.1765E-01	*	2.64	1.4013E+01	7.1361E-02
1.65	5.2069E+00	1.9204E-01	*	2.15	8.5848E+00	1.1648E-01	*	2.65	1.4154E+01	7.0651E-02
1.66	5.2593E+00	1.9013E-01	*	2.16	8.6711E+00	1.1532E-01	*	2.66	1.4296E+01	6.9948E-02
1.67	5.3121E+00	1.8824E-01	*	2.17	8.7582E+00	1.1417E-01	*	2.67	1.4439E+01	6.9252E-02
1.68	5.3655E+00	1.8637E-01	*	2.18	8.8463E+00	1.1304E-01	*	2.68	1.4585E+01	6.8563E-02
1.69	5.4194E+00	1.8451E-01	*	2.19	8.9352E+00	1.1191E-01	*	2.69	1.4731E+01	6.7880E-02
1.70	5.4739E+00	1.8268E-01	*	2.20	9.0250E+00	1.1080E-01	*	2.70	1.4879E+01	6.7205E-02
1.71	5.5289E+00	1.8086E-01	*	2.21	9.1157E+00	1.0970E-01	*	2.71	1.5029E+01	6.6536E-02
1.72	5.5845E+00	1.7906E-01	*	2.22	9.2073E+00	1.0860E-01	*	2.72	1.5180E+01	6.5874E-02
1.73	5.6406E+00	1.7728E-01	*	2.23	9.2998E+00	1.0752E-01	*	2.73	1.5332E+01	6.5219E-02
1.74	5.6973E+00	1.7552E-01	*	2.24	9.3933E+00	1.0645E-01	*	2.74	1.5486E+01	6.4570E-02
1.75	5.7546E+00	1.7377E-01	*	2.25	9.4877E+00	1.0539E-01	*	2.75	1.5642E+01	6.3927E-02
1.76	5.8124E+00	1.7204E-01	*	2.26	9.5830E+00	1.0435E-01	*	2.76	1.5799E+01	6.3291E-02
1.77	5.8708E+00	1.7033E-01	*	2.27	9.6794E+00	1.0331E-01	*	2.77	1.5958E+01	6.2662E-02
1.78	5.9298E+00	1.6863E-01	*	2.28	9.7766E+00	1.0228E-01	*	2.78	1.6119E+01	6.2038E-02
1.79	5.9894E+00	1.6696E-01	*	2.29	9.8749E+00	1.0126E-01	*	2.79	1.6281E+01	6.1421E-02
1.80	6.0496E+00	1.6529E-01	*	2.30	9.9741E+00	1.0025E-01	*	2.80	1.6444E+01	6.0810E-02
1.81	6.1104E+00	1.6365E-01	*	2.31	1.0074E+01	9.9261E-02	*	2.81	1.6609E+01	6.0204E-02
1.82	6.1718E+00	1.6202E-01	*	2.32	1.0175E+01	9.8273E-02	*	2.82	1.6776E+01	5.9605E-02
1.83	6.2338E+00	1.6041E-01	*	2.33	1.0277E+01	9.7295E-02	*	2.83	1.6945E+01	5.9012E-02
1.84	6.2965E+00	1.5881E-01	*	2.34	1.0381E+01	9.6327E-02	*	2.84	1.7115E+01	5.8425E-02
1.85	6.3598E+00	1.5723E-01	*	2.35	1.0485E+01	9.5369E-02	*	2.85	1.7287E+01	5.7844E-02
1.86	6.4237E+00	1.5567E-01	*	2.36	1.0590E+01	9.4420E-02	*	2.86	1.7461E+01	5.7268E-02
1.87	6.4882E+00	1.5412E-01	*	2.37	1.0697E+01	9.3480E-02	*	2.87	1.7637E+01	5.6698E-02
1.88	6.5535E+00	1.5259E-01	*	2.38	1.0804E+01	9.2550E-02	*	2.88	1.7814E+01	5.6134E-02
1.89	6.6193E+00	1.5107E-01	*	2.39	1.0913E+01	9.1629E-02	*	2.89	1.7993E+01	5.5576E-02
1.90	6.6858E+00	1.4956E-01	*	2.40	1.1023E+01	9.0717E-02	*	2.90	1.8174E+01	5.5023E-02
1.91	6.7530E+00	1.4808E-01	*	2.41	1.1133E+01	8.9815E-02	*	2.91	1.8356E+01	5.4475E-02
1.92	6.8209E+00	1.4660E-01	*	2.42	1.1245E+01	8.8921E-02	*	2.92	1.8541E+01	5.3933E-02
1.93	6.8895E+00	1.4514E-01	*	2.43	1.1358E+01	8.8036E-02	*	2.93	1.8727E+01	5.3397E-02
1.94	6.9587E+00	1.4370E-01	*	2.44	1.1473E+01	8.7160E-02	*	2.94	1.8915E+01	5.2865E-02
1.95	7.0286E+00	1.4227E-01	*	2.45	1.1588E+01	8.6293E-02	*	2.95	1.9105E+01	5.2339E-02
1.96	7.0993E+00	1.4085E-01	*	2.46	1.1704E+01	8.5434E-02	*	2.96	1.9297E+01	5.1818E-02
1.97	7.1706E+00	1.3945E-01	*	2.47	1.1822E+01	8.4584E-02	*	2.97	1.9491E+01	5.1303E-02
1.98	7.2427E+00	1.3806E-01	*	2.48	1.1941E+01	8.3743E-02	*	2.98	1.9687E+01	5.0792E-02
1.99	7.3155E+00	1.3669E-01	*	2.49	1.2061E+01	8.2909E-02	*	2.99	1.9885E+01	5.0287E-02

x	E	E̅		x	E	E̅		x	E	E̅
3.00	2.0085E+01	4.9787E-02	*	3.50	3.3115E+01	3.0197E-02	*	4.00	5.4598E+01	1.8315E-02
3.01	2.0287E+01	4.9291E-02	*	3.51	3.3448E+01	2.9896E-02	*	4.01	5.5146E+01	1.8133E-02
3.02	2.0491E+01	4.8801E-02	*	3.52	3.3784E+01	2.9599E-02	*	4.02	5.5701E+01	1.7952E-02
3.03	2.0697E+01	4.8315E-02	*	3.53	3.4123E+01	2.9304E-02	*	4.03	5.6260E+01	1.7774E-02
3.04	2.0905E+01	4.7834E-02	*	3.54	3.4466E+01	2.9013E-02	*	4.04	5.6826E+01	1.7597E-02
3.05	2.1115E+01	4.7358E-02	*	3.55	3.4813E+01	2.8724E-02	*	4.05	5.7397E+01	1.7422E-02
3.06	2.1327E+01	4.6887E-02	*	3.56	3.5163E+01	2.8438E-02	*	4.06	5.7974E+01	1.7249E-02
3.07	2.1541E+01	4.6421E-02	*	3.57	3.5516E+01	2.8155E-02	*	4.07	5.8556E+01	1.7077E-02
3.08	2.1758E+01	4.5959E-02	*	3.58	3.5873E+01	2.7875E-02	*	4.08	5.9145E+01	1.6907E-02
3.09	2.1977E+01	4.5501E-02	*	3.59	3.6234E+01	2.7598E-02	*	4.09	5.9739E+01	1.6739E-02
3.10	2.2197E+01	4.5049E-02	*	3.60	3.6598E+01	2.7323E-02	*	4.10	6.0340E+01	1.6572E-02
3.11	2.2421E+01	4.4600E-02	*	3.61	3.6966E+01	2.7051E-02	*	4.11	6.0946E+01	1.6407E-02
3.12	2.2646E+01	4.4157E-02	*	3.62	3.7337E+01	2.6782E-02	*	4.12	6.1559E+01	1.6244E-02
3.13	2.2873E+01	4.3717E-02	*	3.63	3.7712E+01	2.6516E-02	*	4.13	6.2177E+01	1.6082E-02
3.14	2.3103E+01	4.3282E-02	*	3.64	3.8091E+01	2.6252E-02	*	4.14	6.2802E+01	1.5922E-02
3.15	2.3336E+01	4.2852E-02	*	3.65	3.8474E+01	2.5991E-02	*	4.15	6.3434E+01	1.5764E-02
3.16	2.3570E+01	4.2425E-02	*	3.66	3.8861E+01	2.5732E-02	*	4.16	6.4071E+01	1.5607E-02
3.17	2.3807E+01	4.2003E-02	*	3.67	3.9251E+01	2.5476E-02	*	4.17	6.4715E+01	1.5452E-02
3.18	2.4046E+01	4.1585E-02	*	3.68	3.9646E+01	2.5222E-02	*	4.18	6.5365E+01	1.5298E-02
3.19	2.4288E+01	4.1171E-02	*	3.69	4.0044E+01	2.4972E-02	*	4.19	6.6022E+01	1.5146E-02
3.20	2.4532E+01	4.0762E-02	*	3.70	4.0447E+01	2.4723E-02	*	4.20	6.6686E+01	1.4995E-02
3.21	2.4779E+01	4.0356E-02	*	3.71	4.0853E+01	2.4477E-02	*	4.21	6.7356E+01	1.4846E-02
3.22	2.5028E+01	3.9955E-02	*	3.72	4.1264E+01	2.4233E-02	*	4.22	6.8033E+01	1.4698E-02
3.23	2.5279E+01	3.9557E-02	*	3.73	4.1679E+01	2.3992E-02	*	4.23	6.8717E+01	1.4552E-02
3.24	2.5533E+01	3.9163E-02	*	3.74	4.2097E+01	2.3754E-02	*	4.24	6.9407E+01	1.4407E-02
3.25	2.5790E+01	3.8774E-02	*	3.75	4.2521E+01	2.3517E-02	*	4.25	7.0105E+01	1.4264E-02
3.26	2.6049E+01	3.8388E-02	*	3.76	4.2948E+01	2.3283E-02	*	4.26	7.0809E+01	1.4122E-02
3.27	2.6311E+01	3.8006E-02	*	3.77	4.3380E+01	2.3052E-02	*	4.27	7.1521E+01	1.3981E-02
3.28	2.6575E+01	3.7628E-02	*	3.78	4.3816E+01	2.2822E-02	*	4.28	7.2240E+01	1.3842E-02
3.29	2.6842E+01	3.7253E-02	*	3.79	4.4256E+01	2.2595E-02	*	4.29	7.2966E+01	1.3704E-02
3.30	2.7112E+01	3.6883E-02	*	3.80	4.4701E+01	2.2370E-02	*	4.30	7.3699E+01	1.3568E-02
3.31	2.7385E+01	3.6516E-02	*	3.81	4.5150E+01	2.2148E-02	*	4.31	7.4440E+01	1.3433E-02
3.32	2.7660E+01	3.6152E-02	*	3.82	4.5604E+01	2.1927E-02	*	4.32	7.5188E+01	1.3299E-02
3.33	2.7938E+01	3.5793E-02	*	3.83	4.6062E+01	2.1709E-02	*	4.33	7.5944E+01	1.3167E-02
3.34	2.8219E+01	3.5436E-02	*	3.84	4.6525E+01	2.1493E-02	*	4.34	7.6707E+01	1.3036E-02
3.35	2.8502E+01	3.5084E-02	*	3.85	4.6993E+01	2.1279E-02	*	4.35	7.7478E+01	1.2906E-02
3.36	2.8789E+01	3.4735E-02	*	3.86	4.7465E+01	2.1067E-02	*	4.36	7.8257E+01	1.2778E-02
3.37	2.9078E+01	3.4389E-02	*	3.87	4.7942E+01	2.0858E-02	*	4.37	7.9043E+01	1.2651E-02
3.38	2.9370E+01	3.4047E-02	*	3.88	4.8424E+01	2.0650E-02	*	4.38	7.9838E+01	1.2525E-02
3.39	2.9665E+01	3.3708E-02	*	3.89	4.8910E+01	2.0445E-02	*	4.39	8.0640E+01	1.2400E-02
3.40	2.9964E+01	3.3373E-02	*	3.90	4.9402E+01	2.0241E-02	*	4.40	8.1450E+01	1.2277E-02
3.41	3.0265E+01	3.3041E-02	*	3.91	4.9898E+01	2.0040E-02	*	4.41	8.2269E+01	1.2155E-02
3.42	3.0569E+01	3.2712E-02	*	3.92	5.0400E+01	1.9841E-02	*	4.42	8.3096E+01	1.2034E-02
3.43	3.0876E+01	3.2386E-02	*	3.93	5.0906E+01	1.9643E-02	*	4.43	8.3931E+01	1.1914E-02
3.44	3.1186E+01	3.2064E-02	*	3.94	5.1418E+01	1.9448E-02	*	4.44	8.4774E+01	1.1795E-02
3.45	3.1500E+01	3.1745E-02	*	3.95	5.1935E+01	1.9254E-02	*	4.45	8.5626E+01	1.1678E-02
3.46	3.1816E+01	3.1429E-02	*	3.96	5.2457E+01	1.9063E-02	*	4.46	8.6487E+01	1.1562E-02
3.47	3.2136E+01	3.1117E-02	*	3.97	5.2984E+01	1.8873E-02	*	4.47	8.7356E+01	1.1447E-02
3.48	3.2459E+01	3.0807E-02	*	3.98	5.3517E+01	1.8685E-02	*	4.48	8.8234E+01	1.1333E-02
3.49	3.2785E+01	3.0500E-02	*	3.99	5.4054E+01	1.8499E-02	*	4.49	8.9121E+01	1.1220E-02

x	E (x)	E (-x)		x	E (x)	E (-x)		x	E (x)	E (-x)
4.50	9.0017E+01	1.1108E-02	*	5.00	1.4841E+02	6.7379E-03	*	5.50	2.4469E+02	4.0867E-03
4.51	9.0921E+01	1.0998E-02	*	5.01	1.4990E+02	6.6709E-03	*	5.51	2.4715E+02	4.0461E-03
4.52	9.1835E+01	1.0889E-02	*	5.02	1.5141E+02	6.6045E-03	*	5.52	2.4963E+02	4.0058E-03
4.53	9.2758E+01	1.0780E-02	*	5.03	1.5293E+02	6.5388E-03	*	5.53	2.5214E+02	3.9659E-03
4.54	9.3690E+01	1.0673E-02	*	5.04	1.5447E+02	6.4737E-03	*	5.54	2.5467E+02	3.9265E-03
4.55	9.4632E+01	1.0567E-02	*	5.05	1.5602E+02	6.4093E-03	*	5.55	2.5723E+02	3.8874E-03
4.56	9.5583E+01	1.0462E-02	*	5.06	1.5759E+02	6.3455E-03	*	5.56	2.5982E+02	3.8487E-03
4.57	9.6544E+01	1.0357E-02	*	5.07	1.5917E+02	6.2824E-03	*	5.57	2.6243E+02	3.8104E-03
4.58	9.7514E+01	1.0254E-02	*	5.08	1.6077E+02	6.2199E-03	*	5.58	2.6507E+02	3.7725E-03
4.59	9.8494E+01	1.0152E-02	*	5.09	1.6238E+02	6.1580E-03	*	5.59	2.6773E+02	3.7350E-03
4.60	9.9484E+01	1.0051E-02	*	5.10	1.6402E+02	6.0967E-03	*	5.60	2.7042E+02	3.6978E-03
4.61	1.0048E+02	9.9518E-03	*	5.11	1.6567E+02	6.0360E-03	*	5.61	2.7314E+02	3.6610E-03
4.62	1.0149E+02	9.8527E-03	*	5.12	1.6733E+02	5.9760E-03	*	5.62	2.7588E+02	3.6246E-03
4.63	1.0251E+02	9.7547E-03	*	5.13	1.6901E+02	5.9165E-03	*	5.63	2.7866E+02	3.5885E-03
4.64	1.0354E+02	9.6576E-03	*	5.14	1.7071E+02	5.8576E-03	*	5.64	2.8146E+02	3.5528E-03
4.65	1.0458E+02	9.5616E-03	*	5.15	1.7243E+02	5.7994E-03	*	5.65	2.8429E+02	3.5175E-03
4.66	1.0563E+02	9.4664E-03	*	5.16	1.7416E+02	5.7416E-03	*	5.66	2.8714E+02	3.4825E-03
4.67	1.0669E+02	9.3722E-03	*	5.17	1.7591E+02	5.6845E-03	*	5.67	2.9003E+02	3.4478E-03
4.68	1.0777E+02	9.2790E-03	*	5.18	1.7768E+02	5.6280E-03	*	5.68	2.9294E+02	3.4135E-03
4.69	1.0885E+02	9.1866E-03	*	5.19	1.7946E+02	5.5720E-03	*	5.69	2.9589E+02	3.3795E-03
4.70	1.0994E+02	9.0952E-03	*	5.20	1.8127E+02	5.5165E-03	*	5.70	2.9886E+02	3.3459E-03
4.71	1.1105E+02	9.0047E-03	*	5.21	1.8309E+02	5.4616E-03	*	5.71	3.0187E+02	3.3126E-03
4.72	1.1216E+02	8.9151E-03	*	5.22	1.8493E+02	5.4073E-03	*	5.72	3.0490E+02	3.2797E-03
4.73	1.1329E+02	8.8264E-03	*	5.23	1.8679E+02	5.3535E-03	*	5.73	3.0796E+02	3.2470E-03
4.74	1.1443E+02	8.7386E-03	*	5.24	1.8867E+02	5.3002E-03	*	5.74	3.1106E+02	3.2147E-03
4.75	1.1558E+02	8.6516E-03	*	5.25	1.9056E+02	5.2475E-03	*	5.75	3.1419E+02	3.1827E-03
4.76	1.1674E+02	8.5656E-03	*	5.26	1.9248E+02	5.1953E-03	*	5.76	3.1734E+02	3.1511E-03
4.77	1.1791E+02	8.4803E-03	*	5.27	1.9441E+02	5.1436E-03	*	5.77	3.2053E+02	3.1197E-03
4.78	1.1910E+02	8.3959E-03	*	5.28	1.9636E+02	5.0924E-03	*	5.78	3.2375E+02	3.0887E-03
4.79	1.2030E+02	8.3124E-03	*	5.29	1.9834E+02	5.0417E-03	*	5.79	3.2701E+02	3.0579E-03
4.80	1.2151E+02	8.2297E-03	*	5.30	2.0033E+02	4.9915E-03	*	5.80	3.3029E+02	3.0275E-03
4.81	1.2273E+02	8.1478E-03	*	5.31	2.0235E+02	4.9419E-03	*	5.81	3.3361E+02	2.9974E-03
4.82	1.2396E+02	8.0667E-03	*	5.32	2.0438E+02	4.8927E-03	*	5.82	3.3697E+02	2.9676E-03
4.83	1.2521E+02	7.9865E-03	*	5.33	2.0643E+02	4.8440E-03	*	5.83	3.4035E+02	2.9380E-03
4.84	1.2646E+02	7.9070E-03	*	5.34	2.0851E+02	4.7958E-03	*	5.84	3.4377E+02	2.9088E-03
4.85	1.2774E+02	7.8283E-03	*	5.35	2.1060E+02	4.7481E-03	*	5.85	3.4723E+02	2.8798E-03
4.86	1.2902E+02	7.7504E-03	*	5.36	2.1272E+02	4.7009E-03	*	5.86	3.5072E+02	2.8512E-03
4.87	1.3032E+02	7.6733E-03	*	5.37	2.1486E+02	4.6541E-03	*	5.87	3.5424E+02	2.8228E-03
4.88	1.3163E+02	7.5970E-03	*	5.38	2.1702E+02	4.6078E-03	*	5.88	3.5780E+02	2.7947E-03
4.89	1.3295E+02	7.5214E-03	*	5.39	2.1920E+02	4.5619E-03	*	5.89	3.6140E+02	2.7669E-03
4.90	1.3428E+02	7.4465E-03	*	5.40	2.2140E+02	4.5165E-03	*	5.90	3.6503E+02	2.7394E-03
4.91	1.3563E+02	7.3724E-03	*	5.41	2.2363E+02	4.4716E-03	*	5.91	3.6870E+02	2.7121E-03
4.92	1.3700E+02	7.2991E-03	*	5.42	2.2587E+02	4.4271E-03	*	5.92	3.7241E+02	2.6852E-03
4.93	1.3837E+02	7.2265E-03	*	5.43	2.2814E+02	4.3830E-03	*	5.93	3.7615E+02	2.6584E-03
4.94	1.3977E+02	7.1545E-03	*	5.44	2.3044E+02	4.3394E-03	*	5.94	3.7993E+02	2.6320E-03
4.95	1.4117E+02	7.0834E-03	*	5.45	2.3275E+02	4.2963E-03	*	5.95	3.8375E+02	2.6058E-03
4.96	1.4259E+02	7.0129E-03	*	5.46	2.3509E+02	4.2535E-03	*	5.96	3.8761E+02	2.5799E-03
4.97	1.4402E+02	6.9431E-03	*	5.47	2.3746E+02	4.2112E-03	*	5.97	3.9150E+02	2.5542E-03
4.98	1.4547E+02	6.8740E-03	*	5.48	2.3984E+02	4.1693E-03	*	5.98	3.9544E+02	2.5288E-03
4.99	1.4693E+02	6.8056E-03	*	5.49	2.4225E+02	4.1278E-03	*	5.99	3.9941E+02	2.5036E-03
								6.00	4.0342E+02	2.4787E-03

TABLE B.2

Values of $(1 + i)^j$

J	I =.010	I =.015	I =.020	I =.025	I =.030	I =.035
1	.10100000+01	.10150000+01	.10200000+01	.10250000+01	.10300000+01	.10350000+01
2	.10201000+01	.10302250+01	.10404000+01	.10506250+01	.10609000+01	.10712250+01
3	.10303009+01	.10456783+01	.10612080+01	.10768906+01	.10927269+01	.11087178+01
4	.10406039+01	.10613635+01	.10824321+01	.11038128+01	.11255087+01	.11475230+01
5	.10510100+01	.10772839+01	.11040807+01	.11314081+01	.11592740+01	.11876862+01
6	.10615200+01	.10934431+01	.11261623+01	.11596933+01	.11940521+01	.12292553+01
7	.10721352+01	.11098448+01	.11486856+01	.11886856+01	.12298737+01	.12722792+01
8	.10828566+01	.11264924+01	.11716593+01	.12184027+01	.12667699+01	.13168090+01
9	.10936851+01	.11433898+01	.11950925+01	.12488628+01	.13047729+01	.13628973+01
10	.11046219+01	.11605406+01	.12189943+01	.12800843+01	.13439161+01	.14105987+01
11	.11156681+01	.11779487+01	.12433742+01	.13120864+01	.13842336+01	.14599696+01
12	.11268248+01	.11956179+01	.12682416+01	.13448886+01	.14257605+01	.15110645+01
13	.11380930+01	.12135521+01	.12936065+01	.13785108+01	.14685333+01	.15639559+01
14	.11494740+01	.12317554+01	.13194786+01	.14129735+01	.15125893+01	.16186944+01
15	.11609687+01	.12502317+01	.13458681+01	.14482978+01	.15579669+01	.16753486+01
16	.11725783+01	.12689852+01	.13727855+01	.14845053+01	.16047059+01	.17339858+01
17	.11843041+01	.12880199+01	.14002412+01	.15216179+01	.16528471+01	.17946753+01
18	.11961471+01	.13073402+01	.14282460+01	.15596583+01	.17024325+01	.18574889+01
19	.12081086+01	.13269503+01	.14568109+01	.15986497+01	.17535054+01	.19225010+01
20	.12201897+01	.13468545+01	.14859471+01	.16386160+01	.18061105+01	.19897886+01
21	.12323915+01	.13670573+01	.15156660+01	.16795813+01	.18602938+01	.20594312+01
22	.12447154+01	.13875631+01	.15459794+01	.17215708+01	.19161026+01	.21315112+01
23	.12571626+01	.14083765+01	.15768989+01	.17646101+01	.19735857+01	.22061141+01
24	.12697342+01	.14295021+01	.16084369+01	.18087253+01	.20327932+01	.22833281+01
25	.12824315+01	.14509446+01	.16406056+01	.18539434+01	.20937770+01	.23632445+01
26	.12952558+01	.14727088+01	.16734177+01	.19002920+01	.21565902+01	.24459580+01
27	.13082083+01	.14947994+01	.17068860+01	.19477995+01	.22212879+01	.25315665+01
28	.13212904+01	.15172213+01	.17410237+01	.19964942+01	.22879265+01	.26201714+01
29	.13345033+01	.15399796+01	.17758442+01	.20464066+01	.23565642+01	.27118774+01
30	.13478483+01	.15630793+01	.18113611+01	.20975666+01	.24272611+01	.28067931+01
31	.13613268+01	.15865255+01	.18475883+01	.21500058+01	.25000789+01	.29050308+01
32	.13749400+01	.16103233+01	.18845401+01	.22037559+01	.25750812+01	.30067068+01
33	.13886894+01	.16344781+01	.19222308+01	.22588497+01	.26523336+01	.31119415+01
34	.14025763+01	.16589953+01	.19606754+01	.23153211+01	.27319036+01	.32208595+01
35	.14166020+01	.16838802+01	.19998889+01	.23732039+01	.28138606+01	.33335895+01
36	.14307680+01	.17091383+01	.20398867+01	.24325340+01	.28982764+01	.34502662+01
37	.14450757+01	.17347754+01	.20806844+01	.24933473+01	.29852246+01	.35710244+01
38	.14595264+01	.17607970+01	.21222981+01	.25556809+01	.30747813+01	.36960102+01
39	.14741216+01	.17872089+01	.21647440+01	.26195730+01	.31670246+01	.38253705+01
40	.14888628+01	.18140170+01	.22080349+01	.26850622+01	.32620353+01	.39592584+01
41	.15037514+01	.18412272+01	.22521996+01	.27521847+01	.33598963+01	.40978324+01
42	.15187889+01	.18688456+01	.22972436+01	.28209934+01	.34606931+01	.42412566+01
43	.15339768+01	.18968782+01	.23431884+01	.28915183+01	.35645138+01	.43897005+01
44	.15493165+01	.19253314+01	.23900522+01	.29638062+01	.36714492+01	.45433400+01
45	.15648097+01	.19542113+01	.24378531+01	.30379012+01	.37815926+01	.47023568+01
46	.15804577+01	.19835244+01	.24866102+01	.31138487+01	.38950404+01	.48669393+01
47	.15962623+01	.20132773+01	.25363424+01	.31916949+01	.40118915+01	.50372820+01
48	.16122249+01	.20434764+01	.25870692+01	.32714872+01	.41322482+01	.52135868+01
49	.16283471+01	.20741285+01	.26388106+01	.33532744+01	.42562155+01	.53960624+01
50	.16446306+01	.21052404+01	.26915868+01	.34371062+01	.43839020+01	.55849245+01

TABLE B.2 (continued)

VALUES OF (1+I)^J

J	I =.040	I =.045	I =.050	I =.055	I =.060	I =.065
1	.1040000+01	.1045000+01	.10500000+01	.10550000+01	.10600000+01	.10650000+01
2	.1081600+01	.1092025+01	.11025000+01	.11130250+01	.11236000+01	.11342250+01
3	.1124864+01	.1141166+01	.11576250+01	.11742413+01	.11910159+01	.12079496+01
4	.11698585+01	.11925185+01	.12155062+01	.12388246+01	.12624769+01	.12864663+01
5	.12166528+01	.12461818+01	.12762815+01	.13069599+01	.13382255+01	.13700866+01
6	.12653189+01	.13022600+01	.13400956+01	.13788427+01	.14185190+01	.14591622+01
7	.13159317+01	.13608617+01	.14071003+01	.14546790+01	.15036301+01	.15539864+01
8	.13685689+01	.14221004+01	.14774553+01	.15346864+01	.15938479+01	.16549955+01
9	.14233317+01	.14860949+01	.15513281+01	.16190941+01	.16894787+01	.17625702+01
10	.14802443+01	.15529692+01	.16288945+01	.17081443+01	.17908474+01	.18771373+01
11	.15394543+01	.16228528+01	.17103392+01	.18020922+01	.18982982+01	.19991512+01
12	.16010320+01	.16958811+01	.17958561+01	.19012072+01	.20121961+01	.21290960+01
13	.16650732+01	.17721957+01	.18856489+01	.20057736+01	.21329278+01	.22674873+01
14	.17316762+01	.18519445+01	.19799314+01	.21160912+01	.22609034+01	.24148739+01
15	.18009432+01	.19352820+01	.20789279+01	.22324761+01	.23965576+01	.25718407+01
16	.18729809+01	.20223697+01	.21828743+01	.23552623+01	.25403509+01	.27390103+01
17	.19479001+01	.21133762+01	.22920180+01	.24848017+01	.26927719+01	.29170460+01
18	.20258161+01	.22084781+01	.24066189+01	.26214658+01	.28543382+01	.31066539+01
19	.21068487+01	.23078596+01	.25269498+01	.27656464+01	.30255985+01	.33085864+01
20	.21911226+01	.24117132+01	.26532973+01	.29177568+01	.32071343+01	.35236445+01
21	.22787675+01	.25202402+01	.27859621+01	.30782335+01	.33995623+01	.37526814+01
22	.23699182+01	.26336510+01	.29252601+01	.32475362+01	.36035360+01	.39966056+01
23	.24647149+01	.27521653+01	.30715232+01	.34261507+01	.38197481+01	.42563850+01
24	.25633034+01	.28760127+01	.32250993+01	.36145889+01	.40489329+01	.45330500+01
25	.26658355+01	.30054332+01	.33863542+01	.38133913+01	.42918688+01	.48276982+01
26	.27724689+01	.31406776+01	.35556719+01	.40231277+01	.45493808+01	.51414985+01
27	.28833367+01	.32820081+01	.37334555+01	.42443997+01	.48223436+01	.54756959+01
28	.29987022+01	.34296983+01	.39201283+01	.44778416+01	.51116640+01	.58316161+01
29	.31186503+01	.35840347+01	.41161346+01	.47241227+01	.54183850+01	.62106711+01
30	.32433963+01	.37453162+01	.43219413+01	.49839494+01	.57434879+01	.66143646+01
31	.33731321+01	.39138554+01	.45380383+01	.52580065+01	.60880972+01	.70442983+01
32	.35080573+01	.40899789+01	.47649401+01	.55472601+01	.64533828+01	.75021777+01
33	.36483795+01	.42740278+01	.50031871+01	.58523594+01	.68405857+01	.79898192+01
34	.37943147+01	.44663589+01	.52533464+01	.61742391+01	.72510207+01	.85091573+01
35	.39460872+01	.46673450+01	.55160137+01	.65138222+01	.76860818+01	.90622524+01
36	.41039307+01	.48773754+01	.57918144+01	.68720823+01	.81472466+01	.9651298+01
37	.42680878+01	.50968572+01	.60814051+01	.72500467+01	.86360812+01	.10278633+02
38	.44388112+01	.53262157+01	.63854752+01	.76487993+01	.91542460+01	.10946744+02
39	.46163636+01	.55658954+01	.67047689+01	.80694830+01	.97035005+01	.11658263+02
40	.48010182+01	.58163606+01	.70399863+01	.85133045+01	.10285710+02	.12416077+02
41	.49930586+01	.60760967+01	.73919854+01	.89815362+01	.10902853+02	.13223115+02
42	.51927811+01	.63516109+01	.77615848+01	.94755205+01	.11557024+02	.14062618+02
43	.54004923+01	.66374333+01	.81496640+01	.99966740+01	.12250445+02	.14997988+02
44	.56165119+01	.69361177+01	.85571470+01	.10546491+02	.12985471+02	.15972857+02
45	.58411723+01	.72482429+01	.89850044+01	.11126548+02	.13764600+02	.17011093+02
46	.60748191+01	.75744136+01	.94342544+01	.11738068+02	.14590475+02	.18116813+02
47	.63178118+01	.79152621+01	.99059670+01	.12384125+02	.15465904+02	.19294406+02
48	.65705241+01	.82714488+01	.10401265+02	.13065252+02	.16393857+02	.20548543+02
49	.68333451+01	.86436639+01	.10921328+02	.13783841+02	.17377468+02	.21884198+02
50	.71066788+01	.90326285+01	.11467395+02	.14541952+02	.18420137+02	.23306671+02

VALUES OF (1+I)^J

J	I =.070	I =.075	I =.080	I =.085	I =.090	I =.095
1	.10700000+01	.10750000+01	.10800000+01	.10850000+01	.10900000+01	.10950000+01
2	.11449000+01	.11556250+01	.11664000+01	.11772250+01	.11881000+01	.11990250+01
3	.12250430+01	.12422968+01	.12597120+01	.12772891+01	.12950289+01	.13129324+01
4	.13107960+01	.13354691+01	.13604889+01	.13858587+01	.14115815+01	.14376609+01
5	.14025517+01	.14356292+01	.14693280+01	.15036566+01	.15386238+01	.15742387+01
6	.15007303+01	.15433014+01	.15868743+01	.16314674+01	.16770999+01	.17237914+01
7	.16057814+01	.16590490+01	.17138242+01	.17701421+01	.18280389+01	.18875515+01
8	.17181860+01	.17834776+01	.18509301+01	.19206042+01	.19925624+01	.20668689+01
9	.18384590+01	.19172384+01	.19990045+01	.20838555+01	.21718930+01	.22632215+01
10	.19671512+01	.20613312+01	.21589249+01	.22600832+01	.23673633+01	.24782275+01
11	.21048517+01	.22159680+01	.23316389+01	.24531668+01	.25804260+01	.27136591+01
12	.22521913+01	.23817792+01	.25181700+01	.26616859+01	.28126643+01	.29714567+01
13	.24098448+01	.25604126+01	.27196235+01	.28879292+01	.30658040+01	.32537451+01
14	.25785337+01	.27524435+01	.29371934+01	.31334031+01	.33417263+01	.35628508+01
15	.27590311+01	.29588767+01	.31721688+01	.33997423+01	.36424816+01	.39013217+01
16	.29521632+01	.31807924+01	.34259423+01	.36887204+01	.39703049+01	.42719471+01
17	.31588146+01	.34193517+01	.37000177+01	.40022616+01	.43276323+01	.46777821+01
18	.33799316+01	.36758031+01	.39960191+01	.43424058+01	.47171191+01	.51221714+01
19	.36165268+01	.39514882+01	.43157005+01	.47115623+01	.51416598+01	.56087776+01
20	.38696830+01	.42478596+01	.46609566+01	.51120450+01	.56044091+01	.61416115+01
21	.41405614+01	.45664385+01	.50338330+01	.55465688+01	.61088058+01	.67250645+01
22	.44304007+01	.49089213+01	.54365396+01	.60180270+01	.66585982+01	.73639656+01
23	.47405287+01	.52770902+01	.58714627+01	.65295593+01	.72578719+01	.80635203+01
24	.50723650+01	.56728719+01	.63411798+01	.70845717+01	.79110803+01	.88295547+01
25	.54274311+01	.60983372+01	.68484741+01	.76867603+01	.86230774+01	.96683623+01
26	.58073512+01	.65557124+01	.73963520+01	.83401348+01	.93991542+01	.10586857+02
27	.62138657+01	.70473907+01	.79880601+01	.90490640+01	.10245078+02	.11592608+02
28	.66488363+01	.75759449+01	.86271049+01	.98182149+01	.11167135+02	.12693906+02
29	.71142548+01	.81441406+01	.93172731+01	.10652763+02	.12172177+02	.13899826+02
30	.76122525+01	.87549510+01	.10062655+02	.11558248+02	.13267672+02	.15220310+02
31	.81451102+01	.94115722+01	.10867667+02	.12540699+02	.14461763+02	.16666249+02
32	.87152670+01	.10117440+02	.11737081+02	.13606658+02	.15763321+02	.18249532+02
33	.93253364+01	.10876248+02	.12676047+02	.14763224+02	.17182019+02	.19983237+02
34	.99781098+01	.11691966+02	.13690131+02	.16018097+02	.18728401+02	.21881644+02
35	.10676577+02	.12568863+02	.14785341+02	.17379636+02	.20413957+02	.23960400+02
36	.11423938+02	.13511528+02	.15968168+02	.18856905+02	.22251213+02	.26236638+02
37	.12223613+02	.14524892+02	.17245621+02	.20459741+02	.24253821+02	.28729119+02
38	.13079260+02	.15614259+02	.18625271+02	.22198819+02	.26436665+02	.31458385+02
39	.13994814+02	.16785328+02	.20115293+02	.24085718+02	.28815964+02	.34446932+02
40	.14974451+02	.18044227+02	.21724516+02	.26133004+02	.31409400+02	.37719309+02
41	.16022663+02	.19397544+02	.23462477+02	.28354309+02	.34236646+02	.41302731+02
42	.17144249+02	.20852359+02	.25339475+02	.30764425+02	.37317507+02	.45224490+02
43	.18344349+02	.22416286+02	.27366633+02	.33379401+02	.40676082+02	.49523006+02
44	.19628450+02	.24097507+02	.29553963+02	.36216669+02	.44336929+02	.54227661+02
45	.21002441+02	.25904820+02	.31920400+02	.39295064+02	.48327252+02	.59379322+02
46	.22472612+02	.27847681+02	.34474075+02	.42635144+02	.52676704+02	.65020357+02
47	.24045694+02	.29936256+02	.37232000+02	.46259131+02	.57417606+02	.71197290+02
48	.25728892+02	.32181475+02	.40210560+02	.50191156+02	.62585189+02	.77961033+02
49	.27529914+02	.34595085+02	.43427405+02	.54457403+02	.68217855+02	.85367330+02
50	.29457008+02	.37189716+02	.46901596+02	.59086282+02	.74357460+02	.93477226+02

VALUES OF $(1+I)^J$

J	I =.100	I =.105	I =.110	I =.115	I =.120	I =.125
1	.11000000+01	.11050000+01	.11100000+01	.11150000+01	.11200000+01	.11250000+01
2	.12100000+01	.12210250+01	.12321000+01	.12432250+01	.12544000+01	.12656250+01
3	.13310000+01	.13492326+01	.13676309+01	.13861958+01	.14049279+01	.14238281+01
4	.14640999+01	.14909020+01	.15180703+01	.15456083+01	.15735193+01	.16018065+01
5	.16105099+01	.16474467+01	.16850580+01	.17233533+01	.17623416+01	.18020323+01
6	.17715609+01	.18204285+01	.18704143+01	.19215389+01	.19738225+01	.20272863+01
7	.19487170+01	.20115735+01	.20761599+01	.21425159+01	.22106812+01	.22806970+01
8	.21435887+01	.22227887+01	.23045374+01	.23889051+01	.24759629+01	.25657841+01
9	.23579475+01	.24561814+01	.25580365+01	.26636292+01	.27730785+01	.28865071+01
10	.25937422+01	.27140804+01	.28394205+01	.29699466+01	.31058478+01	.32473204+01
11	.28531164+01	.29990589+01	.31517567+01	.33114903+01	.34785495+01	.36532354+01
12	.31384240+01	.33139600+01	.34984498+01	.36923117+01	.38959754+01	.41098897+01
13	.34522708+01	.36619257+01	.38832793+01	.41169275+01	.43634924+01	.46236259+01
14	.37974978+01	.40464279+01	.43104399+01	.45903742+01	.48871113+01	.52015789+01
15	.41772476+01	.44713027+01	.47845882+01	.51182670+01	.54735646+01	.58517762+01
16	.45949722+01	.49407894+01	.53108928+01	.57068677+01	.61303923+01	.65832481+01
17	.50544693+01	.54595722+01	.58950908+01	.63631574+01	.68660392+01	.74061540+01
18	.55599162+01	.60328272+01	.65435507+01	.70949204+01	.76899638+01	.83319230+01
19	.61159077+01	.66662739+01	.72633412+01	.79108362+01	.86127593+01	.93734132+01
20	.67274984+01	.73662326+01	.80623086+01	.88205823+01	.96462903+01	.10545090+02
21	.74002482+01	.81396870+01	.89491624+01	.98349492+01	.10803845+02	.11863226+02
22	.81402729+01	.89943539+01	.99335700+01	.10965968+02	.12100306+02	.13346129+02
23	.89543001+01	.99387609+01	.11026262+02	.12227054+02	.13552343+02	.15014394+02
24	.98497299+01	.10982331+02	.12239151+02	.13633166+02	.15178623+02	.16891193+02
25	.10834703+02	.12135475+02	.13585458+02	.15200979+02	.17000058+02	.19002592+02
26	.11918173+02	.13409700+02	.15079857+02	.16949092+02	.19040065+02	.21377916+02
27	.13109990+02	.14817718+02	.16738641+02	.18898237+02	.21324872+02	.24050155+02
28	.14420989+02	.16373578+02	.18579892+02	.21071534+02	.23883857+02	.27056424+02
29	.15863086+02	.18092804+02	.20623679+02	.23494760+02	.26749991+02	.30438476+02
30	.17449396+02	.19992547+02	.22892284+02	.26196657+02	.29999909+02	.34243285+02
31	.19194335+02	.22091765+02	.25410435+02	.29209273+02	.33555097+02	.38523695+02
32	.21113769+02	.24411400+02	.28205562+02	.32568339+02	.37581708+02	.43339156+02
33	.23225145+02	.26974596+02	.31308195+02	.36313627+02	.42091512+02	.48756550+02
34	.25547659+02	.29806928+02	.34752095+02	.40489771+02	.47142493+02	.54851117+02
35	.28102425+02	.32936656+02	.38574825+02	.45146095+02	.52799591+02	.61707566+02
36	.30912668+02	.36395004+02	.42818055+02	.50337895+02	.59135541+02	.69420942+02
37	.34003934+02	.40216479+02	.47528040+02	.56126752+02	.66231806+02	.78098558+02
38	.37404327+02	.44439208+02	.52756124+02	.62581328+02	.74179621+02	.87860877+02
39	.41144759+02	.49105325+02	.58559296+02	.69778181+02	.83081175+02	.98843464+02
40	.45259234+02	.54261382+02	.65000818+02	.77802671+02	.93050914+02	.11119892+03
41	.49785157+02	.59958827+02	.72150906+02	.86749978+02	.10421702+03	.12509878+03
42	.54763672+02	.66254502+02	.80087504+02	.96726225+02	.11672306+03	.14073613+03
43	.60240038+02	.73211224+02	.88897128+02	.10784974+03	.13072983+03	.15832814+03
44	.66264042+02	.80898401+02	.98675811+02	.12025246+03	.14641741+03	.17811915+03
45	.72890444+02	.89392731+02	.10953015+03	.13408149+03	.16398750+03	.20038404+03
46	.80179488+02	.98778967+02	.12157846+03	.14950068+03	.18366599+03	.22543205+03
47	.88197430+02	.10915076+03	.13495209+03	.16669346+03	.20570591+03	.25361104+03
48	.97017178+02	.12061158+03	.14979681+03	.18586320+03	.23039062+03	.28531242+03
49	.10671889+03	.13327580+03	.16627447+03	.20723747+03	.25803749+03	.32097647+03
50	.11739078+03	.14726976+03	.18456465+03	.23106978+03	.28900198+03	.36109852+03

VALUES OF $(1+I)^J$

J	I =.130	I =.135	I =.140	I =.145	I =.150	I =.160
1	.11300000+01	.11350000+01	.11400000+01	.11450000+01	.11500000+01	.11600000+01
2	.12769000+01	.12882250+01	.12996000+01	.13110250+01	.13225000+01	.13456000+01
3	.14428970+01	.14621353+01	.14815439+01	.15011236+01	.15208749+01	.15608960+01
4	.16304736+01	.16595236+01	.16889600+01	.17187865+01	.17490062+01	.18106393+01
5	.18424351+01	.18835592+01	.19254144+01	.19680105+01	.20113571+01	.21003416+01
6	.20815116+01	.21378397+01	.21949724+01	.22533720+01	.23130606+01	.24363963+01
7	.23526054+01	.24264480+01	.25022685+01	.25801110+01	.26600196+01	.28262196+01
8	.26584440+01	.27540185+01	.28525861+01	.29542270+01	.30590226+01	.32784147+01
9	.30040417+01	.31258108+01	.32519481+01	.33825899+01	.35178759+01	.38029610+01
10	.33945671+01	.35477953+01	.37072207+01	.38730654+01	.40455572+01	.44114348+01
11	.38358608+01	.40267476+01	.42262316+01	.44346599+01	.46523908+01	.51172642+01
12	.43345227+01	.45703585+01	.48179039+01	.50776855+01	.53502493+01	.59360265+01
13	.48980106+01	.51873569+01	.54924102+01	.58139499+01	.61527665+01	.68857907+01
14	.55347519+01	.58876498+01	.62613476+01	.66569725+01	.70757045+01	.79875172+01
15	.62542696+01	.66824825+01	.71379361+01	.76222334+01	.81370600+01	.92655199+01
16	.70673246+01	.75846175+01	.81372470+01	.87274572+01	.93576189+01	.10748004+02
17	.79860767+01	.86085408+01	.92764614+01	.99929384+01	.10761262+02	.12467685+02
18	.90242666+01	.97706937+01	.10575166+02	.11441914+02	.12375451+02	.14462512+02
19	.10197421+02	.11089737+02	.12055669+02	.13100992+02	.14231768+02	.16765140+02
20	.11523086+02	.12586851+02	.13743485+02	.15000636+02	.16366533+02	.19460756+02
21	.13021087+02	.14286076+02	.15667573+02	.17175727+02	.18821513+02	.22574477+02
22	.14713826+02	.16214696+02	.17861032+02	.19666208+02	.21644739+02	.26186393+02
23	.16622626+02	.18403680+02	.20361576+02	.22517808+02	.24891450+02	.30376216+02
24	.18788087+02	.20888177+02	.23212197+02	.25782889+02	.28625167+02	.35236410+02
25	.21230537+02	.23708080+02	.26461904+02	.29521408+02	.32918941+02	.40874235+02
26	.23990507+02	.26908670+02	.30166570+02	.33802012+02	.37856782+02	.47414113+02
27	.27109274+02	.30541340+02	.34389889+02	.38703303+02	.43535299+02	.55000370+02
28	.30633479+02	.34664421+02	.39204473+02	.44315282+02	.50065593+02	.63800429+02
29	.34615830+02	.39344117+02	.44693098+02	.50740997+02	.57575431+02	.74008497+02
30	.39115886+02	.44655573+02	.50950031+02	.58089841+02	.66211745+02	.85849856+02
31	.44200953+02	.50684074+02	.58083148+02	.66522714+02	.76143505+02	.99585833+02
32	.49947076+02	.57526422+02	.66214788+02	.76168507+02	.87565031+02	.11551956+03
33	.56440549+02	.65292489+02	.75484857+02	.87212940+02	.10069978+03	.13400269+03
34	.63777420+02	.74106973+02	.86052736+02	.99858816+02	.11580047+03	.15544312+03
35	.72068484+02	.84111413+02	.98100118+02	.11433834+03	.13317546+03	.18031402+03
36	.81437387+02	.95466454+02	.11183413+03	.13091740+03	.15315178+03	.20916426+03
37	.92024246+02	.10835442+03	.12749091+03	.14990043+03	.17612454+03	.24263054+03
38	.10397874+03	.12298227+03	.14533964+03	.17163599+03	.20264222+03	.28145143+03
39	.11750576+03	.13958848+03	.16568718+03	.19652320+03	.23292470+03	.32648365+03
40	.13278151+03	.15842883+03	.18888338+03	.22501907+03	.26786341+03	.37872104+03
41	.15004310+03	.17981672+03	.21532705+03	.25764682+03	.30804291+03	.43931640+03
42	.16954871+03	.20409197+03	.24547283+03	.29500561+03	.35424934+03	.50960701+03
43	.19159003+03	.23164439+03	.27983902+03	.33778142+03	.40738674+03	.59114412+03
44	.21649674+03	.26291638+03	.31901648+03	.38675973+03	.46849474+03	.68572718+03
45	.24464131+03	.29841009+03	.36367878+03	.44283988+03	.53876894+03	.79544312+03
46	.27644467+03	.33869544+03	.41459381+03	.50705166+03	.61959427+03	.92271448+03
47	.31238248+03	.38441932+03	.47263693+03	.58057415+03	.71252190+03	.10703684+04
48	.35299220+03	.43631592+03	.53880609+03	.66475739+03	.81940018+03	.12416046+04
49	.39888118+03	.49521858+03	.61423893+03	.76114721+03	.94231020+03	.14402613+04
50	.45073573+03	.56207307+03	.70023236+03	.87151355+03	.10836567+04	.16707031+04

VALUES OF $(1+I)^J$

J	I =.170	I =.180	I =.190	I =.200	I =.210	I =.220
1	.11700000+01	.11800000+01	.11900000+01	.12000000+01	.12100000+01	.12200000+01
2	.13689000+01	.13924000+01	.14161000+01	.14400000+01	.14641000+01	.14884000+01
3	.16016129+01	.16430320+01	.16651590+01	.17279999+01	.17715610+01	.18158479+01
4	.18738871+01	.19387777+01	.20053392+01	.20735999+01	.21435887+01	.22153344+01
5	.21924479+01	.22877576+01	.23863535+01	.24883199+01	.25937423+01	.27027079+01
6	.25651640+01	.26995540+01	.28397607+01	.29859838+01	.31384262+01	.32973035+01
7	.30012418+01	.31854737+01	.33793152+01	.35831805+01	.37974980+01	.40227103+01
8	.35114529+01	.37588589+01	.40213851+01	.42998165+01	.45949726+01	.49077065+01
9	.41083997+01	.44354534+01	.47854482+01	.51597797+01	.55599167+01	.59874018+01
10	.48068276+01	.52338350+01	.56946833+01	.61917356+01	.67274992+01	.73046300+01
11	.56239882+01	.61759252+01	.67766730+01	.74300826+01	.81402739+01	.89116484+01
12	.65800661+01	.72875916+01	.80642410+01	.89160990+01	.98497313+01	.10872211+02
13	.76986772+01	.85993580+01	.95964467+01	.10699318+02	.11918175+02	.13264097+02
14	.90074521+01	.10147242+02	.11419771+02	.12839182+02	.14420991+02	.16182198+02
15	.10538719+02	.11973746+02	.13589528+02	.15407018+02	.17449399+02	.19742261+02
16	.12330301+02	.14129020+02	.16171538+02	.18488421+02	.21113773+02	.24085563+02
17	.14426452+02	.16672243+02	.19241130+02	.22186106+02	.25547665+02	.29384410+02
18	.16878946+02	.19673247+02	.22900514+02	.26623327+02	.30912674+02	.35848980+02
19	.19748369+02	.23214431+02	.27251612+02	.31947991+02	.37404335+02	.43735754+02
20	.23105592+02	.27393028+02	.32429418+02	.38337589+02	.45259245+02	.53357620+02
21	.27033541+02	.32323773+02	.38591007+02	.46005106+02	.54763686+02	.65096294+02
22	.31629243+02	.38142052+02	.45923299+02	.55206126+02	.66264059+02	.79417478+02
23	.37006214+02	.45007620+02	.54648724+02	.66247351+02	.80179510+02	.96889321+02
24	.43297269+02	.53108991+02	.65031981+02	.79496820+02	.97017206+02	.11820497+03
25	.50657804+02	.62668610+02	.77388057+02	.95396182+02	.11739082+03	.14421006+03
26	.59269630+02	.73948958+02	.92091788+02	.11447542+03	.14204289+03	.17593627+03
27	.69345460+02	.87259769+02	.10958923+03	.13737050+03	.17187189+03	.21464225+03
28	.81134194+02	.10296653+03	.13041118+03	.16484459+03	.20796499+03	.26186354+03
29	.94927005+02	.12150050+03	.15518931+03	.19781351+03	.25163764+03	.31947351+03
30	.11106645+03	.14337059+03	.18467527+03	.23737621+03	.30448154+03	.38975767+03
31	.12994558+03	.16917729+03	.21976357+03	.28485145+03	.36842265+03	.47550435+03
32	.15203632+03	.19962920+03	.26151865+03	.34182173+03	.44579140+03	.58011530+03
33	.17788249+03	.23556246+03	.31120771+03	.41018607+03	.53940758+03	.70774064+03
34	.20812251+03	.27796370+03	.37033655+03	.49222329+03	.65268316+03	.86344358+03
35	.24350333+03	.32799716+03	.44070049+03	.59066793+03	.78974663+03	.10534012+04
36	.28489889+03	.38703664+03	.52443358+03	.70880151+03	.95559342+03	.12851494+04
37	.33333170+03	.45670323+03	.62407595+03	.85056180+03	.11562680+04	.15678822+04
38	.38999808+03	.53690980+03	.74265037+03	.10206741+04	.13990843+04	.19128162+04
39	.45629775+03	.63591356+03	.88375394+03	.12248090+04	.16928919+04	.23336358+04
40	.53386835+03	.75037799+03	.10516672+04	.14697707+04	.20483993+04	.28470356+04
41	.62462596+03	.88544602+03	.12514839+04	.17637248+04	.24785631+04	.34733833+04
42	.73081230+03	.10448263+04	.14892659+04	.21164697+04	.29990613+04	.42375276+04
43	.85505045+03	.12328950+04	.17722264+04	.25397637+04	.36288641+04	.51697835+04
44	.10004090+04	.14548161+04	.21089949+04	.30477164+04	.43909255+04	.63071358+04
45	.11704785+04	.17166830+04	.25096498+04	.36572596+04	.53130198+04	.76947056+04
46	.13694599+04	.20256859+04	.29864832+04	.43887115+04	.64287539+04	.93875407+04
47	.16022680+04	.23903093+04	.35539150+04	.52664536+04	.77787922+04	.11452799+05
48	.18746535+04	.28205650+04	.42291588+04	.63197442+04	.94123384+04	.13972615+05
49	.21933446+04	.33282686+04	.50326990+04	.75836930+04	.11388929+05	.17046346+05
50	.25662131+04	.39273546+04	.59889117+04	.91004314+04	.13780604+05	.20796542+05

VALUES OF $(1+I)^J$

J	I =.230	I =.240	I =.250	I =.260	I =.270	I =.280
1	.12300000+01	.12400000+01	.12500000+01	.12600000+01	.12700000+01	.12800000+01
2	.15129000+01	.15376000+01	.15625000+01	.15876000+01	.16129000+01	.16384000+01
3	.18608669+01	.19066240+01	.19531249+01	.20003759+01	.20483830+01	.20971520+01
4	.22888663+01	.23642137+01	.24414061+01	.25204737+01	.26014464+01	.26843544+01
5	.28153055+01	.29316249+01	.30517576+01	.31757968+01	.33038369+01	.34359736+01
6	.34628257+01	.36352149+01	.38146969+01	.40015039+01	.41958728+01	.43980461+01
7	.42592750+01	.45076665+01	.47683711+01	.50418947+01	.53287584+01	.56294990+01
8	.52389089+01	.55895063+01	.59604637+01	.63527873+01	.67675231+01	.72057565+01
9	.64438578+01	.69309877+01	.74505796+01	.80045120+01	.85947543+01	.92233748+01
10	.79259451+01	.85944247+01	.93132242+01	.10085685+02	.10915336+02	.11805914+02
11	.97489122+01	.10657087+02	.11641530+02	.12707963+02	.13862479+02	.15111570+02
12	.11991162+02	.13214787+02	.14551912+02	.16012033+02	.17605348+02	.19342810+02
13	.14749129+02	.16386336+02	.18189890+02	.20175161+02	.22358792+02	.24758796+02
14	.18141429+02	.20319057+02	.22737362+02	.25420703+02	.28395665+02	.31691258+02
15	.22313959+02	.25195630+02	.28421703+02	.32030085+02	.36062495+02	.40564810+02
16	.27446166+02	.31242581+02	.35527128+02	.40357907+02	.45799367+02	.51922956+02
17	.33758784+02	.38740800+02	.44409092+02	.50850962+02	.58165196+02	.66461383+02
18	.41523304+02	.48038591+02	.55511135+02	.64072211+02	.73869798+02	.85070694+02
19	.51073662+02	.59567832+02	.69388918+02	.80730984+02	.93814643+02	.10889033+03
20	.62820600+02	.73864135+02	.86736146+02	.10172004+03	.11914460+03	.13937961+03
21	.77269342+02	.91591527+02	.10842018+03	.12816851+03	.15131364+03	.17840590+03
22	.95041290+02	.11357349+03	.13552523+03	.16149232+03	.19216832+03	.22835956+03
23	.11690079+03	.14083113+03	.16940653+03	.20348032+03	.24405377+03	.29230022+03
24	.14378797+03	.17463060+03	.21175815+03	.25638520+03	.30994828+03	.37414428+03
25	.17685919+03	.21654194+03	.26469769+03	.32304535+03	.39363431+03	.47890467+03
26	.21753681+03	.26851200+03	.33087210+03	.40703714+03	.49991557+03	.61299797+03
27	.26757020+03	.33295488+03	.41359012+03	.51286678+03	.63489277+03	.78463739+03
28	.32911143+03	.41286065+03	.51698764+03	.64621213+03	.80631361+03	.10043358+04
29	.40480705+03	.51195142+03	.64623453+03	.81422728+03	.10240185+04	.12855498+04
30	.49791266+03	.63481975+03	.80779315+03	.10259264+04	.13005035+04	.16455034+04
31	.61243259+03	.78717648+03	.10097414+04	.12926672+04	.16516394+04	.21062448+04
32	.75329205+03	.97609883+03	.12621768+04	.16287606+04	.20975821+04	.26959933+04
33	.92654920+03	.12103625+04	.15777209+04	.20522384+04	.26639292+04	.34508714+04
34	.11396555+04	.15008495+04	.19721511+04	.25858203+04	.33831901+04	.44171153+04
35	.14017762+04	.18610534+04	.24651889+04	.32581335+04	.42966514+04	.56539074+04
36	.17241848+04	.23077062+04	.30814860+04	.41052482+04	.54567472+04	.72370014+04
37	.21207472+04	.28615557+04	.38518574+04	.51726127+04	.69300689+04	.92633617+04
38	.26085190+04	.35483290+04	.48148217+04	.65179919+04	.88011874+04	.11857103+05
39	.32084784+04	.43999279+04	.60185270+04	.82120394+04	.11177508+05	.15177091+05
40	.39464284+04	.54559104+04	.75231586+04	.10347716+05	.14195435+05	.19426673+05
41	.48541066+04	.67653269+04	.94039482+04	.13037434+05	.18028203+05	.24866146+05
42	.59705512+04	.83890078+04	.11754935+05	.16427167+05	.22895817+05	.31828666+05
43	.73437779+04	.10402370+05	.14693668+05	.20698230+05	.29077667+05	.40740692+05
44	.90328468+04	.12898938+05	.18367080+05	.26079769+05	.36928663+05	.52148084+05
45	.11110401+05	.15994683+05	.22958850+05	.32860509+05	.46899461+05	.66749546+05
46	.13665793+05	.19833407+05	.28698570+05	.41404240+05	.59562230+05	.85439418+05
47	.16808926+05	.24593425+05	.35873212+05	.52169342+05	.75644042+05	.10936245+06
48	.20674979+05	.30495846+05	.44841515+05	.65733369+05	.96067933+05	.13998394+06
49	.25430223+05	.37814849+05	.56051892+05	.82824045+05	.12200027+06	.17917944+06
50	.31279174+05	.46890412+05	.70064864+05	.10435829+06	.15494797+06	.22934967+06

J	I =.290	I =.300	I =.350	I =.400	I =.450	I =.500
1	.12900000+01	.13000000+01	.13500000+01	.14000000+01	.14500000+01	.15000000+01
2	.16641000+01	.16900000+01	.18225000+01	.19600000+01	.21025000+01	.22499999+01
3	.21466889+01	.21969999+01	.24603750+01	.27440000+01	.30486249+01	.33749998+01
4	.27692287+01	.28560998+01	.33215062+01	.38415999+01	.44205506+01	.50624997+01
5	.35723050+01	.37129297+01	.44840333+01	.53782398+01	.64097317+01	.75937495+01
6	.46082734+01	.48268086+01	.60534448+01	.75295356+01	.92941137+01	.11390624+02
7	.59446726+01	.62748510+01	.81721504+01	.10541350+02	.13476465+02	.17085936+02
8	.76686276+01	.81573061+01	.11032403+02	.14757889+02	.19540874+02	.25628904+02
9	.98925295+01	.10604498+02	.14893744+02	.20661045+02	.28334266+02	.38443355+02
10	.12761363+02	.13785847+02	.20106554+02	.28925463+02	.41084685+02	.57665031+02
11	.16462158+02	.17921600+02	.27143847+02	.40495647+02	.59572793+02	.86497545+02
12	.21236183+02	.23298080+02	.36644194+02	.56939905+02	.86380548+02	.12974632+03
13	.27394676+02	.30287503+02	.49469661+02	.79371466+02	.12525179+03	.19461947+03
14	.35339132+02	.39373753+02	.66784041+02	.11112005+03	.18161510+03	.29192920+03
15	.45587479+02	.51185878+02	.90158454+02	.15556807+03	.26334189+03	.43789379+03
16	.58807848+02	.66541641+02	.12171391+03	.21779530+03	.38184574+03	.65684067+03
17	.75862122+02	.86504132+02	.16431379+03	.30491342+03	.55367631+03	.98526100+03
18	.97862136+02	.11245537+03	.22182360+03	.42687878+03	.80283064+03	.14778915+04
19	.12624215+03	.14619198+03	.29946186+03	.59763028+03	.11641044+04	.22168372+04
20	.16285238+03	.19004957+03	.40427351+03	.83668238+03	.16879514+04	.33252557+04
21	.21007957+03	.24706443+03	.54576923+03	.11713553+04	.24475294+04	.49878836+04
22	.27100264+03	.32118376+03	.73678846+03	.16398975+04	.35489176+04	.74818252+04
23	.34959339+03	.41753887+03	.99466442+03	.22958564+04	.51459304+04	.11222738+05
24	.45097548+03	.54280053+03	.13427970+04	.32141989+04	.74615991+04	.16834106+05
25	.58175835+03	.70564068+03	.18127759+04	.44998784+04	.10819319+05	.25251159+05
26	.75046827+03	.91733287+03	.24472474+04	.62998297+04	.15688012+05	.37876738+05
27	.96810406+03	.11925327+04	.33037839+04	.88197614+04	.22747617+05	.56815106+05
28	.12488542+04	.15502924+04	.44601083+04	.12347666+05	.32984044+05	.85222658+05
29	.16110219+04	.20153802+04	.60211461+04	.17286732+05	.47826864+05	.12783398+06
30	.20782182+04	.26199992+04	.81285471+04	.24201424+05	.69348951+05	.19175097+06
31	.26809015+04	.34059924+04	.10973538+05	.33881994+05	.10055598+06	.28762646+06
32	.34583629+04	.44277900+04	.14814277+05	.47434791+05	.14580617+06	.43143968+06
33	.44612881+04	.57561269+04	.19999274+05	.66408706+05	.21141894+06	.64715951+06
34	.57550616+04	.74829649+04	.26999020+05	.92972188+05	.30655745+06	.97073926+06
35	.74240293+04	.97278541+04	.36448676+05	.13016106+06	.44450831+06	.14561088+07
36	.95769978+04	.12646210+05	.49205712+05	.18222549+06	.64453702+06	.21841633+07
37	.12354327+05	.16440073+05	.66427710+05	.25511568+06	.93457868+06	.32762448+07
38	.15937082+05	.21372095+05	.89677408+05	.35716195+06	.13551391+07	.49143671+07
39	.20558836+05	.27783722+05	.12106450+06	.50002671+06	.19649516+07	.73715506+07
40	.26520897+05	.36118838+05	.16343708+06	.70003740+06	.28491798+07	.11057326+08
41	.34211957+05	.46954489+05	.22064005+06	.98005234+06	.41313107+07	.16585988+08
42	.44133424+05	.61040834+05	.29786906+06	.13720732+07	.59904003+07	.24878982+08
43	.56932116+05	.79353082+05	.40211664+06	.19209025+07	.86860804+07	.37318473+08
44	.73442429+05	.10315900+06	.54285724+06	.26892635+07	.12594816+08	.55977708+08
45	.94740733+05	.13410670+06	.73285726+06	.37649689+07	.18262484+08	.83966561+08
46	.12221554+06	.17433871+06	.98935730+06	.52709564+07	.26480601+08	.12594984+09
47	.15765805+06	.22664032+06	.13356324+07	.73793389+07	.38396870+08	.18892476+09
48	.20337889+06	.29463241+06	.18031036+07	.10331074+08	.55675461+08	.28338713+09
49	.26235875+06	.38302213+06	.24341899+07	.14463504+08	.80729418+08	.42508069+09
50	.33844279+06	.49792876+06	.32861564+07	.20248905+08	.11759765+09	.63762102+09

TABLE B.3 Values of $\sum_{j=0}^{N} e^{-ri}$

TABULATED VALUES OF E WHEN R =0.000

X	E^{-RX}	SUM OF E^{-RX}	*	X	E^{-RX}	SUM OF E^{-RX}	*
0.	1.0000000E+00	1.0000000E+00	*	50.	1.0000000E+00	5.1000000E+01	*
1.	1.0000000E+00	2.0000000E+00	*	51.	1.0000000E+00	5.2000000E+01	*
2.	1.0000000E+00	3.0000000E+00	*	52.	1.0000000E+00	5.3000000E+01	*
3.	1.0000000E+00	4.0000000E+00	*	53.	1.0000000E+00	5.4000000E+01	*
4.	1.0000000E+00	5.0000000E+00	*	54.	1.0000000E+00	5.5000000E+01	*
5.	1.0000000E+00	6.0000000E+00	*	55.	1.0000000E+00	5.6000000E+01	*
6.	1.0000000E+00	7.0000000E+00	*	56.	1.0000000E+00	5.7000000E+01	*
7.	1.0000000E+00	8.0000000E+00	*	57.	1.0000000E+00	5.8000000E+01	*
8.	1.0000000E+00	9.0000000E+00	*	58.	1.0000000E+00	5.9000000E+01	*
9.	1.0000000E+00	1.0000000E+01	*	59.	1.0000000E+00	6.0000000E+01	*
10.	1.0000000E+00	1.1000000E+01	*	60.	1.0000000E+00	6.1000000E+01	*
11.	1.0000000E+00	1.2000000E+01	*	61.	1.0000000E+00	6.2000000E+01	*
12.	1.0000000E+00	1.3000000E+01	*	62.	1.0000000E+00	6.3000000E+01	*
13.	1.0000000E+00	1.4000000E+01	*	63.	1.0000000E+00	6.4000000E+01	*
14.	1.0000000E+00	1.5000000E+01	*	64.	1.0000000E+00	6.5000000E+01	*
15.	1.0000000E+00	1.6000000E+01	*	65.	1.0000000E+00	6.6000000E+01	*
16.	1.0000000E+00	1.7000000E+01	*	66.	1.0000000E+00	6.7000000E+01	*
17.	1.0000000E+00	1.8000000E+01	*	67.	1.0000000E+00	6.8000000E+01	*
18.	1.0000000E+00	1.9000000E+01	*	68.	1.0000000E+00	6.9000000E+01	*
19.	1.0000000E+00	2.0000000E+01	*	69.	1.0000000E+00	7.0000000E+01	*
20.	1.0000000E+00	2.1000000E+01	*	70.	1.0000000E+00	7.1000000E+01	*
21.	1.0000000E+00	2.2000000E+01	*	71.	1.0000000E+00	7.2000000E+01	*
22.	1.0000000E+00	2.3000000E+01	*	72.	1.0000000E+00	7.3000000E+01	*
23.	1.0000000E+00	2.4000000E+01	*	73.	1.0000000E+00	7.4000000E+01	*
24.	1.0000000E+00	2.5000000E+01	*	74.	1.0000000E+00	7.5000000E+01	*
25.	1.0000000E+00	2.6000000E+01	*	75.	1.0000000E+00	7.6000000E+01	*
26.	1.0000000E+00	2.7000000E+01	*	76.	1.0000000E+00	7.7000000E+01	*
27.	1.0000000E+00	2.8000000E+01	*	77.	1.0000000E+00	7.8000000E+01	*
28.	1.0000000E+00	2.9000000E+01	*	78.	1.0000000E+00	7.9000000E+01	*
29.	1.0000000E+00	3.0000000E+01	*	79.	1.0000000E+00	8.0000000E+01	*
30.	1.0000000E+00	3.1000000E+01	*	80.	1.0000000E+00	8.1000000E+01	*
31.	1.0000000E+00	3.2000000E+01	*	81.	1.0000000E+00	8.2000000E+01	*
32.	1.0000000E+00	3.3000000E+01	*	82.	1.0000000E+00	8.3000000E+01	*
33.	1.0000000E+00	3.4000000E+01	*	83.	1.0000000E+00	8.4000000E+01	*
34.	1.0000000E+00	3.5000000E+01	*	84.	1.0000000E+00	8.5000000E+01	*
35.	1.0000000E+00	3.6000000E+01	*	85.	1.0000000E+00	8.6000000E+01	*
36.	1.0000000E+00	3.7000000E+01	*	86.	1.0000000E+00	8.7000000E+01	*
37.	1.0000000E+00	3.8000000E+01	*	87.	1.0000000E+00	8.8000000E+01	*
38.	1.0000000E+00	3.9000000E+01	*	88.	1.0000000E+00	8.9000000E+01	*
39.	1.0000000E+00	4.0000000E+01	*	89.	1.0000000E+00	9.0000000E+01	*
40.	1.0000000E+00	4.1000000E+01	*	90.	1.0000000E+00	9.1000000E+01	*
41.	1.0000000E+00	4.2000000E+01	*	91.	1.0000000E+00	9.2000000E+01	*
42.	1.0000000E+00	4.3000000E+01	*	92.	1.0000000E+00	9.3000000E+01	*
43.	1.0000000E+00	4.4000000E+01	*	93.	1.0000000E+00	9.4000000E+01	*
44.	1.0000000E+00	4.5000000E+01	*	94.	1.0000000E+00	9.5000000E+01	*
45.	1.0000000E+00	4.6000000E+01	*	95.	1.0000000E+00	9.6000000E+01	*
46.	1.0000000E+00	4.7000000E+01	*	96.	1.0000000E+00	9.7000000E+01	*
47.	1.0000000E+00	4.8000000E+01	*	97.	1.0000000E+00	9.8000000E+01	*
48.	1.0000000E+00	4.9000000E+01	*	98.	1.0000000E+00	9.9000000E+01	*
49.	1.0000000E+00	5.0000000E+01	*	99.	1.0000000E+00	1.0000000E+02	*
50.	1.0000000E+00	5.1000000E+01	*	101.	1.0000000E+00	1.0100000E+02	*

TABULATED VALUES OF E   WHEN R = .001

X	E (−RX)	SUM OF E (−RX)	*	X	E (−RX)	SUM OF E (−RX)	*
0.	1.0000000E+00	1.0000000E+00	*	50.	9.5122942E-01	4.9746173E+01	*
1.	9.9900049E-01	1.9990004E+00	*	51.	9.5027865E-01	5.0696451E+01	*
2.	9.9800199E-01	2.9970023E+00	*	52.	9.4932886E-01	5.1645779E+01	*
3.	9.9700449E-01	3.9940067E+00	*	53.	9.4838001E-01	5.2594159E+01	*
4.	9.9600798E-01	4.9900146E+00	*	54.	9.4743210E-01	5.3541591E+01	*
5.	9.9501247E-01	5.9850270E+00	*	55.	9.4648514E-01	5.4488076E+01	*
6.	9.9401796E-01	6.9790449E+00	*	56.	9.4553913E-01	5.5433615E+01	*
7.	9.9302444E-01	7.9720693E+00	*	57.	9.4459404E-01	5.6378209E+01	*
8.	9.9203191E-01	8.9641012E+00	*	58.	9.4364994E-01	5.7321858E+01	*
9.	9.9104037E-01	9.9551415E+00	*	59.	9.4270676E-01	5.8264564E+01	*
10.	9.9004983E-01	1.0945191E+01	*	60.	9.4176453E-01	5.9206328E+01	*
11.	9.8906027E-01	1.1934251E+01	*	61.	9.4082323E-01	6.0147151E+01	*
12.	9.8807171E-01	1.2922322E+01	*	62.	9.3988288E-01	6.1087033E+01	*
13.	9.8708413E-01	1.3909406E+01	*	63.	9.3894347E-01	6.2025976E+01	*
14.	9.8609754E-01	1.4895503E+01	*	64.	9.3800499E-01	6.2963980E+01	*
15.	9.8511193E-01	1.5880614E+01	*	65.	9.3706746E-01	6.3901047E+01	*
16.	9.8412731E-01	1.6864741E+01	*	66.	9.3613086E-01	6.4837177E+01	*
17.	9.8314368E-01	1.7847884E+01	*	67.	9.3519519E-01	6.5772372E+01	*
18.	9.8216103E-01	1.8830045E+01	*	68.	9.3426047E-01	6.6706632E+01	*
19.	9.8117936E-01	1.9811224E+01	*	69.	9.3332667E-01	6.7639958E+01	*
20.	9.8019867E-01	2.0791422E+01	*	70.	9.3239381E-01	6.8572351E+01	*
21.	9.7921896E-01	2.1770640E+01	*	71.	9.3146188E-01	6.9503812E+01	*
22.	9.7824023E-01	2.2748880E+01	*	72.	9.3053089E-01	7.0434342E+01	*
23.	9.7726248E-01	2.3726142E+01	*	73.	9.2960082E-01	7.1363942E+01	*
24.	9.7628570E-01	2.4702427E+01	*	74.	9.2867169E-01	7.2292613E+01	*
25.	9.7530991E-01	2.5677736E+01	*	75.	9.2774348E-01	7.3220356E+01	*
26.	9.7433508E-01	2.6652071E+01	*	76.	9.2681620E-01	7.4147172E+01	*
27.	9.7336124E-01	2.7625432E+01	*	77.	9.2588985E-01	7.5073061E+01	*
28.	9.7238836E-01	2.8597820E+01	*	78.	9.2496442E-01	7.5998025E+01	*
29.	9.7141646E-01	2.9569236E+01	*	79.	9.2403992E-01	7.6922064E+01	*
30.	9.7044553E-01	3.0539681E+01	*	80.	9.2311634E-01	7.7845180E+01	*
31.	9.6947557E-01	3.1509156E+01	*	81.	9.2219369E-01	7.8767373E+01	*
32.	9.6850658E-01	3.2477662E+01	*	82.	9.2127195E-01	7.9688644E+01	*
33.	9.6753855E-01	3.3445200E+01	*	83.	9.2035114E-01	8.0608995E+01	*
34.	9.6657150E-01	3.4411771E+01	*	84.	9.1943125E-01	8.1528426E+01	*
35.	9.6560541E-01	3.5377376E+01	*	85.	9.1851228E-01	8.2446938E+01	*
36.	9.6464029E-01	3.6342016E+01	*	86.	9.1759422E-01	8.3364532E+01	*
37.	9.6367613E-01	3.7305692E+01	*	87.	9.1667709E-01	8.4281209E+01	*
38.	9.6271293E-01	3.8268404E+01	*	88.	9.1576087E-01	8.5196969E+01	*
39.	9.6175070E-01	3.9230154E+01	*	89.	9.1484557E-01	8.6111814E+01	*
40.	9.6078943E-01	4.0190943E+01	*	90.	9.1393118E-01	8.7025745E+01	*
41.	9.5982912E-01	4.1150772E+01	*	91.	9.1301770E-01	8.7938762E+01	*
42.	9.5886977E-01	4.2109641E+01	*	92.	9.1210514E-01	8.8850867E+01	*
43.	9.5791138E-01	4.3067552E+01	*	93.	9.1119349E-01	8.9762060E+01	*
44.	9.5695395E-01	4.4024505E+01	*	94.	9.1028276E-01	9.0672342E+01	*
45.	9.5599748E-01	4.4980502E+01	*	95.	9.0937293E-01	9.1581714E+01	*
46.	9.5504196E-01	4.5935543E+01	*	96.	9.0846401E-01	9.2490178E+01	*
47.	9.5408739E-01	4.6889630E+01	*	97.	9.0755600E-01	9.3397734E+01	*
48.	9.5313378E-01	4.7842763E+01	*	98.	9.0664890E-01	9.4304382E+01	*
49.	9.5218112E-01	4.8794944E+01	*	99.	9.0574270E-01	9.5210124E+01	*
50.	9.5122942E-01	4.9746173E+01	*	100.	9.0483741E-01	9.6114961E+01	*

TABULATED VALUES OF E   WHEN R = .002

X	E (−RX)	SUM OF E (−RX)	*	X	E (−RX)	SUM OF E (−RX)	*
0.	1.0000000E+00	1.0000000E+00	*	50.	9.0483741E-01	4.8533702E+01	*
1.	9.9800199E-01	1.9980019E+00	*	51.	9.0302954E-01	4.9436731E+01	*
2.	9.9600798E-01	2.9940098E+00	*	52.	9.0122529E-01	5.0337956E+01	*
3.	9.9401796E-01	3.9880277E+00	*	53.	8.9942464E-01	5.1237380E+01	*
4.	9.9203191E-01	4.9800596E+00	*	54.	8.9762759E-01	5.2135007E+01	*
5.	9.9004983E-01	5.9701094E+00	*	55.	8.9583413E-01	5.3030841E+01	*
6.	9.8807171E-01	6.9581811E+00	*	56.	8.9404425E-01	5.3924885E+01	*
7.	9.8609754E-01	7.9442786E+00	*	57.	8.9225795E-01	5.4817142E+01	*
8.	9.8412731E-01	8.9284059E+00	*	58.	8.9047522E-01	5.5707617E+01	*
9.	9.8216103E-01	9.9105669E+00	*	59.	8.8869605E-01	5.6596313E+01	*
10.	9.8019867E-01	1.0890765E+01	*	60.	8.8692043E-01	5.7483233E+01	*
11.	9.7824023E-01	1.1869005E+01	*	61.	8.8514836E-01	5.8368381E+01	*
12.	9.7628570E-01	1.2845290E+01	*	62.	8.8337983E-01	5.9251760E+01	*
13.	9.7433508E-01	1.3819625E+01	*	63.	8.8161484E-01	6.0133374E+01	*
14.	9.7238836E-01	1.4792013E+01	*	64.	8.7985337E-01	6.1013227E+01	*
15.	9.7044553E-01	1.5762458E+01	*	65.	8.7809542E-01	6.1891322E+01	*
16.	9.6850658E-01	1.6730964E+01	*	66.	8.7634099E-01	6.2767662E+01	*
17.	9.6657150E-01	1.7697535E+01	*	67.	8.7459006E-01	6.3642252E+01	*
18.	9.6464029E-01	1.8662175E+01	*	68.	8.7284263E-01	6.4515094E+01	*
19.	9.6271293E-01	1.9624887E+01	*	69.	8.7109869E-01	6.5386192E+01	*
20.	9.6078943E-01	2.0585676E+01	*	70.	8.6935823E-01	6.6255550E+01	*
21.	9.5886977E-01	2.1544545E+01	*	71.	8.6762125E-01	6.7123171E+01	*
22.	9.5695395E-01	2.2501498E+01	*	72.	8.6588774E-01	6.7989058E+01	*
23.	9.5504196E-01	2.3456539E+01	*	73.	8.6415770E-01	6.8853215E+01	*
24.	9.5313378E-01	2.4409672E+01	*	74.	8.6243111E-01	6.9715646E+01	*
25.	9.5122942E-01	2.5360901E+01	*	75.	8.6070797E-01	7.0576353E+01	*
26.	9.4932886E-01	2.6310229E+01	*	76.	8.5898827E-01	7.1435341E+01	*
27.	9.4743210E-01	2.7257661E+01	*	77.	8.5727201E-01	7.2292613E+01	*
28.	9.4553913E-01	2.8203200E+01	*	78.	8.5555918E-01	7.3148172E+01	*
29.	9.4364994E-01	2.9146849E+01	*	79.	8.5384977E-01	7.4002021E+01	*
30.	9.4176453E-01	3.0088613E+01	*	80.	8.5214378E-01	7.4854164E+01	*
31.	9.3988288E-01	3.1028495E+01	*	81.	8.5044120E-01	7.5704605E+01	*
32.	9.3800499E-01	3.1966499E+01	*	82.	8.4874202E-01	7.6553347E+01	*
33.	9.3613086E-01	3.2902629E+01	*	83.	8.4704623E-01	7.7400393E+01	*
34.	9.3426047E-01	3.3836889E+01	*	84.	8.4535383E-01	7.8245746E+01	*
35.	9.3239381E-01	3.4769282E+01	*	85.	8.4366481E-01	7.9089410E+01	*
36.	9.3053089E-01	3.5699812E+01	*	86.	8.4197917E-01	7.9931389E+01	*
37.	9.2867169E-01	3.6628483E+01	*	87.	8.4029689E-01	8.0771685E+01	*
38.	9.2681620E-01	3.7555299E+01	*	88.	8.3861798E-01	8.1610302E+01	*
39.	9.2496442E-01	3.8480263E+01	*	89.	8.3694242E-01	8.2447244E+01	*
40.	9.2311634E-01	3.9403379E+01	*	90.	8.3527020E-01	8.3282514E+01	*
41.	9.2127195E-01	4.0324650E+01	*	91.	8.3360133E-01	8.4116115E+01	*
42.	9.1943125E-01	4.1244081E+01	*	92.	8.3193580E-01	8.4948050E+01	*
43.	9.1759422E-01	4.2161675E+01	*	93.	8.3027359E-01	8.5778323E+01	*
44.	9.1576087E-01	4.3077435E+01	*	94.	8.2861479E-01	8.6606937E+01	*
45.	9.1393118E-01	4.3991366E+01	*	95.	8.2695913E-01	8.7433896E+01	*
46.	9.1210514E-01	4.4903471E+01	*	96.	8.2530686E-01	8.8259202E+01	*
47.	9.1028276E-01	4.5813753E+01	*	97.	8.2365790E-01	8.9082859E+01	*
48.	9.0846401E-01	4.6722217E+01	*	98.	8.2201223E-01	8.9904871E+01	*
49.	9.0664890E-01	4.7628865E+01	*	99.	8.2036985E-01	9.0725240E+01	*
50.	9.0483741E-01	4.8533702E+01	*	100.	8.1873075E-01	9.1543970E+01	*

TABULATED VALUES OF E^{-RX} WHEN R = .003

X	E^{-RX}	SUM OF E^{-RX}	*	X	E^{-RX}	SUM OF E^{-RX}	*
0.	1.0000000E+00	1.0000000E+00		50.	8.6070797E-01	4.7361039E+01	*
1.	9.9700449E-01	1.9970044E+00		51.	8.5812971E-01	4.8219168E+01	*
2.	9.9401796E-01	2.9910223E+00		52.	8.5555918E-01	4.9074727E+01	*
3.	9.9104037E-01	3.9820626E+00		53.	8.5299635E-01	4.9927723E+01	*
4.	9.8807171E-01	4.9701343E+00		54.	8.5044120E-01	5.0777816E+01	*
5.	9.8511193E-01	5.9552462E+00		55.	8.4789370E-01	5.1626057E+01	*
6.	9.8216103E-01	6.9374072E+00		56.	8.4535383E-01	5.2471410E+01	*
7.	9.7921896E-01	7.9166261E+00		57.	8.4282157E-01	5.3314231E+01	*
8.	9.7628570E-01	8.8929118E+00		58.	8.4029689E-01	5.4154527E+01	*
9.	9.7336124E-01	9.8662730E+00		59.	8.3777978E-01	5.4992306E+01	*
10.	9.7044553E-01	1.0836671E+01		60.	8.3527020E-01	5.5827576E+01	*
11.	9.6753855E-01	1.1804256E+01		61.	8.3276815E-01	5.6660344E+01	*
12.	9.6464029E-01	1.2768496E+01		62.	8.3027359E-01	5.7490617E+01	*
13.	9.6175070E-01	1.3730646E+01		63.	8.2778650E-01	5.8318403E+01	*
14.	9.5886977E-01	1.4689515E+01		64.	8.2530686E-01	5.9143709E+01	*
15.	9.5599748E-01	1.5645512E+01		65.	8.2283465E-01	5.9966543E+01	*
16.	9.5313378E-01	1.6598645E+01		66.	8.2036985E-01	6.0786912E+01	*
17.	9.5027866E-01	1.7548923E+01		67.	8.1791242E-01	6.1604824E+01	*
18.	9.4743210E-01	1.8496355E+01		68.	8.1546236E-01	6.2420286E+01	*
19.	9.4459408E-01	1.9440949E+01		69.	8.1301964E-01	6.3233305E+01	*
20.	9.4176403E-01	2.0382713E+01		70.	8.1058424E-01	6.4043889E+01	*
21.	9.3894347E-01	2.1321656E+01		71.	8.0815613E-01	6.4852045E+01	*
22.	9.3613086E-01	2.2257786E+01		72.	8.0573530E-01	6.5657780E+01	*
23.	9.3332667E-01	2.3191112E+01		73.	8.0332171E-01	6.6461101E+01	*
24.	9.3053089E-01	2.4121642E+01		74.	8.0091536E-01	6.7262016E+01	*
25.	9.2774348E-01	2.5049385E+01		75.	7.9851621E-01	6.8060532E+01	*
26.	9.2496442E-01	2.5974349E+01		76.	7.9612425E-01	6.8856656E+01	*
27.	9.2219369E-01	2.6896542E+01		77.	7.9373946E-01	6.9650395E+01	*
28.	9.1943125E-01	2.7815973E+01		78.	7.9136181E-01	7.0441756E+01	*
29.	9.1667709E-01	2.8732650E+01		79.	7.8899128E-01	7.1230747E+01	*
30.	9.1393118E-01	2.9645581E+01		80.	7.8662786E-01	7.2017374E+01	*
31.	9.1119349E-01	3.0557774E+01		81.	7.8427151E-01	7.2801645E+01	*
32.	9.0846401E-01	3.1466238E+01		82.	7.8192222E-01	7.3583567E+01	*
33.	9.0574270E-01	3.2371980E+01		83.	7.7957997E-01	7.4363146E+01	*
34.	9.0302954E-01	3.3275009E+01		84.	7.7724473E-01	7.5140390E+01	*
35.	9.0032452E-01	3.4175333E+01		85.	7.7491649E-01	7.5915306E+01	*
36.	8.9762759E-01	3.5072960E+01		86.	7.7259523E-01	7.6687901E+01	*
37.	8.9493874E-01	3.5967898E+01		87.	7.7028091E-01	7.7458181E+01	*
38.	8.9225795E-01	3.6860155E+01		88.	7.6797353E-01	7.8226154E+01	*
39.	8.8958519E-01	3.7749405E+01		89.	7.6567307E-01	7.8991827E+01	*
40.	8.8692043E-01	3.8636660E+01		90.	7.6337949E-01	7.9755206E+01	*
41.	8.8426365E-01	3.9520923E+01		91.	7.6109278E-01	8.0516298E+01	*
42.	8.8161484E-01	4.0402537E+01		92.	7.5881293E-01	8.1275110E+01	*
43.	8.7897396E-01	4.1281510E+01		93.	7.5653990E-01	8.2031649E+01	*
44.	8.7634099E-01	4.2157850E+01		94.	7.5427368E-01	8.2785922E+01	*
45.	8.7371591E-01	4.3031565E+01		95.	7.5201425E-01	8.3537936E+01	*
46.	8.7109869E-01	4.3902643E+01		96.	7.4976159E-01	8.4287697E+01	*
47.	8.6848931E-01	4.4771152E+01		97.	7.4751567E-01	8.5035212E+01	*
48.	8.6587746E-01	4.5637030E+01		98.	7.4527648E-01	8.5780688E+01	*
49.	8.6329397E-01	4.6500332E+01		99.	7.4304401E-01	8.6523532E+01	*
50.	8.6070797E-01	4.7361039E+01		100.	7.4081821E-01	8.7264350E+01	*

TABULATED VALUES OF E^{-RX} WHEN R = .004

X	E^{-RX}	SUM OF E^{-RX}	*	X	E^{-RX}	SUM OF E^{-RX}	*
0.	1.0000000E+00	1.0000000E+00		50.	8.1873075E-01	4.6226716E+01	*
1.	9.9600798E-01	1.9960079E+00		51.	8.1546236E-01	4.7042178E+01	*
2.	9.9203191E-01	2.9880398E+00		52.	8.1220703E-01	4.7854385E+01	*
3.	9.8807171E-01	3.9761115E+00		53.	8.0896469E-01	4.8663349E+01	*
4.	9.8412731E-01	4.9602388E+00		54.	8.0573530E-01	4.9469084E+01	*
5.	9.8019867E-01	5.9404374E+00		55.	8.0251879E-01	5.0271602E+01	*
6.	9.7628570E-01	6.9167231E+00		56.	7.9931513E-01	5.1070917E+01	*
7.	9.7238836E-01	7.8891114E+00		57.	7.9612425E-01	5.1870414E+01	*
8.	9.6850658E-01	8.8576179E+00		58.	7.9294412E-01	5.2659987E+01	*
9.	9.6464029E-01	9.8222581E+00		59.	7.8977067E-01	5.3449767E+01	*
10.	9.6078943E-01	1.0783047E+01		60.	7.8662786E-01	5.4236394E+01	*
11.	9.5695395E-01	1.1740000E+01		61.	7.8348763E-01	5.5019881E+01	*
12.	9.5313378E-01	1.2693133E+01		62.	7.8035994E-01	5.5800240E+01	*
13.	9.4932886E-01	1.3642461E+01		63.	7.7724473E-01	5.6577484E+01	*
14.	9.4553913E-01	1.4588000E+01		64.	7.7414196E-01	5.7351625E+01	*
15.	9.4176453E-01	1.5529766E+01		65.	7.7105158E-01	5.8122676E+01	*
16.	9.3800499E-01	1.6467768E+01		66.	7.6797353E-01	5.8890469E+01	*
17.	9.3426047E-01	1.7400202E+01		67.	7.6490777E-01	5.9655555E+01	*
18.	9.3053089E-01	1.8332558E+01		68.	7.6185426E-01	6.0417410E+01	*
19.	9.2681620E-01	1.9259374E+01		69.	7.5881293E-01	6.1176222E+01	*
20.	9.2311634E-01	2.0182490E+01		70.	7.5578374E-01	6.1932005E+01	*
21.	9.1943125E-01	2.1101921E+01		71.	7.5276664E-01	6.2684771E+01	*
22.	9.1576087E-01	2.2017681E+01		72.	7.4976159E-01	6.3434532E+01	*
23.	9.1210514E-01	2.2929786E+01		73.	7.4676853E-01	6.4181300E+01	*
24.	9.0846401E-01	2.3838250E+01		74.	7.4378742E-01	6.4925087E+01	*
25.	9.0483741E-01	2.4743037E+01		75.	7.4081821E-01	6.5665905E+01	*
26.	9.0122529E-01	2.5644312E+01		76.	7.3786086E-01	6.6403765E+01	*
27.	8.9762759E-01	2.6541939E+01		77.	7.3491531E-01	6.7138680E+01	*
28.	8.9404425E-01	2.7435983E+01		78.	7.3199152E-01	6.7870661E+01	*
29.	8.9047522E-01	2.8326458E+01		79.	7.2905944E-01	6.8599720E+01	*
30.	8.8692043E-01	2.9213378E+01		80.	7.2614903E-01	6.9325869E+01	*
31.	8.8337983E-01	3.0096757E+01		81.	7.2325024E-01	7.0049119E+01	*
32.	8.7985337E-01	3.0976602E+01		82.	7.2036301E-01	7.0769482E+01	*
33.	8.7634099E-01	3.1852950E+01		83.	7.1747732E-01	7.1486969E+01	*
34.	8.7284263E-01	3.2725792E+01		84.	7.1462310E-01	7.2201592E+01	*
35.	8.6935823E-01	3.3595150E+01		85.	7.1177032E-01	7.2913362E+01	*
36.	8.6588774E-01	3.4461037E+01		86.	7.0892892E-01	7.3622290E+01	*
37.	8.6243111E-01	3.5323468E+01		87.	7.0609887E-01	7.4328838E+01	*
38.	8.5898827E-01	3.6182456E+01		88.	7.0328012E-01	7.5031668E+01	*
39.	8.5555918E-01	3.7038015E+01		89.	7.0047261E-01	7.5732140E+01	*
40.	8.5214378E-01	3.7890158E+01		90.	6.9767632E-01	7.6429816E+01	*
41.	8.4874202E-01	3.8738900E+01		91.	6.9489119E-01	7.7124707E+01	*
42.	8.4535383E-01	3.9584253E+01		92.	6.9211717E-01	7.7816924E+01	*
43.	8.4197917E-01	4.0426232E+01		93.	6.8935424E-01	7.8506178E+01	*
44.	8.3861798E-01	4.1264849E+01		94.	6.8660233E-01	7.9192780E+01	*
45.	8.3527020E-01	4.2100119E+01		95.	6.8386140E-01	7.9876641E+01	*
46.	8.3193580E-01	4.2932054E+01		96.	6.8113142E-01	8.0557772E+01	*
47.	8.2861470E-01	4.3760668E+01		97.	6.7841234E-01	8.1236186E+01	*
48.	8.2530686E-01	4.4585974E+01		98.	6.7570411E-01	8.1911888E+01	*
49.	8.2201223E-01	4.5407986E+01		99.	6.7300669E-01	8.2584894E+01	*
50.	8.1873075E-01	4.6226716E+01		100.	6.7032004E-01	8.3255214E+01	*

139

TABULATED VALUES OF E WHEN R = .005

X	E^{-RX}	SUM OF E^{-RX}	*	X	E^{-RX}	SUM OF E^{-KX}	*
0.	1.0000000E+00	1.0000000E+00	*	50.	7.7880078E-01	4.5129315E+01	*
1.	9.9501247E-01	1.9950124E+00	*	51.	7.7491669E-01	4.5904231E+01	*
2.	9.9004983E-01	2.9850622E+00	*	52.	7.7105158E-01	4.6675282E+01	*
3.	9.8511193E-01	3.9701741E+00	*	53.	7.6720594E-01	4.7442487E+01	*
4.	9.8019867E-01	4.9503727E+00	*	54.	7.6337949E-01	4.8205866E+01	*
5.	9.7530991E-01	5.9256826E+00	*	55.	7.5957212E-01	4.8965438E+01	*
6.	9.7044553E-01	6.8961281E+00	*	56.	7.5578374E-01	4.9721221E+01	*
7.	9.6560541E-01	7.8617335E+00	*	57.	7.5201425E-01	5.0473235E+01	*
8.	9.6078943E-01	8.8225229E+00	*	58.	7.4826356E-01	5.1221499E+01	*
9.	9.5599748E-01	9.7785203E+00	*	59.	7.4453158E-01	5.1966029E+01	*
10.	9.5122942E-01	1.0729744E+01	*	60.	7.4081821E-01	5.2706847E+01	*
11.	9.4648514E-01	1.1676234E+01	*	61.	7.3712337E-01	5.3443970E+01	*
12.	9.4176453E-01	1.2617998E+01	*	62.	7.3344695E-01	5.4177416E+01	*
13.	9.3706746E-01	1.3555065E+01	*	63.	7.2978887E-01	5.4907204E+01	*
14.	9.3239381E-01	1.4487458E+01	*	64.	7.2614903E-01	5.5633353E+01	*
15.	9.2774348E-01	1.5415201E+01	*	65.	7.2252735E-01	5.6355880E+01	*
16.	9.2311634E-01	1.6334317E+01	*	66.	7.1892373E-01	5.7074803E+01	*
17.	9.1851228E-01	1.7256829E+01	*	67.	7.1533808E-01	5.7790141E+01	*
18.	9.1393118E-01	1.8170760E+01	*	68.	7.1177032E-01	5.8501911E+01	*
19.	9.0937293E-01	1.9090132E+01	*	69.	7.0822035E-01	5.9210131E+01	*
20.	9.0483741E-01	1.9984969E+01	*	70.	7.0468808E-01	5.9914819E+01	*
21.	9.0032452E-01	2.0885293E+01	*	71.	7.0117344E-01	6.0615992E+01	*
22.	8.9583413E-01	2.1781127E+01	*	72.	6.9767632E-01	6.1313668E+01	*
23.	8.9136614E-01	2.2672493E+01	*	73.	6.9419664E-01	6.2007864E+01	*
24.	8.8692043E-01	2.3559413E+01	*	74.	6.9073432E-01	6.2698598E+01	*
25.	8.8249690E-01	2.4441909E+01	*	75.	6.8728927E-01	6.3385887E+01	*
26.	8.7809542E-01	2.5320004E+01	*	76.	6.8386140E-01	6.4069748E+01	*
27.	8.7371591E-01	2.6193719E+01	*	77.	6.8045063E-01	6.4750198E+01	*
28.	8.6935823E-01	2.7063077E+01	*	78.	6.7705687E-01	6.5427254E+01	*
29.	8.6502229E-01	2.7928099E+01	*	79.	6.7368003E-01	6.6100934E+01	*
30.	8.6070797E-01	2.8788806E+01	*	80.	6.7032004E-01	6.6771254E+01	*
31.	8.5641517E-01	2.9645221E+01	*	81.	6.6697680E-01	6.7438230E+01	*
32.	8.5214378E-01	3.0497364E+01	*	82.	6.6365024E-01	6.8101880E+01	*
33.	8.4789370E-01	3.1345257E+01	*	83.	6.6034027E-01	6.8762220E+01	*
34.	8.4366481E-01	3.2188921E+01	*	84.	6.5704691E-01	6.9419266E+01	*
35.	8.3945701E-01	3.3028378E+01	*	85.	6.5376978E-01	7.0073035E+01	*
36.	8.3527020E-01	3.3863648E+01	*	86.	6.5050909E-01	7.0723544E+01	*
37.	8.3110428E-01	3.4694752E+01	*	87.	6.4726666E-01	7.1370808E+01	*
38.	8.2695913E-01	3.5521711E+01	*	88.	6.4403641E-01	7.2014844E+01	*
39.	8.2283465E-01	3.6344565E+01	*	89.	6.4082427E-01	7.2655668E+01	*
40.	8.1873075E-01	3.7163275E+01	*	90.	6.3762814E-01	7.3293296E+01	*
41.	8.1464731E-01	3.7977922E+01	*	91.	6.3443796E-01	7.3927743E+01	*
42.	8.1058424E-01	3.8788506E+01	*	92.	6.3128364E-01	7.4559026E+01	*
43.	8.0654143E-01	3.9595047E+01	*	93.	6.2813510E-01	7.5187161E+01	*
44.	8.0251879E-01	4.0397565E+01	*	94.	6.2500226E-01	7.5812163E+01	*
45.	7.9851621E-01	4.1196081E+01	*	95.	6.2188505E-01	7.6434048E+01	*
46.	7.9453359E-01	4.1990614E+01	*	96.	6.1878339E-01	7.7052831E+01	*
47.	7.9057084E-01	4.2781184E+01	*	97.	6.1569719E-01	7.7668528E+01	*
48.	7.8662786E-01	4.3567811E+01	*	98.	6.1262638E-01	7.8281154E+01	*
49.	7.8270453E-01	4.4350515E+01	*	99.	6.0957090E-01	7.8890724E+01	*
50.	7.7880078E-01	4.5129315E+01	*	100.	6.0653065E-01	7.9497254E+01	*

TABULATED VALUES OF E WHEN R = .006

X	E^{-RX}	SUM OF E^{-RX}	*	X	E^{-RX}	SUM OF E^{-RX}	*
0.	1.0000000E+00	1.0000000E+00	*	50.	7.4081821E-01	4.4067479E+01	*
1.	9.9401796E-01	1.9940179E+00	*	51.	7.3638661E-01	4.4803865E+01	*
2.	9.8807171E-01	2.9820896E+00	*	52.	7.3198152E-01	4.5535846E+01	*
3.	9.8216103E-01	3.9642506E+00	*	53.	7.2760278E-01	4.6263444E+01	*
4.	9.7628570E-01	4.9405363E+00	*	54.	7.2325024E-01	4.6986698E+01	*
5.	9.7044553E-01	5.9109818E+00	*	55.	7.1892373E-01	4.7705621E+01	*
6.	9.6464029E-01	6.8756220E+00	*	56.	7.1462310E-01	4.8420244E+01	*
7.	9.5886977E-01	7.8344917E+00	*	57.	7.1034820E-01	4.9130592E+01	*
8.	9.5313378E-01	8.7876254E+00	*	58.	7.0609887E-01	4.9836690E+01	*
9.	9.4743210E-01	9.7350575E+00	*	59.	7.0187496E-01	5.0538564E+01	*
10.	9.4176453E-01	1.0676822E+01	*	60.	6.9767632E-01	5.1236240E+01	*
11.	9.3613086E-01	1.1612952E+01	*	61.	6.9350279E-01	5.1929742E+01	*
12.	9.3053089E-01	1.2543482E+01	*	62.	6.8935424E-01	5.2619098E+01	*
13.	9.2496442E-01	1.3468446E+01	*	63.	6.8523040E-01	5.3304328E+01	*
14.	9.1943125E-01	1.4387877E+01	*	64.	6.8113142E-01	5.3985457E+01	*
15.	9.1393118E-01	1.5301808E+01	*	65.	6.7705687E-01	5.4662513E+01	*
16.	9.0846401E-01	1.6210272E+01	*	66.	6.7300669E-01	5.5335519E+01	*
17.	9.0302954E-01	1.7113301E+01	*	67.	6.6898074E-01	5.6004499E+01	*
18.	8.9762759E-01	1.8010928E+01	*	68.	6.6497887E-01	5.6669477E+01	*
19.	8.9225795E-01	1.8903185E+01	*	69.	6.6100094E-01	5.7330477E+01	*
20.	8.8692043E-01	1.9790105E+01	*	70.	6.5704681E-01	5.7987523E+01	*
21.	8.8161484E-01	2.0671719E+01	*	71.	6.5311633E-01	5.8640639E+01	*
22.	8.7634099E-01	2.1548059E+01	*	72.	6.4920937E-01	5.9289984E+01	*
23.	8.7109869E-01	2.2419157E+01	*	73.	6.4532578E-01	5.9935173E+01	*
24.	8.6588774E-01	2.3285044E+01	*	74.	6.4146541E-01	6.0576638E+01	*
25.	8.6070797E-01	2.4145751E+01	*	75.	6.3762814E-01	6.1214266E+01	*
26.	8.5555918E-01	2.5001310E+01	*	76.	6.3381383E-01	6.1848079E+01	*
27.	8.5044120E-01	2.5851751E+01	*	77.	6.3002233E-01	6.2478101E+01	*
28.	8.4535383E-01	2.6697104E+01	*	78.	6.2625352E-01	6.3104354E+01	*
29.	8.4029689E-01	2.7537400E+01	*	79.	6.2250725E-01	6.3726861E+01	*
30.	8.3527020E-01	2.8372670E+01	*	80.	6.1878339E-01	6.4345644E+01	*
31.	8.3027359E-01	2.9202943E+01	*	81.	6.1508180E-01	6.4960725E+01	*
32.	8.2530686E-01	3.0028249E+01	*	82.	6.1140236E-01	6.5572127E+01	*
33.	8.2036985E-01	3.0848611E+01	*	83.	6.0774603E-01	6.6179871E+01	*
34.	8.1546238E-01	3.1664080E+01	*	84.	6.0410938E-01	6.6783980E+01	*
35.	8.1058424E-01	3.2474664E+01	*	85.	6.0049557E-01	6.7384475E+01	*
36.	8.0573530E-01	3.3280399E+01	*	86.	5.9690330E-01	6.7981378E+01	*
37.	8.0091536E-01	3.4081314E+01	*	87.	5.9333269E-01	6.8574710E+01	*
38.	7.9612425E-01	3.4877743E+01	*	88.	5.8978335E-01	6.9164493E+01	*
39.	7.9136181E-01	3.5668799E+01	*	89.	5.8625525E-01	6.9750744E+01	*
40.	7.8662786E-01	3.6455426E+01	*	90.	5.8274625E-01	7.0333496E+01	*
41.	7.8192222E-01	3.7237348E+01	*	91.	5.7924223E-01	7.0912758E+01	*
42.	7.7724473E-01	3.8014592E+01	*	92.	5.7579706E-01	7.1488555E+01	*
43.	7.7259523E-01	3.8787187E+01	*	93.	5.7235262E-01	7.2060907E+01	*
44.	7.6797353E-01	3.9555160E+01	*	94.	5.6892878E-01	7.2629935E+01	*
45.	7.6337949E-01	4.0318938E+01	*	95.	5.6552543E-01	7.3195360E+01	*
46.	7.5881293E-01	4.1077351E+01	*	96.	5.6214244E-01	7.3757502E+01	*
47.	7.5427368E-01	4.1831624E+01	*	97.	5.5877968E-01	7.4316281E+01	*
48.	7.4976159E-01	4.2581385E+01	*	98.	5.5543704E-01	7.4871718E+01	*
49.	7.4527668E-01	4.3326661E+01	*	99.	5.5211440E-01	7.5423832E+01	*
50.	7.4081821E-01	4.4067479E+01	*	100.	5.4881163E-01	7.5972643E+01	*

TABULATED VALUES OF E   WHEN R = .007

X	E (-RX)	SUM OF E (-RX)	*	X	E (-RX)	SUM OF E (-RX)	*
0.	1.0000000E+00	1.0000000E+00	*	50.	7.0468808E-01	4.3039913E+01	*
1.	9.9302444E-01	1.9930244E+00	*	51.	6.9977249E-01	4.3739685E+01	*
2.	9.8609754E-01	2.9791219E+00	*	52.	6.9489119E-01	4.4434576E+01	*
3.	9.7921896E-01	3.9583408E+00	*	53.	6.9004394E-01	4.5124519E+01	*
4.	9.7238836E-01	4.9307291E+00	*	54.	6.8523049E-01	4.5809849E+01	*
5.	9.6560541E-01	5.8963345E+00	*	55.	6.8045063E-01	4.6490299E+01	*
6.	9.5886977E-01	6.8552042E+00	*	56.	6.7570411E-01	4.7166003E+01	*
7.	9.5218112E-01	7.8073853E+00	*	57.	6.7099069E-01	4.7836993E+01	*
8.	9.4553913E-01	8.7529244E+00	*	58.	6.6631016E-01	4.8503303E+01	*
9.	9.3894347E-01	9.6918678E+00	*	59.	6.6166228E-01	4.9164965E+01	*
10.	9.3239381E-01	1.0624226E+01	*	60.	6.5704681E-01	4.9822011E+01	*
11.	9.2588985E-01	1.1550150E+01	*	61.	6.5246355E-01	5.0474474E+01	*
12.	9.1943125E-01	1.2469581E+01	*	62.	6.4791225E-01	5.1122386E+01	*
13.	9.1301770E-01	1.3382598E+01	*	63.	6.4339270E-01	5.1765778E+01	*
14.	9.0664890E-01	1.4289246E+01	*	64.	6.3890468E-01	5.2404682E+01	*
15.	9.0032452E-01	1.5189570E+01	*	65.	6.3444796E-01	5.3039129E+01	*
16.	8.9404425E-01	1.6083614E+01	*	66.	6.3002233E-01	5.3669151E+01	*
17.	8.8780779E-01	1.6971421E+01	*	67.	6.2562758E-01	5.4294778E+01	*
18.	8.8161484E-01	1.7853035E+01	*	68.	6.2126348E-01	5.4916041E+01	*
19.	8.7546509E-01	1.8728500E+01	*	69.	6.1692982E-01	5.5532970E+01	*
20.	8.6935823E-01	1.9597858E+01	*	70.	6.1262639E-01	5.6145596E+01	*
21.	8.6329397E-01	2.0461151E+01	*	71.	6.0835298E-01	5.6753948E+01	*
22.	8.5727201E-01	2.1318423E+01	*	72.	6.0410938E-01	5.7358057E+01	*
23.	8.5129206E-01	2.2169715E+01	*	73.	5.9989538E-01	5.7957952E+01	*
24.	8.4535383E-01	2.3015068E+01	*	74.	5.9571077E-01	5.8553662E+01	*
25.	8.3945701E-01	2.3854525E+01	*	75.	5.9155536E-01	5.9145217E+01	*
26.	8.3360133E-01	2.4688126E+01	*	76.	5.8742893E-01	5.9732645E+01	*
27.	8.2778650E-01	2.5515912E+01	*	77.	5.8333129E-01	6.0315976E+01	*
28.	8.2201223E-01	2.6337924E+01	*	78.	5.7926223E-01	6.0895238E+01	*
29.	8.1627823E-01	2.7154202E+01	*	79.	5.7522155E-01	6.1470459E+01	*
30.	8.1058424E-01	2.7964786E+01	*	80.	5.7120906E-01	6.2041668E+01	*
31.	8.0492996E-01	2.8769715E+01	*	81.	5.6722456E-01	6.2608892E+01	*
32.	7.9931513E-01	2.9569030E+01	*	82.	5.6326785E-01	6.3172159E+01	*
33.	7.9373946E-01	3.0362769E+01	*	83.	5.5933874E-01	6.3731497E+01	*
34.	7.8820269E-01	3.1150971E+01	*	84.	5.5543704E-01	6.4286934E+01	*
35.	7.8270453E-01	3.1933675E+01	*	85.	5.5156256E-01	6.4838496E+01	*
36.	7.7724473E-01	3.2710919E+01	*	86.	5.4771510E-01	6.5386211E+01	*
37.	7.7182302E-01	3.3482742E+01	*	87.	5.4389449E-01	6.5930105E+01	*
38.	7.6643912E-01	3.4249181E+01	*	88.	5.4010052E-01	6.6470205E+01	*
39.	7.6109278E-01	3.5010273E+01	*	89.	5.3633302E-01	6.7006538E+01	*
40.	7.5578374E-01	3.5766056E+01	*	90.	5.3259179E-01	6.7539129E+01	*
41.	7.5051172E-01	3.6516567E+01	*	91.	5.2887667E-01	6.8068005E+01	*
42.	7.4527648E-01	3.7261843E+01	*	92.	5.2518746E-01	6.8593192E+01	*
43.	7.4007777E-01	3.8001920E+01	*	93.	5.2152399E-01	6.9114715E+01	*
44.	7.3491531E-01	3.8736835E+01	*	94.	5.1788607E-01	6.9632601E+01	*
45.	7.2978887E-01	3.9466623E+01	*	95.	5.1427352E-01	7.0146874E+01	*
46.	7.2469818E-01	4.0191321E+01	*	96.	5.1068618E-01	7.0657560E+01	*
47.	7.1964301E-01	4.0910964E+01	*	97.	5.0712386E-01	7.1164683E+01	*
48.	7.1462310E-01	4.1625587E+01	*	98.	5.0358638E-01	7.1668269E+01	*
49.	7.0963820E-01	4.2335225E+01	*	99.	5.0007359E-01	7.2168342E+01	*
50.	7.0468808E-01	4.3039913E+01	*	100.	4.9658530E-01	7.2664927E+01	*

TABULATED VALUES OF E   WHEN R = .008

X	E (-RX)	SUM OF E (-RX)	*	X	E (-RX)	SUM OF E (-RX)	*
0.	1.0000000E+00	1.0000000E+00	*	50.	6.7032004E-01	4.2045354E+01	*
1.	9.9203191E-01	1.9920319E+00	*	51.	6.6497887E-01	4.2710332E+01	*
2.	9.8412731E-01	2.9761592E+00	*	52.	6.5968026E-01	4.3370012E+01	*
3.	9.7628570E-01	3.9524449E+00	*	53.	6.5442387E-01	4.4024435E+01	*
4.	9.6850658E-01	4.9209514E+00	*	54.	6.4920937E-01	4.4673644E+01	*
5.	9.6078943E-01	5.8817408E+00	*	55.	6.4403641E-01	4.5317680E+01	*
6.	9.5313378E-01	6.8348745E+00	*	56.	6.3890468E-01	4.5956584E+01	*
7.	9.4553913E-01	7.7804136E+00	*	57.	6.3381383E-01	4.6590397E+01	*
8.	9.3800499E-01	8.7184185E+00	*	58.	6.2876355E-01	4.7217160E+01	*
9.	9.3053089E-01	9.6489493E+00	*	59.	6.2375351E-01	4.7842913E+01	*
10.	9.2311634E-01	1.0572065E+01	*	60.	6.1878339E-01	4.8461696E+01	*
11.	9.1576087E-01	1.1487825E+01	*	61.	6.1385287E-01	4.9075548E+01	*
12.	9.0846401E-01	1.2396289E+01	*	62.	6.0896164E-01	4.9684509E+01	*
13.	9.0122529E-01	1.3297514E+01	*	63.	6.0410938E-01	5.0288618E+01	*
14.	8.9404425E-01	1.4191558E+01	*	64.	5.9929578E-01	5.0887913E+01	*
15.	8.8692043E-01	1.5078478E+01	*	65.	5.9452054E-01	5.1482433E+01	*
16.	8.7985337E-01	1.5958331E+01	*	66.	5.8978335E-01	5.2072216E+01	*
17.	8.7284263E-01	1.6831173E+01	*	67.	5.8508391E-01	5.2657299E+01	*
18.	8.6588774E-01	1.7697060E+01	*	68.	5.8042191E-01	5.3237720E+01	*
19.	8.5898827E-01	1.8556048E+01	*	69.	5.7579706E-01	5.3813517E+01	*
20.	8.5214378E-01	1.9408191E+01	*	70.	5.7120906E-01	5.4384726E+01	*
21.	8.4535383E-01	2.0253544E+01	*	71.	5.6665762E-01	5.4951383E+01	*
22.	8.3861798E-01	2.1092161E+01	*	72.	5.6214244E-01	5.5513525E+01	*
23.	8.3193580E-01	2.1924096E+01	*	73.	5.5766324E-01	5.6071188E+01	*
24.	8.2530686E-01	2.2749402E+01	*	74.	5.5321973E-01	5.6624407E+01	*
25.	8.1873073E-01	2.3568132E+01	*	75.	5.4881163E-01	5.7173218E+01	*
26.	8.1220703E-01	2.4380339E+01	*	76.	5.4443865E-01	5.7717656E+01	*
27.	8.0573530E-01	2.5186074E+01	*	77.	5.4010052E-01	5.8257756E+01	*
28.	7.9931513E-01	2.5985389E+01	*	78.	5.3579695E-01	5.8793552E+01	*
29.	7.9294612E-01	2.6778335E+01	*	79.	5.3152768E-01	5.9325079E+01	*
30.	7.8662786E-01	2.7564962E+01	*	80.	5.2729242E-01	5.9852371E+01	*
31.	7.8035994E-01	2.8345321E+01	*	81.	5.2309091E-01	6.0375461E+01	*
32.	7.7414196E-01	2.9119462E+01	*	82.	5.1892287E-01	6.0894383E+01	*
33.	7.6797353E-01	2.9887435E+01	*	83.	5.1478805E-01	6.1409171E+01	*
34.	7.6185426E-01	3.0649289E+01	*	84.	5.1068618E-01	6.1919857E+01	*
35.	7.5578374E-01	3.1405072E+01	*	85.	5.0661699E-01	6.2426473E+01	*
36.	7.4976159E-01	3.2154833E+01	*	86.	5.0258022E-01	6.2929053E+01	*
37.	7.4378742E-01	3.2898620E+01	*	87.	4.9857562E-01	6.3427628E+01	*
38.	7.3786086E-01	3.3636480E+01	*	88.	4.9460292E-01	6.3922230E+01	*
39.	7.3198152E-01	3.4368461E+01	*	89.	4.9066189E-01	6.4412891E+01	*
40.	7.2614903E-01	3.5094610E+01	*	90.	4.8675225E-01	6.4899643E+01	*
41.	7.2036301E-01	3.5814973E+01	*	91.	4.8287377E-01	6.5382516E+01	*
42.	7.1462310E-01	3.6529596E+01	*	92.	4.7902619E-01	6.5861542E+01	*
43.	7.0892892E-01	3.7238524E+01	*	93.	4.7520927E-01	6.6336751E+01	*
44.	7.0328012E-01	3.7941804E+01	*	94.	4.7142276E-01	6.6808173E+01	*
45.	6.9767632E-01	3.8639480E+01	*	95.	4.6766642E-01	6.7275839E+01	*
46.	6.9211717E-01	3.9331597E+01	*	96.	4.6394002E-01	6.7739779E+01	*
47.	6.8660233E-01	4.0018199E+01	*	97.	4.6024330E-01	6.8200022E+01	*
48.	6.8113142E-01	4.0699330E+01	*	98.	4.5657604E-01	6.8656598E+01	*
49.	6.7570411E-01	4.1375034E+01	*	99.	4.5293801E-01	6.9109536E+01	*
50.	6.7032004E-01	4.2045354E+01	*	100.	4.4932896E-01	6.9558864E+01	*

	-RX					-RX		

TABULATED VALUES OF E   WHEN R = .009

	-RX	-RX				-RX	-RX	
x	E	SUM OF E	*	x	E	SUM OF E	*
0.	1.0000000E+00	1.0000000E+00	*	50.	6.3762814E-01	4.1082602E+01	*
1.	9.9104037E-01	1.9910403E+00	*	51.	6.3191524E-01	4.1714517E+01	*
2.	9.8216103E-01	2.9732013E+00	*	52.	6.2625352E-01	4.2340770E+01	*
3.	9.7336124E-01	3.9465625E+00	*	53.	6.2064252E-01	4.2961412E+01	*
4.	9.6464029E-01	4.9112027E+00	*	54.	6.1508180E-01	4.3576493E+01	*
5.	9.5599748E-01	5.8672001E+00	*	55.	6.0957090E-01	4.4186063E+01	*
6.	9.4743210E-01	6.8146322E+00	*	56.	6.0410938E-01	4.4790172E+01	*
7.	9.3894347E-01	7.7535756E+00	*	57.	5.9869678E-01	4.5388868E+01	*
8.	9.3053089E-01	8.6841064E+00	*	58.	5.9333269E-01	4.5982200E+01	*
9.	9.2219369E-01	9.6063000E+00	*	59.	5.8801665E-01	4.6570216E+01	*
10.	9.1393118E-01	1.0520231E+01	*	60.	5.8274825E-01	4.7152964E+01	*
11.	9.0574270E-01	1.1425973E+01	*	61.	5.7752704E-01	4.7730491E+01	*
12.	8.9762759E-01	1.2323600E+01	*	62.	5.7235262E-01	4.8302843E+01	*
13.	8.8958519E-01	1.3213185E+01	*	63.	5.6722456E-01	4.8870067E+01	*
14.	8.8161484E-01	1.4094799E+01	*	64.	5.6214244E-01	4.9432209E+01	*
15.	8.7371591E-01	1.4968514E+01	*	65.	5.5710586E-01	4.9989314E+01	*
16.	8.6588776E-01	1.5834401E+01	*	66.	5.5211440E-01	5.0541428E+01	*
17.	8.5812971E-01	1.6692530E+01	*	67.	5.4716766E-01	5.1088595E+01	*
18.	8.5044120E-01	1.7542971E+01	*	68.	5.4226525E-01	5.1630760E+01	*
19.	8.4282157E-01	1.8385792E+01	*	69.	5.3740676E-01	5.2168266E+01	*
20.	8.3527020E-01	1.9221062E+01	*	70.	5.3259179E-01	5.2700857E+01	*
21.	8.2778650E-01	2.0048848E+01	*	71.	5.2781997E-01	5.3228676E+01	*
22.	8.2036985E-01	2.0869217E+01	*	72.	5.2309091E-01	5.3751766E+01	*
23.	8.1301964E-01	2.1682236E+01	*	73.	5.1840421E-01	5.4270170E+01	*
24.	8.0573509E-01	2.2487971E+01	*	74.	5.1375950E-01	5.4783929E+01	*
25.	7.9851621E-01	2.3286487E+01	*	75.	5.0915641E-01	5.5293085E+01	*
26.	7.9136181E-01	2.4077848E+01	*	76.	5.0459456E-01	5.5797679E+01	*
27.	7.8427151E-01	2.4862119E+01	*	77.	5.0007359E-01	5.6297752E+01	*
28.	7.7724473E-01	2.5639363E+01	*	78.	4.9559312E-01	5.6793345E+01	*
29.	7.7028091E-01	2.6409643E+01	*	79.	4.9115279E-01	5.7284497E+01	*
30.	7.6337949E-01	2.7173022E+01	*	80.	4.8675225E-01	5.7771249E+01	*
31.	7.5653990E-01	2.7929561E+01	*	81.	4.8239113E-01	5.8253640E+01	*
32.	7.4976159E-01	2.8679322E+01	*	82.	4.7806909E-01	5.8731709E+01	*
33.	7.4304401E-01	2.9422366E+01	*	83.	4.7378577E-01	5.9205494E+01	*
34.	7.3638661E-01	3.0158752E+01	*	84.	4.6954083E-01	5.9675034E+01	*
35.	7.2978887E-01	3.0888540E+01	*	85.	4.6533393E-01	6.0140367E+01	*
36.	7.2325024E-01	3.1611790E+01	*	86.	4.6116471E-01	6.0601531E+01	*
37.	7.1677019E-01	3.2328560E+01	*	87.	4.5703285E-01	6.1058563E+01	*
38.	7.1034820E-01	3.3038908E+01	*	88.	4.5293801E-01	6.1511501E+01	*
39.	7.0398375E-01	3.3742891E+01	*	89.	4.4887985E-01	6.1960380E+01	*
40.	6.9767632E-01	3.4440567E+01	*	90.	4.4485806E-01	6.2405238E+01	*
41.	6.9142540E-01	3.5131992E+01	*	91.	4.4087230E-01	6.2846110E+01	*
42.	6.8523049E-01	3.5817222E+01	*	92.	4.3692225E-01	6.3283032E+01	*
43.	6.7909109E-01	3.6496313E+01	*	93.	4.3300759E-01	6.3716039E+01	*
44.	6.7300669E-01	3.7169519E+01	*	94.	4.2912801E-01	6.4145167E+01	*
45.	6.6697680E-01	3.7836295E+01	*	95.	4.2528319E-01	6.4570450E+01	*
46.	6.6100094E-01	3.8497295E+01	*	96.	4.2147281E-01	6.4991922E+01	*
47.	6.5507863E-01	3.9152373E+01	*	97.	4.1769657E-01	6.5409618E+01	*
48.	6.4920937E-01	3.9801562E+01	*	98.	4.1395417E-01	6.5823572E+01	*
49.	6.4339270E-01	4.0444974E+01	*	99.	4.1024530E-01	6.6233817E+01	*
50.	6.3762814E-01	4.1082602E+01	*	100.	4.0656965E-01	6.6640386E+01	*

-RX

TABULATED VALUES OF E   WHEN R = .010

	-RX	-RX				-RX	-RX	
x	E	SUM OF E	*	x	E	SUM OF E	*
0.	1.0000000E+00	1.0000000E+00	*	50.	6.0653065E-01	4.0150507E+01	*
1.	9.9004983E-01	1.9900498E+00	*	51.	6.0049557E-01	4.0751002E+01	*
2.	9.8019867E-01	2.9702484E+00	*	52.	5.9452054E-01	4.1345522E+01	*
3.	9.7044553E-01	3.9406939E+00	*	53.	5.8860496E-01	4.1934126E+01	*
4.	9.6078943E-01	4.9014833E+00	*	54.	5.8274825E-01	4.2516874E+01	*
5.	9.5122942E-01	5.8527127E+00	*	55.	5.7694980E-01	4.3093823E+01	*
6.	9.4176453E-01	6.7944772E+00	*	56.	5.7120906E-01	4.3665032E+01	*
7.	9.3239381E-01	7.7268710E+00	*	57.	5.6552543E-01	4.4230557E+01	*
8.	9.2311634E-01	8.6499873E+00	*	58.	5.5989836E-01	4.4790455E+01	*
9.	9.1393118E-01	9.5639184E+00	*	59.	5.5432728E-01	4.5344782E+01	*
10.	9.0483741E-01	1.0468755E+01	*	60.	5.4881163E-01	4.5893593E+01	*
11.	8.9583413E-01	1.1364589E+01	*	61.	5.4335086E-01	4.6436943E+01	*
12.	8.8692043E-01	1.2251509E+01	*	62.	5.3794443E-01	4.6974887E+01	*
13.	8.7809542E-01	1.3129604E+01	*	63.	5.3259179E-01	4.7507478E+01	*
14.	8.6935823E-01	1.3998962E+01	*	64.	5.2729242E-01	4.8034770E+01	*
15.	8.6070797E-01	1.4859669E+01	*	65.	5.2204577E-01	4.8556815E+01	*
16.	8.5214378E-01	1.5711812E+01	*	66.	5.1685133E-01	4.9073666E+01	*
17.	8.4366481E-01	1.6555476E+01	*	67.	5.1170857E-01	4.9585374E+01	*
18.	8.3527020E-01	1.7390746E+01	*	68.	5.0661699E-01	5.0091990E+01	*
19.	8.2695912E-01	1.8217705E+01	*	69.	5.0157606E-01	5.0593666E+01	*
20.	8.1873075E-01	1.9036435E+01	*	70.	4.9658530E-01	5.1090151E+01	*
21.	8.1058424E-01	1.9847019E+01	*	71.	4.9164419E-01	5.1581795E+01	*
22.	8.0251879E-01	2.0649537E+01	*	72.	4.8675225E-01	5.2068547E+01	*
23.	7.9453359E-01	2.1444070E+01	*	73.	4.8190898E-01	5.2550455E+01	*
24.	7.8662786E-01	2.2230697E+01	*	74.	4.7711391E-01	5.3027568E+01	*
25.	7.7880078E-01	2.3009497E+01	*	75.	4.7236655E-01	5.3499934E+01	*
26.	7.7105158E-01	2.3780548E+01	*	76.	4.6766642E-01	5.3967600E+01	*
27.	7.6337949E-01	2.4543927E+01	*	77.	4.6301306E-01	5.4430613E+01	*
28.	7.5578374E-01	2.5299710E+01	*	78.	4.5840601E-01	5.4889019E+01	*
29.	7.4826356E-01	2.6047973E+01	*	79.	4.5384479E-01	5.5342863E+01	*
30.	7.4081821E-01	2.6788791E+01	*	80.	4.4932896E-01	5.5792191E+01	*
31.	7.3344695E-01	2.7522237E+01	*	81.	4.4485806E-01	5.6237049E+01	*
32.	7.2614903E-01	2.8248366E+01	*	82.	4.4043165E-01	5.6677480E+01	*
33.	7.1892373E-01	2.8967309E+01	*	83.	4.3604928E-01	5.7113529E+01	*
34.	7.1177032E-01	2.9679079E+01	*	84.	4.3171052E-01	5.7545239E+01	*
35.	7.0468808E-01	3.0383767E+01	*	85.	4.2741493E-01	5.7972653E+01	*
36.	6.9767632E-01	3.1081443E+01	*	86.	4.2316208E-01	5.8395815E+01	*
37.	6.9073432E-01	3.1772177E+01	*	87.	4.1895154E-01	5.8814766E+01	*
38.	6.8386140E-01	3.2456038E+01	*	88.	4.1478291E-01	5.9229544E+01	*
39.	6.7705687E-01	3.3133094E+01	*	89.	4.1065575E-01	5.9640203E+01	*
40.	6.7032004E-01	3.3803414E+01	*	90.	4.0656965E-01	6.0046772E+01	*
41.	6.6365024E-01	3.4467064E+01	*	91.	4.0252422E-01	6.0449296E+01	*
42.	6.5704681E-01	3.5124110E+01	*	92.	3.9851903E-01	6.0847815E+01	*
43.	6.5050909E-01	3.5774619E+01	*	93.	3.9455370E-01	6.1242346E+01	*
44.	6.4403641E-01	3.6418655E+01	*	94.	3.9062783E-01	6.1632495E+01	*
45.	6.3762814E-01	3.7056283E+01	*	95.	3.8674102E-01	6.2019736E+01	*
46.	6.3128364E-01	3.7687566E+01	*	96.	3.8289288E-01	6.2402629E+01	*
47.	6.2500226E-01	3.8312568E+01	*	97.	3.7907303E-01	6.2781711E+01	*
48.	6.1878339E-01	3.8931351E+01	*	98.	3.7531109E-01	6.3157022E+01	*
49.	6.1262639E-01	3.9543977E+01	*	99.	3.7157669E-01	6.3528598E+01	*
50.	6.0653065E-01	4.0150507E+01	*	100.	3.6787944E-01	6.3896477E+01	*

TABULATED VALUES OF E^{-RX} WHEN R = .011

X	E^{-RX}	SUM OF E^{-RX}	*	X	E^{-RX}	SUM OF E^{-RX}	*
0.	1.0000000E+00	1.0000000E+00	*	50.	5.7694980E-01	3.9247949E+01	*
1.	9.8906027E-01	1.9890602E+00	*	51.	5.7063813E-01	3.9818587E+01	*
2.	9.7824023E-01	2.9673004E+00	*	52.	5.6439551E-01	4.0382982E+01	*
3.	9.6753855E-01	3.9348389E+00	*	53.	5.5822118E-01	4.0941203E+01	*
4.	9.5695395E-01	4.8917928E+00	*	54.	5.5211440E-01	4.1493317E+01	*
5.	9.4648514E-01	5.8382779E+00	*	55.	5.4607442E-01	4.2039391E+01	*
6.	9.3613086E-01	6.7744087E+00	*	56.	5.4010052E-01	4.2579491E+01	*
7.	9.2588985E-01	7.7002985E+00	*	57.	5.3419197E-01	4.3113682E+01	*
8.	9.1576087E-01	8.6160593E+00	*	58.	5.2834806E-01	4.3642030E+01	*
9.	9.0574270E-01	9.5218020E+00	*	59.	5.2256808E-01	4.4164598E+01	*
10.	8.9583413E-01	1.0417636E+01	*	60.	5.1685133E-01	4.4681449E+01	*
11.	8.8603395E-01	1.1303669E+01	*	61.	5.1119710E-01	4.5192646E+01	*
12.	8.7634099E-01	1.2180009E+01	*	62.	5.0560476E-01	4.5698250E+01	*
13.	8.6675406E-01	1.3046763E+01	*	63.	5.0007359E-01	4.6198323E+01	*
14.	8.5727201E-01	1.3904035E+01	*	64.	4.9460292E-01	4.6692925E+01	*
15.	8.4789370E-01	1.4751928E+01	*	65.	4.8919211E-01	4.7182117E+01	*
16.	8.3861798E-01	1.5590545E+01	*	66.	4.8384048E-01	4.7665957E+01	*
17.	8.2944373E-01	1.6419988E+01	*	67.	4.7854740E-01	4.8144504E+01	*
18.	8.2036985E-01	1.7240357E+01	*	68.	4.7331223E-01	4.8617816E+01	*
19.	8.1139523E-01	1.8051752E+01	*	69.	4.6813432E-01	4.9085950E+01	*
20.	8.0251879E-01	1.8854270E+01	*	70.	4.6301306E-01	4.9548963E+01	*
21.	7.9373946E-01	1.9648009E+01	*	71.	4.5794783E-01	5.0006910E+01	*
22.	7.8505617E-01	2.0433065E+01	*	72.	4.5293801E-01	5.0459848E+01	*
23.	7.7646788E-01	2.1209532E+01	*	73.	4.4798299E-01	5.0907830E+01	*
24.	7.6797353E-01	2.1977505E+01	*	74.	4.4308218E-01	5.1350912E+01	*
25.	7.5957212E-01	2.2737077E+01	*	75.	4.3823499E-01	5.1789146E+01	*
26.	7.5126261E-01	2.3488339E+01	*	76.	4.3344082E-01	5.2222586E+01	*
27.	7.4304401E-01	2.4231383E+01	*	77.	4.2869910E-01	5.2651285E+01	*
28.	7.3491531E-01	2.4966298E+01	*	78.	4.2400925E-01	5.3075294E+01	*
29.	7.2687554E-01	2.5693173E+01	*	79.	4.1937070E-01	5.3494646E+01	*
30.	7.1892373E-01	2.6412096E+01	*	80.	4.1478291E-01	5.3909446E+01	*
31.	7.1105890E-01	2.7123154E+01	*	81.	4.1024530E-01	5.4319691E+01	*
32.	7.0328012E-01	2.7826434E+01	*	82.	4.0575733E-01	5.4725448E+01	*
33.	6.9558643E-01	2.8522020E+01	*	83.	4.0131845E-01	5.5126766E+01	*
34.	6.8797690E-01	2.9209996E+01	*	84.	3.9692814E-01	5.5523694E+01	*
35.	6.8045063E-01	2.9890446E+01	*	85.	3.9258586E-01	5.5916279E+01	*
36.	6.7300669E-01	3.0563452E+01	*	86.	3.8829108E-01	5.6304570E+01	*
37.	6.6564418E-01	3.1229096E+01	*	87.	3.8404328E-01	5.6688613E+01	*
38.	6.5836222E-01	3.1887458E+01	*	88.	3.7984196E-01	5.7068454E+01	*
39.	6.5115992E-01	3.2538617E+01	*	89.	3.7568659E-01	5.7444140E+01	*
40.	6.4403641E-01	3.3182653E+01	*	90.	3.7157669E-01	5.7815716E+01	*
41.	6.3699083E-01	3.3819643E+01	*	91.	3.6751174E-01	5.8183227E+01	*
42.	6.3002233E-01	3.4449665E+01	*	92.	3.6349126E-01	5.8546718E+01	*
43.	6.2313007E-01	3.5072795E+01	*	93.	3.5951477E-01	5.8906232E+01	*
44.	6.1631320E-01	3.5689108E+01	*	94.	3.5558178E-01	5.9261813E+01	*
45.	6.0957090E-01	3.6298678E+01	*	95.	3.5169181E-01	5.9613504E+01	*
46.	6.0290237E-01	3.6901580E+01	*	96.	3.4784440E-01	5.9961348E+01	*
47.	5.9630678E-01	3.7497886E+01	*	97.	3.4403908E-01	6.0305387E+01	*
48.	5.8978335E-01	3.8087669E+01	*	98.	3.4027539E-01	6.0645662E+01	*
49.	5.8333129E-01	3.8671000E+01	*	99.	3.3655287E-01	6.0982214E+01	*
50.	5.7694980E-01	3.9247949E+01	*	100.	3.3287108E-01	6.1315085E+01	*

TABULATED VALUES OF E^{-RX} WHEN R = .012

X	E^{-RX}	SUM OF E^{-RX}	*	X	E^{-RX}	SUM OF E^{-RX}	*
0.	1.0000000E+00	1.0000000E+00	*	50.	5.4881163E-01	3.8373866E+01	*
1.	9.8807171E-01	1.9880717E+00	*	51.	5.4226525E-01	3.8916131E+01	*
2.	9.7628570E-01	2.9643574E+00	*	52.	5.3579695E-01	3.9451927E+01	*
3.	9.6464029E-01	3.9289976E+00	*	53.	5.2940581E-01	3.9981332E+01	*
4.	9.5313378E-01	4.8821313E+00	*	54.	5.2309091E-01	4.0504422E+01	*
5.	9.4176453E-01	5.8238958E+00	*	55.	5.1685133E-01	4.1021273E+01	*
6.	9.3053089E-01	6.7544266E+00	*	56.	5.1068618E-01	4.1531959E+01	*
7.	9.1943125E-01	7.6738578E+00	*	57.	5.0459456E-01	4.2036553E+01	*
8.	9.0846401E-01	8.5823218E+00	*	58.	4.9857562E-01	4.2535128E+01	*
9.	8.9762759E-01	9.4799493E+00	*	59.	4.9262848E-01	4.3027756E+01	*
10.	8.8692043E-01	1.0366889E+01	*	60.	4.8675225E-01	4.3514508E+01	*
11.	8.7634099E-01	1.1243209E+01	*	61.	4.8094613E-01	4.3995454E+01	*
12.	8.6588774E-01	1.2109096E+01	*	62.	4.7520927E-01	4.4470663E+01	*
13.	8.5555918E-01	1.2964655E+01	*	63.	4.6954083E-01	4.4940203E+01	*
14.	8.4535383E-01	1.3810008E+01	*	64.	4.6394002E-01	4.5404143E+01	*
15.	8.3527020E-01	1.4645278E+01	*	65.	4.5840601E-01	4.5862549E+01	*
16.	8.2530686E-01	1.5470584E+01	*	66.	4.5293801E-01	4.6315487E+01	*
17.	8.1546236E-01	1.6286046E+01	*	67.	4.4753523E-01	4.6763022E+01	*
18.	8.0573530E-01	1.7091781E+01	*	68.	4.4219690E-01	4.7205218E+01	*
19.	7.9612425E-01	1.7887905E+01	*	69.	4.3692225E-01	4.7642140E+01	*
20.	7.8662786E-01	1.8674532E+01	*	70.	4.3171052E-01	4.8073850E+01	*
21.	7.7724473E-01	1.9451776E+01	*	71.	4.2656095E-01	4.8500410E+01	*
22.	7.6797353E-01	2.0219749E+01	*	72.	4.2147281E-01	4.8921882E+01	*
23.	7.5881293E-01	2.0978561E+01	*	73.	4.1644536E-01	4.9338327E+01	*
24.	7.4976159E-01	2.1728322E+01	*	74.	4.1147788E-01	4.9749804E+01	*
25.	7.4081821E-01	2.2469140E+01	*	75.	4.0656965E-01	5.0156373E+01	*
26.	7.3198152E-01	2.3201121E+01	*	76.	4.0171997E-01	5.0558092E+01	*
27.	7.2325024E-01	2.3924371E+01	*	77.	3.9692814E-01	5.0955020E+01	*
28.	7.1462301E-01	2.4638994E+01	*	78.	3.9219347E-01	5.1347213E+01	*
29.	7.0609887E-01	2.5345092E+01	*	79.	3.8751527E-01	5.1734728E+01	*
30.	6.9767632E-01	2.6042768E+01	*	80.	3.8289288E-01	5.2117620E+01	*
31.	6.8935424E-01	2.6732122E+01	*	81.	3.7832562E-01	5.2495945E+01	*
32.	6.8113142E-01	2.7413253E+01	*	82.	3.7381285E-01	5.2869757E+01	*
33.	6.7300669E-01	2.8086259E+01	*	83.	3.6935390E-01	5.3239110E+01	*
34.	6.6497887E-01	2.8751237E+01	*	84.	3.6494814E-01	5.3604058E+01	*
35.	6.5704681E-01	2.9408283E+01	*	85.	3.6059493E-01	5.3966652E+01	*
36.	6.4920937E-01	3.0057542E+01	*	86.	3.5629365E-01	5.4320945E+01	*
37.	6.4146541E-01	3.0698957E+01	*	87.	3.5204368E-01	5.4672988E+01	*
38.	6.3381383E-01	3.1332770E+01	*	88.	3.4784440E-01	5.5020832E+01	*
39.	6.2625352E-01	3.1959023E+01	*	89.	3.4369522E-01	5.5364527E+01	*
40.	6.1878339E-01	3.2577806E+01	*	90.	3.3959552E-01	5.5704122E+01	*
41.	6.1140236E-01	3.3189208E+01	*	91.	3.3554473E-01	5.6039666E+01	*
42.	6.0410938E-01	3.3793317E+01	*	92.	3.3154225E-01	5.6371208E+01	*
43.	5.9690339E-01	3.4390220E+01	*	93.	3.2758752E-01	5.6698795E+01	*
44.	5.8978335E-01	3.4980003E+01	*	94.	3.2367996E-01	5.7022476E+01	*
45.	5.8274825E-01	3.5562751E+01	*	95.	3.1981902E-01	5.7342293E+01	*
46.	5.7579706E-01	3.6138548E+01	*	96.	3.1600412E-01	5.7658297E+01	*
47.	5.6892878E-01	3.6707476E+01	*	97.	3.1223474E-01	5.7970531E+01	*
48.	5.6214244E-01	3.7269618E+01	*	98.	3.0851031E-01	5.8279041E+01	*
49.	5.5543704E-01	3.7825055E+01	*	99.	3.0483031E-01	5.8583871E+01	*
50.	5.4881163E-01	3.8373866E+01	*	100.	3.0119421E-01	5.8885065E+01	*

143

TABULATED VALUES OF E WHEN R = .013

X	E $^{-RX}$	SUM OF E $^{-RX}$	*	X	E $^{-RX}$	SUM OF E $^{-RX}$	*
0.	1.0000000E+00	1.0000000E+00	*	50.	5.2204577E-01	3.7527226E+01	*
1.	9.8708413E-01	1.9870841E+00	*	51.	5.1530310E-01	3.8042529E+01	*
2.	9.7433508E-01	2.9614191E+00	*	52.	5.0864751E-01	3.8551176E+01	*
3.	9.6175070E-01	3.9231698E+00	*	53.	5.0207789E-01	3.9053253E+01	*
4.	9.4932888E-01	4.8724986E+00	*	54.	4.9559312E-01	3.9548846E+01	*
5.	9.3706746E-01	5.8095660E+00	*	55.	4.8919211E-01	4.0037803E+01	*
6.	9.2496442E-01	6.7345304E+00	*	56.	4.8287377E-01	4.0520911E+01	*
7.	9.1301770E-01	7.6475481E+00	*	57.	4.7663703E-01	4.0997548E+01	*
8.	9.0122529E-01	8.5487733E+00	*	58.	4.7048085E-01	4.1468028E+01	*
9.	8.8958519E-01	9.4383584E+00	*	59.	4.6440419E-01	4.1932432E+01	*
10.	8.7809542E-01	1.0316453E+01	*	60.	4.5840601E-01	4.2390838E+01	*
11.	8.6675406E-01	1.1183207E+01	*	61.	4.5248530E-01	4.2843323E+01	*
12.	8.5555918E-01	1.2038766E+01	*	62.	4.4664106E-01	4.3289964E+01	*
13.	8.4450890E-01	1.2883274E+01	*	63.	4.4087230E-01	4.3730836E+01	*
14.	8.3360133E-01	1.3716875E+01	*	64.	4.3517805E-01	4.4166014E+01	*
15.	8.2283465E-01	1.4539709E+01	*	65.	4.2955735E-01	4.4595571E+01	*
16.	8.1220703E-01	1.5351916E+01	*	66.	4.2400925E-01	4.5019500E+01	*
17.	8.0171667E-01	1.6153632E+01	*	67.	4.1853280E-01	4.5438112E+01	*
18.	7.9136181E-01	1.6944993E+01	*	68.	4.1312709E-01	4.5851239E+01	*
19.	7.8114069E-01	1.7726133E+01	*	69.	4.0779119E-01	4.6259030E+01	*
20.	7.7105158E-01	1.8497184E+01	*	70.	4.0252422E-01	4.6661554E+01	*
21.	7.6109278E-01	1.9258276E+01	*	71.	3.9732527E-01	4.7058879E+01	*
22.	7.5126261E-01	2.0009538E+01	*	72.	3.9219347E-01	4.7451072E+01	*
23.	7.4155940E-01	2.0751097E+01	*	73.	3.8712795E-01	4.7838199E+01	*
24.	7.3198152E-01	2.1483078E+01	*	74.	3.8212786E-01	4.8220326E+01	*
25.	7.2252735E-01	2.2205605E+01	*	75.	3.7719235E-01	4.8597518E+01	*
26.	7.1319528E-01	2.2918800E+01	*	76.	3.7232058E-01	4.8969838E+01	*
27.	7.0398375E-01	2.3622783E+01	*	77.	3.6751174E-01	4.9337349E+01	*
28.	6.9489119E-01	2.4317674E+01	*	78.	3.6276501E-01	4.9700114E+01	*
29.	6.8591607E-01	2.5003590E+01	*	79.	3.5807958E-01	5.0058193E+01	*
30.	6.7705687E-01	2.5680646E+01	*	80.	3.5345468E-01	5.0411647E+01	*
31.	6.6831209E-01	2.6348958E+01	*	81.	3.4888950E-01	5.0760536E+01	*
32.	6.5968026E-01	2.7008638E+01	*	82.	3.4438329E-01	5.1104919E+01	*
33.	6.5115992E-01	2.7659797E+01	*	83.	3.3993529E-01	5.1444854E+01	*
34.	6.4274963E-01	2.8302546E+01	*	84.	3.3554473E-01	5.1780398E+01	*
35.	6.3444796E-01	2.8936993E+01	*	85.	3.3121088E-01	5.2111608E+01	*
36.	6.2625352E-01	2.9563246E+01	*	86.	3.2693300E-01	5.2438541E+01	*
37.	6.1816491E-01	3.0181410E+01	*	87.	3.2271038E-01	5.2761251E+01	*
38.	6.1018078E-01	3.0791590E+01	*	88.	3.1854229E-01	5.3079793E+01	*
39.	6.0229976E-01	3.1393889E+01	*	89.	3.1442805E-01	5.3394221E+01	*
40.	5.9452054E-01	3.1988409E+01	*	90.	3.1036694E-01	5.3704587E+01	*
41.	5.8684180E-01	3.2575250E+01	*	91.	3.0635828E-01	5.4010945E+01	*
42.	5.7926223E-01	3.3154512E+01	*	92.	3.0240140E-01	5.4313346E+01	*
43.	5.7178055E-01	3.3726292E+01	*	93.	2.9849562E-01	5.4611841E+01	*
44.	5.6439551E-01	3.4290687E+01	*	94.	2.9464029E-01	5.4906481E+01	*
45.	5.5710586E-01	3.4847792E+01	*	95.	2.9083476E-01	5.5197315E+01	*
46.	5.4991035E-01	3.5397702E+01	*	96.	2.8707837E-01	5.5484393E+01	*
47.	5.4280778E-01	3.5940509E+01	*	97.	2.8337051E-01	5.5767763E+01	*
48.	5.3579695E-01	3.6476305E+01	*	98.	2.7971053E-01	5.6047473E+01	*
49.	5.2887667E-01	3.7005181E+01	*	99.	2.7609783E-01	5.6323570E+01	*
50.	5.2204577E-01	3.7527226E+01	*	100.	2.7253179E-01	5.6596101E+01	*

TABULATED VALUES OF E WHEN R = .014

X	E $^{-RX}$	SUM OF E $^{-RX}$	*	X	E $^{-RX}$	SUM OF E $^{-RX}$	*
0.	1.0000000E+00	1.0000000E+00	*	50.	4.9658530E-01	3.6707056E+01	*
1.	9.8609754E-01	1.9860975E+00	*	51.	4.8968154E-01	3.7196737E+01	*
2.	9.7238836E-01	2.9584858E+00	*	52.	4.8287377E-01	3.7679610E+01	*
3.	9.5886977E-01	3.9173555E+00	*	53.	4.7616064E-01	3.8155770E+01	*
4.	9.4553913E-01	4.8628946E+00	*	54.	4.6954083E-01	3.8625310E+01	*
5.	9.3239381E-01	5.7952884E+00	*	55.	4.6301304E-01	3.9088323E+01	*
6.	9.1943125E-01	6.7147196E+00	*	56.	4.5657604E-01	3.9544098E+01	*
7.	9.0664890E-01	7.6213685E+00	*	57.	4.5022852E-01	3.9995127E+01	*
8.	8.9404425E-01	8.5154127E+00	*	58.	4.4396923E-01	4.0439096E+01	*
9.	8.8161484E-01	9.3970275E+00	*	59.	4.3779697E-01	4.0876892E+01	*
10.	8.6935823E-01	1.0266385E+01	*	60.	4.3171052E-01	4.1308602E+01	*
11.	8.5727201E-01	1.1123657E+01	*	61.	4.2570868E-01	4.1734310E+01	*
12.	8.4535383E-01	1.1969010E+01	*	62.	4.1979028E-01	4.2154100E+01	*
13.	8.3360103E-01	1.2802611E+01	*	63.	4.1395417E-01	4.2568054E+01	*
14.	8.2201223E-01	1.3624623E+01	*	64.	4.0819019E-01	4.2976253E+01	*
15.	8.1058424E-01	1.4435207E+01	*	65.	4.0252422E-01	4.3377777E+01	*
16.	7.9931513E-01	1.5234522E+01	*	66.	3.9692814E-01	4.3775705E+01	*
17.	7.8820269E-01	1.6022724E+01	*	67.	3.9140987E-01	4.4167114E+01	*
18.	7.7724473E-01	1.6799968E+01	*	68.	3.8596831E-01	4.4553082E+01	*
19.	7.6643912E-01	1.7566407E+01	*	69.	3.8060240E-01	4.4933684E+01	*
20.	7.5578374E-01	1.8322190E+01	*	70.	3.7531109E-01	4.5308995E+01	*
21.	7.4527648E-01	1.9067466E+01	*	71.	3.7009335E-01	4.5670988E+01	*
22.	7.3491531E-01	1.9802381E+01	*	72.	3.6494814E-01	4.6044036E+01	*
23.	7.2469818E-01	2.0527079E+01	*	73.	3.5987447E-01	4.6403910E+01	*
24.	7.1462310E-01	2.1241702E+01	*	74.	3.5487133E-01	4.6758781E+01	*
25.	7.0468808E-01	2.1946390E+01	*	75.	3.4993774E-01	4.7108718E+01	*
26.	6.9489119E-01	2.2641281E+01	*	76.	3.4507275E-01	4.7453790E+01	*
27.	6.8523044E-01	2.3326511E+01	*	77.	3.4027539E-01	4.7794069E+01	*
28.	6.7570411E-01	2.4002215E+01	*	78.	3.3554473E-01	4.8129609E+01	*
29.	6.6631016E-01	2.4668525E+01	*	79.	3.3087983E-01	4.8460488E+01	*
30.	6.5704681E-01	2.5325571E+01	*	80.	3.2627979E-01	4.8786767E+01	*
31.	6.4791225E-01	2.5973483E+01	*	81.	3.2174370E-01	4.9108510E+01	*
32.	6.3890468E-01	2.6612387E+01	*	82.	3.1727067E-01	4.9425780E+01	*
33.	6.3002233E-01	2.7242409E+01	*	83.	3.1285983E-01	4.9738639E+01	*
34.	6.2126348E-01	2.7863672E+01	*	84.	3.0851031E-01	5.0047149E+01	*
35.	6.1262639E-01	2.8476298E+01	*	85.	3.0422126E-01	5.0351370E+01	*
36.	6.0410938E-01	2.9080407E+01	*	86.	2.9999186E-01	5.0651361E+01	*
37.	5.9571077E-01	2.9678117E+01	*	87.	2.9582121E-01	5.0947182E+01	*
38.	5.8742893E-01	3.0263546E+01	*	88.	2.9170857E-01	5.1238809E+01	*
39.	5.7926223E-01	3.0842807E+01	*	89.	2.8765311E-01	5.1526543E+01	*
40.	5.7120906E-01	3.1414016E+01	*	90.	2.8365402E-01	5.1810197E+01	*
41.	5.6326785E-01	3.1977283E+01	*	91.	2.7971053E-01	5.2099907E+01	*
42.	5.5543704E-01	3.2532720E+01	*	92.	2.7582187E-01	5.2365729E+01	*
43.	5.4771510E-01	3.3080435E+01	*	93.	2.7198727E-01	5.2637715E+01	*
44.	5.4010052E-01	3.3620535E+01	*	94.	2.6820593E-01	5.2905920E+01	*
45.	5.3259179E-01	3.4153126E+01	*	95.	2.6447729E-01	5.3170397E+01	*
46.	5.2518764E-01	3.4678313E+01	*	96.	2.6080037E-01	5.3431197E+01	*
47.	5.1788607E-01	3.5196199E+01	*	97.	2.5717461E-01	5.3688371E+01	*
48.	5.1068618E-01	3.5706265E+01	*	98.	2.5359925E-01	5.3941970E+01	*
49.	5.0358638E-01	3.6210471E+01	*	99.	2.5007340E-01	5.4192243E+01	*
50.	4.9658530E-01	3.6707056E+01	*	100.	2.4659696E-01	5.4438639E+01	*

144

TABULATED VALUES OF E   WHEN R = .015

X	E^{-RX}	SUM OF E^{-RX}	*	X	E^{-RX}	SUM OF E^{-RX}	*
0.	1.0000000E+00	1.0000000E+00	*	50.	4.7236655E-01	3.5912385E+01	*
1.	9.8511193E-01	1.9851119E+00	*	51.	4.6533393E-01	3.6377718E+01	*
2.	9.7044553E-01	2.9555574E+00	*	52.	4.5840601E-01	3.6836124E+01	*
3.	9.5599748E-01	3.9115548E+00	*	53.	4.5158123E-01	3.7287705E+01	*
4.	9.4176453E-01	4.8533193E+00	*	54.	4.4485805E-01	3.7732563E+01	*
5.	9.2774348E-01	5.7810627E+00	*	55.	4.3823499E-01	3.8170797E+01	*
6.	9.1393118E-01	6.6949938E+00	*	56.	4.3171052E-01	3.8602507E+01	*
7.	9.0032452E-01	7.5953183E+00	*	57.	4.2528319E-01	3.9027790E+01	*
8.	8.8692043E-01	8.4823378E+00	*	58.	4.1895154E-01	3.9446741E+01	*
9.	8.7371591E-01	9.3559546E+00	*	59.	4.1271417E-01	3.9859455E+01	*
10.	8.6070797E-01	1.0216662E+01	*	60.	4.0656965E-01	4.0266024E+01	*
11.	8.4789370E-01	1.1064555E+01	*	61.	4.0051662E-01	4.0666540E+01	*
12.	8.3527020E-01	1.1899825E+01	*	62.	3.9455370E-01	4.1061093E+01	*
13.	8.2283465E-01	1.2722659E+01	*	63.	3.8867957E-01	4.1449772E+01	*
14.	8.1058424E-01	1.3533243E+01	*	64.	3.8289288E-01	4.1832664E+01	*
15.	7.9851621E-01	1.4331759E+01	*	65.	3.7719235E-01	4.2209856E+01	*
16.	7.8662786E-01	1.5118386E+01	*	66.	3.7157669E-01	4.2581432E+01	*
17.	7.7491649E-01	1.5893302E+01	*	67.	3.6604463E-01	4.2947676E+01	*
18.	7.6337949E-01	1.6656681E+01	*	68.	3.6059493E-01	4.3308070E+01	*
19.	7.5201425E-01	1.7408695E+01	*	69.	3.5522638E-01	4.3663296E+01	*
20.	7.4081821E-01	1.8149513E+01	*	70.	3.4993774E-01	4.4013233E+01	*
21.	7.2978887E-01	1.8879301E+01	*	71.	3.4472785E-01	4.4357960E+01	*
22.	7.1892373E-01	1.9598224E+01	*	72.	3.3959552E-01	4.4697555E+01	*
23.	7.0822035E-01	2.0306444E+01	*	73.	3.3453960E-01	4.5032094E+01	*
24.	6.9767632E-01	2.1004120E+01	*	74.	3.2955896E-01	4.5361652E+01	*
25.	6.8728927E-01	2.1691409E+01	*	75.	3.2465246E-01	4.5686304E+01	*
26.	6.7705687E-01	2.2368465E+01	*	76.	3.1981902E-01	4.6006123E+01	*
27.	6.6697680E-01	2.3035441E+01	*	77.	3.1505753E-01	4.6321180E+01	*
28.	6.5704681E-01	2.3692487E+01	*	78.	3.1036694E-01	4.6631546E+01	*
29.	6.4726466E-01	2.4339751E+01	*	79.	3.0574617E-01	4.6937292E+01	*
30.	6.3762814E-01	2.4977379E+01	*	80.	3.0119421E-01	4.7238486E+01	*
31.	6.2813510E-01	2.5605514E+01	*	81.	2.9671001E-01	4.7535196E+01	*
32.	6.1878339E-01	2.6224297E+01	*	82.	2.9229257E-01	4.7827488E+01	*
33.	6.0957090E-01	2.6833867E+01	*	83.	2.8794090E-01	4.8115428E+01	*
34.	6.0049557E-01	2.7434362E+01	*	84.	2.8365402E-01	4.8399082E+01	*
35.	5.9155536E-01	2.8025917E+01	*	85.	2.7943096E-01	4.8678512E+01	*
36.	5.8274825E-01	2.8608665E+01	*	86.	2.7527078E-01	4.8953782E+01	*
37.	5.7407226E-01	2.9182737E+01	*	87.	2.7117253E-01	4.9224954E+01	*
38.	5.6552543E-01	2.9748262E+01	*	88.	2.6713530E-01	4.9492089E+01	*
39.	5.5710586E-01	3.0305367E+01	*	89.	2.6315817E-01	4.9755247E+01	*
40.	5.4881163E-01	3.0854178E+01	*	90.	2.5924026E-01	5.0014487E+01	*
41.	5.4064089E-01	3.1394818E+01	*	91.	2.5538067E-01	5.0269867E+01	*
42.	5.3259179E-01	3.1927409E+01	*	92.	2.5157855E-01	5.0521445E+01	*
43.	5.2466254E-01	3.2452071E+01	*	93.	2.4783303E-01	5.0769278E+01	*
44.	5.1685133E-01	3.2968922E+01	*	94.	2.4414328E-01	5.1013421E+01	*
45.	5.0915641E-01	3.3478078E+01	*	95.	2.4050846E-01	5.1253929E+01	*
46.	5.0157606E-01	3.3979654E+01	*	96.	2.3692775E-01	5.1490856E+01	*
47.	4.9410857E-01	3.4473762E+01	*	97.	2.3340363E-01	5.1724256E+01	*
48.	4.8675225E-01	3.4960514E+01	*	98.	2.2992548E-01	5.1954181E+01	*
49.	4.7950545E-01	3.5440019E+01	*	99.	2.2650234E-01	5.2180683E+01	*
50.	4.7236655E-01	3.5912385E+01	*	100.	2.2313015E-01	5.2403813E+01	*

TABULATED VALUES OF E   WHEN R = .016

X	E^{-RX}	SUM OF E^{-RX}	*	X	E^{-RX}	SUM OF E^{-RX}	*
0.	1.0000000E+00	1.0000000E+00	*	50.	4.4932896E-01	3.5142318E+01	*
1.	9.8412731E-01	1.9841273E+00	*	51.	4.4219690E-01	3.5584514E+01	*
2.	9.6850658E-01	2.9526338E+00	*	52.	4.3517805E-01	3.6019692E+01	*
3.	9.5313378E-01	3.9057675E+00	*	53.	4.2827061E-01	3.6447962E+01	*
4.	9.3800499E-01	4.8437724E+00	*	54.	4.2147281E-01	3.6869434E+01	*
5.	9.2311634E-01	5.7668887E+00	*	55.	4.1478291E-01	3.7284216E+01	*
6.	9.0846401E-01	6.6753527E+00	*	56.	4.0819919E-01	3.7692413E+01	*
7.	8.9404425E-01	7.5693969E+00	*	57.	4.0171997E-01	3.8094134E+01	*
8.	8.7985337E-01	8.4492502E+00	*	58.	3.9534360E-01	3.8489477E+01	*
9.	8.6588774E-01	9.3151379E+00	*	59.	3.8906844E-01	3.8878545E+01	*
10.	8.5214378E-01	1.0167281E+01	*	60.	3.8289288E-01	3.9261437E+01	*
11.	8.3861798E-01	1.1005898E+01	*	61.	3.7681534E-01	3.9638252E+01	*
12.	8.2530686E-01	1.1831204E+01	*	62.	3.7083427E-01	4.0009086E+01	*
13.	8.1220703E-01	1.2643411E+01	*	63.	3.6494814E-01	4.0374034E+01	*
14.	7.9931513E-01	1.3442726E+01	*	64.	3.5915544E-01	4.0733189E+01	*
15.	7.8662786E-01	1.4229353E+01	*	65.	3.5345468E-01	4.1086643E+01	*
16.	7.7414196E-01	1.5003494E+01	*	66.	3.4784440E-01	4.1434487E+01	*
17.	7.6185426E-01	1.5765348E+01	*	67.	3.4232318E-01	4.1776810E+01	*
18.	7.4976159E-01	1.6515109E+01	*	68.	3.3688959E-01	4.2113699E+01	*
19.	7.3786086E-01	1.7252969E+01	*	69.	3.3154225E-01	4.2445241E+01	*
20.	7.2614903E-01	1.7979118E+01	*	70.	3.2627979E-01	4.2771520E+01	*
21.	7.1462310E-01	1.8693741E+01	*	71.	3.2110085E-01	4.3092620E+01	*
22.	7.0328012E-01	1.9397021E+01	*	72.	3.1600412E-01	4.3408624E+01	*
23.	6.9211717E-01	2.0089138E+01	*	73.	3.1098829E-01	4.3719612E+01	*
24.	6.8113142E-01	2.0770269E+01	*	74.	3.0605207E-01	4.4025664E+01	*
25.	6.7032004E-01	2.1440589E+01	*	75.	3.0119421E-01	4.4326858E+01	*
26.	6.5968026E-01	2.2100269E+01	*	76.	2.9641345E-01	4.4623271E+01	*
27.	6.4920937E-01	2.2749478E+01	*	77.	2.9170857E-01	4.4914979E+01	*
28.	6.3890468E-01	2.3388382E+01	*	78.	2.8707837E-01	4.5202057E+01	*
29.	6.2876355E-01	2.4017145E+01	*	79.	2.8252167E-01	4.5484578E+01	*
30.	6.1878339E-01	2.4635928E+01	*	80.	2.7803730E-01	4.5762615E+01	*
31.	6.0896164E-01	2.5244889E+01	*	81.	2.7362410E-01	4.6036239E+01	*
32.	5.9929578E-01	2.5844847E+01	*	82.	2.6928095E-01	4.6305519E+01	*
33.	5.8978335E-01	2.6433967E+01	*	83.	2.6500676E-01	4.6570525E+01	*
34.	5.8042191E-01	2.7014388E+01	*	84.	2.6080037E-01	4.6831325E+01	*
35.	5.7120906E-01	2.7585597E+01	*	85.	2.5666077E-01	4.7087985E+01	*
36.	5.6214244E-01	2.8147739E+01	*	86.	2.5258688E-01	4.7340571E+01	*
37.	5.5321973E-01	2.8700958E+01	*	87.	2.4857765E-01	4.7589148E+01	*
38.	5.4443865E-01	2.9245396E+01	*	88.	2.4463205E-01	4.7833780E+01	*
39.	5.3579695E-01	2.9781192E+01	*	89.	2.4074909E-01	4.8074529E+01	*
40.	5.2729242E-01	3.0308484E+01	*	90.	2.3692775E-01	4.8311456E+01	*
41.	5.1892287E-01	3.0827406E+01	*	91.	2.3316707E-01	4.8544623E+01	*
42.	5.1068618E-01	3.1338092E+01	*	92.	2.2946609E-01	4.8774089E+01	*
43.	5.0258022E-01	3.1840672E+01	*	93.	2.2582385E-01	4.8999912E+01	*
44.	4.9460292E-01	3.2335274E+01	*	94.	2.2223942E-01	4.9222151E+01	*
45.	4.8675225E-01	3.2822026E+01	*	95.	2.1871188E-01	4.9440862E+01	*
46.	4.7902619E-01	3.3301052E+01	*	96.	2.1524034E-01	4.9656102E+01	*
47.	4.7142276E-01	3.3772474E+01	*	97.	2.1182390E-01	4.9867925E+01	*
48.	4.6394002E-01	3.4236414E+01	*	98.	2.0846168E-01	5.0076386E+01	*
49.	4.5657604E-01	3.4692990E+01	*	99.	2.0515284E-01	5.0281538E+01	*
50.	4.4932896E-01	3.5142318E+01	*	100.	2.0189651E-01	5.0483434E+01	*

145

TABULATED VALUES OF E^{-RX} WHEN R = .017

X	E^{-RX}	SUM OF E^{-RX}	*	X	E^{-RX}	SUM OF E^{-RX}	*
0.	1.0000000E+00	1.0000000E+00	*	50.	4.2741493E-01	3.4395972E+01	*
1.	9.8314368E-01	1.9831436E+00	*	51.	4.2021029E-01	3.4816182E+01	*
2.	9.6657150E-01	2.9497151E+00	*	52.	4.1312709E-01	3.5229309E+01	*
3.	9.5027866E-01	3.8999937E+00	*	53.	4.0616329E-01	3.5635472E+01	*
4.	9.3426047E-01	4.8342541E+00	*	54.	3.9931687E-01	3.6034788E+01	*
5.	9.1851226E-01	5.7527663E+00	*	55.	3.9258586E-01	3.6427373E+01	*
6.	9.0302954E-01	6.6557958E+00	*	56.	3.8596631E-01	3.6813341E+01	*
7.	8.8780779E-01	7.5436035E+00	*	57.	3.7946231E-01	3.7192803E+01	*
8.	8.7284263E-01	8.4164461E+00	*	58.	3.7306597E-01	3.7565868E+01	*
9.	8.5812971E-01	9.2745758E+00	*	59.	3.6677745E-01	3.7932645E+01	*
10.	8.4366481E-01	1.0118240E+01	*	60.	3.6059493E-01	3.8293239E+01	*
11.	8.2944373E-01	1.0947683E+01	*	61.	3.5451663E-01	3.8647755E+01	*
12.	8.1546236E-01	1.1763145E+01	*	62.	3.4854079E-01	3.8996295E+01	*
13.	8.0171667E-01	1.2564861E+01	*	63.	3.4266567E-01	3.9338960E+01	*
14.	7.8820269E-01	1.3353063E+01	*	64.	3.3688959E-01	3.9675849E+01	*
15.	7.7491649E-01	1.4127979E+01	*	65.	3.3121098E-01	4.0007059E+01	*
16.	7.6185426E-01	1.4889833E+01	*	66.	3.2562788E-01	4.0332686E+01	*
17.	7.4901220E-01	1.5638845E+01	*	67.	3.2013899E-01	4.0652824E+01	*
18.	7.3638661E-01	1.6375231E+01	*	68.	3.1474263E-01	4.0967566E+01	*
19.	7.2397385E-01	1.7099204E+01	*	69.	3.0943723E-01	4.1277003E+01	*
20.	7.1177032E-01	1.7810974E+01	*	70.	3.0422126E-01	4.1581224E+01	*
21.	6.9977249E-01	1.8510746E+01	*	71.	2.9909321E-01	4.1880317E+01	*
22.	6.8797690E-01	1.9198722E+01	*	72.	2.9405160E-01	4.2174368E+01	*
23.	6.7638015E-01	1.9875102E+01	*	73.	2.8909497E-01	4.2463462E+01	*
24.	6.6497887E-01	2.0540080E+01	*	74.	2.8422190E-01	4.2747683E+01	*
25.	6.5376978E-01	2.1193840E+01	*	75.	2.7943096E-01	4.3027113E+01	*
26.	6.4274963E-01	2.1836598E+01	*	76.	2.7472079E-01	4.3301833E+01	*
27.	6.3191524E-01	2.2468513E+01	*	77.	2.7009001E-01	4.3571923E+01	*
28.	6.2126348E-01	2.3089776E+01	*	78.	2.6553728E-01	4.3837460E+01	*
29.	6.1079126E-01	2.3700567E+01	*	79.	2.6106130E-01	4.4098521E+01	*
30.	6.0049557E-01	2.4301062E+01	*	80.	2.5666077E-01	4.4355181E+01	*
31.	5.9037343E-01	2.4851435E+01	*	81.	2.5233442E-01	4.4607515E+01	*
32.	5.8042191E-01	2.5471856E+01	*	82.	2.4808099E-01	4.4855595E+01	*
33.	5.7063813E-01	2.6042494E+01	*	83.	2.4389926E-01	4.5099494E+01	*
34.	5.6101928E-01	2.6603513E+01	*	84.	2.3978801E-01	4.5339282E+01	*
35.	5.5156256E-01	2.7155075E+01	*	85.	2.3574607E-01	4.5575072E+01	*
36.	5.4226525E-01	2.7697340E+01	*	86.	2.3177226E-01	4.5806800E+01	*
37.	5.3312465E-01	2.8230464E+01	*	87.	2.2786543E-01	4.6034665E+01	*
38.	5.2413813E-01	2.8754602E+01	*	88.	2.2402446E-01	4.6258689E+01	*
39.	5.1530310E-01	2.9269905E+01	*	89.	2.2024824E-01	4.6478937E+01	*
40.	5.0661699E-01	2.9776521E+01	*	90.	2.1653566E-01	4.6695472E+01	*
41.	4.9807729E-01	3.0274598E+01	*	91.	2.1288567E-01	4.6908357E+01	*
42.	4.8968154E-01	3.0764279E+01	*	92.	2.0929720E-01	4.7117654E+01	*
43.	4.8142732E-01	3.1245706E+01	*	93.	2.0576922E-01	4.7323423E+01	*
44.	4.7331223E-01	3.1719018E+01	*	94.	2.0230071E-01	4.7525723E+01	*
45.	4.6533393E-01	3.2184351E+01	*	95.	1.9889067E-01	4.7724613E+01	*
46.	4.5749011E-01	3.2641841E+01	*	96.	1.9553810E-01	4.7920151E+01	*
47.	4.4977851E-01	3.3091619E+01	*	97.	1.9224205E-01	4.8112393E+01	*
48.	4.4219690E-01	3.3533815E+01	*	98.	1.8900156E-01	4.8301394E+01	*
49.	4.3474309E-01	3.3968558E+01	*	99.	1.8581569E-01	4.8487209E+01	*
50.	4.2741493E-01	3.4395972E+01	*	100.	1.8268352E-01	4.8669892E+01	*

TABULATED VALUES OF E^{-RX} WHEN R = .018

X	E^{-RX}	SUM OF E^{-RX}	*	X	E^{-RX}	SUM OF E^{-RX}	*
0.	1.0000000E+00	1.0000000E+00	*	50.	4.0656965E-01	3.3672507E+01	*
1.	9.8216103E-01	1.9821610E+00	*	51.	3.9931687E-01	3.4071823E+01	*
2.	9.6464029E-01	2.9468012E+00	*	52.	3.9219347E-01	3.4464016E+01	*
3.	9.4743210E-01	3.8942333E+00	*	53.	3.8519714E-01	3.4849213E+01	*
4.	9.3053089E-01	4.8247641E+00	*	54.	3.7832562E-01	3.5227538E+01	*
5.	9.1393118E-01	5.7386952E+00	*	55.	3.7157669E-01	3.5599114E+01	*
6.	8.9762759E-01	6.6363227E+00	*	56.	3.6494814E-01	3.5964062E+01	*
7.	8.8161484E-01	7.5179375E+00	*	57.	3.5843784E-01	3.6322499E+01	*
8.	8.6588774E-01	8.3838252E+00	*	58.	3.5204368E-01	3.6674542E+01	*
9.	8.5044120E-01	9.2342664E+00	*	59.	3.4576359E-01	3.7020305E+01	*
10.	8.3527020E-01	1.0069536E+01	*	60.	3.3959552E-01	3.7359900E+01	*
11.	8.2036985E-01	1.0889905E+01	*	61.	3.3353749E-01	3.7693437E+01	*
12.	8.0573530E-01	1.1695640E+01	*	62.	3.2758752E-01	3.8021024E+01	*
13.	7.9136181E-01	1.2487001E+01	*	63.	3.2174370E-01	3.8342767E+01	*
14.	7.7724473E-01	1.3264245E+01	*	64.	3.1600412E-01	3.8658771E+01	*
15.	7.6337949E-01	1.4027624E+01	*	65.	3.1036694E-01	3.8969137E+01	*
16.	7.4976159E-01	1.4777385E+01	*	66.	3.0483031E-01	3.9273967E+01	*
17.	7.3638661E-01	1.5513771E+01	*	67.	2.9939245E-01	3.9573359E+01	*
18.	7.2325024E-01	1.6237021E+01	*	68.	2.9405160E-01	3.9867410E+01	*
19.	7.1034820E-01	1.6947369E+01	*	69.	2.8880602E-01	4.0156216E+01	*
20.	6.9767632E-01	1.7645045E+01	*	70.	2.8365402E-01	4.0439870E+01	*
21.	6.8523049E-01	1.8330275E+01	*	71.	2.7859393E-01	4.0718463E+01	*
22.	6.7300669E-01	1.9003281E+01	*	72.	2.7362410E-01	4.0992087E+01	*
23.	6.6100094E-01	1.9664281E+01	*	73.	2.6874293E-01	4.1260829E+01	*
24.	6.4920937E-01	2.0313490E+01	*	74.	2.6394883E-01	4.1524777E+01	*
25.	6.3762814E-01	2.0951118E+01	*	75.	2.5924026E-01	4.1784017E+01	*
26.	6.2625352E-01	2.1577371E+01	*	76.	2.5461568E-01	4.2038632E+01	*
27.	6.1508180E-01	2.2192452E+01	*	77.	2.5007360E-01	4.2288705E+01	*
28.	6.0410938E-01	2.2796561E+01	*	78.	2.4561254E-01	4.2534317E+01	*
29.	5.9333269E-01	2.3389893E+01	*	79.	2.4123107E-01	4.2775548E+01	*
30.	5.8274825E-01	2.3972641E+01	*	80.	2.3692775E-01	4.3012475E+01	*
31.	5.7235226E-01	2.4544993E+01	*	81.	2.3270121E-01	4.3245176E+01	*
32.	5.6214446E-01	2.5107135E+01	*	82.	2.2855006E-01	4.3473726E+01	*
33.	5.5211446E-01	2.5659249E+01	*	83.	2.2447296E-01	4.3698197E+01	*
34.	5.4226525E-01	2.6201514E+01	*	84.	2.2046859E-01	4.3918666E+01	*
35.	5.3259179E-01	2.6734105E+01	*	85.	2.1653566E-01	4.4135201E+01	*
36.	5.2309091E-01	2.7257195E+01	*	86.	2.1267289E-01	4.4347873E+01	*
37.	5.1375950E-01	2.7770954E+01	*	87.	2.0887902E-01	4.4556752E+01	*
38.	5.0459456E-01	2.8275548E+01	*	88.	2.0515284E-01	4.4761904E+01	*
39.	4.9559312E-01	2.8771141E+01	*	89.	2.0149312E-01	4.4963397E+01	*
40.	4.8675225E-01	2.9257893E+01	*	90.	1.9789869E-01	4.5161295E+01	*
41.	4.7806909E-01	2.9735962E+01	*	91.	1.9436839E-01	4.5355663E+01	*
42.	4.6954083E-01	3.0205502E+01	*	92.	1.9090105E-01	4.5546564E+01	*
43.	4.6116471E-01	3.0666666E+01	*	93.	1.8749549E-01	4.5734059E+01	*
44.	4.5293803E-01	3.1119604E+01	*	94.	1.8415055E-01	4.5918209E+01	*
45.	4.4485806E-01	3.1564462E+01	*	95.	1.8086579E-01	4.6099074E+01	*
46.	4.3692225E-01	3.2001384E+01	*	96.	1.7763933E-01	4.6276713E+01	*
47.	4.2912801E-01	3.2430512E+01	*	97.	1.7447043E-01	4.6451183E+01	*
48.	4.2147281E-01	3.2851984E+01	*	98.	1.7135805E-01	4.6622541E+01	*
49.	4.1395417E-01	3.3265938E+01	*	99.	1.6830120E-01	4.6790842E+01	*
50.	4.0656965E-01	3.3672507E+01	*	100.	1.6529888E-01	4.6956140E+01	*

TABULATED VALUES OF E WHEN R = .019

X	E −RX	SUM OF E −RX	*	X	E −RX	SUM OF E −RX	*
0.	1.0000000E+00	1.0000000E+00	*	50.	3.8674102E-01	3.2971108E+01	*
1.	9.8117936E-01	1.9811793E+00	*	51.	3.7946231E-01	3.3350570E+01	*
2.	9.6271293E-01	2.9438922E+00	*	52.	3.7232058E-01	3.3722890E+01	*
3.	9.4459406E-01	3.8884862E+00	*	53.	3.6531327E-01	3.4088203E+01	*
4.	9.2681620E-01	4.8153024E+00	*	54.	3.5843784E-01	3.4446640E+01	*
5.	9.0937293E-01	5.7246753E+00	*	55.	3.5169181E-01	3.4798331E+01	*
6.	8.9225795E-01	6.6169332E+00	*	56.	3.4507275E-01	3.5143403E+01	*
7.	8.7546509E-01	7.4923982E+00	*	57.	3.3857826E-01	3.5481981E+01	*
8.	8.5898827E-01	8.3513864E+00	*	58.	3.3220600E-01	3.5814187E+01	*
9.	8.4282157E-01	9.1942079E+00	*	59.	3.2595367E-01	3.6140140E+01	*
10.	8.2695913E-01	1.0021167E+01	*	60.	3.1981902E-01	3.6459959E+01	*
11.	8.1139523E-01	1.0832562E+01	*	61.	3.1379982E-01	3.6773758E+01	*
12.	7.9612425E-01	1.1628686E+01	*	62.	3.0789391E-01	3.7081651E+01	*
13.	7.8114069E-01	1.2409826E+01	*	63.	3.0209915E-01	3.7383750E+01	*
14.	7.6643912E-01	1.3176265E+01	*	64.	2.9641345E-01	3.7680163E+01	*
15.	7.5201425E-01	1.3928279E+01	*	65.	2.9083476E-01	3.7970997E+01	*
16.	7.3786086E-01	1.4666139E+01	*	66.	2.8536106E-01	3.8256358E+01	*
17.	7.2397385E-01	1.5390112E+01	*	67.	2.7999038E-01	3.8536348E+01	*
18.	7.1034820E-01	1.6100460E+01	*	68.	2.7472079E-01	3.8811068E+01	*
19.	6.9697899E-01	1.6797438E+01	*	69.	2.6955037E-01	3.9080618E+01	*
20.	6.8386140E-01	1.7481299E+01	*	70.	2.6447726E-01	3.9345095E+01	*
21.	6.7099069E-01	1.8152289E+01	*	71.	2.5949962E-01	3.9604594E+01	*
22.	6.5836222E-01	1.8810651E+01	*	72.	2.5461568E-01	3.9859209E+01	*
23.	6.4597142E-01	1.9456622E+01	*	73.	2.4982365E-01	4.0109932E+01	*
24.	6.3381383E-01	2.0090435E+01	*	74.	2.4512181E-01	4.0354153E+01	*
25.	6.2188505E-01	2.0712320E+01	*	75.	2.4050846E-01	4.0594661E+01	*
26.	6.1018078E-01	2.1322500E+01	*	76.	2.3598194E-01	4.0830642E+01	*
27.	5.9869678E-01	2.1921196E+01	*	77.	2.3154060E-01	4.1062182E+01	*
28.	5.8742893E-01	2.2508624E+01	*	78.	2.2718286E-01	4.1289364E+01	*
29.	5.7637314E-01	2.3084997E+01	*	79.	2.2290714E-01	4.1512271E+01	*
30.	5.6552543E-01	2.3650522E+01	*	80.	2.1871188E-01	4.1730982E+01	*
31.	5.5488188E-01	2.4205403E+01	*	81.	2.1459558E-01	4.1945577E+01	*
32.	5.4443865E-01	2.4749841E+01	*	82.	2.1055676E-01	4.2156133E+01	*
33.	5.3419197E-01	2.5284032E+01	*	83.	2.0659395E-01	4.2362726E+01	*
34.	5.2413813E-01	2.5808170E+01	*	84.	2.0270572E-01	4.2565431E+01	*
35.	5.1427352E-01	2.6322443E+01	*	85.	1.9889067E-01	4.2764321E+01	*
36.	5.0459456E-01	2.6827037E+01	*	86.	1.9514742E-01	4.2959468E+01	*
37.	4.9509778E-01	2.7322134E+01	*	87.	1.9147462E-01	4.3150942E+01	*
38.	4.8577972E-01	2.7807913E+01	*	88.	1.8787094E-01	4.3338812E+01	*
39.	4.7663703E-01	2.8284550E+01	*	89.	1.8433509E-01	4.3523147E+01	*
40.	4.6766642E-01	2.8752216E+01	*	90.	1.8086579E-01	4.3704012E+01	*
41.	4.5886464E-01	2.9211080E+01	*	91.	1.7746178E-01	4.3881473E+01	*
42.	4.5022852E-01	2.9661308E+01	*	92.	1.7412183E-01	4.4055594E+01	*
43.	4.4175493E-01	3.0103062E+01	*	93.	1.7084475E-01	4.4226438E+01	*
44.	4.3344082E-01	3.0536502E+01	*	94.	1.6762934E-01	4.4390467E+01	*
45.	4.2528319E-01	3.0961785E+01	*	95.	1.6447445E-01	4.4558541E+01	*
46.	4.1727908E-01	3.1379064E+01	*	96.	1.6137894E-01	4.4719919E+01	*
47.	4.0942563E-01	3.1786480E+01	*	97.	1.5834146E-01	4.4878260E+01	*
48.	4.0171997E-01	3.2190209E+01	*	98.	1.5536159E-01	4.5033621E+01	*
49.	3.9415935E-01	3.2584367E+01	*	99.	1.5243759E-01	4.5186058E+01	*
50.	3.8674102E-01	3.2971108E+01	*	100.	1.4956861E-01	4.5335626E+01	*

TABULATED VALUES OF E WHEN R = .020

X	E −RX	SUM OF E −RX	*	X	E −RX	SUM OF E −RX	*
0.	1.0000000E+00	1.0000000E+00	*	50.	3.6787944E-01	3.2291002E+01	*
1.	9.8019867E-01	1.9801986E+00	*	51.	3.6059493E-01	3.2651596E+01	*
2.	9.6078943E-01	2.9409880E+00	*	52.	3.5345468E-01	3.3005050E+01	*
3.	9.4176453E-01	3.8827525E+00	*	53.	3.4645580E-01	3.3351505E+01	*
4.	9.2311634E-01	4.8058688E+00	*	54.	3.3959552E-01	3.3691100E+01	*
5.	9.0483741E-01	5.7107062E+00	*	55.	3.3287108E-01	3.4023971E+01	*
6.	8.8692043E-01	6.5976266E+00	*	56.	3.2627979E-01	3.4350250E+01	*
7.	8.6935823E-01	7.4669848E+00	*	57.	3.1981902E-01	3.4670069E+01	*
8.	8.5214378E-01	8.3191288E+00	*	58.	3.1348638E-01	3.4983555E+01	*
9.	8.3527020E-01	9.1543987E+00	*	59.	3.0727873E-01	3.5290833E+01	*
10.	8.1873075E-01	9.9731294E+00	*	60.	3.0119421E-01	3.5592027E+01	*
11.	8.0251879E-01	1.0775648E+01	*	61.	2.9523016E-01	3.5887257E+01	*
12.	7.8662786E-01	1.1562275E+01	*	62.	2.8938421E-01	3.6176641E+01	*
13.	7.7105158E-01	1.2333326E+01	*	63.	2.8365402E-01	3.6460295E+01	*
14.	7.5578374E-01	1.3089109E+01	*	64.	2.7803730E-01	3.6738332E+01	*
15.	7.4081821E-01	1.3829927E+01	*	65.	2.7253179E-01	3.7010863E+01	*
16.	7.2614903E-01	1.4556076E+01	*	66.	2.6713530E-01	3.7277998E+01	*
17.	7.1177032E-01	1.5267846E+01	*	67.	2.6184566E-01	3.7539843E+01	*
18.	6.9767632E-01	1.5965522E+01	*	68.	2.5666077E-01	3.7796503E+01	*
19.	6.8386140E-01	1.6649383E+01	*	69.	2.5157855E-01	3.8048081E+01	*
20.	6.7032004E-01	1.7319703E+01	*	70.	2.4659696E-01	3.8294677E+01	*
21.	6.5704681E-01	1.7976749E+01	*	71.	2.4171401E-01	3.8536391E+01	*
22.	6.4403641E-01	1.8620785E+01	*	72.	2.3692775E-01	3.8773318E+01	*
23.	6.3128364E-01	1.9252068E+01	*	73.	2.3223627E-01	3.9005554E+01	*
24.	6.1878339E-01	1.9870851E+01	*	74.	2.2763768E-01	3.9233191E+01	*
25.	6.0653065E-01	2.0477381E+01	*	75.	2.2313015E-01	3.9456321E+01	*
26.	5.9452054E-01	2.1071901E+01	*	76.	2.1871188E-01	3.9675032E+01	*
27.	5.8274829E-01	2.1654649E+01	*	77.	2.1438110E-01	3.9889413E+01	*
28.	5.7120906E-01	2.2225858E+01	*	78.	2.1013607E-01	4.0099549E+01	*
29.	5.5989836E-01	2.2785756E+01	*	79.	2.0597509E-01	4.0305524E+01	*
30.	5.4881163E-01	2.3334567E+01	*	80.	2.0189651E-01	4.0507420E+01	*
31.	5.3794443E-01	2.3872511E+01	*	81.	1.9789869E-01	4.0705318E+01	*
32.	5.2729242E-01	2.4399803E+01	*	82.	1.9398004E-01	4.0899298E+01	*
33.	5.1685133E-01	2.4916654E+01	*	83.	1.9013897E-01	4.1089436E+01	*
34.	5.0661699E-01	2.5423270E+01	*	84.	1.8637397E-01	4.1275809E+01	*
35.	4.9658530E-01	2.5919855E+01	*	85.	1.8268352E-01	4.1458492E+01	*
36.	4.8675225E-01	2.6406607E+01	*	86.	1.7906614E-01	4.1637558E+01	*
37.	4.7711391E-01	2.6883720E+01	*	87.	1.7552040E-01	4.1813078E+01	*
38.	4.6766642E-01	2.7351386E+01	*	88.	1.7204486E-01	4.1985122E+01	*
39.	4.5840601E-01	2.7809792E+01	*	89.	1.6863814E-01	4.2153760E+01	*
40.	4.4932896E-01	2.8259120E+01	*	90.	1.6529888E-01	4.2319058E+01	*
41.	4.4043165E-01	2.8699551E+01	*	91.	1.6202575E-01	4.2481083E+01	*
42.	4.3171052E-01	2.9131261E+01	*	92.	1.5881742E-01	4.2639900E+01	*
43.	4.2316208E-01	2.9554423E+01	*	93.	1.5567263E-01	4.2795572E+01	*
44.	4.1478291E-01	2.9969205E+01	*	94.	1.5259010E-01	4.2948162E+01	*
45.	4.0656965E-01	3.0375791E+01	*	95.	1.4956861E-01	4.3097730E+01	*
46.	3.9851903E-01	3.0774293E+01	*	96.	1.4660696E-01	4.3244334E+01	*
47.	3.9062783E-01	3.1164920E+01	*	97.	1.4370394E-01	4.3388039E+01	*
48.	3.8289288E-01	3.1547812E+01	*	98.	1.4085842E-01	4.3528897E+01	*
49.	3.7531109E-01	3.1923123E+01	*	99.	1.3806923E-01	4.3666966E+01	*
50.	3.6787944E-01	3.2291002E+01	*	100.	1.3533528E-01	4.3802301E+01	*

TABULATED VALUES OF E   WHEN R = .021

X	E^{-RX}	SUM OF E^{-RX}	*	X	E^{-RX}	SUM OF E^{-RX}	*
0.	1.0000000E+00	1.0000000E+00	*	50.	3.4993774E-01	3.1631432E+01	*
1.	9.7921896E-01	1.9792189E+00	*	51.	3.4266567E-01	3.1974097E+01	*
2.	9.5886977E-01	2.9380886E+00	*	52.	3.3554473E-01	3.2309641E+01	*
3.	9.3894347E-01	3.8770320E+00	*	53.	3.2857176E-01	3.2638212E+01	*
4.	9.1943125E-01	4.7964632E+00	*	54.	3.2174370E-01	3.2959955E+01	*
5.	9.0032452E-01	5.6967877E+00	*	55.	3.1505753E-01	3.3275012E+01	*
6.	8.8161484E-01	6.5784025E+00	*	56.	3.0851031E-01	3.3583522E+01	*
7.	8.6329397E-01	7.4416964E+00	*	57.	3.0209915E-01	3.3885621E+01	*
8.	8.4535383E-01	8.2870502E+00	*	58.	2.9582121E-01	3.4181442E+01	*
9.	8.2778650E-01	9.1148367E+00	*	59.	2.8967374E-01	3.4471115E+01	*
10.	8.1058424E-01	9.9254209E+00	*	60.	2.8365402E-01	3.4754769E+01	*
11.	7.9373946E-01	1.0719160E+01	*	61.	2.7775940E-01	3.5032528E+01	*
12.	7.7724473E-01	1.1496404E+01	*	62.	2.7198727E-01	3.5304515E+01	*
13.	7.6109278E-01	1.2257496E+01	*	63.	2.6633509E-01	3.5570850E+01	*
14.	7.4527648E-01	1.3002772E+01	*	64.	2.6080037E-01	3.5831650E+01	*
15.	7.2978887E-01	1.3732560E+01	*	65.	2.5538067E-01	3.6087030E+01	*
16.	7.1462310E-01	1.4447183E+01	*	66.	2.5007360E-01	3.6337103E+01	*
17.	6.9977249E-01	1.5146955E+01	*	67.	2.4487681E-01	3.6581979E+01	*
18.	6.8523049E-01	1.5832185E+01	*	68.	2.3978801E-01	3.6821767E+01	*
19.	6.7099069E-01	1.6503175E+01	*	69.	2.3480497E-01	3.7056571E+01	*
20.	6.5704681E-01	1.7160221E+01	*	70.	2.2992548E-01	3.7286496E+01	*
21.	6.4339270E-01	1.7803613E+01	*	71.	2.2514739E-01	3.7511643E+01	*
22.	6.3002233E-01	1.8433635E+01	*	72.	2.2046859E-01	3.7732111E+01	*
23.	6.1692982E-01	1.9050564E+01	*	73.	2.1588703E-01	3.7947998E+01	*
24.	6.0410938E-01	1.9654673E+01	*	74.	2.1140067E-01	3.8159398E+01	*
25.	5.9155536E-01	2.0246228E+01	*	75.	2.0700755E-01	3.8366405E+01	*
26.	5.7926223E-01	2.0825490E+01	*	76.	2.0270572E-01	3.8569110E+01	*
27.	5.6722456E-01	2.1392714E+01	*	77.	1.9849329E-01	3.8767603E+01	*
28.	5.5543704E-01	2.1948151E+01	*	78.	1.9436839E-01	3.8961971E+01	*
29.	5.4389449E-01	2.2492045E+01	*	79.	1.9032921E-01	3.9152300E+01	*
30.	5.3259179E-01	2.3024636E+01	*	80.	1.8637397E-01	3.9338673E+01	*
31.	5.2152399E-01	2.3546159E+01	*	81.	1.8250093E-01	3.9521173E+01	*
32.	5.1068618E-01	2.4056845E+01	*	82.	1.7870837E-01	3.9699881E+01	*
33.	5.0007359E-01	2.4556918E+01	*	83.	1.7499462E-01	3.9874875E+01	*
34.	4.8968154E-01	2.5046599E+01	*	84.	1.7135805E-01	4.0046233E+01	*
35.	4.7950545E-01	2.5526104E+01	*	85.	1.6779750E-01	4.0214030E+01	*
36.	4.6954083E-01	2.5999644E+01	*	86.	1.6431006E-01	4.0378340E+01	*
37.	4.5978329E-01	2.6455427E+01	*	87.	1.6089553E-01	4.0539235E+01	*
38.	4.5022632E-01	2.6905655E+01	*	88.	1.5755195E-01	4.0696786E+01	*
39.	4.4087230E-01	2.7346527E+01	*	89.	1.5427786E-01	4.0851063E+01	*
40.	4.3171052E-01	2.7782237E+01	*	90.	1.5107180E-01	4.1002134E+01	*
41.	4.2273913E-01	2.8200976E+01	*	91.	1.4793238E-01	4.1150066E+01	*
42.	4.1395417E-01	2.8614930E+01	*	92.	1.4485819E-01	4.1294924E+01	*
43.	4.0535177E-01	2.9020281E+01	*	93.	1.4184788E-01	4.1436771E+01	*
44.	3.9692814E-01	2.9417209E+01	*	94.	1.3890014E-01	4.1575671E+01	*
45.	3.8867957E-01	2.9805888E+01	*	95.	1.3601365E-01	4.1711684E+01	*
46.	3.8060240E-01	3.0186490E+01	*	96.	1.3318714E-01	4.1844871E+01	*
47.	3.7269309E-01	3.0559183E+01	*	97.	1.3041938E-01	4.1975290E+01	*
48.	3.6494814E-01	3.0924131E+01	*	98.	1.2770913E-01	4.2102999E+01	*
49.	3.5736414E-01	3.1281495E+01	*	99.	1.2505520E-01	4.2228055E+01	*
50.	3.4993774E-01	3.1631432E+01	*	100.	1.2245642E-01	4.2350510E+01	*

TABULATED VALUES OF E   WHEN R = .022

X	E^{-RX}	SUM OF E^{-RX}	*	X	E^{-RX}	SUM OF E^{-RX}	*
0.	1.0000000E+00	1.0000000E+00	*	50.	3.3287108E-01	3.0991682E+01	*
1.	9.7824023E-01	1.9782402E+00	*	51.	3.2562788E-01	3.1317309E+01	*
2.	9.5695395E-01	2.9351941E+00	*	52.	3.1854229E-01	3.1635851E+01	*
3.	9.3613086E-01	3.8713249E+00	*	53.	3.1161089E-01	3.1947461E+01	*
4.	9.1576087E-01	4.7870857E+00	*	54.	3.0483031E-01	3.2252291E+01	*
5.	8.9583413E-01	5.6829198E+00	*	55.	2.9819727E-01	3.2550488E+01	*
6.	8.7634099E-01	6.5592607E+00	*	56.	2.9170857E-01	3.2842196E+01	*
7.	8.5727201E-01	7.4165327E+00	*	57.	2.8536106E-01	3.3127557E+01	*
8.	8.3861798E-01	8.2551506E+00	*	58.	2.7915167E-01	3.3406708E+01	*
9.	8.2036985E-01	9.0755204E+00	*	59.	2.7307740E-01	3.3679785E+01	*
10.	8.0251879E-01	9.8780391E+00	*	60.	2.6713530E-01	3.3946920E+01	*
11.	7.8505617E-01	1.0663095E+01	*	61.	2.6132249E-01	3.4208242E+01	*
12.	7.6797353E-01	1.1431068E+01	*	62.	2.5563618E-01	3.4463878E+01	*
13.	7.5126261E-01	1.2182330E+01	*	63.	2.5007360E-01	3.4713951E+01	*
14.	7.3491531E-01	1.2917245E+01	*	64.	2.4463205E-01	3.4958583E+01	*
15.	7.1892373E-01	1.3636168E+01	*	65.	2.3930892E-01	3.5197891E+01	*
16.	7.0328012E-01	1.4339448E+01	*	66.	2.3410161E-01	3.5431992E+01	*
17.	6.8797690E-01	1.5027424E+01	*	67.	2.2900761E-01	3.5660999E+01	*
18.	6.7300669E-01	1.5700430E+01	*	68.	2.2402446E-01	3.5885023E+01	*
19.	6.5836222E-01	1.6358792E+01	*	69.	2.1914974E-01	3.6104172E+01	*
20.	6.4403641E-01	1.7002828E+01	*	70.	2.1438110E-01	3.6318553E+01	*
21.	6.3002233E-01	1.7632850E+01	*	71.	2.0971621E-01	3.6528269E+01	*
22.	6.1631320E-01	1.8249163E+01	*	72.	2.0515284E-01	3.6733421E+01	*
23.	6.0290237E-01	1.8852065E+01	*	73.	2.0068876E-01	3.6934109E+01	*
24.	5.8978335E-01	1.9441848E+01	*	74.	1.9632182E-01	3.7130430E+01	*
25.	5.7694980E-01	2.0018797E+01	*	75.	1.9204990E-01	3.7322470E+01	*
26.	5.6439551E-01	2.0583192E+01	*	76.	1.8787094E-01	3.7510349E+01	*
27.	5.5211440E-01	2.1135306E+01	*	77.	1.8378291E-01	3.7694131E+01	*
28.	5.4010052E-01	2.1675406E+01	*	78.	1.7978384E-01	3.7873914E+01	*
29.	5.2834806E-01	2.2203754E+01	*	79.	1.7587179E-01	3.8049785E+01	*
30.	5.1685133E-01	2.2720605E+01	*	80.	1.7204486E-01	3.8221829E+01	*
31.	5.0560476E-01	2.3226209E+01	*	81.	1.6830120E-01	3.8390130E+01	*
32.	4.9460292E-01	2.3720811E+01	*	82.	1.6463901E-01	3.8554769E+01	*
33.	4.8384048E-01	2.4204651E+01	*	83.	1.6105650E-01	3.8715825E+01	*
34.	4.7331223E-01	2.4677963E+01	*	84.	1.5755195E-01	3.8873376E+01	*
35.	4.6301306E-01	2.5140976E+01	*	85.	1.5412366E-01	3.9027690E+01	*
36.	4.5293801E-01	2.5593914E+01	*	86.	1.5076998E-01	3.9178268E+01	*
37.	4.4308218E-01	2.6036996E+01	*	87.	1.4748924E-01	3.9325757E+01	*
38.	4.3344082E-01	2.6470436E+01	*	88.	1.4427991E-01	3.9470034E+01	*
39.	4.2400925E-01	2.6894445E+01	*	89.	1.4114041E-01	3.9611176E+01	*
40.	4.1478291E-01	2.7309227E+01	*	90.	1.3806923E-01	3.9749245E+01	*
41.	4.0575733E-01	2.7714984E+01	*	91.	1.3506488E-01	3.9884309E+01	*
42.	3.9692814E-01	2.8111912E+01	*	92.	1.3212590E-01	4.0016634E+01	*
43.	3.8829108E-01	2.8500203E+01	*	93.	1.2925087E-01	4.0145684E+01	*
44.	3.7984196E-01	2.8880044E+01	*	94.	1.2643840E-01	4.0272122E+01	*
45.	3.7157669E-01	2.9251620E+01	*	95.	1.2368713E-01	4.0395809E+01	*
46.	3.6349126E-01	2.9615111E+01	*	96.	1.2099573E-01	4.0516804E+01	*
47.	3.5558178E-01	2.9970692E+01	*	97.	1.1836285E-01	4.0635166E+01	*
48.	3.4784440E-01	3.0318453E+01	*	98.	1.1578734E-01	4.0750953E+01	*
49.	3.4027539E-01	3.0658811E+01	*	99.	1.1326783E-01	4.0864220E+01	*
50.	3.3287108E-01	3.0991682E+01	*	100.	1.1080315E-01	4.0975023E+01	*

TABULATED VALUES OF E^{-RX} WHEN R = .023

X	E^{-RX}	SUM OF E^{-RX}	*	X	E^{-RX}	SUM OF E^{-RX}	*
0.	1.0000000E+00	1.0000000E+00		50.	3.1663676E-01	3.0371055E+01	*
1.	9.7726248E-01	1.9772624E+00		51.	3.0943723E-01	3.0680492E+01	*
2.	9.5504196E-01	2.9323043E+00		52.	3.0240140E-01	3.0982893E+01	*
3.	9.3332667E-01	3.8656309E+00		53.	2.9552554E-01	3.1278418E+01	*
4.	9.1210514E-01	4.7777360E+00		54.	2.8880602E-01	3.1567224E+01	*
5.	8.9136614E-01	5.6691021E+00		55.	2.8223929E-01	3.1849463E+01	*
6.	8.7109869E-01	6.5402007E+00		56.	2.7582187E-01	3.2125284E+01	*
7.	8.5129206E-01	7.3914927E+00		57.	2.6955037E-01	3.2394834E+01	*
8.	8.3193580E-01	8.2234285E+00		58.	2.6342146E-01	3.2658255E+01	*
9.	8.1301964E-01	9.0364481E+00		59.	2.5743191E-01	3.2915686E+01	*
10.	7.9453359E-01	9.8309816E+00	*	60.	2.5157855E-01	3.3167264E+01	*
11.	7.7646788E-01	1.0607449E+01		61.	2.4585828E-01	3.3413122E+01	*
12.	7.5881293E-01	1.1366261E+01	*	62.	2.4026807E-01	3.3653390E+01	*
13.	7.4155940E-01	1.2107820E+01		63.	2.3480497E-01	3.3888194E+01	*
14.	7.2469818E-01	1.2832518E+01	*	64.	2.2946609E-01	3.4117660E+01	*
15.	7.0822035E-01	1.3540738E+01	*	65.	2.2424860E-01	3.4341908E+01	*
16.	6.9211717E-01	1.4232855E+01	*	66.	2.1914974E-01	3.4561057E+01	*
17.	6.7638015E-01	1.4909235E+01	*	67.	2.1416682E-01	3.4775223E+01	*
18.	6.6100094E-01	1.5570235E+01	*	68.	2.0929720E-01	3.4984520E+01	*
19.	6.4597142E-01	1.6216206E+01	*	69.	2.0453830E-01	3.5189058E+01	*
20.	6.3128364E-01	1.6847489E+01	*	70.	1.9988761E-01	3.5388945E+01	*
21.	6.1692982E-01	1.7464418E+01	*	71.	1.9534266E-01	3.5584287E+01	*
22.	6.0290227E-01	1.8067320E+01	*	72.	1.9090105E-01	3.5775188E+01	*
23.	5.8919386E-01	1.8656513E+01	*	73.	1.8656044E-01	3.5961748E+01	*
24.	5.7579706E-01	1.9232310E+01	*	74.	1.8231852E-01	3.6144066E+01	*
25.	5.6270486E-01	1.9795014E+01	*	75.	1.7817305E-01	3.6322239E+01	*
26.	5.4991035E-01	2.0344924E+01	*	76.	1.7412183E-01	3.6496360E+01	*
27.	5.3740676E-01	2.0882330E+01	*	77.	1.7016274E-01	3.6666522E+01	*
28.	5.2518746E-01	2.1407517E+01	*	78.	1.6629366E-01	3.6832815E+01	*
29.	5.1324600E-01	2.1920763E+01	*	79.	1.6251255E-01	3.6995327E+01	*
30.	5.0157606E-01	2.2422339E+01	*	80.	1.5881742E-01	3.7154144E+01	*
31.	4.9017147E-01	2.2912510E+01	*	81.	1.5520631E-01	3.7309350E+01	*
32.	4.7902619E-01	2.3391536E+01	*	82.	1.5167730E-01	3.7461027E+01	*
33.	4.6813432E-01	2.3859670E+01	*	83.	1.4822854E-01	3.7609255E+01	*
34.	4.5749011E-01	2.4317160E+01	*	84.	1.4485819E-01	3.7754113E+01	*
35.	4.4708792E-01	2.4764247E+01	*	85.	1.4156447E-01	3.7895677E+01	*
36.	4.3692225E-01	2.5201169E+01	*	86.	1.3834565E-01	3.8034022E+01	*
37.	4.2698773E-01	2.5628156E+01	*	87.	1.3520001E-01	3.8169222E+01	*
38.	4.1727908E-01	2.6045435E+01	*	88.	1.3212590E-01	3.8301347E+01	*
39.	4.0779119E-01	2.6453226E+01	*	89.	1.2912168E-01	3.8430468E+01	*
40.	3.9851903E-01	2.6851745E+01	*	90.	1.2618578E-01	3.8556653E+01	*
41.	3.8945770E-01	2.7241202E+01	*	91.	1.2331663E-01	3.8679969E+01	*
42.	3.8060240E-01	2.7621804E+01	*	92.	1.2051271E-01	3.8800481E+01	*
43.	3.7194845E-01	2.7993752E+01	*	93.	1.1777255E-01	3.8918253E+01	*
44.	3.6349126E-01	2.8357243E+01	*	94.	1.1509470E-01	3.9033347E+01	*
45.	3.5522638E-01	2.8712469E+01	*	95.	1.1247773E-01	3.9145824E+01	*
46.	3.4714941E-01	2.9059618E+01	*	96.	1.0992026E-01	3.9255744E+01	*
47.	3.3925609E-01	2.9398874E+01	*	97.	1.0742095E-01	3.9363164E+01	*
48.	3.3154225E-01	2.9730416E+01	*	98.	1.0497846E-01	3.9468142E+01	*
49.	3.2400381E-01	3.0054419E+01	*	99.	1.0259151E-01	3.9570733E+01	*
50.	3.1663676E-01	3.0371055E+01		100.	1.0025884E-01	3.9670991E+01	*

TABULATED VALUES OF E^{-RX} WHEN R = .024

X	E^{-RX}	SUM OF E^{-RX}	*	X	E^{-RX}	SUM OF E^{-RX}	*
0.	1.0000000E+00	1.0000000E+00		50.	3.0119421E-01	2.9768882E+01	*
1.	9.7628570E-01	1.9762857E+00		51.	2.9405160E-01	3.0062933E+01	*
2.	9.5313378E-01	2.9294194E+00		52.	2.8707837E-01	3.0350011E+01	*
3.	9.3053089E-01	3.8599502E+00		53.	2.8027051E-01	3.0630281E+01	*
4.	9.0846401E-01	4.7684142E+00		54.	2.7362410E-01	3.0903905E+01	*
5.	8.8692043E-01	5.6553346E+00		55.	2.6713530E-01	3.1171040E+01	*
6.	8.6588774E-01	6.5212223E+00		56.	2.6080037E-01	3.1431840E+01	*
7.	8.4535383E-01	7.3665761E+00		57.	2.5461568E-01	3.1686455E+01	*
8.	8.2530686E-01	8.1918829E+00		58.	2.4857765E-01	3.1935032E+01	*
9.	8.0573530E-01	8.9976182E+00		59.	2.4268280E-01	3.2177714E+01	*
10.	7.8662786E-01	9.7842460E+00		60.	2.3692775E-01	3.2414641E+01	*
11.	7.6797353E-01	1.0552219E+01	*	61.	2.3130918E-01	3.2645950E+01	*
12.	7.4976159E-01	1.1301980E+01	*	62.	2.2582385E-01	3.2871773E+01	*
13.	7.3198152E-01	1.2033981E+01	*	63.	2.2046859E-01	3.3092241E+01	*
14.	7.1462310E-01	1.2748584E+01	*	64.	2.1524034E-01	3.3307481E+01	*
15.	6.9767632E-01	1.3446260E+01	*	65.	2.1013607E-01	3.3517617E+01	*
16.	6.8113142E-01	1.4127391E+01	*	66.	2.0515284E-01	3.3722769E+01	*
17.	6.6497887E-01	1.4792369E+01	*	67.	2.0028778E-01	3.3923056E+01	*
18.	6.4920937E-01	1.5441578E+01	*	68.	1.9553810E-01	3.4118594E+01	*
19.	6.3381383E-01	1.6075391E+01	*	69.	1.9090105E-01	3.4309495E+01	*
20.	6.1878339E-01	1.6694174E+01	*	70.	1.8637397E-01	3.4495868E+01	*
21.	6.0410938E-01	1.7298283E+01	*	71.	1.8195424E-01	3.4677822E+01	*
22.	5.8978335E-01	1.7888066E+01	*	72.	1.7763933E-01	3.4855461E+01	*
23.	5.7579706E-01	1.8463863E+01	*	73.	1.7342674E-01	3.5028887E+01	*
24.	5.6214244E-01	1.9026005E+01	*	74.	1.6931405E-01	3.5198201E+01	*
25.	5.4881163E-01	1.9574816E+01	*	75.	1.6529888E-01	3.5363499E+01	*
26.	5.3579695E-01	2.0110612E+01	*	76.	1.6137894E-01	3.5524877E+01	*
27.	5.2309091E-01	2.0633702E+01	*	77.	1.5755195E-01	3.5682428E+01	*
28.	5.1068618E-01	2.1144388E+01	*	78.	1.5381572E-01	3.5836243E+01	*
29.	4.9857562E-01	2.1642963E+01	*	79.	1.5016809E-01	3.5986411E+01	*
30.	4.8675225E-01	2.2129715E+01	*	80.	1.4660696E-01	3.6133017E+01	*
31.	4.7520927E-01	2.2604924E+01	*	81.	1.4313028E-01	3.6276147E+01	*
32.	4.6394002E-01	2.3068864E+01	*	82.	1.3973604E-01	3.6415883E+01	*
33.	4.5293801E-01	2.3521802E+01	*	83.	1.3642230E-01	3.6552305E+01	*
34.	4.4219690E-01	2.3963998E+01	*	84.	1.3318714E-01	3.6685492E+01	*
35.	4.3171052E-01	2.4395708E+01	*	85.	1.3002871E-01	3.6815520E+01	*
36.	4.2147281E-01	2.4817180E+01	*	86.	1.2694517E-01	3.6942465E+01	*
37.	4.1147788E-01	2.5228657E+01	*	87.	1.2393475E-01	3.7066399E+01	*
38.	4.0171997E-01	2.5630376E+01	*	88.	1.2099573E-01	3.7187394E+01	*
39.	3.9219347E-01	2.6022569E+01	*	89.	1.1812640E-01	3.7305520E+01	*
40.	3.8289288E-01	2.6405461E+01	*	90.	1.1532512E-01	3.7420845E+01	*
41.	3.7381285E-01	2.6779273E+01	*	91.	1.1259026E-01	3.7533435E+01	*
42.	3.6494814E-01	2.7144221E+01	*	92.	1.0992026E-01	3.7643355E+01	*
43.	3.5629365E-01	2.7500514E+01	*	93.	1.0731358E-01	3.7750668E+01	*
44.	3.4784440E-01	2.7848358E+01	*	94.	1.0476872E-01	3.7855436E+01	*
45.	3.3959552E-01	2.8187953E+01	*	95.	1.0228420E-01	3.7957720E+01	*
46.	3.3154225E-01	2.8519495E+01	*	96.	9.9858609E-02	3.8057578E+01	*
47.	3.2367996E-01	2.8843174E+01	*	97.	9.7490533E-02	3.8155068E+01	*
48.	3.1600412E-01	2.9159178E+01	*	98.	9.5178614E-02	3.8250246E+01	*
49.	3.0851031E-01	2.9467688E+01	*	99.	9.2921521E-02	3.8343167E+01	*
50.	3.0119421E-01	2.9768882E+01	*	100.	9.0717953E-02	3.8433884E+01	*

TABULATED VALUES OF E^{-RX} WHEN R = .025

X	E^{-RX}	SUM OF E^{-RX}	*	X	E^{-RX}	SUM OF E^{-RX}	*
0.	1.0000000E+00	1.0000000E+00	*	50.	2.8650479E-01	2.9184526E+01	*
1.	9.7530991E-01	1.9753099E+00	*	51.	2.7943096E-01	2.9463956E+01	*
2.	9.5122942E-01	2.9265393E+00	*	52.	2.7253179E-01	2.9736487E+01	*
3.	9.2774348E-01	3.8542827E+00	*	53.	2.6580295E-01	3.0002289E+01	*
4.	9.0483741E-01	4.7591201E+00	*	54.	2.5924026E-01	3.0261529E+01	*
5.	8.8249690E-01	5.6416170E+00	*	55.	2.5283959E-01	3.0514364E+01	*
6.	8.6070797E-01	6.5023249E+00	*	56.	2.4659696E-01	3.0760964E+01	*
7.	8.3945701E-01	7.3417819E+00	*	57.	2.4050846E-01	3.1001472E+01	*
8.	8.1873075E-01	8.1605126E+00	*	58.	2.3457028E-01	3.1236042E+01	*
9.	7.9851621E-01	8.9590288E+00	*	59.	2.2877672E-01	3.1464820E+01	*
10.	7.7880078E-01	9.7378295E+00	*	60.	2.2313015E-01	3.1687950E+01	*
11.	7.5957212E-01	1.0497401E+01	*	61.	2.1762105E-01	3.1905571E+01	*
12.	7.4081821E-01	1.1236219E+01	*	62.	2.1224797E-01	3.2117818E+01	*
13.	7.2252735E-01	1.1960746E+01	*	63.	2.0700755E-01	3.2324825E+01	*
14.	7.0468808E-01	1.2665434E+01	*	64.	2.0189651E-01	3.2526721E+01	*
15.	6.8728927E-01	1.3352723E+01	*	65.	1.9691167E-01	3.2723632E+01	*
16.	6.7032004E-01	1.4023043E+01	*	66.	1.9204990E-01	3.2915681E+01	*
17.	6.5376978E-01	1.4676812E+01	*	67.	1.8730817E-01	3.3102989E+01	*
18.	6.3762814E-01	1.5314440E+01	*	68.	1.8268352E-01	3.3285672E+01	*
19.	6.2188505E-01	1.5936325E+01	*	69.	1.7817305E-01	3.3463845E+01	*
20.	6.0653065E-01	1.6542855E+01	*	70.	1.7377394E-01	3.3637618E+01	*
21.	5.9155368E-01	1.7134410E+01	*	71.	1.6948344E-01	3.3807101E+01	*
22.	5.7694980E-01	1.7711359E+01	*	72.	1.6529888E-01	3.3972399E+01	*
23.	5.6270486E-01	1.8274063E+01	*	73.	1.6121764E-01	3.4133616E+01	*
24.	5.4881163E-01	1.8822874E+01	*	74.	1.5723716E-01	3.4290853E+01	*
25.	5.3526142E-01	1.9358135E+01	*	75.	1.5335649E-01	3.4444207E+01	*
26.	5.2204577E-01	1.9880180E+01	*	76.	1.4956861E-01	3.4593775E+01	*
27.	5.0915641E-01	2.0389336E+01	*	77.	1.4587575E-01	3.4739650E+01	*
28.	4.9658530E-01	2.0885921E+01	*	78.	1.4227407E-01	3.4881924E+01	*
29.	4.8432456E-01	2.1370245E+01	*	79.	1.3876131E-01	3.5020685E+01	*
30.	4.7236655E-01	2.1842611E+01	*	80.	-1.3533528E-01	3.5156020E+01	*
31.	4.6070378E-01	2.2303314E+01	*	81.	1.3199384E-01	3.5288013E+01	*
32.	4.4932846E-01	2.2752642E+01	*	82.	1.2873490E-01	3.5416747E+01	*
33.	4.3823499E-01	2.3190876E+01	*	83.	1.2555642E-01	3.5542303E+01	*
34.	4.2741493E-01	2.3618290E+01	*	84.	1.2245642E-01	3.5664759E+01	*
35.	4.1686201E-01	2.4035152E+01	*	85.	1.1943296E-01	3.5784191E+01	*
36.	4.0656965E-01	2.4441721E+01	*	86.	1.1648415E-01	3.5900675E+01	*
37.	3.9653141E-01	2.4838252E+01	*	87.	1.1360815E-01	3.6014283E+01	*
38.	3.8674102E-01	2.5224993E+01	*	88.	1.1080315E-01	3.6125086E+01	*
39.	3.7719235E-01	2.5601285E+01	*	89.	1.0806741E-01	3.6233153E+01	*
40.	3.6787944E-01	2.5970064E+01	*	90.	1.0539922E-01	3.6338552E+01	*
41.	3.5879646E-01	2.6328860E+01	*	91.	1.0279690E-01	3.6441344E+01	*
42.	3.4993774E-01	2.6678797E+01	*	92.	1.0025884E-01	3.6541606E+01	*
43.	3.4129775E-01	2.7020094E+01	*	93.	9.7783443E-02	3.6639389E+01	*
44.	3.3287108E-01	2.7352965E+01	*	94.	9.5369162E-02	3.6734758E+01	*
45.	3.2465246E-01	2.7677617E+01	*	95.	9.3014489E-02	3.6827772E+01	*
46.	3.1663676E-01	2.7994253E+01	*	96.	9.0717953E-02	3.6918489E+01	*
47.	3.0881897E-01	2.8303071E+01	*	97.	8.8478118E-02	3.7006967E+01	*
48.	3.0119421E-01	2.8604265E+01	*	98.	8.6293586E-02	3.7093260E+01	*
49.	2.9375769E-01	2.8898022E+01	*	99.	8.4162990E-02	3.7177422E+01	*
50.	2.8650479E-01	2.9184526E+01	*	100.	8.2084998E-02	3.7259506E+01	*

TABULATED VALUES OF E^{-RX} WHEN R = .026

X	E^{-RX}	SUM OF E^{-RX}	*	X	E^{-RX}	SUM OF E^{-RX}	*
0.	1.0000000E+00	1.0000000E+00	*	50.	2.7253179E-01	2.8617370E+01	*
1.	9.7433508E-01	1.9743350E+00	*	51.	2.6553728E-01	2.8882907E+01	*
2.	9.4932886E-01	2.9236638E+00	*	52.	2.5872229E-01	2.9141629E+01	*
3.	9.2496442E-01	3.8486282E+00	*	53.	2.5208221E-01	2.9393711E+01	*
4.	9.0122529E-01	4.7498534E+00	*	54.	2.4561254E-01	2.9639323E+01	*
5.	8.7809542E-01	5.6279488E+00	*	55.	2.3930892E-01	2.9878631E+01	*
6.	8.5555918E-01	6.4835079E+00	*	56.	2.3316707E-01	3.0111798E+01	*
7.	8.3360133E-01	7.3171092E+00	*	57.	2.2718286E-01	3.0338980E+01	*
8.	8.1220703E-01	8.1293162E+00	*	58.	2.2135223E-01	3.0560332E+01	*
9.	7.9136181E-01	8.9206780E+00	*	59.	2.1567126E-01	3.0776033E+01	*
10.	7.7105158E-01	9.6917295E+00	*	60.	2.1013607E-01	3.0986139E+01	*
11.	7.5126261E-01	1.0442992E+01	*	61.	2.0474294E-01	3.1190881E+01	*
12.	7.3198152E-01	1.1174973E+01	*	62.	1.9948823E-01	3.1390369E+01	*
13.	7.1319528E-01	1.1888816E+01	*	63.	1.9436839E-01	3.1584737E+01	*
14.	6.9489119E-01	1.2583059E+01	*	64.	1.8937994E-01	3.1774116E+01	*
15.	6.7705687E-01	1.3260115E+01	*	65.	1.8451952E-01	3.1958635E+01	*
16.	6.5968026E-01	1.3919795E+01	*	66.	1.7978384E-01	3.2138418E+01	*
17.	6.4274963E-01	1.4562544E+01	*	67.	1.7516971E-01	3.2313587E+01	*
18.	6.2625352E-01	1.5188797E+01	*	68.	1.7067399E-01	3.2484226E+01	*
19.	6.1018078E-01	1.5798977E+01	*	69.	1.6629366E-01	3.2650553E+01	*
20.	5.9452054E-01	1.6393497E+01	*	70.	1.6202575E-01	3.2812578E+01	*
21.	5.7926223E-01	1.6972759E+01	*	71.	1.5786737E-01	3.2970445E+01	*
22.	5.6439551E-01	1.7537154E+01	*	72.	1.5381572E-01	3.3124260E+01	*
23.	5.4991035E-01	1.8087064E+01	*	73.	1.4986805E-01	3.3274128E+01	*
24.	5.3579645E-01	1.8622860E+01	*	74.	1.4602170E-01	3.3420149E+01	*
25.	5.2204577E-01	1.9144905E+01	*	75.	1.4227407E-01	3.3562423E+01	*
26.	5.0864751E-01	1.9653552E+01	*	76.	1.3862261E-01	3.3701045E+01	*
27.	4.9559312E-01	2.0149145E+01	*	77.	1.3506488E-01	3.3836109E+01	*
28.	4.8287377E-01	2.0632018E+01	*	78.	1.3159845E-01	3.3967707E+01	*
29.	4.7048085E-01	2.1102498E+01	*	79.	1.2822099E-01	3.4095927E+01	*
30.	4.5840401E-01	2.1560904E+01	*	80.	1.2493021E-01	3.4220857E+01	*
31.	4.4664106E-01	2.2007545E+01	*	81.	1.2172368E-01	3.4342580E+01	*
32.	4.3517806E-01	2.2442723E+01	*	82.	1.1859985E-01	3.4461179E+01	*
33.	4.2400925E-01	2.2866732E+01	*	83.	1.1555600E-01	3.4576735E+01	*
34.	4.1312709E-01	2.3279859E+01	*	84.	1.1259026E-01	3.4689325E+01	*
35.	4.0252042E-01	2.3682383E+01	*	85.	1.0970064E-01	3.4799025E+01	*
36.	3.9219347E-01	2.4074576E+01	*	86.	1.0688519E-01	3.4905910E+01	*
37.	3.8212786E-01	2.4456703E+01	*	87.	1.0414199E-01	3.5010051E+01	*
38.	3.7232058E-01	2.4829023E+01	*	88.	1.0146919E-01	3.5111520E+01	*
39.	3.6276501E-01	2.5191788E+01	*	89.	9.8864999E-02	3.5210384E+01	*
40.	3.5345468E-01	2.5545242E+01	*	90.	9.6327638E-02	3.5306711E+01	*
41.	3.4438329E-01	2.5889625E+01	*	91.	9.3855397E-02	3.5400566E+01	*
42.	3.3554473E-01	2.6225169E+01	*	92.	9.1446607E-02	3.5492012E+01	*
43.	3.2693300E-01	2.6552102E+01	*	93.	8.9099638E-02	3.5581111E+01	*
44.	3.1854229E-01	2.6870644E+01	*	94.	8.6812904E-02	3.5667923E+01	*
45.	3.1036694E-01	2.7181010E+01	*	95.	8.4584858E-02	3.5752507E+01	*
46.	3.0240140E-01	2.7483411E+01	*	96.	8.2413995E-02	3.5834920E+01	*
47.	2.9464029E-01	2.7778051E+01	*	97.	8.0298884E-02	3.5915218E+01	*
48.	2.8707837E-01	2.8065129E+01	*	98.	7.8237985E-02	3.5993455E+01	*
49.	2.7971053E-01	2.8344839E+01	*	99.	7.6230014E-02	3.6069695E+01	*
50.	2.7253179E-01	2.8617370E+01	*	100.	7.4273578E-02	3.6143958E+01	*

X	E^{-RX}	SUM OF E^{-RX}	*	X	E^{-RX}	SUM OF E^{-RX}	*
0.	1.0000000E+00	1.0000000E+00	*	50.	2.5924026E-01	2.8066813E+01	*
1.	9.7336124E-01	1.9733612E+00	*	51.	2.5233442E-01	2.8319147E+01	*
2.	9.4743210E-01	2.9207933E+00	*	52.	2.4561254E-01	2.8564759E+01	*
3.	9.2219369E-01	3.8429869E+00	*	53.	2.3906973E-01	2.8803828E+01	*
4.	8.9762759E-01	4.7406144E+00	*	54.	2.3270121E-01	2.9036529E+01	*
5.	8.7371591E-01	5.6143303E+00	*	55.	2.2650234E-01	2.9263031E+01	*
6.	8.5044120E-01	6.4647115E+00	*	56.	2.2046859E-01	2.9483499E+01	*
7.	8.2778650E-01	7.2925580E+00	*	57.	2.1459558E-01	2.9698094E+01	*
8.	8.0573530E-01	8.0982933E+00	*	58.	2.0887902E-01	2.9906973E+01	*
9.	7.8427151E-01	8.8825648E+00	*	59.	2.0331475E-01	3.0110287E+01	*
10.	7.6337949E-01	9.6459442E+00	*	60.	1.9789869E-01	3.0308185E+01	*
11.	7.4304401E-01	1.0388988E+01	*	61.	1.9262692E-01	3.0500811E+01	*
12.	7.2325024E-01	1.1112238E+01	*	62.	1.8749558E-01	3.0688306E+01	*
13.	7.0398375E-01	1.1816221E+01	*	63.	1.8250093E-01	3.0870806E+01	*
14.	6.8523049E-01	1.2501451E+01	*	64.	1.7763933E-01	3.1048445E+01	*
15.	6.6697680E-01	1.3168427E+01	*	65.	1.7290724E-01	3.1221352E+01	*
16.	6.4920937E-01	1.3817636E+01	*	66.	1.6830120E-01	3.1389653E+01	*
17.	6.3191524E-01	1.4449551E+01	*	67.	1.6381787E-01	3.1553470E+01	*
18.	6.1508180E-01	1.5064632E+01	*	68.	1.5945396E-01	3.1712923E+01	*
19.	5.9869678E-01	1.5663328E+01	*	69.	1.5520631E-01	3.1868129E+01	*
20.	5.8274825E-01	1.6246076E+01	*	70.	1.5107180E-01	3.2019200E+01	*
21.	5.6722456E-01	1.6813300E+01	*	71.	1.4704744E-01	3.2166247E+01	*
22.	5.5211440E-01	1.7365414E+01	*	72.	1.4313028E-01	3.2309377E+01	*
23.	5.3740676E-01	1.7902820E+01	*	73.	1.3931746E-01	3.2448694E+01	*
24.	5.2309091E-01	1.8425910E+01	*	74.	1.3560622E-01	3.2584300E+01	*
25.	5.0915641E-01	1.8935066E+01	*	75.	1.3199384E-01	3.2716293E+01	*
26.	4.9559312E-01	1.9430659E+01	*	76.	1.2847769E-01	3.2844770E+01	*
27.	4.8239113E-01	1.9913050E+01	*	77.	1.2505520E-01	3.2969825E+01	*
28.	4.6954083E-01	2.0382590E+01	*	78.	1.2172388E-01	3.3091548E+01	*
29.	4.5703285E-01	2.0839622E+01	*	79.	1.1848131E-01	3.3210029E+01	*
30.	4.4485806E-01	2.1284480E+01	*	80.	1.1532512E-01	3.3325354E+01	*
31.	4.3300759E-01	2.1717487E+01	*	81.	1.1225300E-01	3.3437607E+01	*
32.	4.2147281E-01	2.2138959E+01	*	82.	1.0926272E-01	3.3546869E+01	*
33.	4.1024530E-01	2.2549204E+01	*	83.	1.0635209E-01	3.3653221E+01	*
34.	3.9931687E-01	2.2948520E+01	*	84.	1.0351901E-01	3.3756740E+01	*
35.	3.8867957E-01	2.3337199E+01	*	85.	1.0076139E-01	3.3857501E+01	*
36.	3.7832562E-01	2.3715524E+01	*	86.	9.8077234E-02	3.3955578E+01	*
37.	3.6824750E-01	2.4083771E+01	*	87.	9.5464578E-02	3.4051042E+01	*
38.	3.5843784E-01	2.4442208E+01	*	88.	9.2921521E-02	3.4143963E+01	*
39.	3.4888950E-01	2.4791097E+01	*	89.	9.0446207E-02	3.4234409E+01	*
40.	3.3959552E-01	2.5130692E+01	*	90.	8.8036832E-02	3.4322454E+01	*
41.	3.3054912E-01	2.5461241E+01	*	91.	8.5691640E-02	3.4408136E+01	*
42.	3.2174370E-01	2.5782984E+01	*	92.	8.3408921E-02	3.4491544E+01	*
43.	3.1317285E-01	2.6096156E+01	*	93.	8.1187011E-02	3.4572731E+01	*
44.	3.0483031E-01	2.6400986E+01	*	94.	7.9024290E-02	3.4651755E+01	*
45.	2.9671001E-01	2.6697696E+01	*	95.	7.6919181E-02	3.4728674E+01	*
46.	2.8880602E-01	2.6986502E+01	*	96.	7.4870149E-02	3.4803544E+01	*
47.	2.8111259E-01	2.7267614E+01	*	97.	7.2875702E-02	3.4876419E+01	*
48.	2.7362410E-01	2.7541238E+01	*	98.	7.0934383E-02	3.4947353E+01	*
49.	2.6633509E-01	2.7807573E+01	*	99.	6.9044779E-02	3.5016397E+01	*
50.	2.5924026E-01	2.8066813E+01	*	100.	6.7205512E-02	3.5083602E+01	*

X	E^{-RX}	SUM OF E^{-RX}	*	X	E^{-RX}	SUM OF E^{-RX}	*
0.	1.0000000E+00	1.0000000E+00	*	50.	2.4659696E-01	2.7532289E+01	*
1.	9.7238836E-01	1.9723883E+00	*	51.	2.3978801E-01	2.7772077E+01	*
2.	9.4553913E-01	2.9179274E+00	*	52.	2.3316707E-01	2.8005244E+01	*
3.	9.1943125E-01	3.8373586E+00	*	53.	2.2672895E-01	2.8231972E+01	*
4.	8.9404425E-01	4.7314028E+00	*	54.	2.2046859E-01	2.8452440E+01	*
5.	8.6935823E-01	5.6007610E+00	*	55.	2.1438110E-01	2.8666821E+01	*
6.	8.4535383E-01	6.4461148E+00	*	56.	2.0846168E-01	2.8875282E+01	*
7.	8.2201223E-01	7.2681270E+00	*	57.	2.0270572E-01	2.9077987E+01	*
8.	7.9931513E-01	8.0674421E+00	*	58.	1.9710868E-01	2.9275095E+01	*
9.	7.7724473E-01	8.8446868E+00	*	59.	1.9166619E-01	2.9466761E+01	*
10.	7.5578374E-01	9.6004705E+00	*	60.	1.8637397E-01	2.9653134E+01	*
11.	7.3491531E-01	1.0335385E+01	*	61.	1.8122788E-01	2.9834361E+01	*
12.	7.1462310E-01	1.1050008E+01	*	62.	1.7623388E-01	3.0010584E+01	*
13.	6.9489119E-01	1.1744899E+01	*	63.	1.7135805E-01	3.0181942E+01	*
14.	6.7570411E-01	1.2420603E+01	*	64.	1.6662658E-01	3.0348568E+01	*
15.	6.5704681E-01	1.3077649E+01	*	65.	1.6202575E-01	3.0510593E+01	*
16.	6.3890468E-01	1.3716553E+01	*	66.	1.5755195E-01	3.0668144E+01	*
17.	6.2126348E-01	1.4337816E+01	*	67.	1.5320168E-01	3.0821345E+01	*
18.	6.0410938E-01	1.4941925E+01	*	68.	1.4897153E-01	3.0970316E+01	*
19.	5.8742893E-01	1.5529353E+01	*	69.	1.4485819E-01	3.1115174E+01	*
20.	5.7120906E-01	1.6100562E+01	*	70.	1.4085842E-01	3.1256032E+01	*
21.	5.5543704E-01	1.6655999E+01	*	71.	1.3696908E-01	3.1393001E+01	*
22.	5.4010052E-01	1.7196909E+01	*	72.	1.3318714E-01	3.1526188E+01	*
23.	5.2518746E-01	1.7721286E+01	*	73.	1.2950963E-01	3.1655697E+01	*
24.	5.1068618E-01	1.8231972E+01	*	74.	1.2593366E-01	3.1781630E+01	*
25.	4.9658530E-01	1.8728557E+01	*	75.	1.2245642E-01	3.1904086E+01	*
26.	4.8287377E-01	1.9211430E+01	*	76.	1.1907520E-01	3.2023161E+01	*
27.	4.6954083E-01	1.9680970E+01	*	77.	1.1578734E-01	3.2138948E+01	*
28.	4.5657604E-01	2.0137546E+01	*	78.	1.1259026E-01	3.2251538E+01	*
29.	4.4396923E-01	2.0581515E+01	*	79.	1.0948146E-01	3.2361019E+01	*
30.	4.3171052E-01	2.1013225E+01	*	80.	1.0645850E-01	3.2467470E+01	*
31.	4.1979028E-01	2.1433015E+01	*	81.	1.0351901E-01	3.2570996E+01	*
32.	4.0819919E-01	2.1841214E+01	*	82.	1.0066068E-01	3.2671656E+01	*
33.	3.9692814E-01	2.2238142E+01	*	83.	9.7881276E-02	3.2769537E+01	*
34.	3.8596831E-01	2.2624110E+01	*	84.	9.5178614E-02	3.2864715E+01	*
35.	3.7531109E-01	2.2999421E+01	*	85.	9.2550577E-02	3.2957265E+01	*
36.	3.6494814E-01	2.3364369E+01	*	86.	8.9995104E-02	3.3047260E+01	*
37.	3.5487133E-01	2.3719240E+01	*	87.	8.7510192E-02	3.3134770E+01	*
38.	3.4507275E-01	2.4064312E+01	*	88.	8.5093893E-02	3.3219863E+01	*
39.	3.3554473E-01	2.4399856E+01	*	89.	8.2744317E-02	3.3302607E+01	*
40.	3.2627979E-01	2.4726135E+01	*	90.	8.0459605E-02	3.3383066E+01	*
41.	3.1727067E-01	2.5043405E+01	*	91.	7.8237985E-02	3.3461303E+01	*
42.	3.0851031E-01	2.5351915E+01	*	92.	7.6077706E-02	3.3537380E+01	*
43.	2.9999184E-01	2.5651906E+01	*	93.	7.3977077E-02	3.3611357E+01	*
44.	2.9170857E-01	2.5943614E+01	*	94.	7.1934449E-02	3.3683291E+01	*
45.	2.8365924E-01	2.6227268E+01	*	95.	6.9948221E-02	3.3753239E+01	*
46.	2.7582187E-01	2.6503089E+01	*	96.	6.8016836E-02	3.3821255E+01	*
47.	2.6820590E-01	2.6771294E+01	*	97.	6.6138780E-02	3.3887393E+01	*
48.	2.6080037E-01	2.7032094E+01	*	98.	6.4312581E-02	3.3951705E+01	*
49.	2.5359925E-01	2.7285693E+01	*	99.	6.2536805E-02	3.4014241E+01	*
50.	2.4659696E-01	2.7532289E+01	*	100.	6.0810062E-02	3.4075051E+01	*

TABULATED VALUES OF E WHEN R = .029

X	E	SUM OF E	*	X	E	SUM OF E	*
0.	1.0000000E+00	1.0000000E+00	*	50.	2.3457028E-01	2.7013244E+01	*
1.	9.7141646E-01	1.9714164E+00	*	51.	2.2786543E-01	2.7241109E+01	=
2.	9.4364994E-01	2.9150663E+00	=	52.	2.2135223E-01	2.7462461E+01	*
3.	9.1667709E-01	3.8317433E+00	*	53.	2.1502521E-01	2.7677486E+01	*
4.	8.9047522E-01	4.7222185E+00	*	54.	2.0887902E-01	2.7886365E+01	*
5.	8.6502229E-01	5.5872407E+00	*	55.	2.0290852E-01	2.8089273E+01	*
6.	8.4029689E-01	6.4275375E+00	*	56.	1.9710868E-01	2.8286381E+01	*
7.	8.1627823E-01	7.2438157E+00	*	57.	1.9147462E-01	2.8477855E+01	*
8.	7.9294612E-01	8.0367618E+00	*	58.	1.8600160E-01	2.8663856E+01	*
9.	7.7028091E-01	8.8070427E+00	*	59.	1.8069501E-01	2.8844541E+01	*
10.	7.4826356E-01	9.5553062E+00	*	60.	1.7552040E-01	2.9020061E+01	*
11.	7.2687554E-01	1.0282181E+01	*	61.	1.7050340E-01	2.9190564E+01	*
12.	7.0609887E-01	1.0988279E+01	*	62.	1.6562981E-01	2.9356193E+01	*
13.	6.8591607E-01	1.1674195E+01	*	63.	1.6089553E-01	2.9517088E+01	*
14.	6.6631016E-01	1.2340505E+01	*	64.	1.5629656E-01	2.9673384E+01	*
15.	6.4726466E-01	1.2987769E+01	*	65.	1.5182905E-01	2.9825213E+01	*
16.	6.2876355E-01	1.3616532E+01	*	66.	1.4748924E-01	2.9972702E+01	*
17.	6.1079126E-01	1.4227323E+01	*	67.	1.4327344E-01	3.0115975E+01	*
18.	5.9333269E-01	1.4820655E+01	*	68.	1.3917822E-01	3.0255153E+01	*
19.	5.7637314E-01	1.5397028E+01	*	69.	1.3520001E-01	3.0390353E+01	*
20.	5.5989836E-01	1.5956926E+01	*	70.	1.3133552E-01	3.0521688E+01	*
21.	5.4389449E-01	1.6500820E+01	*	71.	1.2758144E-01	3.0649269E+01	*
22.	5.2834806E-01	1.7029168E+01	*	72.	1.2393475E-01	3.0773203E+01	*
23.	5.1324600E-01	1.7542414E+01	*	73.	1.2039226E-01	3.0893595E+01	*
24.	4.9857562E-01	1.8040989E+01	*	74.	1.1695102E-01	3.1010546E+01	*
25.	4.8432456E-01	1.8525313E+01	*	75.	1.1360815E-01	3.1124154E+01	*
26.	4.7048085E-01	1.8995793E+01	*	76.	1.1036083E-01	3.1234514E+01	*
27.	4.5703285E-01	1.9452825E+01	*	77.	1.0720632E-01	3.1341720E+01	*
28.	4.4396923E-01	1.9896794E+01	*	78.	1.0414199E-01	3.1445861E+01	*
29.	4.3127902E-01	2.0328073E+01	*	79.	1.0116524E-01	3.1547026E+01	*
30.	4.1895154E-01	2.0747024E+01	*	80.	9.8273585E-02	3.1645290E+01	*
31.	4.0697643E-01	2.1154000E+01	*	81.	9.5464579E-02	3.1740763E+01	*
32.	3.9534360E-01	2.1549343E+01	*	82.	9.2735843E-02	3.1833490E+01	*
33.	3.8404328E-01	2.1933386E+01	*	83.	9.0085144E-02	3.1923583E+01	*
34.	3.7306597E-01	2.2306451E+01	*	84.	8.7510192E-02	3.2011093E+01	*
35.	3.6240242E-01	2.2668853E+01	*	85.	8.5008842E-02	3.2096101E+01	*
36.	3.5204388E-01	2.3020896E+01	=	86.	8.2579888E-02	3.2178679E+01	*
37.	3.4198103E-01	2.3362877E+01	*	87.	8.0218589E-02	3.2258897E+01	=
38.	3.3220600E-01	2.3695083E+01	*	88.	7.7925654E-02	3.2336822E+01	*
39.	3.2271038E-01	2.4017793E+01	*	89.	7.5659267E-02	3.2412520E+01	*
40.	3.1348618E-01	2.4331279E+01	*	90.	7.3534543E-02	3.2486054E+01	*
41.	3.0452563E-01	2.4635804E+01	*	91.	7.1432665E-02	3.2557486E+01	*
42.	2.9582121E-01	2.4931625E+01	*	92.	6.9390868E-02	3.2626676E+01	*
43.	2.8736560E-01	2.5218990E+01	*	93.	6.7407431E-02	3.2694283E+01	*
44.	2.7915167E-01	2.5498141E+01	*	94.	6.5480659E-02	3.2759763E+01	*
45.	2.7117253E-01	2.5769313E+01	*	95.	6.3609019E-02	3.2823372E+01	*
46.	2.6342146E-01	2.6032734E+01	*	96.	6.1790848E-02	3.2885162E+01	*
47.	2.5589194E-01	2.6288625E+01	*	97.	6.0024647E-02	3.2945186E+01	*
48.	2.4857765E-01	2.6537202E+01	*	98.	5.8309031E-02	3.3003496E+01	*
49.	2.4147242E-01	2.6778674E+01	*	99.	5.6642255E-02	3.3060130E+01	=
50.	2.3457028E-01	2.7013244E+01	*	100.	5.5023219E-02	3.3115159E+01	=

TABULATED VALUES OF E WHEN R = .030

X	E	SUM OF E	*	X	E	SUM OF E	*
0.	1.0000000E+00	1.0000000E+00	*	50.	2.2313015E-01	2.6509148E+01	*
1.	9.7044553E-01	1.9704455E+00	*	51.	2.1653566E-01	2.6725683E+01	*
2.	9.4176453E-01	2.9122100E+00	=	52.	2.1013607E-01	2.6935819E+01	*
3.	9.1393118E-01	3.8261411E+00	=	53.	2.0392561E-01	2.7139744E+01	*
4.	8.8692043E-01	4.7130615E+00	*	54.	1.9789869E-01	2.7337642E+01	*
5.	8.6070797E-01	5.5737694E+00	*	55.	1.9204990E-01	2.7529691E+01	*
6.	8.3527020E-01	6.4090396E+00	*	56.	1.8637397E-01	2.7716064E+01	*
7.	8.1058424E-01	7.2194623E+00	*	57.	1.8086579E-01	2.7896929E+01	*
8.	7.8662786E-01	8.0062516E+00	*	58.	1.7552040E-01	2.8072449E+01	*
9.	7.6337949E-01	8.7696310E+00	*	59.	1.7033295E-01	2.8242781E+01	*
10.	7.4081821E-01	9.5104492E+00	*	60.	1.6529888E-01	2.8408079E+01	*
11.	7.1892373E-01	1.0229372E+01	*	61.	1.6041356E-01	2.8568492E+01	*
12.	6.9767632E-01	1.0927046E+01	*	62.	1.5567262E-01	2.8724164E+01	*
13.	6.7705687E-01	1.1604104E+01	*	63.	1.5107180E-01	2.8875235E+01	*
14.	6.5704681E-01	1.2261150E+01	*	64.	1.4660696E-01	2.9021841E+01	*
15.	6.3762814E-01	1.2898778E+01	*	65.	1.4227407E-01	2.9164115E+01	*
16.	6.1878339E-01	1.3517561E+01	*	66.	1.3806923E-01	2.9302184E+01	*
17.	6.0049557E-01	1.4118056E+01	*	67.	1.3398867E-01	2.9436172E+01	*
18.	5.8274825E-01	1.4700804E+01	*	68.	1.3002871E-01	2.9566200E+01	*
19.	5.6552543E-01	1.5266329E+01	*	69.	1.2618578E-01	2.9692385E+01	*
20.	5.4881163E-01	1.5815140E+01	*	70.	1.2245642E-01	2.9814841E+01	*
21.	5.3259179E-01	1.6347731E+01	*	71.	1.1883729E-01	2.9933678E+01	*
22.	5.1685133E-01	1.6864582E+01	*	72.	1.1532512E-01	3.0049003E+01	*
23.	5.0157606E-01	1.7366158E+01	*	73.	1.1191674E-01	3.0160919E+01	*
24.	4.8675225E-01	1.7852910E+01	*	74.	1.0860910E-01	3.0269528E+01	*
25.	4.7236655E-01	1.8325276E+01	*	75.	1.0539922E-01	3.0374927E+01	*
26.	4.5840601E-01	1.8783682E+01	*	76.	1.0228420E-01	3.0477211E+01	*
27.	4.4485806E-01	1.9228540E+01	*	77.	9.9261251E-02	3.0576472E+01	*
28.	4.3171052E-01	1.9660250E+01	*	78.	9.6327638E-02	3.0672799E+01	*
29.	4.1895154E-01	2.0079201E+01	*	79.	9.3480726E-02	3.0766279E+01	*
30.	4.0656965E-01	2.0485770E+01	*	80.	9.0717953E-02	3.0856996E+01	*
31.	3.9455370E-01	2.0880323E+01	*	81.	8.8036832E-02	3.0945032E+01	*
32.	3.8289288E-01	2.1263215E+01	*	82.	8.5434950E-02	3.1030468E+01	*
33.	3.7157669E-01	2.1634791E+01	*	83.	8.2909966E-02	3.1113375E+01	*
34.	3.6059493E-01	2.1995385E+01	*	84.	8.0459604E-02	3.1193834E+01	*
35.	3.4993774E-01	2.2345322E+01	*	85.	7.8081665E-02	3.1271915E+01	*
36.	3.3959552E-01	2.2684917E+01	*	86.	7.5774003E-02	3.1347689E+01	=
37.	3.2955896E-01	2.3014475E+01	*	87.	7.3534543E-02	3.1421223E+01	*
38.	3.1981902E-01	2.3334294E+01	*	88.	7.1361269E-02	3.1492584E+01	=
39.	3.1036694E-01	2.3644660E+01	*	89.	6.9252225E-02	3.1561836E+01	=
40.	3.0119421E-01	2.3945854E+01	*	90.	6.7205512E-02	3.1629041E+01	=
41.	2.9229257E-01	2.4231466E+01	*	91.	6.5219289E-02	3.1694260E+01	=
42.	2.8365402E-01	2.4521800E+01	*	92.	6.3291768E-02	3.1757551E+01	*
43.	2.7527078E-01	2.4797073E+01	*	93.	6.1421213E-02	3.1818972E+01	=
44.	2.6713330E-01	2.5064205E+01	*	94.	5.9605942E-02	3.1878577E+01	=
45.	2.5924026E-01	2.5323445E+01	*	95.	5.7844320E-02	3.1936421E+01	*
46.	2.5157855E-01	2.5575023E+01	*	96.	5.6134762E-02	3.1992555E+01	*
47.	2.4414328E-01	2.5819166E+01	=	97.	5.4475729E-02	3.2047030E+01	=
48.	2.3692775E-01	2.6056093E+01	*	98.	5.2865728E-02	3.2099895E+01	=
49.	2.2992568E-01	2.6286018E+01	*	99.	5.1303310E-02	3.2151199E+01	=
50.	2.2313015E-01	2.6509148E+01	*	100.	4.9787068E-02	3.2200985E+01	=

TABULATED VALUES OF E^{-RX} WHEN R = .031

X	E^{-RX}	SUM OF E^{-RX}	*	X	E^{-RX}	SUM OF E^{-RX}	*
0.	1.0000000E+00	1.0000000E+00	*	50.	2.1224797E-01	2.6019495E+01	*
1.	9.6947557E-01	1.9694755E+00	*	51.	2.0576922E-01	2.6225264E+01	*
2.	9.3988288E-01	2.9093583E+00	*	52.	1.9948823E-01	2.6424752E+01	*
3.	9.1119349E-01	3.8205517E+00	*	53.	1.9339497E-01	2.6618150E+01	*
4.	8.8337983E-01	4.7039315E+00	*	54.	1.8749558E-01	2.6805645E+01	*
5.	8.5641517E-01	5.5603466E+00	*	55.	1.8177238E-01	2.6987417E+01	*
6.	8.3027359E-01	6.3906201E+00	*	56.	1.7622388E-01	2.7163640E+01	*
7.	8.0492996E-01	7.1955500E+00	*	57.	1.7084475E-01	2.7334484E+01	*
8.	7.8035994E-01	7.9759099E+00	*	58.	1.6562981E-01	2.7500113E+01	*
9.	7.5653990E-01	8.7324498E+00	*	59.	1.6057406E-01	2.7660687E+01	*
10.	7.3344695E-01	9.4658967E+00	*	60.	1.5567263E-01	2.7816359E+01	*
11.	7.1105890E-01	1.0176955E+01	*	61.	1.5092081E-01	2.7967279E+01	*
12.	6.8935424E-01	1.0866309E+01	*	62.	1.4631404E-01	2.8113593E+01	*
13.	6.6831209E-01	1.1534621E+01	*	63.	1.4184788E-01	2.8255440E+01	*
14.	6.4791225E-01	1.2182533E+01	*	64.	1.3751806E-01	2.8392958E+01	*
15.	6.2813510E-01	1.2810668E+01	*	65.	1.3332040E-01	2.8526278E+01	*
16.	6.0896164E-01	1.3419629E+01	*	66.	1.2925087E-01	2.8655528E+01	*
17.	5.9037343E-01	1.4010002E+01	*	67.	1.2530556E-01	2.8780833E+01	*
18.	5.7235262E-01	1.4582354E+01	*	68.	1.2148068E-01	2.8902313E+01	*
19.	5.5488188E-01	1.5137235E+01	*	69.	1.1777255E-01	2.9020085E+01	*
20.	5.3794443E-01	1.5675179E+01	*	70.	1.1417761E-01	2.9134262E+01	*
21.	5.2152399E-01	1.6196702E+01	*	71.	1.1069241E-01	2.9244954E+01	*
22.	5.0560476E-01	1.6702306E+01	*	72.	1.0731358E-01	2.9352267E+01	*
23.	4.9017147E-01	1.7192477E+01	*	73.	1.0403790E-01	2.9456304E+01	*
24.	4.7520927E-01	1.7667686E+01	*	74.	1.0086220E-01	2.9557166E+01	*
25.	4.6070378E-01	1.8128389E+01	*	75.	9.7783443E-02	2.9654949E+01	*
26.	4.4664106E-01	1.8575030E+01	*	76.	9.4798660E-02	2.9749747E+01	*
27.	4.3300759E-01	1.9008037E+01	*	77.	9.1904985E-02	2.9841651E+01	*
28.	4.1979028E-01	1.9427827E+01	*	78.	8.9099638E-02	2.9930750E+01	*
29.	4.0697643E-01	1.9834803E+01	*	79.	8.6379922E-02	3.0017129E+01	*
30.	3.9455370E-01	2.0229356E+01	*	80.	8.3743225E-02	3.0100872E+01	*
31.	3.8251018E-01	2.0611866E+01	*	81.	8.1187011E-02	3.0182059E+01	*
32.	3.7083427E-01	2.0982700E+01	*	82.	7.8708824E-02	3.0260767E+01	*
33.	3.5951477E-01	2.1342214E+01	*	83.	7.6306282E-02	3.0337073E+01	*
34.	3.4854079E-01	2.1690754E+01	*	84.	7.3977077E-02	3.0411050E+01	*
35.	3.3790178E-01	2.2028655E+01	*	85.	7.1718969E-02	3.0482768E+01	*
36.	3.2758752E-01	2.2356242E+01	*	86.	6.9529788E-02	3.0552297E+01	*
37.	3.1758810E-01	2.2673830E+01	*	87.	6.7407431E-02	3.0619704E+01	*
38.	3.0789391E-01	2.2981723E+01	*	88.	6.5349858E-02	3.0685053E+01	*
39.	2.9849562E-01	2.3280218E+01	*	89.	6.3355091E-02	3.0748408E+01	*
40.	2.8938421E-01	2.3569602E+01	*	90.	6.1421213E-02	3.0809829E+01	*
41.	2.8055092E-01	2.3850152E+01	*	91.	5.9546366E-02	3.0869375E+01	*
42.	2.7198727E-01	2.4122139E+01	*	92.	5.7728747E-02	3.0927103E+01	*
43.	2.6368501E-01	2.4385824E+01	*	93.	5.5966610E-02	3.0983069E+01	*
44.	2.5563618E-01	2.4641460E+01	*	94.	5.4258262E-02	3.1037327E+01	*
45.	2.4783303E-01	2.4889293E+01	*	95.	5.2602059E-02	3.1089929E+01	*
46.	2.4026807E-01	2.5129561E+01	*	96.	5.0996411E-02	3.1140925E+01	*
47.	2.3293402E-01	2.5362495E+01	*	97.	4.9439775E-02	3.1190364E+01	*
48.	2.2582385E-01	2.5588318E+01	*	98.	4.7930654E-02	3.1238294E+01	*
49.	2.1893070E-01	2.5807248E+01	*	99.	4.6467599E-02	3.1284761E+01	*
50.	2.1224797E-01	2.6019495E+01	*	100.	4.5049202E-02	3.1329810E+01	*

TABULATED VALUES OF E^{-RX} WHEN R = .032

X	E^{-RX}	SUM OF E^{-RX}	*	X	E^{-RX}	SUM OF E^{-RX}	*
0.	1.0000000E+00	1.0000000E+00	*	50.	2.0189651E-01	2.5543790E+01	*
1.	9.6850658E-01	1.9685065E+00	*	51.	1.9553810E-01	2.5739328E+01	*
2.	9.3800499E-01	2.9065114E+00	*	52.	1.8937994E-01	2.5928707E+01	*
3.	9.0846401E-01	3.8149754E+00	*	53.	1.8341572E-01	2.6112122E+01	*
4.	8.7985337E-01	4.6948287E+00	*	54.	1.7763933E-01	2.6289761E+01	*
5.	8.5214378E-01	5.5469724E+00	*	55.	1.7204486E-01	2.6461805E+01	*
6.	8.2530686E-01	6.3722792E+00	*	56.	1.6662658E-01	2.6628431E+01	*
7.	7.9931513E-01	7.1715943E+00	*	57.	1.6137894E-01	2.6789809E+01	*
8.	7.7414196E-01	7.9457362E+00	*	58.	1.5629654E-01	2.6946105E+01	*
9.	7.4976159E-01	8.6954977E+00	*	59.	1.5137425E-01	2.7097479E+01	*
10.	7.2614903E-01	9.4216467E+00	*	60.	1.4660694E-01	2.7244085E+01	*
11.	7.0328012E-01	1.0124924E+01	*	61.	1.4198980E-01	2.7386074E+01	*
12.	6.8113142E-01	1.0806057E+01	*	62.	1.3751806E-01	2.7523592E+01	*
13.	6.5968268E-01	1.1465737E+01	*	63.	1.3318714E-01	2.7656779E+01	*
14.	6.3890668E-01	1.2104641E+01	*	64.	1.2899263E-01	2.7785771E+01	*
15.	6.1878339E-01	1.2723424E+01	*	65.	1.2493021E-01	2.7910701E+01	*
16.	5.9929578E-01	1.3322719E+01	*	66.	1.2099553E-01	2.8031696E+01	*
17.	5.8042191E-01	1.3903140E+01	*	67.	1.1718516E-01	2.8148881E+01	*
18.	5.6214244E-01	1.4465282E+01	*	68.	1.1349460E-01	2.8262375E+01	*
19.	5.4443865E-01	1.5009720E+01	*	69.	1.0992026E-01	2.8372295E+01	*
20.	5.2729242E-01	1.5537012E+01	*	70.	1.0645850E-01	2.8478753E+01	*
21.	5.1068618E-01	1.6047698E+01	*	71.	1.0310576E-01	2.8581858E+01	*
22.	4.9460292E-01	1.6542300E+01	*	72.	9.9858609E-02	2.8681716E+01	*
23.	4.7902619E-01	1.7021326E+01	*	73.	9.6713720E-02	2.8778429E+01	*
24.	4.6394002E-01	1.7485266E+01	*	74.	9.3667874E-02	2.8872096E+01	*
25.	4.4932896E-01	1.7934594E+01	*	75.	9.0717953E-02	2.8962813E+01	*
26.	4.3517805E-01	1.8369772E+01	*	76.	8.7860934E-02	2.9050673E+01	*
27.	4.2147281E-01	1.8791244E+01	*	77.	8.5093893E-02	2.9135766E+01	*
28.	4.0819919E-01	1.9199443E+01	*	78.	8.2413995E-02	2.9218179E+01	*
29.	3.9534360E-01	1.9594786E+01	*	79.	7.9818497E-02	2.9297997E+01	*
30.	3.8289288E-01	1.9977678E+01	*	80.	7.7304740E-02	2.9375301E+01	*
31.	3.7083427E-01	2.0348512E+01	*	81.	7.4870149E-02	2.9450171E+01	*
32.	3.5915544E-01	2.0707667E+01	*	82.	7.2512232E-02	2.9522683E+01	*
33.	3.4784405E-01	2.1055511E+01	*	83.	7.0228574E-02	2.9592911E+01	*
34.	3.3688959E-01	2.1392400E+01	*	84.	6.8016836E-02	2.9660927E+01	*
35.	3.2627979E-01	2.1718679E+01	*	85.	6.5874754E-02	2.9726801E+01	*
36.	3.1600412E-01	2.2034683E+01	*	86.	6.3800132E-02	2.9790601E+01	*
37.	3.0605207E-01	2.2340735E+01	*	87.	6.1790848E-02	2.9852391E+01	*
38.	2.9641345E-01	2.2637148E+01	*	88.	5.9844843E-02	2.9912235E+01	*
39.	2.8707837E-01	2.2924226E+01	*	89.	5.7960125E-02	2.9970195E+01	*
40.	2.7803730E-01	2.3202223E+01	*	90.	5.6134762E-02	3.0026329E+01	*
41.	2.6928095E-01	2.3471543E+01	*	91.	5.4366887E-02	3.0080695E+01	*
42.	2.6080037E-01	2.3732343E+01	*	92.	5.2654688E-02	3.0133349E+01	*
43.	2.5258688E-01	2.3984929E+01	*	93.	5.0996411E-02	3.0184345E+01	*
44.	2.4463205E-01	2.4229561E+01	*	94.	4.9390360E-02	3.0233735E+01	*
45.	2.3692775E-01	2.4466488E+01	*	95.	4.7834889E-02	3.0281569E+01	*
46.	2.2946609E-01	2.4695954E+01	*	96.	4.6328405E-02	3.0327897E+01	*
47.	2.2223942E-01	2.4918193E+01	*	97.	4.4869365E-02	3.0372766E+01	*
48.	2.1524034E-01	2.5133433E+01	*	98.	4.3456275E-02	3.0416222E+01	*
49.	2.0846168E-01	2.5341894E+01	*	99.	4.2087689E-02	3.0458309E+01	*
50.	2.0189651E-01	2.5543790E+01	*	100.	4.0762203E-02	3.0499071E+01	*

x	E $(-RX)$	SUM OF E $(-RX)$	∞	x	E $(-RX)$	SUM OF E $(-RX)$	∞
0.	1.0000000E+00	1.0000000E+00	∞	50.	1.9204990E-01	2.5081561E+01	∞
1.	9.6753855E-01	1.9675385E+00	∞	51.	1.8581569E-01	2.5267376E+01	∞
2.	9.3613086E-01	2.9036693E+00	∞	52.	1.7978384E-01	2.5447159E+01	∞
3.	9.0574270E-01	3.8094120E+00	∞	53.	1.7394780E-01	2.5621106E+01	∞
4.	8.7634099E-01	4.6857529E+00	∞	54.	1.6830120E-01	2.5789407E+01	∞
5.	8.4789370E-01	5.5336466E+00	∞	55.	1.6283790E-01	2.5952244E+01	∞
6.	8.2036985E-01	6.3540164E+00	∞	56.	1.5755195E-01	2.6109795E+01	∞
7.	7.9373946E-01	7.1477558E+00	∞	57.	1.5243759E-01	2.6262232E+01	∞
8.	7.6797353E-01	7.9157293E+00	∞	58.	1.4748934E-01	2.6409721E+01	∞
9.	7.4304401E-01	8.6587733E+00	∞	59.	1.4270153E-01	2.6552422E+01	∞
10.	7.1892373E-01	9.3376970E+00	∞	60.	1.3806923E-01	2.6690491E+01	∞
11.	6.9558643E-01	1.0073283E+01	∞	61.	1.3358731E-01	2.6824078E+01	∞
12.	6.7300669E-01	1.0746289E+01	∞	62.	1.2925087E-01	2.6953328E+01	∞
13.	6.5115992E-01	1.1397448E+01	∞	63.	1.2505520E-01	2.7078383E+01	∞
14.	6.3002233E-01	1.2027470E+01	∞	64.	1.2099573E-01	2.7199378E+01	∞
15.	6.0957090E-01	1.2637040E+01	∞	65.	1.1706803E-01	2.7316446E+01	∞
16.	5.8978335E-01	1.3226823E+01	∞	66.	1.1326783E-01	2.7429313E+01	∞
17.	5.7063813E-01	1.3797461E+01	∞	67.	1.0959100E-01	2.7539304E+01	∞
18.	5.5211440E-01	1.4349575E+01	∞	68.	1.0603352E-01	2.7645337E+01	∞
19.	5.3419197E-01	1.4883766E+01	∞	69.	1.0259151E-01	2.7747928E+01	∞
20.	5.1685133E-01	1.5400617E+01	∞	70.	9.9261251E-02	2.7847189E+01	∞
21.	5.0007359E-01	1.5900690E+01	∞	71.	9.6039088E-02	2.7943228E+01	∞
22.	4.8384048E-01	1.6384530E+01	∞	72.	9.2921521E-02	2.8036149E+01	∞
23.	4.6813432E-01	1.6852664E+01	∞	73.	8.9905154E-02	2.8126054E+01	∞
24.	4.5293801E-01	1.7305602E+01	∞	74.	8.6986703E-02	2.8213040E+01	∞
25.	4.3823499E-01	1.7743836E+01	∞	75.	8.4162990E-02	2.8297202E+01	∞
26.	4.2400925E-01	1.8167845E+01	∞	76.	8.1430938E-02	2.8378632E+01	∞
27.	4.1024530E-01	1.8578090E+01	∞	77.	7.8787572E-02	2.8457419E+01	∞
28.	3.9692814E-01	1.8975018E+01	∞	78.	7.6230014E-02	2.8533649E+01	∞
29.	3.8404328E-01	1.9359061E+01	∞	79.	7.3755478E-02	2.8607604E+01	∞
30.	3.7157669E-01	1.9730637E+01	∞	80.	7.1361269E-02	2.8678755E+01	∞
31.	3.5951477E-01	2.0090151E+01	∞	81.	6.9044779E-02	2.8747809E+01	∞
32.	3.4784440E-01	2.0437995E+01	∞	82.	6.6803486E-02	2.8814612E+01	∞
33.	3.3655287E-01	2.0774547E+01	∞	83.	6.4634949E-02	2.8879246E+01	∞
34.	3.2562788E-01	2.1100174E+01	∞	84.	6.2536805E-02	2.8941728E+01	∞
35.	3.1505753E-01	2.1415231E+01	∞	85.	6.0506771E-02	2.9002288E+01	∞
36.	3.0483031E-01	2.1720061E+01	∞	86.	5.8542634E-02	2.9060830E+01	∞
37.	2.9493502E-01	2.2014996E+01	∞	87.	5.6642255E-02	2.9117472E+01	∞
38.	2.8536106E-01	2.2300357E+01	∞	88.	5.4803566E-02	2.9172277E+01	∞
39.	2.7609783E-01	2.2576454E+01	∞	89.	5.3024563E-02	2.9225299E+01	∞
40.	2.6713530E-01	2.2843589E+01	∞	90.	5.1303310E-02	2.9276602E+01	∞
41.	2.5846370E-01	2.3102052E+01	∞	91.	4.9637930E-02	2.9326239E+01	∞
42.	2.5007360E-01	2.3352125E+01	∞	92.	4.8026612E-02	2.9374265E+01	∞
43.	2.4195585E-01	2.3594080E+01	∞	93.	4.6467599E-02	2.9420732E+01	∞
44.	2.3410161E-01	2.3828181E+01	∞	94.	4.4956193E-02	2.9465691E+01	∞
45.	2.2650234E-01	2.4054683E+01	∞	95.	4.3499753E-02	2.9509190E+01	∞
46.	2.1914476E-01	2.4273832E+01	∞	96.	4.2087689E-02	2.9551277E+01	∞
47.	2.1203583E-01	2.4485867E+01	∞	97.	4.0721462E-02	2.9591998E+01	∞
48.	2.0515284E-01	2.4691019E+01	∞	98.	3.9399584E-02	2.9631397E+01	∞
49.	1.9849328E-01	2.4889517E+01	∞	99.	3.8120617E-02	2.9669517E+01	∞
50.	1.9204990E-01	2.5081561E+01	∞	100.	3.6883167E-02	2.9706400E+01	∞

x	E $(-RX)$	SUM OF E $(-RX)$	∞	x	E $(-RX)$	SUM OF E $(-RX)$	∞
0.	1.0000000E+00	1.0000000E+00	∞	50.	1.8268352E-01	2.4632354E+01	∞
1.	9.6657150E-01	1.9665715E+00	∞	51.	1.7657668E-01	2.4808930E+01	∞
2.	9.3426047E-01	2.9008319E+00	∞	52.	1.7067399E-01	2.4979605E+01	∞
3.	9.0302954E-01	3.8038614E+00	∞	53.	1.6496862E-01	2.5144571E+01	∞
4.	8.7284263E-01	4.6767040E+00	∞	54.	1.5945396E-01	2.5304024E+01	∞
5.	8.4366481E-01	5.5203688E+00	∞	55.	1.5412365E-01	2.5458147E+01	∞
6.	8.1546236E-01	6.3358311E+00	∞	56.	1.4897153E-01	2.5607118E+01	∞
7.	7.8820269E-01	7.1240337E+00	∞	57.	1.4399164E-01	2.5751109E+01	∞
8.	7.6185426E-01	7.8858879E+00	∞	58.	1.3917822E-01	2.5890287E+01	∞
9.	7.3638661E-01	8.6222745E+00	∞	59.	1.3452570E-01	2.6024812E+01	∞
10.	7.1177032E-01	9.3340448E+00	∞	60.	1.3002871E-01	2.6154840E+01	∞
11.	6.8797690E-01	1.0022021E+01	∞	61.	1.2568204E-01	2.6280522E+01	∞
12.	6.6497887E-01	1.0686999E+01	∞	62.	1.2148068E-01	2.6402002E+01	∞
13.	6.4274963E-01	1.1329748E+01	∞	63.	1.1741976E-01	2.6519421E+01	∞
14.	6.2126348E-01	1.1951011E+01	∞	64.	1.1349460E-01	2.6632915E+01	∞
15.	6.0049557E-01	1.2551506E+01	∞	65.	1.0970064E-01	2.6742615E+01	∞
16.	5.8042191E-01	1.3131927E+01	∞	66.	1.0603352E-01	2.6848648E+01	∞
17.	5.6101928E-01	1.3692946E+01	∞	67.	1.0248897E-01	2.6951136E+01	∞
18.	5.4226525E-01	1.4235211E+01	∞	68.	9.9062927E-02	2.7050198E+01	∞
19.	5.2413813E-01	1.4759349E+01	∞	69.	9.5751402E-02	2.7145949E+01	∞
20.	5.0661699E-01	1.5265965E+01	∞	70.	9.2550577E-02	2.7238449E+01	∞
21.	4.8968156E-01	1.5755646E+01	∞	71.	8.9467503E-02	2.7327955E+01	∞
22.	4.7331223E-01	1.6229958E+01	∞	72.	8.6463463E-02	2.7414421E+01	∞
23.	4.5749011E-01	1.6686644E+01	∞	73.	8.3575906E-02	2.7497984E+01	∞
24.	4.4219690E-01	1.7128644E+01	∞	74.	8.0782089E-02	2.7578775E+01	∞
25.	4.2741493E-01	1.7556058E+01	∞	75.	7.8081665E-02	2.7656859E+01	∞
26.	4.1312709E-01	1.7969185E+01	∞	76.	7.5471513E-02	2.7732330E+01	∞
27.	3.9931687E-01	1.8368501E+01	∞	77.	7.2948614E-02	2.7805278E+01	∞
28.	3.8596831E-01	1.8754469E+01	∞	78.	7.0510051E-02	2.7875788E+01	∞
29.	3.7306597E-01	1.9127534E+01	∞	79.	6.8153006E-02	2.7943941E+01	∞
30.	3.6059493E-01	1.9488128E+01	∞	80.	6.5874754E-02	2.8009815E+01	∞
31.	3.4854079E-01	1.9836668E+01	∞	81.	6.3672609E-02	2.8073448E+01	∞
32.	3.3688959E-01	2.0173555E+01	∞	82.	6.1544179E-02	2.8135031E+01	∞
33.	3.2562788E-01	2.0499184E+01	∞	83.	5.9486849E-02	2.8194517E+01	∞
34.	3.1474263E-01	2.0813926E+01	∞	84.	5.7499293E-02	2.8252015E+01	∞
35.	3.0422126E-01	2.1118147E+01	∞	85.	5.5576212E-02	2.8307591E+01	∞
36.	2.9405160E-01	2.1412199E+01	∞	86.	5.3718383E-02	2.8361306E+01	∞
37.	2.8422190E-01	2.1696410E+01	∞	87.	5.1922658E-02	2.8413231E+01	∞
38.	2.7472079E-01	2.1971139E+01	∞	88.	5.0186962E-02	2.8463417E+01	∞
39.	2.6553728E-01	2.2236676E+01	∞	89.	4.8509227E-02	2.8511926E+01	∞
40.	2.5666077E-01	2.2493336E+01	∞	90.	4.6887695E-02	2.8558413E+01	∞
41.	2.4804099E-01	2.2741416E+01	∞	91.	4.5320310E-02	2.8604133E+01	∞
42.	2.3978801E-01	2.2981204E+01	∞	92.	4.3805320E-02	2.8647937E+01	∞
43.	2.3177226E-01	2.3212976E+01	∞	93.	4.2340675E-02	2.8690237E+01	∞
44.	2.2402446E-01	2.3437000E+01	∞	94.	4.0925570E-02	2.8731293E+01	∞
45.	2.1653566E-01	2.3653535E+01	∞	95.	3.9557498E-02	2.8770760E+01	∞
46.	2.0929720E-01	2.3862832E+01	∞	96.	3.8235151E-02	2.8808995E+01	∞
47.	2.0230071E-01	2.4065132E+01	∞	97.	3.6957307E-02	2.8845452E+01	∞
48.	1.9553810E-01	2.4260670E+01	∞	98.	3.5721590E-02	2.8881673E+01	∞
49.	1.8900156E-01	2.4449671E+01	∞	99.	3.4527471E-02	2.8916200E+01	∞
50.	1.8268352E-01	2.4632354E+01	∞	100.	3.3373269E-02	2.8949575E+01	∞

TABULATED VALUES OF E WHEN R = .035

X	E $-RX$	SUM OF E $-RX$	*	X	E $-RX$	SUM OF E $-RX$	*
0.	1.0000000E+00	1.0000000E+00	*	50.	1.7377394E-01	2.4195735E+01	*
1.	9.6560541E-01	1.9656054E+00	*	51.	1.6779706E-01	2.4363532E+01	*
2.	9.3239381E-01	2.8979992E+00	*	52.	1.6202575E-01	2.4525557E+01	*
3.	9.0032462E-01	3.7983237E+00	*	53.	1.5645294E-01	2.4682009E+01	*
4.	8.6935823E-01	4.6676819E+00	*	54.	1.5107180E-01	2.4833080E+01	*
5.	8.3945701E-01	5.5071389E+00	*	55.	1.4587575E-01	2.4978955E+01	*
6.	8.1058424E-01	6.3177231E+00	*	56.	1.4085842E-01	2.5119813E+01	*
7.	7.8270453E-01	7.1004276E+00	*	57.	1.3601365E-01	2.5255826E+01	*
8.	7.5578374E-01	7.8562113E+00	*	58.	1.3133552E-01	2.5387161E+01	*
9.	7.2978887E-01	8.5860001E+00	*	59.	1.2681829E-01	2.5513979E+01	*
10.	7.0468808E-01	9.2906881E+00	*	60.	1.2245642E-01	2.5636435E+01	*
11.	6.8045045E-01	9.9711387E+00	*	61.	1.1824459E-01	2.5754679E+01	*
12.	6.5704681E-01	1.0628185E+01	*	62.	1.1417761E-01	2.5868856E+01	*
13.	6.3444796E-01	1.1262632E+01	*	63.	1.1025052E-01	2.5979106E+01	*
14.	6.1262639E-01	1.1875258E+01	*	64.	1.0645850E-01	2.6085564E+01	*
15.	5.9155536E-01	1.2466813E+01	*	65.	1.0279690E-01	2.6188360E+01	*
16.	5.7120906E-01	1.3038022E+01	*	66.	9.9261251E-02	2.6287621E+01	*
17.	5.5156256E-01	1.3589584E+01	*	67.	9.5847202E-02	2.6383468E+01	*
18.	5.3259179E-01	1.4122175E+01	*	68.	9.2550577E-02	2.6476018E+01	*
19.	5.1427352E-01	1.4636448E+01	*	69.	8.9367338E-02	2.6565385E+01	*
20.	4.9658530E-01	1.5133033E+01	*	70.	8.6293586E-02	2.6651678E+01	*
21.	4.7950545E-01	1.5612538E+01	*	71.	8.3325554E-02	2.6735033E+01	*
22.	4.6301306E-01	1.6075551E+01	*	72.	8.0459606E-02	2.6815462E+01	*
23.	4.4708792E-01	1.6522638E+01	*	73.	7.7692231E-02	2.6893154E+01	*
24.	4.3171052E-01	1.6954348E+01	*	74.	7.5020040E-02	2.6968174E+01	*
25.	4.1686201E-01	1.7371210E+01	*	75.	7.2439756E-02	2.7040613E+01	*
26.	4.0252422E-01	1.7773734E+01	*	76.	6.9948221E-02	2.7110561E+01	*
27.	3.8867957E-01	1.8162413E+01	*	77.	6.7542381E-02	2.7178103E+01	*
28.	3.7531109E-01	1.8537724E+01	*	78.	6.5219289E-02	2.7243322E+01	*
29.	3.6240242E-01	1.8900126E+01	*	79.	6.2976099E-02	2.7306298E+01	*
30.	3.4993774E-01	1.9250063E+01	*	80.	6.0810062E-02	2.7367108E+01	*
31.	3.3790178E-01	1.9587964E+01	*	81.	5.8718525E-02	2.7425824E+01	*
32.	3.2627979E-01	1.9914243E+01	*	82.	5.6698926E-02	2.7482524E+01	*
33.	3.1505753E-01	2.0229300E+01	*	83.	5.4748790E-02	2.7537272E+01	*
34.	3.0422126E-01	2.0533521E+01	*	84.	5.2865728E-02	2.7590137E+01	*
35.	2.9375769E-01	2.0827278E+01	*	85.	5.1047433E-02	2.7641184E+01	*
36.	2.8365402E-01	2.1110932E+01	*	86.	4.9291678E-02	2.7690475E+01	*
37.	2.7389786E-01	2.1384829E+01	*	87.	4.7596311E-02	2.7738071E+01	*
38.	2.6447726E-01	2.1649306E+01	*	88.	4.5959256E-02	2.7784030E+01	*
39.	2.5538067E-01	2.1904686E+01	*	89.	4.4378507E-02	2.7828408E+01	*
40.	2.4659696E-01	2.2151282E+01	*	90.	4.2852126E-02	2.7871260E+01	*
41.	2.3811536E-01	2.2389397E+01	*	91.	4.1378245E-02	2.7912638E+01	*
42.	2.2992548E-01	2.2619322E+01	*	92.	3.9955058E-02	2.7952593E+01	*
43.	2.2201729E-01	2.2841339E+01	*	93.	3.8580820E-02	2.7991173E+01	*
44.	2.1438110E-01	2.3055720E+01	*	94.	3.7253849E-02	2.8028426E+01	*
45.	2.0700755E-01	2.3262727E+01	*	95.	3.5972518E-02	2.8064398E+01	*
46.	1.9988761E-01	2.3462614E+01	*	96.	3.4735258E-02	2.8099133E+01	*
47.	1.9301256E-01	2.3655624E+01	*	97.	3.3540554E-02	2.8132673E+01	*
48.	1.8637397E-01	2.3841999E+01	*	98.	3.2386940E-02	2.8165059E+01	*
49.	1.7996372E-01	2.4021962E+01	*	99.	3.1273005E-02	2.8196332E+01	*
50.	1.7377394E-01	2.4195735E+01	*	100.	3.0197383E-02	2.8226529E+01	*

TABULATED VALUES OF E WHEN R = .036

X	E $-RX$	SUM OF E $-RX$	*	X	E $-RX$	SUM OF E $-RX$	*
0.	1.0000000E+00	1.0000000E+00	*	50.	1.6529888E-01	2.3771276E+01	*
1.	9.6464029E-01	1.9646402E+00	*	51.	1.5945396E-01	2.3930729E+01	*
2.	9.3053089E-01	2.8951710E+00	*	52.	1.5381572E-01	2.4084544E+01	*
3.	8.9762759E-01	3.7927985E+00	*	53.	1.4837684E-01	2.4232920E+01	*
4.	8.6588774E-01	4.6586862E+00	*	54.	1.4313028E-01	2.4376050E+01	*
5.	8.3527020E-01	5.4939564E+00	*	55.	1.3806923E-01	2.4514119E+01	*
6.	8.0573530E-01	6.2996917E+00	*	56.	1.3318714E-01	2.4647306E+01	*
7.	7.7724473E-01	7.0769364E+00	*	57.	1.2847769E-01	2.4775783E+01	*
8.	7.4976159E-01	7.8266979E+00	*	58.	1.2393475E-01	2.4899717E+01	*
9.	7.2325024E-01	8.5499481E+00	*	59.	1.1955246E-01	2.5019269E+01	*
10.	6.9767632E-01	9.2476244E+00	*	60.	1.1532512E-01	2.5134594E+01	*
11.	6.7300669E-01	9.9206310E+00	*	61.	1.1124725E-01	2.5245841E+01	*
12.	6.4920937E-01	1.0569840E+01	*	62.	1.0731358E-01	2.5353154E+01	*
13.	6.2625352E-01	1.1196093E+01	*	63.	1.0351901E-01	2.5456673E+01	*
14.	6.0410938E-01	1.1800202E+01	*	64.	9.9858609E-02	2.5556531E+01	*
15.	5.8274825E-01	1.2382950E+01	*	65.	9.6327638E-02	2.5652858E+01	*
16.	5.6214244E-01	1.2945092E+01	*	66.	9.2921521E-02	2.5745779E+01	*
17.	5.4226525E-01	1.3487357E+01	*	67.	8.9635843E-02	2.5835414E+01	*
18.	5.2309091E-01	1.4010447E+01	*	68.	8.6466346E-02	2.5921880E+01	*
19.	5.0459456E-01	1.4515041E+01	*	69.	8.3408921E-02	2.6005288E+01	*
20.	4.8675225E-01	1.5001793E+01	*	70.	8.0459606E-02	2.6085747E+01	*
21.	4.6954083E-01	1.5471333E+01	*	71.	7.7614578E-02	2.6163361E+01	*
22.	4.5293801E-01	1.5924271E+01	*	72.	7.4870149E-02	2.6238231E+01	*
23.	4.3692225E-01	1.6361193E+01	*	73.	7.2222763E-02	2.6310453E+01	*
24.	4.2147281E-01	1.6782665E+01	*	74.	6.9668987E-02	2.6380121E+01	*
25.	4.0656965E-01	1.7189234E+01	*	75.	6.7205512E-02	2.6447326E+01	*
26.	3.9219347E-01	1.7581427E+01	*	76.	6.4829145E-02	2.6512155E+01	*
27.	3.7832562E-01	1.7959752E+01	*	77.	6.2536805E-02	2.6574691E+01	*
28.	3.6494814E-01	1.8324700E+01	*	78.	6.0325522E-02	2.6635016E+01	*
29.	3.5204368E-01	1.8676743E+01	*	79.	5.8192429E-02	2.6693208E+01	*
30.	3.3959552E-01	1.9016338E+01	*	80.	5.6134762E-02	2.6749342E+01	*
31.	3.2758752E-01	1.9343925E+01	*	81.	5.4149853E-02	2.6803491E+01	*
32.	3.1600412E-01	1.9659929E+01	*	82.	5.2235130E-02	2.6855726E+01	*
33.	3.0483031E-01	1.9964759E+01	*	83.	5.0388112E-02	2.6906114E+01	*
34.	2.9405160E-01	2.0258810E+01	*	84.	4.8606403E-02	2.6954720E+01	*
35.	2.8365402E-01	2.0542464E+01	*	85.	4.6887695E-02	2.7001607E+01	*
36.	2.7362410E-01	2.0816088E+01	*	86.	4.5229760E-02	2.7046836E+01	*
37.	2.6394883E-01	2.1080036E+01	*	87.	4.3630448E-02	2.7090466E+01	*
38.	2.5461568E-01	2.1334651E+01	*	88.	4.2087689E-02	2.7132553E+01	*
39.	2.4561254E-01	2.1580263E+01	*	89.	4.0599480E-02	2.7173152E+01	*
40.	2.3692775E-01	2.1817190E+01	*	90.	3.9163895E-02	2.7212315E+01	*
41.	2.2855006E-01	2.2045740E+01	*	91.	3.7779071E-02	2.7250094E+01	*
42.	2.2046859E-01	2.2266208E+01	*	92.	3.6443214E-02	2.7286537E+01	*
43.	2.1267289E-01	2.2478880E+01	*	93.	3.5154592E-02	2.7321691E+01	*
44.	2.0515284E-01	2.2684032E+01	*	94.	3.3911538E-02	2.7355602E+01	*
45.	1.9789869E-01	2.2881930E+01	*	95.	3.2712434E-02	2.7388314E+01	*
46.	1.9090105E-01	2.3072831E+01	*	96.	3.1555732E-02	2.7419869E+01	*
47.	1.8415085E-01	2.3256981E+01	*	97.	3.0439931E-02	2.7450308E+01	*
48.	1.7763933E-01	2.3434620E+01	*	98.	2.9363584E-02	2.7479671E+01	*
49.	1.7135805E-01	2.3605978E+01	*	99.	2.8325296E-02	2.7507996E+01	*
50.	1.6529888E-01	2.3771276E+01	*	100.	2.7323752E-02	2.7535319E+01	*

TABULATED VALUES OF E   WHEN R = .037

x	E −RX	SUM OF E −RX	*	x	E −RX	SUM OF E −RX	*
0.	1.0000000E+00	1.0000000E+00	*	50.	1.5723716E-01	2.3358570E+01	*
1.	9.6367613E-01	1.9636761E+00	*	51.	1.5152570E-01	2.3510095E+01	*
2.	9.2867169E-01	2.8923477E+00	*	52.	1.4602170E-01	2.3656116E+01	*
3.	8.9493874E-01	3.7872864E+00	*	53.	1.4071763E-01	2.3796833E+01	*
4.	8.6243111E-01	4.6497175E+00	*	54.	1.3560622E-01	2.3932439E+01	*
5.	8.3116428E-01	5.4808217E+00	*	55.	1.3068048E-01	2.4063119E+01	*
6.	8.0091538E-01	6.2817370E+00	*	56.	1.2593366E-01	2.4189052E+01	*
7.	7.7182302E-01	7.0535600E+00	*	57.	1.2135926E-01	2.4310411E+01	*
8.	7.4378742E-01	7.7973474E+00	*	58.	1.1695102E-01	2.4427362E+01	*
9.	7.1677019E-01	8.5141175E+00	*	59.	1.1270291E-01	2.4540064E+01	*
10.	6.9073432E-01	9.2048518E+00	*	60.	1.0860910E-01	2.4648673E+01	*
11.	6.6564418E-01	9.8704959E+00	*	61.	1.0466400E-01	2.4753337E+01	*
12.	6.4146541E-01	1.0511961E+01	*	62.	1.0086220E-01	2.4854199E+01	*
13.	6.1816491E-01	1.1130125E+01	*	63.	9.7198499E-02	2.4951397E+01	*
14.	5.9571077E-01	1.1725835E+01	*	64.	9.3667874E-02	2.5045064E+01	*
15.	5.7407226E-01	1.2299907E+01	*	65.	9.0265495E-02	2.5135329E+01	*
16.	5.5321973E-01	1.2853126E+01	*	66.	8.6986703E-02	2.5222315E+01	*
17.	5.3312465E-01	1.3386250E+01	*	67.	8.3827010E-02	2.5306142E+01	*
18.	5.1375950E-01	1.3900009E+01	*	68.	8.0780089E-02	2.5386924E+01	*
19.	4.9509778E-01	1.4395105E+01	*	69.	7.7847771E-02	2.5464771E+01	*
20.	4.7711391E-01	1.4872219E+01	*	70.	7.5020040E-02	2.5539791E+01	*
21.	4.5978329E-01	1.5332002E+01	*	71.	7.2295022E-02	2.5612086E+01	*
22.	4.4308218E-01	1.5775084E+01	*	72.	6.9668987E-02	2.5681754E+01	*
23.	4.2698773E-01	1.6202071E+01	*	73.	6.7138340E-02	2.5748892E+01	*
24.	4.1147788E-01	1.6613548E+01	*	74.	6.4699616E-02	2.5813591E+01	*
25.	3.9653141E-01	1.7010079E+01	*	75.	6.2344476E-02	2.5875940E+01	*
26.	3.8212786E-01	1.7392206E+01	*	76.	6.0084702E-02	2.5936024E+01	*
27.	3.6824750E-01	1.7760453E+01	*	77.	5.7902194E-02	2.5993926E+01	*
28.	3.5487133E-01	1.8115324E+01	*	78.	5.5799962E-02	2.6049724E+01	*
29.	3.4198103E-01	1.8457305E+01	*	79.	5.3772128E-02	2.6103496E+01	*
30.	3.2955896E-01	1.8786863E+01	*	80.	5.1818917E-02	2.6155314E+01	*
31.	3.1758810E-01	1.9104451E+01	*	81.	4.9936653E-02	2.6205250E+01	*
32.	3.0605207E-01	1.9410503E+01	*	82.	4.8122761E-02	2.6253372E+01	*
33.	2.9493508E-01	1.9705438E+01	*	83.	4.6374756E-02	2.6299746E+01	*
34.	2.8422190E-01	1.9989659E+01	*	84.	4.4690246E-02	2.6344436E+01	*
35.	2.7389786E-01	2.0263556E+01	*	85.	4.3066923E-02	2.6387502E+01	*
36.	2.6394883E-01	2.0527504E+01	*	86.	4.1502566E-02	2.6429004E+01	*
37.	2.5436119E-01	2.0781865E+01	*	87.	3.9995033E-02	2.6468999E+01	*
38.	2.4512181E-01	2.1026986E+01	*	88.	3.8542256E-02	2.6507541E+01	*
39.	2.3621803E-01	2.1263204E+01	*	89.	3.7142255E-02	2.6544683E+01	*
40.	2.2763768E-01	2.1490841E+01	*	90.	3.5793105E-02	2.6580474E+01	*
41.	2.1936900E-01	2.1710210E+01	*	91.	3.4492961E-02	2.6614968E+01	*
42.	2.1140067E-01	2.1921610E+01	*	92.	3.3240043E-02	2.6648208E+01	*
43.	2.0372178E-01	2.2125331E+01	*	93.	3.2032636E-02	2.6680240E+01	*
44.	1.9632182E-01	2.2321652E+01	*	94.	3.0869087E-02	2.6711109E+01	*
45.	1.8919065E-01	2.2510842E+01	*	95.	2.9747802E-02	2.6740855E+01	*
46.	1.8231852E-01	2.2693160E+01	*	96.	2.8667247E-02	2.6769523E+01	*
47.	1.7569600E-01	2.2868856E+01	*	97.	2.7625942E-02	2.6797148E+01	*
48.	1.6931405E-01	2.3038170E+01	*	98.	2.6622461E-02	2.6823770E+01	*
49.	1.6316390E-01	2.3201333E+01	*	99.	2.5655430E-02	2.6849425E+01	*
50.	1.5723716E-01	2.3358570E+01	*	100.	2.4723526E-02	2.6874148E+01	*

TABULATED VALUES OF E   WHEN R = .038

x	E −RX	SUM OF E −RX	*	x	E −RX	SUM OF E −RX	*
0.	1.0000000E+00	1.0000000E+00	*	50.	1.4956861E-01	2.2957227E+01	*
1.	9.6271293E-01	1.9627129E+00	*	51.	1.4399164E-01	2.3101211E+01	*
2.	9.2681620E-01	2.8895291E+00	*	52.	1.3862261E-01	2.3239846E+01	*
3.	8.9225795E-01	3.7817870E+00	*	53.	1.3345379E-01	2.3373293E+01	*
4.	8.5898827E-01	4.6407752E+00	*	54.	1.2847769E-01	2.3501770E+01	*
5.	8.2695913E-01	5.4677343E+00	*	55.	1.2368713E-01	2.3625457E+01	*
6.	7.9612425E-01	6.2638585E+00	*	56.	1.1907520E-01	2.3744532E+01	*
7.	7.6643912E-01	7.0302976E+00	*	57.	1.1463524E-01	2.3859167E+01	*
8.	7.3786086E-01	7.7681584E+00	*	58.	1.1036083E-01	2.3969527E+01	*
9.	7.1034820E-01	8.4785066E+00	*	59.	1.0624579E-01	2.4075772E+01	*
10.	6.8386140E-01	9.1623680E+00	*	60.	1.0228420E-01	2.4178056E+01	*
11.	6.5836222E-01	9.8207302E+00	*	61.	9.8470329E-02	2.4276526E+01	*
12.	6.3381383E-01	1.0454544E+01	*	62.	9.4798600E-02	2.4371324E+01	*
13.	6.1018078E-01	1.1064724E+01	*	63.	9.1263897E-02	2.4462587E+01	*
14.	5.8742893E-01	1.1652152E+01	*	64.	8.7860934E-02	2.4550447E+01	*
15.	5.6552543E-01	1.2217677E+01	*	65.	8.4584858E-02	2.4635031E+01	*
16.	5.4443865E-01	1.2762115E+01	*	66.	8.1430938E-02	2.4716461E+01	*
17.	5.2413813E-01	1.3286253E+01	*	67.	7.8394618E-02	2.4794855E+01	*
18.	5.0459466E-01	1.3790847E+01	*	68.	7.5471513E-02	2.4870326E+01	*
19.	4.8577972E-01	1.4276626E+01	*	69.	7.2657402E-02	2.4942983E+01	*
20.	4.6766642E-01	1.4744292E+01	*	70.	6.9948221E-02	2.5012931E+01	*
21.	4.5022852E-01	1.5194520E+01	*	71.	6.7340058E-02	2.5080271E+01	*
22.	4.3344082E-01	1.5627960E+01	*	72.	6.4829145E-02	2.5145100E+01	*
23.	4.1727908E-01	1.6045239E+01	*	73.	6.2411857E-02	2.5207511E+01	*
24.	4.0171997E-01	1.6446958E+01	*	74.	6.0084702E-02	2.5267595E+01	*
25.	3.8674102E-01	1.6833699E+01	*	75.	5.7844320E-02	2.5325439E+01	*
26.	3.7232058E-01	1.7206019E+01	*	76.	5.5687476E-02	2.5381126E+01	*
27.	3.5843784E-01	1.7564456E+01	*	77.	5.3611053E-02	2.5434737E+01	*
28.	3.4507275E-01	1.7909528E+01	*	78.	5.1612055E-02	2.5486349E+01	*
29.	3.3220600E-01	1.8241734E+01	*	79.	4.9687593E-02	2.5536036E+01	*
30.	3.1981902E-01	1.8561553E+01	*	80.	4.7834889E-02	2.5583870E+01	*
31.	3.0789391E-01	1.8869446E+01	*	81.	4.6051267E-02	2.5629921E+01	*
32.	2.9641345E-01	1.9165859E+01	*	82.	4.4334150E-02	2.5674255E+01	*
33.	2.8536106E-01	1.9451220E+01	*	83.	4.2681060E-02	2.5716936E+01	*
34.	2.7472079E-01	1.9725440E+01	*	84.	4.1089609E-02	2.5758025E+01	*
35.	2.6447726E-01	1.9990417E+01	*	85.	3.9557498E-02	2.5797582E+01	*
36.	2.5461568E-01	2.0245032E+01	*	86.	3.8082515E-02	2.5835664E+01	*
37.	2.4512181E-01	2.0490153E+01	*	87.	3.6662530E-02	2.5872326E+01	*
38.	2.3598194E-01	2.0726134E+01	*	88.	3.5295492E-02	2.5907621E+01	*
39.	2.2718286E-01	2.0953331E+01	*	89.	3.3979427E-02	2.5941600E+01	*
40.	2.1871148E-01	2.1172027E+01	*	90.	3.2712434E-02	2.5974312E+01	*
41.	2.1055676E-01	2.1382583E+01	*	91.	3.1492684E-02	2.6005804E+01	*
42.	2.0270572E-01	2.1585288E+01	*	92.	3.0319414E-02	2.6036122E+01	*
43.	1.9514742E-01	2.1780435E+01	*	93.	2.9187930E-02	2.6065309E+01	*
44.	1.8787094E-01	2.1968305E+01	*	94.	2.8099598E-02	2.6093408E+01	*
45.	1.8086579E-01	2.2149170E+01	*	95.	2.7051844E-02	2.6120459E+01	*
46.	1.7412183E-01	2.2323291E+01	*	96.	2.6043162E-02	2.6146502E+01	*
47.	1.6762934E-01	2.2490920E+01	*	97.	2.5072090E-02	2.6171574E+01	*
48.	1.6137894E-01	2.2652229E+01	*	98.	2.4137725E-02	2.6195711E+01	*
49.	1.5536159E-01	2.2807659E+01	*	99.	2.3237219E-02	2.6218948E+01	*
50.	1.4956861E-01	2.2957227E+01	*	100.	2.2370771E-02	2.6241318E+01	*

TABULATED VALUES OF E^{-RX} WHEN R = .039

X	E^{-RX}	SUM OF E^{-RX}	*	X	E^{-RX}	SUM OF E^{-RX}	*
0.	1.0000000E+00	1.0000000E+00	*	50.	1.4227407E-01	2.2566879E+01	*
1.	9.6175070E-01	1.9617507E+00	*	51.	1.3683218E-01	2.2703711E+01	*
2.	9.2496442E-01	2.8867151E+00	*	52.	1.3159845E-01	2.2835309E+01	*
3.	8.8958519E-01	3.7763002E+00	*	53.	1.2656490E-01	2.2961873E+01	*
4.	8.5555918E-01	4.6318593E+00	*	54.	1.2172388E-01	2.3083596E+01	*
5.	8.2283465E-01	5.4546939E+00	*	55.	1.1706803E-01	2.3200664E+01	*
6.	7.9136181E-01	6.2460557E+00	*	56.	1.1259026E-01	2.3313254E+01	*
7.	7.6109278E-01	7.0071484E+00	*	57.	1.0828376E-01	2.3421537E+01	*
8.	7.3198152E-01	7.7391299E+00	*	58.	1.0414199E-01	2.3525678E+01	*
9.	7.0398376E-01	8.4431136E+00	*	59.	1.0015863E-01	2.3625836E+01	*
10.	6.7705687E-01	9.1201704E+00	*	60.	9.6327638E-02	2.3722163E+01	*
11.	6.5115992E-01	9.7713303E+00	*	61.	9.2643174E-02	2.3814806E+01	*
12.	6.2625352E-01	1.0397583E+01	*	62.	8.9099638E-02	2.3903905E+01	*
13.	6.0229976E-01	1.0999882E+01	*	63.	8.5691640E-02	2.3989596E+01	*
14.	5.7926223E-01	1.1579144E+01	*	64.	8.2413995E-02	2.4072009E+01	*
15.	5.5710588E-01	1.2136249E+01	*	65.	7.9261719E-02	2.4151270E+01	*
16.	5.3579695E-01	1.2672045E+01	*	66.	7.6230014E-02	2.4227500E+01	*
17.	5.1530310E-01	1.3187348E+01	*	67.	7.3314270E-02	2.4300814E+01	*
18.	4.9559312E-01	1.3682941E+01	*	68.	7.0510051E-02	2.4371324E+01	*
19.	4.7663703E-01	1.4159578E+01	*	69.	6.7813092E-02	2.4439137E+01	*
20.	4.5840601E-01	1.4617984E+01	*	70.	6.5219289E-02	2.4504356E+01	*
21.	4.4087230E-01	1.5058856E+01	*	71.	6.2724698E-02	2.4567080E+01	*
22.	4.2400925E-01	1.5482865E+01	*	72.	6.0325522E-02	2.4627405E+01	*
23.	4.0779119E-01	1.5890656E+01	*	73.	5.8018114E-02	2.4685423E+01	*
24.	3.9219347E-01	1.6282849E+01	*	74.	5.5798962E-02	2.4741221E+01	*
25.	3.7719235E-01	1.6660041E+01	*	75.	5.3664691E-02	2.4794885E+01	*
26.	3.6276501E-01	1.7022806E+01	*	76.	5.1612055E-02	2.4846497E+01	*
27.	3.4888950E-01	1.7371695E+01	*	77.	4.9637930E-02	2.4896134E+01	*
28.	3.3554473E-01	1.7707239E+01	*	78.	4.7739315E-02	2.4943873E+01	*
29.	3.2271038E-01	1.8029949E+01	*	79.	4.5913320E-02	2.4989786E+01	*
30.	3.1036694E-01	1.8340315E+01	*	80.	4.4157168E-02	2.5033943E+01	*
31.	2.9849562E-01	1.8638810E+01	*	81.	4.2468187E-02	2.5076411E+01	*
32.	2.8707837E-01	1.8925838E+01	*	82.	4.0843809E-02	2.5117254E+01	*
33.	2.7609783E-01	1.9201985E+01	*	83.	3.9281563E-02	2.5156535E+01	*
34.	2.6553728E-01	1.9467522E+01	*	84.	3.7779071E-02	2.5194314E+01	*
35.	2.5538067E-01	1.9722902E+01	*	85.	3.6334048E-02	2.5230648E+01	*
36.	2.4561254E-01	1.9968514E+01	*	86.	3.4944296E-02	2.5265592E+01	*
37.	2.3621803E-01	2.0204732E+01	*	87.	3.3607702E-02	2.5299199E+01	*
38.	2.2718286E-01	2.0431914E+01	*	88.	3.2322231E-02	2.5331521E+01	*
39.	2.1849328E-01	2.0650407E+01	*	89.	3.1085929E-02	2.5362606E+01	*
40.	2.1013607E-01	2.0860543E+01	*	90.	2.9896914E-02	2.5392502E+01	*
41.	2.0209851E-01	2.1062641E+01	*	91.	2.8753378E-02	2.5421255E+01	*
42.	1.9436839E-01	2.1257009E+01	*	92.	2.7653582E-02	2.5448908E+01	*
43.	1.8693393E-01	2.1443942E+01	*	93.	2.6595852E-02	2.5475503E+01	*
44.	1.7978384E-01	2.1623725E+01	*	94.	2.5578579E-02	2.5501081E+01	*
45.	1.7290724E-01	2.1796632E+01	*	95.	2.4600217E-02	2.5525681E+01	*
46.	1.6629366E-01	2.1962925E+01	*	96.	2.3659276E-02	2.5549340E+01	*
47.	1.5993304E-01	2.2122858E+01	*	97.	2.2754325E-02	2.5572094E+01	*
48.	1.5381572E-01	2.2276673E+01	*	98.	2.1883989E-02	2.5593977E+01	*
49.	1.4793238E-01	2.2424605E+01	*	99.	2.1046942E-02	2.5615023E+01	*
50.	1.4227407E-01	2.2566879E+01	*	100.	2.0241911E-02	2.5635264E+01	*

TABULATED VALUES OF E^{-RX} WHEN R = .040

X	E^{-RX}	SUM OF E^{-RX}	*	X	E^{-RX}	SUM OF E^{-RX}	*
0.	1.0000000E+00	1.0000000E+00	*	50.	1.3533528E-01	2.2187147E+01	*
1.	9.6078943E-01	1.9607894E+00	*	51.	1.3002871E-01	2.2317175E+01	*
2.	9.2311634E-01	2.8839057E+00	*	52.	1.2493021E-01	2.2442105E+01	*
3.	8.8692043E-01	3.7708261E+00	*	53.	1.2003162E-01	2.2562136E+01	*
4.	8.5214378E-01	4.6229698E+00	*	54.	1.1532512E-01	2.2677461E+01	*
5.	8.1873075E-01	5.4417005E+00	*	55.	1.1080315E-01	2.2788264E+01	*
6.	7.8662786E-01	6.2283283E+00	*	56.	1.0645850E-01	2.2894722E+01	*
7.	7.5578374E-01	6.9841120E+00	*	57.	1.0228420E-01	2.2997006E+01	*
8.	7.2614903E-01	7.7102610E+00	*	58.	9.8273585E-02	2.3095279E+01	*
9.	6.9767632E-01	8.4079373E+00	*	59.	9.4420222E-02	2.3189699E+01	*
10.	6.7032004E-01	9.0782573E+00	*	60.	9.0717953E-02	2.3280416E+01	*
11.	6.4403641E-01	9.7222937E+00	*	61.	8.7160851E-02	2.3367576E+01	*
12.	6.1878339E-01	1.0341077E+01	*	62.	8.3743225E-02	2.3451319E+01	*
13.	5.9452054E-01	1.0935597E+01	*	63.	8.0459060E-02	2.3531718E+01	*
14.	5.7120906E-01	1.1506806E+01	*	64.	7.7304740E-02	2.3609082E+01	*
15.	5.4881163E-01	1.2055617E+01	*	65.	7.4273578E-02	2.3683355E+01	*
16.	5.2729242E-01	1.2582909E+01	*	66.	7.1361269E-02	2.3754716E+01	*
17.	5.0661699E-01	1.3089525E+01	*	67.	6.8563153E-02	2.3823279E+01	*
18.	4.8675225E-01	1.3576277E+01	*	68.	6.5874754E-02	2.3889153E+01	*
19.	4.6766642E-01	1.4043943E+01	*	69.	6.3291768E-02	2.3952444E+01	*
20.	4.4932956E-01	1.4493271E+01	*	70.	6.0810062E-02	2.4013254E+01	*
21.	4.3171052E-01	1.4924981E+01	*	71.	5.8425665E-02	2.4071679E+01	*
22.	4.1478291E-01	1.5339763E+01	*	72.	5.6134762E-02	2.4127813E+01	*
23.	3.9851903E-01	1.5738282E+01	*	73.	5.3933687E-02	2.4181766E+01	*
24.	3.8289288E-01	1.6121174E+01	*	74.	5.1818917E-02	2.4233564E+01	*
25.	3.6787944E-01	1.6489053E+01	*	75.	4.9787068E-02	2.4283351E+01	*
26.	3.5345468E-01	1.6842507E+01	*	76.	4.7834889E-02	2.4331185E+01	*
27.	3.3959552E-01	1.7182102E+01	*	77.	4.5959256E-02	2.4377144E+01	*
28.	3.2627979E-01	1.7508381E+01	*	78.	4.4157168E-02	2.4421301E+01	*
29.	3.1348618E-01	1.7821867E+01	*	79.	4.2425741E-02	2.4463726E+01	*
30.	3.0119421E-01	1.8123061E+01	*	80.	4.0762203E-02	2.4504488E+01	*
31.	2.8938421E-01	1.8412445E+01	*	81.	3.9163895E-02	2.4543651E+01	*
32.	2.7803730E-01	1.8690482E+01	*	82.	3.7628256E-02	2.4581279E+01	*
33.	2.6713530E-01	1.8957617E+01	*	83.	3.6152831E-02	2.4617431E+01	*
34.	2.5666077E-01	1.9214277E+01	*	84.	3.4735258E-02	2.4652166E+01	*
35.	2.4659696E-01	1.9460873E+01	*	85.	3.3373269E-02	2.4685539E+01	*
36.	2.3692775E-01	1.9697800E+01	*	86.	3.2064685E-02	2.4717603E+01	*
37.	2.2763768E-01	1.9925437E+01	*	87.	3.0807411E-02	2.4748410E+01	*
38.	2.1871188E-01	2.0144148E+01	*	88.	2.9599435E-02	2.4778009E+01	*
39.	2.1013607E-01	2.0354284E+01	*	89.	2.8438824E-02	2.4806447E+01	*
40.	2.0189691E-01	2.0556180E+01	*	90.	2.7323722E-02	2.4833770E+01	*
41.	1.9398004E-01	2.0750160E+01	*	91.	2.6252343E-02	2.4860022E+01	*
42.	1.8637397E-01	2.0936533E+01	*	92.	2.5222974E-02	2.4885244E+01	*
43.	1.7906614E-01	2.1115599E+01	*	93.	2.4233967E-02	2.4909477E+01	*
44.	1.7204486E-01	2.1287643E+01	*	94.	2.3283740E-02	2.4932760E+01	*
45.	1.6529888E-01	2.1452941E+01	*	95.	2.2370771E-02	2.4955130E+01	*
46.	1.5881742E-01	2.1611758E+01	*	96.	2.1493601E-02	2.4976623E+01	*
47.	1.5259010E-01	2.1764348E+01	*	97.	2.0650825E-02	2.4997273E+01	*
48.	1.4660696E-01	2.1910954E+01	*	98.	1.9841094E-02	2.5017114E+01	*
49.	1.4085842E-01	2.2051812E+01	*	99.	1.9063114E-02	2.5036177E+01	*
50.	1.3533528E-01	2.2187147E+01	*	100.	1.8315638E-02	2.5054492E+01	*

TABULATED VALUES OF E   WHEN R = .041

x	−RX E	−RX SUM OF E	*	x	−RX E	−RX SUM OF E	*
0.	1.0000000E+00	1.0000000E+00	*	50.	1.2873490E-01	2.1817692E+01	*
1.	9.5982912E-01	1.9598291E+00	*	51.	1.2356351E-01	2.1941255E+01	*
2.	9.2127195E-01	2.8811010E+00	*	52.	1.1859985E-01	2.2059854E+01	*
3.	8.8426365E-01	3.7653646E+00	*	53.	1.1383559E-01	2.2173689E+01	*
4.	8.4874202E-01	4.6141066E+00	*	54.	1.0926272E-01	2.2282951E+01	*
5.	8.1464731E-01	5.4287539E+00	*	55.	1.0487354E-01	2.2387824E+01	*
6.	7.8192727E-01	6.2106761E+00	*	56.	1.0066068E-01	2.2488484E+01	*
7.	7.5051172E-01	6.9611878E+00	*	57.	9.6617054E-02	2.2585101E+01	*
8.	7.2036301E-01	7.6815508E+00	*	58.	9.2735863E-02	2.2677836E+01	*
9.	6.9142540E-01	8.3729762E+00	*	59.	8.9010583E-02	2.2766846E+01	*
10.	6.6365024E-01	9.0366264E+00	*	60.	8.5434950E-02	2.2852280E+01	*
11.	6.3699083E-01	9.6736172E+00	*	61.	8.2002954E-02	2.2934282E+01	*
12.	6.1140236E-01	1.0285019E+01	*	62.	7.8708824E-02	2.3012990E+01	*
13.	5.8684180E-01	1.0871860E+01	*	63.	7.5547022E-02	2.3088537E+01	*
14.	5.6326785E-01	1.1435127E+01	*	64.	7.2512232E-02	2.3161049E+01	*
15.	5.4064089E-01	1.1975767E+01	*	65.	6.9599353E-02	2.3230648E+01	*
16.	5.1892287E-01	1.2494689E+01	*	66.	6.6803486E-02	2.3297451E+01	*
17.	4.9807729E-01	1.2992766E+01	*	67.	6.4119932E-02	2.3361570E+01	*
18.	4.7806909E-01	1.3470835E+01	*	68.	6.1544179E-02	2.3423114E+01	*
19.	4.5886464E-01	1.3929699E+01	*	69.	5.9071895E-02	2.3482185E+01	*
20.	4.4043165E-01	1.4370130E+01	*	70.	5.6698926E-02	2.3538883E+01	*
21.	4.2273913E-01	1.4792869E+01	*	71.	5.4421281E-02	2.3593304E+01	*
22.	4.0575733E-01	1.5198626E+01	*	72.	5.2235130E-02	2.3645539E+01	*
23.	3.8945770E-01	1.5588083E+01	*	73.	5.0136800E-02	2.3695675E+01	*
24.	3.7381285E-01	1.5961895E+01	*	74.	4.8122761E-02	2.3743797E+01	*
25.	3.5879646E-01	1.6320691E+01	*	75.	4.6189628E-02	2.3789986E+01	*
26.	3.4438329E-01	1.6665074E+01	*	76.	4.4334150E-02	2.3834320E+01	*
27.	3.3054912E-01	1.6995623E+01	*	77.	4.2553209E-02	2.3876873E+01	*
28.	3.1727067E-01	1.7312893E+01	*	78.	4.0843809E-02	2.3917716E+01	*
29.	3.0452563E-01	1.7617418E+01	*	79.	3.9203078E-02	2.3956919E+01	*
30.	2.9229257E-01	1.7909710E+01	*	80.	3.7628256E-02	2.3994547E+01	*
31.	2.8055092E-01	1.8190260E+01	*	81.	3.6116696E-02	2.4030663E+01	*
32.	2.6928095E-01	1.8459540E+01	*	82.	3.4665857E-02	2.4065328E+01	*
33.	2.5846370E-01	1.8718003E+01	*	83.	3.3273300E-02	2.4098601E+01	*
34.	2.4808099E-01	1.8966083E+01	*	84.	3.1936682E-02	2.4130537E+01	*
35.	2.3811536E-01	1.9204198E+01	*	85.	3.0653758E-02	2.4161190E+01	*
36.	2.2855066E-01	1.9432748E+01	*	86.	2.9422370E-02	2.4190612E+01	*
37.	2.1936900E-01	1.9652117E+01	*	87.	2.8240448E-02	2.4218852E+01	*
38.	2.1055676E-01	1.9862673E+01	*	88.	2.7106004E-02	2.4245958E+01	*
39.	2.0209851E-01	2.0064771E+01	*	89.	2.6017132E-02	2.4271975E+01	*
40.	1.9398004E-01	2.0258751E+01	*	90.	2.4972002E-02	2.4296947E+01	*
41.	1.8618769E-01	2.0444938E+01	*	91.	2.3968854E-02	2.4320915E+01	*
42.	1.7870837E-01	2.0623646E+01	*	92.	2.3006005E-02	2.4343921E+01	*
43.	1.7152950E-01	2.0795175E+01	*	93.	2.2081833E-02	2.4366002E+01	*
44.	1.6463901E-01	2.0959814E+01	*	94.	2.1194787E-02	2.4387196E+01	*
45.	1.5802532E-01	2.1117839E+01	*	95.	2.0343374E-02	2.4407539E+01	*
46.	1.5167730E-01	2.1269516E+01	*	96.	1.9526163E-02	2.4427065E+01	*
47.	1.4558429E-01	2.1415100E+01	*	97.	1.8741780E-02	2.4445806E+01	*
48.	1.3973604E-01	2.1554836E+01	*	98.	1.7988906E-02	2.4463794E+01	*
49.	1.3412272E-01	2.1688958E+01	*	99.	1.7266276E-02	2.4481060E+01	*
50.	1.2873490E-01	2.1817692E+01	*	100.	1.6572675E-02	2.4497632E+01	*

TABULATED VALUES OF E   WHEN R = .042

x	−RX E	−RX SUM OF E	*	x	−RX E	−RX SUM OF E	*
0.	1.0000000E+00	1.0000000E+00	*	50.	1.2245642E-01	2.1458177E+01	*
1.	9.5886976E-01	1.9588697E+00	*	51.	1.1741976E-01	2.1575596E+01	*
2.	9.1943125E-01	2.8783009E+00	*	52.	1.1259026E-01	2.1688186E+01	*
3.	8.8161484E-01	3.7599157E+00	*	53.	1.0795940E-01	2.1796145E+01	*
4.	8.4535383E-01	4.6052695E+00	*	54.	1.0351901E-01	2.1899664E+01	*
5.	8.1058424E-01	5.4158537E+00	*	55.	9.9261251E-02	2.1998925E+01	*
6.	7.7724473E-01	6.1930984E+00	*	56.	9.5178614E-02	2.2094103E+01	*
7.	7.4527648E-01	6.9383748E+00	*	57.	9.1263897E-02	2.2185366E+01	*
8.	7.1462310E-01	7.6529979E+00	*	58.	8.7510192E-02	2.2272876E+01	*
9.	6.8523049E-01	8.3382283E+00	*	59.	8.3910879E-02	2.2356786E+01	*
10.	6.5704681E-01	8.9952751E+00	*	60.	8.0459606E-02	2.2437245E+01	*
11.	6.3002233E-01	9.6252974E+00	*	61.	7.7150285E-02	2.2514395E+01	*
12.	6.0410938E-01	1.0229406E+01	*	62.	7.3977077E-02	2.2588372E+01	*
13.	5.7926223E-01	1.0808668E+01	*	63.	7.0934383E-02	2.2659306E+01	*
14.	5.5543704E-01	1.1364105E+01	*	64.	6.8016836E-02	2.2727322E+01	*
15.	5.3259179E-01	1.1896696E+01	*	65.	6.5219289E-02	2.2792541E+01	*
16.	5.1068618E-01	1.2407382E+01	*	66.	6.2536805E-02	2.2855077E+01	*
17.	4.8968154E-01	1.2897063E+01	*	67.	5.9964653E-02	2.2915041E+01	*
18.	4.6954083E-01	1.3366603E+01	*	68.	5.7498293E-02	2.2972593E+01	*
19.	4.5022852E-01	1.3816831E+01	*	69.	5.5133376E-02	2.3027672E+01	*
20.	4.3171052E-01	1.4248541E+01	*	70.	5.2865728E-02	2.3080537E+01	*
21.	4.1395417E-01	1.4662495E+01	*	71.	5.0691349E-02	2.3131228E+01	*
22.	3.9692814E-01	1.5059423E+01	*	72.	4.8606403E-02	2.3179834E+01	*
23.	3.8060240E-01	1.5440025E+01	*	73.	4.6607211E-02	2.3226441E+01	*
24.	3.6494814E-01	1.5804973E+01	*	74.	4.4690246E-02	2.3271131E+01	*
25.	3.4993774E-01	1.6154910E+01	*	75.	4.2852126E-02	2.3313983E+01	*
26.	3.3554473E-01	1.6490454E+01	*	76.	4.1089609E-02	2.3355072E+01	*
27.	3.2174370E-01	1.6812197E+01	*	77.	3.9399584E-02	2.3394471E+01	*
28.	3.0851031E-01	1.7120707E+01	*	78.	3.7779071E-02	2.3432250E+01	*
29.	2.9582121E-01	1.7416528E+01	*	79.	3.6225209E-02	2.3468475E+01	*
30.	2.8365402E-01	1.7700182E+01	*	80.	3.4735258E-02	2.3503210E+01	*
31.	2.7198727E-01	1.7972169E+01	*	81.	3.3306590E-02	2.3536516E+01	*
32.	2.6080037E-01	1.8232969E+01	*	82.	3.1936682E-02	2.3568452E+01	*
33.	2.5007360E-01	1.8483042E+01	*	83.	3.0623119E-02	2.3599075E+01	*
34.	2.3978801E-01	1.8722830E+01	*	84.	2.9363584E-02	2.3628438E+01	*
35.	2.2992548E-01	1.8952755E+01	*	85.	2.8155853E-02	2.3656593E+01	*
36.	2.2046859E-01	1.9173223E+01	*	86.	2.6997797E-02	2.3683590E+01	*
37.	2.1140067E-01	1.9384623E+01	*	87.	2.5887371E-02	2.3709477E+01	*
38.	2.0270572E-01	1.9587328E+01	*	88.	2.4822618E-02	2.3734299E+01	*
39.	1.9436839E-01	1.9781696E+01	*	89.	2.3801658E-02	2.3758100E+01	*
40.	1.8637397E-01	1.9968069E+01	*	90.	2.2822691E-02	2.3780922E+01	*
41.	1.7870837E-01	2.0146777E+01	*	91.	2.1883989E-02	2.3802805E+01	*
42.	1.7135805E-01	2.0318135E+01	*	92.	2.0983895E-02	2.3823788E+01	*
43.	1.6431066E-01	2.0482445E+01	*	93.	2.0120823E-02	2.3843908E+01	*
44.	1.5755195E-01	2.0639996E+01	*	94.	1.9293249E-02	2.3863201E+01	*
45.	1.5107180E-01	2.0791004E+01	*	95.	1.8499714E-02	2.3881700E+01	*
46.	1.4485819E-01	2.0935925E+01	*	96.	1.7738816E-02	2.3899438E+01	*
47.	1.3890014E-01	2.1074825E+01	*	97.	1.7009215E-02	2.3916447E+01	*
48.	1.3318714E-01	2.1208012E+01	*	98.	1.6309622E-02	2.3932756E+01	*
49.	1.2770913E-01	2.1335721E+01	*	99.	1.5638804E-02	2.3948394E+01	*
50.	1.2245642E-01	2.1458177E+01	*	100.	1.4995576E-02	2.3963389E+01	*

TABULATED VALUES OF E^{-RX} WHEN R = .043

X	E^{-RX}	SUM OF E^{-RX}	*	X	E^{-RX}	SUM OF E^{-RX}	*
0.	1.0000000E+00	1.0000000E+00	*	50.	1.1648415E-01	2.1108268E+01	*
1.	9.5791138E-01	1.9579113E+00	*	51.	1.1158150E-01	2.1219849E+01	*
2.	9.1759422E-01	2.8755055E+00	*	52.	1.0688519E-01	2.1326734E+01	*
3.	8.7897396E-01	3.7544794E+00	*	53.	1.0238654E-01	2.1429120E+01	*
4.	8.4197917E-01	4.5964585E+00	*	54.	9.8077234E-02	2.1527197E+01	*
5.	8.0654143E-01	5.4029999E+00	*	55.	9.3949300E-02	2.1621146E+01	*
6.	7.7259523E-01	6.1755951E+00	*	56.	8.9995104E-02	2.1711141E+01	*
7.	7.4007777E-01	6.9156728E+00	*	57.	8.6207335E-02	2.1797348E+01	*
8.	7.0892892E-01	7.6246017E+00	*	58.	8.2578088E-02	2.1879926E+01	*
9.	6.7909109E-01	8.3036927E+00	*	59.	7.9103354E-02	2.1959029E+01	*
10.	6.5050909E-01	8.9542017E+00	*	60.	7.5774003E-02	2.2034803E+01	*
11.	6.2313007E-01	9.5773317E+00	*	61.	7.2584781E-02	2.2107387E+01	*
12.	5.9690339E-01	1.0174235E+01	*	62.	6.9529788E-02	2.2176916E+01	*
13.	5.7178055E-01	1.0746015E+01	*	63.	6.6603376E-02	2.2243519E+01	*
14.	5.4771510E-01	1.1293730E+01	*	64.	6.3800132E-02	2.2307319E+01	*
15.	5.2466254E-01	1.1818392E+01	*	65.	6.1114874E-02	2.2368433E+01	*
16.	5.0258022E-01	1.2320972E+01	*	66.	5.8542634E-02	2.2426975E+01	*
17.	4.8142732E-01	1.2802399E+01	*	67.	5.6078655E-02	2.2483053E+01	*
18.	4.6116471E-01	1.3263563E+01	*	68.	5.3718383E-02	2.2536771E+01	*
19.	4.4175493E-01	1.3705317E+01	*	69.	5.1457451E-02	2.2588228E+01	*
20.	4.2316208E-01	1.4128479E+01	*	70.	4.9291678E-02	2.2637519E+01	*
21.	4.0535177E-01	1.4533830E+01	*	71.	4.7217060E-02	2.2684736E+01	*
22.	3.8829108E-01	1.4922121E+01	*	72.	4.5229760E-02	2.2729965E+01	*
23.	3.7194845E-01	1.5294069E+01	*	73.	4.3326102E-02	2.2773291E+01	*
24.	3.5629365E-01	1.5650362E+01	*	74.	4.1502566E-02	2.2814793E+01	*
25.	3.4129775E-01	1.5991659E+01	*	75.	3.9755781E-02	2.2854548E+01	*
26.	3.2693300E-01	1.6318592E+01	*	76.	3.8082515E-02	2.2892630E+01	*
27.	3.1317285E-01	1.6631764E+01	*	77.	3.6479675E-02	2.2929109E+01	*
28.	2.9999184E-01	1.6931755E+01	*	78.	3.4944296E-02	2.2964053E+01	*
29.	2.8736560E-01	1.7219120E+01	*	79.	3.3473540E-02	2.2997526E+01	*
30.	2.7527078E-01	1.7494390E+01	*	80.	3.2064685E-02	2.3029590E+01	*
31.	2.6368501E-01	1.7758075E+01	*	81.	3.0715127E-02	2.3060305E+01	*
32.	2.5258688E-01	1.8010661E+01	*	82.	2.9422370E-02	2.3089727E+01	*
33.	2.4195585E-01	1.8252616E+01	*	83.	2.8184023E-02	2.3117911E+01	*
34.	2.3177226E-01	1.8484388E+01	*	84.	2.6997797E-02	2.3144908E+01	*
35.	2.2201729E-01	1.8706405E+01	*	85.	2.5861497E-02	2.3170769E+01	*
36.	2.1267289E-01	1.8919077E+01	*	86.	2.4773023E-02	2.3195542E+01	*
37.	2.0372178E-01	1.9122798E+01	*	87.	2.3730360E-02	2.3219272E+01	*
38.	1.9514742E-01	1.9317945E+01	*	88.	2.2731582E-02	2.3242003E+01	*
39.	1.8693393E-01	1.9504878E+01	*	89.	2.1774842E-02	2.3263777E+01	*
40.	1.7906614E-01	1.9683944E+01	*	90.	2.0858369E-02	2.3284635E+01	*
41.	1.7152950E-01	1.9855473E+01	*	91.	1.9980469E-02	2.3304615E+01	*
42.	1.6431006E-01	2.0019783E+01	*	92.	1.9139519E-02	2.3323754E+01	*
43.	1.5739448E-01	2.0177177E+01	*	93.	1.8333963E-02	2.3342087E+01	*
44.	1.5076995E-01	2.0327946E+01	*	94.	1.7562312E-02	2.3359649E+01	*
45.	1.4442426E-01	2.0472370E+01	*	95.	1.6823139E-02	2.3376472E+01	*
46.	1.3834565E-01	2.0610715E+01	*	96.	1.6115076E-02	2.3392587E+01	*
47.	1.3252287E-01	2.0743237E+01	*	97.	1.5436815E-02	2.3408023E+01	*
48.	1.2694517E-01	2.0870182E+01	*	98.	1.4787101E-02	2.3422810E+01	*
49.	1.2160222E-01	2.0991784E+01	*	99.	1.4164732E-02	2.3436974E+01	*
50.	1.1648415E-01	2.1108268E+01	*	100.	1.3568558E-02	2.3450542E+01	*

TABULATED VALUES OF E^{-RX} WHEN R = .044

X	E^{-RX}	SUM OF E^{-RX}	*	X	E^{-RX}	SUM OF E^{-RX}	*
0.	1.0000000E+00	1.0000000E+00	*	50.	1.1080315E-01	2.0767660E+01	*
1.	9.5695395E-01	1.9569539E+00	*	51.	1.0603352E-01	2.0873693E+01	*
2.	9.1576087E-01	2.8727147E+00	*	52.	1.0146919E-01	2.0975162E+01	*
3.	8.7634099E-01	3.7490556E+00	*	53.	9.7101349E-02	2.1072263E+01	*
4.	8.3861798E-01	4.5876735E+00	*	54.	9.2921521E-02	2.1165184E+01	*
5.	8.0251879E-01	5.3901922E+00	*	55.	8.8921617E-02	2.1254105E+01	*
6.	7.6797353E-01	6.1581657E+00	*	56.	8.5093893E-02	2.1339198E+01	*
7.	7.3491531E-01	6.8930810E+00	*	57.	8.1430938E-02	2.1420628E+01	*
8.	7.0328012E-01	7.5963611E+00	*	58.	7.7925658E-02	2.1498553E+01	*
9.	6.7300669E-01	8.2693677E+00	*	59.	7.4571267E-02	2.1573124E+01	*
10.	6.4403641E-01	8.9134041E+00	*	60.	7.1361269E-02	2.1644485E+01	*
11.	6.1631320E-01	9.5297173E+00	*	61.	6.8289449E-02	2.1712774E+01	*
12.	5.8978335E-01	1.0119500E+01	*	62.	6.5349858E-02	2.1778123E+01	*
13.	5.6439551E-01	1.0683895E+01	*	63.	6.2536805E-02	2.1840659E+01	*
14.	5.4010052E-01	1.1223995E+01	*	64.	5.9844843E-02	2.1900503E+01	*
15.	5.1685133E-01	1.1740846E+01	*	65.	5.7268760E-02	2.1957771E+01	*
16.	4.9460292E-01	1.2235448E+01	*	66.	5.4803566E-02	2.2012574E+01	*
17.	4.7331223E-01	1.2708760E+01	*	67.	5.2444489E-02	2.2065018E+01	*
18.	4.5293801E-01	1.3161698E+01	*	68.	5.0186962E-02	2.2115204E+01	*
19.	4.3344082E-01	1.3595138E+01	*	69.	4.8026612E-02	2.2163230E+01	*
20.	4.1478291E-01	1.4009920E+01	*	70.	4.5959256E-02	2.2209189E+01	*
21.	3.9692814E-01	1.4406848E+01	*	71.	4.3980892E-02	2.2253169E+01	*
22.	3.7984196E-01	1.4786689E+01	*	72.	4.2087689E-02	2.2295256E+01	*
23.	3.6349126E-01	1.5150180E+01	*	73.	4.0275980E-02	2.2335531E+01	*
24.	3.4784440E-01	1.5498024E+01	*	74.	3.8542259E-02	2.2374073E+01	*
25.	3.3287108E-01	1.5830895E+01	*	75.	3.6883167E-02	2.2410956E+01	*
26.	3.1854229E-01	1.6149437E+01	*	76.	3.5295492E-02	2.2446251E+01	*
27.	3.0483031E-01	1.6454267E+01	*	77.	3.3776161E-02	2.2480027E+01	*
28.	2.9170857E-01	1.6745975E+01	*	78.	3.2322231E-02	2.2512349E+01	*
29.	2.7915167E-01	1.7025126E+01	*	79.	3.0930887E-02	2.2543279E+01	*
30.	2.6713530E-01	1.7292261E+01	*	80.	2.9599435E-02	2.2572878E+01	*
31.	2.5563618E-01	1.7547897E+01	*	81.	2.8325296E-02	2.2601203E+01	*
32.	2.4463205E-01	1.7792529E+01	*	82.	2.7106004E-02	2.2628309E+01	*
33.	2.3410161E-01	1.8026630E+01	*	83.	2.5939198E-02	2.2654248E+01	*
34.	2.2402446E-01	1.8250654E+01	*	84.	2.4822618E-02	2.2679070E+01	*
35.	2.1438110E-01	1.8465035E+01	*	85.	2.3754103E-02	2.2702824E+01	*
36.	2.0515284E-01	1.8670187E+01	*	86.	2.2731582E-02	2.2725555E+01	*
37.	1.9632182E-01	1.8866508E+01	*	87.	2.1753078E-02	2.2747308E+01	*
38.	1.8787094E-01	1.9054378E+01	*	88.	2.0816694E-02	2.2768124E+01	*
39.	1.7978384E-01	1.9234161E+01	*	89.	1.9920618E-02	2.2788044E+01	*
40.	1.7204486E-01	1.9406205E+01	*	90.	1.9063114E-02	2.2807107E+01	*
41.	1.6463901E-01	1.9570844E+01	*	91.	1.8242522E-02	2.2825349E+01	*
42.	1.5755195E-01	1.9728395E+01	*	92.	1.7457254E-02	2.2842806E+01	*
43.	1.5076996E-01	1.9879164E+01	*	93.	1.6705788E-02	2.2859511E+01	*
44.	1.4427991E-01	2.0023443E+01	*	94.	1.5986670E-02	2.2875497E+01	*
45.	1.3806923E-01	2.0161512E+01	*	95.	1.5298507E-02	2.2890795E+01	*
46.	1.3212590E-01	2.0293637E+01	*	96.	1.4639967E-02	2.2905434E+01	*
47.	1.2643840E-01	2.0420755E+01	*	97.	1.4009774E-02	2.2919443E+01	*
48.	1.2099573E-01	2.0541070E+01	*	98.	1.3406709E-02	2.2932849E+01	*
49.	1.1578734E-01	2.0656857E+01	*	99.	1.2829603E-02	2.2945678E+01	*
50.	1.1080315E-01	2.0767660E+01	*	100.	1.2277339E-02	2.2957955E+01	*

TABULATED VALUES OF E   WHEN R = .045

x	E −RX	SUM OF E −RX	*	x	E −RX	SUM OF E −RX	*
0.	1.0000000E+00	1.0000000E+00	*	50.	1.0539922E-01	2.0436052E+01	*
1.	9.5599748E-01	1.9559974E+00	*	51.	1.0076139E-01	2.0536813E+01	*
2.	9.1393118E-01	2.8699285E+00	*	52.	9.6327638E-02	2.0633140E+01	*
3.	8.7371591E-01	3.7436444E+00	*	53.	9.2088979E-02	2.0725228E+01	*
4.	8.3527020E-01	4.5789146E+00	*	54.	8.8036832E-02	2.0813264E+01	*
5.	7.9851621E-01	5.3774308E+00	*	55.	8.4162990E-02	2.0897426E+01	*
6.	7.6337949E-01	6.1408102E+00	*	56.	8.0459606E-02	2.0977885E+01	*
7.	7.2978387E-01	6.8705990E+00	*	57.	7.6919181E-02	2.1054804E+01	*
8.	6.9767632E-01	7.5682753E+00	*	58.	7.3534543E-02	2.1128338E+01	*
9.	6.6697680E-01	8.2352521E+00	*	59.	7.0298838E-02	2.1198636E+01	*
10.	6.3762814E-01	8.8728802E+00	*	60.	6.7205512E-02	2.1265841E+01	*
11.	6.0957090E-01	9.4824511E+00	*	61.	6.4248300E-02	2.1330089E+01	*
12.	5.8274625E-01	1.0065199E+01	*	62.	6.1421213E-02	2.1391510E+01	*
13.	5.5710586E-01	1.0622304E+01	*	63.	5.8718525E-02	2.1450228E+01	*
14.	5.3259179E-01	1.1154895E+01	*	64.	5.6134762E-02	2.1506362E+01	*
15.	5.0915641E-01	1.1664051E+01	*	65.	5.3664691E-02	2.1560026E+01	*
16.	4.8675225E-01	1.2150803E+01	*	66.	5.1303310E-02	2.1611329E+01	*
17.	4.6533393E-01	1.2616136E+01	*	67.	4.9045835E-02	2.1660374E+01	*
18.	4.4485806E-01	1.3060994E+01	*	68.	4.6887695E-02	2.1707261E+01	*
19.	4.2528319E-01	1.3486277E+01	*	69.	4.4824518E-02	2.1752085E+01	*
20.	4.0656965E-01	1.3892846E+01	*	70.	4.2852126E-02	2.1794937E+01	*
21.	3.8867957E-01	1.4281525E+01	*	71.	4.0966525E-02	2.1835903E+01	*
22.	3.7157669E-01	1.4653101E+01	*	72.	3.9163895E-02	2.1875066E+01	*
23.	3.5522638E-01	1.5008327E+01	*	73.	3.7440585E-02	2.1912506E+01	*
24.	3.3959552E-01	1.5347922E+01	*	74.	3.5793105E-02	2.1948299E+01	*
25.	3.2465246E-01	1.5672574E+01	*	75.	3.4218118E-02	2.1982517E+01	*
26.	3.1036694E-01	1.5982940E+01	*	76.	3.2712434E-02	2.2015229E+01	*
27.	2.9671001E-01	1.6279650E+01	*	77.	3.1273005E-02	2.2046502E+01	*
28.	2.8365402E-01	1.6563304E+01	*	78.	2.9896914E-02	2.2076398E+01	*
29.	2.7117253E-01	1.6834476E+01	*	79.	2.8581374E-02	2.2104979E+01	*
30.	2.5924026E-01	1.7093716E+01	*	80.	2.7323722E-02	2.2132302E+01	*
31.	2.4783303E-01	1.7341549E+01	*	81.	2.6121409E-02	2.2158423E+01	*
32.	2.3692775E-01	1.7578476E+01	*	82.	2.4972002E-02	2.2183395E+01	*
33.	2.2650234E-01	1.7804978E+01	*	83.	2.3873171E-02	2.2207268E+01	*
34.	2.1653566E-01	1.8021513E+01	*	84.	2.2822691E-02	2.2230090E+01	*
35.	2.0700755E-01	1.8228520E+01	*	85.	2.1818435E-02	2.2251908E+01	*
36.	1.9789869E-01	1.8426418E+01	*	86.	2.0858369E-02	2.2272766E+01	*
37.	1.8919065E-01	1.8615608E+01	*	87.	1.9940548E-02	2.2292706E+01	*
38.	1.8086579E-01	1.8796473E+01	*	88.	1.9063114E-02	2.2311769E+01	*
39.	1.7290724E-01	1.8969380E+01	*	89.	1.8224289E-02	2.2329993E+01	*
40.	1.6529888E-01	1.9134678E+01	*	90.	1.7422374E-02	2.2347415E+01	*
41.	1.5802532E-01	1.9292703E+01	*	91.	1.6655746E-02	2.2364070E+01	*
42.	1.5107180E-01	1.9443774E+01	*	92.	1.5922851E-02	2.2379992E+01	*
43.	1.4442426E-01	1.9588198E+01	*	93.	1.5222205E-02	2.2395214E+01	*
44.	1.3806923E-01	1.9726267E+01	*	94.	1.4552390E-02	2.2409766E+01	*
45.	1.3199384E-01	1.9858260E+01	*	95.	1.3912048E-02	2.2423678E+01	*
46.	1.2618578E-01	1.9984445E+01	*	96.	1.3299883E-02	2.2436977E+01	*
47.	1.2063328E-01	2.0105078E+01	*	97.	1.2714655E-02	2.2449691E+01	*
48.	1.1532512E-01	2.0220403E+01	*	98.	1.2155178E-02	2.2461846E+01	*
49.	1.1025052E-01	2.0330653E+01	*	99.	1.1620319E-02	2.2473466E+01	*
50.	1.0539922E-01	2.0436052E+01	*	100.	1.1108996E-02	2.2484574E+01	*

TABULATED VALUES OF E   WHEN R = .046

x	E −RX	SUM OF E −RX	*	x	E −RX	SUM OF E −RX	*
0.	1.0000000E+00	1.0000000E+00	*	50.	1.0025884E-01	2.0113151E+01	*
1.	9.5504196E-01	1.9550419E+00	*	51.	9.5751402E-02	2.0208902E+01	*
2.	9.1210514E-01	2.8671470E+00	*	52.	9.1446607E-02	2.0300348E+01	*
3.	8.7109869E-01	3.7382456E+00	*	53.	8.7335347E-02	2.0387683E+01	*
4.	8.3193580E-01	4.5701814E+00	*	54.	8.3408921E-02	2.0471091E+01	*
5.	7.9453359E-01	5.3647149E+00	*	55.	7.9659019E-02	2.0550750E+01	*
6.	7.5881293E-01	6.1235278E+00	*	56.	7.6077706E-02	2.0626827E+01	*
7.	7.2469818E-01	6.8482259E+00	*	57.	7.2657402E-02	2.0699484E+01	*
8.	6.9211717E-01	7.5403430E+00	*	58.	6.9390868E-02	2.0768874E+01	*
9.	6.6100094E-01	8.2013439E+00	*	59.	6.6271190E-02	2.0835145E+01	*
10.	6.3128364E-01	8.8326275E+00	*	60.	6.3291768E-02	2.0898436E+01	*
11.	6.0290237E-01	9.4355298E+00	*	61.	6.0446294E-02	2.0958882E+01	*
12.	5.7579706E-01	1.0011326E+01	*	62.	5.7728747E-02	2.1016610E+01	*
13.	5.4991035E-01	1.0561236E+01	*	63.	5.5133376E-02	2.1071743E+01	*
14.	5.2518746E-01	1.1086423E+01	*	64.	5.2654688E-02	2.1124397E+01	*
15.	5.0157606E-01	1.1587999E+01	*	65.	5.0287436E-02	2.1174684E+01	*
16.	4.7902619E-01	1.2067025E+01	*	66.	4.8026612E-02	2.1222710E+01	*
17.	4.5749011E-01	1.2524515E+01	*	67.	4.5867429E-02	2.1268577E+01	*
18.	4.3692225E-01	1.2961437E+01	*	68.	4.3805320E-02	2.1312382E+01	*
19.	4.1727908E-01	1.3378716E+01	*	69.	4.1835918E-02	2.1354217E+01	*
20.	3.9851903E-01	1.3777235E+01	*	70.	3.9955058E-02	2.1394172E+01	*
21.	3.8060240E-01	1.4157837E+01	*	71.	3.8158757E-02	2.1432330E+01	*
22.	3.6349126E-01	1.4521328E+01	*	72.	3.6443214E-02	2.1468773E+01	*
23.	3.4714941E-01	1.4868477E+01	*	73.	3.4804798E-02	2.1503577E+01	*
24.	3.3154225E-01	1.5200019E+01	*	74.	3.3240043E-02	2.1536817E+01	*
25.	3.1663676E-01	1.5516655E+01	*	75.	3.1745636E-02	2.1568562E+01	*
26.	3.0240140E-01	1.5819056E+01	*	76.	3.0318414E-02	2.1598880E+01	*
27.	2.8880602E-01	1.6107862E+01	*	77.	2.8955358E-02	2.1627835E+01	*
28.	2.7582187E-01	1.6383683E+01	*	78.	2.7653582E-02	2.1655488E+01	*
29.	2.6342146E-01	1.6647104E+01	*	79.	2.6410331E-02	2.1681898E+01	*
30.	2.5157855E-01	1.6898682E+01	*	80.	2.5222974E-02	2.1707120E+01	*
31.	2.4026807E-01	1.7138950E+01	*	81.	2.4088999E-02	2.1731208E+01	*
32.	2.2946609E-01	1.7368416E+01	*	82.	2.3006003E-02	2.1754214E+01	*
33.	2.1914747E-01	1.7587565E+01	*	83.	2.1971700E-02	2.1776185E+01	*
34.	2.0929720E-01	1.7796862E+01	*	84.	2.0983895E-02	2.1797168E+01	*
35.	1.9988761E-01	1.7996749E+01	*	85.	2.0040500E-02	2.1817208E+01	*
36.	1.9090105E-01	1.8187650E+01	*	86.	1.9139519E-02	2.1836347E+01	*
37.	1.8231852E-01	1.8369968E+01	*	87.	1.8279044E-02	2.1854626E+01	*
38.	1.7412183E-01	1.8544089E+01	*	88.	1.7457254E-02	2.1872083E+01	*
39.	1.6629366E-01	1.8710382E+01	*	89.	1.6672410E-02	2.1888755E+01	*
40.	1.5881742E-01	1.8869199E+01	*	90.	1.5922851E-02	2.1904677E+01	*
41.	1.5167730E-01	1.9020876E+01	*	91.	1.5206991E-02	2.1919883E+01	*
42.	1.4485819E-01	1.9165734E+01	*	92.	1.4523314E-02	2.1934406E+01	*
43.	1.3834565E-01	1.9304079E+01	*	93.	1.3870375E-02	2.1948276E+01	*
44.	1.3212590E-01	1.9436204E+01	*	94.	1.3246790E-02	2.1961522E+01	*
45.	1.2618578E-01	1.9562389E+01	*	95.	1.2651240E-02	2.1974173E+01	*
46.	1.2051271E-01	1.9682901E+01	*	96.	1.2082465E-02	2.1986255E+01	*
47.	1.1509407E-01	1.9797995E+01	*	97.	1.1539261E-02	2.1997794E+01	*
48.	1.0992026E-01	1.9907915E+01	*	98.	1.1020479E-02	2.2008814E+01	*
49.	1.0497846E-01	2.0012893E+01	*	99.	1.0525019E-02	2.2019339E+01	*
50.	1.0025884E-01	2.0113151E+01	*	100.	1.0051835E-02	2.2029390E+01	*

X	E^-RX	SUM OF E^-RX	*	X	E^-RX	SUM OF E^-RX	*
0.	1.0000000E+00	1.0000000E+00	*	50.	9.5369162E-02	1.9798673E+01	*
1.	9.5408739E-01	1.9540873E+00	*	51.	9.0990515E-02	1.9889663E+01	*
2.	9.1028276E-01	2.8643700E+00	*	52.	8.6812904E-02	1.9976475E+01	*
3.	8.6848931E-01	3.7328593E+00	*	53.	8.2827097E-02	2.0059302E+01	*
4.	8.2861470E-01	4.5614740E+00	*	54.	7.9024290E-02	2.0138326E+01	*
5.	7.9057034E-01	5.3520444E+00	*	55.	7.5396079E-02	2.0213722E+01	*
6.	7.5427368E-01	6.1063184E+00	*	56.	7.1934449E-02	2.0285656E+01	*
7.	7.1964301E-01	6.8259614E+00	*	57.	6.8631751E-02	2.0354287E+01	*
8.	6.8660233E-01	7.5125637E+00	*	58.	6.5480689E-02	2.0419767E+01	*
9.	6.5507862E-01	8.1676423E+00	*	59.	6.2474300E-02	2.0482241E+01	*
10.	6.2500226E-01	8.7926445E+00	*	60.	5.9605942E-02	2.0541846E+01	*
11.	5.9630678E-01	9.3889512E+00	*	61.	5.6869278E-02	2.0598715E+01	*
12.	5.6892878E-01	9.9578799E+00	*	62.	5.4258262E-02	2.0652973E+01	*
13.	5.4280778E-01	1.0500687E+01	*	63.	5.1767124E-02	2.0704740E+01	*
14.	5.1788607E-01	1.1018573E+01	*	64.	4.9390360E-02	2.0754130E+01	*
15.	4.9410857E-01	1.1512681E+01	*	65.	4.7122720E-02	2.0801252E+01	*
16.	4.7142276E-01	1.1984103E+01	*	66.	4.4959193E-02	2.0846211E+01	*
17.	4.4977501E-01	1.2433881E+01	*	67.	4.2895000E-02	2.0889106E+01	*
18.	4.2912801E-01	1.2863009E+01	*	68.	4.0925579E-02	2.0930031E+01	*
19.	4.0942563E-01	1.3272434E+01	*	69.	3.9046579E-02	2.0969077E+01	*
20.	3.9062783E-01	1.3663061E+01	*	70.	3.7253849E-02	2.1006330E+01	*
21.	3.7269309E-01	1.4035754E+01	*	71.	3.5543428E-02	2.1041873E+01	*
22.	3.5558178E-01	1.4391335E+01	*	72.	3.3911536E-02	2.1075784E+01	*
23.	3.3925609E-01	1.4730591E+01	*	73.	3.2354569E-02	2.1108138E+01	*
24.	3.2367996E-01	1.5054270E+01	*	74.	3.0869087E-02	2.1139007E+01	*
25.	3.0881897E-01	1.5363088E+01	*	75.	2.9451800E-02	2.1168458E+01	*
26.	2.9464029E-01	1.5657728E+01	*	76.	2.8099598E-02	2.1196557E+01	*
27.	2.8111259E-01	1.5938840E+01	*	77.	2.6809472E-02	2.1223366E+01	*
28.	2.6820598E-01	1.6207045E+01	*	78.	2.5578579E-02	2.1248944E+01	*
29.	2.5589194E-01	1.6462936E+01	*	79.	2.4404200E-02	2.1273348E+01	*
30.	2.4414328E-01	1.6707079E+01	*	80.	2.3283740E-02	2.1296631E+01	*
31.	2.3293402E-01	1.6940013E+01	*	81.	2.2214723E-02	2.1318845E+01	*
32.	2.2223942E-01	1.7162252E+01	*	82.	2.1194787E-02	2.1340039E+01	*
33.	2.1203583E-01	1.7374287E+01	*	83.	2.0221679E-02	2.1360260E+01	*
34.	2.0230071E-01	1.7576587E+01	*	84.	1.9293249E-02	2.1379553E+01	*
35.	1.9301256E-01	1.7769599E+01	*	85.	1.8407446E-02	2.1397960E+01	*
36.	1.8415085E-01	1.7953749E+01	*	86.	1.7562312E-02	2.1415522E+01	*
37.	1.7569600E-01	1.8129445E+01	*	87.	1.6755981E-02	2.1432277E+01	*
38.	1.6762934E-01	1.8297074E+01	*	88.	1.5986670E-02	2.1448263E+01	*
39.	1.5993304E-01	1.8457007E+01	*	89.	1.5252680E-02	2.1463515E+01	*
40.	1.5259010E-01	1.8609597E+01	*	90.	1.4552392E-02	2.1478067E+01	*
41.	1.4558429E-01	1.8755181E+01	*	91.	1.3884252E-02	2.1491951E+01	*
42.	1.3890014E-01	1.8894081E+01	*	92.	1.3246790E-02	2.1505197E+01	*
43.	1.3252287E-01	1.9026603E+01	*	93.	1.2638595E-02	2.1517835E+01	*
44.	1.2643840E-01	1.9153041E+01	*	94.	1.2058324E-02	2.1529893E+01	*
45.	1.2063328E-01	1.9273674E+01	*	95.	1.1504695E-02	2.1541397E+01	*
46.	1.1509470E-01	1.9388768E+01	*	96.	1.0976485E-02	2.1552373E+01	*
47.	1.0981046E-01	1.9498578E+01	*	97.	1.0472526E-02	2.1562845E+01	*
48.	1.0476872E-01	1.9603346E+01	*	98.	9.9917052E-03	2.1572836E+01	*
49.	9.9958517E-02	1.9703304E+01	*	99.	9.5329600E-03	2.1582363E+01	*
50.	9.5369162E-02	1.9798673E+01	*	100.	9.0952770E-03	2.1591463E+01	*

X	E^-RX	SUM OF E^-RX	*	X	E^-RX	SUM OF E^-RX	*
0.	1.0000000E+00	1.0000000E+00	*	50.	9.0717953E-02	1.9492353E+01	*
1.	9.5313378E-01	1.9531337E+00	*	51.	8.6466346E-02	1.9578819E+01	*
2.	9.0846401E-01	2.8615977E+00	*	52.	8.2413995E-02	1.9661232E+01	*
3.	8.6588774E-01	3.7274854E+00	*	53.	7.8551546E-02	1.9739783E+01	*
4.	8.2530686E-01	4.5527922E+00	*	54.	7.4870149E-02	1.9814653E+01	*
5.	7.8662786E-01	5.3394200E+00	*	55.	7.1361269E-02	1.9888604E+01	*
6.	7.4976159E-01	6.0891815E+00	*	56.	6.8016836E-02	1.9956030E+01	*
7.	7.1462310E-01	6.8038046E+00	*	57.	6.4829157E-02	2.0018859E+01	*
8.	6.8113142E-01	7.4849360E+00	*	58.	6.1790848E-02	2.0080649E+01	*
9.	6.4920937E-01	8.1341453E+00	*	59.	5.8894945E-02	2.0139543E+01	*
10.	6.1878339E-01	8.7529286E+00	*	60.	5.6134726E-02	2.0195677E+01	*
11.	5.8978335E-01	9.3427119E+00	*	61.	5.3503938E-02	2.0249180E+01	*
12.	5.6214244E-01	9.9048543E+00	*	62.	5.0996411E-02	2.0300176E+01	*
13.	5.3579695E-01	1.0440651E+01	*	63.	4.8606403E-02	2.0348782E+01	*
14.	5.1068618E-01	1.0951337E+01	*	64.	4.6328405E-02	2.0395110E+01	*
15.	4.8675225E-01	1.1438089E+01	*	65.	4.4157168E-02	2.0439267E+01	*
16.	4.6394002E-01	1.1902029E+01	*	66.	4.2087689E-02	2.0481354E+01	*
17.	4.4219690E-01	1.2344225E+01	*	67.	4.0115198E-02	2.0521469E+01	*
18.	4.2147281E-01	1.2765697E+01	*	68.	3.8235151E-02	2.0559704E+01	*
19.	4.0171997E-01	1.3167416E+01	*	69.	3.6443214E-02	2.0596147E+01	*
20.	3.8289288E-01	1.3550308E+01	*	70.	3.4735258E-02	2.0630882E+01	*
21.	3.6494814E-01	1.3915256E+01	*	71.	3.3107430E-02	2.0663989E+01	*
22.	3.4784440E-01	1.4263100E+01	*	72.	3.1555732E-02	2.0695544E+01	*
23.	3.3154225E-01	1.4594642E+01	*	73.	3.0076835E-02	2.0725620E+01	*
24.	3.1600412E-01	1.4910646E+01	*	74.	2.8667274E-02	2.0754287E+01	*
25.	3.0119421E-01	1.5211840E+01	*	75.	2.7323722E-02	2.0781610E+01	*
26.	2.8707837E-01	1.5498918E+01	*	76.	2.6043162E-02	2.0807653E+01	*
27.	2.7362410E-01	1.5772542E+01	*	77.	2.4822618E-02	2.0832475E+01	*
28.	2.6080037E-01	1.6033342E+01	*	78.	2.3659276E-02	2.0856134E+01	*
29.	2.4857765E-01	1.6281919E+01	*	79.	2.2550455E-02	2.0878684E+01	*
30.	2.3692775E-01	1.6518846E+01	*	80.	2.1493601E-02	2.0900177E+01	*
31.	2.2582385E-01	1.6744669E+01	*	81.	2.0486277E-02	2.0920663E+01	*
32.	2.1524034E-01	1.6959909E+01	*	82.	1.9526163E-02	2.0940189E+01	*
33.	2.0515284E-01	1.7165061E+01	*	83.	1.8610046E-02	2.0958800E+01	*
34.	1.9553810E-01	1.7360599E+01	*	84.	1.7738816E-02	2.0976538E+01	*
35.	1.8637397E-01	1.7546972E+01	*	85.	1.6907465E-02	2.0993445E+01	*
36.	1.7763933E-01	1.7724611E+01	*	86.	1.6115076E-02	2.1009560E+01	*
37.	1.6931405E-01	1.7893925E+01	*	87.	1.5359824E-02	2.1024919E+01	*
38.	1.6137894E-01	1.8055303E+01	*	88.	1.4639967E-02	2.1039558E+01	*
39.	1.5381572E-01	1.8209118E+01	*	89.	1.3953847E-02	2.1053511E+01	*
40.	1.4660696E-01	1.8355724E+01	*	90.	1.3299883E-02	2.1066810E+01	*
41.	1.3973694E-01	1.8495460E+01	*	91.	1.2676568E-02	2.1079486E+01	*
42.	1.3318714E-01	1.8628647E+01	*	92.	1.2082469E-02	2.1091568E+01	*
43.	1.2694517E-01	1.8755592E+01	*	93.	1.1516208E-02	2.1103084E+01	*
44.	1.2099573E-01	1.8876587E+01	*	94.	1.0976485E-02	2.1114060E+01	*
45.	1.1532512E-01	1.8991912E+01	*	95.	1.0462058E-02	2.1124522E+01	*
46.	1.0992026E-01	1.9101832E+01	*	96.	9.9717410E-03	2.1134493E+01	*
47.	1.0476872E-01	1.9206600E+01	*	97.	9.5044040E-03	2.1143997E+01	*
48.	9.9858609E-02	1.9306458E+01	*	98.	9.0589686E-03	2.1153055E+01	*
49.	9.5178614E-02	1.9401636E+01	*	99.	8.6344090E-03	2.1161689E+01	*
50.	9.0717953E-02	1.9492353E+01	*	100.	8.2297470E-03	2.1169918E+01	*

x	E^{-RX}	SUM OF E^{-RX}	°	x	E^{-RX}	SUM OF E^{-RX}	°
0.	1.0000000E+00	1.0000000E+00	°	50.	8.6293586E-02	1.9193931E+01	°
1.	9.5218112E-01	1.9521811E+00	°	51.	8.2167124E-02	1.9276098E+01	°
2.	9.0664490E-01	2.8588300E+00	°	52.	7.8237985E-02	1.9354335E+01	°
3.	8.6329397E-01	3.7221239E+00	°	53.	7.4496733E-02	1.9428831E+01	°
4.	8.2201223E-01	4.5441361E+00	°	54.	7.0934383E-02	1.9499765E+01	°
5.	7.8270453E-01	5.3268406E+00	°	55.	6.7542381E-02	1.9567307E+01	°
6.	7.4527648E-01	6.0721170E+00	°	56.	6.4312581E-02	1.9631619E+01	°
7.	7.0963820E-01	6.7817552E+00	°	57.	6.1237226E-02	1.9692856E+01	°
8.	6.7570411E-01	7.4574593E+00	°	58.	5.8308931E-02	1.9751164E+01	°
9.	6.4339270E-01	8.1008520E+00	°	59.	5.5520664E-02	1.9806684E+01	°
10.	6.1262639E-01	8.7134783E+00	°	60.	5.2865728E-02	1.9859549E+01	°
11.	5.8333129E-01	9.2968095E+00	°	61.	5.0337749E-02	1.9909886E+01	°
12.	5.5543704E-01	9.8522465E+00	°	62.	4.7930654E-02	1.9957816E+01	°
13.	5.2887667E-01	1.0381123E+01	°	63.	4.5638665E-02	2.0003454E+01	°
14.	5.0358638E-01	1.0884709E+01	°	64.	4.3456275E-02	2.0046910E+01	°
15.	4.7950565E-01	1.1364214E+01	°	65.	4.1378245E-02	2.0088288E+01	°
16.	4.5657604E-01	1.1820790E+01	°	66.	3.9399584E-02	2.0127687E+01	°
17.	4.3474309E-01	1.2255533E+01	°	67.	3.7515541E-02	2.0165202E+01	°
18.	4.1395417E-01	1.2669487E+01	°	68.	3.5721590E-02	2.0200923E+01	°
19.	3.9415935E-01	1.3063646E+01	°	69.	3.4013424E-02	2.0234936E+01	°
20.	3.7531109E-01	1.3438957E+01	°	70.	3.2386940E-02	2.0267322E+01	°
21.	3.5736414E-01	1.3796321E+01	°	71.	3.0838233E-02	2.0298160E+01	°
22.	3.4027539E-01	1.4136596E+01	°	72.	2.9363584E-02	2.0327523E+01	°
23.	3.2400381E-01	1.4460599E+01	°	73.	2.7959450E-02	2.0355482E+01	°
24.	3.0851031E-01	1.4769109E+01	°	74.	2.6622461E-02	2.0382104E+01	°
25.	2.9375769E-01	1.5062866E+01	°	75.	2.5349405E-02	2.0407453E+01	°
26.	2.7971053E-01	1.5342576E+01	°	76.	2.4137225E-02	2.0431590E+01	°
27.	2.6633509E-01	1.5608911E+01	°	77.	2.2983010E-02	2.0454573E+01	°
28.	2.5359925E-01	1.5862510E+01	°	78.	2.1883989E-02	2.0476566E+01	°
29.	2.4147242E-01	1.6103982E+01	°	79.	2.0837521E-02	2.0497293E+01	°
30.	2.2992548E-01	1.6333907E+01	°	80.	1.9841094E-02	2.0517134E+01	°
31.	2.1893070E-01	1.6552837E+01	°	81.	1.8892315E-02	2.0536026E+01	°
32.	2.0846168E-01	1.6761298E+01	°	82.	1.7989066E-02	2.0554014E+01	°
33.	1.9849328E-01	1.6959791E+01	°	83.	1.7128697E-02	2.0571142E+01	°
34.	1.8900156E-01	1.7148792E+01	°	84.	1.6309622E-02	2.0587451E+01	°
35.	1.7996372E-01	1.7328755E+01	°	85.	1.5529714E-02	2.0602980E+01	°
36.	1.7135805E-01	1.7500113E+01	°	86.	1.4787101E-02	2.0617767E+01	°
37.	1.6316390E-01	1.7663276E+01	°	87.	1.4079999E-02	2.0631846E+01	°
38.	1.5536159E-01	1.7818637E+01	°	88.	1.3406709E-02	2.0645252E+01	°
39.	1.4793238E-01	1.7966569E+01	°	89.	1.2765615E-02	2.0658017E+01	°
40.	1.4085842E-01	1.8107427E+01	°	90.	1.2155178E-02	2.0670172E+01	°
41.	1.3412272E-01	1.8241549E+01	°	91.	1.1573931E-02	2.0681745E+01	°
42.	1.2770913E-01	1.8369258E+01	°	92.	1.1020479E-02	2.0692765E+01	°
43.	1.2160222E-01	1.8490860E+01	°	93.	1.0493492E-02	2.0703256E+01	°
44.	1.1578734E-01	1.8606647E+01	°	94.	9.9917052E-03	2.0713249E+01	°
45.	1.1025052E-01	1.8716897E+01	°	95.	9.5139132E-03	2.0722762E+01	°
46.	1.0497846E-01	1.8821875E+01	°	96.	9.0586968E-03	2.0731820E+01	°
47.	9.9958517E-02	1.8921833E+01	°	97.	8.6257749E-03	2.0740445E+01	°
48.	9.5178614E-02	1.9017011E+01	°	98.	8.2133039E-03	2.0748665E+01	°
49.	9.0627280E-02	1.9107638E+01	°	99.	7.8205530E-03	2.0756478E+01	°
50.	8.6293586E-02	1.9193931E+01	°	100.	7.4465830E-03	2.0763924E+01	°

x	E^{-RX}	SUM OF E	°	x	E^{-RX}	SUM OF E	°
0.	1.0000000E+00	1.0000000E+00	°	50.	8.2084998E-02	1.8903146E+01	°
1.	9.5122942E-01	1.9512294E+00	°	51.	7.8081665E-02	1.8981227E+01	°
2.	9.0483741E-01	2.8560668E+00	°	52.	7.4273578E-02	1.9055500E+01	°
3.	8.6070797E-01	3.7167747E+00	°	53.	7.0651212E-02	1.9126151E+01	°
4.	8.1873075E-01	4.5355054E+00	°	54.	6.7205512E-02	1.9193356E+01	°
5.	7.7880078E-01	5.3143061E+00	°	55.	6.3927860E-02	1.9257283E+01	°
6.	7.4081821E-01	6.0551243E+00	°	56.	6.0810062E-02	1.9318093E+01	°
7.	7.0468808E-01	6.7598123E+00	°	57.	5.7844320E-02	1.9375937E+01	°
8.	6.7032004E-01	7.4301323E+00	°	58.	5.5023219E-02	1.9430960E+01	°
9.	6.3762814E-01	8.0677604E+00	°	59.	5.2339705E-02	1.9483299E+01	°
10.	6.0653065E-01	8.6742910E+00	°	60.	4.9787068E-02	1.9533086E+01	°
11.	5.7694980E-01	9.2512408E+00	°	61.	4.7359924E-02	1.9580444E+01	°
12.	5.4881163E-01	9.8000524E+00	°	62.	4.5049220E-02	1.9625493E+01	°
13.	5.2204577E-01	1.0322098E+01	°	63.	4.2852126E-02	1.9668345E+01	°
14.	4.9658530E-01	1.0818683E+01	°	64.	4.0762203E-02	1.9709107E+01	°
15.	4.7236655E-01	1.1291049E+01	°	65.	3.8774207E-02	1.9747881E+01	°
16.	4.4932896E-01	1.1740377E+01	°	66.	3.6883167E-02	1.9784764E+01	°
17.	4.2741493E-01	1.2167791E+01	°	67.	3.5084354E-02	1.9819848E+01	°
18.	4.0656965E-01	1.2574360E+01	°	68.	3.3373269E-02	1.9853221E+01	°
19.	3.8674102E-01	1.2961101E+01	°	69.	3.1745636E-02	1.9884966E+01	°
20.	3.6787944E-01	1.3328980E+01	°	70.	3.0197383E-02	1.9915163E+01	°
21.	3.4993774E-01	1.3678917E+01	°	71.	2.8724639E-02	1.9943887E+01	°
22.	3.3287108E-01	1.4011788E+01	°	72.	2.7323722E-02	1.9971210E+01	°
23.	3.1663676E-01	1.4328424E+01	°	73.	2.5991128E-02	1.9997201E+01	°
24.	3.0119421E-01	1.4629618E+01	°	74.	2.4723526E-02	2.0021924E+01	°
25.	2.8650479E-01	1.4916122E+01	°	75.	2.3517745E-02	2.0045441E+01	°
26.	2.7253179E-01	1.5188653E+01	°	76.	2.2370771E-02	2.0067811E+01	°
27.	2.5924026E-01	1.5447893E+01	°	77.	2.1279736E-02	2.0089090E+01	°
28.	2.4659696E-01	1.5694489E+01	°	78.	2.0241911E-02	2.0109331E+01	°
29.	2.3457028E-01	1.5929059E+01	°	79.	1.9254701E-02	2.0128585E+01	°
30.	2.2313015E-01	1.6152189E+01	°	80.	1.8315638E-02	2.0146900E+01	°
31.	2.1224797E-01	1.6364434E+01	°	81.	1.7422374E-02	2.0164322E+01	°
32.	2.0189651E-01	1.6566332E+01	°	82.	1.6572675E-02	2.0180894E+01	°
33.	1.9204990E-01	1.6758381E+01	°	83.	1.5764416E-02	2.0196659E+01	°
34.	1.8268352E-01	1.6941064E+01	°	84.	1.4995576E-02	2.0211653E+01	°
35.	1.7377394E-01	1.7114837E+01	°	85.	1.4264233E-02	2.0225917E+01	°
36.	1.6529888E-01	1.7280135E+01	°	86.	1.3568558E-02	2.0239485E+01	°
37.	1.5723716E-01	1.7437372E+01	°	87.	1.2906812E-02	2.0252391E+01	°
38.	1.4956861E-01	1.7586940E+01	°	88.	1.2277339E-02	2.0264668E+01	°
39.	1.4227407E-01	1.7729214E+01	°	89.	1.1678566E-02	2.0276346E+01	°
40.	1.3533528E-01	1.7864549E+01	°	90.	1.1108996E-02	2.0287454E+01	°
41.	1.2873490E-01	1.7993283E+01	°	91.	1.0567204E-02	2.0298021E+01	°
42.	1.2245642E-01	1.8115739E+01	°	92.	1.0051835E-02	2.0308072E+01	°
43.	1.1648415E-01	1.8232223E+01	°	93.	9.5616019E-03	2.0317633E+01	°
44.	1.1080315E-01	1.8343026E+01	°	94.	9.0952770E-03	2.0326728E+01	°
45.	1.0539922E-01	1.8448425E+01	°	95.	8.6516951E-03	2.0335379E+01	°
46.	1.0025884E-01	1.8548683E+01	°	96.	8.2297470E-03	2.0343608E+01	°
47.	9.5369162E-02	1.8640052E+01	°	97.	7.8283775E-03	2.0351436E+01	°
48.	9.0717953E-02	1.8734769E+01	°	98.	7.4465830E-03	2.0358882E+01	°
49.	8.6293586E-02	1.8821062E+01	°	99.	7.0834089E-03	2.0365965E+01	°
50.	8.2084998E-02	1.8903146E+01	°	100.	6.7379469E-03	2.0372702E+01	°

X	E^{-RX}	SUM OF E^{-RX}	*	X	E^{-RX}	SUM OF E^{-RX}	*
0.	1.0000000E+00	1.0000000E+00	*	50.	7.8081665E-02	1.8619763E+01	*
1.	9.5027866E-01	1.9502786E+00	*	51.	7.4199341E-02	1.8693967E+01	*
2.	9.0302954E-01	2.8533081E+00	*	52.	7.0510051E-02	1.8764477E+01	*
3.	8.5812971E-01	3.7114378E+00	*	53.	6.700419?E-02	1.8831481E+01	*
4.	8.1546236E-01	4.5269001E+00	*	54.	6.3672660E-02	1.8895153E+01	*
5.	7.7491649E-01	5.3018165E+00	*	55.	6.0506771E-02	1.8955659E+01	*
6.	7.3638661E-01	6.0382031E+00	*	56.	5.7498293E-02	1.9013157E+01	*
7.	6.9977249E-01	6.7379755E+00	*	57.	5.4639402E-02	1.9067796E+01	*
8.	6.6497887E-01	7.4029543E+00	*	58.	5.1922658E-02	1.9119719E+01	*
9.	6.3191524E-01	8.0348695E+00	*	59.	4.9340995E-02	1.9169059E+01	*
10.	6.0049557E-01	8.6353650E+00	*	60.	4.6887695E-02	1.9215945E+01	*
11.	5.7063813E-01	9.2060031E+00	*	61.	4.4556376E-02	1.9260501E+01	*
12.	5.4226525E-01	9.7482683E+00	*	62.	4.2340974E-02	1.9302841E+01	*
13.	5.1530310E-01	1.0263571E+01	*	63.	4.0235724E-02	1.9343076E+01	*
14.	4.8968154E-01	1.0753252E+01	*	64.	3.8235151E-02	1.9381311E+01	*
15.	4.6533393E-01	1.1218585E+01	*	65.	3.6334043E-02	1.9417645E+01	*
16.	4.4219690E-01	1.1660781E+01	*	66.	3.4527471E-02	1.9452172E+01	*
17.	4.2021029E-01	1.2080991E+01	*	67.	3.2810719E-02	1.9484982E+01	*
18.	3.9931687E-01	1.2480307E+01	*	68.	3.1179326E-02	1.9516161E+01	*
19.	3.7946231E-01	1.2859769E+01	*	69.	2.9629049E-02	1.9545790E+01	*
20.	3.6059493E-01	1.3220363E+01	*	70.	2.8155853E-02	1.9573945E+01	*
21.	3.4266567E-01	1.3563028E+01	*	71.	2.6755907E-02	1.9600700E+01	*
22.	3.2562788E-01	1.3888655E+01	*	72.	2.5425567E-02	1.9626125E+01	*
23.	3.0943723E-01	1.4198092E+01	*	73.	2.4161374E-02	1.9650286E+01	*
24.	2.9405160E-01	1.4492143E+01	*	74.	2.2960039E-02	1.9673246E+01	*
25.	2.7943096E-01	1.4771573E+01	*	75.	2.1818435E-02	1.9695064E+01	*
26.	2.6553728E-01	1.5037110E+01	*	76.	2.0733593E-02	1.9715797E+01	*
27.	2.5233442E-01	1.5289444E+01	*	77.	1.9702692E-02	1.9735499E+01	*
28.	2.3978801E-01	1.5529232E+01	*	78.	1.8723047E-02	1.9754222E+01	*
29.	2.2786543E-01	1.5757097E+01	*	79.	1.7792113E-02	1.9772014E+01	*
30.	2.1653566E-01	1.5973632E+01	*	80.	1.6907465E-02	1.9788921E+01	*
31.	2.0576922E-01	1.6179401E+01	*	81.	1.6066803E-02	1.9804987E+01	*
32.	1.9553810E-01	1.6374939E+01	*	82.	1.5267941E-02	1.9820254E+01	*
33.	1.8581569E-01	1.6560754E+01	*	83.	1.4508798E-02	1.9834762E+01	*
34.	1.7657640E-01	1.6737330E+01	*	84.	1.3787401E-02	1.9848549E+01	*
35.	1.6779706E-01	1.6905127E+01	*	85.	1.3101874E-02	1.9861650E+01	*
36.	1.5945396E-01	1.7064580E+01	*	86.	1.2450631E-02	1.9874100E+01	*
37.	1.5152570E-01	1.7216105E+01	*	87.	1.1831379E-02	1.9885931E+01	*
38.	1.4399164E-01	1.7360056E+01	*	88.	1.1243107E-02	1.9897174E+01	*
39.	1.3683218E-01	1.7496928E+01	*	89.	1.0684085E-02	1.9907858E+01	*
40.	1.3002871E-01	1.7626956E+01	*	90.	1.0152858E-02	1.9918010E+01	*
41.	1.2356351E-01	1.7750519E+01	*	91.	9.6480447E-03	1.9927658E+01	*
42.	1.1741976E-01	1.7867938E+01	*	92.	9.1683311E-03	1.9936826E+01	*
43.	1.1158150E-01	1.7979519E+01	*	93.	8.7124695E-03	1.9945538E+01	*
44.	1.0603352E-01	1.8085552E+01	*	94.	8.2792739E-03	1.9953817E+01	*
45.	1.0076139E-01	1.8186313E+01	*	95.	7.8676174E-03	1.9961684E+01	*
46.	9.5751402E-02	1.8282064E+01	*	96.	7.4764290E-03	1.9969160E+01	*
47.	9.0990515E-02	1.8373054E+01	*	97.	7.1046910E-03	1.9976264E+01	*
48.	8.6466346E-02	1.8459520E+01	*	98.	6.7514343E-03	1.9983015E+01	*
49.	8.2167124E-02	1.8541687E+01	*	99.	6.4157459E-03	1.9989463E+01	*
50.	7.8081665E-02	1.8619763E+01	*	100.	6.0967465E-03	1.9995526E+01	*

X	E^{-RX}	SUM OF E^{-RX}	*	X	E^{-RX}	SUM OF E^{-RX}	*
0.	1.0000000E+00	1.0000000E+00	*	50.	7.4273578E-02	1.8343559E+01	*
1.	9.4932866E-01	1.9493286E+00	*	51.	7.0510051E-02	1.8414069E+01	*
2.	9.0122529E-01	2.8505540E+00	*	52.	6.6937227E-02	1.8481000E+01	*
3.	8.5555918E-01	3.7061131E+00	*	53.	6.3545424E-02	1.8544551E+01	*
4.	8.1220703E-01	4.5183201E+00	*	54.	6.0325522E-02	1.8604876E+01	*
5.	7.7105158E-01	5.2893716E+00	*	55.	5.7268780E-02	1.8662144E+01	*
6.	7.3198152E-01	6.0213531E+00	*	56.	5.4366887E-02	1.8716510E+01	*
7.	6.9489119E-01	6.7162464E+00	*	57.	5.1612055E-02	1.8768122E+01	*
8.	6.5968026E-01	7.3759244E+00	*	58.	4.8996814E-02	1.8817118E+01	*
9.	6.2625352E-01	8.0021779E+00	*	59.	4.6514089E-02	1.8863632E+01	*
10.	5.9452054E-01	8.5966984E+00	*	60.	4.4157168E-02	1.8907789E+01	*
11.	5.6439551E-01	9.1610939E+00	*	61.	4.1919674E-02	1.8949709E+01	*
12.	5.3579695E-01	9.6968908E+00	*	62.	3.9795557E-02	1.8989503E+01	*
13.	5.0864751E-01	1.0205538E+01	*	63.	3.7779071E-02	1.9027282E+01	*
14.	4.8287377E-01	1.0688411E+01	*	64.	3.5864762E-02	1.9063146E+01	*
15.	4.5840601E-01	1.1146817E+01	*	65.	3.4047454E-02	1.9097193E+01	*
16.	4.3517805E-01	1.1581995E+01	*	66.	3.2322231E-02	1.9129515E+01	*
17.	4.1312709E-01	1.1995122E+01	*	67.	3.0684427E-02	1.9160199E+01	*
18.	3.9219347E-01	1.2387315E+01	*	68.	2.9129612E-02	1.9189328E+01	*
19.	3.7232058E-01	1.2759635E+01	*	69.	2.7653582E-02	1.9216981E+01	*
20.	3.5345468E-01	1.3113089E+01	*	70.	2.6252343E-02	1.9243233E+01	*
21.	3.3554473E-01	1.3448633E+01	*	71.	2.4922107E-02	1.9268155E+01	*
22.	3.1854229E-01	1.3767175E+01	*	72.	2.3659276E-02	1.9291914E+01	*
23.	3.0240140E-01	1.4069576E+01	*	73.	2.2460434E-02	1.9314274E+01	*
24.	2.8707937E-01	1.4356654E+01	*	74.	2.1322334E-02	1.9335596E+01	*
25.	2.7253179E-01	1.4629185E+01	*	75.	2.0241911E-02	1.9355837E+01	*
26.	2.5872229E-01	1.4887907E+01	*	76.	1.9216230E-02	1.9375053E+01	*
27.	2.4561254E-01	1.5133519E+01	*	77.	1.8247522E-02	1.9393295E+01	*
28.	2.3316707E-01	1.5366686E+01	*	78.	1.7318153E-02	1.9410613E+01	*
29.	2.2135223E-01	1.5588038E+01	*	79.	1.6440622E-02	1.9427053E+01	*
30.	2.1013607E-01	1.5798174E+01	*	80.	1.5607557E-02	1.9442660E+01	*
31.	1.9948823E-01	1.5997662E+01	*	81.	1.4816705E-02	1.9457474E+01	*
32.	1.8937994E-01	1.6187041E+01	*	82.	1.4065924E-02	1.9471541E+01	*
33.	1.7978384E-01	1.6366842E+01	*	83.	1.3353189E-02	1.9484804E+01	*
34.	1.7067309E-01	1.6537497E+01	*	84.	1.2676568E-02	1.9497570E+01	*
35.	1.6202575E-01	1.6699522E+01	*	85.	1.2034232E-02	1.9509604E+01	*
36.	1.5381572E-01	1.6853337E+01	*	86.	1.1424444E-02	1.9521028E+01	*
37.	1.4602170E-01	1.6999358E+01	*	87.	1.0845556E-02	1.9531873E+01	*
38.	1.3862261E-01	1.7137980E+01	*	88.	1.0295997E-02	1.9542168E+01	*
39.	1.3159845E-01	1.7269578E+01	*	89.	9.7742861E-03	1.9551942E+01	*
40.	1.2493021E-01	1.7394504E+01	*	90.	9.2790138E-03	1.9561221E+01	*
41.	1.1859985E-01	1.7513107E+01	*	91.	8.8085337E-03	1.9570329E+01	*
42.	1.1259026E-01	1.7625697E+01	*	92.	8.3624829E-03	1.9578301E+01	*
43.	1.0688519E-01	1.7732592E+01	*	93.	7.9387456E-03	1.9586329E+01	*
44.	1.0146919E-01	1.7834051E+01	*	94.	7.5364893E-03	1.9593865E+01	*
45.	9.6327638E-02	1.7930373E+01	*	95.	7.1545983E-03	1.9601019E+01	*
46.	9.1446607E-02	1.8021825E+01	*	96.	6.7920667E-03	1.9607811E+01	*
47.	8.6812904E-02	1.8108636E+01	*	97.	6.4479050E-03	1.9614258E+01	*
48.	8.2413995E-02	1.8191049E+01	*	98.	6.1211823E-03	1.9620379E+01	*
49.	7.8237985E-02	1.8269286E+01	*	99.	5.8110151E-03	1.9626190E+01	*
50.	7.4273578E-02	1.8343559E+01	*	100.	5.5165466E-03	1.9631706E+01	*

163

TABULATED VALUES OF E   WHEN R = .053

X	E⁻ᴿˣ	SUM OF E⁻ᴿˣ	*	X	E⁻ᴿˣ	SUM OF E⁻ᴿˣ	*
0.	1.0000000E+00	1.0000000E+00	*	50.	7.0651212E-02	1.8074289E+01	*
1.	9.4838001E-01	1.9483800E+00	*	51.	6.7004199E-02	1.8141263E+01	*
2.	8.9942444E-01	2.8478046E+00	*	52.	6.3545442E-02	1.8204838E+01	*
3.	8.5299453E-01	3.7008009E+00	*	53.	6.0265227E-02	1.8265103E+01	*
4.	8.0896469E-01	4.5097655E+00	*	54.	5.7154337E-02	1.8322257E+01	*
5.	7.6720594E-01	5.2769714E+00	*	55.	5.4204330E-02	1.8376461E+01	*
6.	7.2760278E-01	6.0045741E+00	*	56.	5.1406019E-02	1.8427867E+01	*
7.	6.9004394E-01	6.6946180E+00	*	57.	4.8752441E-02	1.8476619E+01	*
8.	6.5442387E-01	7.3490418E+00	*	58.	4.6235841E-02	1.8522854E+01	*
9.	6.2064252E-01	7.9696843E+00	*	59.	4.3849147E-02	1.8566703E+01	*
10.	5.8860496E-01	8.5582892E+00	*	60.	4.1585655E-02	1.8608288E+01	*
11.	5.5822118E-01	9.1165103E+00	*	61.	3.9439004E-02	1.8647727E+01	*
12.	5.2940581E-01	9.6459161E+00	*	62.	3.7403163E-02	1.8685130E+01	*
13.	5.0207789E-01	1.0147993E+01	*	63.	3.5472412E-02	1.8720602E+01	*
14.	4.7616064E-01	1.0624153E+01	*	64.	3.3641326E-02	1.8754243E+01	*
15.	4.5158123E-01	1.1075734E+01	*	65.	3.1904761E-02	1.8786147E+01	*
16.	4.2827061E-01	1.1504004E+01	*	66.	3.0257838E-02	1.8816404E+01	*
17.	4.0616329E-01	1.1910167E+01	*	67.	2.8695929E-02	1.8845099E+01	*
18.	3.8519714E-01	1.2295364E+01	*	68.	2.7214645E-02	1.8872313E+01	*
19.	3.6531327E-01	1.2660677E+01	*	69.	2.5809826E-02	1.8898122E+01	*
20.	3.4645580E-01	1.3007132E+01	*	70.	2.4477523E-02	1.8922549E+01	*
21.	3.2857176E-01	1.3335703E+01	*	71.	2.3213993E-02	1.8945812E+01	*
22.	3.1161089E-01	1.3647313E+01	*	72.	2.2015687E-02	1.8967827E+01	*
23.	2.9552554E-01	1.3942834E+01	*	73.	2.0879234E-02	1.8988706E+01	*
24.	2.8027051E-01	1.4223103E+01	*	74.	1.9801452E-02	1.9008507E+01	*
25.	2.6580295E-01	1.4488910E+01	*	75.	1.8779301E-02	1.9027286E+01	*
26.	2.5208221E-01	1.4740992E+01	*	76.	1.7809914E-02	1.9045095E+01	*
27.	2.3906973E-01	1.4980061E+01	*	77.	1.6890566E-02	1.9061985E+01	*
28.	2.2672895E-01	1.5206789E+01	*	78.	1.6018675E-02	1.9078003E+01	*
29.	2.1502521E-01	1.5421814E+01	*	79.	1.5191791E-02	1.9093194E+01	*
30.	2.0392561E-01	1.5625739E+01	*	80.	1.4407591E-02	1.9107601E+01	*
31.	1.9339897E-01	1.5819137E+01	*	81.	1.3663872E-02	1.9121264E+01	*
32.	1.8341572E-01	1.6002552E+01	*	82.	1.2958543E-02	1.9134222E+01	*
33.	1.7394780E-01	1.6176499E+01	*	83.	1.2296623E-02	1.9146511E+01	*
34.	1.6496862E-01	1.6341467E+01	*	84.	1.1655233E-02	1.9158166E+01	*
35.	1.5645294E-01	1.6497919E+01	*	85.	1.1053590E-02	1.9169210E+01	*
36.	1.4837684E-01	1.6646295E+01	*	86.	1.0483003E-02	1.9179702E+01	*
37.	1.4071763E-01	1.6787012E+01	*	87.	9.9418714E-03	1.9189643E+01	*
38.	1.3345379E-01	1.6920465E+01	*	88.	9.4286721E-03	1.9199071E+01	*
39.	1.2656490E-01	1.7047029E+01	*	89.	8.9419642E-03	1.9208012E+01	*
40.	1.2003104E-01	1.7167060E+01	*	90.	8.4803801E-03	1.9216492E+01	*
41.	1.1383559E-01	1.7280895E+01	*	91.	8.0426230E-03	1.9224534E+01	*
42.	1.0795940E-01	1.7388854E+01	*	92.	7.6274629E-03	1.9232161E+01	*
43.	1.0238654E-01	1.7491240E+01	*	93.	7.2337333E-03	1.9239394E+01	*
44.	9.7101349E-02	1.7588341E+01	*	94.	6.8603281E-03	1.9246254E+01	*
45.	9.2088979E-02	1.7680429E+01	*	95.	6.5061980E-03	1.9252760E+01	*
46.	8.7335347E-02	1.7767664E+01	*	96.	6.1703482E-03	1.9258936E+01	*
47.	8.2827097E-02	1.7850591E+01	*	97.	5.8518349E-03	1.9264781E+01	*
48.	7.8551544E-02	1.7929142E+01	*	98.	5.5497632E-03	1.9270330E+01	*
49.	7.4496733E-02	1.8003638E+01	*	99.	5.2632645E-03	1.9275593E+01	*
50.	7.0651212E-02	1.8074289E+01	*	100.	4.9915939E-03	1.9280584E+01	*

TABULATED VALUES OF E   WHEN R = .054

X	E⁻ᴿˣ	SUM OF E⁻ᴿˣ	*	X	E⁻ᴿˣ	SUM OF E⁻ᴿˣ	*
0.	1.0000000E+00	1.0000000E+00	*	50.	6.7205512E-02	1.7811753E+01	*
1.	9.4743210E-01	1.9474321E+00	*	51.	6.3672660E-02	1.7875425E+01	*
2.	8.9762759E-01	2.8450596E+00	*	52.	6.0325522E-02	1.7935750E+01	*
3.	8.5044120E-01	3.6955008E+00	*	53.	5.7154337E-02	1.7992904E+01	*
4.	8.0573530E-01	4.5012361E+00	*	54.	5.4149853E-02	1.8047053E+01	*
5.	7.6337949E-01	5.2646155E+00	*	55.	5.1303310E-02	1.8098356E+01	*
6.	7.2325024E-01	5.9878657E+00	*	56.	4.8606403E-02	1.8146962E+01	*
7.	6.8523049E-01	6.6730961E+00	*	57.	4.6051267E-02	1.8193013E+01	*
8.	6.4920537E-01	7.3223054E+00	*	58.	4.3630448E-02	1.8236643E+01	*
9.	6.1508180E-01	7.9373872E+00	*	59.	4.1336888E-02	1.8277979E+01	*
10.	5.8274825E-01	8.5201354E+00	*	60.	3.9163895E-02	1.8317142E+01	*
11.	5.5211440E-01	9.0722498E+00	*	61.	3.7105131E-02	1.8354247E+01	*
12.	5.2309091E-01	9.5953407E+00	*	62.	3.5154592E-02	1.8389401E+01	*
13.	4.9559312E-01	1.0090933E+01	*	63.	3.3306590E-02	1.8422707E+01	*
14.	4.6954083E-01	1.0560473E+01	*	64.	3.1555732E-02	1.8454262E+01	*
15.	4.4485806E-01	1.1005331E+01	*	65.	2.9896914E-02	1.8484158E+01	*
16.	4.2147281E-01	1.1426803E+01	*	66.	2.8325296E-02	1.8512493E+01	*
17.	3.9931687E-01	1.1826119E+01	*	67.	2.6836295E-02	1.8539196E+01	*
18.	3.7832560E-01	1.2204444E+01	*	68.	2.5425567E-02	1.8564744E+01	*
19.	3.5843784E-01	1.2562881E+01	*	69.	2.4088999E-02	1.8588834E+01	*
20.	3.3959552E-01	1.2902476E+01	*	70.	2.2822691E-02	1.8611654E+01	*
21.	3.2174370E-01	1.3224219E+01	*	71.	2.1622950E-02	1.8633276E+01	*
22.	3.0483031E-01	1.3529049E+01	*	72.	2.0486277E-02	1.8653762E+01	*
23.	2.8880602E-01	1.3817855E+01	*	73.	1.9409357E-02	1.8673171E+01	*
24.	2.7362410E-01	1.4091479E+01	*	74.	1.8389048E-02	1.8691560E+01	*
25.	2.5924026E-01	1.4350719E+01	*	75.	1.7422374E-02	1.8708982E+01	*
26.	2.4561254E-01	1.4596331E+01	*	76.	1.6506517E-02	1.8725488E+01	*
27.	2.3270121E-01	1.4829032E+01	*	77.	1.5638604E-02	1.8741124E+01	*
28.	2.2046659E-01	1.5049500E+01	*	78.	1.4816705E-02	1.8755942E+01	*
29.	2.0887902E-01	1.5258379E+01	*	79.	1.4037822E-02	1.8769973E+01	*
30.	1.9789869E-01	1.5456277E+01	*	80.	1.3299883E-02	1.8783278E+01	*
31.	1.8749558E-01	1.5643772E+01	*	81.	1.2600736E-02	1.8795878E+01	*
32.	1.7763933E-01	1.5821411E+01	*	82.	1.1938342E-02	1.8807916E+01	*
33.	1.6830120E-01	1.5989712E+01	*	83.	1.1310768E-02	1.8819126E+01	*
34.	1.5945396E-01	1.6149165E+01	*	84.	1.0716185E-02	1.8829826E+01	*
35.	1.5107180E-01	1.6300236E+01	*	85.	1.0152858E-02	1.8839994E+01	*
36.	1.4313028E-01	1.6443366E+01	*	86.	9.6191439E-03	1.8849613E+01	*
37.	1.3560622E-01	1.6578972E+01	*	87.	9.1134858E-03	1.8858726E+01	*
38.	1.2847769E-01	1.6707446E+01	*	88.	8.6344009E-03	1.8867360E+01	*
39.	1.2172388E-01	1.6829172E+01	*	89.	8.1803153E-03	1.8875540E+01	*
40.	1.1532512E-01	1.6944497E+01	*	90.	7.7504683E-03	1.8883290E+01	*
41.	1.0926272E-01	1.7053759E+01	*	91.	7.3430572E-03	1.8890633E+01	*
42.	1.0351901E-01	1.7157277E+01	*	92.	6.9570428E-03	1.8897590E+01	*
43.	9.8077234E-02	1.7255355E+01	*	93.	6.5913308E-03	1.8904181E+01	*
44.	9.2921521E-02	1.7348276E+01	*	94.	6.2448384E-03	1.8910425E+01	*
45.	8.8036832E-02	1.7436312E+01	*	95.	5.9165604E-03	1.8916341E+01	*
46.	8.3409921E-02	1.7519720E+01	*	96.	5.6055393E-03	1.8921946E+01	*
47.	7.9024290E-02	1.7598744E+01	*	97.	5.3108679E-03	1.8927256E+01	*
48.	7.4870124E-02	1.7673614E+01	*	98.	5.0316883E-03	1.8932287E+01	*
49.	7.0934383E-02	1.7744568E+01	*	99.	4.7671816E-03	1.8937154E+01	*
50.	6.7205512E-02	1.7811753E+01	*	100.	4.5165809E-03	1.8941570E+01	*

164

$-RX$

TABULATED VALUES OF E   WHEN R = .055

X	E ($-RX$)	SUM OF E ($-RX$)	*	X	E ($-RX$)	SUM OF E ($-RX$)	*
0.	1.0000000E+00	1.0000000E+00	*	50.	6.3927860E-02	1.7555728E+01	*
1.	9.4648514E-01	1.9464851E+00	*	51.	6.0506771E-02	1.7616234E+01	*
2.	8.9583413E-01	2.8423192E+00	*	52.	5.7268760E-02	1.7673502E+01	*
3.	8.4789370E-01	3.6902129E+00	*	53.	5.4204030E-02	1.7727706E+01	*
4.	8.0251879E-01	4.4927316E+00	*	54.	5.1303310E-02	1.7779009E+01	*
5.	7.5957212E-01	5.2523037E+00	*	55.	4.8557821E-02	1.7827566E+01	*
6.	7.1892373E-01	5.9712274E+00	*	56.	4.5959256E-02	1.7873525E+01	*
7.	6.8045063E-01	6.6516780E+00	*	57.	4.3499753E-02	1.7917024E+01	*
8.	6.4403641E-01	7.2957144E+00	*	58.	4.1171870E-02	1.7958195E+01	*
9.	6.0957090E-01	7.9052853E+00	*	59.	3.8968564E-02	1.7997163E+01	*
10.	5.7694980E-01	8.4822351E+00	*	60.	3.6883167E-02	1.8034046E+01	*
11.	5.4607442E-01	9.0283095E+00	*	61.	3.4909370E-02	1.8068955E+01	*
12.	5.1685133E-01	9.5451608E+00	*	62.	3.3041200E-02	1.8101996E+01	*
13.	4.8919211E-01	1.0034352E+01	*	63.	3.1273005E-02	1.8133269E+01	*
14.	4.6301306E-01	1.0497365E+01	*	64.	2.9599435E-02	1.8162868E+01	*
15.	4.3823499E-01	1.0935599E+01	*	65.	2.8015425E-02	1.8190883E+01	*
16.	4.1478291E-01	1.1350381E+01	*	66.	2.6516184E-02	1.8217399E+01	*
17.	3.9258586E-01	1.1742966E+01	*	67.	2.5097174E-02	1.8242496E+01	*
18.	3.7157669E-01	1.2114542E+01	*	68.	2.3754103E-02	1.8266250E+01	*
19.	3.5169181E-01	1.2466233E+01	*	69.	2.2482905E-02	1.8288732E+01	*
20.	3.3287108E-01	1.2799104E+01	*	70.	2.1279735E-02	1.8310011E+01	*
21.	3.1505753E-01	1.3114161E+01	*	71.	2.0140954E-02	1.8330151E+01	*
22.	2.9819727E-01	1.3412358E+01	*	72.	1.9063114E-02	1.8349214E+01	*
23.	2.8223929E-01	1.3694597E+01	*	73.	1.8042954E-02	1.8367256E+01	*
24.	2.6713530E-01	1.3961732E+01	*	74.	1.7077388E-02	1.8384333E+01	*
25.	2.5283959E-01	1.4214571E+01	*	75.	1.6163494E-02	1.8400496E+01	*
26.	2.3930892E-01	1.4453879E+01	*	76.	1.5298507E-02	1.8415794E+01	*
27.	2.2650234E-01	1.4680381E+01	*	77.	1.4479810E-02	1.8430273E+01	*
28.	2.1438110E-01	1.4894762E+01	*	78.	1.3704925E-02	1.8443977E+01	*
29.	2.0290852E-01	1.5097670E+01	*	79.	1.2971508E-02	1.8456948E+01	*
30.	1.9204990E-01	1.5289719E+01	*	80.	1.2277339E-02	1.8469225E+01	*
31.	1.8177238E-01	1.5471491E+01	*	81.	1.1620319E-02	1.8480845E+01	*
32.	1.7204486E-01	1.5643535E+01	*	82.	1.0998460E-02	1.8491843E+01	*
33.	1.6283790E-01	1.5806372E+01	*	83.	1.0409879E-02	1.8502252E+01	*
34.	1.5412366E-01	1.5960495E+01	*	84.	9.8527960E-03	1.8512104E+01	*
35.	1.4587575E-01	1.6106370E+01	*	85.	9.3255251E-03	1.8521429E+01	*
36.	1.3806923E-01	1.6244439E+01	*	86.	8.8264710E-03	1.8530255E+01	*
37.	1.3068048E-01	1.6375119E+01	*	87.	8.3541237E-03	1.8538609E+01	*
38.	1.2368713E-01	1.6498806E+01	*	88.	7.9070540E-03	1.8546516E+01	*
39.	1.1706803E-01	1.6615874E+01	*	89.	7.4839092E-03	1.8553999E+01	*
40.	1.1080315E-01	1.6726677E+01	*	90.	7.0834088E-03	1.8561082E+01	*
41.	1.0487354E-01	1.6831550E+01	*	91.	6.7043413E-03	1.8567786E+01	*
42.	9.9261251E-02	1.6930811E+01	*	92.	6.3455594E-03	1.8574131E+01	*
43.	9.3949300E-02	1.7024760E+01	*	93.	6.0059778E-03	1.8580136E+01	*
44.	8.8921617E-02	1.7113681E+01	*	94.	5.6845688E-03	1.8585820E+01	*
45.	8.4162990E-02	1.7197843E+01	*	95.	5.3803599E-03	1.8591200E+01	*
46.	7.9659019E-02	1.7277502E+01	*	96.	5.0924307E-03	1.8596292E+01	*
47.	7.5396079E-02	1.7352898E+01	*	97.	4.8199101E-03	1.8601111E+01	*
48.	7.1361269E-02	1.7424259E+01	*	98.	4.5619733E-03	1.8605672E+01	*
49.	6.7542381E-02	1.7491801E+01	*	99.	4.3178400E-03	1.8609989E+01	*
50.	6.3927860E-02	1.7555728E+01	*	100.	4.0867714E-03	1.8614075E+01	*

$-RX$

TABULATED VALUES OF E   WHEN R = .056

X	E ($-RX$)	SUM OF E ($-RX$)	*	X	E ($-RX$)	SUM OF E ($-RX$)	*
0.	1.0000000E+00	1.0000000E+00	*	50.	6.0810062E-02	1.7306016E+01	*
1.	9.4553913E-01	1.9455391E+00	*	51.	5.7498293E-02	1.7363514E+01	*
2.	8.9404425E-01	2.8395833E+00	*	52.	5.4366887E-02	1.7417880E+01	*
3.	8.4535383E-01	3.6849371E+00	*	53.	5.1406019E-02	1.7469286E+01	*
4.	7.9931513E-01	4.4842522E+00	*	54.	4.8606403E-02	1.7517892E+01	*
5.	7.5578374E-01	5.2400359E+00	*	55.	4.5959256E-02	1.7563851E+01	*
6.	7.1462310E-01	5.9546590E+00	*	56.	4.3456275E-02	1.7607307E+01	*
7.	6.7570411E-01	6.6303631E+00	*	57.	4.1089609E-02	1.7648396E+01	*
8.	6.3890468E-01	7.2692677E+00	*	58.	3.8851833E-02	1.7687247E+01	*
9.	6.0410938E-01	7.8733770E+00	*	59.	3.6735922E-02	1.7723982E+01	*
10.	5.7120906E-01	8.4445860E+00	*	60.	3.4735258E-02	1.7758717E+01	*
11.	5.4010052E-01	8.9846865E+00	*	61.	3.2843546E-02	1.7791560E+01	*
12.	5.1068618E-01	9.4953726E+00	*	62.	3.1054858E-02	1.7822614E+01	*
13.	4.8287377E-01	9.9782463E+00	*	63.	2.9363584E-02	1.7851977E+01	*
14.	4.5657604E-01	1.0434822E+01	*	64.	2.7764418E-02	1.7879741E+01	*
15.	4.3171052E-01	1.0866532E+01	*	65.	2.6252343E-02	1.7905993E+01	*
16.	4.0819919E-01	1.1274731E+01	*	66.	2.4822618E-02	1.7930815E+01	*
17.	3.8596831E-01	1.1660699E+01	*	67.	2.3470757E-02	1.7954285E+01	*
18.	3.6494814E-01	1.2025647E+01	*	68.	2.2192519E-02	1.7976477E+01	*
19.	3.4507275E-01	1.2370719E+01	*	69.	2.0983895E-02	1.7997460E+01	*
20.	3.2627979E-01	1.2696998E+01	*	70.	1.9841094E-02	1.8017301E+01	*
21.	3.0851031E-01	1.3005508E+01	*	71.	1.8760531E-02	1.8036061E+01	*
22.	2.9170857E-01	1.3297216E+01	*	72.	1.7738816E-02	1.8053799E+01	*
23.	2.7582187E-01	1.3573037E+01	*	73.	1.6772745E-02	1.8070571E+01	*
24.	2.6080037E-01	1.3833837E+01	*	74.	1.5859287E-02	1.8086430E+01	*
25.	2.4659696E-01	1.4080433E+01	*	75.	1.4995576E-02	1.8101425E+01	*
26.	2.3316707E-01	1.4313600E+01	*	76.	1.4178904E-02	1.8115603E+01	*
27.	2.2046859E-01	1.4534068E+01	*	77.	1.3406709E-02	1.8129009E+01	*
28.	2.0846168E-01	1.4742529E+01	*	78.	1.2676568E-02	1.8141685E+01	*
29.	1.9710868E-01	1.4939637E+01	*	79.	1.1986191E-02	1.8153671E+01	*
30.	1.8637397E-01	1.5126010E+01	*	80.	1.1333413E-02	1.8165004E+01	*
31.	1.7622388E-01	1.5302233E+01	*	81.	1.0716185E-02	1.8175720E+01	*
32.	1.6662658E-01	1.5468859E+01	*	82.	1.0132572E-02	1.8185852E+01	*
33.	1.5755195E-01	1.5626410E+01	*	83.	9.5807442E-03	1.8195432E+01	*
34.	1.4897153E-01	1.5775381E+01	*	84.	9.0589686E-03	1.8204490E+01	*
35.	1.4085842E-01	1.5916239E+01	*	85.	8.5656093E-03	1.8213055E+01	*
36.	1.3318714E-01	1.6049426E+01	*	86.	8.0991188E-03	1.8221154E+01	*
37.	1.2593366E-01	1.6175359E+01	*	87.	7.6580338E-03	1.8228812E+01	*
38.	1.1907520E-01	1.6294434E+01	*	88.	7.2409707E-03	1.8236052E+01	*
39.	1.1259026E-01	1.6407024E+01	*	89.	6.8466212E-03	1.8242898E+01	*
40.	1.0645850E-01	1.6513482E+01	*	90.	6.4737483E-03	1.8249371E+01	*
41.	1.0066068E-01	1.6614142E+01	*	91.	6.1211823E-03	1.8255492E+01	*
42.	9.5178614E-02	1.6709320E+01	*	92.	5.7878175E-03	1.8261279E+01	*
43.	8.9995104E-02	1.6799315E+01	*	93.	5.4726079E-03	1.8266751E+01	*
44.	8.5093893E-02	1.6884408E+01	*	94.	5.1745649E-03	1.8271925E+01	*
45.	8.0459606E-02	1.6964867E+01	*	95.	4.8927537E-03	1.8276817E+01	*
46.	7.6077706E-02	1.7040944E+01	*	96.	4.6262901E-03	1.8281443E+01	*
47.	7.1934449E-02	1.7112878E+01	*	97.	4.3743383E-03	1.8285817E+01	*
48.	6.8016836E-02	1.7180894E+01	*	98.	4.1361081E-03	1.8289953E+01	*
49.	6.4312581E-02	1.7245206E+01	*	99.	3.9108520E-03	1.8293863E+01	*
50.	6.0810062E-02	1.7306016E+01	*	100.	3.6978637E-03	1.8297560E+01	*

TABULATED VALUES OF E   WHEN R = .057

x	E $^{-RX}$	SUM OF E $^{-RX}$	*	x	E $^{-RX}$	SUM OF E $^{-RX}$	*
0.	1.0000000E+00	1.0000000E+00	*	50.	5.7844320E-02	1.7062425E+01	*
1.	9.4459406E-01	1.9445940E+00	*	51.	5.4639402E-02	1.7117064E+01	*
2.	8.9225795E-01	2.8368519E+00	*	52.	5.1612055E-02	1.7168676E+01	*
3.	8.4282157E-01	3.6796734E+00	*	53.	4.8752441E-02	1.7217428E+01	*
4.	7.9612425E-01	4.4757976E+00	*	54.	4.6051267E-02	1.7263479E+01	*
5.	7.5201425E-01	5.2278118E+00	*	55.	4.3499753E-02	1.7306978E+01	*
6.	7.1034820E-01	5.9381600E+00	*	56.	4.1089609E-02	1.7348067E+01	=
7.	6.7099069E-01	6.6091506E+00	*	57.	3.8813001E-02	1.7386880E+01	*
8.	6.3381383E-01	7.2429644E+00	*	58.	3.6662530E-02	1.7423542E+01	=
9.	5.9869678E-01	7.8416611E+00	*	59.	3.4631209E-02	1.7458173E+01	*
10.	5.6552543E-01	8.4071865E+00	=	60.	3.2712434E-02	1.7490885E+01	*
11.	5.3419197E-01	8.9413784E+00	*	61.	3.0899972E-02	1.7521784E+01	*
12.	5.0459456E-01	9.4459729E+00	*	62.	2.9187930E-02	1.7550971E+01	*
13.	4.7663703E-01	9.9226099E+00	*	63.	2.7570745E-02	1.7578541E+01	*
14.	4.5022852E-01	1.0372838E+01	*	64.	2.6043162E-02	1.7604584E+01	*
15.	4.2528319E-01	1.0798121E+01	*	65.	2.4600217E-02	1.7629184E+01	*
16.	4.0171997E-01	1.1199840E+01	*	66.	2.3237219E-02	1.7652421E+01	*
17.	3.7946231E-01	1.1579302E+01	*	67.	2.1949739E-02	1.7674370E+01	*
18.	3.5843784E-01	1.1937739E+01	*	68.	2.0733593E-02	1.7695103E+01	*
19.	3.3857826E-01	1.2276317E+01	=	69.	1.9584829E-02	1.7714687E+01	*
20.	3.1981902E-01	1.2596136E+01	*	70.	1.8499714E-02	1.7733186E+01	*
21.	3.0209915E-01	1.2898235E+01	*	71.	1.7474720E-02	1.7750660E+01	*
22.	2.8536106E-01	1.3183596E+01	*	72.	1.6506517E-02	1.7767165E+01	*
23.	2.6955037E-01	1.3453146E+01	*	73.	1.5591958E-02	1.7782757E+01	*
24.	2.5461548E-01	1.3707761E+01	*	74.	1.4728071E-02	1.7797485E+01	*
25.	2.4050848E-01	1.3948269E+01	*	75.	1.3912048E-02	1.7811397E+01	*
26.	2.2718286E-01	1.4175451E+01	*	76.	1.3141238E-02	1.7824538E+01	*
27.	2.1459558E-01	1.4390046E+01	*	77.	1.2413136E-02	1.7836951E+01	*
28.	2.0270572E-01	1.4592751E+01	*	78.	1.1725374E-02	1.7848676E+01	*
29.	1.9147462E-01	1.4784225E+01	*	79.	1.1075719E-02	1.7859751E+01	*
30.	1.8086579E-01	1.4965090E+01	*	80.	1.0462058E-02	1.7870213E+01	*
31.	1.7084475E-01	1.5135934E+01	*	81.	9.8823988E-03	1.7880095E+01	*
32.	1.6137894E-01	1.5297312E+01	*	82.	9.3348553E-03	1.7889429E+01	*
33.	1.5243759E-01	1.5449749E+01	*	83.	8.8176489E-03	1.7898248E+01	*
34.	1.4399164E-01	1.5593740E+01	*	84.	8.3290989E-03	1.7906575E+01	*
35.	1.3601365E-01	1.5729753E+01	*	85.	7.8676174E-03	1.7914442E+01	*
36.	1.2847369E-01	1.5858230E+01	*	86.	7.4317047E-03	1.7921873E+01	*
37.	1.2135926E-01	1.5979589E+01	=	87.	7.0199442E-03	1.7928892E+01	*
38.	1.1463524E-01	1.6094224E+01	*	88.	6.6309977E-03	1.7935522E+01	*
39.	1.0828376E-01	1.6202507E+01	*	89.	6.2636011E-03	1.7941785E+01	*
40.	1.0228420E-01	1.6304791E+01	*	90.	5.9165604E-03	1.7947701E+01	*
41.	9.6617054E-02	1.6401408E+01	*	91.	5.5887479E-03	1.7953289E+01	*
42.	9.1263897E-02	1.6492671E+01	*	92.	5.2790981E-03	1.7958568E+01	*
43.	8.6207335E-02	1.6578878E+01	*	93.	4.9866048E-03	1.7963554E+01	*
44.	8.1430938E-02	1.6660308E+01	*	94.	4.7103173E-03	1.7968264E+01	*
45.	7.6919181E-02	1.6737227E+01	*	95.	4.4493378E-03	1.7972713E+01	*
46.	7.2657402E-02	1.6809884E+01	*	96.	4.2028181E-03	1.7976915E+01	*
47.	6.8631751E-02	1.6878515E+01	*	97.	3.9699570E-03	1.7980884E+01	*
48.	6.4829145E-02	1.6943344E+01	=	98.	3.7499978E-03	1.7984633E+01	*
49.	6.1237226E-02	1.7004581E+01	*	99.	3.5422257E-03	1.7988175E+01	*
50.	5.7844320E-02	1.7062425E+01	*	100.	3.3459654E-03	1.7991520E+01	=

TABULATED VALUES OF E   WHEN R = .058

x	E $^{-RX}$	SUM OF E $^{-RX}$	*	x	E $^{-RX}$	SUM OF E $^{-RX}$	*
0.	1.0000000E+00	1.0000000E+00	*	50.	5.5023219E-02	1.6824761E+01	*
1.	9.4364994E-01	1.9436499E+00	*	51.	5.1922658E-02	1.6876683E+01	*
2.	8.9047522E-01	2.8341251E+00	*	52.	4.8996814E-02	1.6926679E+01	*
3.	8.4029689E-01	3.6744219E+00	*	53.	4.6235841E-02	1.6971914E+01	*
4.	7.9294612E-01	4.4673680E+00	*	54.	4.3630448E-02	1.7015544E+01	*
5.	7.4826356E-01	5.2156315E+00	*	55.	4.1171870E-02	1.7056715E+01	*
6.	7.0609887E-01	5.9217303E+00	*	56.	3.8851833E-02	1.7095566E+01	*
7.	6.6631016E-01	6.5880404E+00	*	57.	3.6662530E-02	1.7132228E+01	*
8.	6.2876355E-01	7.2168039E+00	*	58.	3.4596595E-02	1.7166824E+01	*
9.	5.9333269E-01	7.8101365E+00	*	59.	3.2647075E-02	1.7199471E+01	*
10.	5.5989836E-01	8.3700348E+00	*	60.	3.0807411E-02	1.7230278E+01	*
11.	5.2834806E-01	8.8983828E+00	*	61.	2.9071411E-02	1.7259349E+01	*
12.	4.9857562E-01	9.3969584E+00	*	62.	2.7433236E-02	1.7286782E+01	*
13.	4.7048085E-01	9.8674392E+00	*	63.	2.5887371E-02	1.7312669E+01	*
14.	4.4396923E-01	1.0311408E+01	*	64.	2.4428617E-02	1.7337097E+01	*
15.	4.1895154E-01	1.0730359E+01	*	65.	2.3052063E-02	1.7360149E+01	*
16.	3.9534360E-01	1.1125702E+01	*	66.	2.1753078E-02	1.7381902E+01	*
17.	3.7306597E-01	1.1498767E+01	*	67.	2.0527291E-02	1.7402429E+01	*
18.	3.5204368E-01	1.1850810E+01	*	68.	1.9370577E-02	1.7421799E+01	*
19.	3.3220600E-01	1.2183016E+01	*	69.	1.8279044E-02	1.7440078E+01	*
20.	3.1348618E-01	1.2496502E+01	*	70.	1.7249019E-02	1.7457327E+01	*
21.	2.9582121E-01	1.2792323E+01	*	71.	1.6277035E-02	1.7473604E+01	*
22.	2.7915167E-01	1.3071474E+01	*	72.	1.5359824E-02	1.7488963E+01	*
23.	2.6342146E-01	1.3334895E+01	*	73.	1.4494297E-02	1.7503457E+01	*
24.	2.4857765E-01	1.3583472E+01	*	74.	1.3677542E-02	1.7517134E+01	*
25.	2.3457028E-01	1.3818042E+01	*	75.	1.2906812E-02	1.7530040E+01	*
26.	2.2135223E-01	1.4039394E+01	*	76.	1.2179512E-02	1.7542219E+01	*
27.	2.0887902E-01	1.4248273E+01	*	77.	1.1493196E-02	1.7553712E+01	*
28.	1.9710868E-01	1.4445381E+01	*	78.	1.0845554E-02	1.7564557E+01	*
29.	1.8600160E-01	1.4631382E+01	*	79.	1.0234460E-02	1.7574791E+01	*
30.	1.7552040E-01	1.4806902E+01	*	80.	9.6576976E-03	1.7584448E+01	*
31.	1.6562981E-01	1.4972531E+01	*	81.	9.1134858E-03	1.7593561E+01	*
32.	1.5629656E-01	1.5128627E+01	*	82.	8.5999404E-03	1.7602160E+01	*
33.	1.4748924E-01	1.5276316E+01	*	83.	8.1153333E-03	1.7610275E+01	*
34.	1.3917822E-01	1.5415494E+01	*	84.	7.6580338E-03	1.7617933E+01	*
35.	1.3133552E-01	1.5546829E+01	*	85.	7.2265032E-03	1.7625159E+01	*
36.	1.2393475E-01	1.5670763E+01	*	86.	6.8192894E-03	1.7631978E+01	*
37.	1.1695102E-01	1.5787714E+01	*	87.	6.4350221E-03	1.7638413E+01	*
38.	1.1036083E-01	1.5898074E+01	*	88.	6.0724082E-03	1.7644485E+01	*
39.	1.0414199E-01	1.6002215E+01	*	89.	5.7302277E-03	1.7650215E+01	*
40.	9.8273565E-02	1.6100488E+01	*	90.	5.4073291E-03	1.7655622E+01	*
41.	9.2733663E-02	1.6193223E+01	*	91.	5.1026259E-03	1.7660724E+01	*
42.	8.7510192E-02	1.6280733E+01	*	92.	4.8150926E-03	1.7665539E+01	*
43.	8.2578988E-02	1.6363311E+01	*	93.	4.5437618E-03	1.7670092E+01	*
44.	7.7925658E-02	1.6441236E+01	*	94.	4.2877206E-03	1.7674369E+01	*
45.	7.3534543E-02	1.6514770E+01	*	95.	4.0461073E-03	1.7678415E+01	*
46.	6.9390868E-02	1.6584160E+01	*	96.	3.8181090E-03	1.7682233E+01	*
47.	6.5480689E-02	1.6649640E+01	*	97.	3.6029583E-03	1.7685835E+01	*
48.	6.1790848E-02	1.6711430E+01	*	98.	3.3999314E-03	1.7689234E+01	*
49.	5.8309831E-02	1.6769738E+01	*	99.	3.2083451E-03	1.7692442E+01	*
50.	5.5023219E-02	1.6824761E+01	*	100.	3.0275547E-03	1.7695469E+01	*

X	E (-RX)	SUM OF E (-RX)	*	X	E (-RX)	SUM OF E (-RX)	*
0.	1.0000000E+00	1.0000000E+00	*	50.	5.2339705E-02	1.6592847E+01	*
1.	9.4270676E-01	1.9427067E+00	*	51.	4.9340995E-02	1.6642187E+01	*
2.	8.8696605E-01	2.8314027E+00	*	52.	4.6514089E-02	1.6688701E+01	*
3.	8.3777978E-01	3.6691824E+00	*	53.	4.3849147E-02	1.6732550E+01	*
4.	7.8978067E-01	4.4589630E+00	*	54.	4.1336888E-02	1.6773886E+01	*
5.	7.4453158E-01	5.2034945E+00	*	55.	3.8968564E-02	1.6812854E+01	*
6.	7.0187496E-01	5.9053694E+00	*	56.	3.6735929E-02	1.6849549E+01	*
7.	6.6166228E-01	6.5670316E+00	*	57.	3.4631209E-02	1.6884220E+01	*
8.	6.2375351E-01	7.1907851E+00	*	58.	3.2647075E-02	1.6916867E+01	*
9.	5.8801665E-01	7.7788017E+00	*	59.	3.0776618E-02	1.6947643E+01	*
10.	5.5432728E-01	8.3331289E+00	*	60.	2.9013327E-02	1.6976656E+01	*
11.	5.2256808E-01	8.8556969E+00	*	61.	2.7351059E-02	1.7004407E+01	*
12.	4.9262846E-01	9.3483253E+00	*	62.	2.5784029E-02	1.7029791E+01	*
13.	4.6440419E-01	9.8127294E+00	*	63.	2.4306778E-02	1.7054097E+01	*
14.	4.3779697E-01	1.0250526E+01	*	64.	2.2914164E-02	1.7077011E+01	*
15.	4.1271417E-01	1.0663240E+01	*	65.	2.1601338E-02	1.7098612E+01	*
16.	3.8906844E-01	1.1052308E+01	*	66.	2.0363727E-02	1.7118975E+01	*
17.	3.6677745E-01	1.1419085E+01	*	67.	1.9197024E-02	1.7138172E+01	*
18.	3.4576359E-01	1.1764848E+01	*	68.	1.8097164E-02	1.7156269E+01	*
19.	3.2595367E-01	1.2090801E+01	*	69.	1.7060319E-02	1.7173329E+01	*
20.	3.0727873E-01	1.2398079E+01	*	70.	1.6082878E-02	1.7189411E+01	*
21.	2.8967374E-01	1.2687752E+01	*	71.	1.5161438E-02	1.7204572E+01	*
22.	2.7307740E-01	1.2960829E+01	*	72.	1.4292790E-02	1.7218864E+01	*
23.	2.5743191E-01	1.3218260E+01	*	73.	1.3473910E-02	1.7232337E+01	*
24.	2.4268280E-01	1.3460942E+01	*	74.	1.2701966E-02	1.7245038E+01	*
25.	2.2877872E-01	1.3689720E+01	*	75.	1.1974211E-02	1.7257012E+01	*
26.	2.1567125E-01	1.3905391E+01	*	76.	1.1288170E-02	1.7268300E+01	*
27.	2.0331475E-01	1.4108705E+01	*	77.	1.0641434E-02	1.7278941E+01	*
28.	1.9166619E-01	1.4300371E+01	*	78.	1.0031752E-02	1.7288972E+01	*
29.	1.8068501E-01	1.4481056E+01	*	79.	9.4570006E-03	1.7298429E+01	*
30.	1.7033298E-01	1.4651388E+01	*	80.	8.9151785E-03	1.7307344E+01	*
31.	1.6057406E-01	1.4811962E+01	*	81.	8.4043991E-03	1.7315748E+01	*
32.	1.5137425E-01	1.4963336E+01	*	82.	7.9228439E-03	1.7323670E+01	*
33.	1.4270153E-01	1.5106037E+01	*	83.	7.4689563E-03	1.7331139E+01	*
34.	1.3452570E-01	1.5240562E+01	*	84.	7.0410357E-03	1.7338179E+01	*
35.	1.2681829E-01	1.5367380E+01	*	85.	6.6376320E-03	1.7344816E+01	*
36.	1.1955246E-01	1.5486932E+01	*	86.	6.2573406E-03	1.7351073E+01	*
37.	1.1270291E-01	1.5599634E+01	*	87.	5.8983373E-03	1.7356971E+01	*
38.	1.0624579E-01	1.5705879E+01	*	88.	5.5608739E-03	1.7362531E+01	*
39.	1.0015863E-01	1.5806037E+01	*	89.	5.2422734E-03	1.7367773E+01	*
40.	9.4420222E-02	1.5900457E+01	*	90.	4.9419267E-03	1.7372714E+01	*
41.	8.9010583E-02	1.5989467E+01	*	91.	4.6597871E-03	1.7377372E+01	*
42.	8.3910879E-02	1.6073373E+01	*	92.	4.3918707E-03	1.7381763E+01	*
43.	7.9103354E-02	1.6152480E+01	*	93.	4.1402462E-03	1.7385903E+01	*
44.	7.4571267E-02	1.6227051E+01	*	94.	3.9030382E-03	1.7389806E+01	*
45.	7.0298838E-02	1.6297349E+01	*	95.	3.6794205E-03	1.7393485E+01	*
46.	6.6271190E-02	1.6363620E+01	*	96.	3.4686164E-03	1.7396953E+01	*
47.	6.2474300E-02	1.6426094E+01	*	97.	3.2698865E-03	1.7400222E+01	*
48.	5.8894945E-02	1.6484988E+01	*	98.	3.0825441E-03	1.7403304E+01	*
49.	5.5520664E-02	1.6540508E+01	*	99.	2.9059352E-03	1.7406209E+01	*
50.	5.2339705E-02	1.6592847E+01	*	100.	2.7394448E-03	1.7406948E+01	*

X	E (-RX)	SUM OF E (-RX)	*	X	E (-RX)	SUM OF E (-RX)	*
0.	1.0000000E+00	1.0000000E+00	*	50.	4.9787068E-02	1.6366507E+01	*
1.	9.4176453E-01	1.9417645E+00	#	51.	4.6887695E-02	1.6413394E+01	*
2.	8.8692043E-01	2.8286849E+00	#	52.	4.4157168E-02	1.6457551E+01	*
3.	8.3527020E-01	3.6639551E+00	*	53.	4.1585655E-02	1.6499136E+01	*
4.	7.8662786E-01	4.4505829E+00	*	54.	3.9163895E-02	1.6538299E+01	*
5.	7.4081821E-01	5.1914011E+00	*	55.	3.6883167E-02	1.6575182E+01	*
6.	6.9767632E-01	5.8890774E+00	*	56.	3.4735258E-02	1.6609917E+01	*
7.	6.5704681E-01	6.5461242E+00	*	57.	3.2712434E-02	1.6642629E+01	*
8.	6.1878339E-01	7.1649075E+00	*	58.	3.0807411E-02	1.6673436E+01	*
9.	5.8274825E-01	7.7476557E+00	*	59.	2.9013327E-02	1.6702449E+01	*
10.	5.4881163E-01	8.2964673E+00	*	60.	2.7323722E-02	1.6729772E+01	*
11.	5.1685133E-01	8.8133186E+00	*	61.	2.5732512E-02	1.6755504E+01	*
12.	4.8675225E-01	9.3000707E+00	*	62.	2.4233967E-02	1.6779737E+01	*
13.	4.5840601E-01	9.7584768E+00	*	63.	2.2822691E-02	1.6802559E+01	*
14.	4.3171052E-01	1.0190187E+01	*	64.	2.1493601E-02	1.6824052E+01	*
15.	4.0656965E-01	1.0596756E+01	*	65.	2.0241911E-02	1.6844293E+01	*
16.	3.8289288E-01	1.0979648E+01	*	66.	1.9063114E-02	1.6863356E+01	*
17.	3.6059493E-01	1.1340242E+01	*	67.	1.7952964E-02	1.6881308E+01	*
18.	3.3959552E-01	1.1679837E+01	*	68.	1.6907465E-02	1.6898215E+01	*
19.	3.1981902E-01	1.1999656E+01	*	69.	1.5922851E-02	1.6914137E+01	*
20.	3.0119421E-01	1.2300850E+01	*	70.	1.4995766E-02	1.6929132E+01	*
21.	2.8365402E-01	1.2584504E+01	*	71.	1.4122302E-02	1.6943254E+01	*
22.	2.6713530E-01	1.2851639E+01	*	72.	1.3298983E-02	1.6956553E+01	*
23.	2.5157855E-01	1.3103217E+01	*	73.	1.2525358E-02	1.6969078E+01	*
24.	2.3692775E-01	1.3340144E+01	*	74.	1.1795938E-02	1.6980873E+01	*
25.	2.2313015E-01	1.3563274E+01	*	75.	1.1108996E-02	1.6991981E+01	*
26.	2.1013607E-01	1.3773410E+01	*	76.	1.0462058E-02	1.7002443E+01	*
27.	1.9789869E-01	1.3971308E+01	*	77.	9.8527940E-03	1.7012295E+01	*
28.	1.8637397E-01	1.4157681E+01	*	78.	9.2790138E-03	1.7021574E+01	*
29.	1.7552040E-01	1.4333201E+01	*	79.	8.7386461E-03	1.7030312E+01	*
30.	1.6529888E-01	1.4498499E+01	*	80.	8.2297470E-03	1.7038541E+01	*
31.	1.5567263E-01	1.4654171E+01	*	81.	7.7504483E-03	1.7046291E+01	*
32.	1.4660696E-01	1.4800777E+01	*	82.	7.2991308E-03	1.7053590E+01	*
33.	1.3806923E-01	1.4938846E+01	*	83.	6.8740625E-03	1.7060464E+01	*
34.	1.3002871E-01	1.5068874E+01	*	84.	6.4737483E-03	1.7066937E+01	*
35.	1.2245642E-01	1.5191330E+01	*	85.	6.0967465E-03	1.7073033E+01	*
36.	1.1532512E-01	1.5306655E+01	*	86.	5.7416996E-03	1.7078774E+01	*
37.	1.0860910E-01	1.5415264E+01	*	87.	5.4073291E-03	1.7084181E+01	*
38.	1.0228420E-01	1.5517548E+01	*	88.	5.0925307E-03	1.7089273E+01	*
39.	9.6327638E-02	1.5613875E+01	*	89.	4.7958707E-03	1.7094069E+01	*
40.	9.0717953E-02	1.5704592E+01	*	90.	4.5165809E-03	1.7098584E+01	*
41.	8.5434950E-02	1.5790026E+01	*	91.	4.2535557E-03	1.7102837E+01	*
42.	8.0459606E-02	1.5870485E+01	*	92.	4.0058479E-03	1.7106842E+01	*
43.	7.5774003E-02	1.5946259E+01	*	93.	3.7725655E-03	1.7110614E+01	*
44.	7.1361269E-02	1.6017620E+01	*	94.	3.5528684E-03	1.7114166E+01	*
45.	6.7205512E-02	1.6084825E+01	*	95.	3.3459654E-03	1.7117511E+01	*
46.	6.3291768E-02	1.6148116E+01	*	96.	3.1511115E-03	1.7120662E+01	*
47.	5.9605942E-02	1.6207721E+01	*	97.	2.9676051E-03	1.7123629E+01	*
48.	5.6134762E-02	1.6263855E+01	*	98.	2.7947852E-03	1.7126423E+01	*
49.	5.2865728E-02	1.6316720E+01	*	99.	2.6320296E-03	1.7129055E+01	*
50.	4.9787068E-02	1.6366507E+01	*	100.	2.4787521E-03	1.7131533E+01	*

TABULATED VALUES OF E WHEN R = .061

X	E (−RX)	SUM OF E (−RX)	*	X	E (−RX)	SUM OF E (−RX)	*
0.	1.0000000E+00	1.0000000E+00	*	50.	4.7358924E-02	1.6145569E+01	*
1.	9.4082323E-01	1.9408232E+00	*	51.	4.4556376E-02	1.6190125E+01	*
2.	8.8514836E-01	2.8259715E+00	*	52.	4.1919674E-02	1.6232044E+01	*
3.	8.3276815E-01	3.6587396E+00	*	53.	3.9435004E-02	1.6271493E+01	*
4.	7.8348763E-01	4.4422272E+00	*	54.	3.7105131E-02	1.6308588E+01	*
5.	7.3712337E-01	5.1793505E+00	*	55.	3.4909370E-02	1.6343497E+01	*
6.	6.9350279E-01	5.8728532E+00	*	56.	3.2843568E-02	1.6376340E+01	*
7.	6.5246355E-01	6.5253167E+00	*	57.	3.0899972E-02	1.6407239E+01	*
8.	6.1385287E-01	7.1391695E+00	*	58.	2.9071411E-02	1.6436310E+01	*
9.	5.7752704E-01	7.7166965E+00	*	59.	2.7351059E-02	1.6463661E+01	*
10.	5.4335086E-01	8.2600473E+00	*	60.	2.5732512E-02	1.6489393E+01	*
11.	5.1119712E-01	8.7712444E+00	*	61.	2.4209745E-02	1.6513602E+01	*
12.	4.8094613E-01	9.2521905E+00	*	62.	2.2777091E-02	1.6536379E+01	*
13.	4.5248530E-01	9.7046758E+00	*	63.	2.1429217E-02	1.6557808E+01	*
14.	4.2570868E-01	1.0130384E+01	*	64.	2.0161105E-02	1.6577969E+01	*
15.	4.0051662E-01	1.0530900E+01	*	65.	1.8968036E-02	1.6596937E+01	*
16.	3.7681534E-01	1.0907715E+01	*	66.	1.7845569E-02	1.6614782E+01	*
17.	3.5451663E-01	1.1262231E+01	*	67.	1.6789526E-02	1.6631571E+01	*
18.	3.3353749E-01	1.1595768E+01	*	68.	1.5795976E-02	1.6647366E+01	*
19.	3.1379982E-01	1.1909567E+01	*	69.	1.4861222E-02	1.6662227E+01	*
20.	2.9523016E-01	1.2204797E+01	*	70.	1.3981783E-02	1.6676208E+01	*
21.	2.7775940E-01	1.2482556E+01	*	71.	1.3154386E-02	1.6689362E+01	*
22.	2.6132249E-01	1.2743878E+01	*	72.	1.2375952E-02	1.6701737E+01	*
23.	2.4585828E-01	1.2989736E+01	*	73.	1.1643583E-02	1.6713380E+01	*
24.	2.3130918E-01	1.3221045E+01	*	74.	1.0954554E-02	1.6724334E+01	*
25.	2.1762105E-01	1.3438666E+01	*	75.	1.0306299E-02	1.6734640E+01	*
26.	2.0474294E-01	1.3643408E+01	*	76.	9.6964057E-03	1.6744336E+01	*
27.	1.9262692E-01	1.3836034E+01	*	77.	9.1226038E-03	1.6753458E+01	*
28.	1.8122788E-01	1.4017261E+01	*	78.	8.5827577E-03	1.6762040E+01	*
29.	1.7050340E-01	1.4187764E+01	*	79.	8.0748579E-03	1.6770114E+01	*
30.	1.6041356E-01	1.4348177E+01	*	80.	7.5970140E-03	1.6777711E+01	*
31.	1.5092081E-01	1.4499097E+01	*	81.	7.1474473E-03	1.6784858E+01	*
32.	1.4198980E-01	1.4641086E+01	*	82.	6.7244845E-03	1.6791582E+01	*
33.	1.3358731E-01	1.4774673E+01	*	83.	6.3265513E-03	1.6797908E+01	*
34.	1.2568204E-01	1.4900355E+01	*	84.	5.9521665E-03	1.6803860E+01	*
35.	1.1824469E-01	1.5018599E+01	*	85.	5.5999366E-03	1.6809459E+01	*
36.	1.1124725E-01	1.5129846E+01	*	86.	5.2685504E-03	1.6814727E+01	*
37.	1.0466400E-01	1.5234510E+01	*	87.	4.9567747E-03	1.6819683E+01	*
38.	9.8470329E-02	1.5332980E+01	*	88.	4.6634688E-03	1.6824346E+01	*
39.	9.2643174E-02	1.5425623E+01	*	89.	4.3874810E-03	1.6828733E+01	*
40.	8.7160851E-02	1.5512738E+01	*	90.	4.1278441E-03	1.6832860E+01	*
41.	8.2002954E-02	1.5594785E+01	*	91.	3.8835717E-03	1.6836743E+01	*
42.	7.7150285E-02	1.5671935E+01	*	92.	3.6537545E-03	1.6840396E+01	*
43.	7.2584781E-02	1.5744519E+01	*	93.	3.4375371E-03	1.6843833E+01	*
44.	6.8289449E-02	1.5812808E+01	*	94.	3.2341148E-03	1.6847067E+01	*
45.	6.4248300E-02	1.5877050E+01	*	95.	3.0427304E-03	1.6850109E+01	*
46.	6.0446294E-02	1.5937502E+01	*	96.	2.8626714E-03	1.6852971E+01	*
47.	5.6869278E-02	1.5994371E+01	*	97.	2.6932678E-03	1.6855664E+01	*
48.	5.3503938E-02	1.6047874E+01	*	98.	2.5338898E-03	1.6858197E+01	*
49.	5.0337740E-02	1.6098211E+01	*	99.	2.3839418E-03	1.6860580E+01	*
50.	4.7358924E-02	1.6145569E+01	*	100.	2.2428677E-03	1.6862822E+01	*

TABULATED VALUES OF E WHEN R = .062

X	E (−RX)	SUM OF E (−RX)	*	X	E (−RX)	SUM OF E (−RX)	*
0.	1.0000000E+00	1.0000000E+00	*	50.	4.5049202E-02	1.5929871E+01	*
1.	9.3988288E-01	1.9398829E+00	*	51.	4.2340974E-02	1.5972211E+01	*
2.	8.8337983E-01	2.8232626E+00	*	52.	3.9795557E-02	1.6012006E+01	*
3.	8.3027359E-01	3.6535361E+00	*	53.	3.7403163E-02	1.6049409E+01	*
4.	7.8035994E-01	4.4338960E+00	*	54.	3.5154592E-02	1.6084563E+01	*
5.	7.3344695E-01	5.1673429E+00	*	55.	3.3041200E-02	1.6117604E+01	*
6.	6.8935424E-01	5.8566971E+00	*	56.	3.1054858E-02	1.6148658E+01	*
7.	6.4791225E-01	6.5046093E+00	*	57.	2.9187630E-02	1.6177495E+01	*
8.	6.0896164E-01	7.1135709E+00	*	58.	2.7432365E-02	1.6205279E+01	*
9.	5.7235262E-01	7.6859235E+00	*	59.	2.5784029E-02	1.6231062E+01	*
10.	5.3794443E-01	8.2238679E+00	*	60.	2.4233967E-02	1.6255295E+01	*
11.	5.0560476E-01	8.7294726E+00	*	61.	2.2777091E-02	1.6278072E+01	*
12.	4.7520927E-01	9.2046818E+00	*	62.	2.1407798E-02	1.6299479E+01	*
13.	4.4664010E-01	9.6513229E+00	*	63.	2.0120823E-02	1.6319595E+01	*
14.	4.1979028E-01	1.0071113E+01	*	64.	1.8911217E-02	1.6338510E+01	*
15.	3.9455370E-01	1.0465666E+01	*	65.	1.7774329E-02	1.6356284E+01	*
16.	3.7083427E-01	1.0836500E+01	*	66.	1.6705788E-02	1.6372994E+01	*
17.	3.4854079E-01	1.1185040E+01	*	67.	1.5701484E-02	1.6388690E+01	*
18.	3.2758752E-01	1.1512627E+01	*	68.	1.4757559E-02	1.6403447E+01	*
19.	3.0789391E-01	1.1820520E+01	*	69.	1.3870375E-02	1.6417317E+01	*
20.	2.8938421E-01	1.2109904E+01	*	70.	1.3036525E-02	1.6430353E+01	*
21.	2.7198727E-01	1.2381891E+01	*	71.	1.2252809E-02	1.6442605E+01	*
22.	2.5563618E-01	1.2637527E+01	*	72.	1.1516206E-02	1.6454121E+01	*
23.	2.4026807E-01	1.2877795E+01	*	73.	1.0823885E-02	1.6464946E+01	*
24.	2.2582385E-01	1.3103618E+01	*	74.	1.0173184E-02	1.6475117E+01	*
25.	2.1224797E-01	1.3315865E+01	*	75.	9.5616019E-03	1.6484678E+01	*
26.	1.9948823E-01	1.3515353E+01	*	76.	8.9867860E-03	1.6493666E+01	*
27.	1.8749558E-01	1.3702848E+01	*	77.	8.4465263E-03	1.6502110E+01	*
28.	1.7622388E-01	1.3879071E+01	*	78.	7.9387456E-03	1.6510048E+01	*
29.	1.6562981E-01	1.4044700E+01	*	79.	7.4614911E-03	1.6517509E+01	*
30.	1.5567263E-01	1.4200372E+01	*	80.	7.0129276E-03	1.6524521E+01	*
31.	1.4631404E-01	1.4346668E+01	*	81.	6.5913308E-03	1.6531112E+01	*
32.	1.3751806E-01	1.4484204E+01	*	82.	6.1950790E-03	1.6537307E+01	*
33.	1.2925087E-01	1.4613454E+01	*	83.	5.8226487E-03	1.6543129E+01	*
34.	1.2148068E-01	1.4734943E+01	*	84.	5.4726079E-03	1.6548601E+01	*
35.	1.1417761E-01	1.4849111E+01	*	85.	5.1436105E-03	1.6553744E+01	*
36.	1.0731356E-01	1.4956424E+01	*	86.	4.8343915E-03	1.6558578E+01	*
37.	1.0086220E-01	1.5057286E+01	*	87.	4.5437618E-03	1.6563121E+01	*
38.	9.4798660E-02	1.5152066E+01	*	88.	4.2706040E-03	1.6567391E+01	*
39.	9.0996358E-02	1.5244118E+01	*	89.	4.0138678E-03	1.6571404E+01	*
40.	8.3743225E-02	1.5328692E+01	*	90.	3.7725695E-03	1.6575175E+01	*
41.	7.3708824E-02	1.5403634E+01	*	91.	3.5457697E-03	1.6578721E+01	*
42.	7.3977077E-02	1.5477611E+01	*	92.	3.3326083E-03	1.6582053E+01	*
43.	6.9529788E-02	1.5547140E+01	*	93.	3.1322615E-03	1.6585185E+01	*
44.	6.5349857E-02	1.5612468E+01	*	94.	2.9439591E-03	1.6588128E+01	*
45.	6.1421213E-02	1.5673910E+01	*	95.	2.7669766E-03	1.6590942E+01	*
46.	5.7728747E-02	1.5731638E+01	*	96.	2.6006343E-03	1.6593446E+01	*
47.	5.4258262E-02	1.5785896E+01	*	97.	2.4442901E-03	1.6595903E+01	*
48.	5.0996411E-02	1.5836892E+01	*	98.	2.2973476E-03	1.6598235E+01	*
49.	4.7930654E-02	1.5884622E+01	*	99.	2.1593377E-03	1.6600394E+01	*
50.	4.5049202E-02	1.5929871E+01	*	100.	2.0294336E-03	1.6602425E+01	*

TABULATED VALUES OF E^{-RX} WHEN R = .063

X	E^{-RX}	SUM OF E^{-RX}	☆	X	E^{-RX}	SUM OF E^{-RX}	☆
0.	1.0000000E+00	1.0000000E+00	☆	50.	4.2852126E-02	1.5719256E+01	☆
1.	9.3894347E-01	1.9389434E+00	☆	51.	4.0235724E-02	1.5759491E+01	☆
2.	8.8161484E-01	2.8205582E+00	☆	52.	3.7779071E-02	1.5797270E+01	☆
3.	8.2778650E-01	3.6483447E+00	☆	53.	3.5472412E-02	1.5832742E+01	☆
4.	7.7724473E-01	4.4255894E+00	☆	54.	3.3306590E-02	1.5866048E+01	☆
5.	7.2978887E-01	5.1553782E+00	☆	55.	3.1273005E-02	1.5897321E+01	☆
6.	6.8523049E-01	5.8406086E+00	☆	56.	2.9363584E-02	1.5926684E+01	☆
7.	6.4339270E-01	6.4840013E+00	☆	57.	2.7570745E-02	1.5954254E+01	☆
8.	6.0410938E-01	7.0881106E+00	☆	58.	2.5887371E-02	1.5980141E+01	☆
9.	5.6722456E-01	7.6553331E+00	☆	59.	2.4306778E-02	1.6004447E+01	☆
10.	5.3259179E-01	8.1879268E+00	☆	60.	2.2822691E-02	1.6027269E+01	☆
11.	5.0007359E-01	8.6880003E+00	☆	61.	2.1429217E-02	1.6048698E+01	☆
12.	4.6954083E-01	9.1575411E+00	☆	62.	2.0120823E-02	1.6068818E+01	☆
13.	4.4087230E-01	9.5984134E+00	☆	63.	1.8892315E-02	1.6087710E+01	☆
14.	4.1395417E-01	1.0012367E+01	☆	64.	1.7738816E-02	1.6105448E+01	☆
15.	3.8867957E-01	1.0401046E+01	☆	65.	1.6655746E-02	1.6122103E+01	☆
16.	3.6494814E-01	1.0765994E+01	☆	66.	1.5638804E-02	1.6137741E+01	☆
17.	3.4266567E-01	1.1108659E+01	☆	67.	1.4683953E-02	1.6152424E+01	☆
18.	3.2174370E-01	1.1430402E+01	☆	68.	1.3787401E-02	1.6166211E+01	☆
19.	3.0209915E-01	1.1732501E+01	☆	69.	1.2945591E-02	1.6179156E+01	☆
20.	2.8365402E-01	1.2016155E+01	☆	70.	1.2155178E-02	1.6191311E+01	☆
21.	2.6633509E-01	1.2282490E+01	☆	71.	1.1413025E-02	1.6202724E+01	☆
22.	2.5007360E-01	1.2532563E+01	☆	72.	1.0716185E-02	1.6213440E+01	☆
23.	2.3480497E-01	1.2767367E+01	☆	73.	1.0061843E-02	1.6223501E+01	☆
24.	2.2046859E-01	1.2987835E+01	☆	74.	9.4475483E-03	1.6232944E+01	☆
25.	2.0700755E-01	1.3194842E+01	☆	75.	8.8707138E-03	1.6241818E+01	☆
26.	1.9436879E-01	1.3389210E+01	☆	76.	8.3290980E-03	1.6250147E+01	☆
27.	1.8250093E-01	1.3571710E+01	☆	77.	7.8205530E-03	1.6257967E+01	☆
28.	1.7135805E-01	1.3743068E+01	☆	78.	7.3430572E-03	1.6265310E+01	☆
29.	1.6089553E-01	1.3903963E+01	☆	79.	6.8947156E-03	1.6272204E+01	☆
30.	1.5107180E-01	1.4055034E+01	☆	80.	6.4737483E-03	1.6278677E+01	☆
31.	1.4184788E-01	1.4196881E+01	☆	81.	6.0784837E-03	1.6284755E+01	☆
32.	1.3318714E-01	1.4330068E+01	☆	82.	5.7073526E-03	1.6290462E+01	☆
33.	1.2505520E-01	1.4455123E+01	☆	83.	5.3588814E-03	1.6295820E+01	☆
34.	1.1741976E-01	1.4572542E+01	☆	84.	5.0316867E-03	1.6300851E+01	☆
35.	1.1025052E-01	1.4682792E+01	☆	85.	4.7244694E-03	1.6305575E+01	☆
36.	1.0351901E-01	1.4786311E+01	☆	86.	4.4360097E-03	1.6310011E+01	☆
37.	9.7198499E-02	1.4883509E+01	☆	87.	4.1651624E-03	1.6314176E+01	☆
38.	9.1263897E-02	1.4974772E+01	☆	88.	3.9108520E-03	1.6318046E+01	☆
39.	8.5691640E-02	1.5060683E+01	☆	89.	3.6720690E-03	1.6321758E+01	☆
40.	8.0459606E-02	1.5140922E+01	☆	90.	3.4478652E-03	1.6325205E+01	☆
41.	7.5547022E-02	1.5216469E+01	☆	91.	3.2373505E-03	1.6328442E+01	☆
42.	7.0934383E-02	1.5287403E+01	☆	92.	3.0396892E-03	1.6331416E+01	☆
43.	6.6603376E-02	1.5354006E+01	☆	93.	2.8540963E-03	1.6334335E+01	☆
44.	6.2536805E-02	1.5416542E+01	☆	94.	2.6798351E-03	1.6337014E+01	☆
45.	5.8718525E-02	1.5475260E+01	☆	95.	2.5162137E-03	1.6339530E+01	☆
46.	5.5133376E-02	1.5530393E+01	☆	96.	2.3625824E-03	1.6341892E+01	☆
47.	5.1767124E-02	1.5582160E+01	☆	97.	2.2183313E-03	1.6344110E+01	☆
48.	4.8606403E-02	1.5630766E+01	☆	98.	2.0828877E-03	1.6346192E+01	☆
49.	4.5638665E-02	1.5676404E+01	☆	99.	1.9557138E-03	1.6348147E+01	☆
50.	4.2852126E-02	1.5719256E+01	☆	100.	1.8363047E-03	1.6349983E+01	☆

TABULATED VALUES OF E^{-RX} WHEN R = .064

X	E^{-RX}	SUM OF E^{-RX}	☆	X	E^{-RX}	SUM OF E^{-RX}	☆
0.	1.0000000E+00	1.0000000E+00	☆	50.	4.0762203E-02	1.5513568E+01	☆
1.	9.3800499E-01	1.9380049E+00	☆	51.	3.8235151E-02	1.5551803E+01	☆
2.	8.7953337E-01	2.8178582E+00	☆	52.	3.5864762E-02	1.5587667E+01	☆
3.	8.2530686E-01	3.6431650E+00	☆	53.	3.3641326E-02	1.5621308E+01	☆
4.	7.7414196E-01	4.4173069E+00	☆	54.	3.1555732E-02	1.5652883E+01	☆
5.	7.2614903E-01	5.1434559E+00	☆	55.	2.9599435E-02	1.5682462E+01	☆
6.	6.8113142E-01	5.8245873E+00	☆	56.	2.7764418E-02	1.5710226E+01	☆
7.	6.3890468E-01	6.4634919E+00	☆	57.	2.6043162E-02	1.5736269E+01	☆
8.	5.9929578E-01	7.0627876E+00	☆	58.	2.4429617E-02	1.5760697E+01	☆
9.	5.6214244E-01	7.6249300E+00	☆	59.	2.2914164E-02	1.5783611E+01	☆
10.	5.2729242E-01	8.1522224E+00	☆	60.	2.1493601E-02	1.5805104E+01	☆
11.	4.9460292E-01	8.6468253E+00	☆	61.	2.0161105E-02	1.5825265E+01	☆
12.	4.6394002E-01	9.1107653E+00	☆	62.	1.8911217E-02	1.5844176E+01	☆
13.	4.3517805E-01	9.5459433E+00	☆	63.	1.7738816E-02	1.5861914E+01	☆
14.	4.0819919E-01	9.9541424E+00	☆	64.	1.6639098E-02	1.5878553E+01	☆
15.	3.8289288E-01	1.0337035E+01	☆	65.	1.5607557E-02	1.5894160E+01	☆
16.	3.5915544E-01	1.0696190E+01	☆	66.	1.4639967E-02	1.5908799E+01	☆
17.	3.3688959E-01	1.1033079E+01	☆	67.	1.3732362E-02	1.5922531E+01	☆
18.	3.1600412E-01	1.1349083E+01	☆	68.	1.2881024E-02	1.5935412E+01	☆
19.	2.9641345E-01	1.1645496E+01	☆	69.	1.2082465E-02	1.5947494E+01	☆
20.	2.7803730E-01	1.1923533E+01	☆	70.	1.1333413E-02	1.5958827E+01	☆
21.	2.6080037E-01	1.2184333E+01	☆	71.	1.0630798E-02	1.5969457E+01	☆
22.	2.4463205E-01	1.2428965E+01	☆	72.	9.9717418E-03	1.5979429E+01	☆
23.	2.2946609E-01	1.2658431E+01	☆	73.	9.3535437E-03	1.5988781E+01	☆
24.	2.1524034E-01	1.2873671E+01	☆	74.	8.7735707E-03	1.5997554E+01	☆
25.	2.0189651E-01	1.3075567E+01	☆	75.	8.2297470E-03	1.6005783E+01	☆
26.	1.8937994E-01	1.3264946E+01	☆	76.	7.7195438E-03	1.6013502E+01	☆
27.	1.7763933E-01	1.3442585E+01	☆	77.	7.2409707E-03	1.6020742E+01	☆
28.	1.6662658E-01	1.3609211E+01	☆	78.	6.7920667E-03	1.6027534E+01	☆
29.	1.5629656E-01	1.3765507E+01	☆	79.	6.3709925E-03	1.6033904E+01	☆
30.	1.4660696E-01	1.3912113E+01	☆	80.	5.9760228E-03	1.6039800E+01	☆
31.	1.3751808E-01	1.4049631E+01	☆	81.	5.6055393E-03	1.6045405E+01	☆
32.	1.2899263E-01	1.4178623E+01	☆	82.	5.2580239E-03	1.6050743E+01	☆
33.	1.2099573E-01	1.4299618E+01	☆	83.	4.9320527E-03	1.6055675E+01	☆
34.	1.1349460E-01	1.4413112E+01	☆	84.	4.6262901E-03	1.6060301E+01	☆
35.	1.0645850E-01	1.4519570E+01	☆	85.	4.3394832E-03	1.6064640E+01	☆
36.	9.9858609E-02	1.4619428E+01	☆	86.	4.0704569E-03	1.6068710E+01	☆
37.	9.3667874E-02	1.4713095E+01	☆	87.	3.8181090E-03	1.6072528E+01	☆
38.	8.7860934E-02	1.4800955E+01	☆	88.	3.5814053E-03	1.6076109E+01	☆
39.	8.2413995E-02	1.4883368E+01	☆	89.	3.3593761E-03	1.6079468E+01	☆
40.	7.7304740E-02	1.4960672E+01	☆	90.	3.1511119E-03	1.6082619E+01	☆
41.	7.2512232E-02	1.5033184E+01	☆	91.	2.9557584E-03	1.6085577E+01	☆
42.	6.8016836E-02	1.5101200E+01	☆	92.	2.7725161E-03	1.6088346E+01	☆
43.	6.3800132E-02	1.5165000E+01	☆	93.	2.6006340E-03	1.6090946E+01	☆
44.	5.9844843E-02	1.5224844E+01	☆	94.	2.4394077E-03	1.6093385E+01	☆
45.	5.6134762E-02	1.5280978E+01	☆	95.	2.2881766E-03	1.6095673E+01	☆
46.	5.2654688E-02	1.5333632E+01	☆	96.	2.1463211E-03	1.6097819E+01	☆
47.	4.9390360E-02	1.5383022E+01	☆	97.	2.0132599E-03	1.6099832E+01	☆
48.	4.6328405E-02	1.5429350E+01	☆	98.	1.8884479E-03	1.6101720E+01	☆
49.	4.3456275E-02	1.5472806E+01	☆	99.	1.7713735E-03	1.6103491E+01	☆
50.	4.0762203E-02	1.5513568E+01	☆	100.	1.6615572E-03	1.6105152E+01	☆

169

TABULATED VALUES OF E⁻ᴿˣ   WHEN R = .065

x	E^{-Rx}	SUM OF E^{-Rx}	x	E^{-Rx}	SUM OF E^{-Rx}
0.	1.0000000E+00	1.0000000E+00	50.	3.8774207E-02	1.5312662E+01
1.	9.3706746E-01	1.9370674E+00	51.	3.6334048E-02	1.5348996E+01
2.	8.7809542E-01	2.8151562E+00	52.	3.4047454E-02	1.5383403E+01
3.	8.2283465E-01	3.6379974E+00	53.	3.1904781E-02	1.5414947E+01
4.	7.7105158E-01	4.4090490E+00	54.	2.9896914E-02	1.5444843E+01
5.	7.2252735E-01	5.1315762E+00	55.	2.8015425E-02	1.5472858E+01
6.	6.7705687E-01	5.8086330E+00	56.	2.6252343E-02	1.5499110E+01
7.	6.3444796E-01	6.4430809E+00	57.	2.4600217E-02	1.5523710E+01
8.	5.9452054E-01	7.0376014E+00	58.	2.3052063E-02	1.5546762E+01
9.	5.7105866E-01	7.5947072E+00	59.	2.1601333E-02	1.5568363E+01
10.	5.2204577E-01	8.1167529E+00	60.	2.0241911E-02	1.5588604E+01
11.	4.8919211E-01	8.6059450E+00	61.	1.8968036E-02	1.5607572E+01
12.	4.5840601E-01	9.0643510E+00	62.	1.7774329E-02	1.5625346E+01
13.	4.2955735E-01	9.4939083E+00	63.	1.6655746E-02	1.5642001E+01
14.	4.0252422E-01	9.8964325E+00	64.	1.5607557E-02	1.5657608E+01
15.	3.7719235E-01	1.0273624E+01	65.	1.4625334E-02	1.5672233E+01
16.	3.5345468E-01	1.0627078E+01	66.	1.3704925E-02	1.5686593E+01
17.	3.3121088E-01	1.0958288E+01	67.	1.2842439E-02	1.5698779E+01
18.	3.1036694E-01	1.1268654E+01	68.	1.2034232E-02	1.5710813E+01
19.	2.9083476E-01	1.1559488E+01	69.	1.1276887E-02	1.5722089E+01
20.	2.7253179E-01	1.1832019E+01	70.	1.0567204E-02	1.5732656E+01
21.	2.5538067E-01	1.2087399E+01	71.	9.9021834E-03	1.5742558E+01
22.	2.3930692E-01	1.2326707E+01	72.	9.2790183E-03	1.5751837E+01
23.	2.2424860E-01	1.2550955E+01	73.	8.6950619E-03	1.5760532E+01
24.	2.1013607E-01	1.2761091E+01	74.	8.1478596E-03	1.5768679E+01
25.	1.9691167E-01	1.2958002E+01	75.	7.6350942E-03	1.5776314E+01
26.	1.8451952E-01	1.3142521E+01	76.	7.1545983E-03	1.5783468E+01
27.	1.7290724E-01	1.3315428E+01	77.	6.7043413E-03	1.5790172E+01
28.	1.6202575E-01	1.3477453E+01	78.	6.2824201E-03	1.5796454E+01
29.	1.5182905E-01	1.3629282E+01	79.	5.8870514E-03	1.5802341E+01
30.	1.4227407E-01	1.3771556E+01	80.	5.5165644E-03	1.5807857E+01
31.	1.3332016E-01	1.3904876E+01	81.	5.1693930E-03	1.5813026E+01
32.	1.2493021E-01	1.4029806E+01	82.	4.8440700E-03	1.5817870E+01
33.	1.1706803E-01	1.4146876E+01	83.	4.5392203E-03	1.5822409E+01
34.	1.0970064E-01	1.4256576E+01	84.	4.2535557E-03	1.5826662E+01
35.	1.0279690E-01	1.4359370E+01	85.	3.9858668E-03	1.5830647E+01
36.	9.6327636E-02	1.4455697E+01	86.	3.7350278E-03	1.5834382E+01
37.	9.0265495E-02	1.4545962E+01	87.	3.4999730E-03	1.5837881E+01
38.	8.4584056E-02	1.4630546E+01	88.	3.2797108E-03	1.5841160E+01
39.	7.9261719E-02	1.4709807E+01	89.	3.0733103E-03	1.5844233E+01
40.	7.4273576E-02	1.4784080E+01	90.	2.8798991E-03	1.5847112E+01
41.	6.9599335E-02	1.4853676E+01	91.	2.6986597E-03	1.5849810E+01
42.	6.5219286E-02	1.4918698E+01	92.	2.5288262E-03	1.5852353E+01
43.	6.1114874E-02	1.4980012E+01	93.	2.3696808E-03	1.5854707E+01
44.	5.7268760E-02	1.5037280E+01	94.	2.2205598E-03	1.5856927E+01
45.	5.3664691E-02	1.5090944E+01	95.	2.0808595E-03	1.5859007E+01
46.	5.0287436E-02	1.5141231E+01	96.	1.9498555E-03	1.5860955E+01
47.	4.7122720E-02	1.5188353E+01	97.	1.8271441E-03	1.5862783E+01
48.	4.4157168E-02	1.5232531E+01	98.	1.7121592E-03	1.5864495E+01
49.	4.1378245E-02	1.5273888E+01	99.	1.6044086E-03	1.5866090E+01
50.	3.8774207E-02	1.5312662E+01	100.	1.5034391E-03	1.5867602E+01

TABULATED VALUES OF E⁻ᴿˣ   WHEN R = .066

x	E^{-Rx}	SUM OF E^{-Rx}	x	E^{-Rx}	SUM OF E^{-Rx}
0.	1.0000000E+00	1.0000000E+00	50.	3.6883167E-02	1.5116397E+01
1.	9.3613086E-01	1.9361308E+00	51.	3.4527471E-02	1.5150924E+01
2.	8.7634099E-01	2.8124717E+00	52.	3.2322231E-02	1.5183246E+01
3.	8.2036985E-01	3.6328415E+00	53.	3.0257838E-02	1.5213503E+01
4.	7.6797353E-01	4.4008150E+00	54.	2.8325296E-02	1.5241828E+01
5.	7.1892373E-01	5.1197387E+00	55.	2.6516184E-02	1.5268344E+01
6.	6.7300069E-01	5.7927453E+00	56.	2.4822618E-02	1.5293166E+01
7.	6.3002233E-01	6.4227678E+00	57.	2.3237219E-02	1.5316403E+01
8.	5.8978335E-01	7.0125509E+00	58.	2.1753078E-02	1.5338156E+01
9.	5.5211440E-01	7.5646653E+00	59.	2.0363727E-02	1.5358519E+01
10.	5.1685133E-01	8.0815166E+00	60.	1.9063114E-02	1.5377582E+01
11.	4.8384048E-01	8.5653570E+00	61.	1.7845569E-02	1.5395427E+01
12.	4.5293801E-01	9.0182950E+00	62.	1.6705784E-02	1.5412132E+01
13.	4.2400925E-01	9.4423042E+00	63.	1.5638804E-02	1.5427770E+01
14.	3.9692814E-01	9.8392323E+00	64.	1.4639967E-02	1.5442409E+01
15.	3.7157669E-01	1.0210800E+01	65.	1.3704925E-02	1.5456113E+01
16.	3.4784440E-01	1.0558652E+01	66.	1.2829603E-02	1.5468942E+01
17.	3.2562788E-01	1.0884279E+01	67.	1.2010187E-02	1.5480952E+01
18.	3.0483031E-01	1.1189109E+01	68.	1.1243107E-02	1.5492195E+01
19.	2.8536106E-01	1.1474470E+01	69.	1.0525019E-02	1.5502720E+01
20.	2.6713530E-01	1.1741605E+01	70.	9.8527960E-03	1.5512572E+01
21.	2.5007360E-01	1.1991678E+01	71.	9.2235064E-03	1.5521795E+01
22.	2.3410161E-01	1.2225779E+01	72.	8.6344090E-03	1.5530429E+01
23.	2.1914974E-01	1.2444928E+01	73.	8.0829363E-03	1.5538511E+01
24.	2.0515284E-01	1.2650080E+01	74.	7.5666866E-03	1.5546077E+01
25.	1.9204990E-01	1.2842129E+01	75.	7.0834080E-03	1.5553160E+01
26.	1.7978364E-01	1.3021912E+01	76.	6.6309977E-03	1.5559790E+01
27.	1.6830120E-01	1.3190213E+01	77.	6.2074816E-03	1.5565997E+01
28.	1.5755195E-01	1.3347764E+01	78.	5.8110151E-03	1.5571808E+01
29.	1.4748924E-01	1.3495253E+01	79.	5.4398704E-03	1.5577272E+01
30.	1.3806923E-01	1.3633322E+01	80.	5.0924307E-03	1.5582336E+01
31.	1.2925087E-01	1.3762572E+01	81.	4.7671816E-03	1.5587104E+01
32.	1.2099573E-01	1.3883567E+01	82.	4.4627058E-03	1.5591568E+01
33.	1.1326783E-01	1.3996834E+01	83.	4.1776766E-03	1.5595745E+01
34.	1.0603352E-01	1.4102867E+01	84.	3.9108520E-03	1.5599655E+01
35.	9.9261251E-02	1.4202128E+01	85.	3.6610693E-03	1.5603316E+01
36.	9.2921521E-02	1.4295049E+01	86.	3.4272400E-03	1.5606743E+01
37.	8.6984703E-02	1.4382035E+01	87.	3.2083451E-03	1.5609951E+01
38.	8.1430938E-02	1.4463465E+01	88.	3.0034309E-03	1.5612954E+01
39.	7.6230014E-02	1.4539695E+01	89.	2.8116043E-03	1.5615765E+01
40.	7.1361269E-02	1.4611056E+01	90.	2.6320296E-03	1.5618367E+01
41.	6.6803486E-02	1.4677859E+01	91.	2.4639241E-03	1.5620860E+01
42.	6.2536805E-02	1.4740395E+01	92.	2.3065554E-03	1.5623126E+01
43.	5.8542634E-02	1.4798937E+01	93.	2.1592377E-03	1.5625325E+01
44.	5.4803566E-02	1.4853740E+01	94.	2.0212291E-03	1.5627344E+01
45.	5.1303310E-02	1.4905043E+01	95.	1.8922285E-03	1.5629233E+01
46.	4.8026612E-02	1.4953069E+01	96.	1.7713735E-03	1.5631009E+01
47.	4.4959193E-02	1.4998902E+01	97.	1.6582374E-03	1.5632667E+01
48.	4.2087689E-02	1.5040115E+01	98.	1.5523272E-03	1.5634219E+01
49.	3.9399584E-02	1.5079514E+01	99.	1.4531814E-03	1.5635672E+01
50.	3.6883167E-02	1.5116397E+01	100.	1.3603680E-03	1.5637032E+01

TABULATED VALUES OF E^{-RX} WHEN R = .067

X	E^{-RX}	SUM OF E^{-RX}	*	X	E^{-RX}	SUM OF E^{-RX}	*
0.	1.0000000E+00	1.0000000E+00	*	50.	3.5084354E-02	1.4924636E+01	*
1.	9.3519519E-01	1.9351951E+00	*	51.	3.2810719E-02	1.4957446E+01	*
2.	8.7459006E-01	2.8097851E+00	*	52.	3.0684427E-02	1.4988130E+01	*
3.	8.1791242E-01	3.6276975E+00	*	53.	2.8695929E-02	1.5016825E+01	*
4.	7.6490777E-01	4.3926052E+00	*	54.	2.6836295E-02	1.5043661E+01	*
5.	7.1533808E-01	5.1079432E+00	*	55.	2.5097174E-02	1.5068758E+01	*
6.	6.6898074E-01	5.7769239E+00	*	56.	2.3470757E-02	1.5092228E+01	*
7.	6.2562758E-01	6.4025514E+00	*	57.	2.1949739E-02	1.5114177E+01	*
8.	5.8508391E-01	6.9876353E+00	*	58.	2.0527291E-02	1.5134704E+01	*
9.	5.4716766E-01	7.5348029E+00	*	59.	1.9197024E-02	1.5153901E+01	*
10.	5.1170857E-01	8.0465114E+00	*	60.	1.7952964E-02	1.5171853E+01	*
11.	4.7854740E-01	8.5250588E+00	*	61.	1.6789526E-02	1.5188642E+01	*
12.	4.4753523E-01	8.9725940E+00	*	62.	1.5701484E-02	1.5204343E+01	*
13.	4.1853280E-01	9.3911268E+00	*	63.	1.4683953E-02	1.5219026E+01	*
14.	3.9140987E-01	9.7825366E+00	*	64.	1.3732362E-02	1.5232758E+01	*
15.	3.6604463E-01	1.0148581E+01	*	65.	1.2842439E-02	1.5245600E+01	*
16.	3.4232318E-01	1.0490904E+01	*	66.	1.2010187E-02	1.5257610E+01	*
17.	3.2013899E-01	1.0811042E+01	*	67.	1.1231870E-02	1.5268841E+01	*
18.	2.9939245E-01	1.1110434E+01	*	68.	1.0503990E-02	1.5279344E+01	*
19.	2.7999038E-01	1.1390424E+01	*	69.	9.8232819E-03	1.5289167E+01	*
20.	2.6184566E-01	1.1652269E+01	*	70.	9.1866861E-03	1.5298353E+01	*
21.	2.4487681E-01	1.1897145E+01	*	71.	8.5913447E-03	1.5306944E+01	*
22.	2.2900761E-01	1.2126152E+01	*	72.	8.0345844E-03	1.5314978E+01	*
23.	2.1416682E-01	1.2340318E+01	*	73.	7.5139048E-03	1.5322491E+01	*
24.	2.0028778E-01	1.2540605E+01	*	74.	7.0269677E-03	1.5329517E+01	*
25.	1.8730817E-01	1.2727913E+01	*	75.	6.5715864E-03	1.5336088E+01	*
26.	1.7516971E-01	1.2903082E+01	*	76.	6.1457161E-03	1.5342233E+01	*
27.	1.6381787E-01	1.3066899E+01	*	77.	5.7474442E-03	1.5347980E+01	*
28.	1.5320168E-01	1.3220100E+01	*	78.	5.3749822E-03	1.5353354E+01	*
29.	1.4327348E-01	1.3363373E+01	*	79.	5.0265576E-03	1.5358380E+01	*
30.	1.3398867E-01	1.3497361E+01	*	80.	4.7009061E-03	1.5363080E+01	*
31.	1.2530556E-01	1.3622666E+01	*	81.	4.3962648E-03	1.5367476E+01	*
32.	1.1718516E-01	1.3739851E+01	*	82.	4.1113657E-03	1.5371587E+01	*
33.	1.0959100E-01	1.3849442E+01	*	83.	3.8449295E-03	1.5375431E+01	*
34.	1.0248897E-01	1.3951930E+01	*	84.	3.5957596E-03	1.5379026E+01	*
35.	9.5847202E-02	1.4047777E+01	*	85.	3.3627371E-03	1.5382388E+01	*
36.	8.9635843E-02	1.4137412E+01	*	86.	3.1448156E-03	1.5385532E+01	*
37.	8.3827010E-02	1.4221239E+01	*	87.	2.9410165E-03	1.5388473E+01	*
38.	7.8394618E-02	1.4299633E+01	*	88.	2.7504245E-03	1.5391223E+01	*
39.	7.3314270E-02	1.4372947E+01	*	89.	2.5721838E-03	1.5393795E+01	*
40.	6.8563153E-02	1.4441510E+01	*	90.	2.4054939E-03	1.5396200E+01	*
41.	6.4119932E-02	1.4505629E+01	*	91.	2.2495119E-03	1.5398449E+01	*
42.	5.9964653E-02	1.4565593E+01	*	92.	2.1038211E-03	1.5400552E+01	*
43.	5.6078655E-02	1.4621671E+01	*	93.	1.9674834E-03	1.5402519E+01	*
44.	5.2444489E-02	1.4674115E+01	*	94.	1.8399810E-03	1.5404358E+01	*
45.	4.9045835E-02	1.4723160E+01	*	95.	1.7207414E-03	1.5406078E+01	*
46.	4.5867429E-02	1.4769027E+01	*	96.	1.6092291E-03	1.5407687E+01	*
47.	4.2895000E-02	1.4811922E+01	*	97.	1.5049433E-03	1.5409191E+01	*
48.	4.0115198E-02	1.4852037E+01	*	98.	1.4074158E-03	1.5410598E+01	*
49.	3.7515541E-02	1.4889552E+01	*	99.	1.3162085E-03	1.5411914E+01	*
50.	3.5084354E-02	1.4924636E+01	*	100.	1.2309119E-03	1.5413144E+01	*

TABULATED VALUES OF E^{-RX} WHEN R = .068

X	E^{-RX}	SUM OF E^{-RX}	*	X	E^{-RX}	SUM OF E^{-RX}	*
0.	1.0000000E+00	1.0000000E+00	*	50.	3.3373269E-02	1.4737244E+01	*
1.	9.3426047E-01	1.9342604E+00	*	51.	3.1179326E-02	1.4768423E+01	*
2.	8.7284263E-01	2.8071030E+00	*	52.	2.9129612E-02	1.4797552E+01	*
3.	8.1546236E-01	3.6225653E+00	*	53.	2.7214645E-02	1.4824766E+01	*
4.	7.6185426E-01	4.3844195E+00	*	54.	2.5425567E-02	1.4850191E+01	*
5.	7.1177032E-01	5.0961898E+00	*	55.	2.3754103E-02	1.4873945E+01	*
6.	6.6497788E-01	5.7611686E+00	*	56.	2.2192519E-02	1.4896137E+01	*
7.	6.2126348E-01	6.3824320E+00	*	57.	2.0733593E-02	1.4916870E+01	*
8.	5.8042191E-01	6.9628539E+00	*	58.	1.9370577E-02	1.4936240E+01	*
9.	5.4226525E-01	7.5051191E+00	*	59.	1.8097164E-02	1.4954337E+01	*
10.	5.0661699E-01	8.0117360E+00	*	60.	1.6907465E-02	1.4971244E+01	*
11.	4.7331223E-01	8.4850482E+00	*	61.	1.5795976E-02	1.4987039E+01	*
12.	4.4219690E-01	8.9272451E+00	*	62.	1.4757556E-02	1.5001766E+01	*
13.	4.1312709E-01	9.3403721E+00	*	63.	1.3787401E-02	1.5015583E+01	*
14.	3.8596831E-01	9.7263404E+00	*	64.	1.2881024E-02	1.5028464E+01	*
15.	3.6059493E-01	1.0086935E+01	*	65.	1.2034232E-02	1.5040498E+01	*
16.	3.3688959E-01	1.0423824E+01	*	66.	1.1243107E-02	1.5051741E+01	*
17.	3.1474263E-01	1.0738566E+01	*	67.	1.0503990E-02	1.5062244E+01	*
18.	2.9405160E-01	1.1032617E+01	*	68.	9.8134635E-03	1.5072057E+01	*
19.	2.7472079E-01	1.1307337E+01	*	69.	9.1683311E-03	1.5081225E+01	*
20.	2.5666077E-01	1.1563997E+01	*	70.	8.5656093E-03	1.5089790E+01	*
21.	2.3978801E-01	1.1803785E+01	*	71.	8.0025102E-03	1.5097792E+01	*
22.	2.2402446E-01	1.2027809E+01	*	72.	7.4764290E-03	1.5105268E+01	*
23.	2.0929720E-01	1.2237106E+01	*	73.	6.9849321E-03	1.5112252E+01	*
24.	1.9553810E-01	1.2432644E+01	*	74.	6.5257459E-03	1.5118777E+01	*
25.	1.8268353E-01	1.2615327E+01	*	75.	6.0967465E-03	1.5124873E+01	*
26.	1.7067399E-01	1.2786000E+01	*	76.	5.6959493E-03	1.5130568E+01	*
27.	1.5945396E-01	1.2945453E+01	*	77.	5.3215003E-03	1.5135889E+01	*
28.	1.4897153E-01	1.3094424E+01	*	78.	4.9716674E-03	1.5140860E+01	*
29.	1.3917822E-01	1.3233602E+01	*	79.	4.6448323E-03	1.5145504E+01	*
30.	1.3002871E-01	1.3363630E+01	*	80.	4.3394833E-03	1.5149843E+01	*
31.	1.2148068E-01	1.3485110E+01	*	81.	4.0542076E-03	1.5153897E+01	*
32.	1.1349460E-01	1.3598604E+01	*	82.	3.7876859E-03	1.5157684E+01	*
33.	1.0603352E-01	1.3704637E+01	*	83.	3.5386853E-03	1.5161222E+01	*
34.	9.9062927E-02	1.3803699E+01	*	84.	3.3060538E-03	1.5164528E+01	*
35.	9.2550577E-02	1.3896249E+01	*	85.	3.0887154E-03	1.5167616E+01	*
36.	8.6466340E-02	1.3982715E+01	*	86.	2.8856647E-03	1.5170501E+01	*
37.	8.0782089E-02	1.4063497E+01	*	87.	2.6959624E-03	1.5173196E+01	*
38.	7.5471513E-02	1.4138968E+01	*	88.	2.5187311E-03	1.5175714E+01	*
39.	7.0510051E-02	1.4209478E+01	*	89.	2.3531509E-03	1.5178076E+01	*
40.	6.5874754E-02	1.4275352E+01	*	90.	2.1984559E-03	1.5180265E+01	*
41.	6.1544179E-02	1.4336896E+01	*	91.	2.0539305E-03	1.5182318E+01	*
42.	5.7498293E-02	1.4394394E+01	*	92.	1.9189060E-03	1.5184236E+01	*
43.	5.3718383E-02	1.4448112E+01	*	93.	1.7927581E-03	1.5186028E+01	*
44.	5.0186962E-02	1.4498298E+01	*	94.	1.6749030E-03	1.5187702E+01	*
45.	4.6887695E-02	1.4545185E+01	*	95.	1.5647957E-03	1.5189266E+01	*
46.	4.3805320E-02	1.4588990E+01	*	96.	1.4619267E-03	1.5190727E+01	*
47.	4.0925579E-02	1.4629915E+01	*	97.	1.3658204E-03	1.5192092E+01	*
48.	3.8235151E-02	1.4668150E+01	*	98.	1.2760320E-03	1.5193368E+01	*
49.	3.5721590E-02	1.4703871E+01	*	99.	1.1921462E-03	1.5194560E+01	*
50.	3.3373269E-02	1.4737244E+01	*	100.	1.1137751E-03	1.5195673E+01	*

TABULATED VALUES OF E   WHEN R = .069

x	E (-RX)	SUM OF E (-RX)	*	x	E (-RX)	SUM OF E (-RX)	*
0.	1.0000000E+00	1.0000000E+00	*	50.	3.1745636E-02	1.4554094E+01	*
1.	9.3332667E-01	1.9333266E+00	*	51.	2.9629049E-02	1.4583723E+01	*
2.	8.7109869E-01	2.8044252E+00	*	52.	2.7653582E-02	1.4611376E+01	*
3.	8.1301964E-01	3.6174449E+00	*	53.	2.5809826E-02	1.4637185E+01	*
4.	7.5881293E-01	4.3762577E+00	*	54.	2.4088999E-02	1.4661273E+01	*
5.	7.0822035E-01	5.0844780E+00	*	55.	2.2482905E-02	1.4683755E+01	*
6.	6.6100094E-01	5.7454789E+00	*	56.	2.0983895E-02	1.4704738E+01	*
7.	6.1692982E-01	6.3624087E+00	*	57.	1.9584829E-02	1.4724322E+01	*
8.	5.7579706E-01	6.9382057E+00	*	58.	1.8279044E-02	1.4742601E+01	*
9.	5.3740676E-01	7.4756124E+00	*	59.	1.7060319E-02	1.4759661E+01	*
10.	5.0157606E-01	7.9771884E+00	*	60.	1.5922851E-02	1.4775583E+01	*
11.	4.6813432E-01	8.4453227E+00	*	61.	1.4861222E-02	1.4790444E+01	*
12.	4.3692225E-01	8.8822449E+00	*	62.	1.3870375E-02	1.4804314E+01	*
13.	4.0779119E-01	9.2900360E+00	*	63.	1.2945591E-02	1.4817259E+01	*
14.	3.8060240E-01	9.6706384E+00	*	64.	1.2082465E-02	1.4829341E+01	*
15.	3.5522638E-01	1.0025864E+01	*	65.	1.1276887E-02	1.4840617E+01	*
16.	3.3154225E-01	1.0357406E+01	*	66.	1.0525019E-02	1.4851142E+01	*
17.	3.0943723E-01	1.0666843E+01	*	67.	9.8232819E-03	1.4860965E+01	*
18.	2.8880602E-01	1.0955649E+01	*	68.	9.1683311E-03	1.4870133E+01	*
19.	2.6955037E-01	1.1225199E+01	*	69.	8.5570480E-03	1.4878690E+01	*
20.	2.5157855E-01	1.1476777E+01	*	70.	7.9865212E-03	1.4886676E+01	*
21.	2.3480497E-01	1.1711581E+01	*	71.	7.4540333E-03	1.4894130E+01	*
22.	2.1914974E-01	1.1930730E+01	*	72.	6.9570482E-03	1.4901087E+01	*
23.	2.0453830E-01	1.2135268E+01	*	73.	6.4931987E-03	1.4907580E+01	*
24.	1.9090105E-01	1.2326169E+01	*	74.	6.0602756E-03	1.4913640E+01	*
25.	1.7817305E-01	1.2504342E+01	*	75.	5.6562169E-03	1.4919296E+01	*
26.	1.6629366E-01	1.2670635E+01	*	76.	5.2790981E-03	1.4924575E+01	*
27.	1.5520631E-01	1.2825841E+01	*	77.	4.9271231E-03	1.4929502E+01	*
28.	1.4485819E-01	1.2970699E+01	*	78.	4.5986154E-03	1.4934100E+01	*
29.	1.3520001E-01	1.3105899E+01	*	79.	4.2920105E-03	1.4938392E+01	*
30.	1.2618578E-01	1.3232084E+01	*	80.	4.0058479E-03	1.4942397E+01	*
31.	1.1777255E-01	1.3349856E+01	*	81.	3.7387647E-03	1.4946135E+01	*
32.	1.0992026E-01	1.3459776E+01	*	82.	3.4894888E-03	1.4949624E+01	*
33.	1.0259151E-01	1.3562367E+01	*	83.	3.2568330E-03	1.4952880E+01	*
34.	9.5751402E-02	1.3658113E+01	*	84.	3.0396892E-03	1.4955919E+01	*
35.	8.9367338E-02	1.3747485E+01	*	85.	2.8370230E-03	1.4958756E+01	*
36.	8.3408921E-02	1.3830893E+01	*	86.	2.6478692E-03	1.4961403E+01	*
37.	7.7847771E-02	1.3908740E+01	*	87.	2.4713270E-03	1.4963874E+01	*
38.	7.2657402E-02	1.3981397E+01	*	88.	2.3065554E-03	1.4966180E+01	*
39.	6.7813092E-02	1.4049210E+01	*	89.	2.1527697E-03	1.4968332E+01	*
40.	6.3291768E-02	1.4112501E+01	*	90.	2.0092374E-03	1.4970341E+01	*
41.	5.9071895E-02	1.4171572E+01	*	91.	1.8752749E-03	1.4972216E+01	*
42.	5.5133176E-02	1.4226705E+01	*	92.	1.7502441E-03	1.4973966E+01	*
43.	5.1457451E-02	1.4278162E+01	*	93.	1.6335495E-03	1.4975599E+01	*
44.	4.8026612E-02	1.4326188E+01	*	94.	1.5246335E-03	1.4977123E+01	*
45.	4.4824518E-02	1.4371012E+01	*	95.	1.4229828E-03	1.4978545E+01	*
46.	4.1835918E-02	1.4412847E+01	*	96.	1.3281078E-03	1.4979873E+01	*
47.	3.9046579E-02	1.4451893E+01	*	97.	1.2395585E-03	1.4981112E+01	*
48.	3.6443214E-02	1.4488336E+01	*	98.	1.1569130E-03	1.4982268E+01	*
49.	3.4013424E-02	1.4522349E+01	*	99.	1.0797777E-03	1.4983347E+01	*
50.	3.1745636E-02	1.4554094E+01	*	100.	1.0077854E-03	1.4984354E+01	*

TABULATED VALUES OF E   WHEN R = .070

x	E (-RX)	SUM OF E (-RX)	*	x	E (-RX)	SUM OF E (-RX)	*
0.	1.0000000E+00	1.0000000E+00	*	50.	3.0197383E-02	1.4375061E+01	*
1.	9.3239381E-01	1.9323938E+00	*	51.	2.8155853E-02	1.4403216E+01	*
2.	8.6935823E-01	2.8017520E+00	*	52.	2.6252343E-02	1.4429468E+01	*
3.	8.1058424E-01	3.6123362E+00	*	53.	2.4477523E-02	1.4453945E+01	*
4.	7.5578374E-01	4.3681199E+00	*	54.	2.2822691E-02	1.4476767E+01	*
5.	7.0468808E-01	5.0728079E+00	*	55.	2.1279736E-02	1.4498040E+01	*
6.	6.5704681E-01	5.7298547E+00	*	56.	1.9841094E-02	1.4517887E+01	*
7.	6.1262639E-01	6.3424810E+00	*	57.	1.8499714E-02	1.4536386E+01	*
8.	5.7120906E-01	6.9136900E+00	*	58.	1.7249019E-02	1.4553635E+01	*
9.	5.3259179E-01	7.4462817E+00	*	59.	1.6082878E-02	1.4569717E+01	*
10.	4.9658530E-01	7.9428670E+00	*	60.	1.4995576E-02	1.4584712E+01	*
11.	4.6301306E-01	8.4058800E+00	*	61.	1.3981783E-02	1.4598693E+01	*
12.	4.3171052E-01	8.8375905E+00	*	62.	1.3036528E-02	1.4611729E+01	*
13.	4.0252422E-01	9.2401147E+00	*	63.	1.2155178E-02	1.4623884E+01	*
14.	3.7531109E-01	9.6154257E+00	*	64.	1.1333413E-02	1.4635217E+01	*
15.	3.4993774E-01	9.9653634E+00	*	65.	1.0567204E-02	1.4645784E+01	*
16.	3.2627979E-01	1.0291643E+01	*	66.	9.8527960E-03	1.4655636E+01	*
17.	3.0421126E-01	1.0595864E+01	*	67.	9.1866861E-03	1.4664822E+01	*
18.	2.8365402E-01	1.0879518E+01	*	68.	8.5656093E-03	1.4673387E+01	*
19.	2.6447726E-01	1.1143995E+01	*	69.	7.9865212E-03	1.4681373E+01	*
20.	2.4659696E-01	1.1390591E+01	*	70.	7.4465830E-03	1.4688819E+01	*
21.	2.2992548E-01	1.1620516E+01	*	71.	6.9431480E-03	1.4695762E+01	*
22.	2.1438110E-01	1.1834897E+01	*	72.	6.4737483E-03	1.4702235E+01	*
23.	1.9988761E-01	1.2034784E+01	*	73.	6.0360829E-03	1.4708271E+01	*
24.	1.8637397E-01	1.2221157E+01	*	74.	5.6280063E-03	1.4713899E+01	*
25.	1.7377394E-01	1.2394930E+01	*	75.	5.2475183E-03	1.4719146E+01	*
26.	1.6202575E-01	1.2556955E+01	*	76.	4.8927537E-03	1.4724038E+01	*
27.	1.5107180E-01	1.2708026E+01	*	77.	4.5619733E-03	1.4728599E+01	*
28.	1.4085842E-01	1.2848884E+01	*	78.	4.2535557E-03	1.4732852E+01	*
29.	1.3133552E-01	1.2980219E+01	*	79.	3.9659890E-03	1.4736817E+01	*
30.	1.2245642E-01	1.3102675E+01	*	80.	3.6978637E-03	1.4740514E+01	*
31.	1.1417761E-01	1.3216852E+01	*	81.	3.4478652E-03	1.4743961E+01	*
32.	1.0645850E-01	1.3323310E+01	*	82.	3.2147682E-03	1.4747175E+01	*
33.	9.9261251E-02	1.3422571E+01	*	83.	2.9974300E-03	1.4750172E+01	*
34.	9.2550577E-02	1.3515121E+01	*	84.	2.7947852E-03	1.4752966E+01	*
35.	8.6293586E-02	1.3601414E+01	*	85.	2.6058405E-03	1.4755571E+01	*
36.	8.0459606E-02	1.3681873E+01	*	86.	2.4296695E-03	1.4758000E+01	*
37.	7.5020040E-02	1.3756893E+01	*	87.	2.2654089E-03	1.4760265E+01	*
38.	6.9948221E-02	1.3826841E+01	*	88.	2.1122532E-03	1.4762377E+01	*
39.	6.5219289E-02	1.3892060E+01	*	89.	1.9694518E-03	1.4764346E+01	*
40.	6.0810062E-02	1.3952870E+01	*	90.	1.8363047E-03	1.4766182E+01	*
41.	5.6698926E-02	1.4009568E+01	*	91.	1.7121592E-03	1.4767894E+01	*
42.	5.2865728E-02	1.4062433E+01	*	92.	1.5964066E-03	1.4769490E+01	*
43.	4.9291678E-02	1.4111724E+01	*	93.	1.4884797E-03	1.4770978E+01	*
44.	4.5959256E-02	1.4157683E+01	*	94.	1.3874492E-03	1.4772365E+01	*
45.	4.2852126E-02	1.4200535E+01	*	95.	1.2940221E-03	1.4773659E+01	*
46.	3.9955058E-02	1.4240490E+01	*	96.	1.2065382E-03	1.4774865E+01	*
47.	3.7253445E-02	1.4277743E+01	*	97.	1.1249687E-03	1.4775999E+01	*
48.	3.4735258E-02	1.4312478E+01	*	98.	1.0489139E-03	1.4777037E+01	*
49.	3.2386940E-02	1.4344864E+01	*	99.	9.7800066E-04	1.4778015E+01	*
50.	3.0197383E-02	1.4375061E+01	*	100.	9.1188196E-04	1.4778926E+01	*

$-RX$

X	E $-RX$	SUM OF E $-RX$	*	X	E $-RX$	SUM OF E $-RX$	*
0.	1.0000000E+00	1.0000000E+00	*	50.	2.8724639E-02	1.4200027E+01	*
1.	9.3146188E-01	1.9314618E+00	*	51.	2.6755907E-02	1.4226782E+01	*
2.	8.6762125E-01	2.7990830E+00	*	52.	2.4922107E-02	1.4251704E+01	*
3.	8.0815613E-01	3.6072391E+00	*	53.	2.3213993E-02	1.4274917E+01	*
4.	7.5276664E-01	4.3600057E+00	*	54.	2.1622950E-02	1.4296539E+01	*
5.	7.0117344E-01	5.0611791E+00	*	55.	2.0140954E-02	1.4316679E+01	*
6.	6.5311633E-01	5.7142954E+00	*	56.	1.8760531E-02	1.4335439E+01	*
7.	6.0835298E-01	6.3226483E+00	*	57.	1.7474720E-02	1.4352913E+01	*
8.	5.6665762E-01	6.8893059E+00	*	58.	1.6277035E-02	1.4369190E+01	*
9.	5.2781997E-01	7.4171258E+00	*	59.	1.5161438E-02	1.4384351E+01	*
10.	4.9164419E-01	7.9087699E+00	*	60.	1.4122302E-02	1.4398473E+01	*
11.	4.5794783E-01	8.3667177E+00	*	61.	1.3154386E-02	1.4411627E+01	*
12.	4.2656095E-01	8.7932786E+00	*	62.	1.2252809E-02	1.4423879E+01	*
13.	3.9732527E-01	9.1906038E+00	*	63.	1.1413025E-02	1.4435292E+01	*
14.	3.7009335E-01	9.5606971E+00	*	64.	1.0630798E-02	1.4445922E+01	*
15.	3.4472785E-01	9.9054249E+00	*	65.	9.9021834E-03	1.4455824E+01	*
16.	3.2110085E-01	1.0226525E+01	*	66.	9.2235064E-03	1.4465047E+01	*
17.	2.9909321E-01	1.0525618E+01	*	67.	8.5913447E-03	1.4473638E+01	*
18.	2.7859393E-01	1.0804211E+01	*	68.	8.0025102E-03	1.4481640E+01	*
19.	2.5949962E-01	1.1063710E+01	*	69.	7.4540333E-03	1.4489094E+01	*
20.	2.4171401E-01	1.1305424E+01	*	70.	6.9431480E-03	1.4496037E+01	*
21.	2.2514739E-01	1.1530571E+01	*	71.	6.4672777E-03	1.4502504E+01	*
22.	2.0971621E-01	1.1740287E+01	*	72.	6.0240228E-03	1.4508528E+01	*
23.	1.9534266E-01	1.1935629E+01	*	73.	5.6111476E-03	1.4514139E+01	*
24.	1.8195424E-01	1.2117583E+01	*	74.	5.2265702E-03	1.4519365E+01	*
25.	1.6948344E-01	1.2287066E+01	*	75.	4.8683510E-03	1.4524233E+01	*
26.	1.5786737E-01	1.2444933E+01	*	76.	4.5346834E-03	1.4528767E+01	*
27.	1.4704744E-01	1.2591980E+01	*	77.	4.2238848E-03	1.4532990E+01	*
28.	1.3696908E-01	1.2728949E+01	*	78.	3.9343877E-03	1.4536924E+01	*
29.	1.2758148E-01	1.2856530E+01	*	79.	3.6647322E-03	1.4540588E+01	*
30.	1.1883729E-01	1.2975367E+01	*	80.	3.4135584E-03	1.4544001E+01	*
31.	1.1069241E-01	1.3086059E+01	*	81.	3.1795995E-03	1.4547180E+01	*
32.	1.0310576E-01	1.3189164E+01	*	82.	2.9616758E-03	1.4550141E+01	*
33.	9.6039088E-02	1.3285203E+01	*	83.	2.7586882E-03	1.4552899E+01	*
34.	8.9456750E-02	1.3374659E+01	*	84.	2.5696129E-03	1.4555468E+01	*
35.	8.3325554E-02	1.3457984E+01	*	85.	2.3934965E-03	1.4557861E+01	*
36.	7.7614578E-02	1.3535598E+01	*	86.	2.2294508E-03	1.4560090E+01	*
37.	7.2295022E-02	1.3607893E+01	*	87.	2.0766484E-03	1.4562166E+01	*
38.	6.7340058E-02	1.3675233E+01	*	88.	1.9343189E-03	1.4564100E+01	*
39.	6.2724698E-02	1.3737957E+01	*	89.	1.8017443E-03	1.4565901E+01	*
40.	5.8425665E-02	1.3796382E+01	*	90.	1.6782561E-03	1.4567579E+01	*
41.	5.4421281E-02	1.3850803E+01	*	91.	1.5632316E-03	1.4569142E+01	*
42.	5.0691349E-02	1.3901494E+01	*	92.	1.4560907E-03	1.4570598E+01	*
43.	4.7217060E-02	1.3948711E+01	*	93.	1.3562930E-03	1.4571954E+01	*
44.	4.3980892E-02	1.3992691E+01	*	94.	1.2633352E-03	1.4573217E+01	*
45.	4.0966525E-02	1.4033657E+01	*	95.	1.1767486E-03	1.4574393E+01	*
46.	3.8158757E-02	1.4071815E+01	*	96.	1.0960965E-03	1.4575509E+01	*
47.	3.5543428E-02	1.4107358E+01	*	97.	1.0209721E-03	1.4576509E+01	*
48.	3.3107348E-02	1.4140465E+01	*	98.	9.5099666E-04	1.4577459E+01	*
49.	3.0838233E-02	1.4171303E+01	*	99.	8.8581715E-04	1.4578344E+01	*
50.	2.8724639E-02	1.4200027E+01	*	100.	8.2510492E-04	1.4579169E+01	*

$-RX$

X	E $-RX$	SUM OF E $-RX$	*	X	E $-RX$	SUM OF E $-RX$	*
0.	1.0000000E+00	1.0000000E+00	*	50.	2.7323722E-02	1.4028871E+01	*
1.	9.3053089E-01	1.9305308E+00	*	51.	2.5425567E-02	1.4054296E+01	*
2.	8.6588774E-01	2.7964185E+00	*	52.	2.3659276E-02	1.4077955E+01	*
3.	8.0573530E-01	3.6021538E+00	*	53.	2.2015687E-02	1.4099970E+01	*
4.	7.4976159E-01	4.3519153E+00	*	54.	2.0486277E-02	1.4120456E+01	*
5.	6.9767632E-01	5.0495916E+00	*	55.	1.9063114E-02	1.4139519E+01	*
6.	6.4920937E-01	5.6988009E+00	*	56.	1.7738816E-02	1.4157257E+01	*
7.	6.0410938E-01	6.3029102E+00	*	57.	1.6506517E-02	1.4173763E+01	*
8.	5.6214246E-01	6.8650526E+00	*	58.	1.5359824E-02	1.4189122E+01	*
9.	5.2309091E-01	7.3881435E+00	*	59.	1.4292790E-02	1.4203414E+01	*
10.	4.8675225E-01	7.8748957E+00	*	60.	1.3299883E-02	1.4216713E+01	*
11.	4.5293801E-01	8.3278337E+00	*	61.	1.2375952E-02	1.4229088E+01	*
12.	4.2147281E-01	8.7493065E+00	*	62.	1.1516206E-02	1.4240604E+01	*
13.	3.9219347E-01	9.1414999E+00	*	63.	1.0716185E-02	1.4251320E+01	*
14.	3.6494814E-01	9.5064480E+00	*	64.	9.9717418E-03	1.4261291E+01	*
15.	3.3959552E-01	9.8460435E+00	*	65.	9.2790138E-03	1.4270570E+01	*
16.	3.1600412E-01	1.0162047E+01	*	66.	8.6344090E-03	1.4279204E+01	*
17.	2.9405160E-01	1.0456098E+01	*	67.	8.0345844E-03	1.4287238E+01	*
18.	2.7362410E-01	1.0729722E+01	*	68.	7.4764290E-03	1.4294714E+01	*
19.	2.5461568E-01	1.0984337E+01	*	69.	6.9570482E-03	1.4301671E+01	*
20.	2.3692775E-01	1.1221264E+01	*	70.	6.4737483E-03	1.4308144E+01	*
21.	2.2046859E-01	1.1441732E+01	*	71.	6.0240228E-03	1.4314168E+01	*
22.	2.0515284E-01	1.1646884E+01	*	72.	5.6055393E-03	1.4319773E+01	*
23.	1.9090105E-01	1.1837785E+01	*	73.	5.2161275E-03	1.4324989E+01	*
24.	1.7763933E-01	1.2015424E+01	*	74.	4.8537678E-03	1.4329842E+01	*
25.	1.6529888E-01	1.2180722E+01	*	75.	4.5165809E-03	1.4334358E+01	*
26.	1.5381572E-01	1.2334537E+01	*	76.	4.2028181E-03	1.4338560E+01	*
27.	1.4313028E-01	1.2477667E+01	*	77.	3.9108520E-03	1.4342470E+01	*
28.	1.3318714E-01	1.2610854E+01	*	78.	3.6391687E-03	1.4346109E+01	*
29.	1.2393475E-01	1.2734788E+01	*	79.	3.3863589E-03	1.4349495E+01	*
30.	1.1532512E-01	1.2850113E+01	*	80.	3.1511115E-03	1.4352646E+01	*
31.	1.0731358E-01	1.2957426E+01	*	81.	2.9322066E-03	1.4355578E+01	*
32.	9.9858609E-02	1.3057284E+01	*	82.	2.7285089E-03	1.4358306E+01	*
33.	9.2921521E-02	1.3150205E+01	*	83.	2.5389618E-03	1.4360844E+01	*
34.	8.6466346E-02	1.3236671E+01	*	84.	2.3625824E-03	1.4363206E+01	*
35.	8.0459606E-02	1.3317130E+01	*	85.	2.1984559E-03	1.4365404E+01	*
36.	7.4870149E-02	1.3392000E+01	*	86.	2.0457311E-03	1.4367449E+01	*
37.	6.9668987E-02	1.3461668E+01	*	87.	1.9036160E-03	1.4369352E+01	*
38.	6.4829145E-02	1.3526497E+01	*	88.	1.7713735E-03	1.4371123E+01	*
39.	6.0325522E-02	1.3586822E+01	*	89.	1.6483178E-03	1.4372771E+01	*
40.	5.6134762E-02	1.3642956E+01	*	90.	1.5338106E-03	1.4374304E+01	*
41.	5.2235130E-02	1.3695191E+01	*	91.	1.4272582E-03	1.4375731E+01	*
42.	4.8606403E-02	1.3743797E+01	*	92.	1.3281078E-03	1.4377059E+01	*
43.	4.5229760E-02	1.3789026E+01	*	93.	1.2358454E-03	1.4378294E+01	*
44.	4.2087689E-02	1.3831113E+01	*	94.	1.1499923E-03	1.4379443E+01	*
45.	3.9163895E-02	1.3870276E+01	*	95.	1.0701033E-03	1.4380513E+01	*
46.	3.6443214E-02	1.3906719E+01	*	96.	9.9576427E-04	1.4381508E+01	*
47.	3.3911536E-02	1.3940638E+01	*	97.	9.2658942E-04	1.4382434E+01	*
48.	3.1555732E-02	1.3972185E+01	*	98.	8.6222008E-04	1.4383296E+01	*
49.	2.9363584E-02	1.4001548E+01	*	99.	8.0232242E-04	1.4384098E+01	*
50.	2.7323722E-02	1.4028871E+01	*	100.	7.4658580E-04	1.4384844E+01	*

TABULATED VALUES OF E^{-RX} WHEN R = .073

x	E^{-RX}	SUM OF E^{-RX}	*	x	E^{-RX}	SUM OF E^{-RX}	*
0.	1.0000000E+00	1.0000000E+00	*	50.	2.5991128E-02	1.3861487E+01	*
1.	9.2960082E-01	1.9296008E+00	*	51.	2.4161374E-02	1.3885648E+01	*
2.	8.6415770E-01	2.7937585E+00	*	52.	2.2460434E-02	1.3908108E+01	*
3.	8.0332171E-01	3.5970802E+00	*	53.	2.0879234E-02	1.3928987E+01	*
4.	7.4678853E-01	4.3438487E+00	*	54.	1.9409357E-02	1.3948396E+01	*
5.	6.9419664E-01	5.0380453E+00	*	55.	1.8042954E-02	1.3966643E+01	*
6.	6.4532578E-01	5.6833710E+00	*	56.	1.6772745E-02	1.3983210E+01	*
7.	5.9989538E-01	6.2832663E+00	*	57.	1.5591958E-02	1.3998801E+01	*
8.	5.5766324E-01	6.8409295E+00	*	58.	1.4494297E-02	1.4013295E+01	*
9.	5.1840421E-01	7.3593337E+00	*	59.	1.3473910E-02	1.4026768E+01	*
10.	4.8190898E-01	7.8412426E+00	*	60.	1.2525358E-02	1.4039293E+01	*
11.	4.4798299E-01	8.2892255E+00	*	61.	1.1643583E-02	1.4050936E+01	*
12.	4.1644536E-01	8.7056708E+00	*	62.	1.0823885E-02	1.4061759E+01	*
13.	3.8712795E-01	9.0927987E+00	*	63.	1.0061892E-02	1.4071820E+01	*
14.	3.5987447E-01	9.4526731E+00	*	64.	9.3535437E-03	1.4081173E+01	*
15.	3.3453960E-01	9.7872127E+00	*	65.	8.6950619E-03	1.4089868E+01	*
16.	3.1098829E-01	1.0098200E+01	*	66.	8.0829368E-03	1.4097950E+01	*
17.	2.8909497E-01	1.0387294E+01	*	67.	7.5139048E-03	1.4105463E+01	*
18.	2.6874293E-01	1.0656036E+01	*	68.	6.9849321E-03	1.4112447E+01	*
19.	2.4982365E-01	1.0905859E+01	*	69.	6.4931987E-03	1.4118940E+01	*
20.	2.3223627E-01	1.1138095E+01	*	70.	6.0360829E-03	1.4124976E+01	*
21.	2.1588703E-01	1.1353982E+01	*	71.	5.6111476E-03	1.4130587E+01	*
22.	2.0068876E-01	1.1554670E+01	*	72.	5.2161275E-03	1.4135803E+01	*
23.	1.8656044E-01	1.1741230E+01	*	73.	4.8489165E-03	1.4140651E+01	*
24.	1.7342674E-01	1.1914656E+01	*	74.	4.5075567E-03	1.4145158E+01	*
25.	1.6121764E-01	1.2075873E+01	*	75.	4.1902285E-03	1.4149344E+01	*
26.	1.4986805E-01	1.2225541E+01	*	76.	3.8953399E-03	1.4153243E+01	*
27.	1.3931746E-01	1.2365058E+01	*	77.	3.6210182E-03	1.4156864E+01	*
28.	1.2950963E-01	1.2494567E+01	*	78.	3.3661015E-03	1.4160230E+01	*
29.	1.2039226E-01	1.2614959E+01	*	79.	3.1291308E-03	1.4163359E+01	*
30.	1.1191674E-01	1.2726887E+01	*	80.	2.9088426E-03	1.4166267E+01	*
31.	1.0403790E-01	1.2830912E+01	*	81.	2.7040625E-03	1.4168971E+01	*
32.	9.6713720E-02	1.2927625E+01	*	82.	2.5136987E-03	1.4171484E+01	*
33.	8.9905154E-02	1.3017530E+01	*	83.	2.3367364E-03	1.4173820E+01	*
34.	8.3575906E-02	1.3101105E+01	*	84.	2.1722321E-03	1.4175992E+01	*
35.	7.7692231E-02	1.3178797E+01	*	85.	2.0193088E-03	1.4178011E+01	*
36.	7.2222763E-02	1.3251019E+01	*	86.	1.8771511E-03	1.4179888E+01	*
37.	6.7133408E-02	1.3318157E+01	*	87.	1.7450012E-03	1.4181633E+01	*
38.	6.2411857E-02	1.3380568E+01	*	88.	1.6221546E-03	1.4183255E+01	*
39.	5.8018114E-02	1.3438586E+01	*	89.	1.5079562E-03	1.4184762E+01	*
40.	5.3933687E-02	1.3492519E+01	*	90.	1.4017974E-03	1.4186163E+01	*
41.	5.0136800E-02	1.3542655E+01	*	91.	1.3031120E-03	1.4187466E+01	*
42.	4.6607211E-02	1.3589262E+01	*	92.	1.2113740E-03	1.4188677E+01	*
43.	4.3326102E-02	1.3632588E+01	*	93.	1.1260943E-03	1.4189803E+01	*
44.	4.0275980E-02	1.3672863E+01	*	94.	1.0468181E-03	1.4190849E+01	*
45.	3.7440585E-02	1.3710303E+01	*	95.	9.7312306E-04	1.4191822E+01	*
46.	3.4804798E-02	1.3745107E+01	*	96.	9.0461600E-04	1.4192726E+01	*
47.	3.2354569E-02	1.3777461E+01	*	97.	8.4093179E-04	1.4193566E+01	*
48.	3.0076835E-02	1.3807537E+01	*	98.	7.8173069E-04	1.4194347E+01	*
49.	2.7959450E-02	1.3835496E+01	*	99.	7.2669768E-04	1.4195073E+01	*
50.	2.5991128E-02	1.3861487E+01	*	100.	6.7553677E-04	1.4195748E+01	*

TABULATED VALUES OF E^{-RX} WHEN R = .074

x	E^{-RX}	SUM OF E^{-RX}	*	x	E^{-RX}	SUM OF E^{-RX}	*
0.	1.0000000E+00	1.0000000E+00	*	50.	2.4723526E-02	1.3697769E+01	*
1.	9.2867169E-01	1.9286716E+00	*	51.	2.2960039E-02	1.3720729E+01	*
2.	8.6243111E-01	2.7911027E+00	*	52.	2.1322338E-02	1.3742051E+01	*
3.	8.0091536E-01	3.5920180E+00	*	53.	1.9801452E-02	1.3761852E+01	*
4.	7.4378742E-01	4.3358054E+00	*	54.	1.8389048E-02	1.3780241E+01	*
5.	6.9073432E-01	5.0265397E+00	*	55.	1.7077388E-02	1.3797318E+01	*
6.	6.4146541E-01	5.6680051E+00	*	56.	1.5859287E-02	1.3813177E+01	*
7.	5.9571077E-01	6.2637159E+00	*	57.	1.4728071E-02	1.3827905E+01	*
8.	5.5321973E-01	6.8169355E+00	*	58.	1.3677542E-02	1.3841582E+01	*
9.	5.1375950E-01	7.3306950E+00	*	59.	1.2701946E-02	1.3854283E+01	*
10.	4.7711391E-01	7.8078089E+00	*	60.	1.1795938E-02	1.3866078E+01	*
11.	4.4308218E-01	8.2508910E+00	*	61.	1.0954554E-02	1.3877032E+01	*
12.	4.1147788E-01	8.6623688E+00	*	62.	1.0173184E-02	1.3887205E+01	*
13.	3.8212786E-01	9.0444966E+00	*	63.	9.4475483E-03	1.3896652E+01	*
14.	3.5487133E-01	9.3993679E+00	*	64.	8.7736707E-03	1.3905425E+01	*
15.	3.2955896E-01	9.7289268E+00	*	65.	8.1478596E-03	1.3913572E+01	*
16.	3.0605207E-01	1.0034978E+01	*	66.	7.5666866E-03	1.3921138E+01	*
17.	2.8422190E-01	1.0319199E+01	*	67.	7.0269677E-03	1.3928164E+01	*
18.	2.6394883E-01	1.0583147E+01	*	68.	6.5257459E-03	1.3934689E+01	*
19.	2.4512181E-01	1.0828268E+01	*	69.	6.0602756E-03	1.3940749E+01	*
20.	2.2763766E-01	1.1055905E+01	*	70.	5.6280063E-03	1.3946377E+01	*
21.	2.1140067E-01	1.1267305E+01	*	71.	5.2265702E-03	1.3951603E+01	*
22.	1.9632182E-01	1.1463626E+01	*	72.	4.8537674E-03	1.3956456E+01	*
23.	1.8231852E-01	1.1645944E+01	*	73.	4.5075567E-03	1.3960963E+01	*
24.	1.6931405E-01	1.1815258E+01	*	74.	4.1860404E-03	1.3965149E+01	*
25.	1.5723716E-01	1.1972495E+01	*	75.	3.8874572E-03	1.3969036E+01	*
26.	1.4602170E-01	1.2118516E+01	*	76.	3.6101714E-03	1.3972646E+01	*
27.	1.3560622E-01	1.2254182E+01	*	77.	3.3526640E-03	1.3975998E+01	*
28.	1.2593366E-01	1.2380055E+01	*	78.	3.1135242E-03	1.3979111E+01	*
29.	1.1695102E-01	1.2497006E+01	*	79.	2.8914418E-03	1.3982002E+01	*
30.	1.0860910E-01	1.2605615E+01	*	80.	2.6852001E-03	1.3984687E+01	*
31.	1.0086220E-01	1.2706477E+01	*	81.	2.4936693E-03	1.3987180E+01	*
32.	9.3667874E-02	1.2800144E+01	*	82.	2.3158001E-03	1.3989495E+01	*
33.	8.6986703E-02	1.2887130E+01	*	83.	2.1506180E-03	1.3991645E+01	*
34.	8.0782089E-02	1.2967912E+01	*	84.	1.9972181E-03	1.3993642E+01	*
35.	7.5020040E-02	1.3042932E+01	*	85.	1.8547599E-03	1.3995496E+01	*
36.	6.9668987E-02	1.3112600E+01	*	86.	1.7224630E-03	1.3997218E+01	*
37.	6.4699616E-02	1.3177299E+01	*	87.	1.5996026E-03	1.3998817E+01	*
38.	6.0084702E-02	1.3237383E+01	*	88.	1.4855057E-03	1.4000302E+01	*
39.	5.5798962E-02	1.3293181E+01	*	89.	1.3795471E-03	1.4001681E+01	*
40.	5.1818917E-02	1.3344999E+01	*	90.	1.2811463E-03	1.4002962E+01	*
41.	4.8122761E-02	1.3393121E+01	*	91.	1.1897643E-03	1.4004151E+01	*
42.	4.4690246E-02	1.3437811E+01	*	92.	1.1049004E-03	1.4005255E+01	*
43.	4.1502566E-02	1.3479313E+01	*	93.	1.0260898E-03	1.4006281E+01	*
44.	3.8542359E-02	1.3517855E+01	*	94.	9.5290056E-04	1.4007233E+01	*
45.	3.5793105E-02	1.3553648E+01	*	95.	8.8493177E-04	1.4008117E+01	*
46.	3.3240043E-02	1.3586888E+01	*	96.	8.2181109E-04	1.4008938E+01	*
47.	3.0869087E-02	1.3617757E+01	*	97.	7.6319270E-04	1.4009701E+01	*
48.	2.8667247E-02	1.3646424E+01	*	98.	7.0875545E-04	1.4010409E+01	*
49.	2.6622461E-02	1.3673046E+01	*	99.	6.5820113E-04	1.4011067E+01	*
50.	2.4723526E-02	1.3697769E+01	*	100.	6.1125276E-04	1.4011678E+01	*

TABULATED VALUES OF E^{-RX} WHEN R = .075

X	E^{-RX}	SUM OF E^{-RX}	*	X	E^{-RX}	SUM OF E^{-RX}	*
0.	1.0000000E+00	1.0000000E+00	*	50.	2.3517745E-02	1.3537606E+01	*
1.	9.2774348E-01	1.9277434E+00	*	51.	2.1818435E-02	1.3559424E+01	*
2.	8.6070797E-01	2.7884513E+00	*	52.	2.0241911E-02	1.3579665E+01	*
3.	7.9851621E-01	3.5869675E+00	*	53.	1.8779301E-02	1.3598444E+01	*
4.	7.4081821E-01	4.3277857E+00	*	54.	1.7422374E-02	1.3615866E+01	*
5.	6.8728927E-01	5.0150749E+00	*	55.	1.6163494E-02	1.3632029E+01	*
6.	6.3762814E-01	5.6527030E+00	*	56.	1.4995576E-02	1.3647024E+01	*
7.	5.9155536E-01	6.2442583E+00	*	57.	1.3912048E-02	1.3660936E+01	*
8.	5.4881163E-01	6.7930699E+00	*	58.	1.2906812E-02	1.3673842E+01	*
9.	5.0915641E-01	7.3022263E+00	*	59.	1.1974211E-02	1.3685816E+01	*
10.	4.7236655E-01	7.7745928E+00	*	60.	1.1108996E-02	1.3696924E+01	*
11.	4.3823499E-01	8.2128277E+00	*	61.	1.0306299E-02	1.3707230E+01	*
12.	4.0656965E-01	8.6193973E+00	*	62.	9.5616019E-03	1.3716791E+01	*
13.	3.7719235E-01	8.9965896E+00	*	63.	8.8707138E-03	1.3725661E+01	*
14.	3.4993774E-01	9.3465273E+00	*	64.	8.2297470E-03	1.3733890E+01	*
15.	3.2465246E-01	9.6711797E+00	*	65.	7.6350942E-03	1.3741525E+01	*
16.	3.0119421E-01	9.9723739E+00	*	66.	7.0834089E-03	1.3748608E+01	*
17.	2.7943096E-01	1.0251804E+01	*	67.	6.5715864E-03	1.3755179E+01	*
18.	2.5924026E-01	1.0511044E+01	*	68.	6.0967665E-03	1.3761275E+01	*
19.	2.4050846E-01	1.0751552E+01	*	69.	5.6562169E-03	1.3766931E+01	*
20.	2.2313015E-01	1.0974682E+01	*	70.	5.2475183E-03	1.3772178E+01	*
21.	2.0700755E-01	1.1181689E+01	*	71.	4.8683510E-03	1.3777046E+01	*
22.	1.9204990E-01	1.1373738E+01	*	72.	4.5165809E-03	1.3781562E+01	*
23.	1.7817305E-01	1.1551911E+01	*	73.	4.1902285E-03	1.3785752E+01	*
24.	1.6529888E-01	1.1717209E+01	*	74.	3.8874572E-03	1.3789639E+01	*
25.	1.5335496E-01	1.1870563E+01	*	75.	3.6065631E-03	1.3793245E+01	*
26.	1.4227407E-01	1.2012837E+01	*	76.	3.3459654E-03	1.3796590E+01	*
27.	1.3199384E-01	1.2144830E+01	*	77.	3.1041976E-03	1.3799694E+01	*
28.	1.2245642E-01	1.2267286E+01	*	78.	2.8798991E-03	1.3802573E+01	*
29.	1.1360815E-01	1.2380894E+01	*	79.	2.6718076E-03	1.3805244E+01	*
30.	1.0539922E-01	1.2486293E+01	*	80.	2.4787521E-03	1.3807722E+01	*
31.	9.7783443E-02	1.2584076E+01	*	81.	2.2996461E-03	1.3810021E+01	*
32.	9.0717953E-02	1.2674793E+01	*	82.	2.1334817E-03	1.3812154E+01	*
33.	8.4162990E-02	1.2758955E+01	*	83.	1.9793238E-03	1.3814133E+01	*
34.	7.8081665E-02	1.2837036E+01	*	84.	1.8363047E-03	1.3815969E+01	*
35.	7.2439756E-02	1.2909475E+01	*	85.	1.7036197E-03	1.3817672E+01	*
36.	6.7205512E-02	1.2976680E+01	*	86.	1.5805221E-03	1.3819252E+01	*
37.	6.2349476E-02	1.3039029E+01	*	87.	1.4663191E-03	1.3820718E+01	*
38.	5.7844320E-02	1.3096873E+01	*	88.	1.3603680E-03	1.3822078E+01	*
39.	5.3664691E-02	1.3150537E+01	*	89.	1.2620725E-03	1.3823340E+01	*
40.	4.9787068E-02	1.3200324E+01	*	90.	1.1708796E-03	1.3824510E+01	*
41.	4.6189628E-02	1.3246513E+01	*	91.	1.0862759E-03	1.3825596E+01	*
42.	4.2852126E-02	1.3289365E+01	*	92.	1.0077854E-03	1.3826603E+01	*
43.	3.9755781E-02	1.3329120E+01	*	93.	9.3496636E-04	1.3827537E+01	*
44.	3.6883163E-02	1.3366003E+01	*	94.	8.6740495E-04	1.3828404E+01	*
45.	3.4218118E-02	1.3400221E+01	*	95.	8.0473300E-04	1.3829208E+01	*
46.	3.1745636E-02	1.3431966E+01	*	96.	7.4658580E-04	1.3829954E+01	*
47.	2.9451807E-02	1.3461417E+01	*	97.	6.9264011E-04	1.3830646E+01	*
48.	2.7323722E-02	1.3488740E+01	*	98.	6.4259235E-04	1.3831288E+01	*
49.	2.5349405E-02	1.3514089E+01	*	99.	5.9616087E-04	1.3831884E+01	*
50.	2.3517745E-02	1.3537606E+01	*	100.	5.5308436E-04	1.3832437E+01	*

TABULATED VALUES OF E^{-RX} WHEN R = .076

X	E^{-RX}	SUM OF E^{-RX}	*	X	E^{-RX}	SUM OF E^{-RX}	*
0.	1.0000000E+00	1.0000000E+00	*	50.	2.2370771E-02	1.3380899E+01	*
1.	9.2681620E-01	1.9268162E+00	*	51.	2.0733593E-02	1.3401632E+01	*
2.	8.5898827E-01	2.7858044E+00	*	52.	1.9216230E-02	1.3420848E+01	*
3.	7.9612425E-01	3.5819286E+00	*	53.	1.7809914E-02	1.3438657E+01	*
4.	7.3786066E-01	4.3197894E+00	*	54.	1.6506517E-02	1.3455163E+01	*
5.	6.8381640E-01	5.0036508E+00	*	55.	1.5298507E-02	1.3470461E+01	*
6.	6.3381383E-01	5.6374644E+00	*	56.	1.4178904E-02	1.3484639E+01	*
7.	5.8742893E-01	6.2249935E+00	*	57.	1.3141238E-02	1.3497780E+01	*
8.	5.4443865E-01	6.7693321E+00	*	58.	1.2179512E-02	1.3509955E+01	*
9.	5.0459456E-01	7.2739266E+00	*	59.	1.1288170E-02	1.3521247E+01	*
10.	4.6766642E-01	7.7415930E+00	*	60.	1.0462058E-02	1.3531709E+01	*
11.	4.3344082E-01	8.1750338E+00	*	61.	9.6964057E-03	1.3541405E+01	*
12.	4.0171997E-01	8.5767537E+00	*	62.	8.9867860E-03	1.3550391E+01	*
13.	3.7232058E-01	8.9490742E+00	*	63.	8.3290989E-03	1.3558720E+01	*
14.	3.4507275E-01	9.2941469E+00	*	64.	7.7195438E-03	1.3566439E+01	*
15.	3.1981902E-01	9.6139659E+00	*	65.	7.1545983E-03	1.3573593E+01	*
16.	2.9641345E-01	9.9103793E+00	*	66.	6.6309977E-03	1.3580223E+01	*
17.	2.7472079E-01	1.0185100E+01	*	67.	6.1457161E-03	1.3586368E+01	*
18.	2.5461568E-01	1.0439715E+01	*	68.	5.6959493E-03	1.3592063E+01	*
19.	2.3598194E-01	1.0675696E+01	*	69.	5.2790981E-03	1.3597342E+01	*
20.	2.1871188E-01	1.0894407E+01	*	70.	4.8927543E-03	1.3602234E+01	*
21.	2.0270572E-01	1.1097112E+01	*	71.	4.5346834E-03	1.3606768E+01	*
22.	1.8787094E-01	1.1284982E+01	*	72.	4.2028181E-03	1.3610970E+01	*
23.	1.7412183E-01	1.1459103E+01	*	73.	3.8952399E-03	1.3614865E+01	*
24.	1.6137894E-01	1.1620481E+01	*	74.	3.6101714E-03	1.3618476E+01	*
25.	1.4956861E-01	1.1770049E+01	*	75.	3.3459654E-03	1.3621820E+01	*
26.	1.3862261E-01	1.1908671E+01	*	76.	3.1010950E-03	1.3624921E+01	*
27.	1.2847769E-01	1.2037148E+01	*	77.	2.8741451E-03	1.3627795E+01	*
28.	1.1907520E-01	1.2156223E+01	*	78.	2.6638042E-03	1.3630458E+01	*
29.	1.1036083E-01	1.2266583E+01	*	79.	2.4688569E-03	1.3632926E+01	*
30.	1.0228420E-01	1.2368867E+01	*	80.	2.2881766E-03	1.3635214E+01	*
31.	9.4798660E-02	1.2463665E+01	*	81.	2.1207191E-03	1.3637334E+01	*
32.	8.7860934E-02	1.2551525E+01	*	82.	1.9655169E-03	1.3639299E+01	*
33.	8.1430938E-02	1.2632955E+01	*	83.	1.8216729E-03	1.3641120E+01	*
34.	7.5471513E-02	1.2708426E+01	*	84.	1.6883560E-03	1.3642808E+01	*
35.	6.9948221E-02	1.2778374E+01	*	85.	1.5647957E-03	1.3644372E+01	*
36.	6.4829145E-02	1.2843203E+01	*	86.	1.4502780E-03	1.3645822E+01	*
37.	6.0084702E-02	1.2903287E+01	*	87.	1.3441411E-03	1.3647166E+01	*
38.	5.5687476E-02	1.2958974E+01	*	88.	1.2457718E-03	1.3648411E+01	*
39.	5.1612055E-02	1.3010586E+01	*	89.	1.1546015E-03	1.3649565E+01	*
40.	4.7834889E-02	1.3058420E+01	*	90.	1.0701033E-03	1.3650635E+01	*
41.	4.4334150E-02	1.3102754E+01	*	91.	9.9178917E-04	1.3651627E+01	*
42.	4.1089609E-02	1.3143843E+01	*	92.	9.1920627E-04	1.3652545E+01	*
43.	3.8082515E-02	1.3181925E+01	*	93.	8.5193527E-04	1.3653394E+01	*
44.	3.5295492E-02	1.3217220E+01	*	94.	7.8958742E-04	1.3654185E+01	*
45.	3.2712434E-02	1.3249932E+01	*	95.	7.3180241E-04	1.3654916E+01	*
46.	3.0318414E-02	1.3280250E+01	*	96.	6.7824634E-04	1.3655594E+01	*
47.	2.8099598E-02	1.3308349E+01	*	97.	6.2860970E-04	1.3656222E+01	*
48.	2.6043162E-02	1.3334392E+01	*	98.	5.8260565E-04	1.3656804E+01	*
49.	2.4137225E-02	1.3358529E+01	*	99.	5.3996836E-04	1.3657343E+01	*
50.	2.2370771E-02	1.3380899E+01	*	100.	5.0045143E-04	1.3657843E+01	*

TABULATED VALUES OF E^{−KX}   WHEN R = .077

X	E^{-RX}	SUM OF E^{-RX}	=	X	E^{-RX}	SUM OF E^{-RX}	=
0.	1.0000000E+00	1.0000000E+00	=	50.	2.1279736E-02	1.3227554E+01	=
1.	9.2588985E-01	1.9258898E+00	=	51.	1.9702692E-02	1.3247256E+01	=
2.	8.5727201E-01	2.7831619E+00	=	52.	1.8242522E-02	1.3265498E+01	=
3.	7.9373946E-01	3.5769012E+00	=	53.	1.6890566E-02	1.3282388E+01	=
4.	7.3491531E-01	4.3118165E+00	=	54.	1.5638804E-02	1.3298026E+01	=
5.	6.8045063E-01	4.9922671E+00	=	55.	1.4479810E-02	1.3312505E+01	=
6.	6.3002233E-01	5.6222894E+00	=	56.	1.3406709E-02	1.3325911E+01	=
7.	5.8233129E-01	6.2056206E+00	=	57.	1.2413136E-02	1.3338324E+01	=
8.	5.4010052E-01	6.7457211E+00	=	58.	1.1493196E-02	1.3349817E+01	=
9.	5.0007359E-01	7.2457946E+00	=	59.	1.0641434E-02	1.3360458E+01	=
10.	4.6301306E-01	7.7088076E+00	=	60.	9.8527960E-03	1.3370310E+01	=
11.	4.2869910E-01	8.1375067E+00	=	61.	9.1226031E-03	1.3379432E+01	=
12.	3.9692814E-01	8.5344348E+00	=	62.	8.4465263E-03	1.3387878E+01	=
13.	3.6751174E-01	8.9019465E+00	=	63.	7.8205530E-03	1.3395698E+01	=
14.	3.4027539E-01	9.2422218E+00	=	64.	7.2409707E-03	1.3402938E+01	=
15.	3.1505753E-01	9.5572793E+00	=	65.	6.7043433E-03	1.3409642E+01	=
16.	2.9170857E-01	9.8489878E+00	=	66.	6.2074816E-03	1.3415849E+01	=
17.	2.7009001E-01	1.0119077E+01	=	67.	5.7474442E-03	1.3421596E+01	=
18.	2.5007360E-01	1.0369150E+01	=	68.	5.3215003E-03	1.3426917E+01	=
19.	2.3154060E-01	1.0600690E+01	=	69.	4.9271231E-03	1.3431844E+01	=
20.	2.1438110E-01	1.0815071E+01	=	70.	4.5619733E-03	1.3436405E+01	=
21.	1.9849328E-01	1.1013564E+01	=	71.	4.2238848E-03	1.3440628E+01	=
22.	1.8378291E-01	1.1197346E+01	=	72.	3.9108520E-03	1.3444538E+01	=
23.	1.7016274E-01	1.1367508E+01	=	73.	3.6210182E-03	1.3448159E+01	=
24.	1.5755195E-01	1.1525059E+01	=	74.	3.3526640E-03	1.3451511E+01	=
25.	1.4585755E-01	1.1670934E+01	=	75.	3.1041976E-03	1.3454615E+01	=
26.	1.3506488E-01	1.1805998E+01	=	76.	2.8741451E-03	1.3457489E+01	=
27.	1.2505520E-01	1.1931053E+01	=	77.	2.6611417E-03	1.3460150E+01	=
28.	1.1578734E-01	1.2046840E+01	=	78.	2.4639241E-03	1.3462613E+01	=
29.	1.0720632E-01	1.2154046E+01	=	79.	2.2813224E-03	1.3464894E+01	=
30.	9.9261251E-02	1.2253307E+01	=	80.	2.1122532E-03	1.3467006E+01	=
31.	9.1904985E-02	1.2345211E+01	=	81.	1.955713E-03	1.3468961E+01	=
32.	8.5093893E-02	1.2430304E+01	=	82.	1.8107756E-03	1.3470771E+01	=
33.	7.8787572E-02	1.2509091E+01	=	83.	1.6765787E-03	1.3472447E+01	=
34.	7.2948614E-02	1.2582039E+01	=	84.	1.5523272E-03	1.3473999E+01	=
35.	6.7542381E-02	1.2649581E+01	=	85.	1.4372840E-03	1.3475436E+01	=
36.	6.2536805E-02	1.2712117E+01	=	86.	1.330766E-03	1.3476766E+01	=
37.	5.7902194E-02	1.2770019E+01	=	87.	1.2321434E-03	1.3477998E+01	=
38.	5.3611053E-02	1.2823630E+01	=	88.	1.1408290E-03	1.3479138E+01	=
39.	4.9637930E-02	1.2873267E+01	=	89.	1.0562820E-03	1.3480194E+01	=
40.	4.5959256E-02	1.2919226E+01	=	90.	9.7800086E-04	1.3481172E+01	=
41.	4.2553209E-02	1.2961779E+01	=	91.	9.0552107E-04	1.3482077E+01	=
42.	3.9399584E-02	1.3001178E+01	=	92.	8.3841277E-04	1.3482915E+01	=
43.	3.6479675E-02	1.3037657E+01	=	93.	7.7627788E-04	1.3483691E+01	=
44.	3.3776161E-02	1.3071433E+01	=	94.	7.1874781E-04	1.3484409E+01	=
45.	3.1273005E-02	1.3102706E+01	=	95.	6.6548131E-04	1.3485074E+01	=
46.	2.8955358E-02	1.3131661E+01	=	96.	6.1616239E-04	1.3485690E+01	=
47.	2.6809472E-02	1.3158470E+01	=	97.	5.7049850E-04	1.3486260E+01	=
48.	2.4822618E-02	1.3183292E+01	=	98.	5.2821878E-04	1.3486788E+01	=
49.	2.2983010E-02	1.3206275E+01	=	99.	4.8907241E-04	1.3487277E+01	=
50.	2.1279736E-02	1.3227554E+01	=	100.	4.5282718E-04	1.3487729E+01	=

TABULATED VALUES OF E^{−RX}   WHEN R = .078

X	E^{-RX}	SUM OF E^{-RX}	=	X	E^{-RX}	SUM OF E^{-RX}	=
0.	1.0000000E+00	1.0000000E+00	=	50.	2.0241911E-02	1.3077472E+01	=
1.	9.2496442E-01	1.9249644E+00	=	51.	1.8723047E-02	1.3096195E+01	=
2.	8.5555918E-01	2.7805235E+00	=	52.	1.7318153E-02	1.3113513E+01	=
3.	7.9136191E-01	3.5718853E+00	=	53.	1.6018675E-02	1.3129531E+01	=
4.	7.3198152E-01	4.3038668E+00	=	54.	1.4816705E-02	1.3144347E+01	=
5.	6.7705687E-01	4.9809236E+00	=	55.	1.3704925E-02	1.3158050E+01	=
6.	6.2625352E-01	5.6071771E+00	=	56.	1.2676568E-02	1.3170727E+01	=
7.	5.7926223E-01	6.1864393E+00	=	57.	1.1725374E-02	1.3182452E+01	=
8.	5.3579695E-01	6.7222362E+00	=	58.	1.0845554E-02	1.3193297E+01	=
9.	4.9559312E-01	7.2178293E+00	=	59.	1.0031752E-02	1.3203328E+01	=
10.	4.5840601E-01	7.6762353E+00	=	60.	9.2790130E-03	1.3212607E+01	=
11.	4.2400925E-01	8.1002445E+00	=	61.	8.5827577E-03	1.3221189E+01	=
12.	3.9219347E-01	8.4924379E+00	=	62.	7.9387456E-03	1.3229127E+01	=
13.	3.6276501E-01	8.8552029E+00	=	63.	7.3430572E-03	1.3236470E+01	=
14.	3.3554473E-01	9.1907476E+00	=	64.	6.7920667E-03	1.3243262E+01	=
15.	3.1036694E-01	9.5011145E+00	=	65.	6.2824201E-03	1.3249544E+01	=
16.	2.8707437E-01	9.7881928E+00	=	66.	5.8110151E-03	1.3255355E+01	=
17.	2.6553728E-01	1.0053730E+01	=	67.	5.3749822E-03	1.3260729E+01	=
18.	2.4561254E-01	1.0299342E+01	=	68.	4.9716674E-03	1.3265700E+01	=
19.	2.2718286E-01	1.0526524E+01	=	69.	4.5986154E-03	1.3270298E+01	=
20.	2.1013607E-01	1.0736660E+01	=	70.	4.2535557E-03	1.3274551E+01	=
21.	1.9436839E-01	1.0931028E+01	=	71.	3.9343877E-03	1.3278486E+01	=
22.	1.7978384E-01	1.1110811E+01	=	72.	3.6391687E-03	1.3282124E+01	=
23.	1.6629366E-01	1.1277104E+01	=	73.	3.3661015E-03	1.3285490E+01	=
24.	1.5381572E-01	1.1430919E+01	=	74.	3.1135242E-03	1.3288603E+01	=
25.	1.4227407E-01	1.1573193E+01	=	75.	2.8798991E-03	1.3291482E+01	=
26.	1.3159845E-01	1.1704791E+01	=	76.	2.6638042E-03	1.3294145E+01	=
27.	1.2172388E-01	1.1826514E+01	=	77.	2.4639241E-03	1.3296608E+01	=
28.	1.1259026E-01	1.1939104E+01	=	78.	2.2790422E-03	1.3298887E+01	=
29.	1.0414199E-01	1.2043245E+01	=	79.	2.1080329E-03	1.3300995E+01	=
30.	9.6323995E-02	1.2139572E+01	=	80.	1.9498555E-03	1.3302944E+01	=
31.	8.9099638E-02	1.2228671E+01	=	81.	1.8035469E-03	1.3304747E+01	=
32.	8.2413995E-02	1.2311084E+01	=	82.	1.6682168E-03	1.3306415E+01	=
33.	7.6230014E-02	1.2387314E+01	=	83.	1.5430412E-03	1.3307958E+01	=
34.	7.0510051E-02	1.2457824E+01	=	84.	1.4272582E-03	1.3309385E+01	=
35.	6.5219289E-02	1.2523043E+01	=	85.	1.3201630E-03	1.3310705E+01	=
36.	6.0325522E-02	1.2583368E+01	=	86.	1.2211038E-03	1.3311926E+01	=
37.	5.5798962E-02	1.2639166E+01	=	87.	1.1294776E-03	1.3313055E+01	=
38.	5.1612055E-02	1.2690772E+01	=	88.	1.0447266E-03	1.3314099E+01	=
39.	4.7739315E-02	1.2738517E+01	=	89.	9.6633499E-04	1.3315065E+01	=
40.	4.4157168E-02	1.2782746E+01	=	90.	8.9382549E-04	1.3315958E+01	=
41.	4.0843809E-02	1.2823517E+01	=	91.	8.2676788E-04	1.3316784E+01	=
42.	3.7779071E-02	1.2861296E+01	=	92.	7.6472061E-04	1.3317548E+01	=
43.	3.4944296E-02	1.2896240E+01	=	93.	7.0733936E-04	1.3318255E+01	=
44.	3.2322231E-02	1.2928562E+01	=	94.	6.5426374E-04	1.3318909E+01	=
45.	2.9896914E-02	1.2958458E+01	=	95.	6.0517069E-04	1.3319514E+01	=
46.	2.7653582E-02	1.2986111E+01	=	96.	5.5976136E-04	1.3320073E+01	=
47.	2.5578579E-02	1.3011689E+01	=	97.	5.1775934E-04	1.3320590E+01	=
48.	2.3659276E-02	1.3035345E+01	=	98.	4.7890897E-04	1.3321068E+01	=
49.	2.1883899E-02	1.3057231E+01	=	99.	4.4297376E-04	1.3321510E+01	=
50.	2.0241911E-02	1.3077472E+01	=	100.	4.0973497E-04	1.3321919E+01	=

TABULATED VALUES OF E^-RX   WHEN R = .079

x	E^-RX	SUM OF E^-RX	*	x	E^-RX	SUM OF E^-RX	*
0.	1.0000000E+00	1.0000000E+00	*	50.	1.9254701E-02	1.2930566E+01	*
1.	9.2403992E-01	1.9240399E+00	*	51.	1.7792113E-02	1.2948358E+01	*
2.	8.5384977E-01	2.7778896E+00	*	52.	1.6440622E-02	1.2964798E+01	*
3.	7.8899128E-01	3.5668808E+00	*	53.	1.5191791E-02	1.2979989E+01	*
4.	7.2905944E-01	4.2959402E+00	*	54.	1.4037822E-02	1.2994026E+01	*
5.	6.7368003E-01	4.9696202E+00	*	55.	1.2971508E-02	1.3006997E+01	*
6.	6.2250725E-01	5.5921274E+00	*	56.	1.1986191E-02	1.3018983E+01	*
7.	5.7522155E-01	6.1673489E+00	*	57.	1.1075719E-02	1.3030058E+01	*
8.	5.3152768E-01	6.6988765E+00	*	58.	1.0234406E-02	1.3040292E+01	*
9.	4.9115279E-01	7.1900292E+00	*	59.	9.4570006E-03	1.3049749E+01	*
10.	4.5384479E-01	7.6438739E+00	*	60.	8.7386461E-03	1.3058487E+01	*
11.	4.1937070E-01	8.0632446E+00	*	61.	8.0748579E-03	1.3066561E+01	*
12.	3.8751527E-01	8.4507598E+00	*	62.	7.4614911E-03	1.3074022E+01	*
13.	3.5807958E-01	8.8088393E+00	*	63.	6.8947156E-03	1.3080916E+01	*
14.	3.3087983E-01	9.1397191E+00	*	64.	6.3709925E-03	1.3087286E+01	*
15.	3.0574617E-01	9.4454652E+00	*	65.	5.8870514E-03	1.3093173E+01	*
16.	2.8252167E-01	9.7279868E+00	*	66.	5.4398706E-03	1.3098612E+01	*
17.	2.6106130E-01	9.9890481E+00	*	67.	5.0266576E-03	1.3103638E+01	*
18.	2.4123107E-01	1.0230279E+01	*	68.	4.6448323E-03	1.3108282E+01	*
19.	2.2290714E-01	1.0453186E+01	*	69.	4.2920105E-03	1.3112574E+01	*
20.	2.0597509E-01	1.0659161E+01	*	70.	3.9659890E-03	1.3116539E+01	*
21.	1.9032921E-01	1.0849490E+01	*	71.	3.6647322E-03	1.3120203E+01	*
22.	1.7587179E-01	1.1025361E+01	*	72.	3.3863589E-03	1.3123589E+01	*
23.	1.6251255E-01	1.1187873E+01	*	73.	3.1291308E-03	1.3126718E+01	*
24.	1.5016809E-01	1.1338041E+01	*	74.	2.8914413E-03	1.3129609E+01	*
25.	1.3876131E-01	1.1476802E+01	*	75.	2.6718076E-03	1.3132280E+01	*
26.	1.2822099E-01	1.1605022E+01	*	76.	2.4688569E-03	1.3134748E+01	*
27.	1.1848131E-01	1.1723503E+01	*	77.	2.2813224E-03	1.3137029E+01	*
28.	1.0948146E-01	1.1832984E+01	*	78.	2.1080329E-03	1.3139137E+01	*
29.	1.0116524E-01	1.1934149E+01	*	79.	1.9479061E-03	1.3141084E+01	*
30.	9.3480726E-02	1.2027629E+01	*	80.	1.7999435E-03	1.3142883E+01	*
31.	8.6379922E-02	1.2114008E+01	*	81.	1.6632196E-03	1.3144546E+01	*
32.	7.9818497E-02	1.2193826E+01	*	82.	1.5368813E-03	1.3146082E+01	*
33.	7.3755478E-02	1.2267581E+01	*	83.	1.4201397E-03	1.3147502E+01	*
34.	6.8153006E-02	1.2335734E+01	*	84.	1.3122650E-03	1.3148814E+01	*
35.	6.2976099E-02	1.2398710E+01	*	85.	1.2125860E-03	1.3150026E+01	*
36.	5.8192429E-02	1.2456902E+01	*	86.	1.1204778E-03	1.3151146E+01	*
37.	5.3772128E-02	1.2510674E+01	*	87.	1.0353662E-03	1.3152181E+01	*
38.	4.9687593E-02	1.2560361E+01	*	88.	9.5671979E-04	1.3153137E+01	*
39.	4.5913320E-02	1.2606274E+01	*	89.	8.8404728E-04	1.3154021E+01	*
40.	4.2425741E-02	1.2648699E+01	*	90.	8.1689498E-04	1.3154837E+01	*
41.	3.9203078E-02	1.2687902E+01	*	91.	7.5484358E-04	1.3155591E+01	*
42.	3.6225208E-02	1.2724127E+01	*	92.	6.9750560E-04	1.3156288E+01	*
43.	3.3473540E-02	1.2757600E+01	*	93.	6.4452302E-04	1.3156932E+01	*
44.	3.0930887E-02	1.2788530E+01	*	94.	5.9556501E-04	1.3157527E+01	*
45.	2.8581374E-02	1.2817111E+01	*	95.	5.5032584E-04	1.3158077E+01	*
46.	2.6410331E-02	1.2843521E+01	*	96.	5.0852305E-04	1.3158585E+01	*
47.	2.4404200E-02	1.2867925E+01	*	97.	4.6989560E-04	1.3159054E+01	*
48.	2.2550455E-02	1.2890475E+01	*	98.	4.3420230E-04	1.3159488E+01	*
49.	2.0837521E-02	1.2911312E+01	*	99.	4.0122026E-04	1.3159889E+01	*
50.	1.9254701E-02	1.2930566E+01	*	100.	3.7074353E-04	1.3160259E+01	*

TABULATED VALUES OF E^-RX   WHEN R = .080

x	E^-RX	SUM OF E^-RX	*	x	E^-RX	SUM OF E^-RX	*
0.	1.0000000E+00	1.0000000E+00	*	50.	1.8315638E-02	1.2786737E+01	*
1.	9.2311634E-01	1.9231163E+00	*	51.	1.6907465E-02	1.2803644E+01	*
2.	8.5214378E-01	2.7752600E+00	*	52.	1.5607557E-02	1.2819251E+01	*
3.	7.8662786E-01	3.5618879E+00	*	53.	1.4407591E-02	1.2833658E+01	*
4.	7.2614903E-01	4.2880368E+00	*	54.	1.3299883E-02	1.2846957E+01	*
5.	6.7032004E-01	4.9583568E+00	*	55.	1.2277339E-02	1.2859234E+01	*
6.	6.1878339E-01	5.5771401E+00	*	56.	1.1333413E-02	1.2870567E+01	*
7.	5.7120906E-01	6.1483491E+00	*	57.	1.0462058E-02	1.2881029E+01	*
8.	5.2729242E-01	6.6756415E+00	*	58.	9.6576976E-03	1.2890686E+01	*
9.	4.8675225E-01	7.1623937E+00	*	59.	8.9151785E-03	1.2899601E+01	*
10.	4.4932896E-01	7.6117226E+00	*	60.	8.2297470E-03	1.2907830E+01	*
11.	4.1478291E-01	8.0265055E+00	*	61.	7.5970140E-03	1.2915427E+01	*
12.	3.8289288E-01	8.4093983E+00	*	62.	7.0129278E-03	1.2922439E+01	*
13.	3.5345468E-01	8.7628529E+00	*	63.	6.4737483E-03	1.2928912E+01	*
14.	3.2627979E-01	9.0891326E+00	*	64.	5.9760228E-03	1.2934888E+01	*
15.	3.0119421E-01	9.3903268E+00	*	65.	5.5165644E-03	1.2940404E+01	*
16.	2.7803730E-01	9.6683641E+00	*	66.	5.0924307E-03	1.2945496E+01	*
17.	2.5666077E-01	9.9250248E+00	*	67.	4.7009061E-03	1.2950196E+01	*
18.	2.3692775E-01	1.0161952E+01	*	68.	4.3394832E-03	1.2954535E+01	*
19.	2.1871268E-01	1.0380663E+01	*	69.	4.0058479E-03	1.2958540E+01	*
20.	2.0189651E-01	1.0582559E+01	*	70.	3.6978637E-03	1.2962237E+01	*
21.	1.8637397E-01	1.0768932E+01	*	71.	3.4135584E-03	1.2965650E+01	*
22.	1.7204486E-01	1.0940976E+01	*	72.	3.1511115E-03	1.2968801E+01	*
23.	1.5881742E-01	1.1099793E+01	*	73.	2.9088426E-03	1.2971709E+01	*
24.	1.4660696E-01	1.1246399E+01	*	74.	2.6852001E-03	1.2974394E+01	*
25.	1.3533528E-01	1.1381734E+01	*	75.	2.4787521E-03	1.2976872E+01	*
26.	1.2493021E-01	1.1506664E+01	*	76.	2.2881766E-03	1.2979160E+01	*
27.	1.1532512E-01	1.1621989E+01	*	77.	2.1122532E-03	1.2981272E+01	*
28.	1.0645850E-01	1.1728447E+01	*	78.	1.9498555E-03	1.2983221E+01	*
29.	9.8273585E-02	1.1826720E+01	*	79.	1.7999435E-03	1.2985020E+01	*
30.	9.0717953E-02	1.1917437E+01	*	80.	1.6615572E-03	1.2986681E+01	*
31.	8.3743225E-02	1.2001180E+01	*	81.	1.5338106E-03	1.2988214E+01	*
32.	7.7304740E-02	1.2078484E+01	*	82.	1.4158857E-03	1.2989629E+01	*
33.	7.1361269E-02	1.2149845E+01	*	83.	1.3070272E-03	1.2990936E+01	*
34.	6.5874754E-02	1.2215719E+01	*	84.	1.2065382E-03	1.2992142E+01	*
35.	6.0810062E-02	1.2276529E+01	*	85.	1.1137751E-03	1.2993255E+01	*
36.	5.6134762E-02	1.2332663E+01	*	86.	1.0281440E-03	1.2994283E+01	*
37.	5.1818917E-02	1.2384481E+01	*	87.	9.4909657E-04	1.2995232E+01	*
38.	4.7834889E-02	1.2432315E+01	*	88.	8.7612658E-04	1.2996108E+01	*
39.	4.4157168E-02	1.2476472E+01	*	89.	8.0876674E-04	1.2996916E+01	*
40.	4.0762203E-02	1.2517234E+01	*	90.	7.4658580E-04	1.2997662E+01	*
41.	3.7628256E-02	1.2554862E+01	*	91.	6.8918556E-04	1.2998351E+01	*
42.	3.4735279E-02	1.2589597E+01	*	92.	6.3619845E-04	1.2998987E+01	*
43.	3.2064685E-02	1.2621661E+01	*	93.	5.8728519E-04	1.2999574E+01	*
44.	2.9599435E-02	1.2651260E+01	*	94.	5.4213256E-04	1.3000116E+01	*
45.	2.7323722E-02	1.2678583E+01	*	95.	5.0045143E-04	1.3000616E+01	*
46.	2.5222974E-02	1.2703805E+01	*	96.	4.6197489E-04	1.3001077E+01	*
47.	2.3283740E-02	1.2727088E+01	*	97.	4.2645657E-04	1.3001503E+01	*
48.	2.1493601E-02	1.2748581E+01	*	98.	3.9366904E-04	1.3001890E+01	*
49.	1.9841094E-02	1.2768422E+01	*	99.	3.6340232E-04	1.3002259E+01	*
50.	1.8315638E-02	1.2786737E+01	*	100.	3.3546262E-04	1.3002594E+01	*

x	E^{-RX}	SUM OF E^{-RX}	*	x	E^{-RX}	SUM OF E^{-RX}	*
0.	1.0000000E+00	1.0000000E+00	*	50.	1.7422374E-02	1.2645914E+01	*
1.	9.2219369E-01	1.9221934E+00	*	51.	1.6066803E-02	1.2661980E+01	*
2.	8.5044120E-01	2.7726348E+00	*	52.	1.4816705E-02	1.2676796E+01	*
3.	7.8427151E-01	3.5569063E+00	*	53.	1.3663472E-02	1.2690459E+01	*
4.	7.2325024E-01	4.2801565E+00	*	54.	1.2600736E-02	1.2703059E+01	*
5.	6.6697680E-01	4.9471333E+00	*	55.	1.1620319E-02	1.2714679E+01	*
6.	6.1508180E-01	5.5622151E+00	*	56.	1.0716185E-02	1.2725395E+01	*
7.	5.6722456E-01	6.1294396E+00	*	57.	9.8823988E-03	1.2735277E+01	*
8.	5.2309091E-01	6.6525305E+00	*	58.	9.1134458E-03	1.2744390E+01	*
9.	4.8239113E-01	7.1349216E+00	*	59.	8.4043991E-03	1.2752794E+01	*
10.	4.4485806E-01	7.5797796E+00	*	60.	7.7504838E-03	1.2760544E+01	*
11.	4.1024530E-01	7.9900249E+00	*	61.	7.1474373E-03	1.2767691E+01	*
12.	3.7832562E-01	8.3683505E+00	*	62.	6.5913308E-03	1.2774282E+01	*
13.	3.4888950E-01	8.7172400E+00	*	63.	6.0784837E-03	1.2780360E+01	*
14.	3.2174370E-01	9.0389837E+00	*	64.	5.6055393E-03	1.2785965E+01	*
15.	2.9671001E-01	9.3356937E+00	*	65.	5.1693930E-03	1.2791134E+01	*
16.	2.7362410E-01	9.6093178E+00	*	66.	4.7671816E-03	1.2795901E+01	*
17.	2.5233442E-01	9.8616522E+00	*	67.	4.3962644E-03	1.2800297E+01	*
18.	2.3270121E-01	1.0094353E+01	*	68.	4.0542076E-03	1.2804351E+01	*
19.	2.1459558E-01	1.0308948E+01	*	69.	3.7387647E-03	1.2808089E+01	*
20.	1.9789869E-01	1.0506846E+01	*	70.	3.4478652E-03	1.2811536E+01	*
21.	1.8250093E-01	1.0589346E+01	*	71.	3.1795995E-03	1.2814715E+01	*
22.	1.6830120E-01	1.0857647E+01	*	72.	2.9322066E-03	1.2817647E+01	*
23.	1.5520631E-01	1.1012853E+01	*	73.	2.7040625E-03	1.2820351E+01	*
24.	1.4313028E-01	1.1155983E+01	*	74.	2.4936693E-03	1.2822844E+01	*
25.	1.3199384E-01	1.1287976E+01	*	75.	2.2996461E-03	1.2825143E+01	*
26.	1.2172388E-01	1.1409699E+01	*	76.	2.1207191E-03	1.2827263E+01	*
27.	1.1225300E-01	1.1521952E+01	*	77.	1.9557138E-03	1.2829218E+01	*
28.	1.0351901E-01	1.1625471E+01	*	78.	1.8035469E-03	1.2831021E+01	*
29.	9.5464578E-02	1.1720935E+01	*	79.	1.6632196E-03	1.2832684E+01	*
30.	8.8036832E-02	1.1808971E+01	*	80.	1.5338106E-03	1.2834217E+01	*
31.	8.1187011E-02	1.1890158E+01	*	81.	1.4144705E-03	1.2835631E+01	*
32.	7.4870149E-02	1.1965028E+01	*	82.	1.3044157E-03	1.2836935E+01	*
33.	6.9044779E-02	1.2034072E+01	*	83.	1.2029240E-03	1.2838137E+01	*
34.	6.3672660E-02	1.2097744E+01	*	84.	1.1093289E-03	1.2839246E+01	*
35.	5.8718525E-02	1.2156462E+01	*	85.	1.0230161E-03	1.2840269E+01	*
36.	5.4149853E-02	1.2210611E+01	*	86.	9.4341904E-04	1.2841212E+01	*
37.	4.9936653E-02	1.2260547E+01	*	87.	8.7001508E-04	1.2842082E+01	*
38.	4.6051267E-02	1.2306598E+01	*	88.	8.0232242E-04	1.2842884E+01	*
39.	4.2468187E-02	1.2349066E+01	*	89.	7.3980668E-04	1.2843623E+01	*
40.	3.9163895E-02	1.2388229E+01	*	90.	6.8238805E-04	1.2844305E+01	*
41.	3.6116696E-02	1.2424345E+01	*	91.	6.2923862E-04	1.2844934E+01	*
42.	3.3306590E-02	1.2457651E+01	*	92.	5.8027989E-04	1.2845514E+01	*
43.	3.0715127E-02	1.2488366E+01	*	93.	5.3513045E-04	1.2846049E+01	*
44.	2.8325296E-02	1.2516691E+01	*	94.	4.9349392E-04	1.2846542E+01	*
45.	2.6121409E-02	1.2542812E+01	*	95.	4.5509698E-04	1.2846997E+01	*
46.	2.4089999E-02	1.2566900E+01	*	96.	4.1968757E-04	1.2847416E+01	*
47.	2.2214723E-02	1.2589114E+01	*	97.	3.8703323E-04	1.2847803E+01	*
48.	2.0484627E-02	1.2609600E+01	*	98.	3.5691960E-04	1.2848159E+01	*
49.	1.8892315E-02	1.2628492E+01	*	99.	3.2914900E-04	1.2848488E+01	*
50.	1.7422374E-02	1.2645914E+01	*	100.	3.0353913E-04	1.2848791E+01	*

x	E^{-RX}	SUM OF E^{-RX}	*	x	E^{-RX}	SUM OF E^{-RX}	*
0.	1.0000000E+00	1.0000000E+00	*	50.	1.6572675E-02	1.2508005E+01	*
1.	9.2127195E-01	1.9212719E+00	*	51.	1.5267941E-02	1.2523272E+01	*
2.	8.4874202E-01	2.7700139E+00	*	52.	1.4065926E-02	1.2537337E+01	*
3.	7.8192222E-01	3.5519361E+00	*	53.	1.2958543E-02	1.2550295E+01	*
4.	7.2036301E-01	4.2722991E+00	*	54.	1.1938342E-02	1.2562233E+01	*
5.	6.6365024E-01	4.9359493E+00	*	55.	1.0998460E-02	1.2573231E+01	*
6.	6.1140236E-01	5.5473516E+00	*	56.	1.0132572E-02	1.2583363E+01	*
7.	5.6326785E-01	6.1106194E+00	*	57.	9.3348553E-03	1.2592697E+01	*
8.	5.1892287E-01	6.6295422E+00	*	58.	8.5999404E-03	1.2601296E+01	*
9.	4.7806909E-01	7.1076112E+00	*	59.	7.9228839E-03	1.2609218E+01	*
10.	4.4043165E-01	7.5480428E+00	*	60.	7.2991308E-03	1.2616517E+01	*
11.	4.0575733E-01	7.9538001E+00	*	61.	6.7244645E-03	1.2623241E+01	*
12.	3.7381285E-01	8.3276129E+00	*	62.	6.1950790E-03	1.2629436E+01	*
13.	3.4438329E-01	8.6719961E+00	*	63.	5.7073526E-03	1.2635143E+01	*
14.	3.1727067E-01	8.9892667E+00	*	64.	5.2580239E-03	1.2640401E+01	*
15.	2.9229257E-01	9.2815592E+00	*	65.	4.8440700E-03	1.2645245E+01	*
16.	2.6928095E-01	9.5508401E+00	*	66.	4.4627058E-03	1.2649707E+01	*
17.	2.4808099E-01	9.7989210E+00	*	67.	4.1113657E-03	1.2653818E+01	*
18.	2.2855006E-01	1.0027471E+01	*	68.	3.7876859E-03	1.2657605E+01	*
19.	2.1055676E-01	1.0238027E+01	*	69.	3.4894888E-03	1.2661094E+01	*
20.	1.9398004E-01	1.0432007E+01	*	70.	3.2147682E-03	1.2664308E+01	*
21.	1.7870837E-01	1.0610715E+01	*	71.	2.9616758E-03	1.2667269E+01	*
22.	1.6463901E-01	1.0775354E+01	*	72.	2.7285089E-03	1.2669997E+01	*
23.	1.5167730E-01	1.0927031E+01	*	73.	2.5136987E-03	1.2672510E+01	*
24.	1.3973640E-01	1.1066767E+01	*	74.	2.3158001E-03	1.2674825E+01	*
25.	1.2873490E-01	1.1195501E+01	*	75.	2.1334817E-03	1.2676958E+01	*
26.	1.1859985E-01	1.1314100E+01	*	76.	1.9655169E-03	1.2678923E+01	*
27.	1.0926272E-01	1.1423362E+01	*	77.	1.8107756E-03	1.2680733E+01	*
28.	1.0066068E-01	1.1524022E+01	*	78.	1.6682168E-03	1.2682401E+01	*
29.	9.2735863E-02	1.1616757E+01	*	79.	1.5368813E-03	1.2683937E+01	*
30.	8.5434950E-02	1.1702191E+01	*	80.	1.4158857E-03	1.2685352E+01	*
31.	7.8708824E-02	1.1780899E+01	*	81.	1.3044157E-03	1.2686656E+01	*
32.	7.2512232E-02	1.1853411E+01	*	82.	1.2017216E-03	1.2687857E+01	*
33.	6.6803486E-02	1.1920214E+01	*	83.	1.1071125E-03	1.2688964E+01	*
34.	6.1544179E-02	1.1981758E+01	*	84.	1.0199517E-03	1.2689983E+01	*
35.	5.6698926E-02	1.2038456E+01	*	85.	9.3965290E-04	1.2690922E+01	*
36.	5.2235130E-02	1.2090691E+01	*	86.	8.6567587E-04	1.2691787E+01	*
37.	4.8122761E-02	1.2138813E+01	*	87.	7.9752290E-04	1.2692584E+01	*
38.	4.4334150E-02	1.2183147E+01	*	88.	7.3473548E-04	1.2693318E+01	*
39.	4.0843809E-02	1.2223990E+01	*	89.	6.7689120E-04	1.2693994E+01	*
40.	3.7628256E-02	1.2261618E+01	*	90.	6.2360088E-04	1.2694617E+01	*
41.	3.4665857E-02	1.2296283E+01	*	91.	5.7450600E-04	1.2695191E+01	*
42.	3.1936682E-02	1.2328219E+01	*	92.	5.2927627E-04	1.2695720E+01	*
43.	2.9422370E-02	1.2357641E+01	*	93.	4.8760739E-04	1.2696207E+01	*
44.	2.7106004E-02	1.2384747E+01	*	94.	4.4921901E-04	1.2696656E+01	*
45.	2.4972002E-02	1.2409719E+01	*	95.	4.1385288E-04	1.2697069E+01	*
46.	2.3006005E-02	1.2432725E+01	*	96.	3.8127105E-04	1.2697450E+01	*
47.	2.1194787E-02	1.2453919E+01	*	97.	3.5125433E-04	1.2697801E+01	*
48.	1.9526163E-02	1.2473445E+01	*	98.	3.2360076E-04	1.2698124E+01	*
49.	1.7988906E-02	1.2491433E+01	*	99.	2.9812431E-04	1.2698422E+01	*
50.	1.6572675E-02	1.2508005E+01	*	100.	2.7465356E-04	1.2698696E+01	*

X	E^{-RX}	SUM OF E^{-RX}	*	X	E^{-RX}	SUM OF E^{-RX}	*
0.	1.0000000E+00	1.0000000E+00	*	50.	1.5764416E-02	1.2372934E+01	*
1.	9.2035114E-01	1.9203511E+00	*	51.	1.4508798E-02	1.2387442E+01	*
2.	8.4704623E-01	2.7673973E+00	*	52.	1.3353189E-02	1.2400795E+01	*
3.	7.7957997E-01	3.5469772E+00	*	53.	1.2289623E-02	1.2413084E+01	*
4.	7.1748732E-01	4.2644645E+00	*	54.	1.1310768E-02	1.2424394E+01	*
5.	6.6034027E-01	4.9248047E+00	*	55.	1.0409879E-02	1.2434803E+01	*
6.	6.0774493E-01	5.5325496E+00	*	56.	9.5807442E-03	1.2444383E+01	*
7.	5.5933874E-01	6.0918883E+00	*	57.	8.8176489E-03	1.2453200E+01	*
8.	5.1478805E-01	6.6066763E+00	*	58.	8.1153333E-03	1.2461315E+01	*
9.	4.7378577E-01	7.0804620E+00	*	59.	7.4689563E-03	1.2468783E+01	*
10.	4.3604928E-01	7.5165112E+00	*	60.	6.8740625E-03	1.2475657E+01	*
11.	4.0131845E-01	7.9178296E+00	*	61.	6.3265513E-03	1.2481983E+01	*
12.	3.6935390E-01	8.2871835E+00	*	62.	5.8226487E-03	1.2487805E+01	*
13.	3.3993529E-01	8.6271187E+00	*	63.	5.3588814E-03	1.2493163E+01	*
14.	3.1285983E-01	8.9399785E+00	*	64.	4.9320527E-03	1.2498095E+01	*
15.	2.8794090E-01	9.2279194E+00	*	65.	4.5392203E-03	1.2502634E+01	*
16.	2.6500674E-01	9.4929261E+00	*	66.	4.1776766E-03	1.2506811E+01	*
17.	2.4389926E-01	9.7368253E+00	*	67.	3.8449295E-03	1.2510655E+01	*
18.	2.2447296E-01	9.9612982E+00	*	68.	3.5386853E-03	1.2514193E+01	*
19.	2.0659395E-01	1.0167892E+01	*	69.	3.2568330E-03	1.2517449E+01	*
20.	1.9013897E-01	1.0358030E+01	*	70.	2.9974300E-03	1.2520446E+01	*
21.	1.7499462E-01	1.0533024E+01	*	71.	2.7586882E-03	1.2523204E+01	*
22.	1.6105650E-01	1.0694080E+01	*	72.	2.5389618E-03	1.2525742E+01	*
23.	1.4822854E-01	1.0842308E+01	*	73.	2.3367364E-03	1.2528078E+01	*
24.	1.3642230E-01	1.0978730E+01	*	74.	2.1506180E-03	1.2530228E+01	*
25.	1.2555642E-01	1.1104286E+01	*	75.	1.9793238E-03	1.2532207E+01	*
26.	1.1555600E-01	1.1219842E+01	*	76.	1.8216729E-03	1.2534028E+01	*
27.	1.0635209E-01	1.1326194E+01	*	77.	1.6765787E-03	1.2535704E+01	*
28.	9.7881276E-02	1.1424075E+01	*	78.	1.5430412E-03	1.2537247E+01	*
29.	9.0085144E-02	1.1514160E+01	*	79.	1.4201397E-03	1.2538667E+01	*
30.	8.2909966E-02	1.1597069E+01	*	80.	1.3070272E-03	1.2539974E+01	*
31.	7.6306282E-02	1.1673375E+01	*	81.	1.2029240E-03	1.2541176E+01	*
32.	7.0228574E-02	1.1743634E+01	*	82.	1.1071125E-03	1.2542283E+01	*
33.	6.4634949E-02	1.1808237E+01	*	83.	1.0189322E-03	1.2543301E+01	*
34.	5.9486849E-02	1.1867723E+01	*	84.	9.3777547E-04	1.2544238E+01	*
35.	5.4748790E-02	1.1922471E+01	*	85.	8.6308273E-04	1.2545101E+01	*
36.	5.0388112E-02	1.1972859E+01	*	86.	7.9433918E-04	1.2545895E+01	*
37.	4.6374756E-02	1.2019233E+01	*	87.	7.3107098E-04	1.2546626E+01	*
38.	4.2681060E-02	1.2061914E+01	*	88.	6.7284201E-04	1.2547298E+01	*
39.	3.9281563E-02	1.2101195E+01	*	89.	6.1925092E-04	1.2547917E+01	*
40.	3.6152831E-02	1.2137347E+01	*	90.	5.6992829E-04	1.2548486E+01	*
41.	3.3273300E-02	1.2170620E+01	*	91.	5.2453416E-04	1.2549010E+01	*
42.	3.0623119E-02	1.2201243E+01	*	92.	4.8275561E-04	1.2549492E+01	*
43.	2.8184023E-02	1.2229427E+01	*	93.	4.4430468E-04	1.2549936E+01	*
44.	2.5939198E-02	1.2255366E+01	*	94.	4.0891632E-04	1.2550344E+01	*
45.	2.3873171E-02	1.2279239E+01	*	95.	3.7634661E-04	1.2550720E+01	*
46.	2.1971700E-02	1.2301210E+01	*	96.	3.4637103E-04	1.2551066E+01	*
47.	2.0221679E-02	1.2321431E+01	*	97.	3.1878297E-04	1.2551384E+01	*
48.	1.8611046E-02	1.2340042E+01	*	98.	2.9339228E-04	1.2551677E+01	*
49.	1.7128697E-02	1.2357170E+01	*	99.	2.7002392E-04	1.2551947E+01	*
50.	1.5764416E-02	1.2372934E+01	*	100.	2.4851682E-04	1.2552195E+01	*

X	E^{-RX}	SUM OF E^{-RX}	*	X	E^{-RX}	SUM OF E^{-RX}	*
0.	1.0000000E+00	1.0000000E+00	*	50.	1.4995576E-02	1.2240619E+01	*
1.	9.1943125E-01	1.9194312E+00	*	51.	1.3787401E-02	1.2254406E+01	*
2.	8.4535383E-01	2.7647850E+00	*	52.	1.2676568E-02	1.2267082E+01	*
3.	7.7724473E-01	3.5420297E+00	*	53.	1.1655233E-02	1.2278737E+01	*
4.	7.1462310E-01	4.2566528E+00	*	54.	1.0716185E-02	1.2289453E+01	*
5.	6.5704681E-01	4.9136996E+00	*	55.	9.8527960E-03	1.2299305E+01	*
6.	6.0410938E-01	5.5178089E+00	*	56.	9.0589686E-03	1.2308363E+01	*
7.	5.5543704E-01	6.0732459E+00	*	57.	8.3290989E-03	1.2316692E+01	*
8.	5.1068618E-01	6.5839320E+00	*	58.	7.6580338E-03	1.2324350E+01	*
9.	4.6954083E-01	7.0534728E+00	*	59.	7.0410357E-03	1.2331391E+01	*
10.	4.3171052E-01	7.4851833E+00	*	60.	6.4737483E-03	1.2337864E+01	*
11.	3.9692814E-01	7.8821114E+00	*	61.	5.9521665E-03	1.2343816E+01	*
12.	3.6494814E-01	8.2470595E+00	*	62.	5.4726079E-03	1.2349288E+01	*
13.	3.3554473E-01	8.5826042E+00	*	63.	5.0316867E-03	1.2354319E+01	*
14.	3.0851031E-01	8.8911145E+00	*	64.	4.6262901E-03	1.2358945E+01	*
15.	2.8365402E-01	9.1747685E+00	*	65.	4.2535557E-03	1.2363198E+01	*
16.	2.6080037E-01	9.4355688E+00	*	66.	3.9108520E-03	1.2367108E+01	*
17.	2.3978801E-01	9.6753568E+00	*	67.	3.5957596E-03	1.2370703E+01	*
18.	2.2046859E-01	9.8958253E+00	*	68.	3.3060538E-03	1.2374009E+01	*
19.	2.0270572E-01	1.0098231E+01	*	69.	3.0396892E-03	1.2377048E+01	*
20.	1.8637397E-01	1.0284904E+01	*	70.	2.7947852E-03	1.2379842E+01	*
21.	1.7135805E-01	1.0456202E+01	*	71.	2.5696129E-03	1.2382411E+01	*
22.	1.5755195E-01	1.0613813E+01	*	72.	2.3625824E-03	1.2384773E+01	*
23.	1.4485819E-01	1.0758671E+01	*	73.	2.1722321E-03	1.2386945E+01	*
24.	1.3318714E-01	1.0891858E+01	*	74.	1.9972181E-03	1.2388942E+01	*
25.	1.2245642E-01	1.1014314E+01	*	75.	1.8363047E-03	1.2390778E+01	*
26.	1.1259026E-01	1.1126904E+01	*	76.	1.6883560E-03	1.2392466E+01	*
27.	1.0351901E-01	1.1230423E+01	*	77.	1.5523272E-03	1.2394018E+01	*
28.	9.5178614E-02	1.1325601E+01	*	78.	1.4272582E-03	1.2395445E+01	*
29.	8.7510192E-02	1.1413111E+01	*	79.	1.3122658E-03	1.2396757E+01	*
30.	8.0459606E-02	1.1493570E+01	*	80.	1.2065382E-03	1.2397963E+01	*
31.	7.3977077E-02	1.1567547E+01	*	81.	1.1093289E-03	1.2399072E+01	*
32.	6.8016836E-02	1.1635563E+01	*	82.	1.0199517E-03	1.2400091E+01	*
33.	6.2536805E-02	1.1698099E+01	*	83.	9.3777547E-04	1.2401028E+01	*
34.	5.7498293E-02	1.1755597E+01	*	84.	8.6222008E-04	1.2401890E+01	*
35.	5.2865728E-02	1.1808462E+01	*	85.	7.9275209E-04	1.2402682E+01	*
36.	4.8606403E-02	1.1857068E+01	*	86.	7.2888105E-04	1.2403410E+01	*
37.	4.4690246E-02	1.1901758E+01	*	87.	6.7015602E-04	1.2404080E+01	*
38.	4.1089609E-02	1.1942847E+01	*	88.	6.1616239E-04	1.2404696E+01	*
39.	3.7779071E-02	1.1980626E+01	*	89.	5.6651896E-04	1.2405262E+01	*
40.	3.4735258E-02	1.2015361E+01	*	90.	5.2087524E-04	1.2405782E+01	*
41.	3.1936682E-02	1.2047297E+01	*	91.	4.7890897E-04	1.2406260E+01	*
42.	2.9363584E-02	1.2076660E+01	*	92.	4.4032388E-04	1.2406700E+01	*
43.	2.6997797E-02	1.2103657E+01	*	93.	4.0484754E-04	1.2407104E+01	*
44.	2.4822618E-02	1.2128479E+01	*	94.	3.7222948E-04	1.2407476E+01	*
45.	2.2822691E-02	1.2151301E+01	*	95.	3.4223942E-04	1.2407818E+01	*
46.	2.0983895E-02	1.2172284E+01	*	96.	3.1466562E-04	1.2408132E+01	*
47.	1.9293240E-02	1.2191577E+01	*	97.	2.8931341E-04	1.2408421E+01	*
48.	1.7738816E-02	1.2209315E+01	*	98.	2.6600378E-04	1.2408687E+01	*
49.	1.6309622E-02	1.2225624E+01	*	99.	2.4457219E-04	1.2408931E+01	*
50.	1.4995576E-02	1.2240619E+01	*	100.	2.2486732E-04	1.2409155E+01	*

TABULATED VALUES OF E^(−RX)   WHEN R = .085

X	E^(−RX)	SUM OF E^(−RX)	*	X	E^(−RX)	SUM OF E^(−RX)	*
0.	1.0000000E+00	1.0000000E+00	*	50.	1.4264233E-02	1.2110986E+01	*
1.	9.1851228E-01	1.9185122E+00	*	51.	1.3101874E-02	1.2124087E+01	*
2.	8.4366481E-01	2.7621770E+00	*	52.	1.2034232E-02	1.2136121E+01	*
3.	7.7491649E-01	3.5370934E+00	*	53.	1.1053590E-02	1.2147174E+01	*
4.	7.1177032E-01	4.2488637E+00	*	54.	1.0152858E-02	1.2157326E+01	*
5.	6.5376978E-01	4.9026334E+00	*	55.	9.3255251E-03	1.2166651E+01	*
6.	6.0049557E-01	5.5031289E+00	*	56.	8.5656093E-03	1.2175216E+01	*
7.	5.5156256E-01	6.0546914E+00	*	57.	7.8676174E-03	1.2183083E+01	*
8.	5.0661699E-01	6.5613083E+00	*	58.	7.2265032E-03	1.2190309E+01	*
9.	4.6533393E-01	7.0266422E+00	*	59.	6.6376320E-03	1.2196946E+01	*
10.	4.2741493E-01	7.4540571E+00	*	60.	6.0967465E-03	1.2203042E+01	*
11.	3.9258586E-01	7.8466429E+00	*	61.	5.5999366E-03	1.2208641E+01	*
12.	3.6059493E-01	8.2072378E+00	*	62.	5.1436105E-03	1.2213784E+01	*
13.	3.3121088E-01	8.5384486E+00	*	63.	4.7244694E-03	1.2218508E+01	*
14.	3.0422126E-01	8.8426698E+00	*	64.	4.3394832E-03	1.2222847E+01	*
15.	2.7943096E-01	9.1221007E+00	*	65.	3.9858686E-03	1.2226832E+01	*
16.	2.5666077E-01	9.3787614E+00	*	66.	3.6610693E-03	1.2230493E+01	*
17.	2.3574607E-01	9.6145074E+00	*	67.	3.3627371E-03	1.2233855E+01	*
18.	2.1653566E-01	9.8310430E+00	*	68.	3.0887154E-03	1.2236943E+01	*
19.	1.9889067E-01	1.0029933E+01	*	69.	2.8370230E-03	1.2239780E+01	*
20.	1.8264352E-01	1.0212616E+01	*	70.	2.6058405E-03	1.2242385E+01	*
21.	1.6779706E-01	1.0380413E+01	*	71.	2.3934965E-03	1.2244778E+01	*
22.	1.5412366E-01	1.0534536E+01	*	72.	2.1984559E-03	1.2246976E+01	*
23.	1.4156447E-01	1.0676100E+01	*	73.	2.0193088E-03	1.2248995E+01	*
24.	1.3002871E-01	1.0806128E+01	*	74.	1.8545599E-03	1.2250849E+01	*
25.	1.1943296E-01	1.0925560E+01	*	75.	1.7036197E-03	1.2252552E+01	*
26.	1.0970064E-01	1.1035260E+01	*	76.	1.5647957E-03	1.2254116E+01	*
27.	1.0076139E-01	1.1136021E+01	*	77.	1.4372840E-03	1.2255553E+01	*
28.	9.2550577E-02	1.1228571E+01	*	78.	1.3201630E-03	1.2256873E+01	*
29.	8.5008842E-02	1.1313579E+01	*	79.	1.2125860E-03	1.2258085E+01	*
30.	7.8081665E-02	1.1391660E+01	*	80.	1.1137751E-03	1.2259198E+01	*
31.	7.1718969E-02	1.1463378E+01	*	81.	1.0230161E-03	1.2260221E+01	*
32.	6.5874754E-02	1.1529252E+01	*	82.	9.3965290E-04	1.2261160E+01	*
33.	6.0506771E-02	1.1589758E+01	*	83.	8.6308273E-04	1.2262023E+01	*
34.	5.5576212E-02	1.1645334E+01	*	84.	7.9275209E-04	1.2262815E+01	*
35.	5.1047433E-02	1.1696381E+01	*	85.	7.2815253E-04	1.2263543E+01	*
36.	4.6887695E-02	1.1743268E+01	*	86.	6.6881705E-04	1.2264211E+01	*
37.	4.3066923E-02	1.1786334E+01	*	87.	6.1431667E-04	1.2264825E+01	*
38.	3.9557498E-02	1.1825891E+01	*	88.	5.6425741E-04	1.2265389E+01	*
39.	3.6334048E-02	1.1862225E+01	*	89.	5.1827736E-04	1.2265907E+01	*
40.	3.3373269E-02	1.1895598E+01	*	90.	4.7604412E-04	1.2266383E+01	*
41.	3.0653758E-02	1.1926251E+01	*	91.	4.3725237E-04	1.2266820E+01	*
42.	2.8155853E-02	1.1954406E+01	*	92.	4.0162168E-04	1.2267221E+01	*
43.	2.5861497E-02	1.1980267E+01	*	93.	3.6889444E-04	1.2267589E+01	*
44.	2.3754103E-02	1.2004021E+01	*	94.	3.3883408E-04	1.2267927E+01	*
45.	2.1818435E-02	1.2025839E+01	*	95.	3.1122326E-04	1.2268238E+01	*
46.	2.0040500E-02	1.2045879E+01	*	96.	2.8586239E-04	1.2268523E+01	*
47.	1.8407446E-02	1.2064286E+01	*	97.	2.6256812E-04	1.2268785E+01	*
48.	1.6907465E-02	1.2081193E+01	*	98.	2.4117204E-04	1.2269026E+01	*
49.	1.5529714E-02	1.2096722E+01	*	99.	2.2151948E-04	1.2269247E+01	*
50.	1.4264233E-02	1.2110986E+01	*	100.	2.0346836E-04	1.2269450E+01	*

TABULATED VALUES OF E^(−RX)   WHEN R = .086

X	E^(−RX)	SUM OF E^(−RX)	*	X	E^(−RX)	SUM OF E^(−RX)	*
0.	1.0000000E+00	1.0000000E+00	*	50.	1.3568558E-02	1.1983972E+01	*
1.	9.1759422E-01	1.9175942E+00	*	51.	1.2450431E-02	1.1996422E+01	*
2.	8.4197917E-01	2.7595733E+00	*	52.	1.1424444E-02	1.2007846E+01	*
3.	7.7259523E-01	3.5321685E+00	*	53.	1.0483003E-02	1.2018329E+01	*
4.	7.0892892E-01	4.2410974E+00	*	54.	9.6191439E-03	1.2027948E+01	*
5.	6.5050909E-01	4.8916064E+00	*	55.	8.8264710E-03	1.2036774E+01	*
6.	5.9690339E-01	5.4885097E+00	*	56.	8.0991188E-03	1.2044873E+01	*
7.	5.4771510E-01	6.0362248E+00	*	57.	7.4317047E-03	1.2052304E+01	*
8.	5.0258022E-01	6.5388050E+00	*	58.	6.8192894E-03	1.2059123E+01	*
9.	4.6116471E-01	6.9999697E+00	*	59.	6.2573406E-03	1.2065380E+01	*
10.	4.2316208E-01	7.4231317E+00	*	60.	5.7416996E-03	1.2071121E+01	*
11.	3.8829108E-01	7.8114227E+00	*	61.	5.2685504E-03	1.2076389E+01	*
12.	3.5629365E-01	8.1677163E+00	*	62.	4.8343915E-03	1.2081223E+01	*
13.	3.2693300E-01	8.4946493E+00	*	63.	4.4360097E-03	1.2085659E+01	*
14.	2.9999184E-01	8.7946411E+00	*	64.	4.0704569E-03	1.2089729E+01	*
15.	2.7527078E-01	9.0699118E+00	*	65.	3.7350278E-03	1.2093464E+01	*
16.	2.5258688E-01	9.3224986E+00	*	66.	3.4272400E-03	1.2096891E+01	*
17.	2.3177226E-01	9.5542708E+00	*	67.	3.1448156E-03	1.2100035E+01	*
18.	2.1267289E-01	9.7669436E+00	*	68.	2.8856647E-03	1.2102920E+01	*
19.	1.9514742E-01	9.9620910E+00	*	69.	2.6478692E-03	1.2105567E+01	*
20.	1.7906614E-01	1.0141157E+01	*	70.	2.4296695E-03	1.2107996E+01	*
21.	1.6431006E-01	1.0305467E+01	*	71.	2.2294508E-03	1.2110225E+01	*
22.	1.5076996E-01	1.0456236E+01	*	72.	2.0457311E-03	1.2112270E+01	*
23.	1.3834565E-01	1.0594581E+01	*	73.	1.8771511E-03	1.2114147E+01	*
24.	1.2694517E-01	1.0721526E+01	*	74.	1.7224630E-03	1.2115869E+01	*
25.	1.1648415E-01	1.0838010E+01	*	75.	1.5805221E-03	1.2117449E+01	*
26.	1.0688519E-01	1.0944895E+01	*	76.	1.4502780E-03	1.2118899E+01	*
27.	9.8077224E-02	1.1042972E+01	*	77.	1.3307667E-03	1.2120229E+01	*
28.	8.9995104E-02	1.1132967E+01	*	78.	1.2211038E-03	1.2121450E+01	*
29.	8.2578988E-02	1.1215545E+01	*	79.	1.1204778E-03	1.2122570E+01	*
30.	7.5774003E-02	1.1291319E+01	*	80.	1.0281440E-03	1.2123598E+01	*
31.	6.9529788E-02	1.1360843E+01	*	81.	9.4341904E-04	1.2124541E+01	*
32.	6.3800132E-02	1.1424646E+01	*	82.	8.6567587E-04	1.2125406E+01	*
33.	5.8542634E-02	1.1483190E+01	*	83.	7.9433918E-04	1.2126200E+01	*
34.	5.3718383E-02	1.1536908E+01	*	84.	7.2888105E-04	1.2126928E+01	*
35.	4.9291678E-02	1.1586199E+01	*	85.	6.6881705E-04	1.2127596E+01	*
36.	4.5229760E-02	1.1631428E+01	*	86.	6.1370266E-04	1.2128209E+01	*
37.	4.1502560E-02	1.1672930E+01	*	87.	5.6313002E-04	1.2128772E+01	*
38.	3.8082515E-02	1.1711012E+01	*	88.	5.1672486E-04	1.2129286E+01	*
39.	3.4944296E-02	1.1745956E+01	*	89.	4.7414375E-04	1.2129762E+01	*
40.	3.2064685E-02	1.1778020E+01	*	90.	4.3507157E-04	1.2130197E+01	*
41.	2.9422370E-02	1.1807442E+01	*	91.	3.9921916E-04	1.2130596E+01	*
42.	2.6997797E-02	1.1834439E+01	*	92.	3.6632120E-04	1.2130962E+01	*
43.	2.4773023E-02	1.1859212E+01	*	93.	3.3613422E-04	1.2131298E+01	*
44.	2.2731582E-02	1.1881943E+01	*	94.	3.0843482E-04	1.2131606E+01	*
45.	2.0858369E-02	1.1902801E+01	*	95.	2.8301801E-04	1.2131889E+01	*
46.	1.9139519E-02	1.1921940E+01	*	96.	2.5969569E-04	1.2132148E+01	*
47.	1.7562312E-02	1.1939502E+01	*	97.	2.3829527E-04	1.2132386E+01	*
48.	1.6115076E-02	1.1955617E+01	*	98.	2.1865836E-04	1.2132604E+01	*
49.	1.4787101E-02	1.1970404E+01	*	99.	2.0063965E-04	1.2132804E+01	*
50.	1.3568558E-02	1.1983972E+01	*	100.	1.8410579E-04	1.2132988E+01	*

TABULATED VALUES OF E^{-RX} WHEN R = .087

X	E^{-RX}	SUM OF E^{-RX}	☆	X	E^{-RX}	SUM OF E^{-RX}	☆
0.	1.0000000E+00	1.0000000E+00	☆	50.	1.2906812E-02	1.1859491E+01	☆
1.	9.1667709E-01	1.9166770E+00	☆	51.	1.1831379E-02	1.1871322E+01	☆
2.	8.4029689F-01	2.7569738E+00	☆	52.	1.0845554E-02	1.1882167E+01	☆
3.	7.7028091E-01	3.5272547E+00	☆	53.	9.9418714E-03	1.1892108E+01	☆
4.	7.0609887E-01	4.2333535E+00	☆	54.	9.1134858E-03	1.1901221E+01	☆
5.	6.4726466E-01	4.8806181E+00	☆	55.	8.3541237E-03	1.1909575E+01	☆
6.	5.9333269E-01	5.4739507E+00	☆	56.	7.6580338E-03	1.1917233E+01	☆
7.	5.4389449E-01	6.0178451E+00	☆	57.	7.0199442E-03	1.1924252E+01	☆
8.	4.9857562E-01	6.5164207E+00	☆	58.	6.4350221E-03	1.1930687E+01	☆
9.	4.5703285E-01	6.9734535E+00	☆	59.	5.8988373E-03	1.1936585E+01	☆
10.	4.1895154E-01	7.3924050E+00	☆	60.	5.4073291E-03	1.1941992E+01	☆
11.	3.8404328E-01	7.7764482E+00	☆	61.	4.9567747E-03	1.1946948E+01	☆
12.	3.5204368E-01	8.1284918E+00	☆	62.	4.5437618E-03	1.1951491E+01	☆
13.	3.2271038E-01	8.4512021E+00	☆	63.	4.1651624E-03	1.1955656E+01	☆
14.	2.9582121E-01	8.7470233E+00	☆	64.	3.8181090E-03	1.1959474E+01	☆
15.	2.7117253E-01	9.0181958E+00	☆	65.	3.4999730E-03	1.1962973E+01	☆
16.	2.4857765E-01	9.2667734E+00	☆	66.	3.2083451E-03	1.1966181E+01	☆
17.	2.2786543E-01	9.4946388E+00	☆	67.	2.9410165E-03	1.1969122E+01	☆
18.	2.0887902E-01	9.7035178E+00	☆	68.	2.6959624E-03	1.1971817E+01	☆
19.	1.9147462E-01	9.8949924E+00	☆	69.	2.4713270E-03	1.1974288E+01	☆
20.	1.7552040E-01	1.0070512E+01	☆	70.	2.2654089E-03	1.1976555E+01	☆
21.	1.6089553E-01	1.0231407E+01	☆	71.	2.0766484E-03	1.1978629E+01	☆
22.	1.4748924E-01	1.0378896E+01	☆	72.	1.9036160E-03	1.1980532E+01	☆
23.	1.3520001E-01	1.0514096E+01	☆	73.	1.7450012E-03	1.1982277E+01	☆
24.	1.2393475E-01	1.0638030E+01	☆	74.	1.5996026E-03	1.1983876E+01	☆
25.	1.1360815E-01	1.0751638E+01	☆	75.	1.4663191E-03	1.1985342E+01	☆
26.	1.0414199E-01	1.0855779E+01	☆	76.	1.3441411E-03	1.1986686E+01	☆
27.	9.5464578E-02	1.0951243E+01	☆	77.	1.2321434E-03	1.1987918E+01	☆
28.	8.7510192E-02	1.1038753E+01	☆	78.	1.1294776E-03	1.1989047E+01	☆
29.	8.0218589E-02	1.1118971E+01	☆	79.	1.0353662E-03	1.1990082E+01	☆
30.	7.3534543E-02	1.1192505E+01	☆	80.	9.4909657E-04	1.1991031E+01	☆
31.	6.7407431E-02	1.1259912E+01	☆	81.	8.7001508E-04	1.1991901E+01	☆
32.	6.1790848E-02	1.1321702E+01	☆	82.	7.9752290E-04	1.1992669E+01	☆
33.	5.6642255E-02	1.1378344E+01	☆	83.	7.3107098E-04	1.1993429E+01	☆
34.	5.1922658E-02	1.1430266E+01	☆	84.	6.7015602E-04	1.1994099E+01	☆
35.	4.7596311E-02	1.1477862E+01	☆	85.	6.1431667E-04	1.1994713E+01	☆
36.	4.3630448E-02	1.1521492E+01	☆	86.	5.6313002E-04	1.1995276E+01	☆
37.	3.9995033E-02	1.1561487E+01	☆	87.	5.1620839E-04	1.1995792E+01	☆
38.	3.6662530E-02	1.1598149E+01	☆	88.	4.7319641E-04	1.1996265E+01	☆
39.	3.3607702E-02	1.1631756E+01	☆	89.	4.3376831E-04	1.1996698E+01	☆
40.	3.0807411E-02	1.1662563E+01	☆	90.	3.9762547E-04	1.1997095E+01	☆
41.	2.8240448E-02	1.1690803E+01	☆	91.	3.6449416E-04	1.1997459E+01	☆
42.	2.5887371E-02	1.1716590E+01	☆	92.	3.3412345E-04	1.1997793E+01	☆
43.	2.3730360E-02	1.1740420E+01	☆	93.	3.0628332E-04	1.1998099E+01	☆
44.	2.1753078E-02	1.1762173E+01	☆	94.	2.8076290E-04	1.1998379E+01	☆
45.	1.9940548E-02	1.1782113E+01	☆	95.	2.5736892E-04	1.1998636E+01	☆
46.	1.8279044E-02	1.1800392E+01	☆	96.	2.3592419E-04	1.1998871E+01	☆
47.	1.6755981E-02	1.1817147E+01	☆	97.	2.1626630E-04	1.1999087E+01	☆
48.	1.5359824E-02	1.1832506E+01	☆	98.	1.9824637E-04	1.1999285E+01	☆
49.	1.4079998E-02	1.1846585E+01	☆	99.	1.8172790E-04	1.1999466E+01	☆
50.	1.2906812E-02	1.1859491E+01	☆	100.	1.6658581E-04	1.1999632E+01	☆

TABULATED VALUES OF E^{-RX} WHEN R = .088

X	E^{-RX}	SUM OF E^{-RX}	☆	X	E^{-RX}	SUM OF E^{-RX}	☆
0.	1.0000000E+00	1.0000000E+00	☆	50.	1.2277339E-02	1.1737484E+01	☆
1.	9.1576087E-01	1.9157608E+00	☆	51.	1.1243107E-02	1.1748727E+01	☆
2.	8.3861798E-01	2.7543787E+00	☆	52.	1.0295997E-02	1.1759022E+01	☆
3.	7.6797353E-01	3.5223522E+00	☆	53.	9.4286721E-03	1.1768450E+01	☆
4.	7.0328012E-01	4.2256323E+00	☆	54.	8.6344090E-03	1.1777084E+01	☆
5.	6.4403641E-01	4.8696687E+00	☆	55.	7.9070540E-03	1.1784991E+01	☆
6.	5.8978335E-01	5.4594520E+00	☆	56.	7.2409707E-03	1.1792231E+01	☆
7.	5.4010052E-01	5.9995525E+00	☆	57.	6.6309977E-03	1.1798861E+01	☆
8.	4.9460292E-01	6.4941554E+00	☆	58.	6.0724082E-03	1.1804933E+01	☆
9.	4.5293801E-01	6.9470934E+00	☆	59.	5.5608739E-03	1.1810493E+01	☆
10.	4.1478291E-01	7.3618763E+00	☆	60.	5.0924307E-03	1.1815585E+01	☆
11.	3.7984196E-01	7.7417182E+00	☆	61.	4.6634488E-03	1.1820248E+01	☆
12.	3.4784440E-01	8.0895626E+00	☆	62.	4.2706040E-03	1.1824518E+01	☆
13.	3.1854229E-01	8.4081048E+00	☆	63.	3.9108520E-03	1.1828428E+01	☆
14.	2.9170857E-01	8.6998133E+00	☆	64.	3.5814053E-03	1.1832009E+01	☆
15.	2.6713530E-01	8.9669486E+00	☆	65.	3.2797108E-03	1.1835288E+01	☆
16.	2.4463205E-01	9.2115806E+00	☆	66.	3.0034309E-03	1.1838291E+01	☆
17.	2.2402446E-01	9.4356050E+00	☆	67.	2.7504245E-03	1.1841041E+01	☆
18.	2.0515284E-01	9.6407578E+00	☆	68.	2.5187311E-03	1.1843559E+01	☆
19.	1.8787094E-01	9.8286287E+00	☆	69.	2.3065554E-03	1.1845865E+01	☆
20.	1.7204496E-01	1.0000673E+01	☆	70.	2.1122532E-03	1.1847977E+01	☆
21.	1.5755195E-01	1.0158224E+01	☆	71.	1.9343189E-03	1.1849911E+01	☆
22.	1.4427991E-01	1.0302503E+01	☆	72.	1.7713735E-03	1.1851682E+01	☆
23.	1.3212590E-01	1.0434628E+01	☆	73.	1.6221546E-03	1.1853304E+01	☆
24.	1.2099573E-01	1.0555623E+01	☆	74.	1.4855075E-03	1.1854789E+01	☆
25.	1.1080315E-01	1.0666426E+01	☆	75.	1.3603680E-03	1.1856149E+01	☆
26.	1.0146919E-01	1.0767895E+01	☆	76.	1.2457718E-03	1.1857394E+01	☆
27.	9.2921521E-02	1.0860816E+01	☆	77.	1.1408290E-03	1.1858534E+01	☆
28.	8.5093893E-02	1.0945909E+01	☆	78.	1.0447266E-03	1.1859578E+01	☆
29.	7.7925658E-02	1.1023834E+01	☆	79.	9.5671979E-04	1.1860534E+01	☆
30.	7.1361269E-02	1.1095196E+01	☆	80.	8.7612656E-04	1.1861410E+01	☆
31.	6.5349858E-02	1.1160544E+01	☆	81.	8.0232242E-04	1.1862212E+01	☆
32.	5.9844843E-02	1.1220388E+01	☆	82.	7.3473548E-04	1.1862946E+01	☆
33.	5.4803566E-02	1.1275191E+01	☆	83.	6.7284201E-04	1.1863618E+01	☆
34.	5.0186962E-02	1.1325377E+01	☆	84.	6.1616239E-04	1.1864234E+01	☆
35.	4.5959256E-02	1.1371336E+01	☆	85.	5.6425741E-04	1.1864798E+01	☆
36.	4.2087689E-02	1.1413423E+01	☆	86.	5.1672486E-04	1.1865314E+01	☆
37.	3.8542259E-02	1.1451965E+01	☆	87.	4.7319641E-04	1.1865788E+01	☆
38.	3.5295492E-02	1.1487260E+01	☆	88.	4.3333478E-04	1.1866220E+01	☆
39.	3.2322231E-02	1.1519582E+01	☆	89.	3.9683102E-04	1.1866616E+01	☆
40.	2.9599435E-02	1.1549181E+01	☆	90.	3.6340232E-04	1.1866979E+01	☆
41.	2.7106004E-02	1.1576283E+01	☆	91.	3.3278963E-04	1.1867311E+01	☆
42.	2.4822618E-02	1.1601109E+01	☆	92.	3.0475572E-04	1.1867615E+01	☆
43.	2.2731582E-02	1.1623840E+01	☆	93.	2.7908337E-04	1.1867894E+01	☆
44.	2.0816694E-02	1.1644656E+01	☆	94.	2.5557363E-04	1.1868149E+01	☆
45.	1.9063114E-02	1.1663719E+01	☆	95.	2.3404433E-04	1.1868383E+01	☆
46.	1.7457254E-02	1.1681176E+01	☆	96.	2.1432864E-04	1.1868597E+01	☆
47.	1.5986670E-02	1.1697162E+01	☆	97.	1.9627378E-04	1.1868793E+01	☆
48.	1.4639967E-02	1.1711801E+01	☆	98.	1.7973985E-04	1.1868972E+01	☆
49.	1.3406709E-02	1.1725207E+01	☆	99.	1.6459872E-04	1.1869136E+01	☆
50.	1.2277339E-02	1.1737484E+01	☆	100.	1.5073307E-04	1.1869286E+01	☆

TABULATED VALUES OF E   WHEN R = .089

X	E^−RX	SUM OF E^−RX	*	X	E^−RX	SUM OF E^−RX	*
0.	1.0000000E+00	1.0000000E+00	*	50.	1.1678566E-02	1.1617888E+01	*
1.	9.1484557E-01	1.9148455E+00	*	51.	1.0684085E-02	1.1628572E+01	*
2.	8.3694242E-01	2.7517879E+00	*	52.	9.7742881E-03	1.1638346E+01	*
3.	7.6567307E-01	3.5174609E+00	*	53.	8.9419642E-03	1.1647287E+01	*
4.	7.0047261E-01	4.2179335E+00	*	54.	8.1805163E-03	1.1655467E+01	*
5.	6.4082427E-01	4.8587577E+00	*	55.	7.4839092E-03	1.1662950E+01	*
6.	5.8625525E-01	5.4450129E+00	*	56.	6.8466212E-03	1.1669796E+01	*
7.	5.3633302E-01	5.9813459E+00	*	57.	6.2636011E-03	1.1676059E+01	*
8.	4.9066189E-01	6.4720077E+00	*	58.	5.7302277E-03	1.1681789E+01	*
9.	4.4887985E-01	6.9208875E+00	*	59.	5.2422734E-03	1.1687031E+01	*
10.	4.1065575E-01	7.3315432E+00	*	60.	4.7958707E-03	1.1691826E+01	*
11.	3.7568659E-01	7.7072297E+00	*	61.	4.3874810E-03	1.1696213E+01	*
12.	3.4369522E-01	8.0509249E+00	*	62.	4.0138676E-03	1.1700226E+01	*
13.	3.1442805E-01	8.3653529E+00	*	63.	3.6720690E-03	1.1703898E+01	*
14.	2.8765311E-01	8.6530060E+00	*	64.	3.3593761E-03	1.1707257E+01	*
15.	2.6315817E-01	8.9161641E+00	*	65.	3.0733103E-03	1.1710330E+01	*
16.	2.4074909E-01	9.1569131E+00	*	66.	2.8116043E-03	1.1713141E+01	*
17.	2.2024624E-01	9.3771613E+00	*	67.	2.5721836E-03	1.1715713E+01	*
18.	2.0149312E-01	9.5786544E+00	*	68.	2.3531509E-03	1.1718066E+01	*
19.	1.8433509E-01	9.7629894E+00	*	69.	2.1527697E-03	1.1720218E+01	*
20.	1.6863814E-01	9.9316275E+00	*	70.	1.9694518E-03	1.1722187E+01	*
21.	1.5427786E-01	1.0085905E+01	*	71.	1.8017443E-03	1.1723988E+01	*
22.	1.4114041E-01	1.0227045E+01	*	72.	1.6483178E-03	1.1725636E+01	*
23.	1.2912168E-01	1.0356166E+01	*	73.	1.5079562E-03	1.1727143E+01	*
24.	1.1812640E-01	1.0474292E+01	*	74.	1.3795471E-03	1.1728522E+01	*
25.	1.0806741E-01	1.0582359E+01	*	75.	1.2620725E-03	1.1729784E+01	*
26.	9.8864999E-02	1.0681223E+01	*	76.	1.1546015E-03	1.1730938E+01	*
27.	9.0446207E-02	1.0771669E+01	*	77.	1.0562820E-03	1.1731994E+01	*
28.	8.2744312E-02	1.0854413E+01	*	78.	9.6633499E-04	1.1732960E+01	*
29.	7.5698267E-02	1.0930111E+01	*	79.	8.8404728E-04	1.1733844E+01	*
30.	6.9252225E-02	1.0999363E+01	*	80.	8.0876674E-04	1.1734652E+01	*
31.	6.3355091E-02	1.1062718E+01	*	81.	7.3989668E-04	1.1735391E+01	*
32.	5.7960125E-02	1.1120678E+01	*	82.	6.7689120E-04	1.1736067E+01	*
33.	5.3024563E-02	1.1173702E+01	*	83.	6.1925092E-04	1.1736686E+01	*
34.	4.8509287E-02	1.1222211E+01	*	84.	5.6651896E-04	1.1737252E+01	*
35.	4.4378507E-02	1.1266589E+01	*	85.	5.1827736E-04	1.1737770E+01	*
36.	4.0599480E-02	1.1307188E+01	*	86.	4.7414375E-04	1.1738244E+01	*
37.	3.7142255E-02	1.1344330E+01	*	87.	4.3376831E-04	1.1738677E+01	*
38.	3.3979427E-02	1.1378309E+01	*	88.	3.9683102E-04	1.1739073E+01	*
39.	3.1085929E-02	1.1409394E+01	*	89.	3.6303910E-04	1.1739436E+01	*
40.	2.8438824E-02	1.1437832E+01	*	90.	3.3212471E-04	1.1739768E+01	*
41.	2.6017132E-02	1.1463849E+01	*	91.	3.0384282E-04	1.1740071E+01	*
42.	2.3801658E-02	1.1487650E+01	*	92.	2.7796926E-04	1.1740348E+01	*
43.	2.1774842E-02	1.1509424E+01	*	93.	2.5429895E-04	1.1740602E+01	*
44.	1.9920618E-02	1.1529344E+01	*	94.	2.3264427E-04	1.1740834E+01	*
45.	1.8224289E-02	1.1547568E+01	*	95.	2.1283358E-04	1.1741046E+01	*
46.	1.6672410E-02	1.1564240E+01	*	96.	1.9470986E-04	1.1741240E+01	*
47.	1.5252680E-02	1.1579492E+01	*	97.	1.7812945E-04	1.1741418E+01	*
48.	1.3953847E-02	1.1593445E+01	*	98.	1.6296094E-04	1.1741580E+01	*
49.	1.2765615E-02	1.1606210E+01	*	99.	1.4908409E-04	1.1741729E+01	*
50.	1.1678566E-02	1.1617888E+01	*	100.	1.3638892E-04	1.1741865E+01	*

TABULATED VALUES OF E^−RX   WHEN R = .090

X	E^−RX	SUM OF E^−RX	*	X	E^−RX	SUM OF E^−RX	*
0.	1.0000000E+00	1.0000000E+00	*	50.	1.1108996E-02	1.1500632E+01	*
1.	9.1393118E-01	1.9139311E+00	*	51.	1.0152858E-02	1.1510784E+01	*
2.	8.3527020E-01	2.7492013E+00	*	52.	9.2790138E-03	1.1520063E+01	*
3.	7.6337949E-01	3.5125807E+00	*	53.	8.4803801E-03	1.1528543E+01	*
4.	6.9767632E-01	4.2102570E+00	*	54.	7.7504838E-03	1.1536293E+01	*
5.	6.3762814E-01	4.8478851E+00	*	55.	7.0834089E-03	1.1543376E+01	*
6.	5.8274825E-01	5.4306333E+00	*	56.	6.4737483E-03	1.1549849E+01	*
7.	5.3259179E-01	5.9632250E+00	*	57.	5.9165604E-03	1.1555765E+01	*
8.	4.8675225E-01	6.4499772E+00	*	58.	5.4073291E-03	1.1561172E+01	*
9.	4.4485806E-01	6.8948352E+00	*	59.	4.9419267E-03	1.1566113E+01	*
10.	4.0656965E-01	7.3014048E+00	*	60.	4.5165809E-03	1.1570629E+01	*
11.	3.7157669E-01	7.6729814E+00	*	61.	4.1278441E-03	1.1574756E+01	*
12.	3.3959552E-01	8.0125769E+00	*	62.	3.7725655E-03	1.1578528E+01	*
13.	3.1036694E-01	8.3229433E+00	*	63.	3.4478652E-03	1.1581975E+01	*
14.	2.8365402E-01	8.6065978E+00	*	64.	3.1511115E-03	1.1585126E+01	*
15.	2.5924026E-01	8.8658380E+00	*	65.	2.8798991E-03	1.1588005E+01	*
16.	2.3692775E-01	9.1027657E+00	*	66.	2.6320296E-03	1.1590637E+01	*
17.	2.1653566E-01	9.3193013E+00	*	67.	2.4054939E-03	1.1593042E+01	*
18.	1.9789869E-01	9.5171999E+00	*	68.	2.1984559E-03	1.1595240E+01	*
19.	1.8086579E-01	9.6980656E+00	*	69.	2.0092374E-03	1.1597249E+01	*
20.	1.6529888E-01	9.8633644E+00	*	70.	1.8363047E-03	1.1599085E+01	*
21.	1.5107180E-01	1.0014436E+01	*	71.	1.6782561E-03	1.1600763E+01	*
22.	1.3806923E-01	1.0152505E+01	*	72.	1.5338106E-03	1.1602296E+01	*
23.	1.2618578E-01	1.0278690E+01	*	73.	1.4017974E-03	1.1603697E+01	*
24.	1.1532512E-01	1.0394015E+01	*	74.	1.2811463E-03	1.1604978E+01	*
25.	1.0539922E-01	1.0499414E+01	*	75.	1.1708796E-03	1.1606148E+01	*
26.	9.6327638E-02	1.0595741E+01	*	76.	1.0701033E-03	1.1607218E+01	*
27.	8.8036832E-02	1.0683777E+01	*	77.	9.7800086E-04	1.1608196E+01	*
28.	8.0459606E-02	1.0764236E+01	*	78.	8.9382549E-04	1.1609089E+01	*
29.	7.3534543E-02	1.0837770E+01	*	79.	8.1689498E-04	1.1609905E+01	*
30.	6.7205512E-02	1.0904975E+01	*	80.	7.4658580E-04	1.1610651E+01	*
31.	6.1421213E-02	1.0963366E+01	*	81.	6.8232805E-04	1.1611333E+01	*
32.	5.6134762E-02	1.1022530E+01	*	82.	6.2360088E-04	1.1611956E+01	*
33.	5.1303310E-02	1.1073693E+01	*	83.	5.6992829E-04	1.1612525E+01	*
34.	4.6887695E-02	1.1120720E+01	*	84.	5.2087524E-04	1.1613045E+01	*
35.	4.2852126E-02	1.1163572E+01	*	85.	4.7604412E-04	1.1613521E+01	*
36.	3.9163895E-02	1.1202735E+01	*	86.	4.3507157E-04	1.1613956E+01	*
37.	3.5793105E-02	1.1238528E+01	*	87.	3.9762547E-04	1.1614353E+01	*
38.	3.2712434E-02	1.1271240E+01	*	88.	3.6340232E-04	1.1614716E+01	*
39.	2.9896914E-02	1.1301136E+01	*	89.	3.3212471E-04	1.1615048E+01	*
40.	2.7323722E-02	1.1328459E+01	*	90.	3.0353913E-04	1.1615351E+01	*
41.	2.4972002E-02	1.1353431E+01	*	91.	2.7741388E-04	1.1615628E+01	*
42.	2.2822691E-02	1.1376253E+01	*	92.	2.5353719E-04	1.1615881E+01	*
43.	2.0858369E-02	1.1397111E+01	*	93.	2.3171555E-04	1.1616112E+01	*
44.	1.9063114E-02	1.1416174E+01	*	94.	2.1177207E-04	1.1616323E+01	*
45.	1.7422374E-02	1.1433596E+01	*	95.	1.9354509E-04	1.1616516E+01	*
46.	1.5922851E-02	1.1449518E+01	*	96.	1.7688690E-04	1.1616692E+01	*
47.	1.4552390E-02	1.1464070E+01	*	97.	1.6166245E-04	1.1616853E+01	*
48.	1.3299883E-02	1.1477369E+01	*	98.	1.4774835E-04	1.1617000E+01	*
49.	1.2155178E-02	1.1489524E+01	*	99.	1.3503183E-04	1.1617135E+01	*
50.	1.1108996E-02	1.1500632E+01	*	100.	1.2340980E-04	1.1617258E+01	*

TABULATED VALUES OF E   WHEN R = .091

X	E $^{-RX}$	SUM OF E $^{-RX}$	*	X	E $^{-RX}$	SUM OF E $^{-RX}$	*
0.	1.0000000E+00	1.0000000E+00	*	50.	1.0567204E-02	1.1385655E+01	*
1.	9.1301770E-01	1.9130177E+00	*	51.	9.6480447E-03	1.1395303E+01	*
2.	8.3360133E-01	2.7466190E+00	*	52.	8.8088357E-03	1.1404111E+01	*
3.	7.6109278E-01	3.5077117E+00	*	53.	8.0426230E-03	1.1412153E+01	*
4.	6.9489119E-01	4.2026028E+00	*	54.	7.3430572E-03	1.1419496E+01	*
5.	6.3444796E-01	4.8370507E+00	*	55.	6.7043413E-03	1.1426200E+01	*
6.	5.7926223E-01	5.4163129E+00	*	56.	6.1211823E-03	1.1432321E+01	*
7.	5.2887667E-01	5.9451895E+00	*	57.	5.5887479E-03	1.1437909E+01	*
8.	4.8287377E-01	6.4280632E+00	*	58.	5.1026258E-03	1.1443011E+01	*
9.	4.4087230E-01	6.8689355E+00	*	59.	4.6587877E-03	1.1447669E+01	*
10.	4.0252422E-01	7.2714597E+00	*	60.	4.2535557E-03	1.1451922E+01	*
11.	3.6751174E-01	7.6389714E+00	*	61.	3.8835717E-03	1.1455805E+01	*
12.	3.3554473E-01	7.9745161E+00	*	62.	3.5457697E-03	1.1459350E+01	*
13.	3.0635828E-01	8.2808743E+00	*	63.	3.2373505E-03	1.1462587E+01	*
14.	2.7971053E-01	8.5605848E+00	*	64.	2.9557584E-03	1.1465542E+01	*
15.	2.5538067E-01	8.8159546E+00	*	65.	2.6986597E-03	1.1468240E+01	*
16.	2.3316707E-01	9.0491324E+00	*	66.	2.4639241E-03	1.1470703E+01	*
17.	2.1288567E-01	9.2620180E+00	*	67.	2.2496064E-03	1.1472952E+01	*
18.	1.9436839E-01	9.4563863E+00	*	68.	2.0539305E-03	1.1475005E+01	*
19.	1.7746178E-01	9.6338480E+00	*	69.	1.8752749E-03	1.1476880E+01	*
20.	1.6202575E-01	9.7958737E+00	*	70.	1.7121592E-03	1.1478592E+01	*
21.	1.4793238E-01	9.9438060E+00	*	71.	1.5632316E-03	1.1480155E+01	*
22.	1.3506488E-01	1.0078870E+01	*	72.	1.4272582E-03	1.1481582E+01	*
23.	1.2331663E-01	1.0202186E+01	*	73.	1.3031120E-03	1.1482885E+01	* .
24.	1.1259026E-01	1.0314776E+01	*	74.	1.1897643E-03	1.1484074E+01	*
25.	1.0279690E-01	1.0417572E+01	*	75.	1.0862759E-03	1.1485160E+01	*
26.	9.3855397E-02	1.0511427E+01	*	76.	9.9178917E-04	1.1486151E+01	*
27.	8.5691640E-02	1.0597118E+01	*	77.	9.0552107E-04	1.1487056E+01	*
28.	7.8237985E-02	1.0675355E+01	*	78.	8.2675678E-04	1.1487882E+01	*
29.	7.1432666E-02	1.0746787E+01	*	79.	7.5484358E-04	1.1488636E+01	*
30.	6.5219289E-02	1.0812006E+01	*	80.	6.8918556E-04	1.1489325E+01	*
31.	5.9546366E-02	1.0871552E+01	*	81.	6.2923862E-04	1.1489954E+01	*
32.	5.4366887E-02	1.0925918E+01	*	82.	5.7450600E-04	1.1490528E+01	*
33.	4.9637930E-02	1.0975555E+01	*	83.	5.2453416E-04	1.1491052E+01	*
34.	4.5320310E-02	1.1020875E+01	*	84.	4.7890897E-04	1.1491530E+01	*
35.	4.1378245E-02	1.1062253E+01	*	85.	4.3725237E-04	1.1491967E+01	*
36.	3.7779071E-02	1.1100032E+01	*	86.	3.9921916E-04	1.1492366E+01	*
37.	3.4492961E-02	1.1134524E+01	*	87.	3.6449416E-04	1.1492730E+01	*
38.	3.1492684E-02	1.1166016E+01	*	88.	3.3278963E-04	1.1493062E+01	*
39.	2.8753378E-02	1.1194769E+01	*	89.	3.0384282E-04	1.1493365E+01	*
40.	2.6252343E-02	1.1221021E+01	*	90.	2.7741388E-04	1.1493642E+01	*
41.	2.3968854E-02	1.1244989E+01	*	91.	2.5323378E-04	1.1493895E+01	*
42.	2.1883989E-02	1.1266872E+01	*	92.	2.3125258E-04	1.1494126E+01	*
43.	1.9980469E-02	1.1286852E+01	*	93.	2.1113770E-04	1.1494337E+01	*
44.	1.8242522E-02	1.1305094E+01	*	94.	1.9277246E-04	1.1494529E+01	*
45.	1.6655746E-02	1.1321749E+01	*	95.	1.7600467E-04	1.1494705E+01	*
46.	1.5206991E-02	1.1336955E+01	*	96.	1.6069538E-04	1.1494865E+01	*
47.	1.3884252E-02	1.1350839E+01	*	97.	1.4671773E-04	1.1495011E+01	*
48.	1.2676568E-02	1.1363515E+01	*	98.	1.3395588E-04	1.1495144E+01	*
49.	1.1573931E-02	1.1375088E+01	*	99.	1.2230409E-04	1.1495266E+01	*
50.	1.0567204E-02	1.1385655E+01	*	100.	1.1166580E-04	1.1495377E+01	*

TABULATED VALUES OF E   WHEN R = .092

X	E $^{-RX}$	SUM OF E $^{-RX}$	*	X	E $^{-RX}$	SUM OF E $^{-RX}$	*
0.	1.0000000E+00	1.0000000E+00	*	50.	1.0051835E-02	1.1272903E+01	*
1.	9.1210514E-01	1.9121051E+00	*	51.	9.1683311E-03	1.1282071E+01	*
2.	8.3193580E-01	2.7440409E+00	*	52.	8.3624820E-03	1.1290433E+01	*
3.	7.5881293E-01	3.5028538E+00	*	53.	7.6274629E-03	1.1298060E+01	*
4.	6.9211717E-01	4.1949705E+00	*	54.	6.9570482E-03	1.1305017E+01	*
5.	6.3128364E-01	4.8262545E+00	*	55.	6.3455594E-03	1.1311362E+01	*
6.	5.7579706E-01	5.4020515E+00	*	56.	5.7878175E-03	1.1317149E+01	*
7.	5.2518746E-01	5.9272389E+00	*	57.	5.2790981E-03	1.1322428E+01	*
8.	4.7902619E-01	6.4062650E+00	*	58.	4.8150926E-03	1.1327243E+01	*
9.	4.3692225E-01	6.8431872E+00	*	59.	4.3918707E-03	1.1331634E+01	*
10.	3.9851903E-01	7.2417062E+00	*	60.	4.0058479E-03	1.1335639E+01	*
11.	3.6349126E-01	7.6051974E+00	*	61.	3.6537545E-03	1.1339292E+01	*
12.	3.3154225E-01	7.9367396E+00	*	62.	3.3326083E-03	1.1342624E+01	*
13.	3.0240140E-01	8.2391410E+00	*	63.	3.0396892E-03	1.1345663E+01	*
14.	2.7582187E-01	8.5149628E+00	*	64.	2.7725161E-03	1.1348435E+01	*
15.	2.5157855E-01	8.7665413E+00	*	65.	2.5288262E-03	1.1350963E+01	*
16.	2.2946609E-01	8.9960073E+00	*	66.	2.3065554E-03	1.1353269E+01	*
17.	2.0929720E-01	9.2053045E+00	*	67.	2.1038211E-03	1.1355372E+01	*
18.	1.9090105E-01	9.3962055E+00	*	68.	1.9189060E-03	1.1357290E+01	*
19.	1.7412183E-01	9.5703273E+00	*	69.	1.7502441E-03	1.1359040E+01	*
20.	1.5881742E-01	9.7291447E+00	*	70.	1.5964066E-03	1.1360636E+01	*
21.	1.4485819E-01	9.8740028E+00	*	71.	1.4560907E-03	1.1362092E+01	*
22.	1.3212590E-01	1.0006128E+01	*	72.	1.3281078E-03	1.1363420E+01	*
23.	1.2051271E-01	1.0126640E+01	*	73.	1.2113740E-03	1.1364631E+01	*
24.	1.0992026E-01	1.0236560E+01	*	74.	1.1049004E-03	1.1365735E+01	*
25.	1.0025884E-01	1.0336818E+01	*	75.	1.0077854E-03	1.1366742E+01	*
26.	9.1446607E-02	1.0428264E+01	*	76.	9.1920627E-04	1.1367661E+01	*
27.	8.3408921E-02	1.0511672E+01	*	77.	8.3841277E-04	1.1368499E+01	*
28.	7.6077706E-02	1.0587749E+01	*	78.	7.6472061E-04	1.1369263E+01	*
29.	6.9390868E-02	1.0657139E+01	*	79.	6.9750560E-04	1.1369960E+01	*
30.	6.3291768E-02	1.0720430E+01	*	80.	6.3619845E-04	1.1370596E+01	*
31.	5.7728747E-02	1.0778158E+01	*	81.	5.8027989E-04	1.1371176E+01	*
32.	5.2654688E-02	1.0830812E+01	*	82.	5.2927627E-04	1.1371705E+01	*
33.	4.8026612E-02	1.0878838E+01	*	83.	4.8275561E-04	1.1372187E+01	*
34.	4.3805320E-02	1.0922643E+01	*	84.	4.4032388E-04	1.1372627E+01	*
35.	3.9955058E-02	1.0962598E+01	*	85.	4.0162168E-04	1.1373028E+01	*
36.	3.6443214E-02	1.0999041E+01	*	86.	3.6632120E-04	1.1373394E+01	*
37.	3.3240043E-02	1.1032281E+01	*	87.	3.3412345E-04	1.1373728E+01	*
38.	3.0318414E-02	1.1062599E+01	*	88.	3.0475572E-04	1.1374032E+01	*
39.	2.7653582E-02	1.1090225E+01	*	89.	2.7796926E-04	1.1374309E+01	*
40.	2.5222974E-02	1.1115474E+01	*	90.	2.5353719E-04	1.1374562E+01	*
41.	2.3006005E-02	1.1138480E+01	*	91.	2.3125258E-04	1.1374793E+01	*
42.	2.0983895E-02	1.1159463E+01	*	92.	2.1092667E-04	1.1375003E+01	*
43.	1.9139519E-02	1.1178602E+01	*	93.	1.9238730E-04	1.1375195E+01	*
44.	1.7457254E-02	1.1196059E+01	*	94.	1.7547745E-04	1.1375370E+01	*
45.	1.5922851E-02	1.1211981E+01	*	95.	1.6005388E-04	1.1375530E+01	*
46.	1.4523314E-02	1.1226504E+01	*	96.	1.4598597E-04	1.1375675E+01	*
47.	1.3246790E-02	1.1239750E+01	*	97.	1.3315455E-04	1.1375808E+01	*
48.	1.2082465E-02	1.1251832E+01	*	98.	1.2145095E-04	1.1375929E+01	*
49.	1.1020479E-02	1.1262852E+01	*	99.	1.1077604E-04	1.1376039E+01	*
50.	1.0051835E-02	1.1272903E+01	*	100.	1.0103940E-04	1.1376140E+01	*

X	E ($-RX$)	SUM OF E ($-RX$)	°	X	E ($-RX$)	SUM OF E ($-RX$)	°
0.	1.0000000E+00	1.0000000E+00	°	50.	9.5616019E-03	1.1162313E+01	°
1.	9.1119349E-01	1.9111934E+00	°	51.	8.7124695E-03	1.1171025E+01	°
2.	8.3027359E-01	2.7414669E+00	°	52.	7.9387456E-03	1.1178963E+01	°
3.	7.5653990E-01	3.4980068E+00	°	53.	7.2337333E-03	1.1186196E+01	°
4.	6.8935424E-01	4.1873610E+00	°	54.	6.5913308E-03	1.1192787E+01	°
5.	6.2813510E-01	4.8154961E+00	°	55.	6.0059778E-03	1.1198792E+01	°
6.	5.7235262E-01	5.3878487E+00	°	56.	5.4726079E-03	1.1204264E+01	°
7.	5.2152399E-01	5.9093726E+00	°	57.	4.9866048E-03	1.1209250E+01	°
8.	4.7520927E-01	6.3845818E+00	°	58.	4.5437618E-03	1.1213793E+01	°
9.	4.3300759E-01	6.8175893E+00	°	59.	4.1402462E-03	1.1217933E+01	°
10.	3.9455370E-01	7.2121430E+00	°	60.	3.7725655E-03	1.1221705E+01	°
11.	3.5951477E-01	7.5716577E+00	°	61.	3.4375371E-03	1.1225142E+01	°
12.	3.2758752E-01	7.8992452E+00	°	62.	3.1322615E-03	1.1228274E+01	°
13.	2.9849562E-01	8.1977408E+00	°	63.	2.8540963E-03	1.1231128E+01	°
14.	2.7198727E-01	8.4697208E+00	°	64.	2.6006340E-03	1.1233728E+01	°
15.	2.4783303E-01	8.7175610E+00	°	65.	2.3696808E-03	1.1236097E+01	°
16.	2.2582385E-01	8.9433848E+00	°	66.	2.1592377E-03	1.1238256E+01	°
17.	2.0576922E-01	9.1491540E+00	°	67.	1.9674834E-03	1.1240223E+01	°
18.	1.8749558E-01	9.3366495E+00	°	68.	1.7927581E-03	1.1242015E+01	°
19.	1.7084475E-01	9.5074942E+00	°	69.	1.6335495E-03	1.1243648E+01	°
20.	1.5567263E-01	9.6631668E+00	°	70.	1.4884797E-03	1.1245136E+01	°
21.	1.4184788E-01	9.8050146E+00	°	71.	1.3562930E-03	1.1246492E+01	°
22.	1.2925087E-01	9.9342654E+00	°	72.	1.2358454E-03	1.1247727E+01	°
23.	1.1777255E-01	1.0052037E+01	°	73.	1.1260943E-03	1.1248853E+01	°
24.	1.0731358E-01	1.0159350E+01	°	74.	1.0260898E-03	1.1249879E+01	°
25.	9.7783443E-02	1.0257133E+01	°	75.	9.3496636E-04	1.1250813E+01	°
26.	8.9099638E-02	1.0346232E+01	°	76.	8.5193527E-04	1.1251664E+01	°
27.	8.1187011E-02	1.0427419E+01	°	77.	7.7627788E-04	1.1252440E+01	°
28.	7.3977077E-02	1.0501396E+01	°	78.	7.0733936E-04	1.1253147E+01	°
29.	6.7407431E-02	1.0568803E+01	°	79.	6.4452302E-04	1.1253791E+01	°
30.	6.1421213E-02	1.0630224E+01	°	80.	5.8728519E-04	1.1254378E+01	°
31.	5.5966610E-02	1.0686190E+01	°	81.	5.3513045E-04	1.1254913E+01	°
32.	5.0996611E-02	1.0737186E+01	°	82.	4.8760739E-04	1.1255400E+01	°
33.	4.6467599E-02	1.0783653E+01	°	83.	4.4430468E-04	1.1255844E+01	°
34.	4.2340094E-02	1.0825993E+01	°	84.	4.0484754E-04	1.1256248E+01	°
35.	3.8580820E-02	1.0864573E+01	°	85.	3.6889444E-04	1.1256616E+01	°
36.	3.5154592E-02	1.0899727E+01	°	86.	3.3613422E-04	1.1256952E+01	°
37.	3.2032636E-02	1.0931759E+01	°	87.	3.0628332E-04	1.1257258E+01	°
38.	2.9187930E-02	1.0960946E+01	°	88.	2.7908337E-04	1.1257537E+01	°
39.	2.6595852E-02	1.0987541E+01	°	89.	2.5429895E-04	1.1257791E+01	°
40.	2.4233967E-02	1.1011774E+01	°	90.	2.3171555E-04	1.1258022E+01	°
41.	2.2081833E-02	1.1033855E+01	°	91.	2.1113770E-04	1.1258233E+01	°
42.	2.0120823E-02	1.1053975E+01	°	92.	1.9238730E-04	1.1258425E+01	°
43.	1.8333963E-02	1.1072308E+01	°	93.	1.7530206E-04	1.1258600E+01	°
44.	1.6705788E-02	1.1089013E+01	°	94.	1.5973409E-04	1.1258759E+01	°
45.	1.5222205E-02	1.1104235E+01	°	95.	1.4554867E-04	1.1258904E+01	°
46.	1.3870375E-02	1.1118105E+01	°	96.	1.3262300E-04	1.1259036E+01	°
47.	1.2638595E-02	1.1130743E+01	°	97.	1.2084522E-04	1.1259156E+01	°
48.	1.1516206E-02	1.1142259E+01	°	98.	1.1011337E-04	1.1259266E+01	°
49.	1.0493492E-02	1.1152752E+01	°	99.	1.0033459E-04	1.1259366E+01	°
50.	9.5616019E-03	1.1162313E+01	°	100.	9.1424231E-05	1.1259457E+01	°

X	E ($-RX$)	SUM OF E ($-RX$)	°	X	E ($-RX$)	SUM OF E ($-RX$)	°
0.	1.0000000E+00	1.0000000E+00	°	50.	9.0952770E-03	1.1053833E+01	°
1.	9.1028276E-01	1.9102827E+00	°	51.	8.2792739E-03	1.1062112E+01	°
2.	8.2861470E-01	2.7388974E+00	°	52.	7.5364803E-03	1.1069648E+01	°
3.	7.5427368E-01	3.4931710E+00	°	53.	6.8603281E-03	1.1076508E+01	°
4.	6.8660233E-01	4.1797733E+00	°	54.	6.2448384E-03	1.1082752E+01	°
5.	6.2500226E-01	4.8047755E+00	°	55.	5.6845688E-03	1.1088436E+01	°
6.	5.6892878E-01	5.3737042E+00	°	56.	5.1745649E-03	1.1093610E+01	°
7.	5.1788607E-01	5.8915902E+00	°	57.	4.7103173E-03	1.1098382E+01	°
8.	4.7142276E-01	6.3630129E+00	°	58.	4.2877206E-03	1.1102607E+01	°
9.	4.2912801E-01	6.7921409E+00	°	59.	3.9030382E-03	1.1106510E+01	°
10.	3.9062783E-01	7.1827687E+00	°	60.	3.5528684E-03	1.1110062E+01	°
11.	3.5558178E-01	7.5383504E+00	°	61.	3.2341148E-03	1.1113296E+01	°
12.	3.2367996E-01	7.8620303E+00	°	62.	2.9439590E-03	1.1116239E+01	°
13.	2.9464029E-01	8.1566705E+00	°	63.	2.6798351E-03	1.1118918E+01	°
14.	2.6820598E-01	8.4248764E+00	°	64.	2.4394077E-03	1.1121357E+01	°
15.	2.4414328E-01	8.6690196E+00	°	65.	2.2205508E-03	1.1123577E+01	°
16.	2.2223942E-01	8.8912590E+00	°	66.	2.0213291E-03	1.1125598E+01	°
17.	2.0230071E-01	9.0935597E+00	°	67.	1.8399810E-03	1.1127437E+01	°
18.	1.8415085E-01	9.2777105E+00	°	68.	1.6749030E-03	1.1129111E+01	°
19.	1.6762934E-01	9.4453398E+00	°	69.	1.5246353E-03	1.1130635E+01	°
20.	1.5259010E-01	9.5979299E+00	°	70.	1.3878492E-03	1.1132022E+01	°
21.	1.3890014E-01	9.7368300E+00	°	71.	1.2633352E-03	1.1133285E+01	°
22.	1.2643840E-01	9.8632684E+00	°	72.	1.1499923E-03	1.1134434E+01	°
23.	1.1509470E-01	9.9783631E+00	°	73.	1.0468181E-03	1.1135480E+01	°
24.	1.0476872E-01	1.0083131E+01	°	74.	9.5290056E-04	1.1136432E+01	°
25.	9.5369162E-02	1.0178500E+01	°	75.	8.6740895E-04	1.1137299E+01	°
26.	8.6812904E-02	1.0265312E+01	°	76.	7.8958742E-04	1.1138088E+01	°
27.	7.9024290E-02	1.0344336E+01	°	77.	7.1874781E-04	1.1138806E+01	°
28.	7.1934449E-02	1.0416270E+01	°	78.	6.5426374E-04	1.1139460E+01	°
29.	6.5480689E-02	1.0481750E+01	°	79.	5.9556501E-04	1.1140055E+01	°
30.	5.9605942E-02	1.0541355E+01	°	80.	5.4213256E-04	1.1140597E+01	°
31.	5.4258262E-02	1.0595613E+01	°	81.	4.9349392E-04	1.1141090E+01	°
32.	4.9390360E-02	1.0645003E+01	°	82.	4.4921901E-04	1.1141539E+01	°
33.	4.4959193E-02	1.0689962E+01	°	83.	4.0891632E-04	1.1141947E+01	°
34.	4.0925579E-02	1.0730887E+01	°	84.	3.7222948E-04	1.1142319E+01	°
35.	3.7253849E-02	1.0768140E+01	°	85.	3.3883408E-04	1.1142657E+01	°
36.	3.3911536E-02	1.0802051E+01	°	86.	3.0843462E-04	1.1142965E+01	°
37.	3.0869087E-02	1.0832920E+01	°	87.	2.8076290E-04	1.1143245E+01	°
38.	2.8099559E-02	1.0861019E+01	°	88.	2.5557363E-04	1.1143500E+01	°
39.	2.5578579E-02	1.0886597E+01	°	89.	2.3264427E-04	1.1143732E+01	°
40.	2.3283740E-02	1.0909880E+01	°	90.	2.1177207E-04	1.1143943E+01	°
41.	2.1194787E-02	1.0931074E+01	°	91.	1.9277246E-04	1.1144135E+01	°
42.	1.9293249E-02	1.0950367E+01	°	92.	1.7547745E-04	1.1144310E+01	°
43.	1.7562312E-02	1.0967929E+01	°	93.	1.5973409E-04	1.1144469E+01	°
44.	1.5986670E-02	1.0983915E+01	°	94.	1.4540319E-04	1.1144614E+01	°
45.	1.4552390E-02	1.0998467E+01	°	95.	1.3235802E-04	1.1144746E+01	°
46.	1.3246790E-02	1.1011713E+01	°	96.	1.2048322E-04	1.1144866E+01	°
47.	1.2058324E-02	1.1023771E+01	°	97.	1.0967380E-04	1.1144975E+01	°
48.	1.0976485E-02	1.1034747E+01	°	98.	9.9834174E-05	1.1145074E+01	°
49.	9.9917052E-03	1.1044738E+01	°	99.	9.0877328E-05	1.1145164E+01	°
50.	9.0952770E-03	1.1053833E+01	°	100.	8.2724065E-05	1.1145246E+01	°

X	E^{-RX}	SUM OF E^{-RX}	*	X	E^{-RX}	SUM OF E^{-RX}	*
0.	1.0000000E+00	1.0000000E+00	*	50.	8.6516951E-03	1.0947404E+01	*
1.	9.0937293E-01	1.9093729E+00	*	51.	7.8676174E-03	1.0955271E+01	*
2.	8.2695913E-01	2.7363320E+00	*	52.	7.1545983E-03	1.0962425E+01	*
3.	7.5201425E-01	3.4883462E+00	*	53.	6.5061980E-03	1.0968931E+01	*
4.	6.8386140E-01	4.1722076E+00	*	54.	5.9165604E-03	1.0974847E+01	*
5.	6.2188505E-01	4.7940926E+00	*	55.	5.3803599E-03	1.0980227E+01	*
6.	5.6552543E-01	5.3596180E+00	*	56.	4.8927553E-03	1.0985119E+01	*
7.	5.1427352E-01	5.8738915E+00	*	57.	4.4493378E-03	1.0989568E+01	*
8.	4.6766642E-01	6.3415579E+00	*	58.	4.0461073E-03	1.0993614E+01	*
9.	4.2528319E-01	6.7668410E+00	*	59.	3.6794205E-03	1.0997293E+01	*
10.	3.8674102E-01	7.1535820E+00	*	60.	3.3459654E-03	1.1000638E+01	*
11.	3.5169181E-01	7.5052738E+00	*	61.	3.0427304E-03	1.1003680E+01	*
12.	3.1981902E-01	7.8250928E+00	*	62.	2.7669766E-03	1.1006446E+01	*
13.	2.9083476E-01	8.1159275E+00	*	63.	2.5162137E-03	1.1008962E+01	*
14.	2.6447726E-01	8.3804047E+00	*	64.	2.2881766E-03	1.1011250E+01	*
15.	2.4050846E-01	8.6209131E+00	*	65.	2.0808059E-03	1.1013330E+01	*
16.	2.1871188E-01	8.8396240E+00	*	66.	1.8922285E-03	1.1015222E+01	*
17.	1.9889067E-01	9.0385155E+00	*	67.	1.7207414E-03	1.1016942E+01	*
18.	1.8086579E-01	9.2193812E+00	*	68.	1.5647957E-03	1.1018506E+01	*
19.	1.6447445E-01	9.3838556E+00	*	69.	1.4229828E-03	1.1019928E+01	*
20.	1.4956861E-01	9.5334242E+00	*	70.	1.2940221E-03	1.1021222E+01	*
21.	1.3601365E-01	9.6694378E+00	*	71.	1.1767486E-03	1.1022398E+01	*
22.	1.2368713E-01	9.7931249E+00	*	72.	1.0701033E-03	1.1023468E+01	*
23.	1.1247773E-01	9.9056026E+00	*	73.	9.7312306E-04	1.1024441E+01	*
24.	1.0228420E-01	1.0007886E+01	*	74.	8.8493177E-04	1.1025325E+01	*
25.	9.3014489E-02	1.0100900E+01	*	75.	8.0473300E-04	1.1026129E+01	*
26.	8.4584858E-02	1.0185484E+01	*	76.	7.3180241E-04	1.1026860E+01	*
27.	7.6919181E-02	1.0262403E+01	*	77.	6.6548131E-04	1.1027525E+01	*
28.	6.9948221E-02	1.0332351E+01	*	78.	6.0517069E-04	1.1028130E+01	*
29.	6.3609019E-02	1.0395960E+01	*	79.	5.5032584E-04	1.1028680E+01	*
30.	5.7844320E-02	1.0453804E+01	*	80.	5.0045143E-04	1.1029180E+01	*
31.	5.2602059E-02	1.0506406E+01	*	81.	4.5509698E-04	1.1029635E+01	*
32.	4.7834889E-02	1.0554240E+01	*	82.	4.1385288E-04	1.1030048E+01	*
33.	4.3499753E-02	1.0597739E+01	*	83.	3.7634661E-04	1.1030424E+01	*
34.	3.9557498E-02	1.0637296E+01	*	84.	3.4223942E-04	1.1030766E+01	*
35.	3.5972518E-02	1.0673268E+01	*	85.	3.1122326E-04	1.1031077E+01	*
36.	3.2712434E-02	1.0705980E+01	*	86.	2.8301801E-04	1.1031360E+01	*
37.	2.9747802E-02	1.0735727E+01	*	87.	2.5736892E-04	1.1031617E+01	*
38.	2.7051846E-02	1.0762778E+01	*	88.	2.3404433E-04	1.1031851E+01	*
39.	2.4600217E-02	1.0787378E+01	*	89.	2.1283358E-04	1.1032063E+01	*
40.	2.2370771E-02	1.0809748E+01	*	90.	1.9354509E-04	1.1032256E+01	*
41.	2.0343374E-02	1.0830091E+01	*	91.	1.7600467E-04	1.1032432E+01	*
42.	1.8499714E-02	1.0848590E+01	*	92.	1.6005388E-04	1.1032592E+01	*
43.	1.6823139E-02	1.0865413E+01	*	93.	1.4554867E-04	1.1032737E+01	*
44.	1.5298507E-02	1.0880711E+01	*	94.	1.3235802E-04	1.1032869E+01	*
45.	1.3912048E-02	1.0894623E+01	*	95.	1.2036280E-04	1.1032989E+01	*
46.	1.2651240E-02	1.0907274E+01	*	96.	1.0945467E-04	1.1033098E+01	*
47.	1.1504695E-02	1.0918778E+01	*	97.	9.9535121E-05	1.1033197E+01	*
48.	1.0462058E-02	1.0929240E+01	*	98.	9.0514545E-05	1.1033287E+01	*
49.	9.5139132E-03	1.0938753E+01	*	99.	8.2311477E-05	1.1033369E+01	*
50.	8.6516951E-03	1.0947404E+01	*	100.	7.4851829E-05	1.1033443E+01	*

X	E^{-RX}	SUM OF E^{-RX}	*	X	E^{-RX}	SUM OF E^{-RX}	*
0.	1.0000000E+00	1.0000000E+00	*	50.	8.2297470E-03	1.0842972E+01	*
1.	9.0846401E-01	1.9084640E+00	*	51.	7.4764290E-03	1.0850448E+01	*
2.	8.2530686E-01	2.7337708E+00	*	52.	6.7920667E-03	1.0857240E+01	*
3.	7.4976159E-01	3.4835323E+00	*	53.	6.1703482E-03	1.0863410E+01	*
4.	6.8113142E-01	4.1646637E+00	*	54.	5.6055393E-03	1.0869015E+01	*
5.	6.1878339E-01	4.7834470E+00	*	55.	5.0924307E-03	1.0874107E+01	*
6.	5.6212444E-01	5.3455894E+00	*	56.	4.6262901E-03	1.0878733E+01	*
7.	5.1068618E-01	5.8562755E+00	*	57.	4.2028181E-03	1.0882935E+01	*
8.	4.6394002E-01	6.3202155E+00	*	58.	3.8181090E-03	1.0886753E+01	*
9.	4.2147281E-01	6.7416883E+00	*	59.	3.4686146E-03	1.0890221E+01	*
10.	3.8289288E-01	7.1245811E+00	*	60.	3.1511115E-03	1.0893372E+01	*
11.	3.4784440E-01	7.4724255E+00	*	61.	2.8626714E-03	1.0896234E+01	*
12.	3.1600412E-01	7.7884296E+00	*	62.	2.6006340E-03	1.0898834E+01	*
13.	2.8707837E-01	8.0755079E+00	*	63.	2.3625824E-03	1.0901196E+01	*
14.	2.6080037E-01	8.3363082E+00	*	64.	2.1463211E-03	1.0903342E+01	*
15.	2.3692775E-01	8.5732359E+00	*	65.	1.9498555E-03	1.0905291E+01	*
16.	2.1524034E-01	8.7884762E+00	*	66.	1.7713735E-03	1.0907062E+01	*
17.	1.9553810E-01	8.9840143E+00	*	67.	1.6092291E-03	1.0908671E+01	*
18.	1.7763933E-01	9.1616536E+00	*	68.	1.4619267E-03	1.0910132E+01	*
19.	1.6137894E-01	9.3230325E+00	*	69.	1.3281078E-03	1.0911460E+01	*
20.	1.4660696E-01	9.4696394E+00	*	70.	1.2065382E-03	1.0912666E+01	*
21.	1.3318714E-01	9.6028265E+00	*	71.	1.0960965E-03	1.0913762E+01	*
22.	1.2099573E-01	9.7238222E+00	*	72.	9.9576427E-04	1.0914757E+01	*
23.	1.0992026E-01	9.8337424E+00	*	73.	9.0461600E-04	1.0915661E+01	*
24.	9.9858609E-02	9.9336010E+00	*	74.	8.2181109E-04	1.0916482E+01	*
25.	9.0717953E-02	1.0024318E+01	*	75.	7.4658580E-04	1.0917228E+01	*
26.	8.2413995E-02	1.0106731E+01	*	76.	6.7824634E-04	1.0917906E+01	*
27.	7.4870149E-02	1.0181601E+01	*	77.	6.1616239E-04	1.0918522E+01	*
28.	6.8016836E-02	1.0249617E+01	*	78.	5.5976136E-04	1.0919081E+01	*
29.	6.1790848E-02	1.0311407E+01	*	79.	5.0852305E-04	1.0919589E+01	*
30.	5.6134762E-02	1.0367541E+01	*	80.	4.6197489E-04	1.0920050E+01	*
31.	5.0996411E-02	1.0418530E+01	*	81.	4.1968757E-04	1.0920469E+01	*
32.	4.6328405E-02	1.0464865E+01	*	82.	3.8127105E-04	1.0920850E+01	*
33.	4.2087689E-02	1.0506952E+01	*	83.	3.4637103E-04	1.0921196E+01	*
34.	3.8235151E-02	1.0545187E+01	*	84.	3.1466562E-04	1.0921510E+01	*
35.	3.4735258E-02	1.0579922E+01	*	85.	2.8586239E-04	1.0921795E+01	*
36.	3.1555732E-02	1.0611477E+01	*	86.	2.5969569E-04	1.0922054E+01	*
37.	2.8667247E-02	1.0640144E+01	*	87.	2.3592419E-04	1.0922289E+01	*
38.	2.6043162E-02	1.0666187E+01	*	88.	2.1432864E-04	1.0922503E+01	*
39.	2.3659276E-02	1.0689846E+01	*	89.	1.9470986E-04	1.0922697E+01	*
40.	2.1493601E-02	1.0711339E+01	*	90.	1.7688690E-04	1.0922873E+01'	*
41.	1.9526163E-02	1.0730865E+01	*	91.	1.6069538E-04	1.0923033E+01	*
42.	1.7738816E-02	1.0748603E+01	*	92.	1.4598597E-04	1.0923178E+01	*
43.	1.6115076E-02	1.0764718E+01	*	93.	1.3262300E-04	1.0923310E+01	*
44.	1.4639967E-02	1.0779357E+01	*	94.	1.2048322E-04	1.0923430E+01	*
45.	1.3299883E-02	1.0792656E+01	*	95.	1.0945467E-04	1.0923539E+01	*
46.	1.2082465E-02	1.0804738E+01	*	96.	9.9435635E-05	1.0923638E+01	*
47.	1.0976458E-02	1.0815714E+01	*	97.	9.0333696E-05	1.0923728E+01	*
48.	9.9717418E-03	1.0825685E+01	*	98.	8.2064912E-05	1.0923810E+01	*
49.	9.0589686E-03	1.0834743E+01	*	99.	7.4553020E-05	1.0923884E+01	*
50.	8.2297470E-03	1.0842972E+01	*	100.	6.7728736E-05	1.0923951E+01	*

x	E^{-RX}	SUM OF E^{-RX}	*	x	E^{-RX}	SUM OF E^{-RX}	*
0.	1.0000000E+00	1.0000000E+00	*	50.	7.8283775E-03	1.0740491E+01	*
1.	9.0755600E-01	1.9075560E+00	*	51.	7.1046910E-03	1.0747595E+01	*
2.	8.2365790E-01	2.7312139E+00	*	52.	6.4447905E-03	1.0754042E+01	*
3.	7.4751557E-01	3.4787295E+00	*	53.	5.8518349E-03	1.0759893E+01	*
4.	6.7841234E-01	4.1571418E+00	*	54.	5.3108679E-03	1.0765203E+01	*
5.	6.1569719E-01	4.7728389E+00	*	55.	4.8199101E-03	1.0770022E+01	*
6.	5.5877968E-01	5.3316185E+00	*	56.	4.3743383E-03	1.0774396E+01	*
7.	5.0712336E-01	5.8387423E+00	*	57.	3.9699570E-03	1.0778365E+01	*
8.	4.6024330E-01	6.2989856E+00	*	58.	3.6029583E-03	1.0781967E+01	*
9.	4.1769657E-01	6.7166821E+00	*	59.	3.2698650E-03	1.0785236E+01	*
10.	3.7908303E-01	7.0957651E+00	*	60.	2.9676051E-03	1.0788203E+01	*
11.	3.4403908E-01	7.4398041E+00	*	61.	2.6932678E-03	1.0790896E+01	*
12.	3.1223474E-01	7.7520388E+00	*	62.	2.4442914E-03	1.0793340E+01	*
13.	2.8337051E-01	8.0354093E+00	*	63.	2.2183313E-03	1.0795558E+01	*
14.	2.5717461E-01	8.2925839E+00	*	64.	2.0132599E-03	1.0797571E+01	*
15.	2.3340036E-01	8.5259842E+00	*	65.	1.8271461E-03	1.0799398E+01	*
16.	2.1182390E-01	8.7378081E+00	*	66.	1.6582374E-03	1.0801056E+01	*
17.	1.9224205E-01	8.9300501E+00	*	67.	1.5049433E-03	1.0802560E+01	*
18.	1.7447043E-01	9.1045205E+00	*	68.	1.3658204E-03	1.0803925E+01	*
19.	1.5834168E-01	9.2628621E+00	*	69.	1.2395585E-03	1.0805164E+01	*
20.	1.4370394E-01	9.4065660E+00	*	70.	1.1249687E-03	1.0806288E+01	*
21.	1.3041938E-01	9.5369853E+00	*	71.	1.0209721E-03	1.0807308E+01	*
22.	1.1836289E-01	9.6553481E+00	*	72.	9.2658942E-04	1.0808234E+01	*
23.	1.0742095E-01	9.7627690E+00	*	73.	8.4093179E-04	1.0809074E+01	*
24.	9.7490533E-02	9.8602595E+00	*	74.	7.6319270E-04	1.0809837E+01	*
25.	8.8478118E-02	9.9487376E+00	*	75.	6.9264011E-04	1.0810529E+01	*
26.	8.0298848E-02	1.0029036E+01	*	76.	6.2860970E-04	1.0811157E+01	*
27.	7.2875702E-02	1.0101911E+01	*	77.	5.7049850E-04	1.0811727E+01	*
28.	6.6138780E-02	1.0168049E+01	*	78.	5.1775934E-04	1.0812244E+01	*
29.	6.0024647E-02	1.0228073E+01	*	79.	4.6989560E-04	1.0812713E+01	*
30.	5.4475729E-02	1.0282548E+01	*	80.	4.2645657E-04	1.0813139E+01	*
31.	4.9439775E-02	1.0331987E+01	*	81.	3.8703323E-04	1.0813526E+01	*
32.	4.4869365E-02	1.0376856E+01	*	82.	3.5125433E-04	1.0813877E+01	*
33.	4.0721462E-02	1.0417577E+01	*	83.	3.1878297E-04	1.0814195E+01	*
34.	3.6957007E-02	1.0454534E+01	*	84.	2.8931340E-04	1.0814484E+01	*
35.	3.3540554E-02	1.0488074E+01	*	85.	2.6256812E-04	1.0814746E+01	*
36.	3.0439931E-02	1.0518513E+01	*	86.	2.3829527E-04	1.0814984E+01	*
37.	2.7625942E-02	1.0546138E+01	*	87.	2.1626630E-04	1.0815200E+01	*
38.	2.5072090E-02	1.0571210E+01	*	88.	1.9627378E-04	1.0815396E+01	*
39.	2.2754325E-02	1.0593964E+01	*	89.	1.7812945E-04	1.0815574E+01	*
40.	2.0650825E-02	1.0614614E+01	*	90.	1.6166245E-04	1.0815735E+01	*
41.	1.8741780E-02	1.0633355E+01	*	91.	1.4671773E-04	1.0815881E+01	*
42.	1.7009215E-02	1.0650364E+01	*	92.	1.3315455E-04	1.0816014E+01	*
43.	1.5436815E-02	1.0665800E+01	*	93.	1.2084522E-04	1.0816134E+01	*
44.	1.4009774E-02	1.0679809E+01	*	94.	1.0967380E-04	1.0816243E+01	*
45.	1.2714655E-02	1.0692523E+01	*	95.	9.9535121E-05	1.0816342E+01	*
46.	1.1539261E-02	1.0704062E+01	*	96.	9.0335696E-05	1.0816432E+01	*
47.	1.0472526E-02	1.0714534E+01	*	97.	8.1982889E-05	1.0816513E+01	*
48.	9.5044040E-03	1.0724030E+01	*	98.	7.4404063E-05	1.0816587E+01	*
49.	8.6257789E-03	1.0732663E+01	*	99.	6.7525854E-05	1.0816654E+01	*
50.	7.8283775E-03	1.0740491E+01	*	100.	6.1283494E-05	1.0816715E+01	*

x	E^{-RX}	SUM OF E^{-RX}	*	x	E^{-RX}	SUM OF E^{-RX}	*
0.	1.0000000E+00	1.0000000E+00	*	50.	7.4465830E-03	1.0639909E+01	*
1.	9.0664890E-01	1.9066489E+00	*	51.	6.7514363E-03	1.0646660E+01	*
2.	8.2201223E-01	2.7286611E+00	*	52.	6.1211823E-03	1.0652781E+01	*
3.	7.4527648E-01	3.4739375E+00	*	53.	5.5497632E-03	1.0658330E+01	*
4.	6.7570411E-01	4.1496416E+00	*	54.	5.0316867E-03	1.0663361E+01	*
5.	6.1262639E-01	4.7622679E+00	*	55.	4.5619733E-03	1.0667922E+01	*
6.	5.5543704E-01	5.3177049E+00	*	56.	4.1361081E-03	1.0672058E+01	*
7.	5.0358638E-01	5.8212912E+00	*	57.	3.7499788E-03	1.0675807E+01	*
8.	4.5657604E-01	6.2778672E+00	*	58.	3.3999314E-03	1.0679206E+01	*
9.	4.1395417E-01	6.6918213E+00	*	59.	3.0825441E-03	1.0682288E+01	*
10.	3.7531109E-01	7.0671323E+00	*	60.	2.7947852E-03	1.0685082E+01	*
11.	3.4027539E-01	7.4074076E+00	*	61.	2.5338889E-03	1.0687615E+01	*
12.	3.0851031E-01	7.7159179E+00	*	62.	2.2973476E-03	1.0689912E+01	*
13.	2.7971053E-01	7.9956284E+00	*	63.	2.0828877E-03	1.0691994E+01	*
14.	2.5359925E-01	8.2492276E+00	*	64.	1.8884797E-03	1.0693882E+01	*
15.	2.2992548E-01	8.4791530E+00	*	65.	1.7121592E-03	1.0695594E+01	*
16.	2.0846168E-01	8.6876146E+00	*	66.	1.5523272E-03	1.0697146E+01	*
17.	1.8900156E-01	8.8766161E+00	*	67.	1.4074158E-03	1.0698553E+01	*
18.	1.7135805E-01	9.0479741E+00	*	68.	1.2760320E-03	1.0699829E+01	*
19.	1.5536159E-01	9.2033356E+00	*	69.	1.1569130E-03	1.0700985E+01	*
20.	1.4085842E-01	9.3441940E+00	*	70.	1.0489139E-03	1.0702033E+01	*
21.	1.2770913E-01	9.4719031E+00	*	71.	9.5099666E-04	1.0702983E+01	*
22.	1.1578734E-01	9.5876904E+00	*	72.	8.6222008E-04	1.0703845E+01	*
23.	1.0497846E-01	9.6926688E+00	*	73.	7.8173089E-04	1.0704626E+01	*
24.	9.5178614E-02	9.7878474E+00	*	74.	7.0875545E-04	1.0705334E+01	*
25.	8.6293586E-02	9.8741409E+00	*	75.	6.4259235E-04	1.0705976E+01	*
26.	7.8237985E-02	9.9523788E+00	*	76.	5.8260565E-04	1.0706558E+01	*
27.	7.0934383E-02	1.0023313E+01	*	77.	5.2821878E-04	1.0707086E+01	*
28.	6.4312581E-02	1.0087625E+01	*	78.	4.7890897E-04	1.0707564E+01	*
29.	5.8308931E-02	1.0145933E+01	*	79.	4.3420230E-04	1.0707998E+01	*
30.	5.2865728E-02	1.0198798E+01	*	80.	3.9366904E-04	1.0708391E+01	*
31.	4.7930654E-02	1.0246728E+01	*	81.	3.5691960E-04	1.0708747E+01	*
32.	4.3456275E-02	1.0290184E+01	*	82.	3.2360076E-04	1.0709070E+01	*
33.	3.9399584E-02	1.0329583E+01	*	83.	2.9339222E-04	1.0709363E+01	*
34.	3.5721590E-02	1.0365304E+01	*	84.	2.6600378E-04	1.0709629E+01	*
35.	3.2386940E-02	1.0397690E+01	*	85.	2.4117204E-04	1.0709870E+01	*
36.	2.9363584E-02	1.0427053E+01	*	86.	2.1865836E-04	1.0710088E+01	*
37.	2.6622461E-02	1.0453675E+01	*	87.	1.9824637E-04	1.0710286E+01	*
38.	2.4137225E-02	1.0477812E+01	*	88.	1.7973985E-04	1.0710465E+01	*
39.	2.1883989E-02	1.0499695E+01	*	89.	1.6296094E-04	1.0710627E+01	*
40.	1.9841094E-02	1.0519536E+01	*	90.	1.4774835E-04	1.0710774E+01	*
41.	1.7988906E-02	1.0537524E+01	*	91.	1.3395588E-04	1.0710907E+01	*
42.	1.6309622E-02	1.0553833E+01	*	92.	1.2145095E-04	1.0711028E+01	*
43.	1.4787101E-02	1.0568620E+01	*	93.	1.1011337E-04	1.0711138E+01	*
44.	1.3406709E-02	1.0582026E+01	*	94.	9.9834174E-05	1.0711237E+01	*
45.	1.2155178E-02	1.0594181E+01	*	95.	9.0514545E-05	1.0711327E+01	*
46.	1.1020479E-02	1.0605201E+01	*	96.	8.2064912E-05	1.0711409E+01	*
47.	9.9917052E-03	1.0615192E+01	*	97.	7.4404063E-05	1.0711483E+01	*
48.	9.0589686E-03	1.0624250E+01	*	98.	6.7458362E-05	1.0711550E+01	*
49.	8.2133039E-03	1.0632463E+01	*	99.	6.1161050E-05	1.0711611E+01	*
50.	7.4465830E-03	1.0639909E+01	*	100.	5.5451599E-05	1.0711666E+01	*

TABULATED VALUES OF E^{-RX} WHEN R = .099

X	E^{-RX}	SUM OF E^{-RX}	✿	X	E^{-RX}	SUM OF E^{-RX}	✿
0.	1.0000000E+00	1.0000000E+00	✿	50.	7.0834089E-03	1.0541181E+01	✿
1.	9.0574270E-01	1.9057427E+00	✿	51.	6.4157459E-03	1.0547596E+01	✿
2.	8.2036985E-01	2.7261125E+00	✿	52.	5.8110151E-03	1.0553407E+01	✿
3.	7.4304401E-01	3.4691565E+00	✿	53.	5.2632845E-03	1.0558670E+01	✿
4.	6.7300669E-01	4.1421631E+00	✿	54.	4.7671816E-03	1.0563437E+01	✿
5.	6.0957090E-01	4.7517340E+00	✿	55.	4.3178400E-03	1.0567754E+01	✿
6.	5.5211440E-01	5.3038484E+00	✿	56.	3.9108520E-03	1.0571664E+01	✿
7.	5.0007359E-01	5.8039219E+00	✿	57.	3.5422257E-03	1.0575206E+01	✿
8.	4.5293801E-01	6.2568599E+00	✿	58.	3.2083451E-03	1.0578414E+01	✿
9.	4.1024530E-01	6.6671052E+00	✿	59.	2.9059352E-03	1.0581319E+01	✿
10.	3.7157669E-01	7.0386818E+00	✿	60.	2.6320296E-03	1.0583951E+01	✿
11.	3.3655287E-01	7.3752346E+00	✿	61.	2.3839416E-03	1.0586334E+01	✿
12.	3.0483031E-01	7.6800649E+00	✿	62.	2.1592377E-03	1.0588493E+01	✿
13.	2.7609783E-01	7.9561627E+00	✿	63.	1.9557130E-03	1.0590448E+01	✿
14.	2.5007360E-01	8.2062363E+00	✿	64.	1.7713735E-03	1.0592219E+01	✿
15.	2.2650234E-01	8.4327386E+00	✿	65.	1.6044036E-03	1.0593823E+01	✿
16.	2.0515284E-01	8.6378914E+00	✿	66.	1.4531814E-03	1.0595276E+01	✿
17.	1.8581569E-01	8.8237070E+00	✿	67.	1.3162085E-03	1.0596592E+01	✿
18.	1.6830120E-01	8.9920082E+00	✿	68.	1.1921462E-03	1.0597784E+01	✿
19.	1.5243759E-01	9.1144457E+00	✿	69.	1.0797777E-03	1.0598863E+01	✿
20.	1.3806923E-01	9.2825149E+00	✿	70.	9.7800086E-04	1.0599841E+01	✿
21.	1.2505520E-01	9.4075701E+00	✿	71.	8.8581715E-04	1.0600726E+01	✿
22.	1.1326783E-01	9.5208379E+00	✿	72.	8.0232274E-04	1.0601528E+01	✿
23.	1.0259151E-01	9.6234294E+00	✿	73.	7.2669768E-04	1.0602254E+01	✿
24.	9.2921521E-02	9.7163509E+00	✿	74.	6.5820113E-04	1.0602912E+01	✿
25.	8.4162990E-02	9.8005138E+00	✿	75.	5.9616087E-04	1.0603508E+01	✿
26.	7.6230014E-02	9.8767438E+00	✿	76.	5.3996836E-04	1.0604047E+01	✿
27.	6.9044779E-02	9.9457885E+00	✿	77.	4.8907241E-04	1.0604536E+01	✿
28.	6.2536805E-02	1.0008325E+01	✿	78.	4.4297376E-04	1.0604978E+01	✿
29.	5.6642255E-02	1.0064967E+01	✿	79.	4.0122024E-04	1.0605379E+01	✿
30.	5.1303310E-02	1.0116270E+01	✿	80.	3.6340232E-04	1.0605742E+01	✿
31.	4.6467599E-02	1.0162737E+01	✿	81.	3.2914900E-04	1.0606071E+01	✿
32.	4.2087689E-02	1.0204824E+01	✿	82.	2.9812431E-04	1.0606369E+01	✿
33.	3.8120617E-02	1.0242944E+01	✿	83.	2.7002392E-04	1.0606639E+01	✿
34.	3.4527471E-02	1.0277471E+01	✿	84.	2.4457219E-04	1.0606883E+01	✿
35.	3.1273005E-02	1.0308744E+01	✿	85.	2.2151948E-04	1.0607104E+01	✿
36.	2.8325296E-02	1.0337069E+01	✿	86.	2.0063965E-04	1.0607304E+01	✿
37.	2.5655430E-02	1.0362724E+01	✿	87.	1.8172790E-04	1.0607485E+01	✿
38.	2.3237219E-02	1.0385961E+01	✿	88.	1.6459872E-04	1.0607649E+01	✿
39.	2.1046942E-02	1.0407007E+01	✿	89.	1.4908409E-04	1.0607798E+01	✿
40.	1.9063114E-02	1.0426070E+01	✿	90.	1.3503183E-04	1.0607933E+01	✿
41.	1.7266276E-02	1.0443336E+01	✿	91.	1.2230409E-04	1.0608055E+01	✿
42.	1.5638804E-02	1.0458974E+01	✿	92.	1.1077609E-04	1.0608165E+01	✿
43.	1.4164732E-02	1.0473138E+01	✿	93.	1.0033459E-04	1.0608265E+01	✿
44.	1.2829603E-02	1.0485967E+01	✿	94.	9.0877328E-05	1.0608355E+01	✿
45.	1.1620319E-02	1.0497587E+01	✿	95.	8.2311477E-05	1.0608437E+01	✿
46.	1.0525019E-02	1.0508112E+01	✿	96.	7.4553020E-05	1.0608511E+01	✿
47.	9.5329600E-03	1.0517644E+01	✿	97.	6.7525854E-05	1.0608578E+01	✿
48.	8.6344090E-03	1.0526278E+01	✿	98.	6.1161050E-05	1.0608639E+01	✿
49.	7.8205530E-03	1.0534098E+01	✿	99.	5.5396175E-05	1.0608694E+01	✿
50.	7.0834089E-03	1.0541181E+01	✿	100.	5.0174681E-05	1.0608744E+01	✿

TABULATED VALUES OF E^{-RX} WHEN R = .100

X	E^{-RX}	SUM OF E^{-RX}	✿	X	E^{-RX}	SUM OF E^{-RX}	✿
0.	1.0000000E+00	1.0000000E+00	✿	50.	6.7379469E-03	1.0444252E+01	✿
1.	9.0483741E-01	1.9048374E+00	✿	51.	6.0967465E-03	1.0450344E+01	✿
2.	8.1873075E-01	2.7235681E+00	✿	52.	5.5165644E-03	1.0455864E+01	✿
3.	7.4081821E-01	3.4643863E+00	✿	53.	4.9915939E-03	1.0460855E+01	✿
4.	6.7032004E-01	4.1347063E+00	✿	54.	4.5165809E-03	1.0465371E+01	✿
5.	6.0653065E-01	4.7412369E+00	✿	55.	4.0867714E-03	1.0469457E+01	✿
6.	5.4881163E-01	5.2900485E+00	✿	56.	3.6978637E-03	1.0473154E+01	✿
7.	4.9658530E-01	5.7866338E+00	✿	57.	3.3459654E-03	1.0476499E+01	✿
8.	4.4932896E-01	6.2359627E+00	✿	58.	3.0275547E-03	1.0479526E+01	✿
9.	4.0656965E-01	6.6425323E+00	✿	59.	2.7394448E-03	1.0482265E+01	✿
10.	3.6787944E-01	7.0104117E+00	✿	60.	2.4787521E-03	1.0484743E+01	✿
11.	3.3287108E-01	7.3432827E+00	✿	61.	2.2428677E-03	1.0486985E+01	✿
12.	3.0119421E-01	7.6444769E+00	✿	62.	2.0294306E-03	1.0489014E+01	✿
13.	2.7253179E-01	7.9170086E+00	✿	63.	1.8363045E-03	1.0490850E+01	✿
14.	2.4659696E-01	8.1630556E+00	✿	64.	1.6615572E-03	1.0492511E+01	✿
15.	2.2313015E-01	8.3861835E+00	✿	65.	1.5034391E-03	1.0494014E+01	✿
16.	2.0189651E-01	8.5880800E+00	✿	66.	1.3603680E-03	1.0495374E+01	✿
17.	1.8268352E-01	8.7713156E+00	✿	67.	1.2309119E-03	1.0496604E+01	✿
18.	1.6529888E-01	8.9366144E+00	✿	68.	1.1137751E-03	1.0497717E+01	✿
19.	1.4956861E-01	9.0861830E+00	✿	69.	1.0077864E-03	1.0498724E+01	✿
20.	1.3533528E-01	9.2215182E+00	✿	70.	9.1188196E-04	1.0499635E+01	✿
21.	1.2245642E-01	9.3439746E+00	✿	71.	8.2510490E-04	1.0500460E+01	✿
22.	1.1080315E-01	9.4547777E+00	✿	72.	7.4658580E-04	1.0501206E+01	✿
23.	1.0025884E-01	9.5550365E+00	✿	73.	6.7553877E-04	1.0501881E+01	✿
24.	9.0717953E-02	9.6457544E+00	✿	74.	6.1125274E-04	1.0502492E+01	✿
25.	8.2084998E-02	9.7278393E+00	✿	75.	5.5308436E-04	1.0503045E+01	✿
26.	7.4273578E-02	9.8021128E+00	✿	76.	5.0045143E-04	1.0503545E+01	✿
27.	6.7205512E-02	9.8693183E+00	✿	77.	4.5282718E-04	1.0503997E+01	✿
28.	6.0810062E-02	9.9301283E+00	✿	78.	4.0973497E-04	1.0504406E+01	✿
29.	5.5023219E-02	9.9851515E+00	✿	79.	3.7074356E-04	1.0504776E+01	✿
30.	4.9787068E-02	1.0034934E+01	✿	80.	3.3546262E-04	1.0505111E+01	✿
31.	4.5049202E-02	1.0079987E+01	✿	81.	3.0353913E-04	1.0505414E+01	✿
32.	4.0762203E-02	1.0120749E+01	✿	82.	2.7465356E-04	1.0505688E+01	✿
33.	3.6883167E-02	1.0157662E+01	✿	83.	2.4851682E-04	1.0505936E+01	✿
34.	3.3373269E-02	1.0191005E+01	✿	84.	2.2486732E-04	1.0506160E+01	✿
35.	3.0197383E-02	1.0221202E+01	✿	85.	2.0346836E-04	1.0506363E+01	✿
36.	2.7323722E-02	1.0248525E+01	✿	86.	1.8410570E-04	1.0506547E+01	✿
37.	2.4723526E-02	1.0273248E+01	✿	87.	1.6658581E-04	1.0506713E+01	✿
38.	2.2370771E-02	1.0295618E+01	✿	88.	1.5073537E-04	1.0506863E+01	✿
39.	2.0241911E-02	1.0315859E+01	✿	89.	1.3638892E-04	1.0506999E+01	✿
40.	1.8315638E-02	1.0334174E+01	✿	90.	1.2340980E-04	1.0507122E+01	✿
41.	1.6572675E-02	1.0350746E+01	✿	91.	1.1166580E-04	1.0507233E+01	✿
42.	1.4995576E-02	1.0365741E+01	✿	92.	1.0103940E-04	1.0507334E+01	✿
43.	1.3568558E-02	1.0379309E+01	✿	93.	9.1426231E-05	1.0507425E+01	✿
44.	1.2277335E-02	1.0391586E+01	✿	94.	8.2724065E-05	1.0507507E+01	✿
45.	1.1108996E-02	1.0402694E+01	✿	95.	7.4851829E-05	1.0507581E+01	✿
46.	1.0051835E-02	1.0412745E+01	✿	96.	6.7728730E-05	1.0507648E+01	✿
47.	9.0952770E-03	1.0421840E+01	✿	97.	6.1283494E-05	1.0507709E+01	✿
48.	8.2297470E-03	1.0430069E+01	✿	98.	5.5451599E-05	1.0507764E+01	✿
49.	7.4465830E-03	1.0437515E+01	✿	99.	5.0174681E-05	1.0507814E+01	✿
50.	6.7379469E-03	1.0444252E+01	✿	100.	4.5399929E-05	1.0507859E+01	✿

X	E^{-RX}	SUM OF E^{-RX}	*	X	E^{-RX}	SUM OF E^{-RX}	*
0.	1.0000000E+00	1.0000000E+00	*	50.	5.2475183E-03	9.9851571E+00	*
1.	9.0032452E-01	1.9003245E+00	*	51.	4.7244694E-03	9.9898815E+00	*
2.	8.1058424E-01	2.7109087E+00	*	52.	4.2535557E-03	9.9941350E+00	*
3.	7.2978887E-01	3.4406975E+00	*	53.	3.8295805E-03	9.9979645E+00	*
4.	6.5704681E-01	4.0977443E+00	*	54.	3.4478652E-03	1.0001412E+01	*
5.	5.9155536E-01	4.6892996E+00	*	55.	3.1041976E-03	1.0004516E+01	*
6.	5.3259179E-01	5.2218913E+00	*	56.	2.7947852E-03	1.0007310E+01	*
7.	4.7950545E-01	5.7013967E+00	*	57.	2.5162137E-03	1.0009826E+01	*
8.	4.3171052E-01	6.1331072E+00	*	58.	2.2654089E-03	1.0012091E+01	*
9.	3.8867957E-01	6.5217867E+00	*	59.	2.0396031E-03	1.0014130E+01	*
10.	3.4993774E-01	6.8717244E+00	*	60.	1.8363047E-03	1.0015966E+01	*
11.	3.1505753E-01	7.1867819E+00	*	61.	1.6532702E-03	1.0017619E+01	*
12.	2.8365402E-01	7.4704359E+00	*	62.	1.4884797E-03	1.0019107E+01	*
13.	2.5538067E-01	7.7258165E+00	*	63.	1.3401147E-03	1.0020447E+01	*
14.	2.2992548E-01	7.9557419E+00	*	64.	1.2065382E-03	1.0021653E+01	*
15.	2.0700755E-01	8.1627494E+00	*	65.	1.0862759E-03	1.0022739E+01	*
16.	1.8637397E-01	8.3491233E+00	*	66.	9.7800086E-04	1.0023711E+01	*
17.	1.6779706E-01	8.5169203E+00	*	67.	8.8051816E-04	1.0024597E+01	*
18.	1.5107180E-01	8.6679921E+00	*	68.	7.9275209E-04	1.0025389E+01	*
19.	1.3601365E-01	8.8040057E+00	*	69.	7.1373415E-04	1.0026102E+01	*
20.	1.2245642E-01	8.9264621E+00	*	70.	6.4259235E-04	1.0026744E+01	*
21.	1.1025052E-01	9.0367126E+00	*	71.	5.7854165E-04	1.0027322E+01	*
22.	9.9261251E-02	9.1359738E+00	*	72.	5.2087524E-04	1.0027842E+01	*
23.	8.9367338E-02	9.2253411E+00	*	73.	4.6895675E-04	1.0028310E+01	*
24.	8.0459606E-02	9.3058007E+00	*	74.	4.2221326E-04	1.0028732E+01	*
25.	7.2439756E-02	9.3782404E+00	*	75.	3.8012895E-04	1.0029112E+01	*
26.	6.5219289E-02	9.4434596E+00	*	76.	3.4223942E-04	1.0029454E+01	*
27.	5.8718525E-02	9.5021781E+00	*	77.	3.0812654E-04	1.0029762E+01	*
28.	5.2865728E-02	9.5550438E+00	*	78.	2.7741388E-04	1.0030039E+01	*
29.	4.7596311E-02	9.6026401E+00	*	79.	2.4976252E-04	1.0030288E+01	*
30.	4.2852126E-02	9.6454922E+00	*	80.	2.2486732E-04	1.0030512E+01	*
31.	3.8580820E-02	9.6840730E+00	*	81.	2.0245356E-04	1.0030714E+01	*
32.	3.4735258E-02	9.7188082E+00	*	82.	1.8227391E-04	1.0030896E+01	*
33.	3.1273005E-02	9.7500812E+00	*	83.	1.6410567E-04	1.0031060E+01	*
34.	2.8155853E-02	9.7782370E+00	*	84.	1.4774835E-04	1.0031207E+01	*
35.	2.5349405E-02	9.8035864E+00	*	85.	1.3302147E-04	1.0031340E+01	*
36.	2.2822691E-02	9.8264090E+00	*	86.	1.1976249E-04	1.0031459E+01	*
37.	2.0547828E-02	9.8469568E+00	*	87.	1.0782510E-04	1.0031566E+01	*
38.	1.8499714E-02	9.8654565E+00	*	88.	9.7077590E-05	1.0031663E+01	*
39.	1.6655746E-02	9.8821122E+00	*	89.	8.7401334E-05	1.0031750E+01	*
40.	1.4995576E-02	9.8971077E+00	*	90.	7.8689565E-05	1.0031828E+01	*
41.	1.3500885E-02	9.9106085E+00	*	91.	7.0846145E-05	1.0031898E+01	*
42.	1.2155178E-02	9.9227636E+00	*	92.	6.3784521E-05	1.0031961E+01	*
43.	1.0943605E-02	9.9337072E+00	*	93.	5.7426769E-05	1.0032018E+01	*
44.	9.8527960E-03	9.9435599E+00	*	94.	5.1702728E-05	1.0032069E+01	*
45.	8.8707138E-03	9.9524306E+00	*	95.	4.6549234E-05	1.0032115E+01	*
46.	7.9865212E-03	9.9604171E+00	*	96.	4.1909417E-05	1.0032156E+01	*
47.	7.1904609E-03	9.9676075E+00	*	97.	3.7732076E-05	1.0032193E+01	*
48.	6.4737483E-03	9.9740812E+00	*	98.	3.3971113E-05	1.0032226E+01	*
49.	5.8284743E-03	9.9799096E+00	*	99.	3.0585026E-05	1.0032256E+01	*
50.	5.2475183E-03	9.9851571E+00	*	100.	2.7536449E-05	1.0032283E+01	*

X	E^{-RX}	SUM OF E^{-RX}	*	X	E^{-RX}	SUM OF E^{-RX}	*
0.	1.0000000E+00	1.0000000E+00	*	50.	4.0867714E-03	9.5649251E+00	*
1.	8.9583413E-01	1.8958341E+00	*	51.	3.6610693E-03	9.5685861E+00	*
2.	8.0251879E-01	2.6983528E+00	*	52.	3.2797108E-03	9.5718658E+00	*
3.	7.1892373E-01	3.4172765E+00	*	53.	2.9380769E-03	9.5748038E+00	*
4.	6.4403641E-01	4.0613129E+00	*	54.	2.6320296E-03	9.5774358E+00	*
5.	5.7694980E-01	4.6382627E+00	*	55.	2.3578620E-03	9.5797936E+00	*
6.	5.1685133E-01	5.1551140E+00	*	56.	2.1122532E-03	9.5819058E+00	*
7.	4.6301306E-01	5.6181270E+00	*	57.	1.8922285E-03	9.5837980E+00	*
8.	4.1478291E-01	6.0329099E+00	*	58.	1.6951229E-03	9.5854931E+00	*
9.	3.7157669E-01	6.4044865E+00	*	59.	1.5185490E-03	9.5870116E+00	*
10.	3.3287108E-01	6.7373575E+00	*	60.	1.3603680E-03	9.5883719E+00	*
11.	2.9819727E-01	7.0355547E+00	*	61.	1.2186641E-03	9.5895905E+00	*
12.	2.6713530E-01	7.3026900E+00	*	62.	1.0917209E-03	9.5906822E+00	*
13.	2.3930892E-01	7.5419989E+00	*	63.	9.7800086E-04	9.5916602E+00	*
14.	2.1438110E-01	7.7563800E+00	*	64.	8.7612656E-04	9.5925363E+00	*
15.	1.9204990E-01	7.9484299E+00	*	65.	7.8486408E-04	9.5933211E+00	*
16.	1.7204486E-01	8.1204747E+00	*	66.	7.0310803E-04	9.5940242E+00	*
17.	1.5412366E-01	8.2745983E+00	*	67.	6.2986817E-04	9.5946540E+00	*
18.	1.3806273E-01	8.4126675E+00	*	68.	5.6425741E-04	9.5952182E+00	*
19.	1.2368713E-01	8.5363546E+00	*	69.	5.0548105E-04	9.5957236E+00	*
20.	1.1080315E-01	8.6471577E+00	*	70.	4.5282718E-04	9.5961764E+00	*
21.	9.9261251E-02	8.7464189E+00	*	71.	4.0565804E-04	9.5965820E+00	*
22.	8.8921617E-02	8.8353405E+00	*	72.	3.6340232E-04	9.5969454E+00	*
23.	7.9659019E-02	8.9149995E+00	*	73.	3.2554820E-04	9.5972709E+00	*
24.	7.1361269E-02	8.9863607E+00	*	74.	2.9163719E-04	9.5975625E+00	*
25.	6.3927860E-02	9.0502885E+00	*	75.	2.6125855E-04	9.5978237E+00	*
26.	5.7268760E-02	9.1075572E+00	*	76.	2.3404433E-04	9.5980577E+00	*
27.	5.1303310E-02	9.1588605E+00	*	77.	2.0966490E-04	9.5982673E+00	*
28.	4.5959256E-02	9.2048197E+00	*	78.	1.8782497E-04	9.5984551E+00	*
29.	4.1171870E-02	9.2459915E+00	*	79.	1.6826002E-04	9.5986233E+00	*
30.	3.6883167E-02	9.2828746E+00	*	80.	1.5073307E-04	9.5987740E+00	*
31.	3.3041200E-02	9.3159158E+00	*	81.	1.3503183E-04	9.5989090E+00	*
32.	2.9599435E-02	9.3455152E+00	*	82.	1.2096612E-04	9.5990299E+00	*
33.	2.6516184E-02	9.3720313E+00	*	83.	1.0836558E-04	9.5991382E+00	*
34.	2.3754103E-02	9.3957854E+00	*	84.	9.7077590E-05	9.5992352E+00	*
35.	2.1279736E-02	9.4170651E+00	*	85.	8.6965418E-05	9.5993221E+00	*
36.	1.9063114E-02	9.4361282E+00	*	86.	7.7906590E-05	9.5994000E+00	*
37.	1.7077388E-02	9.4532055E+00	*	87.	6.9791383E-05	9.5994697E+00	*
38.	1.5298507E-02	9.4685040E+00	*	88.	6.2521503E-05	9.5995322E+00	*
39.	1.3704925E-02	9.4822089E+00	*	89.	5.6008897E-05	9.5995882E+00	*
40.	1.2277339E-02	9.4944862E+00	*	90.	5.0174681E-05	9.5996383E+00	*
41.	1.0998466E-02	9.5054846E+00	*	91.	4.4948192E-05	9.5996832E+00	*
42.	9.8527960E-03	9.5153373E+00	*	92.	4.0266125E-05	9.5997234E+00	*
43.	8.8264710E-03	9.5241637E+00	*	93.	3.6071769E-05	9.5997594E+00	*
44.	7.9070540E-03	9.5320707E+00	*	94.	3.2314322E-05	9.5997917E+00	*
45.	7.0834089E-03	9.5391541E+00	*	95.	2.8948273E-05	9.5998206E+00	*
46.	6.3455594E-03	9.5454996E+00	*	96.	2.5932851E-05	9.5998465E+00	*
47.	5.6845688E-03	9.5511841E+00	*	97.	2.3231533E-05	9.5998697E+00	*
48.	5.0924307E-03	9.5562765E+00	*	98.	2.0811600E-05	9.5998905E+00	*
49.	4.5619733E-03	9.5608384E+00	*	99.	1.8643742E-05	9.5999091E+00	*
50.	4.0867714E-03	9.5649251E+00	*	100.	1.6701700E-05	9.5999258E+00	*

TABULATED VALUES OF E^{-RX} WHEN R = .115

X	E^{-RX}	SUM OF E^{-RX}	*	X	E^{-RX}	SUM OF E^{-RX}	*
0.	1.0000000E+00	1.0000000E+00	*	50.	3.1827807E-03	9.1791154E+00	*
1.	8.9136614E-01	1.8913661E+00	*	51.	2.8370230E-03	9.1819524E+00	*
2.	7.9453359E-01	2.6858996E+00	*	52.	2.5288262E-03	9.1844812E+00	*
3.	7.0822035E-01	3.3941199E+00	*	53.	2.2541101E-03	9.1867353E+00	*
4.	6.3128364E-01	4.0254035E+00	*	54.	2.0092374E-03	9.1887445E+00	*
5.	5.6270406E-01	4.5881083E+00	*	55.	1.7909662E-03	9.1905354E+00	*
6.	5.0157606E-01	5.0896843E+00	*	56.	1.5964066E-03	9.1921318E+00	*
7.	4.4708792E-01	5.5367722E+00	*	57.	1.4229828E-03	9.1935547E+00	*
8.	3.9851903E-01	5.9352512E+00	*	58.	1.2683987E-03	9.1948230E+00	*
9.	3.5522638E-01	6.2905175E+00	*	59.	1.1306077E-03	9.1959536E+00	*
10.	3.1663676E-01	6.6071542E+00	*	60.	1.0077854E-03	9.1969613E+00	*
11.	2.8223929E-01	6.8893934E+00	*	61.	8.9830581E-04	9.1978596E+00	*
12.	2.5157855E-01	7.1409719E+00	*	62.	8.0071938E-04	9.1986603E+00	*
13.	2.2424860E-01	7.3652205E+00	*	63.	7.1373415E-04	9.1993740E+00	*
14.	1.9988761E-01	7.5651081E+00	*	64.	6.3619845E-04	9.2000101E+00	*
15.	1.7817305E-01	7.7432811E+00	*	65.	5.6708576E-04	9.2005771E+00	*
16.	1.5881742E-01	7.9020985E+00	*	66.	5.0548105E-04	9.2010825E+00	*
17.	1.4156447E-01	8.0436629E+00	*	67.	4.5056869E-04	9.2015330E+00	*
18.	1.2618578E-01	8.1698486E+00	*	68.	4.0162168E-04	9.2019346E+00	*
19.	1.1247773E-01	8.2823263E+00	*	69.	3.5799197E-04	9.2022925E+00	*
20.	1.0025884E-01	8.3825851E+00	*	70.	3.1910192E-04	9.2026116E+00	*
21.	8.9367338E-02	8.4719524E+00	*	71.	2.8443664E-04	9.2028960E+00	*
22.	7.9659019E-02	8.5516114E+00	*	72.	2.5353719E-04	9.2031495E+00	*
23.	7.1005353E-02	8.6226167E+00	*	73.	2.2599447E-04	9.2033754E+00	*
24.	6.3291768E-02	8.6859084E+00	*	74.	2.0144382E-04	9.2035768E+00	*
25.	5.6416139E-02	8.7423245E+00	*	75.	1.7956020E-04	9.2037563E+00	*
26.	5.0287436E-02	8.7926119E+00	*	76.	1.6005388E-04	9.2039163E+00	*
27.	4.4824518E-02	8.8374364E+00	*	77.	1.4266661E-04	9.2040589E+00	*
28.	3.9955058E-02	8.8773914E+00	*	78.	1.2716819E-04	9.2041860E+00	*
29.	3.5614586E-02	8.9130059E+00	*	79.	1.1335342E-04	9.2042993E+00	*
30.	3.1745636E-02	8.9447515E+00	*	80.	1.0103940E-04	9.2044003E+00	*
31.	2.8296985E-02	8.9730484E+00	*	81.	9.0063101E-05	9.2044903E+00	*
32.	2.5222974E-02	8.9982713E+00	*	82.	8.0279199E-05	9.2045705E+00	*
33.	2.2482905E-02	9.0207542E+00	*	83.	7.1558160E-05	9.2046420E+00	*
34.	2.0040500E-02	9.0407947E+00	*	84.	6.3784521E-05	9.2047057E+00	*
35.	1.7863424E-02	9.0586581E+00	*	85.	5.6855363E-05	9.2047625E+00	*
36.	1.5922851E-02	9.0745809E+00	*	86.	5.0678945E-05	9.2048131E+00	*
37.	1.4193090E-02	9.0887739E+00	*	87.	4.5173496E-05	9.2048582E+00	*
38.	1.2651240E-02	9.1014251E+00	*	88.	4.0266125E-05	9.2048984E+00	*
39.	1.1276887E-02	9.1127019E+00	*	89.	3.5891860E-05	9.2049342E+00	*
40.	1.0051835E-02	9.1227537E+00	*	90.	3.1992789E-05	9.2049661E+00	*
41.	8.9598660E-03	9.1317135E+00	*	91.	2.8517289E-05	9.2049946E+00	*
42.	7.9865212E-03	9.1397000E+00	*	92.	2.5419346E-05	9.2050200E+00	*
43.	7.1189146E-03	9.1468189E+00	*	93.	2.2657944E-05	9.2050426E+00	*
44.	6.3455594E-03	9.1531644E+00	*	94.	2.0196524E-05	9.2050627E+00	*
45.	5.6562169E-03	9.1588206E+00	*	95.	1.8002498E-05	9.2050807E+00	*
46.	5.0417602E-03	9.1638623E+00	*	96.	1.6046817E-05	9.2050967E+00	*
47.	4.4940543E-03	9.1683563E+00	*	97.	1.4303590E-05	9.2051110E+00	*
48.	4.0058479E-03	9.1723621E+00	*	98.	1.2749735E-05	9.2051237E+00	*
49.	3.5706772E-03	9.1759327E+00	*	99.	1.1364482E-05	9.2051350E+00	*
50.	3.1827807E-03	9.1791154E+00	*	100.	1.0130093E-05	9.2051451E+00	*

TABULATED VALUES OF E^{-RX} WHEN R = .120

X	E^{-RX}	SUM OF E^{-RX}	*	X	E^{-RX}	SUM OF E^{-RX}	*
0.	1.0000000E+00	1.0000000E+00	*	50.	2.4787521E-03	8.8238868E+00	*
1.	8.8692043E-01	1.8869204E+00	*	51.	2.1984559E-03	8.8260852E+00	*
2.	7.8662786E-01	2.6735482E+00	*	52.	1.9498555E-03	8.8280350E+00	*
3.	6.9767632E-01	3.3712245E+00	*	53.	1.7293667E-03	8.8297643E+00	*
4.	6.1878339E-01	3.9900078E+00	*	54.	1.5338106E-03	8.8312981E+00	*
5.	5.4881163E-01	4.5388194E+00	*	55.	1.3603680E-03	8.8326584E+00	*
6.	4.8675225E-01	5.0255716E+00	*	56.	1.2065382E-03	8.8338649E+00	*
7.	4.3171052E-01	5.4572821E+00	*	57.	1.0701033E-03	8.8349350E+00	*
8.	3.8289288E-01	5.8401749E+00	*	58.	9.4909657E-04	8.8358840E+00	*
9.	3.3959552E-01	6.1797704E+00	*	59.	8.4177314E-04	8.8367257E+00	*
10.	3.0119421E-01	6.4809646E+00	*	60.	7.4658580E-04	8.8374722E+00	*
11.	2.6713530E-01	6.7480999E+00	*	61.	6.6216220E-04	8.8381343E+00	*
12.	2.3692775E-01	6.9850276E+00	*	62.	5.8728519E-04	8.8387215E+00	*
13.	2.1013607E-01	7.1951636E+00	*	63.	5.2087524E-04	8.8392423E+00	*
14.	1.8637397E-01	7.3815375E+00	*	64.	4.6197849E-04	8.8397042E+00	*
15.	1.6529888E-01	7.5468363E+00	*	65.	4.0973497E-04	8.8401139E+00	*
16.	1.4660696E-01	7.6934432E+00	*	66.	3.6340232E-04	8.8404773E+00	*
17.	1.3002871E-01	7.8234719E+00	*	67.	3.2230894E-04	8.8407996E+00	*
18.	1.1532512E-01	7.9387970E+00	*	68.	2.8586239E-04	8.8410854E+00	*
19.	1.0228420E-01	8.0410812E+00	*	69.	2.5353719E-04	8.8413389E+00	*
20.	9.0717953E-02	8.1317991E+00	*	70.	2.2486732E-04	8.8415637E+00	*
21.	8.0459606E-02	8.2122587E+00	*	71.	1.9943942E-04	8.8417631E+00	*
22.	7.1361269E-02	8.2836199E+00	*	72.	1.7688690E-04	8.8419399E+00	*
23.	6.3291768E-02	8.3469116E+00	*	73.	1.5688460E-04	8.8420967E+00	*
24.	5.6134762E-02	8.4030463E+00	*	74.	1.3914416E-04	8.8422358E+00	*
25.	4.9787068E-02	8.4528333E+00	*	75.	1.2340980E-04	8.8423592E+00	*
26.	4.4157168E-02	8.4969904E+00	*	76.	1.0945467E-04	8.8424686E+00	*
27.	3.9163895E-02	8.5361542E+00	*	77.	9.7077590E-05	8.8425656E+00	*
28.	3.4735258E-02	8.5708894E+00	*	78.	8.6100098E-05	8.8426517E+00	*
29.	3.0807411E-02	8.6016968E+00	*	79.	7.6363937E-05	8.8427280E+00	*
30.	2.7323722E-02	8.6290205E+00	*	80.	6.7728736E-05	8.8427957E+00	*
31.	2.4233967E-02	8.6532544E+00	*	81.	6.0070000E-05	8.8428557E+00	*
32.	2.1493601E-02	8.6747480E+00	*	82.	5.3277311E-05	8.8429090E+00	*
33.	1.9063114E-02	8.6938111E+00	*	83.	4.7252735E-05	8.8429561E+00	*
34.	1.6907465E-02	8.7107185E+00	*	84.	4.1909417E-05	8.8429980E+00	*
35.	1.4995576E-02	8.7257140E+00	*	85.	3.7170318E-05	8.8430351E+00	*
36.	1.3299883E-02	8.7390138E+00	*	86.	3.2967115E-05	8.8430680E+00	*
37.	1.1795938E-02	8.7508097E+00	*	87.	2.9239208E-05	8.8430972E+00	*
38.	1.0462058E-02	8.7612717E+00	*	88.	2.5932851E-05	8.8431231E+00	*
39.	9.2790138E-03	8.7705507E+00	*	89.	2.3000375E-05	8.8431461E+00	*
40.	8.2297470E-03	8.7787804E+00	*	90.	2.0399503E-05	8.8431664E+00	*
41.	7.2991308E-03	8.7860795E+00	*	91.	1.8092736E-05	8.8431844E+00	*
42.	6.4737483E-03	8.7925532E+00	*	92.	1.6046817E-05	8.8432004E+00	*
43.	5.7416996E-03	8.7982948E+00	*	93.	1.4232250E-05	8.8432146E+00	*
44.	5.0924307E-03	8.8033872E+00	*	94.	1.2622873E-05	8.8432272E+00	*
45.	4.5165809E-03	8.8079037E+00	*	95.	1.1195484E-05	8.8432383E+00	*
46.	4.0058479E-03	8.8119095E+00	*	96.	9.9295042E-06	8.8432482E+00	*
47.	3.5528684E-03	8.8154623E+00	*	97.	8.8066802E-06	8.8432570E+00	*
48.	3.1511115E-03	8.8186134E+00	*	98.	7.8108247E-06	8.8432648E+00	*
49.	2.7947852E-03	8.8214081E+00	*	99.	6.9275800E-06	8.8432717E+00	*
50.	2.4787521E-03	8.8238868E+00	*	100.	6.1442123E-06	8.8432778E+00	*

x	E^{-RX}	SUM OF E^{-RX}	*	x	E^{-RX}	SUM OF E^{-RX}	*
0.	1.0000000E+00	1.0000000E+00	*	50.	1.9304541E-03	8.4959125E+00	*
1.	8.8249690E-01	1.8824969E+00	*	51.	1.7036197E-03	8.4976161E+00	*
2.	7.7880078E-01	2.6612976E+00	*	52.	1.5034391E-03	8.4991195E+00	*
3.	6.8724927E-01	3.3485468E+00	*	53.	1.3267804E-03	8.5004462E+00	*
4.	6.0653065E-01	3.9551174E+00	*	54.	1.1708796E-03	8.5016170E+00	*
5.	5.3526142E-01	4.4903788E+00	*	55.	1.0332976E-03	8.5026502E+00	*
6.	4.7236655E-01	4.9627453E+00	*	56.	9.1188196E-04	8.5035620E+00	*
7.	4.1686201E-01	5.3796073E+00	*	57.	8.0473300E-04	8.5043667E+00	*
8.	3.6787944E-01	5.7474867E+00	*	58.	7.1017438E-04	8.5050768E+00	*
9.	3.2465246E-01	6.0721391E+00	*	59.	6.2672669E-04	8.5057035E+00	*
10.	2.8650479E-01	6.3586436E+00	*	60.	5.5308436E-04	8.5062565E+00	*
11.	2.5283959E-01	6.6114833E+00	*	61.	4.8809524E-04	8.5067445E+00	*
12.	2.2313015E-01	6.8346134E+00	*	62.	4.3074253E-04	8.5071752E+00	*
13.	1.9691167E-01	7.0315250E+00	*	63.	3.8012895E-04	8.5075553E+00	*
14.	1.7377394E-01	7.2052989E+00	*	64.	3.3546262E-04	8.5078907E+00	*
15.	1.5335496E-01	7.3586538E+00	*	65.	2.9604472E-04	8.5081867E+00	*
16.	1.3533528E-01	7.4939890E+00	*	66.	2.6125855E-04	8.5084479E+00	*
17.	1.1943296E-01	7.6134219E+00	*	67.	2.3055986E-04	8.5086784E+00	*
18.	1.05399228E-01	7.7188211E+00	*	68.	2.0346836E-04	8.5088818E+00	*
19.	9.3014449E-02	7.8118355E+00	*	69.	1.7954020E-04	8.5090613E+00	*
20.	8.2084998E-02	7.8939204E+00	*	70.	1.5846132E-04	8.5092197E+00	*
21.	7.2439756E-02	7.9663601E+00	*	71.	1.3984162E-04	8.5093595E+00	*
22.	6.3927860E-02	8.0302879E+00	*	72.	1.2340980E-04	8.5094829E+00	*
23.	5.6416139E-02	8.0867040E+00	*	73.	1.0890876E-04	8.5095918E+00	*
24.	4.9787068E-02	8.1364910E+00	*	74.	9.6111651E-05	8.5096879E+00	*
25.	4.3936933E-02	8.1804279E+00	*	75.	8.4818235E-05	8.5097727E+00	*
26.	3.8774207E-02	8.2192021E+00	*	76.	7.4851829E-05	8.5098475E+00	*
27.	3.4218118E-02	8.2534202E+00	*	77.	6.6056507E-05	8.5099135E+00	*
28.	3.0197383E-02	8.2836175E+00	*	78.	5.8294663E-05	8.5099717E+00	*
29.	2.6649097E-02	8.3102665E+00	*	79.	5.1444860E-05	8.5100231E+00	*
30.	2.3517745E-02	8.3337642E+00	*	80.	4.5399929E-05	8.5100684E+00	*
31.	2.0754337E-02	8.3545385E+00	*	81.	4.0065297E-05	8.5101084E+00	*
32.	1.8315638E-02	8.3728541E+00	*	82.	3.5357500E-05	8.5101437E+00	*
33.	1.6163494E-02	8.3890175E+00	*	83.	3.1202884E-05	8.5101749E+00	*
34.	1.4264233E-02	8.4032817E+00	*	84.	2.7536449E-05	8.5102024E+00	*
35.	1.2588142E-02	8.4158608E+00	*	85.	2.4300831E-05	8.5102267E+00	*
36.	1.1108996E-02	8.4269787E+00	*	86.	2.1445408E-05	8.5102481E+00	*
37.	9.8036550E-03	8.4367823E+00	*	87.	1.8925506E-05	8.5102670E+00	*
38.	8.6516951E-03	8.4454339E+00	*	88.	1.6701700E-05	8.5102837E+00	*
39.	7.6350942E-03	8.4530689E+00	*	89.	1.4739199E-05	8.5102984E+00	*
40.	6.7379469E-03	8.4598068E+00	*	90.	1.3007296E-05	8.5103114E+00	*
41.	5.9462173E-03	8.4657530E+00	*	91.	1.1478899E-05	8.5103228E+00	*
42.	5.2475183E-03	8.4710005E+00	*	92.	1.0130093E-05	8.5103329E+00	*
43.	4.6309187E-03	8.4756314E+00	*	93.	8.9397762E-06	8.5103418E+00	*
44.	4.0867714E-03	8.4797181E+00	*	94.	7.8893248E-06	8.5103496E+00	*
45.	3.6065631E-03	8.4833246E+00	*	95.	6.9623047E-06	8.5103565E+00	*
46.	3.1827607E-03	8.4865073E+00	*	96.	6.1442123E-06	8.5103626E+00	*
47.	2.8087941E-03	8.4893160E+00	*	97.	5.4222483E-06	8.5103680E+00	*
48.	2.4787521E-03	8.4917947E+00	*	98.	4.7851173E-06	8.5103727E+00	*
49.	2.1874911E-03	8.4939821E+00	*	99.	4.2228512E-06	8.5103769E+00	*
50.	1.9304541E-03	8.4959125E+00	*	100.	3.7266531E-06	8.5103806E+00	*

x	E^{-RX}	SUM OF E^{-RX}	*	x	E^{-RX}	SUM OF E^{-RX}	*
0.	1.0000000E+00	1.0000000E+00	*	50.	1.5034391E-03	8.1923061E+00	*
1.	8.7809542E-01	1.8780954E+00	*	51.	1.3201630E-03	8.1936262E+00	*
2.	7.7105158E-01	2.6491469E+00	*	52.	1.1592291E-03	8.1947854E+00	*
3.	6.7705687E-01	3.3262037E+00	*	53.	1.0179138E-03	8.1958033E+00	*
4.	5.9452054E-01	3.9207242E+00	*	54.	8.9382540E-04	8.1966971E+00	*
5.	5.2204577E-01	4.4427699E+00	*	55.	7.8484408E-04	8.1974819E+00	*
6.	4.5840601E-01	4.9011759E+00	*	56.	6.8918556E-04	8.1981710E+00	*
7.	4.0252422E-01	5.3037001E+00	*	57.	6.0517069E-04	8.1987761E+00	*
8.	3.5345468E-01	5.6571547E+00	*	58.	5.3139762E-04	8.1993074E+00	*
9.	3.1036694E-01	5.9675216E+00	*	59.	4.6661782E-04	8.1997740E+00	*
10.	2.7253179E-01	6.2400533E+00	*	60.	4.0973497E-04	8.2001837E+00	*
11.	2.3930892E-01	6.4793622E+00	*	61.	3.5978641E-04	8.2005434E+00	*
12.	2.1013607E-01	6.6894982E+00	*	62.	3.1592680E-04	8.2008593E+00	*
13.	1.8451952E-01	6.8740177E+00	*	63.	2.7741388E-04	8.2011367E+00	*
14.	1.6202575E-01	7.0360434E+00	*	64.	2.4359584E-04	8.2013802E+00	*
15.	1.4227407E-01	7.1783174E+00	*	65.	2.1390041E-04	8.2015941E+00	*
16.	1.2493021E-01	7.3032476E+00	*	66.	1.8782497E-04	8.2017819E+00	*
17.	1.0970064E-01	7.4129482E+00	*	67.	1.6492825E-04	8.2019468E+00	*
18.	9.6327638E-02	7.5092758E+00	*	68.	1.4482274E-04	8.2020916E+00	*
19.	8.4584858E-02	7.5938606E+00	*	69.	1.2716819E-04	8.2022187E+00	*
20.	7.4273578E-02	7.6681341E+00	*	70.	1.1166580E-04	8.2023303E+00	*
21.	6.5219289E-02	7.7333533E+00	*	71.	9.8053236E-05	8.2024283E+00	*
22.	5.7268760E-02	7.7906220E+00	*	72.	8.6100098E-05	8.2025144E+00	*
23.	5.0287436E-02	7.8409094E+00	*	73.	7.5604103E-05	8.2025900E+00	*
24.	4.4157168E-02	7.8850665E+00	*	74.	6.6387617E-05	8.2026563E+00	*
25.	3.8774207E-02	7.9238407E+00	*	75.	5.8294663E-05	8.2027145E+00	*
26.	3.4047544E-02	7.9578881E+00	*	76.	5.1188277E-05	8.2027656E+00	*
27.	2.9896914E-02	7.9877850E+00	*	77.	4.4948192E-05	8.2028105E+00	*
28.	2.6252343E-02	8.0140373E+00	*	78.	3.9468802E-05	8.2028499E+00	*
29.	2.3052063E-02	8.0370893E+00	*	79.	3.4657375E-05	8.2028845E+00	*
30.	2.0241911E-02	8.0573312E+00	*	80.	3.0432482E-05	8.2029149E+00	*
31.	1.7774329E-02	8.0751055E+00	*	81.	2.6722624E-05	8.2029416E+00	*
32.	1.5607557E-02	8.0907130E+00	*	82.	2.3465014E-05	8.2029650E+00	*
33.	1.3704925E-02	8.1044179E+00	*	83.	2.0604521E-05	8.2029856E+00	*
34.	1.2034232E-02	8.1164521E+00	*	84.	1.8092736E-05	8.2030036E+00	*
35.	1.0567204E-02	8.1270193E+00	*	85.	1.5887149E-05	8.2030194E+00	*
36.	9.2790138E-03	8.1362983E+00	*	86.	1.3950433E-05	8.2030333E+00	*
37.	8.1478596E-03	8.1444461E+00	*	87.	1.2249811E-05	8.2030456E+00	*
38.	7.1545983E-03	8.1516006E+00	*	88.	1.0756503E-05	8.2030562E+00	*
39.	6.2824201E-03	8.1578830E+00	*	89.	9.4452366E-06	8.2030656E+00	*
40.	5.5165644E-03	8.1633995E+00	*	90.	8.2930191E-06	8.2030738E+00	*
41.	4.8440700E-03	8.1682435E+00	*	91.	7.2827647E-06	8.2030810E+00	*
42.	4.2535557E-03	8.1724970E+00	*	92.	6.3949623E-06	8.2030873E+00	*
43.	3.7350278E-03	8.1762320E+00	*	93.	5.6153872E-06	8.2030929E+00	*
44.	3.2797108E-03	8.1795117E+00	*	94.	4.9308459E-06	8.2030978E+00	*
45.	2.8798991E-03	8.1823915E+00	*	95.	4.3297532E-06	8.2031021E+00	*
46.	2.5288262E-03	8.1849203E+00	*	96.	3.8019365E-06	8.2031059E+00	*
47.	2.2205508E-03	8.1871408E+00	*	97.	3.3384631E-06	8.2031092E+00	*
48.	1.9498555E-03	8.1890906E+00	*	98.	2.9314892E-06	8.2031121E+00	*
49.	1.7121592E-03	8.1908027E+00	*	99.	2.5741272E-06	8.2031146E+00	*
50.	1.5034391E-03	8.1923061E+00	*	100.	2.2603294E-06	8.2031168E+00	*

TABULATED VALUES OF E   WHEN R = .135

x	E (-RX)	SUM OF E (-RX)	*	x	E (-RX)	SUM OF E (-RX)	*
0.	1.0000000E+00	1.0000000E+00	*	50.	1.1708796E-03	7.9105509E+00	*
1.	8.7371591E-01	1.8737159E+00	*	51.	1.0230161E-03	7.9115739E+00	*
2.	7.6337949E-01	2.6370953E+00	*	52.	8.9382549E-04	7.9124677E+00	*
3.	6.6697680E-01	3.3040721E+00	*	53.	7.8094955E-04	7.9132486E+00	*
4.	5.8274825E-01	3.8868203E+00	*	54.	6.8232805E-04	7.9139309E+00	*
5.	5.0915641E-01	4.3959767E+00	*	55.	5.9616087E-04	7.9145270E+00	*
6.	4.4485806E-01	4.8408347E+00	*	56.	5.2087524E-04	7.9150478E+00	*
7.	3.8867957E-01	5.2295142E+00	*	57.	4.5509698E-04	7.9155028E+00	*
8.	3.3959552E-01	5.5691097E+00	*	58.	3.9762547E-04	7.9159004E+00	*
9.	2.9671001E-01	5.8658197E+00	*	59.	3.4741170E-04	7.9162478E+00	*
10.	2.5924026E-01	6.1250599E+00	*	60.	3.0353913E-04	7.9165513E+00	*
11.	2.2650234E-01	6.3515622E+00	*	61.	2.6520697E-04	7.9168165E+00	*
12.	1.9789869E-01	6.5494608E+00	*	62.	2.3171555E-04	7.9170482E+00	*
13.	1.7290724E-01	6.7223680E+00	*	63.	2.0245356E-04	7.9172506E+00	*
14.	1.5107180E-01	6.8734398E+00	*	64.	1.7688690E-04	7.9174274E+00	*
15.	1.3199384E-01	7.0054336E+00	*	65.	1.5454890E-04	7.9175819E+00	*
16.	1.1532512E-01	7.1207587E+00	*	66.	1.3503183E-04	7.9177169E+00	*
17.	1.0076139E-01	7.2215200E+00	*	67.	1.1797946E-04	7.9178348E+00	*
18.	8.8036832E-02	7.3095568E+00	*	68.	1.0308053E-04	7.9179378E+00	*
19.	7.6919181E-02	7.3864759E+00	*	69.	9.0063101E-05	7.9180278E+00	*
20.	6.7205512E-02	7.4536814E+00	*	70.	7.8689565E-05	7.9181064E+00	*
21.	5.8718525E-02	7.5123999E+00	*	71.	6.8752325E-05	7.9181751E+00	*
22.	5.1303310E-02	7.5637032E+00	*	72.	6.0070000E-05	7.9182351E+00	*
23.	4.4824518E-02	7.6085277E+00	*	73.	5.2484115E-05	7.9182875E+00	*
24.	3.9163895E-02	7.6476915E+00	*	74.	4.5856206E-05	7.9183333E+00	*
25.	3.4218118E-02	7.6819096E+00	*	75.	4.0065297E-05	7.9183733E+00	*
26.	2.9896914E-02	7.7118065E+00	*	76.	3.5005687E-05	7.9184083E+00	*
27.	2.6121409E-02	7.7379279E+00	*	77.	3.0585026E-05	7.9184388E+00	*
28.	2.2822691E-02	7.7607505E+00	*	78.	2.6722624E-05	7.9184655E+00	*
29.	1.9940548E-02	7.7806910E+00	*	79.	2.3347981E-05	7.9184888E+00	*
30.	1.7422374E-02	7.7981133E+00	*	80.	2.0399503E-05	7.9185091E+00	*
31.	1.5222205E-02	7.8133355E+00	*	81.	1.7823370E-05	7.9185269E+00	*
32.	1.3299883E-02	7.8266353E+00	*	82.	1.5572562E-05	7.9185424E+00	*
33.	1.1620319E-02	7.8382556E+00	*	83.	1.3605995E-05	7.9185560E+00	*
34.	1.0152858E-02	7.8484084E+00	*	84.	1.1887774E-05	7.9185678E+00	*
35.	8.8707138E-03	7.8572791E+00	*	85.	1.0386538E-05	7.9185781E+00	*
36.	7.7504838E-03	7.8650295E+00	*	86.	9.0748836E-06	7.9185871E+00	*
37.	6.7717210E-03	7.8718012E+00	*	87.	7.9288702E-06	7.9185950E+00	*
38.	5.9165604E-03	7.8777177E+00	*	88.	6.9275800E-06	7.9186019E+00	*
39.	5.1693930E-03	7.8828807E+00	*	89.	6.0527369E-06	7.9186079E+00	*
40.	4.5165809E-03	7.8874035E+00	*	90.	5.2883725E-06	7.9186131E+00	*
41.	3.9462086E-03	7.8913497E+00	*	91.	4.6205352E-06	7.9186177E+00	*
42.	3.4478652E-03	7.8947975E+00	*	92.	4.0370351E-06	7.9186217E+00	*
43.	3.0124547E-03	7.8978099E+00	*	93.	3.5272218E-06	7.9186252E+00	*
44.	2.6320296E-03	7.9004419E+00	*	94.	3.0817898E-06	7.9186282E+00	*
45.	2.2996441E-03	7.9027415E+00	*	95.	2.6926088E-06	7.9186308E+00	*
46.	2.0092374E-03	7.9047507E+00	*	96.	2.3525751E-06	7.9186331E+00	*
47.	1.7555027E-03	7.9065062E+00	*	97.	2.0554823E-06	7.9186351E+00	*
48.	1.5338106E-03	7.9080400E+00	*	98.	1.7959076E-06	7.9186368E+00	*
49.	1.3401147E-03	7.9093801E+00	*	99.	1.5691131E-06	7.9186383E+00	*
50.	1.1708796E-03	7.9105509E+00	*	100.	1.3709590E-06	7.9186396E+00	*

TABULATED VALUES OF E   WHEN R = .140

x	E (-RX)	SUM OF E (-RX)	*	x	E (-RX)	SUM OF E (-RX)	*
0.	1.0000000E+00	1.0000000E+00	*	50.	9.1188196E-04	7.6484495E+00	*
1.	8.6935823E-01	1.8693582E+00	*	51.	7.9275209E-04	7.6492422E+00	*
2.	7.5578374E-01	2.6251419E+00	*	52.	6.8918556E-04	7.6499313E+00	*
3.	6.5704681E-01	3.2821887E+00	*	53.	5.9914914E-04	7.6505304E+00	*
4.	5.7120906E-01	3.8533977E+00	*	54.	5.2087524E-04	7.6510512E+00	*
5.	4.9658530E-01	4.3499830E+00	*	55.	4.5282718E-04	7.6515040E+00	*
6.	4.3171052E-01	4.7816935E+00	*	56.	3.9369046E-04	7.6518976E+00	*
7.	3.7531109E-01	5.1570045E+00	*	57.	3.4223942E-04	7.6522398E+00	*
8.	3.2627979E-01	5.4832842E+00	*	58.	2.9752866E-04	7.6525373E+00	*
9.	2.8365402E-01	5.7669382E+00	*	59.	2.5865899E-04	7.6527959E+00	*
10.	2.4659696E-01	6.0135351E+00	*	60.	2.2486732E-04	7.6530207E+00	*
11.	2.1438110E-01	6.2279162E+00	*	61.	1.9549025E-04	7.6532161E+00	*
12.	1.8637397E-01	6.4142901E+00	*	62.	1.6995106E-04	7.6533860E+00	*
13.	1.6202575E-01	6.5763158E+00	*	63.	1.4774835E-04	7.6535337E+00	*
14.	1.4085842E-01	6.7171742E+00	*	64.	1.2844625E-04	7.6536621E+00	*
15.	1.2245642E-01	6.8396306E+00	*	65.	1.1166580E-04	7.6537737E+00	*
16.	1.0645850E-01	6.9460891E+00	*	66.	9.7077590E-05	7.6538707E+00	*
17.	9.2550577E-02	7.0386396E+00	*	67.	8.4395202E-05	7.6539550E+00	*
18.	8.0459606E-02	7.1190992E+00	*	68.	7.3369664E-05	7.6540283E+00	*
19.	6.9948221E-02	7.1890474E+00	*	69.	6.3784521E-05	7.6540920E+00	*
20.	6.0810062E-02	7.2498574E+00	*	70.	5.5451599E-05	7.6541474E+00	*
21.	5.2865728E-02	7.3027231E+00	*	71.	4.8207304E-05	7.6541956E+00	*
22.	4.5959256E-02	7.3486823E+00	*	72.	4.1909417E-05	7.6542375E+00	*
23.	3.9955058E-02	7.3886373E+00	*	73.	3.6434297E-05	7.6542739E+00	*
24.	3.4735258E-02	7.4233725E+00	*	74.	3.1674456E-05	7.6543055E+00	*
25.	3.0197383E-02	7.4535698E+00	*	75.	2.7536449E-05	7.6543333E+00	*
26.	2.6252343E-02	7.4798221E+00	*	76.	2.3939038E-05	7.6543569E+00	*
27.	2.2822691E-02	7.5026644E+00	*	77.	2.0811600E-05	7.6543777E+00	*
28.	1.9841094E-02	7.5224857E+00	*	78.	1.8092736E-05	7.6543957E+00	*
29.	1.7249019E-02	7.5397347E+00	*	79.	1.5729069E-05	7.6544114E+00	*
30.	1.4995576E-02	7.5547302E+00	*	80.	1.3674196E-05	7.6544250E+00	*
31.	1.3036528E-02	7.5677667E+00	*	81.	1.1887774E-05	7.6544368E+00	*
32.	1.1333413E-02	7.5791001E+00	*	82.	1.0334735E-05	7.6544471E+00	*
33.	9.8527960E-03	7.5889528E+00	*	83.	8.9845870E-06	7.6544560E+00	*
34.	8.5656093E-03	7.5975184E+00	*	84.	7.8108247E-06	7.6544638E+00	*
35.	7.4465830E-03	7.6049649E+00	*	85.	6.7904047E-06	7.6544705E+00	*
36.	6.4737483E-03	7.6114386E+00	*	86.	5.9032943E-06	7.6544764E+00	*
37.	5.6280063E-03	7.6170666E+00	*	87.	5.1320775E-06	7.6544815E+00	*
38.	4.8927537E-03	7.6219593E+00	*	88.	4.4616138E-06	7.6544859E+00	*
39.	4.2535557E-03	7.6262128E+00	*	89.	3.8787407E-06	7.6544897E+00	*
40.	3.6978637E-03	7.6299106E+00	*	90.	3.3720152E-06	7.6544930E+00	*
41.	3.2147682E-03	7.6331253E+00	*	91.	2.9314892E-06	7.6544959E+00	*
42.	2.7947852E-03	7.6359200E+00	*	92.	2.5485142E-06	7.6544984E+00	*
43.	2.4296695E-03	7.6383496E+00	*	93.	2.2155718E-06	7.6545004E+00	*
44.	2.1122532E-03	7.6404618E+00	*	94.	1.9261256E-06	7.6545025E+00	*
45.	1.8363047E-03	7.6422981E+00	*	95.	1.6744932E-06	7.6545041E+00	*
46.	1.5964066E-03	7.6438945E+00	*	96.	1.4557344E-06	7.6545055E+00	*
47.	1.3878492E-03	7.6452823E+00	*	97.	1.2655547E-06	7.6545067E+00	*
48.	1.2065382E-03	7.6464888E+00	*	98.	1.1002204E-06	7.6545078E+00	*
49.	1.0489139E-03	7.6475377E+00	*	99.	9.5648569E-07	7.6545087E+00	*
50.	9.1188196E-04	7.6484495E+00	*	100.	8.3152871E-07	7.6545095E+00	*

TABULATED VALUES OF E^{-RX} WHEN R = .145

X	E^{-RX}	SUM OF E^{-RX}	*	X	E^{-RX}	SUM OF E^{-RX}	*
0.	1.0000000E+00	1.0000000E+00	*	50.	7.1017438E-04	7.4040770E+00	*
1.	8.6502229E-01	1.8650222E+00	*	51.	6.1431667E-04	7.4046913E+00	*
2.	7.4826356E-01	2.6132857E+00	*	52.	5.3139762E-04	7.4052226E+00	*
3.	6.4726466E-01	3.2605503E+00	*	53.	4.5967078E-04	7.4056822E+00	*
4.	5.5989836E-01	3.8204486E+00	*	54.	3.9762547E-04	7.4060798E+00	*
5.	4.843245AE-01	4.3047731E+00	*	55.	3.4395490E-04	7.4064237E+00	*
6.	4.1895154E-01	4.7237246E+00	*	56.	2.9752866E-04	7.4067212E+00	*
7.	3.6240242E-01	5.0861270E+00	*	57.	2.5736892E-04	7.4069785E+00	*
8.	3.1348118E-01	5.3996131E+00	*	58.	2.2262985E-04	7.4072011E+00	*
9.	2.7117253E-01	5.6707856E+00	*	59.	1.9257978E-04	7.4073936E+00	*
10.	2.3457028E-01	5.9053558E+00	*	60.	1.6658581E-04	7.4075601E+00	*
11.	2.0290852E-01	6.1082643E+00	*	61.	1.4410044E-04	7.4077042E+00	*
12.	1.7552040E-01	6.2837847E+00	*	62.	1.2465009E-04	7.4078288E+00	*
13.	1.51A2905E-01	6.4356137E+00	*	63.	1.0782510E-04	7.4079366E+00	*
14.	1.3133552E-01	6.5669492E+00	*	64.	9.3271123E-05	7.4080298E+00	*
15.	1.1360815E-01	6.6805573E+00	*	65.	8.0681600E-05	7.4081104E+00	*
16.	9.8273585E-02	6.7788308E+00	*	66.	6.9791383E-05	7.4081801E+00	*
17.	R.5008842E-02	6.8638396E+00	*	67.	6.0371102E-05	7.4082404E+00	*
18.	7.3534543E-02	6.9373741E+00	*	68.	5.2222349E-05	7.4082926E+00	*
19.	6.3609019E-02	7.0009831E+00	*	69.	4.5173496E-05	7.4083377E+00	*
20.	5.5023219E-02	7.0560063E+00	*	70.	3.9076081E-05	7.4083767E+00	*
21.	4.7596311E-02	7.1036026E+00	*	71.	3.3801681E-05	7.4084105E+00	*
22.	4.1171870E-02	7.1447744E+00	*	72.	2.9239208E-05	7.4084397E+00	*
23.	3.561458bE-02	7.1803889E+00	*	73.	2.5292566E-05	7.4084649E+00	*
24.	3.0807411E-02	7.2111963E+00	*	74.	2.1878634E-05	7.4084867E+00	*
25.	2.6649097E-02	7.2378453E+00	*	75.	1.8925506E-05	7.4085056E+00	*
26.	2.3052063E-02	7.2608973E+00	*	76.	1.6370984E-05	7.4085219E+00	*
27.	1.9940543E-02	7.2808378E+00	*	77.	1.4161266E-05	7.4085360E+00	*
28.	1.7249019E-02	7.2980608E+00	*	78.	1.2249811E-05	7.4085482E+00	*
29.	1.4920786E-02	7.3130075E+00	*	79.	1.0596360E-05	7.4085587E+00	*
30.	1.2906812E-02	7.3259143E+00	*	80.	9.1660877E-06	7.4085678E+00	*
31.	1.1164680E-02	7.3370789E+00	*	81.	7.9288702E-06	7.4085757E+00	*
32.	9.6576976E-03	7.3467365E+00	*	82.	6.8586494E-06	7.4085825E+00	*
33.	8.3541237E-03	7.3550906E+00	*	83.	5.9328847E-06	7.4085884E+00	*
34.	7.2265032E-03	7.3623171E+00	*	84.	5.1320775E-06	7.4085935E+00	*
35.	6.2510864E-03	7.36856R1E+00	*	85.	4.4393614E-06	7.4085979E+00	*
36.	5.4073291E-03	7.3739754E+00	*	86.	3.8401466E-06	7.4086017E+00	*
37.	4.6774602E-03	7.37R6652RE+00	*	87.	3.3218124E-06	7.4086050E+00	*
38.	4.04610 73E-03	7.3826989E+00	*	88.	2.8734418E-06	7.4086078E+00	*
39.	3.4997730E-03	7.3861988E+00	*	89.	2.4855912E-06	7.4086102E+00	*
40.	3.0275547E-03	7.3892263E+00	*	90.	2.1500918E-06	7.4086123E+00	*
41.	2.6189023E-03	7.3918452E+00	*	91.	1.8598773E-06	7.4086141E+00	*
42.	2.2654089E-03	7.3941106E+00	*	92.	1.6088353E-06	7.4086157E+00	*
43.	1.9596292E-03	7.3960702E+00	*	93.	1.3916784E-06	7.4086170E+00	*
44.	1.6951229E-03	7.3577653E+00	*	94.	1.2038329E-06	7.4086182E+00	*
45.	1.4663191E-03	7.3992316E+00	*	95.	1.0413423E-06	7.4086192E+00	*
46.	1.2683987E-03	7.4004999E+00	*	96.	9.0078430E-07	7.4086201E+00	*
47.	1.0971931E-03	7.4015970E+00	*	97.	7.7919850E-07	7.4086208E+00	*
48.	9.4909657E-04	7.4025460E+00	*	98.	6.7402407E-07	7.4086214E+00	*
49.	R.2098969E-04	7.4033669E+00	*	99.	5.8304585E-07	7.4086219E+00	*
50.	7.1017438E-04	7.4040770E+00	*	100.	5.0434766E-07	7.40R6224E+00	*

TABULATED VALUES OF E^{-RX} WHEN R = .150

X	E^{-RX}	SUM OF E^{-RX}	*	X	E^{-RX}	SUM OF E^{-RX}	*
0.	1.0000000E+00	1.0000000E+00	*	50.	5.5308436E-04	7.1757419E+00	*
1.	8.6070797E-01	1.8607079E+00	*	51.	4.7604412E-04	7.1762179E+00	*
2.	7.4081821E-01	2.6015261E+00	*	52.	4.0973497E-04	7.1766276E+00	*
3.	6.3762814E-01	3.2391542E+00	*	53.	3.5266216E-04	7.1769802E+00	*
4.	5.4881163E-01	3.7879658E+00	*	54.	3.0353913E-04	7.1772837E+00	*
5.	4.7236655E-01	4.2603323E+00	*	55.	2.6125855E-04	7.1775449E+00	*
6.	4.0656965E-01	4.6669019E+00	*	56.	2.2486723E-04	7.1777697E+00	*
7.	3.4993774E-01	5.0168396E+00	*	57.	1.9354509E-04	7.1779632E+00	*
8.	3.0119421E-01	5.3180338E+00	*	58.	1.6658581E-04	7.1781297E+00	*
9.	2.5924026E-01	5.5772740E+00	*	59.	1.4338173E-04	7.1782730E+00	*
10.	2.2313015E-01	5.8004041E+00	*	60.	1.2340980E-04	7.1783964E+00	*
11.	1.9204990E-01	5.9924540E+00	*	61.	1.0621980E-04	7.1785026E+00	*
12.	1.6529888E-01	6.1577528E+00	*	62.	9.1424231E-05	7.1785940E+00	*
13.	1.4227407E-01	6.3000268E+00	*	63.	7.8689565E-05	7.1786726E+00	*
14.	1.2245642E-01	6.4224832E+00	*	64.	6.7728736E-05	7.1787403E+00	*
15.	1.0539922E-01	6.5278824E+00	*	65.	5.8294663E-05	7.1787985E+00	*
16.	9.0717953E-02	6.6186003E+00	*	66.	5.0174681E-05	7.1788486E+00	*
17.	7.8081665E-02	6.6966819E+00	*	67.	4.3185749E-05	7.1788917E+00	*
18.	6.7205512E-02	6.7638874E+00	*	68.	3.7170318E-05	7.1789288E+00	*
19.	5.7844320E-02	6.8217317E+00	*	69.	3.1992789E-05	7.1789607E+00	*
20.	4.9787068E-02	6.8715187E+00	*	70.	2.7536449E-05	7.1789882E+00	*
21.	4.2852126E-02	6.9143708E+00	*	71.	2.3700841E-05	7.1790119E+00	*
22.	3.688316 7E-02	6.9512539E+00	*	72.	2.0399503E-05	7.1790322E+00	*
23.	3.1745636E-02	6.9829995E+00	*	73.	1.7558019E-05	7.1790497E+00	*
24.	2.7323722E-02	7.0103232E+00	*	74.	1.5112323E-05	7.1790648E+00	*
25.	2.3517745E-02	7.0338409E+00	*	75.	1.3007297E-05	7.1790778E+00	*
26.	2.0241911E-02	7.0540828E+00	*	76.	1.1195484E-05	7.1790889E+00	*
27.	1.7422374E-02	7.0715051E+00	*	77.	9.6360430E-06	7.1790985E+00	*
28.	1.4995576E-02	7.0865006E+00	*	78.	8.2938191E-06	7.1791067E+00	*
29.	1.2908812E-02	7.0994074E+00	*	79.	7.1385562E-06	7.1791138E+00	*
30.	1.1108996E-02	7.1105163E+00	*	80.	6.1442123E-06	7.1791199E+00	*
31.	9.5616019E-03	7.1200779E+00	*	81.	5.2883725E-06	7.1791251E+00	*
32.	8.2297470E-03	7.1283076E+00	*	82.	4.5517444E-06	7.1791296E+00	*
33.	7.0834089E-03	7.1353910E+00	*	83.	3.9177227E-06	7.1791335E+00	*
34.	6.0967465E-03	7.1414877E+00	*	84.	3.3720152E-06	7.1791368E+00	*
35.	5.2475183E-03	7.1467352E+00	*	85.	2.9023204E-06	7.1791397E+00	*
36.	4.5165809E-03	7.1512517E+00	*	86.	2.4980503E-06	7.1791421E+00	*
37.	3.8874572E-03	7.1551391E+00	*	87.	2.1500918E-06	7.1791442E+00	*
38.	3.3459654E-03	7.1584850E+00	*	88.	1.8506011E-06	7.1791460E+00	*
39.	2.8798991E-03	7.1613648E+00	*	89.	1.5928272E-06	7.1791475E+00	*
40.	2.4787521E-03	7.1638435E+00	*	90.	1.3709590E-06	7.1791488E+00	*
41.	2.1334817E-03	7.1659769E+00	*	91.	1.1799954E-06	7.1791499E+00	*
42.	1.8363047E-03	7.1678132E+00	*	92.	1.0156314E-06	7.1791509E+00	*
43.	1.5805221E-03	7.1693937E+00	*	93.	8.7416210E-07	7.1791517E+00	*
44.	1.3603680E-03	7.1707540E+00	*	94.	7.5239829E-07	7.1791524E+00	*
45.	1.1708796E-03	7.1719248E+00	*	95.	6.4759521E-07	7.1791530E+00	*
46.	1.0077854E-03	7.1729325E+00	*	96.	5.5739036E-07	7.1791535E+00	*
47.	8.6740895E-04	7.1737999E+00	*	97.	4.7975033E-07	7.1791539E+00	*
48.	7.4658580E-04	7.1745464E+00	*	98.	4.1292494E-07	7.1791543E+00	*
49.	6.4259235E-04	7.1751889E+00	*	99.	3.5540778E-07	7.1791546E+00	*
50.	5.5308436E-04	7.1757419E+00	*	100.	3.0590232E-07	7.1791549E+00	*

TABULATED VALUES OF E $^{-RX}$ WHEN R = .155

X	E^{-RX}	SUM OF E^{-RX}	☼	X	E^{-RX}	SUM OF E^{-RX}	☼
0.	1.0000000E+00	1.0000000E+00	☼	50.	4.3074253E-04	6.9619530E+00	☼
1.	8.5645177E-01	1.8564151E+00	☼	51.	3.6889444E-04	6.9623218E+00	☼
2.	7.3344695E-01	2.5898620E+00	☼	52.	3.1592680E-04	6.9626377E+00	☼
3.	6.2813510E-01	3.2179971E+00	☼	53.	2.7056451E-04	6.9629082E+00	☼
4.	5.3794443E-01	3.7559415E+00	☼	54.	2.3171555E-04	6.9631399E+00	☼
5.	4.6070378E-01	4.2166452E+00	☼	55.	1.9844471E-04	6.9633383E+00	☼
6.	3.9455370E-01	4.6111989E+00	☼	56.	1.6995106E-04	6.9635082E+00	☼
7.	3.3790178E-01	4.9491006E+00	☼	57.	1.4554867E-04	6.9636537E+00	☼
8.	2.8938421E-01	5.2384848E+00	☼	58.	1.2465009E-04	6.9637783E+00	☼
9.	2.4783303E-01	5.4863178E+00	☼	59.	1.0675223E-04	6.9638850E+00	☼
10.	2.1224797E-01	5.6985657E+00	☼	60.	9.1424231E-05	6.9639764E+00	☼
11.	1.8177238E-01	5.8803380E+00	☼	61.	7.8297099E-05	6.9640546E+00	☼
12.	1.5567263E-01	6.0360106E+00	☼	62.	6.7054824E-05	6.9641216E+00	☼
13.	1.3332040E-01	6.1693310E+00	☼	63.	5.7426769E-05	6.9641790E+00	☼
14.	1.1417761E-01	6.2835086E+00	☼	64.	4.9181156E-05	6.9642281E+00	☼
15.	9.7783443E-02	6.3812920E+00	☼	65.	4.2119488E-05	6.9642702E+00	☼
16.	8.3743225E-02	6.4650352E+00	☼	66.	3.6071769E-05	6.9643062E+00	☼
17.	7.1718969E-02	6.5367541E+00	☼	67.	3.0892411E-05	6.9643370E+00	☼
18.	6.1421213E-02	6.5981753E+00	☼	68.	2.6456729E-05	6.9643634E+00	☼
19.	5.2602059E-02	6.6507773E+00	☼	69.	2.2657944E-05	6.9643860E+00	☼
20.	4.5049202E-02	6.6958265E+00	☼	70.	1.9404607E-05	6.9644054E+00	☼
21.	3.8580820E-02	6.7344073E+00	☼	71.	1.6618400E-05	6.9644220E+00	☼
22.	3.3041200E-02	6.7674485E+00	☼	72.	1.4232250E-05	6.9644362E+00	☼
23.	2.8296985E-02	6.7957454E+00	☼	73.	1.2188715E-05	6.9644483E+00	☼
24.	2.4233967E-02	6.8199793E+00	☼	74.	1.0438600E-05	6.9644587E+00	☼
25.	2.0754337E-02	6.8407336E+00	☼	75.	8.9397760E-06	6.9644676E+00	☼
26.	1.7774329E-02	6.8585079E+00	☼	76.	7.6561600E-06	6.9644752E+00	☼
27.	1.5222205E-02	6.8737301E+00	☼	77.	6.5568516E-06	6.9644817E+00	☼
28.	1.3036528E-02	6.8867666E+00	☼	78.	5.6153872E-06	6.9644873E+00	☼
29.	1.1164680E-02	6.8979312E+00	☼	79.	4.8091028E-06	6.9644921E+00	☼
30.	9.5616019E-03	6.9074928E+00	☼	80.	4.1185886E-06	6.9644962E+00	☼
31.	8.1887009E-03	6.9156815E+00	☼	81.	3.5272218E-06	6.9644997E+00	☼
32.	7.0129278E-03	6.9226944E+00	☼	82.	3.0207663E-06	6.9645027E+00	☼
33.	6.0059778E-03	6.9287003E+00	☼	83.	2.5870301E-06	6.9645052E+00	☼
34.	5.1436105E-03	6.9338439E+00	☼	84.	2.2155718E-06	6.9645074E+00	☼
35.	4.4050661E-03	6.9382489E+00	☼	85.	1.8974493E-06	6.9645092E+00	☼
36.	3.7725655E-03	6.9420214E+00	☼	86.	1.6250044E-06	6.9645108E+00	☼
37.	3.2308823E-03	6.9452522E+00	☼	87.	1.3916784E-06	6.9645121E+00	☼
38.	2.7669766E-03	6.9480191E+00	☼	88.	1.1918545E-06	6.9645132E+00	☼
39.	2.3696808E-03	6.9503887E+00	☼	89.	1.0207223E-06	6.9645142E+00	☼
40.	2.0294306E-03	6.9524181E+00	☼	90.	8.7416210E-07	6.9645150E+00	☼
41.	1.7380351E-03	6.9541561E+00	☼	91.	7.4864569E-07	6.9645157E+00	☼
42.	1.4884797E-03	6.9556445E+00	☼	92.	6.4115153E-07	6.9645163E+00	☼
43.	1.2747566E-03	6.9569192E+00	☼	93.	5.4909190E-07	6.9645168E+00	☼
44.	1.0917209E-03	6.9580109E+00	☼	94.	4.7025064E-07	6.9645172E+00	☼
45.	9.3496636E-04	6.9589458E+00	☼	95.	4.0272978E-07	6.9645176E+00	☼
46.	8.0071938E-04	6.9597465E+00	☼	96.	3.4490390E-07	6.9645179E+00	☼
47.	6.8574823E-04	6.9604322E+00	☼	97.	2.9538093E-07	6.9645181E+00	☼
48.	5.8728519E-04	6.9610194E+00	☼	98.	2.5296871E-07	6.9645183E+00	☼
49.	5.0295995E-04	6.9615223E+00	☼	99.	2.1664624E-07	6.9645185E+00	☼
50.	4.3074253E-04	6.9619530E+00	☼	100.	1.8553913E-07	6.9645186E+00	☼

TABULATED VALUES OF E $^{-RX}$ WHEN R = .160

X	E^{-RX}	SUM OF E^{-RX}	☼	X	E^{-RX}	SUM OF E^{-RX}	☼
0.	1.0000000E+00	1.0000000E+00	☼	50.	3.3546262E-04	6.7613917E+00	☼
1.	8.5214378E-01	1.8521437E+00	☼	51.	2.8586239E-04	6.7616775E+00	☼
2.	7.2614903E-01	2.5782927E+00	☼	52.	2.4359586E-04	6.7619210E+00	☼
3.	6.1878339E-01	3.1970760E+00	☼	53.	2.0757870E-04	6.7621285E+00	☼
4.	5.2729242E-01	3.7243684E+00	☼	54.	1.7688690E-04	6.7623053E+00	☼
5.	4.4932896E-01	4.1736973E+00	☼	55.	1.5073307E-04	6.7624560E+00	☼
6.	3.8289288E-01	4.5565901E+00	☼	56.	1.2844625E-04	6.7625844E+00	☼
7.	3.2627979E-01	4.8828698E+00	☼	57.	1.0945467E-04	6.7626938E+00	☼
8.	2.7803730E-01	5.1609071E+00	☼	58.	9.3271123E-05	6.7627870E+00	☼
9.	2.3692775E-01	5.3978348E+00	☼	59.	7.9480408E-05	6.7628664E+00	☼
10.	2.0189651E-01	5.5997313E+00	☼	60.	6.7728736E-05	6.7629341E+00	☼
11.	1.7204486E-01	5.7717761E+00	☼	61.	5.7714621E-05	6.7629918E+00	☼
12.	1.4660696E-01	5.9183830E+00	☼	62.	4.9181156E-05	6.7630409E+00	☼
13.	1.2493021E-01	6.0433132E+00	☼	63.	4.1909417E-05	6.7630828E+00	☼
14.	1.0645850E-01	6.1497717E+00	☼	64.	3.5712849E-05	6.7631185E+00	☼
15.	9.0717953E-02	6.2404896E+00	☼	65.	3.0432428E-05	6.7631489E+00	☼
16.	7.7304740E-02	6.3177943E+00	☼	66.	2.5932851E-05	6.7631748E+00	☼
17.	6.5874754E-02	6.3836690E+00	☼	67.	2.2098518E-05	6.7631968E+00	☼
18.	5.6134762E-02	6.4398037E+00	☼	68.	1.8831115E-05	6.7632156E+00	☼
19.	4.7834889E-02	6.4876385E+00	☼	69.	1.6044817E-05	6.7632316E+00	☼
20.	4.0762203E-02	6.5284007E+00	☼	70.	1.3674196E-05	6.7632452E+00	☼
21.	3.4735258E-02	6.5631359E+00	☼	71.	1.1652381E-05	6.7632568E+00	☼
22.	2.9599435E-02	6.5927353E+00	☼	72.	9.9295042E-06	6.7632667E+00	☼
23.	2.5222974E-02	6.6179582E+00	☼	73.	8.4613654E-06	6.7632751E+00	☼
24.	2.1493601E-02	6.6394518E+00	☼	74.	7.2102999E-06	6.7632823E+00	☼
25.	1.8315308E-02	6.6577674E+00	☼	75.	6.1442123E-06	6.7632884E+00	☼
26.	1.5607557E-02	6.6733749E+00	☼	76.	5.2357526E-06	6.7632936E+00	☼
27.	1.3299883E-02	6.6866747E+00	☼	77.	4.4616138E-06	6.7632980E+00	☼
28.	1.1333413E-02	6.6980081E+00	☼	78.	3.8019365E-06	6.7633018E+00	☼
29.	9.6576976E-03	6.7076657E+00	☼	79.	3.2397965E-06	6.7633050E+00	☼
30.	8.2297470E-03	6.7158954E+00	☼	80.	2.7607225E-06	6.7633077E+00	☼
31.	7.0129278E-03	6.7229083E+00	☼	81.	2.3525751E-06	6.7633100E+00	☼
32.	5.9760228E-03	6.7288843E+00	☼	82.	2.0047322E-06	6.7633120E+00	☼
33.	5.0924307E-03	6.7339767E+00	☼	83.	1.7083202E-06	6.7633137E+00	☼
34.	4.3394832E-03	6.7383161E+00	☼	84.	1.4557344E-06	6.7633151E+00	☼
35.	3.6978637E-03	6.7420139E+00	☼	85.	1.2404950E-06	6.7633163E+00	☼
36.	3.1511115E-03	6.7451650E+00	☼	86.	1.0570801E-06	6.7633173E+00	☼
37.	2.6852001E-03	6.7478502E+00	☼	87.	9.0078430E-07	6.7633182E+00	☼
38.	2.2881766E-03	6.7501383E+00	☼	88.	7.6759775E-07	6.7633189E+00	☼
39.	1.9498555E-03	6.7520881E+00	☼	89.	6.5410365E-07	6.7633195E+00	☼
40.	1.6615572E-03	6.7537496E+00	☼	90.	5.5739036E-07	6.7633200E+00	☼
41.	1.4158857E-03	6.7551654E+00	☼	91.	4.7497670E-07	6.7633204E+00	☼
42.	1.2065382E-03	6.7563719E+00	☼	92.	4.0474847E-07	6.7633208E+00	☼
43.	1.0281440E-03	6.7574000E+00	☼	93.	3.4490390E-07	6.7633211E+00	☼
44.	8.7612656E-04	6.7582761E+00	☼	94.	2.9390771E-07	6.7633213E+00	☼
45.	7.4658580E-04	6.7590226E+00	☼	95.	2.5045163E-07	6.7633215E+00	☼
46.	6.3619845E-04	6.7596587E+00	☼	96.	2.1342080E-07	6.7633217E+00	☼
47.	5.4213256E-04	6.7602008E+00	☼	97.	1.8186521E-07	6.7633218E+00	☼
48.	4.6197489E-04	6.7606627E+00	☼	98.	1.5497531E-07	6.7633219E+00	☼
49.	3.9366904E-04	6.7610563E+00	☼	99.	1.3206125E-07	6.7633220E+00	☼
50.	3.3546262E-04	6.7613917E+00	☼	100.	1.1253517E-07	6.7633221E+00	☼

X	E^{-RX}	SUM OF E^{-RX}	*	X	E^{-RX}	SUM OF E^{-RX}	*
0.	1.0000000E+00	1.0000000E+00	*	50.	2.6125855E-04	6.5728913E+00	*
1.	8.4789370E-01	1.8478937E+00	*	51.	2.2151948E-04	6.5731128E+00	*
2.	7.1892373E-01	2.5668174E+00	*	52.	1.8782497E-04	6.5733006E+00	*
3.	6.0957090E-01	3.1763883E+00	*	53.	1.5925561E-04	6.5734598E+00	*
4.	5.1685133E-01	3.6932396E+00	*	54.	1.3503183E-04	6.5735948E+00	*
5.	4.3823499E-01	4.1314745E+00	*	55.	1.1449264E-04	6.5737092E+00	*
6.	3.7157669E-01	4.5030511E+00	*	56.	9.7077590E-05	6.5738062E+00	*
7.	3.1505753E-01	4.8181086E+00	*	57.	8.2311477E-05	6.5738885E+00	*
8.	2.6713530E-01	5.0852439E+00	*	58.	6.9791383E-05	6.5739582E+00	*
9.	2.2650234E-01	5.3117462E+00	*	59.	5.9175674E-05	6.5740173E+00	*
10.	1.9204990E-01	5.5037961E+00	*	60.	5.0174681E-05	6.5740674E+00	*
11.	1.6283790E-01	5.6666340E+00	.	61.	4.2542796E-05	6.5741099E+00	*
12.	1.3806923E-01	5.8047032E+00	*	62.	3.6071769E-05	6.5741459E+00	*
13.	1.1706803E-01	5.9217712E+00	*	63.	3.0585026E-05	6.5741764E+00	*
14.	9.9241251E-02	6.0210324E+00	*	64.	2.5932851E-05	6.5742023E+00	*
15.	8.4162990E-02	6.1051953E+00	*	65.	2.1988301E-05	6.5742242E+00	*
16.	7.1361269E-02	6.1765565E+00	*	66.	1.8643742E-05	6.5742428E+00	*
17.	6.0506771E-02	6.2370632E+00	*	67.	1.5807911E-05	6.5742586E+00	*
18.	5.1303310E-02	6.2883665E+00	*	68.	1.3403428E-05	6.5742720E+00	*
19.	4.3499753E-02	6.3318662E+00	*	69.	1.1364682E-05	6.5742833E+00	*
20.	3.6883167E-02	6.3687493E+00	*	70.	9.6360430E-06	6.5742929E+00	*
21.	3.1273005E-02	6.4000223E+00	*	71.	8.1703042E-06	6.5743010E+00	*
22.	2.6516184E-02	6.4265384E+00	*	72.	6.9275800E-06	6.5743079E+00	*
23.	2.2482905E-02	6.4490213E+00	*	73.	5.8738515E-06	6.5743137E+00	*
24.	1.9063114E-02	6.4680844E+00	*	74.	4.9804017E-06	6.5743186E+00	*
25.	1.6163494E-02	6.4842478E+00	*	75.	4.2228512E-06	6.5743228E+00	*
26.	1.3704925E-02	6.4979527E+00	*	76.	3.5805290E-06	6.5743263E+00	*
27.	1.1620319E-02	6.5095730E+00	*	77.	3.0359080E-06	6.5743293E+00	*
28.	9.8527960E-03	6.5194257E+00	*	78.	2.5741272E-06	6.5743318E+00	*
29.	8.3541237E-03	6.5277798E+00	*	79.	2.1825863E-06	6.5743339E+00	*
30.	7.0834089E-03	6.5348632E+00	*	80.	1.8506011E-06	6.5743357E+00	*
31.	6.0059778E-03	6.5408691E+00	*	81.	1.5691131E-06	6.5743372E+00	*
32.	5.0924307E-03	6.5459615E+00	*	82.	1.3304411E-06	6.5743385E+00	*
33.	4.3178400E-03	6.5502793E+00	*	83.	1.1280726E-06	6.5743396E+00	*
34.	3.6610693E-03	6.5539403E+00	*	84.	9.5648569E-07	6.5743405E+00	*
35.	3.1041976E-03	6.5570444E+00	*	85.	8.1099819E-07	6.5743413E+00	*
36.	2.6320296E-03	6.5596764E+00	*	86.	6.8764026E-07	6.5743419E+00	*
37.	2.2316813E-03	6.5619080E+00	*	87.	5.8304585E-07	6.5743424E+00	*
38.	1.8922285E-03	6.5638002E+00	*	88.	4.9436009E-07	6.5743428E+00	*
39.	1.6044086E-03	6.5654046E+00	*	89.	4.1916550E-07	6.5743432E+00	*
40.	1.3603680E-03	6.5667649E+00	*	90.	3.5546778E-07	6.5743435E+00	*
41.	1.1534474E-03	6.5679183E+00	*	91.	3.0134802E-07	6.5743438E+00	*
42.	9.7800061E-04	6.5688963E+00	*	92.	2.5551109E-07	6.5743440E+00	*
43.	8.2924077E-04	6.5697255E+00	*	93.	2.1664624E-07	6.5743442E+00	*
44.	7.0310803E-04	6.5704286E+00	*	94.	1.8369299E-07	6.5743443E+00	*
45.	5.9616087E-04	6.5710247E+00	*	95.	1.5575213E-07	6.5743444E+00	*
46.	5.0548105E-04	6.5715301E+00	*	96.	1.3206125E-07	6.5743445E+00	*
47.	4.2859420E-04	6.5719586E+00	*	97.	1.1197390E-07	6.5743446E+00	*
48.	3.6340232E-04	6.5723220E+00	*	98.	9.4941967E-08	6.5743446E+00	*
49.	3.0812654E-04	6.5726301E+00	*	99.	8.0500696E-08	6.5743446E+00	*
50.	2.6125855E-04	6.5728913E+00	*	100.	6.8256033E-08	6.5743446E+00	*

X	E^{-RX}	SUM OF E^{-RX}	*	X	E^{-RX}	SUM OF E^{-RX}	*
0.	1.0000000E+00	1.0000000E+00	*	50.	2.0346836E-04	6.3954123E+00	*
1.	8.4364481E-01	1.8436648E+00	*	51.	1.7165910E-04	6.3955839E+00	*
2.	7.1177032E-01	2.5554351E+00	*	52.	1.4482274E-04	6.3957287E+00	*
3.	6.0049557E-01	3.1559306E+00	*	53.	1.2218185E-04	6.3958508E+00	*
4.	5.0661699E-01	3.6625475E+00	*	54.	1.0308053E-04	6.3959538E+00	*
5.	4.2741493E-01	4.0899624E+00	*	55.	8.6965418E-05	6.3960407E+00	*
6.	3.6059493E-01	4.4505573E+00	*	56.	7.3369664E-05	6.3961140E+00	*
7.	3.0422126E-01	4.7547785E+00	*	57.	6.1899404E-05	6.3961758E+00	*
8.	2.5666077E-01	5.0114392E+00	*	58.	5.2223349E-05	6.3962280E+00	*
9.	2.1653566E-01	5.2279748E+00	*	59.	4.4058158E-05	6.3962720E+00	*
10.	1.8268352E-01	5.4106583E+00	*	60.	3.7170318E-05	6.3963091E+00	*
11.	1.5412366E-01	5.5647819E+00	*	61.	3.1359290E-05	6.3963404E+00	*
12.	1.3002871E-01	5.6948106E+00	*	62.	2.6456729E-05	6.3963668E+00	*
13.	1.0970064E-01	5.8045112E+00	*	63.	2.2320611E-05	6.3963891E+00	*
14.	9.2550577E-02	5.8970617E+00	*	64.	1.8831115E-05	6.3964079E+00	*
15.	7.8081665E-02	5.9751433E+00	*	65.	1.5887149E-05	6.3964237E+00	*
16.	6.5874754E-02	6.0410180E+00	*	66.	1.3403428E-05	6.3964371E+00	*
17.	5.5576212E-02	6.0965942E+00	*	67.	1.1304001E-05	6.3964484E+00	*
18.	4.6887695E-02	6.1434818E+00	*	68.	9.5401628E-06	6.3964579E+00	*
19.	3.9557498E-02	6.1830392E+00	*	69.	8.0486997E-06	6.3964659E+00	*
20.	3.3373269E-02	6.2164124E+00	*	70.	6.7904047E-06	6.3964726E+00	*
21.	2.8155853E-02	6.2445682E+00	*	71.	5.7288256E-06	6.3964783E+00	*
22.	2.3754103E-02	6.2683223E+00	*	72.	4.8332086E-06	6.3964831E+00	*
23.	2.0040500E-02	6.2883628E+00	*	73.	4.0776080E-06	6.3964871E+00	*
24.	1.6907465E-02	6.3052702E+00	*	74.	3.4401344E-06	6.3964905E+00	*
25.	1.4264233E-02	6.3195344E+00	*	75.	2.9023204E-06	6.3964934E+00	*
26.	1.2034232E-02	6.3315686E+00	*	76.	2.4485856E-06	6.3964958E+00	*
27.	1.0152886E-02	6.3417214E+00	*	77.	2.0657855E-06	6.3964978E+00	*
28.	8.5656093E-03	6.3502870E+00	*	78.	1.7423036E-06	6.3964995E+00	*
29.	7.2265032E-03	6.3575135E+00	*	79.	1.4703648E-06	6.3965009E+00	*
30.	6.0967465E-03	6.3636102E+00	*	80.	1.2404950E-06	6.3965021E+00	*
31.	5.1436105E-03	6.3687538E+00	*	81.	1.0465620E-06	6.3965031E+00	*
32.	4.3394832E-03	6.3730932E+00	*	82.	8.8294758E-07	6.3965040E+00	*
33.	3.6610693E-03	6.3767542E+00	*	83.	7.4491180E-07	6.3965046E+00	*
34.	3.0887154E-03	6.3798429E+00	*	84.	6.2845588E-07	6.3965052E+00	*
35.	2.6058405E-03	6.3824487E+00	*	85.	5.3020611E-07	6.3965057E+00	*
36.	2.1984559E-03	6.3846471E+00	*	86.	4.4731624E-07	6.3965061E+00	*
37.	1.8547599E-03	6.3865018E+00	*	87.	3.7734948E-07	6.3965064E+00	*
38.	1.5647957E-03	6.3880665E+00	*	88.	3.1838642E-07	6.3965067E+00	*
39.	1.3201630E-03	6.3893866E+00	*	89.	2.6861142E-07	6.3965069E+00	*
40.	1.1137751E-03	6.3905003E+00	*	90.	2.2661801E-07	6.3965071E+00	*
41.	9.3965290E-04	6.3914399E+00	*	91.	1.9118964E-07	6.3965072E+00	*
42.	7.9275209E-04	6.3922326E+00	*	92.	1.6129997E-07	6.3965073E+00	*
43.	6.6881705E-04	6.3929014E+00	*	93.	1.3608311E-07	6.3965074E+00	*
44.	5.6425741E-04	6.3934656E+00	*	94.	1.1480853E-07	6.3965075E+00	*
45.	4.7604412E-04	6.3939416E+00	*	95.	9.6859922E-08	6.3965075E+00	*
46.	4.0162168E-04	6.3943432E+00	*	96.	8.1717308E-08	6.3965075E+00	*
47.	3.3883408E-04	6.3946820E+00	*	97.	6.8942018E-08	6.3965075E+00	*
48.	2.8586239E-04	6.3949678E+00	*	98.	5.8163955E-08	6.3965075E+00	*
49.	2.4117204E-04	6.3952089E+00	*	99.	4.9070882E-08	6.3965075E+00	*
50.	2.0346836E-04	6.3954123E+00	*	100.	4.1399377E-08	6.3965075E+00	*

X	E^−RX	SUM OF E^−RX	✩	X	E^−RX	SUM OF E^−RX	✩
0.	1.0000000E+00	1.0000000E+00	✩	50.	1.5846132E-04	6.2280305E+00	✩
1.	8.3945701E-01	1.8394570E+00	✩	51.	1.3302147E-04	6.2281635E+00	✩
2.	7.0488808E-01	2.5443450E+00	✩	52.	1.1166580E-04	6.2282751E+00	✩
3.	5.9155536E-01	3.1357003E+00	✩	53.	9.3738646E-05	6.2283688E+00	✩
4.	4.9658530E-01	3.6322856E+00	✩	54.	7.8689565E-05	6.2284474E+00	✩
5.	4.1686201E-01	4.0491476E+00	✩	55.	6.6056507E-05	6.2285134E+00	✩
6.	3.4993774E-01	4.3990853E+00	✩	56.	5.5451599E-05	6.2285688E+00	✩
7.	2.9375769E-01	4.6928429E+00	✩	57.	4.6549234E-05	6.2286153E+00	✩
8.	2.4659696E-01	4.9394398E+00	✩	58.	3.9070581E-05	6.2286543E+00	✩
9.	2.0700755E-01	5.1464473E+00	✩	59.	3.2802690E-05	6.2286871E+00	✩
10.	1.7373394E-01	5.3202212E+00	✩	60.	2.7536449E-05	6.2287146E+00	✩
11.	1.4585755E-01	5.4660969E+00	✩	61.	2.3115665E-05	6.2287377E+00	✩
12.	1.2245642E-01	5.5885533E+00	✩	62.	1.9404607E-05	6.2287571E+00	✩
13.	1.0279690E-01	5.6913502E+00	✩	63.	1.6289334E-05	6.2287733E+00	✩
14.	8.6293586E-02	5.7776437E+00	✩	64.	1.3674196E-05	6.2287869E+00	✩
15.	7.2439756E-02	5.8500834E+00	✩	65.	1.1478899E-05	6.2287983E+00	✩
16.	6.0810062E-02	5.9108934E+00	✩	66.	9.6360430E-06	6.2288079E+00	✩
17.	5.1047433E-02	5.9619408E+00	✩	67.	8.0890440E-06	6.2288159E+00	✩
18.	4.2852126E-02	6.0047929E+00	✩	68.	6.7904047E-06	6.2288226E+00	✩
19.	3.5972518E-02	6.0407654E+00	✩	69.	5.7002529E-06	6.2288283E+00	✩
20.	3.0197383E-02	6.0709627E+00	✩	70.	4.7851173E-06	6.2288330E+00	✩
21.	2.5349405E-02	6.0963121E+00	✩	71.	4.0169003E-06	6.2288370E+00	✩
22.	2.1279736E-02	6.1175918E+00	✩	72.	3.3720152E-06	6.2288403E+00	✩
23.	1.7863424E-02	6.1354552E+00	✩	73.	2.8306618E-06	6.2288431E+00	✩
24.	1.4995576E-02	6.1504507E+00	✩	74.	2.3762189E-06	6.2288454E+00	✩
25.	1.2588142E-02	6.1630388E+00	✩	75.	1.9947336E-06	6.2288473E+00	✩
26.	1.0567204E-02	6.1736060E+00	✩	76.	1.6744932E-06	6.2288489E+00	✩
27.	8.8707138E-03	6.1824767E+00	✩	77.	1.4056603E-06	6.2288503E+00	✩
28.	7.4465830E-03	6.1899232E+00	✩	78.	1.1799954E-06	6.2288514E+00	✩
29.	6.2510864E-03	6.1961742E+00	✩	79.	9.9055543E-07	6.2288523E+00	✩
30.	5.2475183E-03	6.2014217E+00	✩	80.	8.3152871E-07	6.2288531E+00	✩
31.	4.4050661E-03	6.2058267E+00	✩	81.	6.9803261E-07	6.2288538E+00	✩
32.	3.6978637E-03	6.2095245E+00	✩	82.	5.8596838E-07	6.2288542E+00	✩
33.	3.1041976E-03	6.2126286E+00	✩	83.	4.9189527E-07	6.2288546E+00	✩
34.	2.6058405E-03	6.2152344E+00	✩	84.	4.1292494E-07	6.2288550E+00	✩
35.	2.1874911E-03	6.2174218E+00	✩	85.	3.4663274E-07	6.2288553E+00	✩
36.	1.8363047E-03	6.2192581E+00	✩	86.	2.9098328E-07	6.2288555E+00	✩
37.	1.5414989E-03	6.2207995E+00	✩	87.	2.4426796E-07	6.2288558E+00	✩
38.	1.2940221E-03	6.2220935E+00	✩	88.	2.0505245E-07	6.2288559E+00	✩
39.	1.0862759E-03	6.2231797E+00	✩	89.	1.7213272E-07	6.2288560E+00	✩
40.	9.1188196E-04	6.2240915E+00	✩	90.	1.4449802E-07	6.2288561E+00	✩
41.	7.6548571E-04	6.2248569E+00	✩	91.	1.2129988E-07	6.2288562E+00	✩
42.	6.4259235E-04	6.2254994E+00	✩	92.	1.0182603E-07	6.2288563E+00	✩
43.	5.3942866E-04	6.2260388E+00	✩	93.	8.5478581E-08	6.2288563E+00	✩
44.	4.5282718E-04	6.2264916E+00	✩	94.	7.1755595E-08	6.2288563E+00	✩
45.	3.8012895E-04	6.2268717E+00	✩	95.	6.0235738E-08	6.2288563E+00	✩
46.	3.1910192E-04	6.2271908E+00	✩	96.	5.0565313E-08	6.2288563E+00	✩
47.	2.6787234E-04	6.2274586E+00	✩	97.	4.2447407E-08	6.2288563E+00	✩
48.	2.2486732E-04	6.2276834E+00	✩	98.	3.5632774E-08	6.2288563E+00	✩
49.	1.8876645E-04	6.2278721E+00	✩	99.	2.9912182E-08	6.2288563E+00	✩
50.	1.5846132E-04	6.2280305E+00	✩	100.	2.5109991E-08	6.2288563E+00	✩

X	E^−RX	SUM OF E^−RX	✩	X	E^−RX	SUM OF E^−RX	✩
0.	1.0000000E+00	1.0000000E+00	✩	50.	1.2340980E-04	6.0699194E+00	✩
1.	8.3527020E-01	1.8352702E+00	✩	51.	1.0308053E-04	6.0700224E+00	✩
2.	6.9767632E-01	2.5329465E+00	✩	52.	8.6100098E-05	6.0701085E+00	✩
3.	5.8274825E-01	3.1156947E+00	✩	53.	7.1916847E-05	6.0701804E+00	✩
4.	4.8675225E-01	3.6024469E+00	✩	54.	6.0070000E-05	6.0702404E+00	✩
5.	4.0656965E-01	4.0090165E+00	✩	55.	5.0176681E-05	6.0702905E+00	✩
6.	3.3959552E-01	4.3486120E+00	✩	56.	4.1904176E-05	6.0703324E+00	✩
7.	2.8365402E-01	4.6322660E+00	✩	57.	3.5005687E-05	6.0703674E+00	✩
8.	2.3692775E-01	4.8691937E+00	✩	58.	2.9239208E-05	6.0703966E+00	✩
9.	1.9789869E-01	5.0670923E+00	✩	59.	2.4422639E-05	6.0704210E+00	✩
10.	1.6529888E-01	5.2323911E+00	✩	60.	2.0399503E-05	6.0704413E+00	✩
11.	1.3806923E-01	5.3704603E+00	✩	61.	1.7039097E-05	6.0704583E+00	✩
12.	1.1532512E-01	5.4857854E+00	✩	62.	1.4232250E-05	6.0704725E+00	✩
13.	9.6327638E-02	5.5821130E+00	✩	63.	1.1887774E-05	6.0704843E+00	✩
14.	8.0459606E-02	5.6625726E+00	✩	64.	9.9295042E-06	6.0704942E+00	✩
15.	6.7205512E-02	5.7297781E+00	✩	65.	8.2938191E-06	6.0705024E+00	✩
16.	5.6134762E-02	5.7859128E+00	✩	66.	6.9275800E-06	6.0705093E+00	✩
17.	4.6887695E-02	5.8328004E+00	✩	67.	5.7864012E-06	6.0705150E+00	✩
18.	3.9163895E-02	5.8719642E+00	✩	68.	4.8332086E-06	6.0705198E+00	✩
19.	3.2712434E-02	5.9046766E+00	✩	69.	4.0370351E-06	6.0705238E+00	✩
20.	2.7323722E-02	5.9320003E+00	✩	70.	3.3720152E-06	6.0705271E+00	✩
21.	2.2822691E-02	5.9548229E+00	✩	71.	2.8165438E-06	6.0705299E+00	✩
22.	1.9063114E-02	5.9738860E+00	✩	72.	2.3525751E-06	6.0705322E+00	✩
23.	1.5922851E-02	5.9898088E+00	✩	73.	1.9650359E-06	6.0705341E+00	✩
24.	1.3299883E-02	6.0031086E+00	✩	74.	1.6413360E-06	6.0705357E+00	✩
25.	1.1108996E-02	6.0142175E+00	✩	75.	1.3709590E-06	6.0705370E+00	✩
26.	9.2790138E-03	6.0234965E+00	✩	76.	1.1451212E-06	6.0705381E+00	✩
27.	7.7504838E-03	6.0312606E+00	✩	77.	9.5648569E-07	6.0705390E+00	✩
28.	6.4737483E-03	6.0377206E+00	✩	78.	7.9892400E-07	6.0705397E+00	✩
29.	5.4073291E-03	6.0431279E+00	✩	79.	6.6731742E-07	6.0705404E+00	✩
30.	4.5165809E-03	6.0476444E+00	✩	80.	5.5739036E-07	6.0705408E+00	✩
31.	3.7725655E-03	6.0514169E+00	✩	81.	4.6557157E-07	6.0705412E+00	✩
32.	3.1511115E-03	6.0545680E+00	✩	82.	3.8887806E-07	6.0705415E+00	✩
33.	2.6320296E-03	6.0572004E+00	✩	83.	3.2481826E-07	6.0705418E+00	✩
34.	2.1984559E-03	6.0593984E+00	✩	84.	2.7131101E-07	6.0705420E+00	✩
35.	1.8363047E-03	6.0612347E+00	✩	85.	2.2661801E-07	6.0705422E+00	✩
36.	1.5338106E-03	6.0627685E+00	✩	86.	1.8928727E-07	6.0705423E+00	✩
37.	1.2811463E-03	6.0640496E+00	✩	87.	1.5810602E-07	6.0705424E+00	✩
38.	1.0701033E-03	6.0651197E+00	✩	88.	1.3206125E-07	6.0705425E+00	✩
39.	8.9382549E-04	6.0660135E+00	✩	89.	1.1030682E-07	6.0705425E+00	✩
40.	7.4658580E-04	6.0667600E+00	✩	90.	9.2136008E-08	6.0705426E+00	✩
41.	6.2360088E-04	6.0673836E+00	✩	91.	7.6958463E-08	6.0705426E+00	✩
42.	5.2087524E-04	6.0679046E+00	✩	92.	6.4281111E-08	6.0705426E+00	✩
43.	4.3507157E-04	6.0683396E+00	✩	93.	5.3692097E-08	6.0705426E+00	✩
44.	3.6340232E-04	6.0687029E+00	✩	94.	4.4847409E-08	6.0705426E+00	✩
45.	3.0353913E-04	6.0690063E+00	✩	95.	3.7459705E-08	6.0705426E+00	✩
46.	2.5353719E-04	6.0692598E+00	✩	96.	3.1288976E-08	6.0705426E+00	✩
47.	2.1177207E-04	6.0694715E+00	✩	97.	2.6134749E-08	6.0705426E+00	✩
48.	1.7684690E-04	6.0696483E+00	✩	98.	2.1829577E-08	6.0705426E+00	✩
49.	1.4774835E-04	6.0697960E+00	✩	99.	1.8233596E-08	6.0705426E+00	✩
50.	1.2340980E-04	6.0699194E+00	✩	100.	1.5229979E-08	6.0705426E+00	✩

TABULATED VALUES OF E^{-RX} WHEN R = .185

X	E^{-RX}	SUM OF E^{-RX}	X	E^{-RX}	SUM OF E^{-RX}
0.	1.0000000E+00	1.0000000E+00	50.	9.6111651E-05	5.9203380E+00
1.	8.3110428E-01	1.8311042E+00	51.	7.9878805E-05	5.9204178E+00
2.	6.9073432E-01	2.5218385E+00	52.	6.6387617E-05	5.9204841E+00
3.	5.7407226E-01	3.0959107E+00	53.	5.5175033E-05	5.9205392E+00
4.	4.7711391E-01	3.5730246E+00	54.	4.5856206E-05	5.9205850E+00
5.	3.9653141E-01	3.9695560E+00	55.	3.8111289E-05	5.9206231E+00
6.	3.2955896E-01	4.2991149E+00	56.	3.1676456E-05	5.9206547E+00
7.	2.7389786E-01	4.5730127E+00	57.	2.6324776E-05	5.9206810E+00
8.	2.2763768E-01	4.8006503E+00	58.	2.1878634E-05	5.9207029E+00
9.	1.8919065E-01	4.9898409E+00	59.	1.8183426E-05	5.9207209E+00
10.	1.5723716E-01	5.1470780E+00	60.	1.5112323E-05	5.9207360E+00
11.	1.3068048E-01	5.2777584E+00	61.	1.2559917E-05	5.9207485E+00
12.	1.0860910E-01	5.3863675E+00	62.	1.0438600E-05	5.9207589E+00
13.	9.0265495E-02	5.4766239E+00	63.	8.6755565E-06	5.9207675E+00
14.	7.5020040E-02	5.5516524E+00	64.	7.2102999E-06	5.9207747E+00
15.	6.2349476E-02	5.6140023E+00	65.	5.9925111E-06	5.9207806E+00
16.	5.1818917E-02	5.6658212E+00	66.	4.9804017E-06	5.9207855E+00
17.	4.3066923E-02	5.7088881E+00	67.	4.1392332E-06	5.9207896E+00
18.	3.5793105E-02	5.7446812E+00	68.	3.4401344E-06	5.9207930E+00
19.	2.9747802E-02	5.7744290E+00	69.	2.8591104E-06	5.9207958E+00
20.	2.4723526E-02	5.7991525E+00	70.	2.3762189E-06	5.9207981E+00
21.	2.0547828E-02	5.8197003E+00	71.	1.9748857E-06	5.9208000E+00
22.	1.7077388E-02	5.8367776E+00	72.	1.6413360E-06	5.9208016E+00
23.	1.4198090E-02	5.8509706E+00	73.	1.3641213E-06	5.9208029E+00
24.	1.1795938E-02	5.8627665E+00	74.	1.1337271E-06	5.9208040E+00
25.	9.8036550E-03	5.8725701E+00	75.	9.4224547E-07	5.9208049E+00
26.	8.1478596E-03	5.8807179E+00	76.	7.8310425E-07	5.9208056E+00
27.	6.7717210E-03	5.8874896E+00	77.	6.5084130E-07	5.9208062E+00
28.	5.6280063E-03	5.8931176E+00	78.	5.4091699E-07	5.9208067E+00
29.	4.6774602E-03	5.8977950E+00	79.	4.4955843E-07	5.9208071E+00
30.	3.8874572E-03	5.9016824E+00	80.	3.7362993E-07	5.9208074E+00
31.	3.2308823E-03	5.9049132E+00	81.	3.1052544E-07	5.9208077E+00
32.	2.6852001E-03	5.9075984E+00	82.	2.5807902E-07	5.9208079E+00
33.	2.2316813E-03	5.9098300E+00	83.	2.144905E-07	5.9208081E+00
34.	1.8547599E-03	5.9116847E+00	84.	1.7826404E-07	5.9208082E+00
35.	1.5414989E-03	5.9132261E+00	85.	1.4815600E-07	5.9208083E+00
36.	1.2811463E-03	5.9145072E+00	86.	1.2313309E-07	5.9208084E+00
37.	1.0647662E-03	5.9155719E+00	87.	1.0233644E-07	5.9208085E+00
38.	8.8493177E-04	5.9164568E+00	88.	8.5052255E-08	5.9208085E+00
39.	7.3547059E-04	5.9171922E+00	89.	7.0687293E-08	5.9208085E+00
40.	6.1125276E-04	5.9178034E+00	90.	5.8748512E-08	5.9208085E+00
41.	5.0801478E-04	5.9183114E+00	91.	4.8826140E-08	5.9208085E+00
42.	4.2221326E-04	5.9187336E+00	92.	4.0579614E-08	5.9208085E+00
43.	3.5090325E-04	5.9190845E+00	93.	3.3725891E-08	5.9208085E+00
44.	2.9163719E-04	5.9193761E+00	94.	2.8029732E-08	5.9208085E+00
45.	2.4238092E-04	5.9196186E+00	95.	2.3295631E-08	5.9208085E+00
46.	2.0144382E-04	5.9198198E+00	96.	1.9361094E-08	5.9208085E+00
47.	1.6742082E-04	5.9199872E+00	97.	1.6091092E-08	5.9208085E+00
48.	1.3914165E-04	5.9201263E+00	98.	1.3373375E-08	5.9208085E+00
49.	1.1564331E-04	5.9202419E+00	99.	1.1116669E-08	5.9208085E+00
50.	9.6111651E-05	5.9203380E+00	100.	9.2374496E-09	5.9208085E+00

TABULATED VALUES OF E^{-RX} WHEN R = .190

X	E^{-RX}	SUM OF E^{-RX}	X	E^{-RX}	SUM OF E^{-RX}
0.	1.0000000E+00	1.0000000E+00	50.	7.4851829E-05	5.7786217E+00
1.	8.2695913E-01	1.8269591E+00	51.	6.1899404E-05	5.7786835E+00
2.	6.8366140E-01	2.5108205E+00	52.	5.1186277E-05	5.7787346E+00
3.	5.6552543E-01	3.0763459E+00	53.	4.2330613E-05	5.7787769E+00
4.	4.6766602E-01	3.5440123E+00	54.	3.5005687E-05	5.7788119E+00
5.	3.8674102E-01	3.9307533E+00	55.	2.8948273E-05	5.7788408E+00
6.	3.1981902E-01	4.2505723E+00	56.	2.3939038E-05	5.7788647E+00
7.	2.6447726E-01	4.5150495E+00	57.	1.9796606E-05	5.7788844E+00
8.	2.1871186E-01	4.7337613E+00	58.	1.6370984E-05	5.7789007E+00
9.	1.8086570E-01	4.9146270E+00	59.	1.3538135E-05	5.7789142E+00
10.	1.4956861E-01	5.0641956E+00	60.	1.1195484E-05	5.7789253E+00
11.	1.2368713E-01	5.1878827E+00	61.	9.2582084E-06	5.7789345E+00
12.	1.0228420E-01	5.2901669E+00	62.	7.6561600E-06	5.7789421E+00
13.	8.4584858E-02	5.3747517E+00	63.	6.3313314E-06	5.7789484E+00
14.	6.9948221E-02	5.4446999E+00	64.	5.2357523E-06	5.7789536E+00
15.	5.7844320E-02	5.5025442E+00	65.	4.3297532E-06	5.7789579E+00
16.	4.7834889E-02	5.5503790E+00	66.	3.5805290E-06	5.7789614E+00
17.	3.9557498E-02	5.5899364E+00	67.	2.9609511E-06	5.7789643E+00
18.	3.2712434E-02	5.6226488E+00	68.	2.4485856E-06	5.7789667E+00
19.	2.7051446E-02	5.6497006E+00	69.	2.0248802E-06	5.7789687E+00
20.	2.2370771E-02	5.6720713E+00	70.	1.6744932E-06	5.7789703E+00
21.	1.8499714E-02	5.6905710E+00	71.	1.3847374E-06	5.7789716E+00
22.	1.5298507E-02	5.7058695E+00	72.	1.1451212E-06	5.7789727E+00
23.	1.2651240E-02	5.7185207E+00	73.	9.4696850E-07	5.7789736E+00
24.	1.0462056E-02	5.7289827E+00	74.	7.8310425E-07	5.7789743E+00
25.	8.6516951E-03	5.7376343E+00	75.	6.4759521E-07	5.7789749E+00
26.	7.1545983E-03	5.7447888E+00	76.	5.3553477E-07	5.7789754E+00
27.	5.9165604E-03	5.7507053E+00	77.	4.4286537E-07	5.7789758E+00
28.	4.8927537E-03	5.7555980E+00	78.	3.6623156E-07	5.7789761E+00
29.	4.0461073E-03	5.7596441E+00	79.	3.0285854E-07	5.7789764E+00
30.	3.3459654E-03	5.7629900E+00	80.	2.5045163E-07	5.7789766E+00
31.	2.7669766E-03	5.7657569E+00	81.	2.0711326E-07	5.7789768E+00
32.	2.2881766E-03	5.7680450E+00	82.	1.7127420E-07	5.7789769E+00
33.	1.8922285E-03	5.7699372E+00	83.	1.4163677E-07	5.7789770E+00
34.	1.5647957E-03	5.7715019E+00	84.	1.1712782E-07	5.7789771E+00
35.	1.2940221E-03	5.7727959E+00	85.	9.6859922E-08	5.7789771E+00
36.	1.0701033E-03	5.7738660E+00	86.	8.0099197E-08	5.7789771E+00
37.	8.8493177E-04	5.7747509E+00	87.	6.6238762E-08	5.7789771E+00
38.	7.3180241E-04	5.7754827E+00	88.	5.4776750E-08	5.7789771E+00
39.	6.0517069E-04	5.7760878E+00	89.	4.5298133E-08	5.7789771E+00
40.	5.0045143E-04	5.7765882E+00	90.	3.7459705E-08	5.7789771E+00
41.	4.1385288E-04	5.7770020E+00	91.	3.0977645E-08	5.7789771E+00
42.	3.4223942E-04	5.7773442E+00	92.	2.5617246E-08	5.7789771E+00
43.	2.8301801E-04	5.7776272E+00	93.	2.1184416E-08	5.7789771E+00
44.	2.3404335E-04	5.7778612E+00	94.	1.7518646E-08	5.7789771E+00
45.	1.9354509E-04	5.7780547E+00	95.	1.4487204E-08	5.7789771E+00
46.	1.6005388E-04	5.7782147E+00	96.	1.1980326E-08	5.7789771E+00
47.	1.3235802E-04	5.7783470E+00	97.	9.9072403E-09	5.7789771E+00
48.	1.0945455E-04	5.7784564E+00	98.	8.1928828E-09	5.7789771E+00
49.	9.0514545E-05	5.7785469E+00	99.	6.7751793E-09	5.7789771E+00
50.	7.4851829E-05	5.7786217E+00	100.	5.6027964E-09	5.7789771E+00

TABULATED VALUES OF E^{-RX} WHEN R = .195

X	E^{-RX}	SUM OF E^{-RX}	X	E^{-RX}	SUM OF E^{-RX}
0.	1.0000000E+00	1.0000000E+00	50.	5.8294663E-05	5.6441715E+00
1.	8.2283465E-01	1.8228346E+00	51.	4.7966869E-05	5.6442194E+00
2.	6.7705687E-01	2.4998914E+00	52.	3.9468802E-05	5.6442588E+00
3.	5.5710586E-01	3.0569972E+00	53.	3.2476298E-05	5.6442912E+00
4.	4.5840601E-01	3.5154032E+00	54.	2.6722624E-05	5.6443179E+00
5.	3.7719235E-01	3.8925955E+00	55.	2.2188301E-05	5.6443398E+00
6.	3.1036694E-01	4.2029624E+00	56.	1.8092736E-05	5.6443578E+00
7.	2.5538067E-01	4.4583430E+00	57.	1.4887330E-05	5.6443726E+00
8.	2.1013607E-01	4.6684790E+00	58.	1.2249811E-05	5.6443848E+00
9.	1.7290724E-01	4.8413862E+00	59.	1.0079569E-05	5.6443948E+00
10.	1.4227407E-01	4.9836602E+00	60.	8.2938191E-06	5.6444030E+00
11.	1.1706803E-01	5.1007282E+00	61.	6.8244418E-06	5.6444098E+00
12.	9.6327638E-02	5.1970558E+00	62.	5.6153872E-06	5.6444154E+00
13.	7.9261719E-02	5.2763175E+00	63.	4.6205352E-06	5.6444200E+00
14.	6.5219289E-02	5.3415367E+00	64.	3.8019365E-06	5.6444238E+00
15.	5.3664691E-02	5.3952013E+00	65.	3.1283651E-06	5.6444269E+00
16.	4.4157168E-02	5.4393584E+00	66.	2.5741272E-06	5.6444294E+00
17.	3.6334048E-02	5.4756924E+00	67.	2.1180811E-06	5.6444315E+00
18.	2.9896914E-02	5.5055893E+00	68.	1.7428305E-06	5.6444332E+00
19.	2.4600217E-02	5.5301895E+00	69.	1.4340613E-06	5.6444346E+00
20.	2.0241911E-02	5.5504314E+00	70.	1.1799954E-06	5.6444357E+00
21.	1.6655746E-02	5.5670871E+00	71.	9.7094112E-07	5.6444366E+00
22.	1.3704925E-02	5.5807920E+00	72.	7.9892400E-07	5.6444373E+00
23.	1.1276887E-02	5.5920688E+00	73.	6.5738236E-07	5.6444379E+00
24.	9.2790138E-03	5.6013478E+00	74.	5.4091699E-07	5.6444384E+00
25.	7.6350942E-03	5.6089828E+00	75.	4.4508524E-07	5.6444388E+00
26.	6.2824201E-03	5.6152652E+00	76.	3.6623156E-07	5.6444391E+00
27.	5.1693930E-03	5.6204345E+00	77.	3.0134802E-07	5.6444394E+00
28.	4.2535557E-03	5.6246880E+00	78.	2.4795960E-07	5.6444396E+00
29.	3.4999730E-03	5.6281879E+00	79.	2.0402975E-07	5.6444398E+00
30.	2.8798991E-03	5.6310677E+00	80.	1.6788275E-07	5.6444399E+00
31.	2.3696808E-03	5.6334373E+00	81.	1.3813974E-07	5.6444400E+00
32.	1.9498555E-03	5.6353871E+00	82.	1.1366617E-07	5.6444401E+00
33.	1.6044084E-03	5.6369915E+00	83.	9.3528465E-08	5.6444401E+00
34.	1.3201630E-03	5.6383116E+00	84.	7.6958463E-08	5.6444401E+00
35.	1.0862759E-03	5.6393978E+00	85.	6.3324090E-08	5.6444401E+00
36.	8.9382549E-04	5.6402916E+00	86.	5.2105256E-08	5.6444401E+00
37.	7.3547059E-04	5.6410270E+00	87.	4.2874010E-08	5.6444401E+00
38.	6.0517069E-04	5.6416321E+00	88.	3.5278222E-08	5.6444401E+00
39.	4.9795542E-04	5.6421300E+00	89.	2.9028143E-08	5.6444401E+00
40.	4.0973497E-04	5.6425397E+00	90.	2.3885362E-08	5.6444401E+00
41.	3.3714414E-04	5.6428768E+00	91.	1.9653704E-08	5.6444401E+00
42.	2.7741388E-04	5.6431542E+00	92.	1.6171749E-08	5.6444401E+00
43.	2.2826575E-04	5.6433824E+00	93.	1.3306675E-08	5.6444401E+00
44.	1.8782497E-04	5.6435702E+00	94.	1.0949193E-08	5.6444401E+00
45.	1.5454890E-04	5.6437247E+00	95.	9.0093761E-09	5.6444401E+00
46.	1.2716819E-04	5.6438518E+00	96.	7.4132269E-09	5.6444401E+00
47.	1.0463839E-04	5.6439564E+00	97.	6.0998600E-09	5.6444401E+00
48.	8.6100098E-05	5.6440425E+00	98.	5.0191762E-09	5.6444401E+00
49.	7.0846145E-05	5.6441133E+00	99.	4.1299522E-09	5.6444401E+00
50.	5.8294663E-05	5.6441715E+00	100.	3.3982678E-09	5.6444401E+00

TABULATED VALUES OF E^{-RX} WHEN R = .200

X	E^{-RX}	SUM OF E^{-RX}	X	E^{-RX}	SUM OF E^{-RX}
0.	1.0000000E+00	1.0000000E+00	50.	4.5399929E-05	5.5164479E+00
1.	8.1873075E-01	1.8187307E+00	51.	3.7170318E-05	5.5164850E+00
2.	6.7032004E-01	2.4890507E+00	52.	3.0432482E-05	5.5165154E+00
3.	5.4881163E-01	3.0378623E+00	53.	2.4916009E-05	5.5165403E+00
4.	4.4932896E-01	3.4871912E+00	54.	2.0399503E-05	5.5165606E+00
5.	3.6787944E-01	3.8550706E+00	55.	1.6701700E-05	5.5165773E+00
6.	3.0119421E-01	4.1562648E+00	56.	1.3674196E-05	5.5165909E+00
7.	2.4659696E-01	4.4028617E+00	57.	1.1195484E-05	5.5166020E+00
8.	2.0189651E-01	4.6047582E+00	58.	9.1660877E-06	5.5166111E+00
9.	1.6529888E-01	4.7700570E+00	59.	7.5045579E-06	5.5166186E+00
10.	1.3533528E-01	4.9053922E+00	60.	6.1442123E-06	5.5166247E+00
11.	1.1080315E-01	5.0161953E+00	61.	5.0304555E-06	5.5166297E+00
12.	9.0717953E-02	5.1069132E+00	62.	4.1185886E-06	5.5166338E+00
13.	7.4273578E-02	5.1811867E+00	63.	3.3720152E-06	5.5166371E+00
14.	6.0810062E-02	5.2419967E+00	64.	2.7607725E-06	5.5166398E+00
15.	4.9787068E-02	5.2917837E+00	65.	2.2603294E-06	5.5166420E+00
16.	4.0762203E-02	5.3325459E+00	66.	1.8506011E-06	5.5166438E+00
17.	3.3373269E-02	5.3659191E+00	67.	1.5151441E-06	5.5166453E+00
18.	2.7323722E-02	5.3932428E+00	68.	1.2404950E-06	5.5166465E+00
19.	2.2370771E-02	5.4156135E+00	69.	1.0156314E-06	5.5166475E+00
20.	1.8315638E-02	5.4339291E+00	70.	8.3152871E-07	5.5166484E+00
21.	1.4995576E-02	5.4489246E+00	71.	6.8079813E-07	5.5166489E+00
22.	1.2277339E-02	5.4612019E+00	72.	5.5739036E-07	5.5166494E+00
23.	1.0051835E-02	5.4712537E+00	73.	4.5635263E-07	5.5166498E+00
24.	8.2297470E-03	5.4794834E+00	74.	3.7362993E-07	5.5166501E+00
25.	6.7379469E-03	5.4862213E+00	75.	3.0590232E-07	5.5166504E+00
26.	5.5165644E-03	5.4917378E+00	76.	2.5045163E-07	5.5166506E+00
27.	4.5165809E-03	5.4962543E+00	77.	2.0505245E-07	5.5166508E+00
28.	3.6978637E-03	5.4999521E+00	78.	1.6788275E-07	5.5166509E+00
29.	3.0275547E-03	5.5029796E+00	79.	1.3745077E-07	5.5166510E+00
30.	2.4787521E-03	5.5054583E+00	80.	1.1253517E-07	5.5166511E+00
31.	2.0294306E-03	5.5074877E+00	81.	9.2136008E-08	5.5166511E+00
32.	1.6615572E-03	5.5091492E+00	82.	7.5434583E-08	5.5166511E+00
33.	1.3603680E-03	5.5105095E+00	83.	6.1760613E-08	5.5166511E+00
34.	1.1137751E-03	5.5116232E+00	84.	5.0565313E-08	5.5166511E+00
35.	9.1188196E-04	5.5125350E+00	85.	4.1399377E-08	5.5166511E+00
36.	7.4658580E-04	5.5132815E+00	86.	3.3894943E-08	5.5166511E+00
37.	6.1125276E-04	5.5138927E+00	87.	2.7750832E-08	5.5166511E+00
38.	5.0045143E-04	5.5143931E+00	88.	2.2720459E-08	5.5166511E+00
39.	4.0973497E-04	5.5148028E+00	89.	1.8601939E-08	5.5166511E+00
40.	3.3546262E-04	5.5151382E+00	90.	1.5229979E-08	5.5166511E+00
41.	2.7465356E-04	5.5154128E+00	91.	1.2469252E-08	5.5166511E+00
42.	2.2486732E-04	5.5156376E+00	92.	1.0208960E-08	5.5166511E+00
43.	1.8410579E-04	5.5158217E+00	93.	8.3583900E-09	5.5166511E+00
44.	1.5073307E-04	5.5159724E+00	94.	6.8432710E-09	5.5166511E+00
45.	1.2340980E-04	5.5160958E+00	95.	5.6027964E-09	5.5166511E+00
46.	1.0103940E-04	5.5161968E+00	96.	4.5871817E-09	5.5166511E+00
47.	8.2724065E-05	5.5162795E+00	97.	3.7556667E-09	5.5166511E+00
48.	6.7728736E-05	5.5163472E+00	98.	3.0748798E-09	5.5166511E+00
49.	5.5451599E-05	5.5164026E+00	99.	2.5174987E-09	5.5166511E+00
50.	4.5399929E-05	5.5164479E+00	100.	2.0611536E-09	5.5166511E+00

x	E −Rλ	SUM OF E −Rλ	*	x	E −RX	SUM OF E −RX	*
0.	1.0000000E+00	1.0000000E+00	*	50.	3.5357500E-05	5.3949622E+00	*
1.	7.1464731E-01	1.8146473E+00	*	51.	2.8803893E-05	5.3949910E+00	*
2.	6.6365024E-01	2.4782975E+00	*	52.	2.3465014E-05	5.3950144E+00	*
3.	5.4066089E-01	3.0189383E+00	*	53.	1.9115710E-05	5.3950335E+00	*
4.	4.4043165E-01	3.4593699E+00	*	54.	1.5572562E-05	5.3950490E+00	*
5.	3.5879646E-01	3.8181663E+00	*	55.	1.2686146E-05	5.3950616E+00	*
6.	2.9229257E-01	4.1104588E+00	*	56.	1.0334735E-05	5.3950719E+00	*
7.	2.3811536E-01	4.3485741E+00	*	57.	8.4191641E-06	5.3950803E+00	*
8.	1.9398004E-01	4.5425541E+00	*	58.	6.8586494E-06	5.3950871E+00	*
9.	1.5802532E-01	4.7005794E+00	*	59.	5.5873804E-06	5.3950926E+00	*
10.	1.2873490E-01	4.8293143E+00	*	60.	4.5517444E-06	5.3950971E+00	*
11.	1.0487354E-01	4.9341878E+00	*	61.	3.7080664E-06	5.3951008E+00	*
12.	8.5434050E-02	5.0196227E+00	*	62.	3.0207663E-06	5.3951038E+00	*
13.	6.9599353E-02	5.0892220E+00	*	63.	2.4604591E-06	5.3951062E+00	*
14.	5.6698926E-02	5.1459209E+00	*	64.	2.0047323E-06	5.3951082E+00	*
15.	4.6189628E-02	5.1921105E+00	*	65.	1.6331498E-06	5.3951098E+00	*
16.	3.7628256E-02	5.2297387E+00	*	66.	1.3304411E-06	5.3951111E+00	*
17.	3.0653758E-02	5.2603924E+00	*	67.	1.0838402E-06	5.3951121E+00	*
18.	2.4972002E-02	5.2853644E+00	*	68.	8.8294758E-07	5.3951129E+00	*
19.	2.0343374E-02	5.3057077E+00	*	69.	7.1929087E-07	5.3951136E+00	*
20.	1.6572675E-02	5.3222803E+00	*	70.	5.8596838E-07	5.3951141E+00	*
21.	1.3500855E-02	5.3357811E+00	*	71.	4.7735757E-07	5.3951145E+00	*
22.	1.0998460E-02	5.3467795E+00	*	72.	3.8887066E-07	5.3951148E+00	*
23.	8.9598660E-03	5.3557393E+00	*	73.	3.1679847E-07	5.3951151E+00	*
24.	7.2991308E-03	5.3630384E+00	*	74.	2.5807902E-07	5.3951153E+00	*
25.	5.9462173E-03	5.3689846E+00	*	75.	2.102433E-07	5.3951155E+00	*
26.	4.8440700E-03	5.3738286E+00	*	76.	1.7127420E-07	5.3951156E+00	*
27.	3.9462086E-03	5.3777748E+00	*	77.	1.3952807E-07	5.3951157E+00	*
28.	3.2147682E-03	5.3809895E+00	*	78.	1.1366617E-07	5.3951158E+00	*
29.	2.6189023E-03	5.3836084E+00	*	79.	9.2597841E-08	5.3951158E+00	*
30.	2.1334817E-03	5.3857418E+00	*	80.	7.5434583E-08	5.3951158E+00	*
31.	1.7380351E-03	5.3874799E+00	*	81.	6.1452580E-08	5.3951158E+00	*
32.	1.4158857E-03	5.3888956E+00	*	82.	5.0062180E-08	5.3951158E+00	*
33.	1.1534474E-03	5.3900490E+00	*	83.	4.0783020E-08	5.3951158E+00	*
34.	9.3965290E-04	5.3909886E+00	*	84.	3.3223778E-08	5.3951158E+00	*
35.	7.6548571E-04	5.3917540E+00	*	85.	2.7065661E-08	5.3951158E+00	*
36.	6.2360088E-04	5.3923776E+00	*	86.	2.2048968E-08	5.3951158E+00	*
37.	5.0801479E-04	5.3928856E+00	*	87.	1.7962133E-08	5.3951158E+00	*
38.	4.1385288E-04	5.3932994E+00	*	88.	1.4632803E-08	5.3951158E+00	*
39.	3.3714414E-04	5.3936365E+00	*	89.	1.1920574E-08	5.3951158E+00	*
40.	2.7465356E-04	5.3939111E+00	*	90.	9.7110638E-09	5.3951158E+00	*
41.	2.2374579E-04	5.3941348E+00	*	91.	7.9110920E-09	5.3951158E+00	*
42.	1.8227391E-04	5.3943170E+00	*	92.	6.4447490E-09	5.3951158E+00	*
43.	1.4848895E-04	5.3944654E+00	*	93.	5.2501982E-09	5.3951158E+00	*
44.	1.2096612E-04	5.3945863E+00	*	94.	4.2770598E-09	5.3951158E+00	*
45.	9.8544730E-05	5.3946848E+00	*	95.	3.4842953E-09	5.3951158E+00	*
46.	8.0279199E-05	5.3947650E+00	*	96.	2.8384718E-09	5.3951158E+00	*
47.	6.5399234E-05	5.3948303E+00	*	97.	2.3123534E-09	5.3951158E+00	*
48.	5.3277311E-05	5.3948835E+00	*	98.	1.8837525E-09	5.3951158E+00	*
49.	4.3402218E-05	5.3949269E+00	*	99.	1.5345939E-09	5.3951158E+00	*
50.	3.5357500E-05	5.3949622E+00	*	100.	1.2501528E-09	5.3951158E+00	*

x	E −RX	SUM OF E −RX	*	x	E −RX	SUM OF E −RX	*
0.	1.0000000E+00	1.0000000E+00	*	50.	2.7536449E-05	5.2792716E+00	*
1.	8.1058424E-01	1.8105842E+00	*	51.	2.2320611E-05	5.2792939E+00	*
2.	6.5704681E-01	2.4676310E+00	*	52.	1.8092736E-05	5.2793119E+00	*
3.	5.3259179E-01	3.0002227E+00	*	53.	1.4665887E-05	5.2793265E+00	*
4.	4.3171052E-01	3.4319332E+00	*	54.	1.1887774E-05	5.2793383E+00	*
5.	3.4993774E-01	3.7818709E+00	*	55.	9.6360430E-06	5.2793479E+00	*
6.	2.8365402E-01	4.0655248E+00	*	56.	7.8106247E-06	5.2793557E+00	*
7.	2.2992548E-01	4.2954503E+00	*	57.	6.3313316E-06	5.2793620E+00	*
8.	1.8637397E-01	4.4818242E+00	*	58.	5.1320775E-06	5.2793671E+00	*
9.	1.5107180E-01	4.6328960E+00	*	59.	4.1599812E-06	5.2793712E+00	*
10.	1.2245642E-01	4.7553524E+00	*	60.	3.3720152E-06	5.2793745E+00	*
11.	9.9261251E-02	4.8546136E+00	*	61.	2.7333024E-06	5.2793772E+00	*
12.	8.0459606E-02	4.9350732E+00	*	62.	2.2155718E-06	5.2793794E+00	*
13.	6.5219289E-02	5.0002924E+00	*	63.	1.7959076E-06	5.2793811E+00	*
14.	5.2865728E-02	5.0531581E+00	*	64.	1.4557344E-06	5.2793825E+00	*
15.	4.2852126E-02	5.0960102E+00	*	65.	1.1799954E-06	5.2793836E+00	*
16.	3.4735258E-02	5.1307454E+00	*	66.	9.5648569E-07	5.2793845E+00	*
17.	2.8155853E-02	5.1589012E+00	*	67.	7.7531223E-07	5.2793852E+00	*
18.	2.2822691E-02	5.1817238E+00	*	68.	6.2845588E-07	5.2793858E+00	*
19.	1.8499714E-02	5.2002235E+00	*	69.	5.0941643E-07	5.2793863E+00	*
20.	1.4995576E-02	5.2152190E+00	*	70.	4.1292494E-07	5.2793867E+00	*
21.	1.2155178E-02	5.2273741E+00	*	71.	3.3471045E-07	5.2793870E+00	*
22.	9.8527960E-03	5.2372268E+00	*	72.	2.7131101E-07	5.2793872E+00	*
23.	7.9865212E-03	5.2452133E+00	*	73.	2.1992043E-07	5.2793874E+00	*
24.	6.4737483E-03	5.2516870E+00	*	74.	1.7826404E-07	5.2793876E+00	*
25.	5.2475183E-03	5.2569345E+00	*	75.	1.4449802E-07	5.2793876E+00	*
26.	4.2535557E-03	5.2611880E+00	*	76.	1.1712782E-07	5.2793877E+00	*
27.	3.4478652E-03	5.2646358E+00	*	77.	9.4941967E-08	5.2793877E+00	*
28.	2.7947852E-03	5.2674305E+00	*	78.	7.6958463E-08	5.2793877E+00	*
29.	2.2654089E-03	5.2696959E+00	*	79.	6.2381317E-08	5.2793877E+00	*
30.	1.8363047E-03	5.2715322E+00	*	80.	5.0565313E-08	5.2793877E+00	*
31.	1.4884797E-03	5.2730206E+00	*	81.	4.0987446E-08	5.2793877E+00	*
32.	1.2065382E-03	5.2742271E+00	*	82.	3.3223778E-08	5.2793877E+00	*
33.	9.7800086E-04	5.2752051E+00	*	83.	2.6930671E-08	5.2793877E+00	*
34.	7.9275209E-04	5.2759978E+00	*	84.	2.1829577E-08	5.2793877E+00	*
35.	6.4259235E-04	5.2766403E+00	*	85.	1.7694711E-08	5.2793877E+00	*
36.	5.2087524E-04	5.2771611E+00	*	86.	1.4343054E-08	5.2793877E+00	*
37.	4.2221326E-04	5.2775833E+00	*	87.	1.1626254E-08	5.2793877E+00	*
38.	3.4223942E-04	5.2779255E+00	*	88.	9.4240585E-09	5.2793877E+00	*
39.	2.7741388E-04	5.2782029E+00	*	89.	7.6389933E-09	5.2793877E+00	*
40.	2.2486732E-04	5.2784277E+00	*	90.	6.1920476E-09	5.2793877E+00	*
41.	1.8227391E-04	5.2786099E+00	*	91.	5.0191762E-09	5.2793877E+00	*
42.	1.4774835E-04	5.2787576E+00	*	92.	4.0684652E-09	5.2793877E+00	*
43.	1.1976249E-04	5.2788773E+00	*	93.	3.2978338E-09	5.2793877E+00	*
44.	9.7077590E-05	5.2789743E+00	*	94.	2.6731721E-09	5.2793877E+00	*
45.	7.8689565E-05	5.2790529E+00	*	95.	2.1668312E-09	5.2793877E+00	*
46.	6.3784521E-05	5.2791166E+00	*	96.	1.7563992E-09	5.2793877E+00	*
47.	5.1702728E-05	5.2791683E+00	*	97.	1.4237095E-09	5.2793877E+00	*
48.	4.1909417E-05	5.2792102E+00	*	98.	1.1540365E-09	5.2793877E+00	*
49.	3.3971113E-05	5.2792441E+00	*	99.	9.3544384E-10	5.2793877E+00	*
50.	2.7536449E-05	5.2792716E+00	*	100.	7.5825604E-10	5.2793877E+00	*

X	E^{-RX}	SUM OF E^{-RX}	*	X	E^{-RX}	SUM OF E^{-RX}	*
0.	1.0000000E+00	1.0000000E+00	*	50.	2.1445408E-05	5.1689736E+00	*
1.	8.0654143E-01	1.8065414E+00	*	51.	1.7296610E-05	5.1689908E+00	*
2.	6.5050909E-01	2.4570504E+00	*	52.	1.3950433E-05	5.1690047E+00	*
3.	5.2466254E-01	2.9817129E+00	*	53.	1.1251602E-05	5.1690159E+00	*
4.	4.2316208E-01	3.4048749E+00	*	54.	9.0748836E-06	5.1690249E+00	*
5.	3.4129775E-01	3.7461726E+00	*	55.	7.3192696E-06	5.1690322E+00	*
6.	2.7527078E-01	4.0214433E+00	*	56.	5.9032943E-06	5.1690381E+00	*
7.	2.2201729E-01	4.2434605E+00	*	57.	4.7612515E-06	5.1690428E+00	*
8.	1.7906614E-01	4.4225266E+00	*	58.	3.8401466E-06	5.1690466E+00	*
9.	1.4442426E-01	4.5669508E+00	*	59.	3.0972374E-06	5.1690496E+00	*
10.	1.1648415E-01	4.6834349E+00	*	60.	2.4980503E-06	5.1690520E+00	*
11.	9.3949300E-02	4.7773842E+00	*	61.	2.0147811E-06	5.1690540E+00	*
12.	7.5774003E-02	4.8531582E+00	*	62.	1.6250044E-06	5.1690556E+00	*
13.	6.1114874E-02	4.9142730E+00	*	63.	1.3106334E-06	5.1690569E+00	*
14.	4.9291678E-02	4.9635646E+00	*	64.	1.0570801E-06	5.1690579E+00	*
15.	3.9755781E-02	5.0033203E+00	*	65.	8.5257896E-07	5.1690587E+00	*
16.	3.2064685E-02	5.0353849E+00	*	66.	6.8764026E-07	5.1690593E+00	*
17.	2.5861497E-02	5.0612463E+00	*	67.	5.5461037E-07	5.1690598E+00	*
18.	2.0858369E-02	5.0821046E+00	*	68.	4.4731624E-07	5.1690602E+00	*
19.	1.6823139E-02	5.0989277E+00	*	69.	3.6077909E-07	5.1690605E+00	*
20.	1.3568558E-02	5.1124962E+00	*	70.	2.9098328E-07	5.1690607E+00	*
21.	1.0943605E-02	5.1234398E+00	*	71.	2.3469007E-07	5.1690609E+00	*
22.	8.8264710E-03	5.1322662E+00	*	72.	1.8928727E-07	5.1690610E+00	*
23.	7.1189146E-03	5.1393851E+00	*	73.	1.5266803E-07	5.1690611E+00	*
24.	5.7416996E-03	5.1451267E+00	*	74.	1.2313309E-07	5.1690612E+00	*
25.	4.6309187E-03	5.1497576E+00	*	75.	9.9311943E-08	5.1690612E+00	*
26.	3.7350278E-03	5.1534926E+00	*	76.	8.0099197E-08	5.1690612E+00	*
27.	3.0124547E-03	5.1565050E+00	*	77.	6.4603322E-08	5.1690612E+00	*
28.	2.4296695E-03	5.1589346E+00	*	78.	5.2105256E-08	5.1690612E+00	*
29.	1.9596292E-03	5.1608942E+00	*	79.	4.2025048E-08	5.1690612E+00	*
30.	1.5805221E-03	5.1624747E+00	*	80.	3.3894943E-08	5.1690612E+00	*
31.	1.2747566E-03	5.1637494E+00	*	81.	2.7337676E-08	5.1690612E+00	*
32.	1.0281440E-03	5.1647775E+00	*	82.	2.2048968E-08	5.1690612E+00	*
33.	8.2924077E-04	5.1656067E+00	*	83.	1.7783407E-08	5.1690612E+00	*
34.	6.6881705E-04	5.1662755E+00	*	84.	1.4343054E-08	5.1690612E+00	*
35.	5.3942866E-04	5.1668149E+00	*	85.	1.1568268E-08	5.1690612E+00	*
36.	4.3507157E-04	5.1672499E+00	*	86.	9.3302875E-09	5.1690612E+00	*
37.	3.5090325E-04	5.1676008E+00	*	87.	7.5252635E-09	5.1690612E+00	*
38.	2.8301801E-04	5.1678838E+00	*	88.	6.0694369E-09	5.1690612E+00	*
39.	2.2826575E-04	5.1681120E+00	*	89.	4.8952523E-09	5.1690612E+00	*
40.	1.8410579E-04	5.1682961E+00	*	90.	3.9482239E-09	5.1690612E+00	*
41.	1.4848895E-04	5.1684445E+00	*	91.	3.1844061E-09	5.1690612E+00	*
42.	1.1976249E-04	5.1685642E+00	*	92.	2.5683555E-09	5.1690612E+00	*
43.	9.6593413E-05	5.1686607E+00	*	93.	2.071485E-09	5.1690612E+00	*
44.	7.7906590E-05	5.1687386E+00	*	94.	1.6707386E-09	5.1690612E+00	*
45.	6.2834894E-05	5.1688014E+00	*	95.	1.3475199E-09	5.1690612E+00	*
46.	5.0678945E-05	5.1688520E+00	*	96.	1.0868306E-09	5.1690612E+00	*
47.	4.0874669E-05	5.1688928E+00	*	97.	8.7657398E-10	5.1690612E+00	*
48.	3.2967115E-05	5.1689257E+00	*	98.	7.0699324E-10	5.1690612E+00	*
49.	2.6589344E-05	5.1689522E+00	*	99.	5.7021935E-10	5.1690612E+00	*
50.	2.1445408E-05	5.1689736E+00	*	100.	4.5990553E-10	5.1690612E+00	*

X	E^{-RX}	SUM OF E^{-RX}	*	X	E^{-RX}	SUM OF E^{-RX}	*
0.	1.0000000E+00	1.0000000E+00	*	50.	1.6701700E-05	5.0637033E+00	*
1.	8.0251879E-01	1.8025187E+00	*	51.	1.3403428E-05	5.0637167E+00	*
2.	6.4403641E-01	2.4465551E+00	*	52.	1.0756503E-05	5.0637274E+00	*
3.	5.1685133E-01	2.9634064E+00	*	53.	8.6322963E-06	5.0637360E+00	*
4.	4.1478291E-01	3.3781893E+00	*	54.	6.9275800E-06	5.0637429E+00	*
5.	3.3287108E-01	3.7110603E+00	*	55.	5.5595132E-06	5.0637484E+00	*
6.	2.6713530E-01	3.9781956E+00	*	56.	4.4616138E-06	5.0637528E+00	*
7.	2.1438110E-01	4.1925767E+00	*	57.	3.5805290E-06	5.0637563E+00	*
8.	1.7204486E-01	4.3646215E+00	*	58.	2.8734448E-06	5.0637591E+00	*
9.	1.3806923E-01	4.5026907E+00	*	59.	2.3059910E-06	5.0637614E+00	*
10.	1.1080315E-01	4.6134938E+00	*	60.	1.8506011E-06	5.0637632E+00	*
11.	8.8921617E-02	4.7024154E+00	*	61.	1.4851422E-06	5.0637646E+00	*
12.	7.1361269E-02	4.7737766E+00	*	62.	1.1918545E-06	5.0637657E+00	*
13.	5.7268760E-02	4.8310453E+00	*	63.	9.5648569E-07	5.0637666E+00	*
14.	4.5959256E-02	4.8770045E+00	*	64.	7.6759775E-07	5.0637673E+00	*
15.	3.6883167E-02	4.9138786E+00	*	65.	6.1601162E-07	5.0637679E+00	*
16.	2.9599435E-02	4.9434870E+00	*	66.	4.9436090E-07	5.0637683E+00	*
17.	2.3754103E-02	4.9672411E+00	*	67.	3.9673392E-07	5.0637686E+00	*
18.	1.9063114E-02	4.9863042E+00	*	68.	3.1838642E-07	5.0637689E+00	*
19.	1.5298507E-02	5.0016027E+00	*	69.	2.5551109E-07	5.0637691E+00	*
20.	1.2277339E-02	5.0138800E+00	*	70.	2.0505245E-07	5.0637693E+00	*
21.	9.8527960E-03	5.0237327E+00	*	71.	1.6455845E-07	5.0637694E+00	*
22.	7.9070540E-03	5.0316397E+00	*	72.	1.3206125E-07	5.0637695E+00	*
23.	6.3455594E-03	5.0379852E+00	*	73.	1.0598163E-07	5.0637696E+00	*
24.	5.0924307E-03	5.0430776E+00	*	74.	8.5052558E-08	5.0637696E+00	*
25.	4.0867714E-03	5.0471643E+00	*	75.	6.8256033E-08	5.0637696E+00	*
26.	3.2797108E-03	5.0504440E+00	*	76.	5.4776750E-08	5.0637696E+00	*
27.	2.6320296E-03	5.0530760E+00	*	77.	4.3959371E-08	5.0637696E+00	*
28.	2.1122532E-03	5.0551882E+00	*	78.	3.5278222E-08	5.0637696E+00	*
29.	1.6951229E-03	5.0568833E+00	*	79.	2.8311436E-08	5.0637696E+00	*
30.	1.3603680E-03	5.0582436E+00	*	80.	2.2720459E-08	5.0637696E+00	*
31.	1.0917209E-03	5.0593353E+00	*	81.	1.8233596E-08	5.0637696E+00	*
32.	8.7612656E-04	5.0602114E+00	*	82.	1.4632803E-08	5.0637696E+00	*
33.	7.0310803E-04	5.0609145E+00	*	83.	1.1743100E-08	5.0637696E+00	*
34.	5.6425741E-04	5.0614787E+00	*	84.	9.4240585E-09	5.0637696E+00	*
35.	4.5282718E-04	5.0619315E+00	*	85.	7.5629841E-09	5.0637696E+00	*
36.	3.6340232E-04	5.0622949E+00	*	86.	6.0694369E-09	5.0637696E+00	*
37.	2.9163719E-04	5.0625865E+00	*	87.	4.8708372E-09	5.0637696E+00	*
38.	2.3404433E-04	5.0628205E+00	*	88.	3.9089384E-09	5.0637696E+00	*
39.	1.8782497E-04	5.0630083E+00	*	89.	3.1369965E-09	5.0637696E+00	*
40.	1.5073307E-04	5.0631590E+00	*	90.	2.5174987E-09	5.0637696E+00	*
41.	1.2096612E-04	5.0632799E+00	*	91.	2.0203600E-09	5.0637696E+00	*
42.	9.7077590E-05	5.0633769E+00	*	92.	1.6213600E-09	5.0637696E+00	*
43.	7.7906590E-05	5.0634548E+00	*	93.	1.3011725E-09	5.0637696E+00	*
44.	6.2521503E-05	5.0635173E+00	*	94.	1.0442154E-09	5.0637696E+00	*
45.	5.0176681E-05	5.0635674E+00	*	95.	8.3800252E-10	5.0637696E+00	*
46.	4.0266125E-05	5.0636076E+00	*	96.	6.7251277E-10	5.0637696E+00	*
47.	3.2314322E-05	5.0636399E+00	*	97.	5.3970414E-10	5.0637696E+00	*
48.	2.5932851E-05	5.0636658E+00	*	98.	4.3312272E-10	5.0637696E+00	*
49.	2.0811600E-05	5.0636866E+00	*	99.	3.4758912E-10	5.0637696E+00	*
50.	1.6701700E-05	5.0637033E+00	*	100.	2.7894680E-10	5.0637696E+00	*

X	E^{-RX}	SUM OF E^{-RX}	*	X	E^{-RX}	SUM OF E^{-RX}	*
0.	1.0000000E+00	1.0000000E+00	*	50.	1.3007297E-05	4.9631245E+00	*
1.	7.9851621E-01	1.7985162E+00	*	51.	1.0386538E-05	4.9631348E+00	*
2.	6.3762814E-01	2.4361443E+00	*	52.	8.2938191E-06	4.9631430E+00	*
3.	5.0915641E-01	2.9453007E+00	*	53.	6.6227490E-06	4.9631496E+00	*
4.	4.0656965E-01	3.3518703E+00	*	54.	5.2863725E-06	4.9631548E+00	*
5.	3.2465246E-01	3.6765227E+00	*	55.	4.2228512E-06	4.9631590E+00	*
6.	2.5924026E-01	3.9357629E+00	*	56.	3.3720152E-06	4.9631623E+00	*
7.	2.0700755E-01	4.1427704E+00	*	57.	2.6926088E-06	4.9631649E+00	*
8.	1.6528388E-01	4.3080692E+00	*	58.	2.1500918E-06	4.9631670E+00	*
9.	1.3199384E-01	4.4400630E+00	*	59.	1.7168832E-06	4.9631687E+00	*
10.	1.0539922E-01	4.5454622E+00	*	60.	1.3709590E-06	4.9631700E+00	*
11.	8.4162990E-02	4.6296251E+00	*	61.	1.0947330E-06	4.9631710E+00	*
12.	6.7205512E-02	4.6968306E+00	*	62.	8.7416210E-07	4.9631718E+00	*
13.	5.3664691E-02	4.7504952E+00	*	63.	6.9803261E-07	4.9631724E+00	*
14.	4.2852126E-02	4.7933473E+00	*	64.	5.5739036E-07	4.9631729E+00	*
15.	3.4218110E-02	4.8275654E+00	*	65.	4.4508524E-07	4.9631733E+00	*
16.	2.7323722E-02	4.8548891E+00	*	66.	3.5540778E-07	4.9631736E+00	*
17.	2.1818435E-02	4.8767075E+00	*	67.	2.8379888E-07	4.9631738E+00	*
18.	1.7422374E-02	4.8941298E+00	*	68.	2.2661801E-07	4.9631740E+00	*
19.	1.3912048E-02	4.9080418E+00	*	69.	1.8095815E-07	4.9631741E+00	*
20.	1.1108996E-02	4.9191507E+00	*	70.	1.4449802E-07	4.9631742E+00	*
21.	8.8707138E-03	4.9280214E+00	*	71.	1.1538401E-07	4.9631743E+00	*
22.	7.0834089E-03	4.9351048E+00	*	72.	9.2136008E-08	4.9631743E+00	*
23.	5.6562169E-03	4.9407610E+00	*	73.	7.3572096E-08	4.9631743E+00	*
24.	4.5165809E-03	4.9452775E+00	*	74.	5.8748512E-08	4.9631743E+00	*
25.	3.6065631E-03	4.9488840E+00	*	75.	4.6911640E-08	4.9631743E+00	*
26.	2.8795991E-03	4.9517638E+00	*	76.	3.7459705E-08	4.9631743E+00	*
27.	2.2996461E-03	4.9540634E+00	*	77.	2.9912182E-08	4.9631743E+00	*
28.	1.8363047E-03	4.9558997E+00	*	78.	2.3885362E-08	4.9631743E+00	*
29.	1.4663191E-03	4.9573660E+00	*	79.	1.9072849E-08	4.9631743E+00	*
30.	1.1708796E-03	4.9585368E+00	*	80.	1.5229979E-08	4.9631743E+00	*
31.	9.3496636E-04	4.9594717E+00	*	81.	1.2161385E-08	4.9631743E+00	*
32.	7.4659580E-04	4.9602182E+00	*	82.	9.7110638E-09	4.9631743E+00	*
33.	5.9616087E-04	4.9608143E+00	*	83.	7.7544419E-09	4.9631743E+00	*
34.	4.7604412E-04	4.9612903E+00	*	84.	6.1920476E-09	4.9631743E+00	*
35.	3.8012895E-04	4.9616704E+00	*	85.	4.9446504E-09	4.9631743E+00	*
36.	3.0353913E-04	4.9619739E+00	*	86.	3.9482239E-09	4.9631743E+00	*
37.	2.4236092E-04	4.9622162E+00	*	87.	3.1527208E-09	4.9631743E+00	*
38.	1.9354509E-04	4.9624097E+00	*	88.	2.5174987E-09	4.9631743E+00	*
39.	1.5454590E-04	4.9625642E+00	*	89.	2.0102635E-09	4.9631743E+00	*
40.	1.2340930E-04	4.9626876E+00	*	90.	1.6052280E-09	4.9631743E+00	*
41.	9.8544730E-05	4.9627861E+00	*	91.	1.2818006E-09	4.9631743E+00	*
42.	7.8689565E-05	4.9628647E+00	*	92.	1.0235385E-09	4.9631743E+00	*
43.	6.2834894E-05	4.9629275E+00	*	93.	8.1731216E-10	4.9631743E+00	*
44.	5.0174681E-05	4.9629777E+00	*	94.	6.5263702E-10	4.9631743E+00	*
45.	4.0065297E-05	4.9630176E+00	*	95.	5.2114124E-10	4.9631743E+00	*
46.	3.1992789E-05	4.9630495E+00	*	96.	4.1613973E-10	4.9631743E+00	*
47.	2.5546761E-05	4.9630750E+00	*	97.	3.3229433E-10	4.9631743E+00	*
48.	2.0399503E-05	4.9630955E+00	*	98.	2.6534241E-10	4.9631743E+00	*
49.	1.6239334E-05	4.9631115E+00	*	99.	2.1189021E-10	4.9631743E+00	*
50.	1.3007297E-05	4.9631245E+00	*	100.	1.6918979E-10	4.9631743E+00	*

X	E^{-RX}	SUM OF E^{-RX}	*	X	E^{-RX}	SUM OF E^{-RX}	*
0.	1.0000000E+00	1.0000000E+00	*	50.	1.0130093E-05	4.8669341E+00	*
1.	7.9453359E-01	1.7945335E+00	*	51.	8.0486997E-06	4.8669421E+00	*
2.	6.3128364E-01	2.4258171E+00	*	52.	6.3949623E-06	4.8669484E+00	*
3.	5.0157606E-01	2.9273931E+00	*	53.	5.0810125E-06	4.8669534E+00	*
4.	3.9851903E-01	3.3259121E+00	*	54.	4.0370351E-06	4.8669574E+00	*
5.	3.1663676E-01	3.6425488E+00	*	55.	3.2075601E-06	4.8669606E+00	*
6.	2.5157855E-01	3.8941273E+00	*	56.	2.5485142E-06	4.8669631E+00	*
7.	1.9987761E-01	4.0940149E+00	*	57.	2.0248802E-06	4.8669651E+00	*
8.	1.5881742E-01	4.2528323E+00	*	58.	1.6084353E-06	4.8669667E+00	*
9.	1.2618578E-01	4.3790180E+00	*	59.	1.2782737E-06	4.8669679E+00	*
10.	1.0025884E-01	4.4792768E+00	*	60.	1.0156314E-06	4.8669689E+00	*
11.	7.9659019E-02	4.5589358E+00	*	61.	8.0695332E-07	4.8669697E+00	*
12.	6.3291768E-02	4.6222275E+00	*	62.	6.4115153E-07	4.8669703E+00	*
13.	5.0287436E-02	4.6725149E+00	*	63.	5.0941643E-07	4.8669708E+00	*
14.	3.9955058E-02	4.7124699E+00	*	64.	4.0474847E-07	4.8669712E+00	*
15.	3.1745636E-02	4.7442155E+00	*	65.	3.2158626E-07	4.8669715E+00	*
16.	2.5222974E-02	4.7694384E+00	*	66.	2.5551109E-07	4.8669717E+00	*
17.	2.0040500E-02	4.7894789E+00	*	67.	2.0301215E-07	4.8669719E+00	*
18.	1.5922851E-02	4.8054017E+00	*	68.	1.6129997E-07	4.8669720E+00	*
19.	1.2651240E-02	4.8180529E+00	*	69.	1.2815825E-07	4.8669721E+00	*
20.	1.0051835E-02	4.8281047E+00	*	70.	1.0182603E-07	4.8669722E+00	*
21.	7.9865212E-03	4.8360912E+00	*	71.	8.0904207E-08	4.8669722E+00	*
22.	6.3455594E-03	4.8424367E+00	*	72.	6.4281111E-08	4.8669722E+00	*
23.	5.0417602E-03	4.8474784E+00	*	73.	5.1073503E-08	4.8669722E+00	*
24.	4.0058479E-03	4.8514842E+00	*	74.	4.0579614E-08	4.8669722E+00	*
25.	3.1827807E-03	4.8546669E+00	*	75.	3.2241867E-08	4.8669722E+00	*
26.	2.5288262E-03	4.8571957E+00	*	76.	2.5617246E-08	4.8669722E+00	*
27.	2.0092374E-03	4.8592049E+00	*	77.	2.0353763E-08	4.8669722E+00	*
28.	1.5964066E-03	4.8608013E+00	*	78.	1.6171749E-08	4.8669722E+00	*
29.	1.2683987E-03	4.8620696E+00	*	79.	1.2848998E-08	4.8669722E+00	*
30.	1.0077854E-03	4.8630773E+00	*	80.	1.0208960E-08	4.8669722E+00	*
31.	8.0071936E-04	4.8638780E+00	*	81.	8.1113623E-09	4.8669722E+00	*
32.	6.3619845E-04	4.8645141E+00	*	82.	6.4447499E-09	4.8669722E+00	*
33.	5.0548105E-04	4.8650195E+00	*	83.	5.1205703E-09	4.8669722E+00	*
34.	4.0162168E-04	4.8654211E+00	*	84.	4.0684652E-09	4.8669722E+00	*
35.	3.1910192E-04	4.8657402E+00	*	85.	3.2325323E-09	4.8669722E+00	*
36.	2.5353719E-04	4.8659937E+00	*	86.	2.5683555E-09	4.8669722E+00	*
37.	2.0144382E-04	4.8661951E+00	*	87.	2.0406447E-09	4.8669722E+00	*
38.	1.6005388E-04	4.8663551E+00	*	88.	1.6213606E-09	4.8669722E+00	*
39.	1.2716819E-04	4.8664822E+00	*	89.	1.2882256E-09	4.8669722E+00	*
40.	1.0103940E-04	4.8665832E+00	*	90.	1.0235385E-09	4.8669722E+00	*
41.	8.0279199E-05	4.8666634E+00	*	91.	8.1323580E-10	4.8669722E+00	*
42.	6.3784521E-05	4.8667271E+00	*	92.	6.4614317E-10	4.8669722E+00	*
43.	5.0678945E-05	4.8667777E+00	*	93.	5.1338246E-10	4.8669722E+00	*
44.	4.0266125E-05	4.8668179E+00	*	94.	4.0789961E-10	4.8669722E+00	*
45.	3.1992789E-05	4.8668499E+00	*	95.	3.2408995E-10	4.8669722E+00	*
46.	2.5419346E-05	4.8668752E+00	*	96.	2.5750035E-10	4.8669722E+00	*
47.	2.0196524E-05	4.8668953E+00	*	97.	2.0459269E-10	4.8669722E+00	*
48.	1.6046817E-05	4.8669113E+00	*	98.	1.6255576E-10	4.8669722E+00	*
49.	1.2749735E-05	4.8669240E+00	*	99.	1.2915601E-10	4.8669722E+00	*
50.	1.0130093E-05	4.8669341E+00	*	100.	1.0261879E-10	4.8669722E+00	*

TABULATED VALUES OF F   WHEN R = .235

X	E (-RX)	SUM OF F (-RX)	*	X	E (-RX)	SUM OF F (-RX)	*
0.	1.0000000E+00	1.0000000E+00	*	50.	7.8893248E-06	4.7748519E+00	*
1.	7.9057084E-01	1.7905708E+00	*	51.	6.2370702E-06	4.7748581E+00	*
2.	6.2500226E-01	2.4155730E+00	*	52.	4.9308459E-06	4.7748630E+00	*
3.	4.9410857E-01	2.9096815E+00	*	53.	3.8981830E-06	4.7748668E+00	*
4.	3.9062783E-01	3.3003093E+00	*	54.	3.0817848E-06	4.7748698E+00	*
5.	3.0881897E-01	3.6091292E+00	*	55.	2.4363732E-06	4.7748722E+00	*
6.	2.4414328E-01	3.8532714E+00	*	56.	1.9261256E-06	4.7748741E+00	*
7.	1.9301256E-01	4.0462839E+00	*	57.	1.5227388E-06	4.7748756E+00	*
8.	1.5259010E-01	4.1988740E+00	*	58.	1.2038329E-06	4.7748768E+00	*
9.	1.2063328E-01	4.3195072E+00	*	59.	9.5171520E-07	4.7748777E+00	*
10.	9.5369162E-02	4.4148763E+00	*	60.	7.5239829E-07	4.7748784E+00	*
11.	7.5396079E-02	4.4902723E+00	*	61.	5.9642416E-07	4.7748790E+00	*
12.	5.9605942E-02	4.5498782E+00	*	62.	4.7025066E-07	4.7748793E+00	*
13.	4.7122720E-02	4.5970009E+00	*	63.	3.7176665E-07	4.7748796E+00	*
14.	3.7253849E-02	4.6342547E+00	*	64.	2.9390771E-07	4.7748798E+00	*
15.	2.9451807E-02	4.6637065E+00	*	65.	2.3235487E-07	4.7748800E+00	*
16.	2.3283740E-02	4.6869902E+00	*	66.	1.8369299E-07	4.7748801E+00	*
17.	1.8407446E-02	4.7053976E+00	*	67.	1.4522232E-07	4.7748802E+00	*
18.	1.4552390E-02	4.7199499E+00	*	68.	1.1480853E-07	4.7748803E+00	*
19.	1.1504695E-02	4.7314545E+00	*	69.	9.0764281E-08	4.7748803E+00	*
20.	9.0952770E-03	4.7405497E+00	*	70.	7.1755595E-08	4.7748803E+00	*
21.	7.1904609E-03	4.7477401E+00	*	71.	5.6727881E-08	4.7748803E+00	*
22.	5.6845688E-03	4.7534246E+00	*	72.	4.4847409E-08	4.7748803E+00	*
23.	4.4940543E-03	4.7579186E+00	*	73.	3.5455054E-08	4.7748803E+00	*
24.	3.5528684E-03	4.7614714E+00	*	74.	2.8029732E-08	4.7748803E+00	*
25.	2.8087941E-03	4.7642801E+00	*	75.	2.2159489E-08	4.7748803E+00	*
26.	2.2205508E-03	4.7665006E+00	*	76.	1.7518644E-08	4.7748803E+00	*
27.	1.7555027E-03	4.7682561E+00	*	77.	1.3849731E-08	4.7748803E+00	*
28.	1.3878492E-03	4.7696439E+00	*	78.	1.0949193E-08	4.7748803E+00	*
29.	1.0971931E-03	4.7707410E+00	*	79.	8.6561135E-09	4.7748803E+00	*
30.	8.6740895E-04	4.7716084E+00	*	80.	6.8432710E-09	4.7748803E+00	*
31.	6.8574723E-04	4.7722941E+00	*	81.	5.4100905E-09	4.7748803E+00	*
32.	5.4213256E-04	4.7728362E+00	*	82.	4.2705598E-09	4.7748803E+00	*
33.	4.2859420E-04	4.7732647E+00	*	83.	3.3813188E-09	4.7748803E+00	*
34.	3.3883408E-04	4.7736035E+00	*	84.	2.6731721E-09	4.7748803E+00	*
35.	2.6787234E-04	4.7738713E+00	*	85.	2.1133319E-09	4.7748803E+00	*
36.	2.1177207E-04	4.7740830E+00	*	86.	1.6707338E-09	4.7748803E+00	*
37.	1.6742082E-04	4.7742504E+00	*	87.	1.3208372E-09	4.7748803E+00	*
38.	1.3235802E-04	4.7743827E+00	*	88.	1.0442154E-09	4.7748803E+00	*
39.	1.0463839E-04	4.7744873E+00	*	89.	8.2552629E-10	4.7748803E+00	*
40.	8.2724065E-05	4.7745700E+00	*	90.	6.5263702E-10	4.7748803E+00	*
41.	6.5399234E-05	4.7746355E+00	*	91.	5.1595580E-10	4.7748803E+00	*
42.	5.1702728E-05	4.7746870E+00	*	92.	4.0789961E-10	4.7748803E+00	*
43.	4.0874669E-05	4.7747278E+00	*	93.	3.2247354E-10	4.7748803E+00	*
44.	3.2314322E-05	4.7747601E+00	*	94.	2.5493818E-10	4.7748803E+00	*
45.	2.5546761E-05	4.7747856E+00	*	95.	2.0154669E-10	4.7748803E+00	*
46.	2.0196524E-05	4.7748057E+00	*	96.	1.5933694E-10	4.7748803E+00	*
47.	1.5966783E-05	4.7748216E+00	*	97.	1.2596714E-10	4.7748803E+00	*
48.	1.2622873E-05	4.7748342E+00	*	98.	9.9585952E-11	4.7748803E+00	*
49.	9.9792761E-06	4.7748441E+00	*	99.	7.8729751E-11	4.7748803E+00	*
50.	7.8893248E-06	4.7748519E+00	*	100.	6.2241446E-11	4.7748803E+00	*

TABULATED VALUES OF F   WHEN R = .240

X	E (-RX)	SUM OF F (-RX)	*	X	E (-RX)	SUM OF F (-RX)	*
0.	1.0000000E+00	1.0000000E+00	*	50.	6.1442123E-06	4.6866223E+00	*
1.	7.8662786E-01	1.7866278E+00	*	51.	4.8332086E-06	4.6866271E+00	*
2.	6.1878339E-01	2.4054111E+00	*	52.	3.8019365E-06	4.6866309E+00	*
3.	4.8675225E-01	2.8921633E+00	*	53.	2.9907092E-06	4.6866338E+00	*
4.	3.8292888E-01	3.2750561E+00	*	54.	2.3525751E-06	4.6866361E+00	*
5.	3.0119421E-01	3.5762503E+00	*	55.	1.8506011E-06	4.6866379E+00	*
6.	2.3692775E-01	3.8131780E+00	*	56.	1.4557346E-06	4.6866393E+00	*
7.	1.8637397E-01	3.9995519E+00	*	57.	1.1451212E-06	4.6866404E+00	*
8.	1.4660696E-01	4.1461588E+00	*	58.	9.0078430E-07	4.6866413E+00	*
9.	1.1532512E-01	4.2614839E+00	*	59.	7.0858203E-07	4.6866420E+00	*
10.	9.0717953E-02	4.3522018E+00	*	60.	5.5730034E-07	4.6866425E+00	*
11.	7.1361269E-02	4.4235630E+00	*	61.	4.3845879E-07	4.6866429E+00	*
12.	5.6134762E-02	4.4796977E+00	*	62.	3.4490390E-07	4.6866432E+00	*
13.	4.4157168E-02	4.5238548E+00	*	63.	2.7131101E-07	4.6866434E+00	*
14.	3.4735258E-02	4.5585900E+00	*	64.	2.1342080E-07	4.6866436E+00	*
15.	2.7323722E-02	4.5859137E+00	*	65.	1.6788275E-07	4.6866437E+00	*
16.	2.1493601E-02	4.6074073E+00	*	66.	1.3206250E-07	4.6866438E+00	*
17.	1.6907465E-02	4.6243147E+00	*	67.	1.0388305E-07	4.6866439E+00	*
18.	1.3299883E-02	4.6376145E+00	*	68.	8.1717308E-08	4.6866439E+00	*
19.	1.0462058E-02	4.6480765E+00	*	69.	6.4281111E-08	4.6866439E+00	*
20.	8.2297470E-03	4.6563062E+00	*	70.	5.0565313E-08	4.6866439E+00	*
21.	6.4737483E-03	4.6627799E+00	*	71.	3.9776084E-08	4.6866439E+00	*
22.	5.0924307E-03	4.6678723E+00	*	72.	3.1288976E-08	4.6866439E+00	*
23.	4.0058479E-03	4.6718781E+00	*	73.	2.4612780E-08	4.6866439E+00	*
24.	3.1511115E-03	4.6750292E+00	*	74.	1.9361098E-08	4.6866439E+00	*
25.	2.4787521E-03	4.6775079E+00	*	75.	1.5229979E-08	4.6866439E+00	*
26.	1.9498555E-03	4.6794577E+00	*	76.	1.1980326E-08	4.6866439E+00	*
27.	1.5338106E-03	4.6809915E+00	*	77.	9.4240585E-09	4.6866439E+00	*
28.	1.2065384E-03	4.6821980E+00	*	78.	7.4132269E-09	4.6866439E+00	*
29.	9.4909657E-04	4.6831470E+00	*	79.	5.8314508E-09	4.6866439E+00	*
30.	7.4658580E-04	4.6838935E+00	*	80.	4.5871817E-09	4.6866439E+00	*
31.	5.8728519E-04	4.6844807E+00	*	81.	3.6084049E-09	4.6866439E+00	*
32.	4.6197489E-04	4.6849426E+00	*	82.	2.8384731E-09	4.6866439E+00	*
33.	3.6340232E-04	4.6853060E+00	*	83.	2.2328210E-09	4.6866439E+00	*
34.	2.8586239E-04	4.6855918E+00	*	84.	1.7563992E-09	4.6866439E+00	*
35.	2.2486732E-04	4.6858166E+00	*	85.	1.3816325E-09	4.6866439E+00	*
36.	1.7688690E-04	4.6859934E+00	*	86.	1.0868308E-09	4.6866439E+00	*
37.	1.3914416E-04	4.6861325E+00	*	87.	8.5493120E-10	4.6866439E+00	*
38.	1.0945467E-04	4.6862419E+00	*	88.	6.7251277E-10	4.6866439E+00	*
39.	8.6100098E-05	4.6863280E+00	*	89.	5.2901728E-10	4.6866439E+00	*
40.	6.7728736E-05	4.6863957E+00	*	90.	4.1613973E-10	4.6866439E+00	*
41.	5.3277311E-05	4.6864489E+00	*	91.	3.2734711E-10	4.6866439E+00	*
42.	4.1909417E-05	4.6864908E+00	*	92.	2.5750003E-10	4.6866439E+00	*
43.	3.2967115E-05	4.6865237E+00	*	93.	2.0255695E-10	4.6866439E+00	*
44.	2.5932851E-05	4.6865496E+00	*	94.	1.5933694E-10	4.6866439E+00	*
45.	2.0399503E-05	4.6865699E+00	*	95.	1.2533888E-10	4.6866439E+00	*
46.	1.6046817E-05	4.6865858E+00	*	96.	9.8595055E-11	4.6866439E+00	*
47.	1.2622873E-05	4.6865985E+00	*	97.	7.7557617E-11	4.6866439E+00	*
48.	9.3295042E-06	4.6866084E+00	*	98.	6.1008927E-11	4.6866439E+00	*
49.	7.8108247E-06	4.6866162E+00	*	99.	4.7991365E-11	4.6866439E+00	*
50.	6.1442123E-06	4.6866223E+00	*	100.	3.7751345E-11	4.6866439E+00	*

TABULATED VALUES OF E WHEN R = .245

x	E	SUM OF E		x	E	SUM OF E	
0.	1.0000000E+00	1.0000000E+00		50.	4.7851173E-06	4.6020089E+00	
1.	7.8270453E-01	1.7827045E+00		51.	3.7453330E-06	4.6020124E+00	
2.	6.1262635E-01	2.3953308E+00		52.	2.9314892E-06	4.6020155E+00	
3.	4.7950545E-01	2.8748362E+00		53.	2.2944899E-06	4.6020177E+00	
4.	3.7531109E-01	3.2501472E+00		54.	1.7959076E-06	4.6020194E+00	
5.	2.9375769E-01	3.5438048E+00		55.	1.4056650E-06	4.6020208E+00	
6.	2.2992548E-01	3.7738302E+00		56.	1.1002204E-06	4.6020219E+00	
7.	1.7996372E-01	3.9537939E+00		57.	8.6114752E-07	4.6020227E+00	
8.	1.4085642E-01	4.0946523E+00		58.	6.7402407E-07	4.6020233E+00	
9.	1.1025052E-01	4.2049027E+00		59.	5.2754170E-07	4.6020238E+00	
10.	8.6293586E-02	4.2911963E+00		60.	4.1292446E-07	4.6020242E+00	
11.	6.7542381E-02	4.3587384E+00		61.	3.2319625E-07	4.6020245E+00	
12.	5.2865728E-02	4.4116043E+00		62.	2.5296871E-07	4.6020247E+00	
13.	4.1378245E-02	4.4529825E+00		63.	1.9799976E-07	4.6020248E+00	
14.	3.2386940E-02	4.4853694E+00		64.	1.5497531E-07	4.6020249E+00	
15.	2.5349405E-02	4.5107188E+00		65.	1.2129988E-07	4.6020250E+00	
16.	1.9841094E-02	4.5305598E+00		66.	9.4941967E-08	4.6020250E+00	
17.	1.5529714E-02	4.5460895E+00		67.	7.4311508E-08	4.6020250E+00	
18.	1.2155178E-02	4.5582446E+00		68.	5.8163955E-08	4.6020250E+00	
19.	9.5139132E-03	4.5677585E+00		69.	4.5525191E-08	4.6020250E+00	
20.	7.4465830E-03	4.5752050E+00		70.	3.5632774E-08	4.6020250E+00	
21.	5.8284743E-03	4.5810334E+00		71.	2.7889934E-08	4.6020250E+00	
22.	4.5619733E-03	4.5855953E+00		72.	2.1829577E-08	4.6020250E+00	
23.	3.5706772E-03	4.5891659E+00		73.	1.7086109E-08	4.6020250E+00	
24.	2.7947852E-03	4.5919606E+00		74.	1.3373375E-08	4.6020250E+00	
25.	2.1874911E-03	4.5941480E+00		75.	1.0467401E-08	4.6020250E+00	
26.	1.7121592E-03	4.5958601E+00		76.	8.1928228E-09	4.6020250E+00	
27.	1.3401147E-03	4.5972002E+00		77.	6.4126066E-09	4.6020250E+00	
28.	1.0489139E-03	4.5982491E+00		78.	5.0191762E-09	4.6020250E+00	
29.	8.2098969E-04	4.5990700E+00		79.	3.9285320E-09	4.6020250E+00	
30.	6.4259235E-04	4.5997125E+00		80.	3.0748798E-09	4.6020250E+00	
31.	5.0295995E-04	4.6002154E+00		81.	2.4067224E-09	4.6020250E+00	
32.	3.9366904E-04	4.6006090E+00		82.	1.8837525E-09	4.6020250E+00	
33.	3.0812654E-04	4.6009171E+00		83.	1.4744216E-09	4.6020250E+00	
34.	2.4117204E-04	4.6011582E+00		84.	1.1540365E-09	4.6020250E+00	
35.	1.8876645E-04	4.6013469E+00		85.	9.0326964E-10	4.6020250E+00	
36.	1.4774835E-04	4.6014946E+00		86.	7.0699324E-10	4.6020250E+00	
37.	1.1564331E-04	4.6016102E+00		87.	5.5336682E-10	4.6020250E+00	
38.	9.0514545E-05	4.6017007E+00		88.	4.3312272E-10	4.6020250E+00	
39.	7.0846145E-05	4.6017715E+00		89.	3.3900712E-10	4.6020250E+00	
40.	5.5451599E-05	4.6018269E+00		90.	2.6534241E-10	4.6020250E+00	
41.	4.3402218E-05	4.6018703E+00		91.	2.0764471E-10	4.6020250E+00	
42.	3.3971113E-05	4.6019042E+00		92.	1.6255576E-10	4.6020250E+00	
43.	2.6589344E-05	4.6019307E+00		93.	1.2723313E-10	4.6020250E+00	
44.	2.0811600E-05	4.6019515E+00		94.	9.9585952E-11	4.6020250E+00	
45.	1.6289334E-05	4.6019677E+00		95.	7.7946376E-11	4.6020250E+00	
46.	1.2749735E-05	4.6019804E+00		96.	6.1008982E-11	4.6020250E+00	
47.	9.9792761E-06	4.6019903E+00		97.	4.7752007E-11	4.6020250E+00	
48.	7.8108247E-06	4.6019981E+00		98.	3.7375713E-11	4.6020250E+00	
49.	6.1135679E-06	4.6020042E+00		99.	2.9254149E-11	4.6020250E+00	
50.	4.7851173E-06	4.6020089E+00		100.	2.2890734E-11	4.6020250E+00	

TABULATED VALUES OF E WHEN R = .250

x	E	SUM OF E		x	E	SUM OF E	
0.	1.0000000E+00	1.0000000E+00		50.	3.7266531E-06	4.5207957E+00	
1.	7.8880078E-01	1.7888007E+00		51.	2.9023204E-06	4.5207986E+00	
2.	6.0653065E-01	2.3853313E+00		52.	2.2603294E-06	4.5208008E+00	
3.	4.7236453E-01	2.8576978E+00		53.	1.7603463E-06	4.5208025E+00	
4.	3.6787944E-01	3.2255772E+00		54.	1.3709590E-06	4.5208038E+00	
5.	2.8650479E-01	3.5120819E+00		55.	1.0677045E-06	4.5208048E+00	
6.	2.2313015E-01	3.7352120E+00		56.	8.3152871E-07	4.5208056E+00	
7.	1.7377394E-01	3.9089859E+00		57.	6.4759521E-07	4.5208062E+00	
8.	1.3533528E-01	4.0443211E+00		58.	5.0434766E-07	4.5208067E+00	
9.	1.0539922E-01	4.1497203E+00		59.	3.9278635E-07	4.5208070E+00	
10.	8.2084998E-02	4.2318052E+00		60.	3.0590232E-07	4.5208073E+00	
11.	6.3927860E-02	4.2957330E+00		61.	2.3823696E-07	4.5208075E+00	
12.	4.9787068E-02	4.3455200E+00		62.	1.8553913E-07	4.5208076E+00	
13.	3.8774207E-02	4.3842942E+00		63.	1.4449802E-07	4.5208077E+00	
14.	3.0197383E-02	4.4144915E+00		64.	1.1253517E-07	4.5208078E+00	
15.	2.3517745E-02	4.4380092E+00		65.	8.7642482E-08	4.5208078E+00	
16.	1.8315633E-02	4.4563248E+00		66.	6.8256033E-08	4.5208078E+00	
17.	1.4264233E-02	4.4705890E+00		67.	5.3157852E-08	4.5208078E+00	
18.	1.1108996E-02	4.4816979E+00		68.	4.1399377E-08	4.5208078E+00	
19.	8.6516951E-03	4.4903495E+00		69.	3.2241867E-08	4.5208078E+00	
20.	6.7379469E-03	4.4970874E+00		70.	2.5109991E-08	4.5208078E+00	
21.	5.2475183E-03	4.5023349E+00		71.	1.9555681E-08	4.5208078E+00	
22.	4.0867714E-03	4.5064216E+00		72.	1.5229979E-08	4.5208078E+00	
23.	3.1827807E-03	4.5096043E+00		73.	1.1861120E-08	4.5208078E+00	
24.	2.4787521E-03	4.5120830E+00		74.	9.2374496E-09	4.5208078E+00	
25.	1.9304541E-03	4.5140134E+00		75.	7.1941330E-09	4.5208078E+00	
26.	1.5034391E-03	4.5155168E+00		76.	5.6027964E-09	4.5208078E+00	
27.	1.1708796E-03	4.5166876E+00		77.	4.3634622E-09	4.5208078E+00	
28.	9.1188196E-04	4.5175994E+00		78.	3.3982678E-09	4.5208078E+00	
29.	7.1017438E-04	4.5183095E+00		79.	2.6465736E-09	4.5208078E+00	
30.	5.5308436E-04	4.5188625E+00		80.	2.0611536E-09	4.5208078E+00	
31.	4.3074253E-04	4.5192932E+00		81.	1.6052220E-09	4.5208078E+00	
32.	3.3546262E-04	4.5196286E+00		82.	1.2501529E-09	4.5208078E+00	
33.	2.6125855E-04	4.5198898E+00		83.	9.7362002E-10	4.5208078E+00	
34.	2.0346836E-04	4.5200932E+00		84.	7.5825604E-10	4.5208078E+00	
35.	1.5846132E-04	4.5202516E+00		85.	5.9053039E-10	4.5208078E+00	
36.	1.2340980E-04	4.5203750E+00		86.	4.5990553E-10	4.5208078E+00	
37.	9.6111651E-05	4.5204711E+00		87.	3.5817479E-10	4.5208078E+00	
38.	7.4851829E-05	4.5205459E+00		88.	2.7894680E-10	4.5208078E+00	
39.	5.8294663E-05	4.5206041E+00		89.	2.1724399E-10	4.5208078E+00	
40.	4.5399929E-05	4.5206494E+00		90.	1.6918979E-10	4.5208078E+00	
41.	3.5357500E-05	4.5206847E+00		91.	1.3176514E-10	4.5208078E+00	
42.	2.7536449E-05	4.5207122E+00		92.	1.0261879E-10	4.5208078E+00	
43.	2.1445408E-05	4.5207336E+00		93.	7.9919598E-11	4.5208078E+00	
44.	1.6701700E-05	4.5207503E+00		94.	6.2241446E-11	4.5208078E+00	
45.	1.3007297E-05	4.5207633E+00		95.	4.8473687E-11	4.5208078E+00	
46.	1.0130093E-05	4.5207734E+00		96.	3.7751345E-11	4.5208078E+00	
47.	7.8893248E-06	4.5207812E+00		97.	2.9400777E-11	4.5208078E+00	
48.	6.1442122E-06	4.5207873E+00		98.	2.2937340E-11	4.5208078E+00	
49.	4.7851173E-06	4.5207920E+00		99.	1.7832472E-11	4.5208078E+00	
50.	3.7266531E-06	4.5207957E+00		100.	1.3887943E-11	4.5208078E+00	

TABULATED VALUES OF E   WHEN R = .255

X	E^{-RX}	SUM OF E^{-RX}	*	X	E^{-RX}	SUM OF E^{-RX}	*
0.	1.0000000E+00	1.0000000E+00	*	50.	2.9023204E-06	4.4427830E+00	*
1.	7.7491649E-01	1.7749166E+00	*	51.	2.2490559E-06	4.4427852E+00	*
2.	6.0049557E-01	2.3754119E+00	*	52.	1.7428305E-06	4.4427869E+00	*
3.	4.6533393E-01	2.8407458E+00	*	53.	1.3505481E-06	4.4427882E+00	*
4.	3.6059493E-01	3.2013407E+00	*	54.	1.0465620E-06	4.4427892E+00	*
5.	2.7943096E-01	3.4807716E+00	*	55.	8.1099819E-07	4.4427900E+00	*
6.	2.1653566E-01	3.6973072E+00	*	56.	6.2845588E-07	4.4427906E+00	*
7.	1.6779706E-01	3.8651042E+00	*	57.	4.8700083E-07	4.4427910E+00	*
8.	1.3002871E-01	3.9951329E+00	*	58.	3.7738498E-07	4.4427913E+00	*
9.	1.0076139E-01	4.0958942E+00	*	59.	2.9244184E-07	4.4427915E+00	*
10.	7.8081665E-02	4.1739758E+00	*	60.	2.2661801E-07	4.4427917E+00	*
11.	6.0506771E-02	4.2344825E+00	*	61.	1.7561003E-07	4.4427918E+00	*
12.	4.6887695E-02	4.2813701E+00	*	62.	1.3608311E-07	4.4427919E+00	*
13.	3.6334048E-02	4.3177041E+00	*	63.	1.0545305E-07	4.4427920E+00	*
14.	2.8155853E-02	4.3458599E+00	*	64.	8.1717730E-08	4.4427920E+00	*
15.	2.1818435E-02	4.3676783E+00	*	65.	6.3324090E-08	4.4427920E+00	*
16.	1.6907465E-02	4.3845857E+00	*	66.	4.9070882E-08	4.4427920E+00	*
17.	1.3101874E-02	4.3976875E+00	*	67.	3.8025363E-08	4.4427920E+00	*
18.	1.0152858E-02	4.4078403E+00	*	68.	2.9466847E-08	4.4427920E+00	*
19.	7.8676174E-03	4.4157079E+00	*	69.	2.2834346E-08	4.4427920E+00	*
20.	6.0967465E-03	4.4218046E+00	*	70.	1.7694711E-08	4.4427920E+00	*
21.	4.7244694E-03	4.4265290E+00	*	71.	1.3711924E-08	4.4427920E+00	*
22.	3.6610693E-03	4.4301900E+00	*	72.	1.0625596E-08	4.4427920E+00	*
23.	2.8370230E-03	4.4330270E+00	*	73.	8.2339498E-09	4.4427920E+00	*
24.	2.1984559E-03	4.4352254E+00	*	74.	6.3806235E-09	4.4427920E+00	*
25.	1.7036197E-03	4.4369290E+00	*	75.	4.9444504E-09	4.4427920E+00	*
26.	1.3201630E-03	4.4382491E+00	*	76.	3.8315362E-09	4.4427920E+00	*
27.	1.0230161E-03	4.4392721E+00	*	77.	2.9691206E-09	4.4427920E+00	*
28.	7.9275209E-04	4.4400648E+00	*	78.	2.3008205E-09	4.4427920E+00	*
29.	6.1431667E-04	4.4406791E+00	*	79.	1.7829437E-09	4.4427920E+00	*
30.	4.7604412E-04	4.4411551E+00	*	80.	1.3816325E-09	4.4427920E+00	*
31.	3.6889444E-04	4.4415239E+00	*	81.	1.0706498E-09	4.4427920E+00	*
32.	2.8586239E-04	4.4418097E+00	*	82.	8.2966426E-10	4.4427920E+00	*
33.	2.2151948E-04	4.4420312E+00	*	83.	6.4292052E-10	4.4427920E+00	*
34.	1.7165910E-04	4.4422028E+00	*	84.	4.9820972E-10	4.4427920E+00	*
35.	1.3302147E-04	4.4423358E+00	*	85.	3.8607093E-10	4.4427920E+00	*
36.	1.0308053E-04	4.4424388E+00	*	86.	2.9917273E-10	4.4427920E+00	*
37.	7.9878805E-05	4.4425186E+00	*	87.	2.3183388E-10	4.4427920E+00	*
38.	6.1899404E-05	4.4425804E+00	*	88.	1.7965190E-10	4.4427920E+00	*
39.	4.7966869E-05	4.4426283E+00	*	89.	1.3921524E-10	4.4427920E+00	*
40.	3.7170318E-05	4.4426654E+00	*	90.	1.0788017E-10	4.4427920E+00	*
41.	2.8803893E-05	4.4426942E+00	*	91.	8.3598124E-11	4.4427920E+00	*
42.	2.2320611E-05	4.4427165E+00	*	92.	6.4781567E-11	4.4427920E+00	*
43.	1.7296610E-05	4.4427337E+00	*	93.	5.0200305E-11	4.4427920E+00	*
44.	1.3403428E-05	4.4427471E+00	*	94.	3.8901045E-11	4.4427920E+00	*
45.	1.0386538E-05	4.4427574E+00	*	95.	3.0145061E-11	4.4427920E+00	*
46.	8.0486997E-06	4.4427654E+00	*	96.	2.3359905E-11	4.4427920E+00	*
47.	6.2370702E-06	4.4427716E+00	*	97.	1.8101976E-11	4.4427920E+00	*
48.	4.8332086E-06	4.4427764E+00	*	98.	1.4027520E-11	4.4427920E+00	*
49.	3.7453330E-06	4.4427801E+00	*	99.	1.0870156E-11	4.4427920E+00	*
50.	2.9023204E-06	4.4427830E+00	*	100.	8.4234637E-12	4.4427920E+00	*

TABULATED VALUES OF E   WHEN R = .260

X	E^{-RX}	SUM OF E^{-RX}	*	X	E^{-RX}	SUM OF E^{-RX}	*
0.	1.0000000E+00	1.0000000E+00	*	50.	2.2603294E-06	4.3677859E+00	*
1.	7.7105158E-01	1.7710515E+00	*	51.	1.7428305E-06	4.3677876E+00	*
2.	5.9452054E-01	2.3655720E+00	*	52.	1.3438122E-06	4.3677889E+00	*
3.	4.5840601E-01	2.8239780E+00	*	53.	1.0361485E-06	4.3677899E+00	*
4.	3.5345468E-01	3.1774326E+00	*	54.	7.9892400E-07	4.3677906E+00	*
5.	2.7253179E-01	3.4499643E+00	*	55.	6.1601162E-07	4.3677912E+00	*
6.	2.1013607E-01	3.6601003E+00	*	56.	4.7497676E-07	4.3677916E+00	*
7.	1.6202575E-01	3.8221260E+00	*	57.	3.6623156E-07	4.3677919E+00	*
8.	1.2493021E-01	3.9470562E+00	*	58.	2.8238343E-07	4.3677921E+00	*
9.	9.6327638E-02	4.0433838E+00	*	59.	2.1773219E-07	4.3677923E+00	*
10.	7.4273578E-02	4.1176573E+00	*	60.	1.6788275E-07	4.3677924E+00	*
11.	5.7268760E-02	4.1749260E+00	*	61.	1.2944626E-07	4.3677925E+00	*
12.	4.4157168E-02	4.2190831E+00	*	62.	9.9809746E-08	4.3677925E+00	*
13.	3.4047454E-02	4.2531305E+00	*	63.	7.6958463E-08	4.3677925E+00	*
14.	2.6252343E-02	4.2793828E+00	*	64.	5.9338944E-08	4.3677925E+00	*
15.	2.0241911E-02	4.2996247E+00	*	65.	4.5753387E-08	4.3677925E+00	*
16.	1.5607557E-02	4.3152322E+00	*	66.	3.5278222E-08	4.3677925E+00	*
17.	1.2034232E-02	4.3272664E+00	*	67.	2.7201329E-08	4.3677925E+00	*
18.	9.2790138E-03	4.3365454E+00	*	68.	2.0973627E-08	4.3677925E+00	*
19.	7.1545983E-03	4.3436999E+00	*	69.	1.6171749E-08	4.3677925E+00	*
20.	5.5165644E-03	4.3492164E+00	*	70.	1.2469252E-08	4.3677925E+00	*
21.	4.2535557E-03	4.3534699E+00	*	71.	9.6144371E-09	4.3677925E+00	*
22.	3.2797108E-03	4.3567496E+00	*	72.	7.4132269E-09	4.3677925E+00	*
23.	2.5288262E-03	4.3592784E+00	*	73.	5.7159804E-09	4.3677925E+00	*
24.	1.9498555E-03	4.3612282E+00	*	74.	4.4073157E-09	4.3677925E+00	*
25.	1.5034391E-03	4.3627316E+00	*	75.	3.3982678E-09	4.3677925E+00	*
26.	1.1592291E-03	4.3638908E+00	*	76.	2.6202397E-09	4.3677925E+00	*
27.	8.9382549E-04	4.3647846E+00	*	77.	2.0203400E-09	4.3677925E+00	*
28.	6.8918556E-04	4.3654737E+00	*	78.	1.5577863E-09	4.3677925E+00	*
29.	5.3139762E-04	4.3660050E+00	*	79.	1.2011336E-09	4.3677925E+00	*
30.	4.0973497E-04	4.3664147E+00	*	80.	9.2613602E-10	4.3677925E+00	*
31.	3.1592680E-04	4.3667306E+00	*	81.	7.1409864E-10	4.3677925E+00	*
32.	2.4359586E-04	4.3669741E+00	*	82.	5.5060689E-10	4.3677925E+00	*
33.	1.8782497E-04	4.3671919E+00	*	83.	4.2466631E-10	4.3677925E+00	*
34.	1.4482274E-04	4.3673067E+00	*	84.	3.2734711E-10	4.3677925E+00	*
35.	1.1166580E-04	4.3674183E+00	*	85.	2.5240150E-10	4.3677925E+00	*
36.	8.6100098E-05	4.3675044E+00	*	86.	1.9461458E-10	4.3677925E+00	*
37.	6.6387617E-05	4.3675707E+00	*	87.	1.5005788E-10	4.3677925E+00	*
38.	5.1188277E-05	4.3676218E+00	*	88.	1.1570236E-10	4.3677925E+00	*
39.	3.9468802E-05	4.3676612E+00	*	89.	8.9212495E-11	4.3677925E+00	*
40.	3.0432482E-05	4.3676916E+00	*	90.	6.8787436E-11	4.3677925E+00	*
41.	2.3465014E-05	4.3677150E+00	*	91.	5.3033661E-11	4.3677925E+00	*
42.	1.8092736E-05	4.3677330E+00	*	92.	4.0895544E-11	4.3677925E+00	*
43.	1.3950433E-05	4.3677469E+00	*	93.	3.1532574E-11	4.3677925E+00	*
44.	1.0756503E-05	4.3677576E+00	*	94.	2.4313241E-11	4.3677925E+00	*
45.	8.2938191E-06	4.3677658E+00	*	95.	1.8746763E-11	4.3677925E+00	*
46.	6.3949623E-06	4.3677721E+00	*	96.	1.4454721E-11	4.3677925E+00	*
47.	4.9308459E-06	4.3677770E+00	*	97.	1.1145335E-11	4.3677925E+00	*
48.	3.8019365E-06	4.3677808E+00	*	98.	8.5936290E-12	4.3677925E+00	*
49.	2.9314892E-06	4.3677837E+00	*	99.	6.6261312E-12	4.3677925E+00	*
50.	2.2603294E-06	4.3677859E+00	*	100.	5.1090890E-12	4.3677925E+00	*

TABULATED VALUES OF E^{-RX} WHEN R = .265

X	E^{-RX}	SUM OF E^{-RX}	°	X	E^{-RX}	SUM OF E^{-RX}	°
0.	1.0000000E+00	1.0000000E+00	°	50.	1.7603463E-06	4.2956339E+00	°
1.	7.6720594E-01	1.7672059E+00	°	51.	1.3505481E-06	4.2956352E+00	°
2.	5.8860496E-01	2.3558109E+00	°	52.	1.0361485E-06	4.2956362E+00	°
3.	4.5158123E-01	2.8073920E+00	°	53.	7.9603935E-07	4.2956369E+00	°
4.	3.4645580E-01	3.1538478E+00	°	54.	6.0988220E-07	4.2956375E+00	°
5.	2.6580295E-01	3.4196507E+00	°	55.	4.6790525E-07	4.2956379E+00	°
6.	2.0392561E-01	3.6235763E+00	°	56.	3.5897969E-07	4.2956382E+00	°
7.	1.5645294E-01	3.7800292E+00	°	57.	2.7541136E-07	4.2956384E+00	°
8.	1.2003162E-01	3.9000608E+00	°	58.	2.1129723E-07	4.2956386E+00	°
9.	9.2088979E-02	3.9921497E+00	°	59.	1.6210849E-07	4.2956387E+00	°
10.	7.0651212E-02	4.0626009E+00	°	60.	1.2437060E-07	4.2956388E+00	°
11.	5.4204030E-02	4.1170049E+00	°	61.	9.5417865E-08	4.2956388E+00	°
12.	4.1583655E-02	4.1585905E+00	°	62.	7.3205154E-08	4.2956388E+00	°
13.	3.1904761E-02	4.1904952E+00	°	63.	5.6163430E-08	4.2956388E+00	°
14.	2.4477523E-02	4.2149727E+00	°	64.	4.3088917E-08	4.2956388E+00	°
15.	1.8779301E-02	4.2337520E+00	°	65.	3.3058074E-08	4.2956388E+00	°
16.	1.4407591E-02	4.2481595E+00	°	66.	2.5362351E-08	4.2956388E+00	°
17.	1.1053590E-02	4.2592130E+00	°	67.	1.9458146E-08	4.2956388E+00	°
18.	8.4803801E-03	4.2676933E+00	°	68.	1.4928405E-08	4.2956388E+00	°
19.	6.5061980E-03	4.2741994E+00	°	69.	1.1453161E-08	4.2956388E+00	°
20.	4.9915939E-03	4.2791909E+00	°	70.	8.7869339E-09	4.2956388E+00	°
21.	3.8295805E-03	4.2830204E+00	°	71.	6.7413879E-09	4.2956388E+00	°
22.	2.9380769E-03	4.2859584E+00	°	72.	5.1720329E-09	4.2956388E+00	°
23.	2.2541101E-03	4.2882125E+00	°	73.	3.9680144E-09	4.2956388E+00	°
24.	1.7293667E-03	4.2899418E+00	°	74.	3.0442843E-09	4.2956388E+00	°
25.	1.3267804E-03	4.2912685E+00	°	75.	2.3355930E-09	4.2956388E+00	°
26.	1.0179138E-03	4.2922864E+00	°	76.	1.7918808E-09	4.2956388E+00	°
27.	7.8094955E-04	4.2930673E+00	°	77.	1.3747416E-09	4.2956388E+00	°
28.	5.9914914E-04	4.2936664E+00	°	78.	1.0547099E-09	4.2956388E+00	°
29.	4.5967078E-04	4.2941260E+00	°	79.	8.0917977E-10	4.2956388E+00	°
30.	3.5266216E-04	4.2944786E+00	°	80.	6.2080754E-10	4.2956388E+00	°
31.	2.7056451E-04	4.2947491E+00	°	81.	4.7628723E-10	4.2956388E+00	°
32.	2.0757870E-04	4.2949566E+00	°	82.	3.6541040E-10	4.2956388E+00	°
33.	1.5925561E-04	4.2951158E+00	°	83.	2.8034503E-10	4.2956388E+00	°
34.	1.2218185E-04	4.2952379E+00	°	84.	2.1508237E-10	4.2956388E+00	°
35.	9.3738646E-05	4.2953316E+00	°	85.	1.6501264E-10	4.2956388E+00	°
36.	7.1916847E-05	4.2954035E+00	°	86.	1.2659455E-10	4.2956388E+00	°
37.	5.5175033E-05	4.2954586E+00	°	87.	9.7127166E-11	4.2956388E+00	°
38.	4.2330613E-05	4.2955009E+00	°	88.	7.4516540E-11	4.2956388E+00	°
39.	3.2476298E-05	4.2955333E+00	°	89.	5.7169532E-11	4.2956388E+00	°
40.	2.4916009E-05	4.2955582E+00	°	90.	4.3860805E-11	4.2956388E+00	°
41.	1.9115710E-05	4.2955773E+00	°	91.	3.3650271E-11	4.2956388E+00	°
42.	1.4665687E-05	4.2955919E+00	°	92.	2.5816688E-11	4.2956388E+00	°
43.	1.1251602E-05	4.2956031E+00	°	93.	1.9906716E-11	4.2956388E+00	°
44.	8.6322763E-06	4.2956117E+00	°	94.	1.5195832E-11	4.2956388E+00	°
45.	6.6227490E-06	4.2956183E+00	°	95.	1.1659331E-11	4.2956388E+00	°
46.	5.0810125E-06	4.2956233E+00	°	96.	8.9443416E-12	4.2956388E+00	°
47.	3.8981830E-06	4.2956271E+00	°	97.	6.8621521E-12	4.2956388E+00	°
48.	2.9907092E-06	4.2956300E+00	°	98.	5.2646639E-12	4.2956388E+00	°
49.	2.2944899E-06	4.2956322E+00	°	99.	4.0390968E-12	4.2956388E+00	°
50.	1.7603463E-06	4.2956339E+00	°	100.	3.0988191E-12	4.2956388E+00	°

TABULATED VALUES OF E^{-RX} WHEN R = .270

X	E^{-RX}	SUM OF E^{-RX}	°	X	E^{-RX}	SUM OF E^{-RX}	°
0.	1.0000000E+00	1.0000000E+00	°	50.	1.3709590E-06	4.2261692E+00	°
1.	7.6337949E-01	1.7633794E+00	°	51.	1.0465620E-06	4.2261702E+00	°
2.	5.8274825E-01	2.3461276E+00	°	52.	7.9892400E-07	4.2261709E+00	°
3.	4.4485806E-01	2.7909856E+00	°	53.	6.0988220E-07	4.2261715E+00	°
4.	3.3959552E-01	3.1305811E+00	°	54.	4.6557157E-07	4.2261719E+00	°
5.	2.5924026E-01	3.3898213E+00	°	55.	3.5540778E-07	4.2261722E+00	°
6.	1.9789869E-01	3.5877199E+00	°	56.	2.7131101E-07	4.2261724E+00	°
7.	1.5107160E-01	3.7387917E+00	°	57.	2.0712132E-07	4.2261726E+00	°
8.	1.1532512E-01	3.8541168E+00	°	58.	1.5810602E-07	4.2261727E+00	°
9.	8.8036832E-02	3.9421536E+00	°	59.	1.2069489E-07	4.2261728E+00	°
10.	6.7205512E-02	4.0093591E+00	°	60.	9.2136020E-08	4.2261728E+00	°
11.	5.1303310E-02	4.0606624E+00	°	61.	7.0334739E-08	4.2261728E+00	°
12.	3.9163895E-02	4.0998262E+00	°	62.	5.3692097E-08	4.2261728E+00	°
13.	2.9896914E-02	4.1297231E+00	°	63.	4.0987446E-08	4.2261728E+00	°
14.	2.2822691E-02	4.1525457E+00	°	64.	3.1288976E-08	4.2261728E+00	°
15.	1.7422374E-02	4.1699680E+00	°	65.	2.3885362E-08	4.2261728E+00	°
16.	1.3299883E-02	4.1832678E+00	°	66.	1.8233596E-08	4.2261728E+00	°
17.	1.0152858E-02	4.1934206E+00	°	67.	1.3919153E-08	4.2261728E+00	°
18.	7.7504838E-03	4.2011710E+00	°	68.	1.0625594E-08	4.2261728E+00	°
19.	5.9165604E-03	4.2070875E+00	°	69.	8.1113623E-09	4.2261728E+00	°
20.	4.5165809E-03	4.2116040E+00	°	70.	6.1920476E-09	4.2261728E+00	°
21.	3.4478652E-03	4.2150518E+00	°	71.	4.7268822E-09	4.2261728E+00	°
22.	2.6320296E-03	4.2176836E+00	°	72.	3.6084049E-09	4.2261728E+00	°
23.	2.0092374E-03	4.2196930E+00	°	73.	2.7545823E-09	4.2261728E+00	°
24.	1.5338106E-03	4.2212266E+00	°	74.	2.1027916E-09	4.2261728E+00	°
25.	1.1708796E-03	4.2223976E+00	°	75.	1.6052280E-09	4.2261728E+00	°
26.	8.9382549E-04	4.2232914E+00	°	76.	1.2253981E-09	4.2261728E+00	°
27.	6.8232805E-04	4.2239737E+00	°	77.	9.3544384E-10	4.2261728E+00	°
28.	5.2087524E-04	4.2244945E+00	°	78.	7.1409864E-10	4.2261728E+00	°
29.	3.9762547E-04	4.2248921E+00	°	79.	5.4512824E-10	4.2261728E+00	°
30.	3.0353913E-04	4.2251956E+00	°	80.	4.1613973E-10	4.2261728E+00	°
31.	2.3171555E-04	4.2254273E+00	°	81.	3.1767254E-10	4.2261728E+00	°
32.	1.7688690E-04	4.2256041E+00	°	82.	2.4250470E-10	4.2261728E+00	°
33.	1.3503183E-04	4.2257391E+00	°	83.	1.8512311E-10	4.2261728E+00	°
34.	1.0308053E-04	4.2258421E+00	°	84.	1.4131919E-10	4.2261728E+00	°
35.	7.8689545E-05	4.2259207E+00	°	85.	1.0788017E-10	4.2261728E+00	°
36.	6.0070000E-05	4.2259807E+00	°	86.	8.2353512E-11	4.2261728E+00	°
37.	4.5856206E-05	4.2260265E+00	°	87.	6.2866983E-11	4.2261728E+00	°
38.	3.5005583E-05	4.2260615E+00	°	88.	4.7991365E-11	4.2261728E+00	°
39.	2.6722624E-05	4.2260882E+00	°	89.	3.6635624E-11	4.2261728E+00	°
40.	2.0399503E-05	4.2261085E+00	°	90.	2.7966884E-11	4.2261728E+00	°
41.	1.5572562E-05	4.2261240E+00	°	91.	2.1349364E-11	4.2261728E+00	°
42.	1.1887774E-05	4.2261358E+00	°	92.	1.6297653E-11	4.2261728E+00	°
43.	9.0748836E-06	4.2261448E+00	°	93.	1.2441294E-11	4.2261728E+00	°
44.	6.9275800E-06	4.2261517E+00	°	94.	9.4974288E-12	4.2261728E+00	°
45.	5.2883725E-06	4.2261569E+00	°	95.	7.2591424E-12	4.2261728E+00	°
46.	4.0370351E-06	4.2261609E+00	°	96.	5.5344100E-12	4.2261728E+00	°
47.	3.0817898E-06	4.2261639E+00	°	97.	4.2250078E-12	4.2261728E+00	°
48.	2.3525751E-06	4.2261662E+00	°	98.	3.2252843E-12	4.2261728E+00	°
49.	1.7959076E-06	4.2261679E+00	°	99.	2.4621150E-12	4.2261728E+00	°
50.	1.3709590E-06	4.2261692E+00	°	100.	1.8795285E-12	4.2261728E+00	°

X	E^{-RX}	SUM OF E^{-RX}	☆	X	E^{-RX}	SUM OF E^{-RX}	☆
0.	1.0000000E+00	1.0000000E+00	☆	50.	1.0677040E-06	4.1592455E+00	☆
1.	7.5957212E-01	1.7595721E+00	☆	51.	8.1099819E-07	4.1592463E+00	☆
2.	5.7694980E-01	2.3365219E+00	☆	52.	6.1601162E-07	4.1592469E+00	☆
3.	4.3823499E-01	2.7747568E+00	☆	53.	4.6790525E-07	4.1592473E+00	☆
4.	3.3287108E-01	3.1076278E+00	☆	54.	3.5540778E-07	4.1592476E+00	☆
5.	2.5283959E-01	3.3604673E+00	☆	55.	2.6995782E-07	4.1592478E+00	☆
6.	1.9204990E-01	3.5525172E+00	☆	56.	2.0505245E-07	4.1592480E+00	☆
7.	1.4587575E-01	3.6983929E+00	☆	57.	1.5575213E-07	4.1592481E+00	☆
8.	1.1080315E-01	3.8091960E+00	☆	58.	1.1830497E-07	4.1592482E+00	☆
9.	8.4162990E-02	3.8933589E+00	☆	59.	8.9861162E-08	4.1592482E+00	☆
10.	6.3927860E-02	3.9572867E+00	☆	60.	6.8256033E-08	4.1592482E+00	☆
11.	4.8557821E-02	4.0058445E+00	☆	61.	5.1845380E-08	4.1592482E+00	☆
12.	3.6883167E-02	4.0427276E+00	☆	62.	3.9380305E-08	4.1592482E+00	☆
13.	2.8015425E-02	4.0707430E+00	☆	63.	2.9912182E-08	4.1592482E+00	☆
14.	2.1279736E-02	4.0920227E+00	☆	64.	2.2720459E-08	4.1592482E+00	☆
15.	1.6163494E-02	4.1081861E+00	☆	65.	1.7257827E-08	4.1592482E+00	☆
16.	1.2277339E-02	4.1204634E+00	☆	66.	1.3108565E-08	4.1592482E+00	☆
17.	9.3255251E-03	4.1297889E+00	☆	67.	9.9569005E-09	4.1592482E+00	☆
18.	7.0834089E-03	4.1368723E+00	☆	68.	7.5629841E-09	4.1592482E+00	☆
19.	5.3803599E-03	4.1422526E+00	☆	69.	5.7446319E-09	4.1592482E+00	☆
20.	4.0867714E-03	4.1463393E+00	☆	70.	4.3634622E-09	4.1592482E+00	☆
21.	3.1041976E-03	4.1494434E+00	☆	71.	3.3143642E-09	4.1592482E+00	☆
22.	2.3578620E-03	4.1518012E+00	☆	72.	2.5174987E-09	4.1592482E+00	☆
23.	1.7909662E-03	4.1535921E+00	☆	73.	1.9122216E-09	4.1592482E+00	☆
24.	1.3603680E-03	4.1549524E+00	☆	74.	1.4524704E-09	4.1592482E+00	☆
25.	1.0332976E-03	4.1559856E+00	☆	75.	1.1032560E-09	4.1592482E+00	☆
26.	7.8486408E-04	4.1567704E+00	☆	76.	8.3800252E-10	4.1592482E+00	☆
27.	5.9616087E-04	4.1573665E+00	☆	77.	6.3652335E-10	4.1592482E+00	☆
28.	4.5282718E-04	4.1578193E+00	☆	78.	4.8348539E-10	4.1592482E+00	☆
29.	3.4395490E-04	4.1581632E+00	☆	79.	3.6724202E-10	4.1592482E+00	☆
30.	2.6125855E-04	4.1584244E+00	☆	80.	2.7894680E-10	4.1592482E+00	☆
31.	1.9844471E-04	4.1586228E+00	☆	81.	2.1188021E-10	4.1592482E+00	☆
32.	1.5073307E-04	4.1587735E+00	☆	82.	1.6093830E-10	4.1592482E+00	☆
33.	1.1449264E-04	4.1588879E+00	☆	83.	1.2224425E-10	4.1592482E+00	☆
34.	8.6965418E-05	4.1589748E+00	☆	84.	9.2853326E-11	4.1592482E+00	☆
35.	6.6056507E-05	4.1590408E+00	☆	85.	7.0528798E-11	4.1592482E+00	☆
36.	5.0174681E-05	4.1590909E+00	☆	86.	5.3571709E-11	4.1592482E+00	☆
37.	3.8111289E-05	4.1591290E+00	☆	87.	4.0691576E-11	4.1592482E+00	☆
38.	2.8948273E-05	4.1591579E+00	☆	88.	3.0908187E-11	4.1592482E+00	☆
39.	2.1983301E-05	4.1591798E+00	☆	89.	2.3476591E-11	4.1592482E+00	☆
40.	1.6701700E-05	4.1591965E+00	☆	90.	1.7832472E-11	4.1592482E+00	☆
41.	1.2686146E-05	4.1592091E+00	☆	91.	1.3545049E-11	4.1592482E+00	☆
42.	9.6360430E-06	4.1592187E+00	☆	92.	1.0288441E-11	4.1592482E+00	☆
43.	7.3192696E-06	4.1592260E+00	☆	93.	7.8148136E-12	4.1592482E+00	☆
44.	5.5595132E-06	4.1592315E+00	☆	94.	5.9359145E-12	4.1592482E+00	☆
45.	4.2228512E-06	4.1592357E+00	☆	95.	4.5087552E-12	4.1592482E+00	☆
46.	3.2075601E-06	4.1592389E+00	☆	96.	3.4247247E-12	4.1592482E+00	☆
47.	2.4363732E-06	4.1592413E+00	☆	97.	2.6013254E-12	4.1592482E+00	☆
48.	1.8506011E-06	4.1592431E+00	☆	98.	1.9758943E-12	4.1592482E+00	☆
49.	1.4056650E-06	4.1592445E+00	☆	99.	1.5008342E-12	4.1592482E+00	☆
50.	1.0677040E-06	4.1592455E+00	☆	100.	1.1399918E-12	4.1592482E+00	☆

X	E^{-RX}	SUM OF E^{-RX}	☆	X	E^{-RX}	SUM OF E^{-RX}	☆
0.	1.0000000E+00	1.0000000E+00	☆	50.	8.3152871E-07	4.0947264E+00	☆
1.	7.5578374E-01	1.7557837E+00	☆	51.	6.2845588E-07	4.0947270E+00	☆
2.	5.7120906E-01	2.3269927E+00	☆	52.	4.7497674E-07	4.0947274E+00	☆
3.	4.3171052E-01	2.7587032E+00	☆	53.	3.5897969E-07	4.0947277E+00	☆
4.	3.2627979E-01	3.0849829E+00	☆	54.	2.7131101E-07	4.0947279E+00	☆
5.	2.4659696E-01	3.3315798E+00	☆	55.	2.0505245E-07	4.0947281E+00	☆
6.	1.8637397E-01	3.5179537E+00	☆	56.	1.5497531E-07	4.0947282E+00	☆
7.	1.4085842E-01	3.6588121E+00	☆	57.	1.1712782E-07	4.0947283E+00	☆
8.	1.0645850E-01	3.7652706E+00	☆	58.	8.8523303E-08	4.0947283E+00	☆
9.	8.0459606E-02	3.8457302E+00	☆	59.	6.6904433E-08	4.0947283E+00	☆
10.	6.0810062E-02	3.9065402E+00	☆	60.	5.0565313E-08	4.0947283E+00	☆
11.	4.5959256E-02	3.9524994E+00	☆	61.	3.8216441E-08	4.0947283E+00	☆
12.	3.4735258E-02	3.9872346E+00	☆	62.	2.8883365E-08	4.0947283E+00	☆
13.	2.6252343E-02	4.0134869E+00	☆	63.	2.1829577E-08	4.0947283E+00	☆
14.	1.9841094E-02	4.0333279E+00	☆	64.	1.6498440E-08	4.0947283E+00	☆
15.	1.4995576E-02	4.0483234E+00	☆	65.	1.2469252E-08	4.0947283E+00	☆
16.	1.1333413E-02	4.0596568E+00	☆	66.	9.4240585E-09	4.0947283E+00	☆
17.	8.5656093E-03	4.0682224E+00	☆	67.	7.1225501E-09	4.0947283E+00	☆
18.	6.4737483E-03	4.0746981E+00	☆	68.	5.3831076E-09	4.0947283E+00	☆
19.	4.8927537E-03	4.0795888E+00	☆	69.	4.0684652E-09	4.0947283E+00	☆
20.	3.6978637E-03	4.0832866E+00	☆	70.	3.0748798E-09	4.0947283E+00	☆
21.	2.7947852E-03	4.0860813E+00	☆	71.	2.3239442E-09	4.0947283E+00	☆
22.	2.1122532E-03	4.0881935E+00	☆	72.	1.7563992E-09	4.0947283E+00	☆
23.	1.5964066E-03	4.0897899E+00	☆	73.	1.3274580E-09	4.0947283E+00	☆
24.	1.2065382E-03	4.0909964E+00	☆	74.	1.0032711E-09	4.0947283E+00	☆
25.	9.1188196E-04	4.0919082E+00	☆	75.	7.5825604E-10	4.0947283E+00	☆
26.	6.8918556E-04	4.0925973E+00	☆	76.	5.7307758E-10	4.0947283E+00	☆
27.	5.2087524E-04	4.0931181E+00	☆	77.	4.3312272E-10	4.0947283E+00	☆
28.	3.9366904E-04	4.0935117E+00	☆	78.	3.2734711E-10	4.0947283E+00	☆
29.	2.9752866E-04	4.0938092E+00	☆	79.	2.4740362E-10	4.0947283E+00	☆
30.	2.2486732E-04	4.0940340E+00	☆	80.	1.8698363E-10	4.0947283E+00	☆
31.	1.6995106E-04	4.0942039E+00	☆	81.	1.4131919E-10	4.0947283E+00	☆
32.	1.2844625E-04	4.0943323E+00	☆	82.	1.0680674E-10	4.0947283E+00	☆
33.	9.7077590E-05	4.0944293E+00	☆	83.	8.0722803E-11	4.0947283E+00	☆
34.	7.3369664E-05	4.0945026E+00	☆	84.	6.1008982E-11	4.0947283E+00	☆
35.	5.5451599E-05	4.0945580E+00	☆	85.	4.6109597E-11	4.0947283E+00	☆
36.	4.1909417E-05	4.0945999E+00	☆	86.	3.4848803E-11	4.0947283E+00	☆
37.	3.1674456E-05	4.0946315E+00	☆	87.	2.6338219E-11	4.0947283E+00	☆
38.	2.3939038E-05	4.0946554E+00	☆	88.	1.9905998E-11	4.0947283E+00	☆
39.	1.8092736E-05	4.0946734E+00	☆	89.	1.5044629E-11	4.0947283E+00	☆
40.	1.3674196E-05	4.0946870E+00	☆	90.	1.1370486E-11	4.0947283E+00	☆
41.	1.0334735E-05	4.0946973E+00	☆	91.	8.5936290E-12	4.0947283E+00	☆
42.	7.8108247E-06	4.0947051E+00	☆	92.	6.4949250E-12	4.0947283E+00	☆
43.	5.9032943E-06	4.0947110E+00	☆	93.	4.9087587E-12	4.0947283E+00	☆
44.	4.4616138E-06	4.0947154E+00	☆	94.	3.7099600E-12	4.0947283E+00	☆
45.	3.3720152E-06	4.0947187E+00	☆	95.	2.8039275E-12	4.0947283E+00	☆
46.	2.5485142E-06	4.0947212E+00	☆	96.	2.1191628E-12	4.0947283E+00	☆
47.	1.9261256E-06	4.0947231E+00	☆	97.	1.6016288E-12	4.0947283E+00	☆
48.	1.4557344E-06	4.0947245E+00	☆	98.	1.2104850E-12	4.0947283E+00	☆
49.	1.1002204E-06	4.0947256E+00	☆	99.	9.1486488E-13	4.0947283E+00	☆
50.	8.3152871E-07	4.0947264E+00	☆	100.	6.9144000E-13	4.0947283E+00	☆

X	E^{-RX}	SUM OF E^{-RX}	σ	X	E^{-RX}	SUM OF E^{-RX}	σ
0.	1.0000000E+00	1.0000000E+00	∞	50.	6.4759521E-07	4.0324854E+00	∞
1.	7.5201425E-01	1.7520142E+00	∞	51.	4.8700083E-07	4.0324858E+00	∞
2.	5.6552543E-01	2.3175396E+00	∞	52.	3.6623156E-07	4.0324861E+00	∞
3.	4.2528319E-01	2.7428227E+00	∞	53.	2.7541136E-07	4.0324863E+00	∞
4.	3.1981902E-01	3.0626417E+00	∞	54.	2.0711326E-07	4.0324865E+00	∞
5.	2.4050846E-01	3.3031501E+00	∞	55.	1.5575213E-07	4.0324866E+00	∞
6.	1.8086579E-01	3.4840158E+00	∞	56.	1.1712782E-07	4.0324867E+00	∞
7.	1.3601345E-01	3.6200294E+00	∞	57.	8.8081791E-08	4.0324867E+00	∞
8.	1.0228420E-01	3.7223136E+00	∞	58.	6.6238762E-08	4.0324867E+00	∞
9.	7.6919181E-02	3.7992327E+00	∞	59.	4.9812494E-08	4.0324867E+00	∞
10.	5.7844320E-02	3.8570770E+00	∞	60.	3.7459705E-08	4.0324867E+00	∞
11.	4.3495753E-02	3.9005767E+00	∞	61.	2.8170232E-08	4.0324867E+00	∞
12.	3.2712434E-02	3.9332891E+00	∞	62.	2.1184416E-08	4.0324867E+00	∞
13.	2.4600217E-02	3.9578893E+00	∞	63.	1.5930983E-08	4.0324867E+00	∞
14.	1.8499714E-02	3.9763690E+00	∞	64.	1.1980326E-08	4.0324867E+00	∞
15.	1.3912045E-02	3.9903010E+00	∞	65.	9.0093761E-09	4.0324867E+00	∞
16.	1.0462056E-02	4.0007630E+00	∞	66.	6.7751763E-09	4.0324867E+00	∞
17.	7.6676174E-03	4.0084306E+00	∞	67.	5.0950314E-09	4.0324867E+00	∞
18.	5.9165604E-03	4.0145471E+00	∞	68.	3.8315362E-09	4.0324867E+00	∞
19.	4.4493378E-03	4.0189664E+00	∞	69.	2.8813698E-09	4.0324867E+00	∞
20.	3.3459654E-03	4.0223423E+00	∞	70.	2.1668312E-09	4.0324867E+00	∞
21.	2.5162137E-03	4.0248585E+00	∞	71.	1.6294879E-09	4.0324867E+00	∞
22.	1.8922285E-03	4.0267507E+00	∞	72.	1.2253981E-09	4.0324867E+00	∞
23.	1.4229828E-03	4.0281736E+00	∞	73.	9.2151689E-10	4.0324867E+00	∞
24.	1.0701033E-03	4.0292437E+00	∞	74.	6.9299364E-10	4.0324867E+00	∞
25.	8.0473300E-04	4.0300484E+00	∞	75.	5.2114124E-10	4.0324867E+00	∞
26.	6.0517069E-04	4.0306535E+00	∞	76.	3.9190564E-10	4.0324867E+00	∞
27.	4.5509698E-04	4.0311085E+00	∞	77.	2.9471863E-10	4.0324867E+00	∞
28.	3.4223942E-04	4.0314507E+00	∞	78.	2.2163261E-10	4.0324867E+00	∞
29.	2.5736892E-04	4.0317080E+00	∞	79.	1.6667088E-10	4.0324867E+00	∞
30.	1.9354509E-04	4.0319015E+00	∞	80.	1.2533888E-10	4.0324867E+00	∞
31.	1.4554867E-04	4.0320470E+00	∞	81.	9.4256624E-11	4.0324867E+00	∞
32.	1.0945467E-04	4.0321564E+00	∞	82.	7.0882325E-11	4.0324867E+00	∞
33.	8.2311477E-05	4.0322387E+00	∞	83.	5.3304519E-11	4.0324867E+00	∞
34.	6.1899404E-05	4.0323005E+00	∞	84.	4.0085758E-11	4.0324867E+00	∞
35.	4.6549234E-05	4.0323470E+00	∞	85.	3.0145061E-11	4.0324867E+00	∞
36.	3.5005667E-05	4.0323820E+00	∞	86.	2.2669515E-11	4.0324867E+00	∞
37.	2.6324776E-05	4.0324083E+00	∞	87.	1.7047799E-11	4.0324867E+00	∞
38.	1.9796606E-05	4.0324280E+00	∞	88.	1.2820187E-11	4.0324867E+00	∞
39.	1.4887330E-05	4.0324428E+00	∞	89.	9.6409641E-12	4.0324867E+00	∞
40.	1.1195484E-05	4.0324539E+00	∞	90.	7.2501424E-12	4.0324867E+00	∞
41.	8.4191641E-06	4.0324623E+00	∞	91.	5.4522104E-12	4.0324867E+00	∞
42.	6.3313314E-06	4.0324686E+00	∞	92.	4.1001399E-12	4.0324867E+00	∞
43.	4.7612515E-06	4.0324733E+00	∞	93.	3.0833637E-12	4.0324867E+00	∞
44.	3.5805290E-06	4.0324768E+00	∞	94.	2.3187334E-12	4.0324867E+00	∞
45.	2.6926088E-06	4.0324794E+00	∞	95.	1.7437206E-12	4.0324867E+00	∞
46.	2.0248802E-06	4.0324814E+00	∞	96.	1.3113027E-12	4.0324867E+00	∞
47.	1.5227386E-06	4.0324829E+00	∞	97.	9.8611836E-13	4.0324867E+00	∞
48.	1.1451212E-06	4.0324840E+00	∞	98.	7.4157505E-13	4.0324867E+00	∞
49.	8.6114752E-07	4.0324848E+00	∞	99.	5.5767502E-13	4.0324867E+00	∞
50.	6.4759521E-07	4.0324854E+00	∞	100.	4.1937956E-13	4.0324867E+00	∞

X	E^{-RX}	SUM OF E^{-RX}	σ	X	E^{-RX}	SUM OF E^{-RX}	σ
0.	1.0000000E+00	1.0000000E+00	∞	50.	5.0434766E-07	3.9724048E+00	∞
1.	7.4826356E-01	1.7482635E+00	∞	51.	3.7738498E-07	3.9724051E+00	∞
2.	5.5989836E-01	2.3081618E+00	∞	52.	2.8238343E-07	3.9724053E+00	∞
3.	4.1895154E-01	2.7271133E+00	∞	53.	2.1129723E-07	3.9724055E+00	∞
4.	3.1348618E-01	3.0405994E+00	∞	54.	1.5810602E-07	3.9724056E+00	∞
5.	2.3457028E-01	3.2751696E+00	∞	55.	1.1830497E-07	3.9724057E+00	∞
6.	1.7552040E-01	3.4506900E+00	∞	56.	8.8523303E-08	3.9724057E+00	∞
7.	1.3132552E-01	3.5820255E+00	∞	57.	6.6238762E-08	3.9724057E+00	∞
8.	9.8273585E-02	3.6802990E+00	∞	58.	4.9564053E-08	3.9724057E+00	∞
9.	7.3534543E-02	3.7538335E+00	∞	59.	3.7086975E-08	3.9724057E+00	∞
10.	5.5023215E-02	3.8088567E+00	∞	60.	2.7750432E-08	3.9724057E+00	∞
11.	4.1171870E-02	3.8500285E+00	∞	61.	2.0764936E-08	3.9724057E+00	∞
12.	3.0807411E-02	3.8808359E+00	∞	62.	1.5537645E-08	3.9724057E+00	∞
13.	2.3052063E-02	3.9038879E+00	∞	63.	1.1626254E-08	3.9724057E+00	∞
14.	1.7249019E-02	3.9211369E+00	∞	64.	8.6995024E-09	3.9724057E+00	∞
15.	1.2906812E-02	3.9340437E+00	∞	65.	6.5095207E-09	3.9724057E+00	∞
16.	9.6576976E-03	3.9437013E+00	∞	66.	4.8708372E-09	3.9724057E+00	∞
17.	7.2265032E-03	3.9509278E+00	∞	67.	3.6446700E-09	3.9724057E+00	∞
18.	5.4073291E-03	3.9563351E+00	∞	68.	2.7271738E-09	3.9724057E+00	∞
19.	4.0461073E-03	3.9603812E+00	∞	69.	2.0406447E-09	3.9724057E+00	∞
20.	3.0275554E-03	3.9634087E+00	∞	70.	1.5269401E-09	3.9724057E+00	∞
21.	2.2654089E-03	3.9656741E+00	∞	71.	1.1425536E-09	3.9724057E+00	∞
22.	1.6951229E-03	3.9673692E+00	∞	72.	8.5493129E-10	3.9724057E+00	∞
23.	1.2683987E-03	3.9686375E+00	∞	73.	6.3971394E-10	3.9724057E+00	∞
24.	9.4909657E-04	3.9695865E+00	∞	74.	4.7867463E-10	3.9724057E+00	∞
25.	7.1017438E-04	3.9702966E+00	∞	75.	3.5817479E-10	3.9724057E+00	∞
26.	5.3139762E-04	3.9708279E+00	∞	76.	2.6800914E-10	3.9724057E+00	∞
27.	3.9762547E-04	3.9712255E+00	∞	77.	2.0054148E-10	3.9724057E+00	∞
28.	2.9752866E-04	3.9715230E+00	∞	78.	1.5005788E-10	3.9724057E+00	∞
29.	2.2262905E-04	3.9717456E+00	∞	79.	1.1228284E-10	3.9724057E+00	∞
30.	1.6658581E-04	3.9719121E+00	∞	80.	8.4017164E-11	3.9724057E+00	∞
31.	1.2465009E-04	3.9720367E+00	∞	81.	6.2866983E-11	3.9724057E+00	∞
32.	9.3271123E-05	3.9721299E+00	∞	82.	4.7041073E-11	3.9724057E+00	∞
33.	6.9791383E-05	3.9721996E+00	∞	83.	3.5199121E-11	3.9724057E+00	∞
34.	5.2222349E-05	3.9722518E+00	∞	84.	2.6338219E-11	3.9724057E+00	∞
35.	3.9076081E-05	3.9722908E+00	∞	85.	1.9707930E-11	3.9724057E+00	∞
36.	2.9239208E-05	3.9723200E+00	∞	86.	1.4746726E-11	3.9724057E+00	∞
37.	2.1878634E-05	3.9723418E+00	∞	87.	1.1034438E-11	3.9724057E+00	∞
38.	1.6370894E-05	3.9723581E+00	∞	88.	8.2566679E-12	3.9724057E+00	∞
39.	1.2249811E-05	3.9723703E+00	∞	89.	6.1781638E-12	3.9724057E+00	∞
40.	9.1660877E-06	3.9723794E+00	∞	90.	4.6228949E-12	3.9724057E+00	∞
41.	6.8586494E-06	3.9723862E+00	∞	91.	3.4591438E-12	3.9724057E+00	∞
42.	5.1320775E-06	3.9723913E+00	∞	92.	2.5883513E-12	3.9724057E+00	∞
43.	3.8401466E-06	3.9723951E+00	∞	93.	1.9367689E-12	3.9724057E+00	∞
44.	2.8734418E-06	3.9723979E+00	∞	94.	1.4492136E-12	3.9724057E+00	∞
45.	2.1500918E-06	3.9724000E+00	∞	95.	1.0843937E-12	3.9724057E+00	∞
46.	1.6088353E-06	3.9724016E+00	∞	96.	8.1141234E-13	3.9724057E+00	∞
47.	1.2038329E-06	3.9724028E+00	∞	97.	6.0715031E-13	3.9724057E+00	∞
48.	9.0078430E-07	3.9724037E+00	∞	98.	4.5430845E-13	3.9724057E+00	∞
49.	6.7402407E-07	3.9724043E+00	∞	99.	3.3994246E-13	3.9724057E+00	∞
50.	5.0434766E-07	3.9724048E+00	∞	100.	2.5436656E-13	3.9724057E+00	∞

X	E $^{-RX}$	SUM OF E $^{-RX}$		X	E $^{-RX}$	SUM OF E $^{-RX}$	
0.	1.0000000E+00	1.0000000E+00	◦	50.	3.9278635E-07	3.9143747E+00	◦
1.	7.4453158E-01	1.7445315E+00		51.	2.9244184E-07	3.9143749E+00	◦
2.	5.5432728E-01	2.2988587E+00	◦	52.	2.1773219E-07	3.9143751E+00	◦
3.	4.1271417E-01	2.7115728E+00	◦	53.	1.6210849E-07	3.9143752E+00	◦
4.	3.0727873E-01	3.0188515E+00	◦	54.	1.2069449E-07	3.9143753E+00	◦
5.	2.2877872E-01	3.2476302E+00	◦	55.	8.9861162E-08	3.9143753E+00	◦
6.	1.7033298E-01	3.4179631E+00	◦	56.	6.6904473E-08	3.9143753E+00	◦
7.	1.2681829E-01	3.5447813E+00	◦	57.	4.9812494E-08	3.9143753E+00	◦
8.	9.4420222E-02	3.6392015E+00	◦	58.	3.7086975E-08	3.9143753E+00	◦
9.	7.0298838E-02	3.7095003E+00		59.	2.7612424E-08	3.9143753E+00	◦
10.	5.2339705E-02	3.7618400E+00	◦	60.	2.0558322E-08	3.9143753E+00	◦
11.	3.8968564E-02	3.8008085E+00	◦	61.	1.5306320E-08	3.9143753E+00	◦
12.	2.9013327E-02	3.8298218E+00	◦	62.	1.1396038E-08	3.9143753E+00	◦
13.	2.1601338E-02	3.8514231E+00	◦	63.	8.4847109E-09	3.9143753E+00	◦
14.	1.6082878E-02	3.8675059E+00	◦	64.	6.3171335E-09	3.9143753E+00	◦
15.	1.1974211E-02	3.8794801E+00	◦	65.	4.7033067E-09	3.9143753E+00	◦
16.	8.9151785E-03	3.8883952E+00	◦	66.	3.5017604E-09	3.9143753E+00	◦
17.	6.6376320E-03	3.8950328E+00	◦	67.	2.6071712E-09	3.9143753E+00	◦
18.	4.9419267E-03	3.8999747E+00	◦	68.	1.9411213E-09	3.9143753E+00	◦
19.	3.6794205E-03	3.9036541E+00	◦	69.	1.4452261E-09	3.9143753E+00	◦
20.	2.7394448E-03	3.9063935E+00	◦	70.	1.0760165E-09	3.9143753E+00	◦
21.	2.0396031E-03	3.9084331E+00	◦	71.	8.0112830E-10	3.9143753E+00	◦
22.	1.5185490E-03	3.9099516E+00	◦	72.	5.9646532E-10	3.9143753E+00	◦
23.	1.1306077E-03	3.9110822E+00	◦	73.	4.4408727E-10	3.9143753E+00	◦
24.	8.4177314E-04	3.9119239E+00	◦	74.	3.3063700E-10	3.9143753E+00	◦
25.	6.2672669E-04	3.9125506E+00	◦	75.	2.4616969E-10	3.9143753E+00	◦
26.	4.6661782E-04	3.9130172E+00	◦	76.	1.8328111E-10	3.9143753E+00	◦
27.	3.4741170E-04	3.9133646E+00	◦	77.	1.3645857E-10	3.9143753E+00	◦
28.	2.5865899E-04	3.9136232E+00	◦	78.	1.0159772E-10	3.9143753E+00	◦
29.	1.9257978E-04	3.9138157E+00	◦	79.	7.5642713E-11	3.9143753E+00	◦
30.	1.4338173E-04	3.9139590E+00	◦	80.	5.6318389E-11	3.9143753E+00	◦
31.	1.0675223E-04	3.9140657E+00	◦	81.	4.1930819E-11	3.9143753E+00	◦
32.	7.9480408E-05	3.9141451E+00	◦	82.	3.1218819E-11	3.9143753E+00	◦
33.	5.9175674E-05	3.9142042E+00	◦	83.	2.3243397E-11	3.9143753E+00	◦
34.	4.4058158E-05	3.9142482E+00	◦	84.	1.7305443E-11	3.9143753E+00	◦
35.	3.2802690E-05	3.9142810E+00	◦	85.	1.2884449E-11	3.9143753E+00	◦
36.	2.4422639E-05	3.9143054E+00	◦	86.	9.5928795E-12	3.9143753E+00	◦
37.	1.8183426E-05	3.9143235E+00	◦	87.	7.1422018E-12	3.9143753E+00	◦
38.	1.3538135E-05	3.9143370E+00	◦	88.	5.3175948E-12	3.9143753E+00	◦
39.	1.0079569E-05	3.9143470E+00	◦	89.	3.9591173E-12	3.9143753E+00	◦
40.	7.5045579E-06	3.9143545E+00	◦	90.	2.9476879E-12	3.9143753E+00	◦
41.	5.5873804E-06	3.9143600E+00	◦	91.	2.1946467E-12	3.9143753E+00	◦
42.	4.1599812E-06	3.9143641E+00	◦	92.	1.6339838E-12	3.9143753E+00	◦
43.	3.0972374E-06	3.9143671E+00	◦	93.	1.2165525E-12	3.9143753E+00	◦
44.	2.3059910E-06	3.9143694E+00	◦	94.	9.0576183E-13	3.9143753E+00	◦
45.	1.7168832E-06	3.9143711E+00	◦	95.	6.7436829E-13	3.9143753E+00	◦
46.	1.2782737E-06	3.9143723E+00	◦	96.	5.0208849E-13	3.9143753E+00	◦
47.	9.5171520E-07	3.9143732E+00	◦	97.	3.7382074E-13	3.9143753E+00	◦
48.	7.0858203E-07	3.9143739E+00	◦	98.	2.7832135E-13	3.9143753E+00	◦
49.	5.2756170E-07	3.9143744E+00	◦	99.	2.0721903E-13	3.9143753E+00	◦
50.	3.9278635E-07	3.9143747E+00	◦	100.	1.5428112E-13	3.9143753E+00	◦

X	E $^{-RX}$	SUM OF E $^{-RX}$		X	E $^{-RX}$	SUM OF E $^{-RX}$	
0.	1.0000000E+00	1.0000000E+00	◦	50.	3.0590232E-07	3.8582924E+00	◦
1.	7.4081821E-01	1.7408182E+00	◦	51.	2.2661801E-07	3.8582926E+00	◦
2.	5.4881163E-01	2.2896298E+00	◦	52.	1.6788275E-07	3.8582927E+00	◦
3.	4.0656965E-01	2.6961994E+00	◦	53.	1.2437060E-07	3.8582928E+00	◦
4.	3.0119421E-01	2.9973936E+00	◦	54.	9.2136000E-08	3.8582928E+00	◦
5.	2.2313015E-01	3.2205237E+00	◦	55.	6.8256033E-08	3.8582928E+00	◦
6.	1.6529888E-01	3.3858225E+00	◦	56.	5.0565313E-08	3.8582928E+00	◦
7.	1.2245642E-01	3.5082789E+00	◦	57.	3.7459705E-08	3.8582928E+00	◦
8.	9.0717953E-02	3.5989968E+00	◦	58.	2.7750832E-08	3.8582928E+00	◦
9.	6.7205512E-02	3.6662023E+00	◦	59.	2.0558322E-08	3.8582928E+00	◦
10.	4.9787068E-02	3.7159893E+00	◦	60.	1.5229979E-08	3.8582928E+00	◦
11.	3.6883167E-02	3.7528724E+00	◦	61.	1.1282646E-08	3.8582928E+00	◦
12.	2.7323722E-02	3.7801961E+00	◦	62.	8.3583900E-09	3.8582928E+00	◦
13.	2.0241911E-02	3.8004380E+00	◦	63.	6.1920476E-09	3.8582928E+00	◦
14.	1.4995576E-02	3.8154335E+00	◦	64.	4.5871817E-09	3.8582928E+00	◦
15.	1.1108996E-02	3.8265424E+00	◦	65.	3.3982678E-09	3.8582928E+00	◦
16.	8.2297470E-03	3.8347721E+00	◦	66.	2.5174987E-09	3.8582928E+00	◦
17.	6.0967465E-03	3.8408688E+00	◦	67.	1.8650089E-09	3.8582928E+00	◦
18.	4.5165809E-03	3.8453853E+00	◦	68.	1.3816325E-09	3.8582928E+00	◦
19.	3.3459654E-03	3.8487312E+00	◦	69.	1.0235385E-09	3.8582928E+00	◦
20.	2.4787521E-03	3.8512099E+00	◦	70.	7.5825604E-10	3.8582928E+00	◦
21.	1.8363047E-03	3.8530462E+00	◦	71.	5.6172989E-10	3.8582928E+00	◦
22.	1.3603680E-03	3.8544065E+00	◦	72.	4.1613973E-10	3.8582928E+00	◦
23.	1.0077854E-03	3.8554142E+00	◦	73.	3.0828390E-10	3.8582928E+00	◦
24.	7.4658580E-04	3.8561607E+00	◦	74.	2.2838233E-10	3.8582928E+00	◦
25.	5.5308436E-04	3.8567137E+00	◦	75.	1.6918979E-10	3.8582928E+00	◦
26.	4.0973497E-04	3.8571234E+00	◦	76.	1.2533888E-10	3.8582928E+00	◦
27.	3.0353913E-04	3.8574269E+00	◦	77.	9.2853326E-11	3.8582928E+00	◦
28.	2.2486732E-04	3.8576517E+00	◦	78.	6.8787436E-11	3.8582928E+00	◦
29.	1.6658581E-04	3.8578182E+00	◦	79.	5.0954986E-11	3.8582928E+00	◦
30.	1.2340980E-04	3.8579416E+00	◦	80.	3.7751345E-11	3.8582928E+00	◦
31.	9.1424231E-05	3.8580330E+00	◦	81.	2.7966884E-11	3.8582928E+00	◦
32.	6.7728736E-05	3.8581007E+00	◦	82.	2.0718377E-11	3.8582928E+00	◦
33.	5.0174681E-05	3.8581508E+00	◦	83.	1.5348551E-11	3.8582928E+00	◦
34.	3.7170318E-05	3.8581879E+00	◦	84.	1.1370486E-11	3.8582928E+00	◦
35.	2.7536449E-05	3.8582154E+00	◦	85.	8.4234637E-12	3.8582928E+00	◦
36.	2.0399503E-05	3.8582357E+00	◦	86.	6.2402554E-12	3.8582928E+00	◦
37.	1.5112323E-05	3.8582508E+00	◦	87.	4.6228944E-12	3.8582928E+00	◦
38.	1.1195484E-05	3.8582619E+00	◦	88.	3.4247247E-12	3.8582928E+00	◦
39.	8.2938191E-06	3.8582701E+00	◦	89.	2.5370985E-12	3.8582928E+00	◦
40.	6.1442123E-06	3.8582762E+00	◦	90.	1.8795288E-12	3.8582928E+00	◦
41.	4.5517444E-06	3.8582807E+00	◦	91.	1.3923891E-12	3.8582928E+00	◦
42.	3.3720152E-06	3.8582840E+00	◦	92.	1.0315072E-12	3.8582928E+00	◦
43.	2.4980503E-06	3.8582864E+00	◦	93.	7.6415939E-13	3.8582928E+00	◦
44.	1.8506011E-06	3.8582882E+00	◦	94.	5.6610319E-13	3.8582928E+00	◦
45.	1.3709590E-06	3.8582895E+00	◦	95.	4.1937956E-13	3.8582928E+00	◦
46.	1.0156314E-06	3.8582905E+00	◦	96.	3.1068402E-13	3.8582928E+00	◦
47.	7.5239829E-07	3.8582912E+00	◦	97.	2.3016034E-13	3.8582928E+00	◦
48.	5.5739036E-07	3.8582918E+00	◦	98.	1.7050700E-13	3.8582928E+00	◦
49.	4.1292494E-07	3.8582921E+00	◦	99.	1.2631469E-13	3.8582928E+00	◦
50.	3.0590232E-07	3.8582924E+00	◦	100.	9.3576229E-14	3.8582928E+00	◦

TABULATED VALUES OF E   WHEN R = .305

X	−RX E	−RX SUM OF E	*	X	−RX E	−RX SUM OF E	*
0.	1.0000000E+00	1.0000000E+00	*	50.	2.3823696E-07	3.8040628E+00	*
1.	7.3712337E-01	1.7371233E+00	*	51.	1.7561003E-07	3.8040629E+00	*
2.	5.4333086E-01	2.2804741E+00	*	52.	1.2944626E-07	3.8040630E+00	*
3.	4.0051662E-01	2.6809907E+00	*	53.	9.5417865E-08	3.8040630E+00	*
4.	2.9523016E-01	2.9762208E+00	*	54.	7.0334739E-08	3.8040630E+00	*
5.	2.1762105E-01	3.1938418E+00	*	55.	5.1845305E-08	3.8040630E+00	*
6.	1.6041356E-01	3.3542553E+00	*	56.	3.8216441E-08	3.8040630E+00	*
7.	1.1824459E-01	3.4724998E+00	*	57.	2.8170232E-08	3.8040630E+00	*
8.	8.7160851E-02	3.5596606E+00	*	58.	2.0764936E-08	3.8040630E+00	*
9.	6.4249300E-02	3.6239089E+00	*	59.	1.5306320E-08	3.8040630E+00	*
10.	4.7358924E-02	3.6712678E+00	*	60.	1.1282646E-08	3.8040630E+00	*
11.	3.4909370E-02	3.7061771E+00	*	61.	8.3167024E-09	3.8040630E+00	*
12.	2.5732512E-02	3.7319046E+00	*	62.	6.1304357E-09	3.8040630E+00	*
13.	1.8968036E-02	3.7508776E+00	*	63.	4.5188875E-09	3.8040630E+00	*
14.	1.3981783E-02	3.7648593E+00	*	64.	3.3309775E-09	3.8040630E+00	*
15.	1.0306299E-02	3.7751655E+00	*	65.	2.4553414E-09	3.8040630E+00	*
16.	7.5970140E-03	3.7827625E+00	*	66.	1.8098895E-09	3.8040630E+00	*
17.	5.5999366E-03	3.7883624E+00	*	67.	1.3341119E-09	3.8040630E+00	*
18.	4.1278441E-03	3.7924902E+00	*	68.	9.8340507E-10	3.8040630E+00	*
19.	3.0427304E-03	3.7955329E+00	*	69.	7.2489086E-10	3.8040630E+00	*
20.	2.2428677E-03	3.7977757E+00	*	70.	5.3433400E-10	3.8040630E+00	*
21.	1.6532702E-03	3.7994289E+00	*	71.	3.9387008E-10	3.8040630E+00	*
22.	1.2186641E-03	3.8006475E+00	*	72.	2.9033084E-10	3.8040630E+00	*
23.	8.9830581E-04	3.8015458E+00	*	73.	2.1400965E-10	3.8040630E+00	*
24.	6.6216220E-04	3.8022079E+00	*	74.	1.5775151E-10	3.8040630E+00	*
25.	4.8809524E-04	3.8026959E+00	*	75.	1.1628233E-10	3.8040630E+00	*
26.	3.5978641E-04	3.8030556E+00	*	76.	8.5714423E-11	3.8040630E+00	*
27.	2.6520697E-04	3.8033220E+00	*	77.	6.3182104E-11	3.8040630E+00	*
28.	1.9549025E-04	3.8035162E+00	*	78.	4.6573006E-11	3.8040630E+00	*
29.	1.4410044E-04	3.8036603E+00	*	79.	3.4330051E-11	3.8040630E+00	*
30.	1.0621980E-04	3.8037665E+00	*	80.	2.5305483E-11	3.8040630E+00	*
31.	7.8297099E-05	3.8038447E+00	*	81.	1.8653263E-11	3.8040630E+00	*
32.	5.7714621E-05	3.8039024E+00	*	82.	1.3749756E-11	3.8040630E+00	*
33.	4.2542796E-05	3.8039449E+00	*	83.	1.0135266E-11	3.8040630E+00	*
34.	3.1359290E-05	3.8039762E+00	*	84.	7.4709421E-12	3.8040630E+00	*
35.	2.3115665E-05	3.8039993E+00	*	85.	5.5070060E-12	3.8040630E+00	*
36.	1.7039097E-05	3.8040163E+00	*	86.	4.0593428E-12	3.8040630E+00	*
37.	1.2559917E-05	3.8040288E+00	*	87.	2.9922365E-12	3.8040630E+00	*
38.	9.2562084E-06	3.8040380E+00	*	88.	2.2056474E-12	3.8040630E+00	*
39.	6.8244418E-06	3.8040448E+00	*	89.	1.6258343E-12	3.8040630E+00	*
40.	5.0304555E-06	3.8040498E+00	*	90.	1.1984404E-12	3.8040630E+00	*
41.	3.7080664E-06	3.8040535E+00	*	91.	8.8339849E-13	3.8040630E+00	*
42.	2.7333024E-06	3.8040562E+00	*	92.	6.5117367E-13	3.8040630E+00	*
43.	2.0147811E-06	3.8040582E+00	*	93.	4.7999533E-13	3.8040630E+00	*
44.	1.4851422E-06	3.8040596E+00	*	94.	3.5381578E-13	3.8040630E+00	*
45.	1.0947330E-06	3.8040606E+00	*	95.	2.6080588E-13	3.8040630E+00	*
46.	8.0695332E-07	3.8040614E+00	*	96.	1.9224611E-13	3.8040630E+00	*
47.	5.9482416E-07	3.8040619E+00	*	97.	1.4170910E-13	3.8040630E+00	*
48.	4.3845879E-07	3.8040623E+00	*	98.	1.0445709E-13	3.8040630E+00	*
49.	3.2319822E-07	3.8040626E+00	*	99.	7.6997764E-14	3.8040630E+00	*
50.	2.3823696E-07	3.8040628E+00	*	100.	5.6756852E-14	3.8040630E+00	*

TABULATED VALUES OF E   WHEN R = .310

X	−RX E	−RX SUM OF E	*	X	−RX E	−RX SUM OF E	*
0.	1.0000000E+00	1.0000000E+00	*	50.	1.8553913E-07	3.7515960E+00	*
1.	7.3344695E-01	1.7334469E+00	*	51.	1.3608315E-07	3.7515961E+00	*
2.	5.3794443E-01	2.2713913E+00	*	52.	9.9809766E-08	3.7515961E+00	*
3.	3.9455370E-01	2.6659450E+00	*	53.	7.3205154E-08	3.7515961E+00	*
4.	2.8938421E-01	2.9553292E+00	*	54.	5.3692097E-08	3.7515961E+00	*
5.	2.1224797E-01	3.1675771E+00	*	55.	3.9380305E-08	3.7515961E+00	*
6.	1.5567263E-01	3.3232497E+00	*	56.	2.8883365E-08	3.7515961E+00	*
7.	1.1417761E-01	3.4374273E+00	*	57.	2.1184616E-08	3.7515961E+00	*
8.	8.3743225E-02	3.5211705E+00	*	58.	1.5537645E-08	3.7515961E+00	*
9.	6.1421213E-02	3.5825917E+00	*	59.	1.1396038E-08	3.7515961E+00	*
10.	4.5049202E-02	3.6276409E+00	*	60.	8.3583900E-09	3.7515961E+00	*
11.	3.3041200E-02	3.6606821E+00	*	61.	6.1304357E-09	3.7515961E+00	*
12.	2.4233967E-02	3.6849160E+00	*	62.	4.4963496E-09	3.7515961E+00	*
13.	1.7774329E-02	3.7026903E+00	*	63.	3.2978338E-09	3.7515961E+00	*
14.	1.3036528E-02	3.7157268E+00	*	64.	2.4187861E-09	3.7515961E+00	*
15.	9.5616019E-03	3.7252884E+00	*	65.	1.7740513E-09	3.7515961E+00	*
16.	7.0129278E-03	3.7323013E+00	*	66.	1.3011725E-09	3.7515961E+00	*
17.	5.1436105E-03	3.7374449E+00	*	67.	9.5434106E-10	3.7515961E+00	*
18.	3.7725655E-03	3.7412174E+00	*	68.	6.9995854E-10	3.7515961E+00	*
19.	2.7669766E-03	3.7439843E+00	*	69.	5.1338246E-10	3.7515961E+00	*
20.	2.0294306E-03	3.7460137E+00	*	70.	3.7653880E-10	3.7515961E+00	*
21.	1.4884797E-03	3.7475021E+00	*	71.	2.7617124E-10	3.7515961E+00	*
22.	1.0917209E-03	3.7485938E+00	*	72.	2.0255695E-10	3.7515961E+00	*
23.	8.0071938E-04	3.7493945E+00	*	73.	1.4856478E-10	3.7515961E+00	*
24.	5.8728519E-04	3.7499817E+00	*	74.	1.0896438E-10	3.7515961E+00	*
25.	4.3074253E-04	3.7504124E+00	*	75.	7.9919598E-11	3.7515961E+00	*
26.	3.1592680E-04	3.7507283E+00	*	76.	5.8616786E-11	3.7515961E+00	*
27.	2.3171555E-04	3.7509600E+00	*	77.	4.2992303E-11	3.7515961E+00	*
28.	1.6995106E-04	3.7511299E+00	*	78.	3.1532574E-11	3.7515961E+00	*
29.	1.2465009E-04	3.7512545E+00	*	79.	2.3127470E-11	3.7515961E+00	*
30.	9.1424231E-05	3.7513459E+00	*	80.	1.6962772E-11	3.7515961E+00	*
31.	6.7054824E-05	3.7514129E+00	*	81.	1.2441294E-11	3.7515961E+00	*
32.	4.9181156E-05	3.7514620E+00	*	82.	9.1250293E-12	3.7515961E+00	*
33.	3.6071769E-05	3.7514980E+00	*	83.	6.6927249E-12	3.7515961E+00	*
34.	2.6456729E-05	3.7515246E+00	*	84.	4.9087587E-12	3.7515961E+00	*
35.	1.9404605E-05	3.7515438E+00	*	85.	3.6003141E-12	3.7515961E+00	*
36.	1.4232250E-05	3.7515580E+00	*	86.	2.6406394E-12	3.7515961E+00	*
37.	1.0438600E-05	3.7515684E+00	*	87.	1.9367689E-12	3.7515961E+00	*
38.	7.6561600E-06	3.7515760E+00	*	88.	1.4205173E-12	3.7515961E+00	*
39.	5.6153872E-06	3.7515816E+00	*	89.	1.0418741E-12	3.7515961E+00	*
40.	4.1185866E-06	3.7515857E+00	*	90.	7.6415939E-13	3.7515961E+00	*
41.	3.0207663E-06	3.7515887E+00	*	91.	5.6047037E-13	3.7515961E+00	*
42.	2.2155718E-06	3.7515909E+00	*	92.	4.1107529E-13	3.7515961E+00	*
43.	1.6250044E-06	3.7515925E+00	*	93.	3.0150192E-13	3.7515961E+00	*
44.	1.1918525E-06	3.7515936E+00	*	94.	2.2113566E-13	3.7515961E+00	*
45.	8.7416210E-07	3.7515944E+00	*	95.	1.6219128E-13	3.7515961E+00	*
46.	6.4115153E-07	3.7515950E+00	*	96.	1.1895870E-13	3.7515961E+00	*
47.	4.7025044E-07	3.7515954E+00	*	97.	8.7249898E-14	3.7515961E+00	*
48.	3.4490390E-07	3.7515957E+00	*	98.	6.3993172E-14	3.7515961E+00	*
49.	2.5296871E-07	3.7515959E+00	*	99.	4.6935597E-14	3.7515961E+00	*
50.	1.8553913E-07	3.7515960E+00	*	100.	3.4424771E-14	3.7515961E+00	*

X	E^{-RX}	SUM OF E^{-RX}	*	X	E^{-RX}	SUM OF E^{-RX}	*
0.	1.0000000E+00	1.0000000E+00	*	50.	1.0545305E-07	3.7008072E+00	*
1.	7.2978887E-01	1.7297888E+00	*	51.	7.6954637E-08	3.7008072E+00	*
2.	5.3259179E-01	2.2623805E+00	*	52.	5.6163430E-08	3.7008072E+00	*
3.	3.8867957E-01	2.6510600E+00	*	53.	4.0987446E-08	3.7008072E+00	*
4.	2.8365402E-01	2.9347140E+00	*	54.	2.9912182E-08	3.7008072E+00	*
5.	2.0700755E-01	3.1417215E+00	*	55.	2.1829577E-08	3.7008072E+00	*
6.	1.5107180E-01	3.2927933E+00	*	56.	1.5930943E-08	3.7008072E+00	*
7.	1.1025052E-01	3.4030438E+00	*	57.	1.1626254E-08	3.7008072E+00	*
8.	8.0459606E-02	3.4835034E+00	*	58.	8.4847109E-09	3.7008072E+00	*
9.	5.8718525E-02	3.5422219E+00	*	59.	6.1920476E-09	3.7008072E+00	*
10.	4.2852126E-02	3.5850740E+00	*	60.	4.5188875E-09	3.7008072E+00	*
11.	3.1273005E-02	3.6163470E+00	*	61.	3.2978338E-09	3.7008072E+00	*
12.	2.2822691E-02	3.6391696E+00	*	62.	2.4067224E-09	3.7008072E+00	*
13.	1.6655746E-02	3.6558253E+00	*	63.	1.7563992E-09	3.7008072E+00	*
14.	1.2155178E-02	3.6679804E+00	*	64.	1.2818006E-09	3.7008072E+00	*
15.	8.8707138E-03	3.6768511E+00	*	65.	9.3544384E-10	3.7008072E+00	*
16.	6.4737483E-03	3.6833248E+00	*	66.	6.8267650E-10	3.7008072E+00	*
17.	4.7244694E-03	3.6880492E+00	*	67.	4.9820972E-10	3.7008072E+00	*
18.	3.4478652E-03	3.6914970E+00	*	68.	3.6358791E-10	3.7008072E+00	*
19.	2.5162137E-03	3.6940132E+00	*	69.	2.6534241E-10	3.7008072E+00	*
20.	1.8363047E-03	3.6958495E+00	*	70.	1.9364394E-10	3.7008072E+00	*
21.	1.3401147E-03	3.6971896E+00	*	71.	1.4131919E-10	3.7008072E+00	*
22.	9.7800086E-04	3.6981676E+00	*	72.	1.0313317E-10	3.7008072E+00	*
23.	7.1373415E-04	3.6988813E+00	*	73.	7.5265443E-11	3.7008072E+00	*
24.	5.2087524E-04	3.6994022E+00	*	74.	5.4927883E-11	3.7008072E+00	*
25.	3.8012895E-04	3.6997822E+00	*	75.	4.0085758E-11	3.7008072E+00	*
26.	2.7741388E-04	3.7000596E+00	*	76.	2.9254140E-11	3.7008072E+00	*
27.	2.0245356E-04	3.7002620E+00	*	77.	2.1349346E-11	3.7008072E+00	*
28.	1.4774835E-04	3.7004097E+00	*	78.	1.5580515E-11	3.7008072E+00	*
29.	1.0782510E-04	3.7005175E+00	*	79.	1.1370486E-11	3.7008072E+00	*
30.	7.8689565E-05	3.7005961E+00	*	80.	8.2980546E-12	3.7008072E+00	*
31.	5.7426769E-05	3.7006535E+00	*	81.	6.0558280E-12	3.7008072E+00	*
32.	4.1909417E-05	3.7006954E+00	*	82.	4.4194758E-12	3.7008072E+00	*
33.	3.0585026E-05	3.7007259E+00	*	83.	3.2252843E-12	3.7008072E+00	*
34.	2.2320611E-05	3.7007482E+00	*	84.	2.3537766E-12	3.7008072E+00	*
35.	1.6289334E-05	3.7007644E+00	*	85.	1.7177599E-12	3.7008072E+00	*
36.	1.1887774E-05	3.7007762E+00	*	86.	1.2536021E-12	3.7008072E+00	*
37.	8.6755658E-06	3.7007848E+00	*	87.	9.1486488E-13	3.7008072E+00	*
38.	6.3313314E-06	3.7007911E+00	*	88.	6.6765821E-13	3.7008072E+00	*
39.	4.6205352E-06	3.7007957E+00	*	89.	4.8724954E-13	3.7008072E+00	*
40.	3.3720152E-06	3.7007990E+00	*	90.	3.5558929E-13	3.7008072E+00	*
41.	2.4608591E-06	3.7008014E+00	*	91.	2.5950510E-13	3.7008072E+00	*
42.	1.7959076E-06	3.7008031E+00	*	92.	1.8938394E-13	3.7008072E+00	*
43.	1.3106334E-06	3.7008044E+00	*	93.	1.3821029E-13	3.7008072E+00	*
44.	9.5648569E-07	3.7008053E+00	*	94.	1.0086433E-13	3.7008072E+00	*
45.	6.9803261E-07	3.7008060E+00	*	95.	7.3609669E-14	3.7008072E+00	*
46.	5.0941643E-07	3.7008064E+00	*	96.	5.3719517E-14	3.7008072E+00	*
47.	3.7176645E-07	3.7008067E+00	*	97.	3.9203906E-14	3.7008072E+00	*
48.	2.7131101E-07	3.7008069E+00	*	98.	2.8610574E-14	3.7008072E+00	*
49.	1.9799976E-07	3.7008070E+00	*	99.	2.0879679E-14	3.7008072E+00	*
50.	1.4449802E-07	3.7008071E+00	*	100.			

X	E^{-RX}	SUM OF E^{-RX}	*	X	E^{-RX}	SUM OF E^{-RX}	*
0.	1.0000000E+00	1.0000000E+00	*	50.	1.1253517E-07	3.6516188E+00	*
1.	7.2614903E-01	1.7261490E+00	*	51.	8.1717308E-08	3.6516188E+00	*
2.	5.2729242E-01	2.2534414E+00	*	52.	5.9338944E-08	3.6516188E+00	*
3.	3.8289288E-01	2.6363342E+00	*	53.	4.3088917E-08	3.6516188E+00	*
4.	2.7803730E-01	2.9143715E+00	*	54.	3.1288976E-08	3.6516188E+00	*
5.	2.0189651E-01	3.1162680E+00	*	55.	2.2720459E-08	3.6516188E+00	*
6.	1.4660696E-01	3.2628749E+00	*	56.	1.6498440E-08	3.6516188E+00	*
7.	1.0645850E-01	3.3693334E+00	*	57.	1.1980326E-08	3.6516188E+00	*
8.	7.7304740E-02	3.4466381E+00	*	58.	8.6995024E-09	3.6516188E+00	*
9.	5.6134762E-02	3.5027728E+00	*	59.	6.3171353E-09	3.6516188E+00	*
10.	4.0762203E-02	3.5435350E+00	*	60.	4.5871817E-09	3.6516188E+00	*
11.	2.9599435E-02	3.5731344E+00	*	61.	3.3309775E-09	3.6516188E+00	*
12.	2.1493601E-02	3.5946280E+00	*	62.	2.4187861E-09	3.6516188E+00	*
13.	1.5607557E-02	3.6102355E+00	*	63.	1.7563992E-09	3.6516188E+00	*
14.	1.1333413E-02	3.6215689E+00	*	64.	1.2750476E-09	3.6516188E+00	*
15.	8.2297470E-03	3.6297986E+00	*	65.	9.2613602E-10	3.6516188E+00	*
16.	5.9760228E-03	3.6357746E+00	*	66.	6.7251277E-10	3.6516188E+00	*
17.	4.3394832E-03	3.6401140E+00	*	67.	4.8834450E-10	3.6516188E+00	*
18.	3.1511115E-03	3.6432651E+00	*	68.	3.5461089E-10	3.6516188E+00	*
19.	2.2881766E-03	3.6455532E+00	*	69.	2.5750035E-10	3.6516188E+00	*
20.	1.6615572E-03	3.6472147E+00	*	70.	1.8698363E-10	3.6516188E+00	*
21.	1.2065382E-03	3.6484212E+00	*	71.	1.3577798E-10	3.6516188E+00	*
22.	8.7612656E-04	3.6492973E+00	*	72.	9.8595055E-11	3.6516188E+00	*
23.	6.3619845E-04	3.6499334E+00	*	73.	7.1594704E-11	3.6516188E+00	*
24.	4.6197489E-04	3.6503953E+00	*	74.	5.1988425E-11	3.6516188E+00	*
25.	3.3546262E-04	3.6507307E+00	*	75.	3.7751345E-11	3.6516188E+00	*
26.	2.4359586E-04	3.6509742E+00	*	76.	2.7413103E-11	3.6516188E+00	*
27.	1.7688690E-04	3.6511510E+00	*	77.	1.9905998E-11	3.6516188E+00	*
28.	1.2844625E-04	3.6512794E+00	*	78.	1.4454721E-11	3.6516188E+00	*
29.	9.3271123E-05	3.6513726E+00	*	79.	1.0496282E-11	3.6516188E+00	*
30.	6.7728736E-05	3.6514402E+00	*	80.	7.6218651E-12	3.6516188E+00	*
31.	4.9181156E-05	3.6514894E+00	*	81.	5.5346100E-12	3.6516188E+00	*
32.	3.5712849E-05	3.6515251E+00	*	82.	4.0189517E-12	3.6516188E+00	*
33.	2.5932851E-05	3.6515510E+00	*	83.	2.9183579E-12	3.6516188E+00	*
34.	1.8831115E-05	3.6515698E+00	*	84.	2.1191628E-12	3.6516188E+00	*
35.	1.3674196E-05	3.6515834E+00	*	85.	1.5388280E-12	3.6516188E+00	*
36.	9.9295042E-06	3.6515933E+00	*	86.	1.1174184E-12	3.6516188E+00	*
37.	7.2102999E-06	3.6516005E+00	*	87.	8.1142236E-13	3.6516188E+00	*
38.	5.2357523E-06	3.6516057E+00	*	88.	5.8920630E-13	3.6516188E+00	*
39.	3.8019365E-06	3.6516095E+00	*	89.	4.2785159E-13	3.6516188E+00	*
40.	2.7607725E-06	3.6516122E+00	*	90.	3.1068402E-13	3.6516188E+00	*
41.	2.0047323E-06	3.6516142E+00	*	91.	2.2560290E-13	3.6516188E+00	*
42.	1.4557344E-06	3.6516156E+00	*	92.	1.6382133E-13	3.6516188E+00	*
43.	1.0570801E-06	3.6516166E+00	*	93.	1.1895870E-13	3.6516188E+00	*
44.	7.6759775E-07	3.6516173E+00	*	94.	8.6381747E-14	3.6516188E+00	*
45.	5.5739036E-07	3.6516178E+00	*	95.	6.2726022E-14	3.6516188E+00	*
46.	4.0474847E-07	3.6516182E+00	*	96.	4.5564460E-14	3.6516188E+00	*
47.	2.9390771E-07	3.6516185E+00	*	97.	3.3074956E-14	3.6516188E+00	*
48.	2.1342080E-07	3.6516186E+00	*	98.	2.4017347E-14	3.6516188E+00	*
49.	1.5497531E-07	3.6516187E+00	*	99.	1.7440173E-14	3.6516188E+00	*
50.	1.1253517E-07	3.6516188E+00	*	100.	1.2664165E-14	3.6516188E+00	*

X	E^{-RX}	SUM OF E^{-RX}	*	X	E^{-RX}	SUM OF E^{-RX}	*
0.	1.0000000E+00	1.0000000E+00	*	50.	8.7642482E-08	3.6039559E+00	*
1.	7.2252735E-01	1.7225273E+00	*	51.	6.3324090E-08	3.6039559E+00	*
2.	5.2204577E-01	2.2445730E+00	*	52.	4.5753387E-08	3.6039559E+00	*
3.	3.7719235E-01	2.6217653E+00	*	53.	3.3058074E-08	3.6039559E+00	*
4.	2.7253179E-01	2.8942970E+00	*	54.	2.3885362E-08	3.6039559E+00	*
5.	1.9691167E-01	3.0912086E+00	*	55.	1.7257627E-08	3.6039559E+00	*
6.	1.4227407E-01	3.2334826E+00	*	56.	1.2469252E-08	3.6039559E+00	*
7.	1.0279690E-01	3.3362795E+00	*	57.	9.0093741E-09	3.6039559E+00	*
8.	7.4273557E-02	3.4105530E+00	*	58.	6.5095207E-09	3.6039559E+00	*
9.	5.3664691E-02	3.4642176E+00	*	59.	4.7033067E-09	3.6039559E+00	*
10.	3.8774207E-02	3.5029918E+00	*	60.	3.3982678E-09	3.6039559E+00	*
11.	2.8015425E-02	3.5310072E+00	*	61.	2.4553414E-09	3.6039559E+00	*
12.	2.0241911E-02	3.5512491E+00	*	62.	1.7740513E-09	3.6039559E+00	*
13.	1.4625334E-02	3.5658744E+00	*	63.	1.2818006E-09	3.6039559E+00	*
14.	1.0567204E-02	3.5764416E+00	*	64.	9.2613602E-10	3.6039559E+00	*
15.	7.6350942E-03	3.5840766E+00	*	65.	6.6915860E-10	3.6039559E+00	*
16.	5.5165644E-03	3.5895931E+00	*	66.	4.8348533E-10	3.6039559E+00	*
17.	3.9858686E-03	3.5935789E+00	*	67.	3.4933142E-10	3.6039559E+00	*
18.	2.8799991E-03	3.5964587E+00	*	68.	2.5240150E-10	3.6039559E+00	*
19.	2.0808059E-03	3.5985395E+00	*	69.	1.8236699E-10	3.6039559E+00	*
20.	1.5034391E-03	3.6000429E+00	*	70.	1.3176514E-10	3.6039559E+00	*
21.	1.0862759E-03	3.6011291E+00	*	71.	9.5203919E-11	3.6039559E+00	*
22.	7.8486408E-04	3.6019139E+00	*	72.	6.8787436E-11	3.6039559E+00	*
23.	5.6705766E-04	3.6024809E+00	*	73.	4.9700804E-11	3.6039559E+00	*
24.	4.0973497E-04	3.6028906E+00	*	74.	3.5910190E-11	3.6039559E+00	*
25.	2.9604472E-04	3.6031866E+00	*	75.	2.5946094E-11	3.6039559E+00	*
26.	2.1390041E-04	3.6034005E+00	*	76.	1.8746763E-11	3.6039559E+00	*
27.	1.5454890E-04	3.6035550E+00	*	77.	1.3545049E-11	3.6039559E+00	*
28.	1.1166580E-04	3.6036666E+00	*	78.	9.7866686E-12	3.6039559E+00	*
29.	8.0681600E-05	3.6037472E+00	*	79.	7.0711357E-12	3.6039559E+00	*
30.	5.8294663E-05	3.6038054E+00	*	80.	5.1090890E-12	3.6039559E+00	*
31.	4.2119488E-05	3.6038475E+00	*	81.	3.6914565E-12	3.6039559E+00	*
32.	3.0432482E-05	3.6038779E+00	*	82.	2.6671783E-12	3.6039559E+00	*
33.	2.1988301E-05	3.6038998E+00	*	83.	1.9271093E-12	3.6039559E+00	*
34.	1.5887149E-05	3.6039156E+00	*	84.	1.3923891E-12	3.6039559E+00	*
35.	1.1478499E-05	3.6039270E+00	*	85.	1.0060392E-12	3.6039559E+00	*
36.	8.2938191E-06	3.6039352E+00	*	86.	7.2689089E-13	3.6039559E+00	*
37.	5.9925111E-06	3.6039411E+00	*	87.	5.2519855E-13	3.6039559E+00	*
38.	4.3297532E-06	3.6039454E+00	*	88.	3.7947032E-13	3.6039559E+00	*
39.	3.1283651E-06	3.6039485E+00	*	89.	2.7417768E-13	3.6039559E+00	*
40.	2.2603294E-06	3.6039507E+00	*	90.	1.9810087E-13	3.6039559E+00	*
41.	1.6331498E-06	3.6039523E+00	*	91.	1.4313330E-13	3.6039559E+00	*
42.	1.1799954E-06	3.6039534E+00	*	92.	1.0341772E-13	3.6039559E+00	*
43.	8.5257896E-07	3.6039542E+00	*	93.	7.4722136E-14	3.6039559E+00	*
44.	6.1601762E-07	3.6039548E+00	*	94.	5.3988787E-14	3.6039559E+00	*
45.	4.4508524E-07	3.6039552E+00	*	95.	3.9008376E-14	3.6039559E+00	*
46.	3.2158626E-07	3.6039555E+00	*	96.	2.8184618E-14	3.6039559E+00	*
47.	2.3235487E-07	3.6039557E+00	*	97.	2.0364157E-14	3.6039559E+00	*
48.	1.6786275E-07	3.6039558E+00	*	98.	1.4713661E-14	3.6039559E+00	*
49.	1.2129988E-07	3.6039559E+00	*	99.	1.0631022E-14	3.6039559E+00	*
50.	8.7642482E-08	3.6039559E+00	*	100.	7.6812044E-15	3.6039559E+00	*

X	E^{-RX}	SUM OF E^{-RX}	=	X	E^{-RX}	SUM OF E^{-RX}	*
0.	1.0000000E+00	1.0000000E+00	=	50.	6.8256033E-08	3.5577506E+00	*
1.	7.1892373E-01	1.7189237E+00	=	51.	4.9070882E-08	3.5577506E+00	*
2.	5.1685133E-01	2.2357750E+00	=	52.	3.5278222E-08	3.5577506E+00	*
3.	3.7157669E-01	2.6073516E+00	=	53.	2.5362351E-08	3.5577506E+00	*
4.	2.6713530E-01	2.8744869E+00	=	54.	1.8233596E-08	3.5577506E+00	*
5.	1.9204990E-01	3.0665368E+00	=	55.	1.3108565E-08	3.5577506E+00	*
6.	1.3806923E-01	3.2046060E+00	=	56.	9.4240585E-09	3.5577506E+00	*
7.	9.9261251E-02	3.3038672E+00	=	57.	6.7751793E-09	3.5577506E+00	*
8.	7.1361269E-02	3.3752284E+00	=	58.	4.8708372E-09	3.5577506E+00	*
9.	5.1303310E-02	3.4265317E+00	=	59.	3.5017604E-09	3.5577506E+00	*
10.	3.6883167E-02	3.4634148E+00	=	60.	2.5174987E-09	3.5577506E+00	*
11.	2.6516184E-02	3.4899309E+00	=	61.	1.8098895E-09	3.5577506E+00	*
12.	1.9063114E-02	3.5089940E+00	=	62.	1.3011725E-09	3.5577506E+00	*
13.	1.3704925E-02	3.5226989E+00	=	63.	9.3544384E-10	3.5577506E+00	*
14.	9.8527960E-03	3.5325516E+00	=	64.	6.7251277E-10	3.5577506E+00	*
15.	7.0834089E-03	3.5396350E+00	=	65.	4.8348539E-10	3.5577506E+00	*
16.	5.0924307E-03	3.5447274E+00	=	66.	3.4758912E-10	3.5577506E+00	*
17.	3.6610693E-03	3.5483884E+00	=	67.	2.4989007E-10	3.5577506E+00	*
18.	2.6320296E-03	3.5510204E+00	=	68.	1.7965190E-10	3.5577506E+00	*
19.	1.8922285E-03	3.5529126E+00	=	69.	1.2915601E-10	3.5577506E+00	*
20.	1.3603680E-03	3.5542729E+00	=	70.	9.2853326E-11	3.5577506E+00	*
21.	9.7800086E-04	3.5552509E+00	=	71.	6.6754460E-11	3.5577506E+00	*
22.	7.0310803E-04	3.5559540E+00	=	72.	4.7991365E-11	3.5577506E+00	*
23.	5.0548105E-04	3.5564594E+00	=	73.	3.4502131E-11	3.5577506E+00	*
24.	3.6340232E-04	3.5568228E+00	=	74.	2.4804401E-11	3.5577506E+00	*
25.	2.6125855E-04	3.5570840E+00	=	75.	1.7832472E-11	3.5577506E+00	*
26.	1.8782497E-04	3.5572718E+00	=	76.	1.2820187E-11	3.5577506E+00	*
27.	1.3503183E-04	3.5574068E+00	=	77.	9.2167374E-12	3.5577506E+00	*
28.	9.7077590E-05	3.5575038E+00	=	78.	6.6261312E-12	3.5577506E+00	*
29.	6.9791383E-05	3.5575735E+00	=	79.	4.7636830E-12	3.5577506E+00	*
30.	5.0174681E-05	3.5576236E+00	=	80.	3.4247247E-12	3.5577506E+00	*
31.	3.6071769E-05	3.5576596E+00	=	81.	2.4621159E-12	3.5577506E+00	*
32.	2.5932851E-05	3.5576855E+00	=	82.	1.7700735E-12	3.5577506E+00	*
33.	1.8643742E-05	3.5577041E+00	=	83.	1.2725479E-12	3.5577506E+00	*
34.	1.3403428E-05	3.5577175E+00	=	84.	9.1486488E-13	3.5577506E+00	*
35.	9.6360430E-06	3.5577271E+00	=	85.	6.5771808E-13	3.5577506E+00	*
36.	6.9275800E-06	3.5577340E+00	=	86.	4.7284913E-13	3.5577506E+00	*
37.	4.9804017E-06	3.5577389E+00	=	87.	3.3994246E-13	3.5577506E+00	*
38.	3.5805290E-06	3.5577424E+00	=	88.	2.4439270E-13	3.5577506E+00	*
39.	2.5741272E-06	3.5577449E+00	=	89.	1.7569971E-13	3.5577506E+00	*
40.	1.8506011E-06	3.5577467E+00	=	90.	1.2631469E-13	3.5577506E+00	*
41.	1.3304411E-06	3.5577480E+00	=	91.	9.0810634E-14	3.5577506E+00	*
42.	9.5648569E-07	3.5577489E+00	=	92.	6.5285619E-14	3.5577506E+00	*
43.	6.8764026E-07	3.5577495E+00	=	93.	4.6938597E-14	3.5577506E+00	*
44.	4.9436090E-07	3.5577499E+00	=	94.	3.3743114E-14	3.5577506E+00	*
45.	3.5540778E-07	3.5577502E+00	=	95.	2.4258726E-14	3.5577506E+00	*
46.	2.5551109E-07	3.5577504E+00	=	96.	1.7440173E-14	3.5577506E+00	*
47.	1.8369299E-07	3.5577505E+00	=	97.	1.2538154E-14	3.5577506E+00	*
48.	1.3206125E-07	3.5577506E+00	=	98.	9.0139771E-15	3.5577506E+00	*
49.	9.4941967E-08	3.5577506E+00	=	99.	6.4803621E-15	3.5577506E+00	*
50.	6.8256033E-08	3.5577506E+00	=	100.	4.6588861E-15	3.5577506E+00	*

X	E^{-RX}	SUM OF E^{-RX}		X	E^{-RX}	SUM OF E^{-RX}	
0.	1.0000000E+00	1.0000000E+00	☆	50.	5.3157852E-08	3.5129363E+00	☆
1.	7.1533808E-01	1.7153380E+00		51.	3.8025836E-08	3.5129363E+00	☆
2.	5.1170857E-01	2.2270465E+00		52.	2.7201329E-08	3.5129363E+00	☆
3.	3.6604463E-01	2.5930911E+00		53.	1.9458146E-08	3.5129363E+00	☆
4.	2.6184566E-01	2.8549367E+00		54.	1.3919153E-08	3.5129363E+00	☆
5.	1.8730817E-01	3.0422448E+00		55.	9.9569005E-09	3.5129363E+00	☆
6.	1.3398867E-01	3.1762334E+00		56.	7.1225501E-09	3.5129363E+00	☆
7.	9.5847202E-02	3.2720806E+00		57.	5.0950314E-09	3.5129363E+00	☆
8.	6.8563153E-02	3.3406437E+00		58.	3.6446700E-09	3.5129363E+00	☆
9.	4.9045835E-02	3.3896895E+00		59.	2.6071712E-09	3.5129363E+00	☆
10.	3.5084354E-02	3.4247738E+00		60.	1.8650089E-09	3.5129363E+00	☆
11.	2.5097174E-02	3.4498709E+00		61.	1.3341119E-09	3.5129363E+00	☆
12.	1.7952964E-02	3.4678238E+00		62.	9.5434100E-10	3.5129363E+00	☆
13.	1.2842439E-02	3.4806662E+00		63.	6.8267650E-10	3.5129363E+00	☆
14.	9.1866861E-03	3.4898528E+00		64.	4.8834450E-10	3.5129363E+00	☆
15.	6.5715864E-03	3.4964243E+00		65.	3.4933142E-10	3.5129363E+00	☆
16.	4.7009061E-03	3.5011252E+00		66.	2.4989007E-10	3.5129363E+00	☆
17.	3.3627371E-03	3.5044879E+00		67.	1.7879588E-10	3.5129363E+00	☆
18.	2.4054939E-03	3.5068933E+00		68.	1.2787089E-10	3.5129363E+00	☆
19.	1.7207414E-03	3.5086140E+00		69.	9.1470920E-11	3.5129363E+00	☆
20.	1.2309119E-03	3.5098449E+00		70.	6.5432633E-11	3.5129363E+00	☆
21.	8.8051816E-04	3.5107254E+00		71.	4.6806454E-11	3.5129363E+00	☆
22.	6.2986817E-04	3.5113552E+00		72.	3.3482439E-11	3.5129363E+00	☆
23.	4.5056869E-04	3.5118057E+00		73.	2.3951264E-11	3.5129363E+00	☆
24.	3.2230894E-04	3.5121280E+00		74.	1.7133251E-11	3.5129363E+00	☆
25.	2.3055986E-04	3.5123585E+00		75.	1.2256067E-11	3.5129363E+00	☆
26.	1.6492825E-04	3.5125234E+00		76.	8.7672318E-12	3.5129363E+00	☆
27.	1.1797946E-04	3.5126413E+00		77.	6.2715348E-12	3.5129363E+00	☆
28.	8.4395202E-05	3.5127256E+00		78.	4.4862677E-12	3.5129363E+00	☆
29.	6.0371102E-05	3.5127859E+00		79.	3.2091981E-12	3.5129363E+00	☆
30.	4.3185749E-05	3.5128290E+00		80.	2.2956616E-12	3.5129363E+00	☆
31.	3.0892411E-05	3.5128598E+00		81.	1.6421742E-12	3.5129363E+00	☆
32.	2.2098518E-05	3.5128818E+00		82.	1.1747097E-12	3.5129363E+00	☆
33.	1.5807911E-05	3.5128976E+00		83.	8.4031463E-13	3.5129363E+00	☆
34.	1.1308001E-05	3.5129089E+00		84.	6.0110906E-13	3.5129363E+00	☆
35.	8.0890440E-06	3.5129169E+00		85.	4.2999620E-13	3.5129363E+00	☆
36.	5.7864012E-06	3.5129226E+00		86.	3.0759266E-13	3.5129363E+00	☆
37.	4.1392332E-06	3.5129267E+00		87.	2.2003274E-13	3.5129363E+00	☆
38.	2.9609511E-06	3.5129296E+00		88.	1.5739780E-13	3.5129363E+00	☆
39.	2.1180811E-06	3.5129317E+00		89.	1.1259264E-13	3.5129363E+00	☆
40.	1.5151441E-06	3.5129332E+00		90.	8.0541806E-14	3.5129363E+00	☆
41.	1.0838402E-06	3.5129342E+00		91.	5.7614622E-14	3.5129363E+00	☆
42.	7.7531223E-07	3.5129349E+00		92.	4.1213933E-14	3.5129363E+00	☆
43.	5.5461037E-07	3.5129354E+00		93.	2.9481896E-14	3.5129363E+00	☆
44.	3.9673392E-07	3.5129357E+00		94.	2.1089523E-14	3.5129363E+00	☆
45.	2.8379888E-07	3.5129359E+00		95.	1.5086139E-14	3.5129363E+00	☆
46.	2.0301215E-07	3.5129361E+00		96.	1.0791689E-14	3.5129363E+00	☆
47.	1.4522232E-07	3.5129362E+00		97.	7.7197068E-15	3.5129363E+00	☆
48.	1.0388305E-07	3.5129363E+00		98.	5.5222003E-15	3.5129363E+00	☆
49.	7.4311508E-08	3.5129363E+00		99.	3.9502412E-15	3.5129363E+00	☆
50.	5.3157852E-08	3.5129363E+00		100.	2.8257572E-15	3.5129363E+00	☆

X	E^{-RX}	SUM OF E^{-RX}		X	E^{-RX}	SUM OF E^{-RX}	
0.	1.0000000E+00	1.0000000E+00	☆	50.	4.1399377E-08	3.4694528E+00	☆
1.	7.1177032E-01	1.7117703E+00		51.	2.9466847E-08	3.4694528E+00	☆
2.	5.0661699E-01	2.2183872E+00		52.	2.0973627E-08	3.4694528E+00	☆
3.	3.6059493E-01	2.5789821E+00		53.	1.4922405E-08	3.4694528E+00	☆
4.	2.5666077E-01	2.8356428E+00		54.	1.0625596E-08	3.4694528E+00	☆
5.	1.8268352E-01	3.0183263E+00		55.	7.5629841E-09	3.4694528E+00	☆
6.	1.3002871E-01	3.1483550E+00		56.	5.3831076E-09	3.4694528E+00	☆
7.	9.2550577E-02	3.2409055E+00		57.	3.8315362E-09	3.4694528E+00	☆
8.	6.5874754E-02	3.3067802E+00		58.	2.7271738E-09	3.4694528E+00	☆
9.	4.6887695E-02	3.3536678E+00		59.	1.9411213E-09	3.4694528E+00	☆
10.	3.3373269E-02	3.3870410E+00		60.	1.3816325E-09	3.4694528E+00	☆
11.	2.3754103E-02	3.4107951E+00		61.	9.8340507E-10	3.4694528E+00	☆
12.	1.6907465E-02	3.4277025E+00		62.	6.9995854E-10	3.4694528E+00	☆
13.	1.2034232E-02	3.4397367E+00		63.	4.9820972E-10	3.4694528E+00	☆
14.	8.5656093E-03	3.4483023E+00		64.	3.5461089E-10	3.4694528E+00	☆
15.	6.0967465E-03	3.4543990E+00		65.	2.5240150E-10	3.4694528E+00	☆
16.	4.3394832E-03	3.4587384E+00		66.	1.7965190E-10	3.4694528E+00	☆
17.	3.0887154E-03	3.4618271E+00		67.	1.2787089E-10	3.4694528E+00	☆
18.	2.1984559E-03	3.4640255E+00		68.	9.1014707E-11	3.4694528E+00	☆
19.	1.5647957E-03	3.4655902E+00		69.	6.4781567E-11	3.4694528E+00	☆
20.	1.1137751E-03	3.4667039E+00		70.	4.6109597E-11	3.4694528E+00	☆
21.	7.9275209E-04	3.4674966E+00		71.	3.2819443E-11	3.4694528E+00	☆
22.	5.6425741E-04	3.4680609E+00		72.	2.3359905E-11	3.4694528E+00	☆
23.	4.0162168E-04	3.4684624E+00		73.	1.6626887E-11	3.4694528E+00	☆
24.	2.8586239E-04	3.4687482E+00		74.	1.1834525E-11	3.4694528E+00	☆
25.	2.0346836E-04	3.4689516E+00		75.	8.4234637E-12	3.4694528E+00	☆
26.	1.4482274E-04	3.4690964E+00		76.	5.9955715E-12	3.4694528E+00	☆
27.	1.0308053E-04	3.4691994E+00		77.	4.2674698E-12	3.4694528E+00	☆
28.	7.3369664E-05	3.4692727E+00		78.	3.0374584E-12	3.4694528E+00	☆
29.	5.2222349E-05	3.4693249E+00		79.	2.1619727E-12	3.4694528E+00	☆
30.	3.7170318E-05	3.4693620E+00		80.	1.5382290E-12	3.4694528E+00	☆
31.	2.6456729E-05	3.4693884E+00		81.	1.0952921E-12	3.4694528E+00	☆
32.	1.8831115E-05	3.4694072E+00		82.	7.7959643E-13	3.4694528E+00	☆
33.	1.3403428E-05	3.4694206E+00		83.	5.5489360E-13	3.4694528E+00	☆
34.	9.5401628E-06	3.4694301E+00		84.	3.9495680E-13	3.4694528E+00	☆
35.	6.7904047E-06	3.4694368E+00		85.	2.8111852E-13	3.4694528E+00	☆
36.	4.8332086E-06	3.4694416E+00		86.	2.0009182E-13	3.4694528E+00	☆
37.	3.4401344E-06	3.4694450E+00		87.	1.4241942E-13	3.4694528E+00	☆
38.	2.4485856E-06	3.4694474E+00		88.	1.0136991E-13	3.4694528E+00	☆
39.	1.7428305E-06	3.4694491E+00		89.	7.2152100E-14	3.4694528E+00	☆
40.	1.2404950E-06	3.4694503E+00		90.	5.1355723E-14	3.4694528E+00	☆
41.	8.8294758E-07	3.4694511E+00		91.	3.6553479E-14	3.4694528E+00	☆
42.	6.2845588E-07	3.4694517E+00		92.	2.6017682E-14	3.4694528E+00	☆
43.	4.4731624E-07	3.4694521E+00		93.	1.8518614E-14	3.4694528E+00	☆
44.	3.1838642E-07	3.4694524E+00		94.	1.3180999E-14	3.4694528E+00	☆
45.	2.2661801E-07	3.4694526E+00		95.	9.3818445E-15	3.4694528E+00	☆
46.	1.6129997E-07	3.4694527E+00		96.	6.6777185E-15	3.4694528E+00	☆
47.	1.1480853E-07	3.4694528E+00		97.	4.7530018E-15	3.4694528E+00	☆
48.	8.1717308E-08	3.4694528E+00		98.	3.3830456E-15	3.4694528E+00	☆
49.	5.8163955E-08	3.4694528E+00		99.	2.4070515E-15	3.4694528E+00	☆
50.	4.1399377E-08	3.4694528E+00		100.	1.7139084E-15	3.4694528E+00	☆

TABULATED VALUES OF E   WHEN R = .345

X	E^{-RX}	SUM OF E^{-RX}	*	X	E^{-RX}	SUM OF E^{-RX}	*
0.	1.0000000E+00	1.0000000E+00	*	50.	3.2241867E-08	3.4272412E+00	*
1.	7.0322035E-01	1.7032203E+00	*	51.	2.2834346E-08	3.4272412E+00	*
2.	5.0157600E-01	2.2097663E+00	*	52.	1.6171749E-08	3.4272412E+00	*
3.	3.5522632E-01	2.5650222E+00	*	53.	1.1453141E-08	3.4272412E+00	*
4.	2.5157855E-01	2.8166011E+00	*	54.	8.1113623E-09	3.4272412E+00	*
5.	1.7817305E-01	2.9947741E+00	*	55.	5.7446319E-09	3.4272412E+00	*
6.	1.2618578E-01	3.1209598E+00	*	56.	4.0684652E-09	3.4272412E+00	*
7.	8.9367338E-02	3.2103271E+00	*	57.	2.8813698E-09	3.4272412E+00	*
8.	6.3291768E-02	3.2732418E+00	*	58.	2.0403447E-09	3.4272412E+00	*
9.	4.4924510E-02	3.3184433E+00	*	59.	1.4452261E-09	3.4272412E+00	*
10.	3.1745636E-02	3.3501169E+00	*	60.	1.0235325E-09	3.4272412E+00	*
11.	2.2482905E-02	3.3726718E+00	*	61.	7.2489086E-10	3.4272412E+00	*
12.	1.5922851E-02	3.3885946E+00	*	62.	5.1332466E-10	3.4272412E+00	*
13.	1.1276837E-02	3.3995714E+00	*	63.	3.6354791E-10	3.4272412E+00	*
14.	7.9865212E-03	3.4075796E+00	*	64.	2.5750035E-10	3.4272412E+00	*
15.	5.6562169E-03	3.4135141E+00	*	65.	1.8236699E-10	3.4272412E+00	*
16.	4.0054479E-03	3.4175146E+00	*	66.	1.2915601E-10	3.4272412E+00	*
17.	2.8370230E-03	3.4203569E+00	*	67.	9.1470920E-11	3.4272412E+00	*
18.	2.0092374E-03	3.4223661E+00	*	68.	6.4761547E-11	3.4272412E+00	*
19.	1.4229628E-03	3.4237893E+00	*	69.	4.5879624E-11	3.4272412E+00	*
20.	1.0077854E-03	3.4247967E+00	*	70.	3.2492484E-11	3.4272412E+00	*
21.	7.1373415E-04	3.4255104E+00	*	71.	2.3112121E-11	3.4272412E+00	*
22.	5.0548105E-04	3.4260158E+00	*	72.	1.6297653E-11	3.4272412E+00	*
23.	3.5796197E-04	3.4263737E+00	*	73.	1.1542320E-11	3.4272412E+00	*
24.	2.5353719E-04	3.4266272E+00	*	74.	8.1745127E-12	3.4272412E+00	*
25.	1.7956020E-04	3.4268067E+00	*	75.	5.7893563E-12	3.4272412E+00	*
26.	1.2716819E-04	3.4269339E+00	*	76.	4.1001399E-12	3.4272412E+00	*
27.	9.0063101E-05	3.4270235E+00	*	77.	2.9038025E-12	3.4272412E+00	*
28.	6.3784521E-05	3.4270875E+00	*	78.	2.0565320E-12	3.4272412E+00	*
29.	4.5173446E-05	3.4271326E+00	*	79.	1.4564778E-12	3.4272412E+00	*
30.	3.1992789E-05	3.4271645E+00	*	80.	1.0315072E-12	3.4272412E+00	*
31.	2.2657944E-05	3.4271871E+00	*	81.	7.3055445E-13	3.4272412E+00	*
32.	1.6046617E-05	3.4272031E+00	*	82.	5.1737936E-13	3.4272412E+00	*
33.	1.1364682E-05	3.4272144E+00	*	83.	3.6641859E-13	3.4272412E+00	*
34.	8.0486997E-06	3.4272224E+00	*	84.	2.5950510E-13	3.4272412E+00	*
35.	5.7002529E-06	3.4272281E+00	*	85.	1.8378689E-13	3.4272412E+00	*
36.	4.0370351E-06	3.4272321E+00	*	86.	1.3016155E-13	3.4272412E+00	*
37.	2.8591104E-06	3.4272349E+00	*	87.	5.2193060E-14	3.4272412E+00	*
38.	2.0248802E-06	3.4272369E+00	*	88.	6.5284619E-14	3.4272412E+00	*
39.	1.4340613E-06	3.4272383E+00	*	89.	4.6238617E-14	3.4272412E+00	*
40.	1.0156314E-06	3.4272393E+00	*	90.	3.2745855E-14	3.4272412E+00	*
41.	7.1929087E-07	3.4272400E+00	*	91.	2.3191281E-14	3.4272412E+00	*
42.	5.0941643E-07	3.4272405E+00	*	92.	1.6424537E-14	3.4272412E+00	*
43.	3.6077909E-07	3.4272408E+00	*	93.	1.1632191E-14	3.4272412E+00	*
44.	2.5551109E-07	3.4272410E+00	*	94.	8.2361548E-15	3.4272412E+00	*
45.	1.9095815E-07	3.4272411E+00	*	95.	5.8344289E-15	3.4272412E+00	*
46.	1.2815275E-07	3.4272412E+00	*	96.	4.1320613E-15	3.4272412E+00	*
47.	9.0764281E-08	3.4272412E+00	*	97.	2.9264090E-15	3.4272412E+00	*
48.	6.4281111E-08	3.4272412E+00	*	98.	2.0725430E-15	3.4272412E+00	*
49.	4.5525161E-08	3.4272412E+00	*	99.	1.4679171E-15	3.4272412E+00	*
50.	3.2241867E-08	3.4272412E+00	*	100.	1.0363380E-15	3.4272412E+00	*

TABULATED VALUES OF E   WHEN R = .350

X	E^{-RX}	SUM OF E^{-RX}	*	X	E^{-RX}	SUM OF E^{-RX}	*
0.	1.0000000E+00	1.0000000E+00	*	50.	2.5109091E-08	3.3862475E+00	*
1.	7.0468808E-01	1.7046880E+00	*	51.	1.7694711E-08	3.3862475E+00	*
2.	4.9458530E-01	2.2012733E+00	*	52.	1.2469252E-08	3.3862475E+00	*
3.	3.4993774E-01	2.5512110E+00	*	53.	8.7860339E-09	3.3862475E+00	*
4.	2.4659696E-01	2.7978079E+00	*	54.	6.1920476E-09	3.3862475E+00	*
5.	1.7377394E-01	2.9715818E+00	*	55.	4.3634622E-09	3.3862475E+00	*
6.	1.2245642E-01	3.0940382E+00	*	56.	3.0748799E-09	3.3862475E+00	*
7.	8.6293556E-02	3.1803317E+00	*	57.	2.1668312E-09	3.3862475E+00	*
8.	6.0810042E-02	3.2411417E+00	*	58.	1.5269401E-09	3.3862475E+00	*
9.	4.2852126E-02	3.2839938E+00	*	59.	1.0760165E-09	3.3862475E+00	*
10.	3.0197353E-02	3.3141911E+00	*	60.	7.5825604E-10	3.3862475E+00	*
11.	2.1279736E-02	3.3354707E+00	*	61.	5.3433400E-10	3.3862475E+00	*
12.	1.4995576E-02	3.3504663E+00	*	62.	3.7653890E-10	3.3862475E+00	*
13.	1.0567204E-02	3.3610335E+00	*	63.	2.6534241E-10	3.3862475E+00	*
14.	7.4465830E-03	3.3684800E+00	*	64.	1.8698363E-10	3.3862475E+00	*
15.	5.2475183E-03	3.3737275E+00	*	65.	1.3176514E-10	3.3862475E+00	*
16.	3.6978637E-03	3.3774253E+00	*	66.	9.2853326E-11	3.3862475E+00	*
17.	2.6058405E-03	3.3800311E+00	*	67.	6.5436233E-11	3.3862475E+00	*
18.	1.8363047E-03	3.3818674E+00	*	68.	4.6109597E-11	3.3862475E+00	*
19.	1.2940221E-03	3.3831614E+00	*	69.	3.2492884E-11	3.3862475E+00	*
20.	9.1188194E-04	3.3840732E+00	*	70.	2.2897348E-11	3.3862475E+00	*
21.	6.4259235E-04	3.3847157E+00	*	71.	1.6135488E-11	3.3862475E+00	*
22.	4.5282718E-04	3.3851685E+00	*	72.	1.1370488E-11	3.3862475E+00	*
23.	3.1910192E-04	3.3854876E+00	*	73.	8.0126465E-12	3.3862475E+00	*
24.	2.2486732E-04	3.3857124E+00	*	74.	5.6464165E-12	3.3862475E+00	*
25.	1.5846132E-04	3.3858709E+00	*	75.	3.9784625E-12	3.3862475E+00	*
26.	1.1166580E-04	3.3859824E+00	*	76.	2.8039275E-12	3.3862475E+00	*
27.	7.8689565E-05	3.3860610E+00	*	77.	1.9758943E-12	3.3862475E+00	*
28.	5.5451599E-05	3.3861164E+00	*	78.	1.3923691E-12	3.3862475E+00	*
29.	3.9076081E-05	3.3861554E+00	*	79.	9.8120007E-13	3.3862475E+00	*
30.	2.7536449E-05	3.3861829E+00	*	80.	6.9144000E-13	3.3862475E+00	*
31.	1.9404607E-05	3.3862023E+00	*	81.	4.8724954E-13	3.3862475E+00	*
32.	1.3674196E-05	3.3862159E+00	*	82.	3.4335846E-13	3.3862475E+00	*
33.	9.6369430E-06	3.3862255E+00	*	83.	2.4196098E-13	3.3862475E+00	*
34.	6.7904047E-06	3.3862327E+00	*	84.	1.7051730E-13	3.3862475E+00	*
35.	4.7851173E-06	3.3862365E+00	*	85.	1.2015425E-13	3.3862475E+00	*
36.	3.3720152E-06	3.3862402E+00	*	86.	8.4651273E-14	3.3862475E+00	*
37.	2.3762189E-06	3.3862425E+00	*	87.	5.9666739E-14	3.3862475E+00	*
38.	1.6744932E-06	3.3862441E+00	*	88.	4.2045105E-14	3.3862475E+00	*
39.	1.1799994E-06	3.3862452E+00	*	89.	2.9626674E-14	3.3862475E+00	*
40.	8.3152871E-07	3.3862460E+00	*	90.	2.0879679E-14	3.3862475E+00	*
41.	5.8596292E-07	3.3862465E+00	*	91.	1.4713661E-14	3.3862475E+00	*
42.	4.1292404E-07	3.3862469E+00	*	92.	1.0369545E-14	3.3862475E+00	*
43.	2.9099320E-07	3.3862471E+00	*	93.	7.3065870E-15	3.3862475E+00	*
44.	2.0505245E-07	3.3862473E+00	*	94.	5.1496565E-15	3.3862475E+00	*
45.	1.4449802E-07	3.3862474E+00	*	95.	3.6283440E-15	3.3862475E+00	*
46.	1.0182603E-07	3.3862475E+00	*	96.	2.5565090E-15	3.3862475E+00	*
47.	7.1755955E-08	3.3862475E+00	*	97.	1.8017923E-15	3.3862475E+00	*
48.	5.0565313E-08	3.3862475E+00	*	98.	1.2694545E-15	3.3862475E+00	*
49.	3.5632274E-08	3.3862475E+00	*	99.	8.9473865E-16	3.3862475E+00	*
50.	2.5109091E-08	3.3862475E+00	*	100.	6.3051167E-16	3.3862475E+00	*

TABULATED VALUES OF E^{-RX} WHEN R = .355

X	E^{-RX}	SUM OF E^{-RX}	☆	X	E^{-RX}	SUM OF E^{-RX}	☆
0.	1.0000000E+00	1.0000000E+00	☆	50.	1.9555681E-08	3.3464204E+00	☆
1.	7.0117344E-01	1.7011734E+00	☆	51.	1.3711924E-08	3.3464204E+00	☆
2.	4.9164419E-01	2.1928175E+00	☆	52.	9.6144371E-09	3.3464204E+00	☆
3.	3.4472785E-01	2.5375453E+00	☆	53.	6.7413879E-09	3.3464204E+00	☆
4.	2.4171401E-01	2.7792593E+00	☆	54.	4.7268822E-09	3.3464204E+00	☆
5.	1.6948344E-01	2.9487427E+00	☆	55.	3.3143642E-09	3.3464204E+00	☆
6.	1.1883729E-01	3.0675799E+00	☆	56.	2.3239442E-09	3.3464204E+00	☆
7.	8.3325554E-02	3.1509054E+00	☆	57.	1.6294879E-09	3.3464204E+00	☆
8.	5.8425665E-02	3.2093310E+00	☆	58.	1.1425536E-09	3.3464204E+00	☆
9.	4.0966525E-02	3.2502975E+00	☆	59.	8.0112830E-10	3.3464204E+00	☆
10.	2.8724639E-02	3.2790221E+00	☆	60.	5.6172989E-10	3.3464204E+00	☆
11.	2.0140954E-02	3.2991630E+00	☆	61.	3.9387008E-10	3.3464204E+00	☆
12.	1.4122302E-02	3.3132853E+00	☆	62.	2.7617124E-10	3.3464204E+00	☆
13.	9.9021834E-03	3.3231874E+00	☆	63.	1.9364394E-10	3.3464204E+00	☆
14.	6.9431480E-03	3.3301305E+00	☆	64.	1.3577798E-10	3.3464204E+00	☆
15.	4.8683510E-03	3.3349988E+00	☆	65.	9.5203919E-11	3.3464204E+00	☆
16.	3.4135584E-03	3.3384123E+00	☆	66.	6.6754460E-11	3.3464204E+00	☆
17.	2.3934965E-03	3.3408057E+00	☆	67.	4.6806454E-11	3.3464204E+00	☆
18.	1.6782561E-03	3.3424839E+00	☆	68.	3.2819443E-11	3.3464204E+00	☆
19.	1.1767486E-03	3.3436606E+00	☆	69.	2.3012121E-11	3.3464204E+00	☆
20.	8.2510492E-04	3.3444857E+00	☆	70.	1.6135488E-11	3.3464204E+00	☆
21.	5.7854165E-04	3.3450642E+00	☆	71.	1.1313776E-11	3.3464204E+00	☆
22.	4.0565804E-04	3.3454698E+00	☆	72.	7.9329194E-12	3.3464204E+00	☆
23.	2.8443664E-04	3.3457542E+00	☆	73.	5.5623524E-12	3.3464204E+00	☆
24.	1.9943942E-04	3.3459536E+00	☆	74.	3.9001737E-12	3.3464204E+00	☆
25.	1.3984162E-04	3.3460934E+00	☆	75.	2.7346982E-12	3.3464204E+00	☆
26.	9.8053236E-05	3.3461914E+00	☆	76.	1.9174978E-12	3.3464204E+00	☆
27.	6.8752325E-05	3.3462601E+00	☆	77.	1.3444985E-12	3.3464204E+00	☆
28.	4.8207304E-05	3.3463083E+00	☆	78.	9.4272667E-13	3.3464204E+00	☆
29.	3.3801681E-05	3.3463421E+00	☆	79.	6.6101490E-13	3.3464204E+00	☆
30.	2.3700841E-05	3.3463658E+00	☆	80.	4.6348609E-13	3.3464204E+00	☆
31.	1.6618400E-05	3.3463824E+00	☆	81.	3.2498414E-13	3.3464204E+00	☆
32.	1.1652381E-05	3.3463940E+00	☆	82.	2.2787025E-13	3.3464204E+00	☆
33.	8.1703402E-06	3.3464021E+00	☆	83.	1.5977656E-13	3.3464204E+00	☆
34.	5.7288256E-06	3.3464078E+00	☆	84.	1.1203108E-13	3.3464204E+00	☆
35.	4.0169003E-06	3.3464118E+00	☆	85.	7.8553222E-14	3.3464204E+00	☆
36.	2.8165438E-06	3.3464146E+00	☆	86.	5.5079433E-14	3.3464204E+00	☆
37.	1.9748857E-06	3.3464165E+00	☆	87.	3.8620236E-14	3.3464204E+00	☆
38.	1.3847374E-06	3.3464178E+00	☆	88.	2.7079483E-14	3.3464204E+00	☆
39.	9.7094112E-07	3.3464187E+00	☆	89.	1.8987415E-14	3.3464204E+00	☆
40.	6.8079813E-07	3.3464193E+00	☆	90.	1.3313471E-14	3.3464204E+00	☆
41.	4.7735757E-07	3.3464197E+00	☆	91.	9.3350524E-15	3.3464204E+00	☆
42.	3.3471005E-07	3.3464200E+00	☆	92.	6.5454906E-15	3.3464204E+00	☆
43.	2.3469007E-07	3.3464202E+00	☆	93.	4.5895243E-15	3.3464204E+00	☆
44.	1.6455845E-07	3.3464203E+00	☆	94.	3.2180525E-15	3.3464204E+00	☆
45.	1.1538401E-07	3.3464204E+00	☆	95.	2.2564130E-15	3.3464204E+00	☆
46.	8.0904207E-08	3.3464204E+00	☆	96.	1.5821368E-15	3.3464204E+00	☆
47.	5.6727881E-08	3.3464204E+00	☆	97.	1.1093523E-15	3.3464204E+00	☆
48.	3.9776084E-08	3.3464204E+00	☆	98.	7.7784842E-16	3.3464204E+00	☆
49.	2.7889934E-08	3.3464204E+00	☆	99.	5.4540665E-16	3.3464204E+00	☆
50.	1.9555681E-08	3.3464204E+00	☆	100.	3.8242466E-16	3.3464204E+00	☆

TABULATED VALUES OF E^{-RX} WHEN R = .360

X	E^{-RX}	SUM OF E^{-RX}	☆	X	E^{-RX}	SUM OF E^{-RX}	☆
0.	1.0000000E+00	1.0000000E+00	☆	50.	1.5229979E-08	3.307710E+00	☆
1.	6.9767632E-01	1.6976763E+00	☆	51.	1.0625596E-08	3.307710E+00	☆
2.	4.8675225E-01	2.1844285E+00	☆	52.	7.4132269E-09	3.307710E+00	☆
3.	3.3959552E-01	2.5240240E+00	☆	53.	5.1720329E-09	3.307710E+00	☆
4.	2.3692775E-01	2.7609517E+00	☆	54.	3.6084049E-09	3.307710E+00	☆
5.	1.6529888E-01	2.9262505E+00	☆	55.	2.5174987E-09	3.307710E+00	☆
6.	1.1532512E-01	3.0415756E+00	☆	56.	1.7563992E-09	3.307710E+00	☆
7.	8.0459606E-02	3.1220352E+00	☆	57.	1.2253981E-09	3.307710E+00	☆
8.	5.6134762E-02	3.1781699E+00	☆	58.	8.5493129E-10	3.307710E+00	☆
9.	3.9163895E-02	3.2173337E+00	☆	59.	5.9646532E-10	3.307710E+00	☆
10.	2.7323722E-02	3.2446574E+00	☆	60.	4.1613973E-10	3.307710E+00	☆
11.	1.9063114E-02	3.2637205E+00	☆	61.	2.9033084E-10	3.307710E+00	☆
12.	1.3299883E-02	3.2770203E+00	☆	62.	2.0255695E-10	3.307710E+00	☆
13.	9.2790138E-03	3.2862993E+00	☆	63.	1.4131919E-10	3.307710E+00	☆
14.	6.4737483E-03	3.2927730E+00	☆	64.	9.8590555E-11	3.307710E+00	☆
15.	4.5165809E-03	3.2972895E+00	☆	65.	6.8787436E-11	3.307710E+00	☆
16.	3.1511115E-03	3.3004406E+00	☆	66.	4.7991365E-11	3.307710E+00	☆
17.	2.1984559E-03	3.3026390E+00	☆	67.	3.3482439E-11	3.307710E+00	☆
18.	1.5338106E-03	3.3041728E+00	☆	68.	2.3359905E-11	3.307710E+00	☆
19.	1.0701033E-03	3.3052429E+00	☆	69.	1.6297653E-11	3.307710E+00	☆
20.	7.4658580E-04	3.3059894E+00	☆	70.	1.1370486E-11	3.307710E+00	☆
21.	5.2087524E-04	3.3065102E+00	☆	71.	7.9329194E-12	3.307710E+00	☆
22.	3.6340232E-04	3.3068736E+00	☆	72.	5.5346100E-12	3.307710E+00	☆
23.	2.5353719E-04	3.3071271E+00	☆	73.	3.8613664E-12	3.307710E+00	☆
24.	1.7688690E-04	3.3073039E+00	☆	74.	2.6939839E-12	3.307710E+00	☆
25.	1.2340980E-04	3.3074273E+00	☆	75.	1.8795288E-12	3.307710E+00	☆
26.	8.6100098E-05	3.3075134E+00	☆	76.	1.3113027E-12	3.307710E+00	☆
27.	6.0070000E-05	3.3075734E+00	☆	77.	9.1486488E-13	3.307710E+00	☆
28.	4.1909417E-05	3.3076153E+00	☆	78.	6.3827957E-13	3.307710E+00	☆
29.	2.9239208E-05	3.3076445E+00	☆	79.	4.4531254E-13	3.307710E+00	☆
30.	2.0399503E-05	3.3076649E+00	☆	80.	3.1068402E-13	3.307710E+00	☆
31.	1.4232250E-05	3.3076790E+00	☆	81.	2.1675688E-13	3.307710E+00	☆
32.	9.9295042E-06	3.3076889E+00	☆	82.	1.5122614E-13	3.307710E+00	☆
33.	6.9275802E-06	3.3076958E+00	☆	83.	1.0550690E-13	3.307710E+00	☆
34.	4.8332086E-06	3.3077006E+00	☆	84.	7.3609669E-14	3.307710E+00	☆
35.	3.3720152E-06	3.3077039E+00	☆	85.	5.1355723E-14	3.307710E+00	☆
36.	2.3525751E-06	3.3077062E+00	☆	86.	3.5829672E-14	3.307710E+00	☆
37.	1.6413360E-06	3.3077078E+00	☆	87.	2.4997514E-14	3.307710E+00	☆
38.	1.1451212E-06	3.3077089E+00	☆	88.	1.7440173E-14	3.307710E+00	☆
39.	7.9892400E-07	3.3077096E+00	☆	89.	1.2167596E-14	3.307710E+00	☆
40.	5.5739036E-07	3.3077101E+00	☆	90.	8.4890440E-15	3.307710E+00	☆
41.	3.8887806E-07	3.3077104E+00	☆	91.	5.9226050E-15	3.307710E+00	☆
42.	2.7131101E-07	3.3077106E+00	☆	92.	4.1320613E-15	3.307710E+00	☆
43.	1.8928727E-07	3.3077107E+00	☆	93.	2.8828413E-15	3.307710E+00	☆
44.	1.3206125E-07	3.3077108E+00	☆	94.	2.0112901E-15	3.307710E+00	☆
45.	9.2136008E-08	3.3077108E+00	☆	95.	1.4032295E-15	3.307710E+00	☆
46.	6.4281111E-08	3.3077108E+00	☆	96.	9.7900002E-16	3.307710E+00	☆
47.	4.4847409E-08	3.3077108E+00	☆	97.	6.8302514E-16	3.307710E+00	☆
48.	3.1288976E-08	3.3077108E+00	☆	98.	4.7653047E-16	3.307710E+00	☆
49.	2.1829577E-08	3.3077108E+00	☆	99.	3.3246402E-16	3.307710E+00	☆
50.	1.5229979E-08	3.3077108E+00	☆	100.	2.3195228E-16	3.307710E+00	☆

X	E	SUM OF E		X	E	SUM OF E	
0.	1.0000000E+00	1.0000000E+00		50.	1.1161123E-15	3.2700724E+00	
1.	6.9419666E-01	1.6941966E+00		51.	5.2320696E-16	3.2700724E+00	
2.	6.3160865E-01	2.1761055E+00		52.	5.7150936E-16	3.2700724E+00	
3.	9.3453965E-01	2.5104451E+00		53.	3.9660144E-16	3.2700724E+00	
4.	2.3223627E-01	2.7426513E+00		54.	2.7545623E-16	3.2700724E+00	
5.	1.6121744E-01	2.9043654E+00		55.	1.9127218E-16	3.2700724E+00	
6.	1.1191674E-01	3.0162815E+00		56.	1.3274505E-16	3.2700724E+00	
7.	7.7692231E-02	3.0939707E+00		57.	9.2151690E-10	3.2700724E+00	
8.	5.3923687E-02	3.1476414E+00		58.	6.3971304E-10	3.2700724E+00	
9.	3.7440585E-02	3.1850815E+00		59.	4.4413727E-10	3.2700724E+00	
10.	2.5991128E-02	3.2110730E+00		60.	3.0828390E-10	3.2700724E+00	
11.	1.8042964E-02	3.2291159E+00		61.	2.1410965E-10	3.2700724E+00	
12.	1.2525352E-02	3.2416412E+00		62.	1.4856479E-10	3.2700724E+00	
13.	8.6950619E-03	3.2503362E+00		63.	1.0313317E-10	3.2700724E+00	
14.	6.0360829E-03	3.2563722E+00		64.	7.1604704E-11	3.2700724E+00	
15.	4.1902275E-03	3.2605624E+00		65.	4.9700834E-11	3.2700724E+00	
16.	2.9088426E-03	3.2634712E+00		66.	3.4507131E-11	3.2700724E+00	
17.	2.0193088E-03	3.2654905E+00		67.	2.3951266E-11	3.2700724E+00	
18.	1.4017974E-03	3.2668922E+00		68.	1.6626687E-11	3.2700724E+00	
19.	9.7312306E-04	3.2678653E+00		69.	1.1543329E-11	3.2700724E+00	
20.	6.7553477E-04	3.2685408E+00		70.	8.0126665E-12	3.2700724E+00	
21.	4.6895675E-04	3.2690097E+00		71.	5.5623524E-12	3.2700724E+00	
22.	3.2554870E-04	3.2693352E+00		72.	3.8613662E-12	3.2700724E+00	
23.	2.2599467E-04	3.2695611E+00		73.	2.6805476E-12	3.2700724E+00	
24.	1.5688460E-04	3.2697179E+00		74.	1.8608271E-12	3.2700724E+00	
25.	1.0590876E-04	3.2698286E+00		75.	1.2917630E-12	3.2700724E+00	
26.	7.5604103E-05	3.2699024E+00		76.	8.9676535E-13	3.2700724E+00	
27.	5.2474115E-05	3.2699546E+00		77.	6.2252030E-13	3.2700724E+00	
28.	3.6434297E-05	3.2699912E+00		78.	4.3215157E-13	3.2700724E+00	
29.	2.5292540E-05	3.2700164E+00		79.	2.9999817E-13	3.2700724E+00	
30.	1.7558015E-05	3.2700339E+00		80.	2.0825772E-13	3.2700724E+00	
31.	1.2188715E-05	3.2700460E+00		81.	1.4457121E-13	3.2700724E+00	
32.	8.4613856E-06	3.2700545E+00		82.	1.0034127E-13	3.2700724E+00	
33.	5.8738515E-06	3.2700602E+00		83.	6.9670459E-14	3.2700724E+00	
34.	4.0776040E-06	3.2700642E+00		84.	4.8364909E-14	3.2700724E+00	
35.	2.8306618E-06	3.2700670E+00		85.	3.3574820E-14	3.2700724E+00	
36.	1.9650309E-06	3.2700689E+00		86.	2.3307527E-14	3.2700724E+00	
37.	1.3641213E-06	3.2700702E+00		87.	1.6120075E-14	3.2700724E+00	
38.	9.4689350E-07	3.2700711E+00		88.	1.1252107E-14	3.2700724E+00	
39.	6.5732236E-07	3.2700717E+00		89.	7.7972912E-15	3.2700724E+00	
40.	4.5635263E-07	3.2700721E+00		90.	5.4128534E-15	3.2700724E+00	
41.	3.1679847E-07	3.2700724E+00		91.	3.7575476E-15	3.2700724E+00	
42.	2.1992043E-07	3.2700726E+00		92.	2.6075027E-15	3.2700724E+00	
43.	1.5266603E-07	3.2700726E+00		93.	1.8109138E-15	3.2700724E+00	
44.	1.0598163E-07	3.2700727E+00		94.	1.2570034E-15	3.2700724E+00	
45.	7.3572096E-08	3.2700728E+00		95.	8.7264764E-16	3.2700724E+00	
46.	5.1073655E-08	3.2700728E+00		96.	6.0578665E-16	3.2700724E+00	
47.	3.5455054E-08	3.2700728E+00		97.	4.2155664E-16	3.2700724E+00	
48.	2.4612706E-08	3.2700728E+00		98.	2.6143514E-16	3.2700724E+00	
49.	1.7081009E-08	3.2700728E+00		99.	2.0266039E-16	3.2700724E+00	
50.	1.1961120E-08	3.2700728E+00		100.	1.4060617E-16	3.2700724E+00	

X	E	SUM OF E		X	E	SUM OF E	
0.	1.0000000E+00	1.0000000E+00		50.	6.2374966E-09	3.2334637E+00	
1.	6.9073432E-01	1.6907343E+00		51.	6.3816235E-09	3.2334637E+00	
2.	4.7711391E-01	2.1678452E+00		52.	4.4073157E-09	3.2334637E+00	
3.	3.2855806E-01	2.4974071E+00		53.	3.0442603E-09	3.2334637E+00	
4.	2.2763766E-01	2.7250447E+00		54.	2.1027916E-09	3.2334637E+00	
5.	1.5723716E-01	2.8822818E+00		55.	1.4524704E-09	3.2334637E+00	
6.	1.0680910E-01	2.9904905E+00		56.	1.0032711E-09	3.2334637E+00	
7.	7.5020040E-02	3.0659109E+00		57.	6.9290364E-10	3.2334637E+00	
8.	5.1818917E-02	3.1177290E+00		58.	4.7867435E-10	3.2334637E+00	
9.	3.5793305E-02	3.1535229E+00		59.	3.3053701E-10	3.2334637E+00	
10.	2.4725260E-02	3.1782466E+00		60.	2.2837233E-10	3.2334637E+00	
11.	1.7077388E-02	3.1953237E+00		61.	1.5775151E-10	3.2334637E+00	
12.	1.1795937E-02	3.2071196E+00		62.	1.0904435E-10	3.2334637E+00	
13.	8.1478590E-03	3.2152674E+00		63.	7.5245663E-11	3.2334637E+00	
14.	5.6280063E-03	3.2209954E+00		64.	5.1984425E-11	3.2334637E+00	
15.	3.8874572E-03	3.2247828E+00		65.	3.5910130E-11	3.2334637E+00	
16.	2.6852001E-03	3.2274600E+00		66.	2.4804401E-11	3.2334637E+00	
17.	1.8547599E-03	3.2295227E+00		67.	1.7133251E-11	3.2334637E+00	
18.	1.2811463E-03	3.2308038E+00		68.	1.1534255E-11	3.2334637E+00	
19.	8.8493177E-04	3.2316887E+00		69.	8.1745127E-12	3.2334637E+00	
20.	6.1112526E-04	3.2320999E+00		70.	5.6446144E-12	3.2334637E+00	
21.	4.2221326E-04	3.2325221E+00		71.	3.9001737E-12	3.2334637E+00	
22.	2.9163719E-04	3.2328137E+00		72.	2.6938630E-12	3.2334637E+00	
23.	2.0144382E-04	3.2330151E+00		73.	1.8608271E-12	3.2334637E+00	
24.	1.3914416E-04	3.2331542E+00		74.	1.2853372E-12	3.2334637E+00	
25.	9.6111651E-05	3.2332503E+00		75.	8.8752654E-13	3.2334637E+00	
26.	6.6387617E-05	3.2333166E+00		76.	6.1325227E-13	3.2334637E+00	
27.	4.5856206E-05	3.2333624E+00		77.	4.2350430E-13	3.2334637E+00	
28.	3.1674456E-05	3.2333940E+00		78.	2.9259110E-13	3.2334637E+00	
29.	2.1878634E-05	3.2334158E+00		79.	2.0210271E-13	3.2334637E+00	
30.	1.5112323E-05	3.2334309E+00		80.	1.3959953E-13	3.2334637E+00	
31.	1.0438600E-05	3.2334413E+00		81.	9.6426050E-14	3.2334637E+00	
32.	7.2102069E-06	3.2334485E+00		82.	6.6604783E-14	3.2334637E+00	
33.	4.9804017E-06	3.2334534E+00		83.	4.6006210E-14	3.2334637E+00	
34.	3.4401344E-06	3.2334568E+00		84.	3.1778064E-14	3.2334637E+00	
35.	2.3762189E-06	3.2334591E+00		85.	2.1950203E-14	3.2334637E+00	
36.	1.6413360E-06	3.2334607E+00		86.	1.5161753E-14	3.2334637E+00	
37.	1.1337271E-06	3.2334618E+00		87.	1.0472747E-14	3.2334637E+00	
38.	7.8317425E-07	3.2334625E+00		88.	7.2336618E-15	3.2334637E+00	
39.	5.4091699E-07	3.2334630E+00		89.	4.9966835E-15	3.2334637E+00	
40.	3.7362903E-07	3.2334633E+00		90.	3.4513677E-15	3.2334637E+00	
41.	2.5807902E-07	3.2334635E+00		91.	2.3838019E-15	3.2334637E+00	
42.	1.7824404E-07	3.2334636E+00		92.	1.6647051E-15	3.2334637E+00	
43.	1.2313309E-07	3.2334637E+00		93.	1.1374357E-15	3.2334637E+00	
44.	8.5052255E-08	3.2334637E+00		94.	7.8556392E-16	3.2334637E+00	
45.	5.8749512E-08	3.2334637E+00		95.	5.4268642E-16	3.2334637E+00	
46.	4.0579614E-08	3.2334637E+00		96.	5.7495214E-16	3.2334637E+00	
47.	2.8029732E-08	3.2334637E+00		97.	2.5857324E-16	3.2334637E+00	
48.	1.9361098E-08	3.2334637E+00		98.	1.7847179E-16	3.2334637E+00	
49.	1.3373375E-08	3.2334637E+00		99.	1.2355584E-16	3.2334637E+00	
50.	9.2374486E-09	3.2334637E+00		100.	8.5330475E-17	3.2334637E+00	

X	E^{-RX}	SUM OF E^{-RX}	*	X	E^{-RX}	SUM OF E^{-RX}	*
0.	1.0000000E+00	1.0000000E+00	*	50.	7.1941330E-09	3.1978413E+00	*
1.	6.8728927E-01	1.6872892E+00	*	51.	4.9444504E-09	3.1978413E+00	*
2.	4.7236655E-01	2.1596557E+00	*	52.	3.3982678E-09	3.1978413E+00	*
3.	3.2465246E-01	2.4843081E+00	*	53.	2.3355930E-09	3.1978413E+00	*
4.	2.2313015E-01	2.7074382E+00	*	54.	1.6052280E-09	3.1978413E+00	*
5.	1.5335496E-01	2.8607931E+00	*	55.	1.1032560E-09	3.1978413E+00	*
6.	1.0539922E-01	2.9661923E+00	*	56.	7.5825604E-10	3.1978413E+00	*
7.	7.2439756E-02	3.0386320E+00	*	57.	5.2114124E-10	3.1978413E+00	*
8.	4.9787068E-02	3.0884190E+00	*	58.	3.5817479E-10	3.1978413E+00	*
9.	3.4218118E-02	3.1226371E+00	*	59.	2.4616969E-10	3.1978413E+00	*
10.	2.3517745E-02	3.1461548E+00	*	60.	1.6918979E-10	3.1978413E+00	*
11.	1.6163494E-02	3.1623182E+00	*	61.	1.1628233E-10	3.1978413E+00	*
12.	1.1108996E-02	3.1734271E+00	*	62.	7.9919598E-11	3.1978413E+00	*
13.	7.6350942E-03	3.1810621E+00	*	63.	5.4927883E-11	3.1978413E+00	*
14.	5.2475183E-03	3.1863096E+00	*	64.	3.7751345E-11	3.1978413E+00	*
15.	3.6065631E-03	3.1899161E+00	*	65.	2.5946094E-11	3.1978413E+00	*
16.	2.4787521E-03	3.1923948E+00	*	66.	1.7832472E-11	3.1978413E+00	*
17.	1.7036197E-03	3.1940984E+00	*	67.	1.2256067E-11	3.1978413E+00	*
18.	1.1708796E-03	3.1952692E+00	*	68.	8.4234637E-12	3.1978413E+00	*
19.	8.0473300E-04	3.1960739E+00	*	69.	5.7893563E-12	3.1978413E+00	*
20.	5.5308436E-04	3.1966269E+00	*	70.	3.9796225E-12	3.1978413E+00	*
21.	3.8012895E-04	3.1970070E+00	*	71.	2.7346982E-12	3.1978413E+00	*
22.	2.6125855E-04	3.1972682E+00	*	72.	1.8795288E-12	3.1978413E+00	*
23.	1.7956020E-04	3.1974477E+00	*	73.	1.2917800E-12	3.1978413E+00	*
24.	1.2340980E-04	3.1975711E+00	*	74.	8.8782654E-13	3.1978413E+00	*
25.	8.4818235E-05	3.1976559E+00	*	75.	6.1019366E-13	3.1978413E+00	*
26.	5.8294663E-05	3.1977141E+00	*	76.	4.1937956E-13	3.1978413E+00	*
27.	4.0065297E-05	3.1977541E+00	*	77.	2.8823507E-13	3.1978413E+00	*
28.	2.7536449E-05	3.1977816E+00	*	78.	1.9810087E-13	3.1978413E+00	*
29.	1.8925506E-05	3.1978005E+00	*	79.	1.3615261E-13	3.1978413E+00	*
30.	1.3007297E-05	3.1978135E+00	*	80.	9.3576229E-14	3.1978413E+00	*
31.	8.9397762E-06	3.1978224E+00	*	81.	6.4313939E-14	3.1978413E+00	*
32.	6.1442123E-06	3.1978285E+00	*	82.	4.4202280E-14	3.1978413E+00	*
33.	4.2228512E-06	3.1978327E+00	*	83.	3.0379753E-14	3.1978413E+00	*
34.	2.9023204E-06	3.1978356E+00	*	84.	2.0879679E-14	3.1978413E+00	*
35.	1.9947336E-06	3.1978375E+00	*	85.	1.4350379E-14	3.1978413E+00	*
36.	1.3709590E-06	3.1978388E+00	*	86.	9.8628620E-15	3.1978413E+00	*
37.	9.4224547E-07	3.1978397E+00	*	87.	6.7786393E-15	3.1978413E+00	*
38.	6.4759521E-07	3.1978403E+00	*	88.	4.6588861E-15	3.1978413E+00	*
39.	4.4508524E-07	3.1978407E+00	*	89.	3.2020024E-15	3.1978413E+00	*
40.	3.0590232E-07	3.1978410E+00	*	90.	2.2007019E-15	3.1978413E+00	*
41.	2.1024338E-07	3.1978412E+00	*	91.	1.5125188E-15	3.1978413E+00	*
42.	1.4449802E-07	3.1978413E+00	*	92.	1.0395380E-15	3.1978413E+00	*
43.	9.9311943E-08	3.1978413E+00	*	93.	7.1446332E-16	3.1978413E+00	*
44.	6.8256033E-08	3.1978413E+00	*	94.	4.9104298E-16	3.1978413E+00	*
45.	4.6911640E-08	3.1978413E+00	*	95.	3.3748857E-16	3.1978413E+00	*
46.	3.2241867E-08	3.1978413E+00	*	96.	2.3195228E-16	3.1978413E+00	*
47.	2.2159489E-08	3.1978413E+00	*	97.	1.5941831E-16	3.1978413E+00	*
48.	1.5229979E-08	3.1978413E+00	*	98.	1.0956650E-16	3.1978413E+00	*
49.	1.0467401E-08	3.1978413E+00	*	99.	7.5303880E-17	3.1978413E+00	*
50.	7.1941330E-09	3.1978413E+00	*	100.	5.1755549E-17	3.1978413E+00	*

X	E^{-RX}	SUM OF E^{-RX}	*	X	E^{-RX}	SUM OF E^{-RX}	*
0.	1.0000000E+00	1.0000000E+00	*	50.	5.6027964E-09	3.1631673E+00	*
1.	6.8386140E-01	1.6838614E+00	*	51.	3.8315362E-09	3.1631673E+00	*
2.	4.6766642E-01	2.1515278E+00	*	52.	2.6202397E-09	3.1631673E+00	*
3.	3.1981902E-01	2.4713468E+00	*	53.	1.7918808E-09	3.1631673E+00	*
4.	2.1871188E-01	2.6900586E+00	*	54.	1.2253981E-09	3.1631673E+00	*
5.	1.4956861E-01	2.8396272E+00	*	55.	8.3800252E-10	3.1631673E+00	*
6.	1.0228420E-01	2.9419114E+00	*	56.	5.7307758E-10	3.1631673E+00	*
7.	6.9948221E-02	3.0118596E+00	*	57.	3.9190564E-10	3.1631673E+00	*
8.	4.7834889E-02	3.0596944E+00	*	58.	2.6800914E-10	3.1631673E+00	*
9.	3.2712434E-02	3.0924068E+00	*	59.	1.8328111E-10	3.1631673E+00	*
10.	2.2370771E-02	3.1147775E+00	*	60.	1.2533888E-10	3.1631673E+00	*
11.	1.5298507E-02	3.1300760E+00	*	61.	8.5714423E-11	3.1631673E+00	*
12.	1.0462058E-02	3.1405380E+00	*	62.	5.8616786E-11	3.1631673E+00	*
13.	7.1545983E-03	3.1476925E+00	*	63.	4.0085758E-11	3.1631673E+00	*
14.	4.892753E-03	3.1525852E+00	*	64.	2.7413103E-11	3.1631673E+00	*
15.	3.3459654E-03	3.1559311E+00	*	65.	1.8746763E-11	3.1631673E+00	*
16.	2.2881766E-03	3.1582192E+00	*	66.	1.2820187E-11	3.1631673E+00	*
17.	1.5647957E-03	3.1597839E+00	*	67.	8.7672318E-12	3.1631673E+00	*
18.	1.0701033E-03	3.1608540E+00	*	68.	5.9955715E-12	3.1631673E+00	*
19.	7.3180241E-04	3.1615858E+00	*	69.	4.1001399E-12	3.1631673E+00	*
20.	5.0045143E-04	3.1620862E+00	*	70.	2.8039275E-12	3.1631673E+00	*
21.	3.4223942E-04	3.1624284E+00	*	71.	1.9174978E-12	3.1631673E+00	*
22.	2.3404433E-04	3.1626624E+00	*	72.	1.3113027E-12	3.1631673E+00	*
23.	1.6005388E-04	3.1628224E+00	*	73.	8.9674935E-13	3.1631673E+00	*
24.	1.0945467E-04	3.1629318E+00	*	74.	6.1325227E-13	3.1631673E+00	*
25.	7.4851829E-05	3.1630066E+00	*	75.	4.1937956E-13	3.1631673E+00	*
26.	5.1188277E-05	3.1630577E+00	*	76.	2.8679750E-13	3.1631673E+00	*
27.	3.5005687E-05	3.1630927E+00	*	77.	1.9612974E-13	3.1631673E+00	*
28.	2.3939038E-05	3.1631166E+00	*	78.	1.3412556E-13	3.1631673E+00	*
29.	1.6370984E-05	3.1631329E+00	*	79.	9.1723295E-14	3.1631673E+00	*
30.	1.1195484E-05	3.1631440E+00	*	80.	6.2726022E-14	3.1631673E+00	*
31.	7.6561600E-06	3.1631516E+00	*	81.	4.2895906E-14	3.1631673E+00	*
32.	5.2357523E-06	3.1631568E+00	*	82.	2.9334854E-14	3.1631673E+00	*
33.	3.5805290E-06	3.1631603E+00	*	83.	2.0060975E-14	3.1631673E+00	*
34.	2.4485856E-06	3.1631627E+00	*	84.	1.3718926E-14	3.1631673E+00	*
35.	1.6744932E-06	3.1631643E+00	*	85.	9.3818445E-15	3.1631673E+00	*
36.	1.1451212E-06	3.1631654E+00	*	86.	6.4158814E-15	3.1631673E+00	*
37.	7.8310425E-07	3.1631661E+00	*	87.	4.3875737E-15	3.1631673E+00	*
38.	5.3353477E-07	3.1631666E+00	*	88.	3.0004923E-15	3.1631673E+00	*
39.	3.6623156E-07	3.1631669E+00	*	89.	2.0519209E-15	3.1631673E+00	*
40.	2.5045163E-07	3.1631671E+00	*	90.	1.4032295E-15	3.1631673E+00,	*
41.	1.7127420E-07	3.1631672E+00	*	91.	9.5961453E-16	3.1631673E+00	*
42.	1.1712782E-07	3.1631673E+00	*	92.	6.5624334E-16	3.1631673E+00	*
43.	8.0099197E-08	3.1631673E+00	*	93.	4.4877949E-16	3.1631673E+00	*
44.	5.4776750E-08	3.1631673E+00	*	94.	3.0690298E-16	3.1631673E+00	*
45.	3.7459705E-08	3.1631673E+00	*	95.	2.0987910E-16	3.1631673E+00	*
46.	2.5617246E-08	3.1631673E+00	*	96.	1.4352822E-16	3.1631673E+00	*
47.	1.7518646E-08	3.1631673E+00	*	97.	9.8153411E-17	3.1631673E+00	*
48.	1.1980326E-08	3.1631673E+00	*	98.	6.7123329E-17	3.1631673E+00	*
49.	8.1928328E-09	3.1631673E+00	*	99.	4.5903055E-17	3.1631673E+00	*
50.	5.6027964E-09	3.1631673E+00	*	100.	3.1391327E-17	3.1631673E+00	*

X	$-RX$ E	$-RX$ SUM OF E	σ	X	$-RX$ E	$-RX$ SUM OF E	σ
0.	1.0000000E+00	1.0000000E+00	σ	50.	4.3636622E-09	3.1294047E+00	σ
1.	6.8045063E-01	1.6804506E+00	σ	51.	2.9661204E-09	3.1294047E+00	σ
2.	4.6501306E-01	2.1434636E+00	σ	52.	2.0213400E-09	3.1294047E+00	σ
3.	3.1505753E-01	2.4585211E+00	σ	53.	1.3747416E-09	3.1294047E+00	σ
4.	2.1438110E-01	2.6729022E+00	σ	54.	6.3564324E-10	3.1294047E+00	σ
5.	1.4527575E-01	2.8187770E+00	σ	55.	6.3652235E-10	3.1294047E+00	σ
6.	9.9261251E-02	2.9180391E+00	σ	56.	4.3312272E-10	3.1294047E+00	σ
7.	6.7562381E-02	2.9855814E+00	σ	57.	2.9471863E-10	3.1294047E+00	σ
8.	4.5950925E-02	3.0315414E+00	σ	58.	2.0046412E-10	3.1294047E+00	σ
9.	3.1273005E-02	3.0627213E+00	σ	59.	1.3645857E-10	3.1294047E+00	σ
10.	2.1279736E-02	3.0840933E+00	σ	60.	9.2853332E-11	3.1294047E+00	σ
11.	1.4479310E-02	3.0985731E+00	σ	61.	6.3182104E-11	3.1294047E+00	σ
12.	9.8529060E-03	3.1084259E+00	σ	62.	4.2992303E-11	3.1294047E+00	σ
13.	6.7043413E-03	3.1151301E+00	σ	63.	2.9254343E-11	3.1294047E+00	σ
14.	4.5619073E-03	3.1196923E+00	σ	64.	1.9905908E-11	3.1294047E+00	σ
15.	3.1041976E-03	3.1227961E+00	σ	65.	1.3545040E-11	3.1294047E+00	σ
16.	2.1122532E-03	3.1249083E+00	σ	66.	9.2147376E-12	3.1294047E+00	σ
17.	1.4372860E-03	3.1263455E+00	σ	67.	6.2715344E-12	3.1294047E+00	σ
18.	9.7800068E-04	3.1273235E+00	σ	68.	4.2674605E-12	3.1294047E+00	σ
19.	6.6564131E-04	3.1279889E+00	σ	69.	2.9038025E-12	3.1294047E+00	σ
20.	4.5282718E-04	3.1284417E+00	σ	70.	1.9758943E-12	3.1294047E+00	σ
21.	3.0812654E-04	3.1287498E+00	σ	71.	1.3446985E-12	3.1294047E+00	σ
22.	2.0964490E-04	3.1289594E+00	σ	72.	9.1486488E-13	3.1294047E+00	σ
23.	1.4266661E-04	3.1291020E+00	σ	73.	6.2252039E-13	3.1294047E+00	σ
24.	9.7077590E-05	3.1291990E+00	σ	74.	4.2356430E-13	3.1294047E+00	σ
25.	6.6056507E-05	3.1292650E+00	σ	75.	2.8823507E-13	3.1294047E+00	σ
26.	4.4948192E-05	3.1293099E+00	σ	76.	1.9612974E-13	3.1294047E+00	σ
27.	3.0589026E-05	3.1293404E+00	σ	77.	1.3345660E-13	3.1294047E+00	σ
28.	2.0811600E-05	3.1293612E+00	σ	78.	9.0810634E-14	3.1294047E+00	σ
29.	1.4161266E-05	3.1293753E+00	σ	79.	6.1752153E-14	3.1294047E+00	σ
30.	9.6360436E-06	3.1293849E+00	σ	80.	4.2044310E-14	3.1294047E+00	σ
31.	6.5568516E-06	3.1293914E+00	σ	81.	2.8610574E-14	3.1294047E+00	σ
32.	4.4614138E-06	3.1293958E+00	σ	82.	1.9468083E-14	3.1294047E+00	σ
33.	3.0359080E-06	3.1293988E+00	σ	83.	1.3247069E-14	3.1294047E+00	σ
34.	2.0657855E-06	3.1294008E+00	σ	84.	9.0139771E-15	3.1294047E+00	σ
35.	1.4056650E-06	3.1294022E+00	σ	85.	6.1335665E-15	3.1294047E+00	σ
36.	9.5648569E-07	3.1294031E+00	σ	86.	4.1735892E-15	3.1294047E+00	σ
37.	6.5084130E-07	3.1294037E+00	σ	87.	2.8398214E-15	3.1294047E+00	σ
38.	4.4286537E-07	3.1294041E+00	σ	88.	1.9324245E-15	3.1294047E+00	σ
39.	3.0134802E-07	3.1294044E+00	σ	89.	1.3149207E-15	3.1294047E+00	σ
40.	2.0505245E-07	3.1294046E+00	σ	90.	8.9473658E-16	3.1294047E+00	σ
41.	1.3952807E-07	3.1294047E+00	σ	91.	6.0922564E-16	3.1294047E+00	σ
42.	9.4941957E-08	3.1294047E+00	σ	92.	4.1427660E-16	3.1294047E+00	σ
43.	6.4603322E-08	3.1294047E+00	σ	93.	2.7194156E-16	3.1294047E+00	σ
44.	4.3959371E-08	3.1294047E+00	σ	94.	1.6191565E-16	3.1294047E+00	σ
45.	2.9912182E-08	3.1294047E+00	σ	95.	1.3052067E-16	3.1294047E+00	σ
46.	2.0353742E-08	3.1294047E+00	σ	96.	8.8812678E-17	3.1294047E+00	σ
47.	1.3849731E-08	3.1294047E+00	σ	97.	6.0437770E-17	3.1294047E+00	σ
48.	9.4240569E-09	3.1294047E+00	σ	98.	4.1121527E-17	3.1294047E+00	σ
49.	6.4126062E-09	3.1294047E+00	σ	99.	2.7911665E-17	3.1294047E+00	σ
50.	4.3636622E-09	3.1294047E+00	σ	100.	1.9930692E-17	3.1294047E+00	σ

X	$-RX$ E	$-RX$ SUM OF E	σ	X	$-RX$ E	$-RX$ SUM OF E	σ
0.	1.0000000E+00	1.0000000E+00	σ	50.	3.3942672E-09	3.0965182E+00	σ
1.	5.7056687E-01	1.6770586E+00	σ	51.	2.3019521E-09	3.0965182E+00	σ
2.	4.5540601E-01	2.1334627E+00	σ	52.	1.5577063E-09	3.0965182E+00	σ
3.	3.1036945E-01	2.4465707E+00	σ	53.	1.0547994E-09	3.0965182E+00	σ
4.	2.1013607E-01	2.6559657E+00	σ	54.	7.1498264E-10	3.0965182E+00	σ
5.	1.4227407E-01	2.7982397E+00	σ	55.	4.8368539E-10	3.0965182E+00	σ
6.	9.6327630E-02	2.8945673E+00	σ	56.	3.2734711E-10	3.0965182E+00	σ
7.	6.5219285E-02	2.9597665E+00	σ	57.	2.2163261E-10	3.0965182E+00	σ
8.	4.4157160E-02	3.0039436E+00	σ	58.	1.5005788E-10	3.0965182E+00	σ
9.	2.9894914E-02	3.0338405E+00	σ	59.	1.0155077E-10	3.0965182E+00	σ
10.	2.0241911E-02	3.0540624E+00	σ	60.	6.8757436E-11	3.0965182E+00	σ
11.	1.3704925E-02	3.0677873E+00	σ	61.	4.6573004E-11	3.0965182E+00	σ
12.	9.2790139E-03	3.0770663E+00	σ	62.	3.1535574E-11	3.0965182E+00	σ
13.	6.2824201E-03	3.0833467E+00	σ	63.	2.1349574E-11	3.0965182E+00	σ
14.	4.2533557E-03	3.0876022E+00	σ	64.	1.4454721E-11	3.0965182E+00	σ
15.	2.8798991E-03	3.0904820E+00	σ	65.	9.7866868E-12	3.0965182E+00	σ
16.	1.9498555E-03	3.0924318E+00	σ	66.	6.6261312E-12	3.0965182E+00	σ
17.	1.3201630E-03	3.0937519E+00	σ	67.	4.4862677E-12	3.0965182E+00	σ
18.	8.9382549E-04	3.0946457E+00	σ	68.	3.3745964E-12	3.0965182E+00	σ
19.	6.0517069E-04	3.0952509E+00	σ	69.	2.0565320E-12	3.0965182E+00	σ
20.	4.0973497E-04	3.0956605E+00	σ	70.	1.3923891E-12	3.0965182E+00	σ
21.	2.7741388E-04	3.0959379E+00	σ	71.	9.4272647E-13	3.0965182E+00	σ
22.	1.8782497E-04	3.0961257E+00	σ	72.	6.3829794E-13	3.0965182E+00	σ
23.	1.2716810E-04	3.0962528E+00	σ	73.	4.3215157E-13	3.0965182E+00	σ
24.	8.6100094E-05	3.0963386E+00	σ	74.	2.9250110E-13	3.0965182E+00	σ
25.	5.8294963E-05	3.0963971E+00	σ	75.	1.9810675E-13	3.0965182E+00	σ
26.	3.9468902E-05	3.0964365E+00	σ	76.	1.3412556E-13	3.0965182E+00	σ
27.	2.6722624E-05	3.0964632E+00	σ	77.	9.0810634E-14	3.0965182E+00	σ
28.	1.8092736E-05	3.0964812E+00	σ	78.	6.1438364E-14	3.0965182E+00	σ
29.	1.2249031E-05	3.0964934E+00	σ	79.	4.1620145E-14	3.0965182E+00	σ
30.	8.2933191E-06	3.0965018E+00	σ	80.	2.8146618E-14	3.0965182E+00	σ
31.	5.6153872E-06	3.0965072E+00	σ	81.	1.9025806E-14	3.0965182E+00	σ
32.	3.8019365E-06	3.0965110E+00	σ	82.	1.2986066E-14	3.0965182E+00	σ
33.	2.5741272E-06	3.0965135E+00	σ	83.	8.7475730E-15	3.0965182E+00	σ
34.	1.7428305E-06	3.0965152E+00	σ	84.	5.9226050E-15	3.0965182E+00	σ
35.	1.1799054E-06	3.0965163E+00	σ	85.	4.0000603E-15	3.0965182E+00	σ
36.	7.9892406E-07	3.0965170E+00	σ	86.	2.7146577E-15	3.0965182E+00	σ
37.	5.4091699E-07	3.0965175E+00	σ	87.	1.8381809E-15	3.0965182E+00	σ
38.	5.6623156E-07	3.0965180E+00	σ	88.	1.2465526E-15	3.0965182E+00	σ
39.	2.4795660E-07	3.0965180E+00	σ	89.	8.4243313E-16	3.0965182E+00	σ
40.	1.6780275E-07	3.0965182E+00	σ	90.	5.7151055E-16	3.0965182E+00	σ
41.	1.1346617E-07	3.0965182E+00	σ	91.	3.5626800E-16	3.0965182E+00	σ
42.	7.6954463E-08	3.0965182E+00	σ	92.	2.6152646E-16	3.0965182E+00	σ
43.	5.2105254E-08	3.0965182E+00	σ	93.	1.7736765E-16	3.0965182E+00	σ
44.	3.5278222E-08	3.0965182E+00	σ	94.	1.1892626E-16	3.0965182E+00	σ
45.	2.3895362E-08	3.0965182E+00	σ	95.	8.1169854E-17	3.0965182E+00	σ
46.	1.6171769E-08	3.0965182E+00	σ	96.	5.4945042E-17	3.0965182E+00	σ
47.	1.0949192E-08	3.0965182E+00	σ	97.	3.7218262E-17	3.0965182E+00	σ
48.	7.4132766E-09	3.0965182E+00	σ	98.	2.5162135E-17	3.0965182E+00	σ
49.	5.0191762E-09	3.0965182E+00	σ	99.	1.7046565E-17	3.0965182E+00	σ
50.	3.3982672E-09	3.0965182E+00	σ	100.	1.1603224E-17	3.0965182E+00	σ

X	E^{-RX}	SUM OF E^{-RX}	☆	X	E^{-RX}	SUM OF E^{-RX}	☆
0.	1.0000000E+00	1.0000000E+00	☆	50.	2.6465736E-09	3.0644746E+00	☆
1.	6.7368003E-01	1.6736800E+00	☆	51.	1.782943RE-09	3.0644746E+00	☆
2.	4.5384479E-01	2.1275247E+00	☆	52.	1.2011336E-09	3.0644746E+00	☆
3.	3.0574617E-01	2.4332708E+00	☆	53.	8.0917977E-10	3.0644746E+00	☆
4.	2.0597509E-01	2.6392458E+00	☆	54.	5.4512826E-10	3.0644746E+00	☆
5.	1.3876131E-01	2.7780071E+00	☆	55.	3.6724202E-10	3.0644746E+00	☆
6.	9.3480726E-02	2.871487RE+00	☆	56.	2.4740362E-10	3.0644746E+00	☆
7.	6.2976099E-02	2.9344638E+00	☆	57.	1.6667088E-10	3.0644746E+00	☆
8.	4.2425741E-02	2.9768895E+00	☆	58.	1.1228284E-10	3.0644746E+00	☆
9.	2.8581374E-02	3.0054708E+00	☆	59.	7.5642713E-11	3.0644746E+00	☆
10.	1.9254701E-02	3.0247255E+00	☆	60.	5.0958986E-11	3.0644746E+00	☆
11.	1.2971508E-02	3.0376970E+00	☆	61.	3.4330051E-11	3.0644746E+00	☆
12.	8.7386461E-03	3.0464356E+00	☆	62.	2.3127470E-11	3.0644746E+00	☆
13.	5.8870514E-03	3.0523226E+00	☆	63.	1.5580515E-11	3.0644746E+00	☆
14.	3.9659890E-03	3.0562885E+00	☆	64.	1.0496282E-11	3.0644746E+00	☆
15.	2.6718076E-03	3.0589603E+00	☆	65.	7.0711357E-12	3.0644746E+00	☆
16.	1.7999435E-03	3.0607602E+00	☆	66.	4.7636830E-12	3.0644746E+00	☆
17.	1.2125860E-03	3.0619727E+00	☆	67.	3.2091981E-12	3.0644746E+00	☆
18.	8.1689498E-04	3.0627895E+00	☆	68.	2.1619727E-12	3.0644746E+00	☆
19.	5.5032584E-04	3.0633398E+00	☆	69.	1.4564778E-12	3.0644746E+00	☆
20.	3.7074353E-04	3.0637105E+00	☆	70.	9.8120007E-13	3.0644746E+00	☆
21.	2.4976252E-04	3.0639602E+00	☆	71.	6.6101490E-13	3.0644746E+00	☆
22.	1.6826002E-04	3.0641284E+00	☆	72.	4.4531294E-13	3.0644746E+00	☆
23.	1.1335342E-04	3.0642417E+00	☆	73.	2.9999817E-13	3.0644746E+00	☆
24.	7.6363937E-05	3.0643180E+00	☆	74.	2.0210278E-13	3.0644746E+00	☆
25.	5.1444860E-05	3.0643694E+00	☆	75.	1.3615261E-13	3.0644746E+00	☆
26.	3.4657375E-05	3.0644040E+00	☆	76.	9.1723295E-14	3.0644746E+00	☆
27.	2.3347981E-05	3.0644273E+00	☆	77.	6.1792153E-14	3.0644746E+00	☆
28.	1.5729069E-05	3.0644430E+00	☆	78.	4.1628140E-14	3.0644746E+00	☆
29.	1.0596360E-05	3.0644535E+00	☆	79.	2.8044047E-14	3.0644746E+00	☆
30.	7.1385562E-06	3.0644606E+00	☆	80.	1.8892714E-14	3.0644746E+00	☆
31.	4.8091028E-06	3.0644654E+00	☆	81.	1.2727644E-14	3.0644746E+00	☆
32.	3.2397966E-06	3.0644686E+00	☆	82.	8.5743603E-15	3.0644746E+00	☆
33.	2.1825863E-06	3.0644707E+00	☆	83.	5.7763705E-15	3.0644746E+00	☆
34.	1.4703648E-06	3.0644721E+00	☆	84.	3.8914288E-15	3.0644746E+00	☆
35.	9.9055543E-07	3.0644730E+00	☆	85.	2.6215779E-15	3.0644746E+00	☆
36.	6.6731742E-07	3.0644736E+00	☆	86.	1.7661041E-15	3.0644746E+00	☆
37.	4.4955843E-07	3.0644740E+00	☆	87.	1.1897894E-15	3.0644746E+00	☆
38.	3.0285854E-07	3.0644743E+00	☆	88.	8.0153714E-16	3.0644746E+00	☆
39.	2.0402975E-07	3.0644745E+00	☆	89.	5.3997976E-16	3.0644746E+00	☆
40.	1.3745077E-07	3.0644746E+00	☆	90.	3.6377359E-16	3.0644746E+00	☆
41.	9.2597841E-08	3.0644746E+00	☆	91.	2.4506700E-16	3.0644746E+00	☆
42.	6.2381317E-08	3.0644746E+00	☆	92.	1.6509675E-16	3.0644746E+00	☆
43.	4.2025048E-08	3.0644746E+00	☆	93.	1.1122283E-16	3.0644746E+00	☆
44.	2.8311436E-08	3.0644746E+00	☆	94.	7.4928301E-17	3.0644746E+00	☆
45.	1.9072849E-08	3.0644746E+00	☆	95.	5.0477700E-17	3.0644746E+00	☆
46.	1.2848998E-08	3.0644746E+00	☆	96.	3.4005819E-17	3.0644746E+00	☆
47.	8.6561135E-09	3.0644746E+00	☆	97.	2.2909041E-17	3.0644746E+00	☆
48.	5.8314508E-09	3.0644746E+00	☆	98.	1.5433366E-17	3.0644746E+00	☆
49.	3.9285320E-09	3.0644746E+00	☆	99.	1.0397149E-17	3.0644746E+00	☆
50.	2.6465736E-09	3.0644746E+00	☆	100.	7.0043520E-18	3.0644746E+00	☆

X	E^{-RX}	SUM OF E^{-RX}	☆	X	E^{-RX}	SUM OF E^{-RX}	☆
0.	1.0000000E+00	1.0000000E+00	☆	50.	2.0611536E-09	3.0332425E+00	☆
1.	6.7032004E-01	1.6703200E+00	☆	51.	1.3816325E-09	3.0332425E+00	☆
2.	4.4932896E-01	2.1196489E+00	☆	52.	9.2613602E-10	3.0332425E+00	☆
3.	3.0119421E-01	2.4208431E+00	☆	53.	6.2080754E-10	3.0332425E+00	☆
4.	2.0189651E-01	2.6227396E+00	☆	54.	4.1613973E-10	3.0332425E+00	☆
5.	1.3533528E-01	2.7580748E+00	☆	55.	2.7894680E-10	3.0332425E+00	☆
6.	9.0717953E-02	2.8487927E+00	☆	56.	1.8698363E-10	3.0332425E+00	☆
7.	6.0810062E-02	2.9096027E+00	☆	57.	1.2533888E-10	3.0332425E+00	☆
8.	4.0762203E-02	2.9503649E+00	☆	58.	8.4017164E-11	3.0332425E+00	☆
9.	2.7323722E-02	2.9776886E+00	☆	59.	5.6318389E-11	3.0332425E+00	☆
10.	1.8315638E-02	2.9960042E+00	☆	60.	3.7751345E-11	3.0332425E+00	☆
11.	1.2277339E-02	3.0082815E+00	☆	61.	2.5305483E-11	3.0332425E+00	☆
12.	8.2297470E-03	3.0165112E+00	☆	62.	1.6962772E-11	3.0332425E+00	☆
13.	5.5165644E-03	3.0220277E+00	☆	63.	1.1370486E-11	3.0332425E+00	☆
14.	3.6978637E-03	3.0257255E+00	☆	64.	7.6218651E-12	3.0332425E+00	☆
15.	2.4787521E-03	3.0282042E+00	☆	65.	5.1090890E-12	3.0332425E+00	☆
16.	1.6615572E-03	3.0298657E+00	☆	66.	3.4247247E-12	3.0332425E+00	☆
17.	1.1137751E-03	3.0309794E+00	☆	67.	2.2956616E-12	3.0332425E+00	☆
18.	7.4658580E-04	3.0317259E+00	☆	68.	1.5388280E-12	3.0332425E+00	☆
19.	5.0045143E-04	3.0322263E+00	☆	69.	1.0315072E-12	3.0332425E+00	☆
20.	3.3546262E-04	3.0325617E+00	☆	70.	6.9144000E-13	3.0332425E+00	☆
21.	2.2486732E-04	3.0327865E+00	☆	71.	4.6348609E-13	3.0332425E+00	☆
22.	1.5073307E-04	3.0329372E+00	☆	72.	3.1068402E-13	3.0332425E+00	☆
23.	1.0103940E-04	3.0330382E+00	☆	73.	2.0825772E-13	3.0332425E+00	☆
24.	6.7728736E-05	3.0331059E+00	☆	74.	1.3959933E-13	3.0332425E+00	☆
25.	4.5399929E-05	3.0331512E+00	☆	75.	9.3576229E-14	3.0332425E+00	☆
26.	3.0432482E-05	3.0331816E+00	☆	76.	6.2726022E-14	3.0332425E+00	☆
27.	2.0399503E-05	3.0332019E+00	☆	77.	4.2046510E-14	3.0332425E+00	☆
28.	1.3674196E-05	3.0332155E+00	☆	78.	2.8184618E-14	3.0332425E+00	☆
29.	9.1660877E-06	3.0332246E+00	☆	79.	1.8892714E-14	3.0332425E+00	☆
30.	6.1442123E-06	3.0332307E+00	☆	80.	1.2664165E-14	3.0332425E+00	☆
31.	4.1185886E-06	3.0332348E+00	☆	81.	8.4890440E-15	3.0332425E+00	☆
32.	2.7607725E-06	3.0332375E+00	☆	82.	5.6903762E-15	3.0332425E+00	☆
33.	1.8506011E-06	3.0332393E+00	☆	83.	3.8143733E-15	3.0332425E+00	☆
34.	1.2404950E-06	3.0332405E+00	☆	84.	2.5568509E-15	3.0332425E+00	☆
35.	8.3152871E-07	3.0332413E+00	☆	85.	1.7139084E-15	3.0332425E+00	☆
36.	5.5739036E-07	3.0332418E+00	☆	86.	1.1488671E-15	3.0332425E+00	☆
37.	3.7362993E-07	3.0332421E+00	☆	87.	7.7010869E-16	3.0332425E+00	☆
38.	2.5045163E-07	3.0332423E+00	☆	88.	5.1621929E-16	3.0332425E+00	☆
39.	1.6788275E-07	3.0332424E+00	☆	89.	3.4603214E-16	3.0332425E+00	☆
40.	1.1253517E-07	3.0332425E+00	☆	90.	2.3195222E-16	3.0332425E+00	☆
41.	7.5434583E-08	3.0332425E+00	☆	91.	1.5547224E-16	3.0332425E+00	☆
42.	5.0565313E-08	3.0332425E+00	☆	92.	1.0422228E-16	3.0332425E+00	☆
43.	3.3894943E-08	3.0332425E+00	☆	93.	6.9862684E-17	3.0332425E+00	☆
44.	2.2720459E-08	3.0332425E+00	☆	94.	4.6830358E-17	3.0332425E+00	☆
45.	1.5229979E-08	3.0332425E+00	☆	95.	3.1391327E-17	3.0332425E+00	☆
46.	1.0208960E-08	3.0332425E+00	☆	96.	2.1042236E-17	3.0332425E+00	☆
47.	6.8432710E-09	3.0332425E+00	☆	97.	1.4105032E-17	3.0332425E+00	☆
48.	4.5871817E-09	3.0332425E+00	☆	98.	9.4548862E-18	3.0332425E+00	☆
49.	3.0748798E-09	3.0332425E+00	☆	99.	6.3377097E-18	3.0332425E+00	☆
50.	2.0611536E-09	3.0332425E+00	☆	100.	4.2483542E-18	3.0332425E+00	☆

INDEX

ABOUT THE AUTHORS

JON D. CLARK is Associate Professor of Information Systems in the College of Business at North Texas State University. Until 1979 he was Assistant Professor of Management Information Systems at the University of Texas at Dallas. Dr. Clark has numerous articles on data base and computer system evaluation. These have appeared in *Data Management, Performance Evaluation Review,* and various ACM Conference Proceedings.

Dr. Clark holds a B.A. in Industrial Administration from Michigan State University, an M.B.A. in Finance from Eastern Michigan University, and a Ph.D. in Management Information Systems from Case Western Reserve University.

ARNOLD REISMAN is Professor of Operations Research in the Weatherhead School of Management at Case Western Reserve University. He also holds joint appointments in the Schools of Library Science, Medicine, and Engineering, and has taught at the University of Wisconsin, University of Hawaii, and the Hebrew University of Jerusalem.

Professor Reisman is author of nine books and monographs and has published over 90 articles ranging from health care to data processing. Dr. Reisman holds a B.S., M.S. and Ph.D. in Engineering from the University of California, Los Angeles.